# BRIAN AND PETER
# A RIGHT PAIR
## 21 YEARS WITH CLOUGH AND TAYLOR

# BRIAN AND PETER
# A RIGHT PAIR
## 21 YEARS WITH CLOUGH AND TAYLOR

# MAURICE EDWARDS

First published in Great Britain in 2010 by The Derby Books Publishing Company Limited,
3 The Parker Centre, Derby, DE21 4SZ.

ISBN 978-1-85983-771-9

Printed and bound by Cromwell Press Group, Trowbridge, Wiltshire.

# CONTENTS

# FOREWORD

No one is better qualified to write a book about Brian Clough and Peter Taylor than Maurice Edwards. They both trusted Maurice as managers and took him to their various clubs, and he has had an insight into both their football and private lives. Maurice was their chief scout through the highs and lows of Derby, Brighton, Leeds United and Nottingham Forest. No one in football knew Brian and Peter better.

Like me, you will enjoy the inside track on the many stories and situations involving this brilliant pair. The fascination about the Clough and Taylor partnership, Brian's larger-than-life outspoken personality and the incredible successes at Derby and Forest ensures their names will live on in the fables of football history. But just when you think there is no more to discover, along comes this book from Maurice.

Brian, as manager, was the public face. His TV interviews were always unpredictable; he was literally a show-stopper. Football grounds hosted packed, noisy match-day social clubs in those days, but when Brian suddenly appeared on the lunchtime TV football programme it all went quiet. You could have heard a pin drop. He understood the media; he knew how to make the headlines.

Peter was the quieter one in public. But they were a partnership. Peter was both the talent spotter and the calming influence.

Brian and Peter fell out with each other in the end; however, it never worked out for either of them on their own. It was a shame but it should never take the shine and wonderful memories off their tremendous rollercoaster ride together through football: the titles, the Cups and the back-to-back European Cup triumphs.

It is scandalous that we have to say 'they were the best that England never had'. I will always believe England could have won the World Cup under Clough and Taylor. That is to take nothing away from the likes of Sir Bobby Robson, however. It is just that I always believed together they could achieve anything.

I miss them both in football and in life. Brian was always good to me. His lovely wife Barbara kindly tells me that Brian was always very fond of me. The feeling was mutual. I felt privileged when Barbara asked me to do the public compèring for the unveiling of Brian's statue in Nottingham.

Peter, like Brian, was a great family man. I worked with his son-in-law John Dickinson, a TV producer, for many years and got to learn a lot about Peter. He would be a good card-marker and contributed to the wit that was in abundance in their company.

Peter brought Maurice into football in their Burton upon Trent days. Not so much has been written before about Peter. Maurice restores that balance. He is the third man with, as he rightly describes it, 'A right pair'.

**Gary Newbon,**
**December 2009**

# TIMELINE

## Burton Albion

1962      Peter Taylor signed as goalkeeper in the Southern League.

1963–64      Appointed manager, finished in eighth position.

1964–65      Won Southern League Cup.

## Hartlepools United

1965–66      Joined manager Brian Clough, finished 18th position, Division Four.

1966–67      Finished fourth position, Division Four.

## Derby County

1967–68      Brian appointed manager, Peter appointed assistant manager.

1968–69      Division Two Champions.

1969–70      Finished fourth position, Division One.

1970      Watney Cup winners (beat Manchester United 4–1).

1970–71      Finished ninth position, Division One.

1971–72      Won Texaco Cup (26 April), Division One Champions.

1972–73      European Cup semi-finalists (lost to Juventus), finished seventh position Division One.

1973–74      Beat Manchester United away 1–0 (13 October), Brian and Peter resigned following week.

## Brighton and Hove Albion

1973–74      Brian appointed manager, Peter appointed assistant manager, finished 19th position, Division Three.

1974–75      Finished 16th position, Division Three.

1975–76      Peter appointed manager, finished fourth position, Division Three.

**Leeds United**

1975        Don Revie appointed England manager, Brian appointed Leeds manager, sacked after 44 days.

**Nottingham Forest**

1975        Brian appointed manager (January), finished 16th position, Division Two.

1975–76     Finished eighth position Division Two.

1976–77     Peter appointed assistant manager, won Anglo-Scottish Cup.

1977–78     Won League Cup at Wembley, Division One Champions.

1978–79     Won Charity Shield at Wembley, won League Cup at Wembley, runners-up (to Liverpool) in Division One, won European Cup in Munich.

1979–80     Won League Cup at Wembley, won European Cup in Madrid, won Super Cup in Barcelona, finished fifth position, Division One.

1980–81     Super Cup Finalists (lost to Valencia on away goals), Intercontinental Cup Finalists in Tokyo (lost to National Montevideo), finished in seventh position, Division One.

1981–82     Finished in 12th position, Division One.

1982–83     Finished in fifth position, Division One, Peter retires through ill-health.

**Derby County**

1982–83     Peter Taylor appointed manager (November), finished 13th position, Division Two.

1983–84     Severe financial troubles, Peter retires through ill-health (April), relegated to Division Three after finishing 20th position, Division Two.

# PREFACE
# HOW IT ALL BEGAN

I have often been approached by sports journalists with national newspapers for stories of my 21 years (1963–84) working with Peter Taylor and Brian Clough as part of their very successful management team.

I have put Peter and Brian's names in that order because it was Peter's arrival at Burton Albion that started it all. From Peter's conversations, I soon realised what a close friend of his Brian Clough was, from their playing days together at Middlesbrough. Peter talked about Brian as a prolific scorer of goals and bemoaned the loss to the game after his unfortunate collision with the Bury goalkeeper on Boxing Day in 1962, while playing for Sunderland. That season he had scored 28 goals in 28 appearances. His goalscoring record is there for all to see: in eight seasons (1955–63) playing in League Division Two and Cup, he made 293 appearances scoring 266 goals, a strike rate of 90 per cent. I would have liked to have seen him play, but I was refereeing on most of the match days. After two years on the injured list at Sunderland, who were by then in the First Division, he attempted to resume his career, but after only three games he had to call it a day. Brian told me that he had tremendous respect for Alan Brown, the Sunderland manager, for his patience and giving him the chance to play again.

I was introduced to Brian when he and Peter were in charge together at Hartlepools United. I fully appreciate how fortunate I was to have been taken on board by these two football geniuses. I never imagined that I would meet and work with so many different well-known personalities, and be able to enhance their careers, allowing them in many cases to go on to win trophies and become household names. With Peter and Brian my life took off in a completely different direction to what I had anticipated.

I was to be the only person to work with Brian and Peter at all the League clubs that they managed together: Hartlepools United, Derby County, Brighton and Hove Albion, Leeds United and Nottingham Forest. I also worked again at Derby County with Peter on his own.

Although I had been in professional football since 1951, at the beginning I knew of them only through what I had read in the national press. I had not seen either of them play as I was involved in football myself on match days. I was, however, able to see one or two Division One matches in midweek after floodlighting had been introduced.

As Peter and Brian have now both passed away, far too early, I have decided to put pen to paper to record my memories of them, among which there are many stories that have not been told before.

Once I got to know Peter and Brian really well, I realised that they were two quite different people. I have heard it said many times that two complete opposites can make a great team. Their aim in football was exactly the same – to be highly successful – and there is no doubt that they achieved this. Together they could solve most problems and resolve difficult situations, making sound decisions that were promptly carried out. When Brian and Peter were working in football management separately each of them achieved only partial success at the top level. The manager is only as good as his immediate staff in this wonderful game, and this pair had a tremendous belief in each other. Their different temperaments meant that they were not always on the same wavelength and arguments, even serious ones, did ensue, but they listened to one another and always steered their way out of trouble. On occasion when there was a serious difference of opinion, with neither man prepared to give way, Peter would leave the ground to cool off, ring me to pour out the trouble, then either ring Brian from home or leave it until the next morning. At Derby these spats were usually resolved within 24 hours.

Where one fell short in running a successful Football League side, the other excelled. Brian's leadership was excellent and his handling of playing staff was exceptional. He got the best out of them, and whatever problems arose, no matter how serious or upsetting, he could handle it and sort things out before the situation worsened. Peter had a natural footballing brain and was a keen judge of players' ability and potential. He had a vital role in the recruitment of players. The two men shared the same vision of how the game should be played, and together they achieved many outstanding successes.

Peter Taylor was born in Nottingham on 2 July 1928. I was 17 months his senior. His football career started off at Nottingham Forest as a teenage goalkeeper. Harry Storer, manager of Coventry City, signed him in 1950, part-time, until he had completed his apprenticeship in the building trade. Coventry were then playing in Division Two of the Football League, but were relegated to Division Three South in 1952. After making 86 appearances Peter was transferred to Middlesbrough in 1955, playing in Division Two as goalkeeper cover for Bob Dennison, their manager. He made 140 appearances before leaving in 1959. During this time Peter had become the best of friends with Brian Clough. Jimmy Gordon was then coaching at Middlesbrough and was later to become an integral part of the Brian and Peter team.

Having spent time with Peter I discovered that he was a highly nervous character and impetuous. When he decided on a course of action it had to be carried out straight away. He was a very heavy smoker when I first knew him, but I think he used to chew more cigarettes than smoke them. He never enjoyed the crowds and the celebrity of football, and he was at his best remaining in the background. Peter liked a bet on football and horse racing and would enjoy an afternoon at the races, but he always kept away from the crowd. At horse race meetings celebrities recognised by the public are rarely pestered as the horses and bookmakers take pride of place. Peter was never very willing to discuss football with people not actually in the game. He had no interest in their opinions, and he was serious about his own view of how the game should be played.

Harry Storer was Peter's great mentor. Harry spent 30 years managing in the Football League, twice with Coventry City and also with Birmingham City and Derby County. Peter always said that Harry knew more about the game than anyone else he had ever met, and the two men spent hours talking football. While playing with Middlesbrough Peter introduced Brian to Harry. I never had the opportunity to speak to Harry, and he passed away shortly before Brian and Peter were appointed at Derby County.

Many of the club directors that Brian and Peter worked for did not appreciate how much input Peter had to the partnership, but he preferred it that way. Much of his work was done away from the home ground. Several times questions were asked about Peter's role, but he declined to give details of the hours that were spent on fruitless scouting journeys which went largely unrecorded. It was important that his missions were kept close to his chest, as scouting and signings are sensitive operations. It is a complete waste of time recording scouting missions with no end product. Peter warned me at a very early date not to disclose to directors anything that I was doing; he thought that the less they knew about possibilities at the early stage the better, as sometimes a player being targeted might not appear, for a variety of reasons.

Brian, however, was the ideal front man, full of confidence in his own ability and not afraid to make decisions promptly. He was almost always in full control of the sporting press, and television interviewers often felt that he had finished up by interviewing them. He was controversial at times and knew how to court publicity. He was always of the opinion that two in management were better than one, if compatible, and in this case he and Peter had contrasting talents, which complemented each other. Almost every player that they took on to the staff, no matter the fee or how experienced they were, improved their standard of play considerably under Brian and Peter. If they did not, they were soon moved on.

Brian did not like to be on his own for long; he preferred company and he was almost always accompanied when out. Most of his close friends were not involved in football. Brian enjoyed eating out in restaurants in company and did not mind the public attention, but if someone was rude to him he could easily shut them up without causing a scene. He enjoyed squash, and he would find time for a game when at work if it was possible. Only on rare occasions did I know him to gamble, and that was a bet on football. He always seemed to have time for and affection for children and the elderly.

Away from football Peter and Brian spent little time together socially. Their private lives were very separate and they both enjoyed time with their families and were very attached to their pet dogs. I hardly ever met up with either of them away from football duties, but occasionally Peter would accompany me to a race meeting in an afternoon. I did not socialise with him in the evenings.

I always did and still do hold both Peter and Brian in high esteem. They brought into my life something that I could never have even dreamt about, and I thoroughly enjoyed every minute of it. The amount of knowledge that I gleaned from them both was immense. I took it all on board and it helped me greatly in my judgement of players. I learned how to deal with and spot talent, and how to analyse games and team performances. Any scouting and dealing with prospective recruits was carried out with the utmost secrecy between the three of us, as any publicity that revealed my involvement would have restricted my activities. More often than not I was completely on my own at matches, which suited me as I was then able to concentrate on the job in hand.

Fortunately for me, football did not interfere with the business I ran. I was able to cope with both occupations alongside each other as the jobs took place at different times of day. With the football I had only Brian and Peter to satisfy and I never feared being sacked: they were my only bosses. I was never put under any pressure from them, and their confidence helped me to achieve results. I cannot recall ever being reprimanded by either of them during our working association. I never refused to go anywhere I was asked, and never skimped a duty assigned to me.

In the many books that have been published about Brian and Peter, my name is mentioned as their chief scout in only a couple. This is probably because I was always able to operate without anyone connecting me with them. The national press reporters that knew who I was never quizzed me on the subject, knowing that they would be wasting their time.

Peter and Brian were ruthless at work. Any players, or non-playing and backroom members of staff, who were not up to the standard that they required, or anyone rocking the boat, were soon despatched. There was no room for passengers in the quest for footballing success.

# INTRODUCTION

# AN INSIGHT INTO
# TALENT DISCOVERY

E
ach club in the Football League uses a scouting system, the depth and intensity of which varies with each club. Mostly scouts are employed on a part-time basis, working from home, and have other full-time employment.

Premier League clubs have the whole of the British Isles covered. The area covered by each scout varies, usually depending on how many League grounds are in the vicinity of where their own homes are situated. The majority of scouts are ex-Football League players. Obviously the payments received for doing this work vary from club to club, with the larger clubs usually paying a monthly retainer plus travelling expenses. Many scouts operate on expenses only. An example of how the country might be split into scouting areas might be: the North West stretching from Manchester to Carlisle, the North East from Sheffield to Newcastle, the North Midlands stretching from the West to the East, the South Midlands down as far as Cheltenham, Wales as a whole, the Eastern Counties covering the North London area, the South Eastern counties with the rest of the London area, the South West from Bristol, one or possibly two in Scotland and the same in Ireland. Many clubs have one or two scouts in Europe; the larger and wealthier clubs have many more representatives and go further afield. Arsenal are having considerable success with recruiting through this avenue. Manchester United, I understand, currently have two full-time scouts operating in Brazil, and the 2008 acquisition of the twins Rafael and Fabio da Silva shows that this operation is proving well worthwhile. In most countries clubs are not allowed to sign boys as professionals until they are 18. This is the reason that more and more of these teenagers are creeping into our academies. The majority of these young lads are under the guidance of agents, but no transfer fees are payable to the clubs that they are attached to. This means that youngsters with great potential can be bought for much less money than similar teenagers in the British Isles.

In practically all cases scouts are instructed by a chief scout, employed at the parent club; although there are odd chief scouts who operate from their homes and are not full-time. In midweek some full-time coaches carry out scouting missions, and as expenses are cheaper for these visits, which use company transport, they are becoming more common.

Scouts are given instructions about which games to visit, and possibly the names of the players on which to make a special report. I personally prefer to keep an open mind about which players to pass judgement on. Nowadays, more than ever before, great emphasis is placed on scouts completing 'match reports', as one or both teams may be due to play the home club in the near future. To do a report on both teams efficiently is a difficult task, simply because of the amount of work and sketching and writing to be done, although you are provided with pitch diagrams and markings. Included in the report are sketches of the line up formation, details of the attacking and defending positions, whether the defensive marking is zonal or man-for-man is used, how dead-ball situations are handled, including corners, any weaknesses in line ups and individual performances by players. All this entails a tremendous amount of work and you are tied up for the whole of the 90 minutes, as well as having over three hours work to do later at home. Today laptops, fax machines and dictaphones are in general use and speed up the operation, which is often essential as some clubs expect to receive the report by 11am the next day.

Another difficulty today is that many clubs will only provide one ticket for each scout, so you cannot take along anyone to help you observe the match. There are now one or two private sporting agencies that provide match reports. I do not know how this compares, either cost-wise or in the standard of the information provided, with clubs instructing their own representatives. I was approached some years ago to join a private agency, but after looking into it I gave the excuse of my age to turn it down, although the money was good.

When assessing a player I ideally prefer to see him playing on three occasions, once on his home ground and twice away. You should have firmly made up your mind by then. Often, if you see that a player has some serious faults in his game, you are wasting your time returning after your first look. Today scouts use an A B C D code to grade players, A being the best and D the worst. If prior to going I know nothing about the lad, or his history, I refer to the *Sky Sports Football Yearbook*, or check the internet before I set out. The age of the player is also an important factor.

Premier League scouts visiting clubs to complete match reports are mostly specialists in this kind of work and they normally stick to it. They become very proficient and fully understand what their management are looking for, which varies from club to club. Brian Clough did not want a lot of this information: he used to remark, when it was suggested to him, 'Let the b******s worry about us, not us them'.

Nowadays there are fewer scouts than there used to be. The rise of agents and the close season for making signings are just two of the reasons. In the two lower divisions managers are restricted because of the costs involved. I am firmly convinced that the quality of players and the type of game played in the two lower divisions of the Football League has dropped markedly, and that the gap between each League has widened. It seems more difficult today for a player to step up to reach the higher grade very quickly. Nevertheless, in spring 2008 I was present at Shrewsbury for the England Under-19s versus the Dutch Under-19s. There were over 50 of us there on scouting missions, together with one or two managers, and for once I came away with a very good impression of the standard of the English lads. I feel sure that in only a few years time we will see several of these players emerging in top football to make their mark.

Premier League reserve-team matches now command a lot of attention from the lower Leagues. Players who cannot make the first-team squads and youngsters coming through are the targets, particularly early in the season. The loan system is now very popular both with the borrowing clubs and the parent clubs. The top club players are gaining vital playing experience while going out on loan and they are usually monitored at intervals to check their progress. Playing at a senior level certainly increases their maturity.

From my own experience I can tell you that you can cover thousands of miles without finding a player who catches your eye and is within your buying range. The luck in it is being there watching on the right day. Never let the fact that you have not recommended anyone for some time cloud your judgement; if you are in doubt, recommending a failure will soon rebound on you. When you are successful in bringing a player to your club and he blossoms, it is a wonderful feeling. Non-League professional clubs, such as those playing in the Blue Square, Ryman, and Unibond Leagues do get attention, but not on such a large scale. However, word rapidly spreads when any player under 23 years of age is showing good potential. Odd players from these leagues do arrive on the scene. Michael Kightly, in his early 20s, now at Wolverhampton Wanderers, having joined them from Grays United, is a fine example. Nigel Clough at Derby picked up three good recruits from non-League clubs in 2008–09. In the past when I had no special instructions I would go along to a fairly local game, as you never know who you might see. My special claim to fame was Garry Birtles, who I spotted and who we bought for £2,000. He was later sold for £1.25 million.

Good scouting comes with experience and knowledge of what is required. Most of those doing it are loaded with experience and have been doing it for a very long time. Over time you get to know them reasonably well. Managers and chief scouts change clubs fairly regularly and tend to take their trusted and seasoned scouts with them.

There are about 12 qualities that we scouts are looking for in a player. I do not recall ever having seen a player with them all. With the modern ball and the speed of the game played today the priorities have changed somewhat since I first started scouting. I look for his first touch when receiving the ball, from any direction, how quickly he gets the ball under control, his first-time passing and shooting (how accurate is he and how strong), his pace, the strength of his tackling, what he is like in the air, his reading of the game, whether he ball-watches, has he made himself ready to receive a pass...this is about half of what I am looking for in total. Attacking players and defenders obviously differ with their brain work. Goalkeepers for me preferably have to be tall, brave, have body strength, be quick off the mark, have a good pair of hands and ideally kick with both feet, which saves vital time. They need positional sense and to be fully awake at all times and vocally very active. I often see a lack of sound communication from the back: goalkeepers should remember that often that they are the only player facing the play. Nowadays kicking the ball a fair distance is not a problem, but when I was a player kicking against the wind on a very wet day was difficult and goalkeepers could hardly kick the ball out of their own penalty area. Full-backs would often take goal-kicks for the 'keeper.

Most professional players today have agents. Generally speaking I am of the opinion that this has not been good for the game as a whole. In 2008–09 payments to agents, in the Premier League alone, amounted to £12 million. When agents were first allowed in Brian Clough was totally against the use of them and would not deal with them. Dennis Roach was the first to persuade Brian otherwise, but my recollection is that the players he brought to him were never great buys. Agents come armed with tapes of the players that they represent, and it is obvious that any inadequacies the player may have will have been edited. I am fully aware that players come from different educational backgrounds, and that given the complexity of contracts and salaries representatives can be required to assist, but the rewards reaped by the agents seem over the top. I was recently surprised to learn that even some of the younger players in the Blue Square Leagues have their own agents.

A friend of mine has a son who has recently become old enough to sign as a professional. He had been with a Premier League club since the age of 12 and he has now signed a professional contract and is being allowed to go to university to continue his education. On the afternoon of his birthday he went with his parents to a meeting with the chairman of the club and he duly signed his professional forms. All, quite rightly, were extremely proud. That same evening, after they got home, an agent called at the house. I am not prepared to mention any names as no rules have been broken, and the agent, on signing him up, agreed not to take a percentage of his salary until it reaches a certain figure, but the question I have asked myself is how did the agent know that the lad was signing his contract that day?

We constantly hear and read that the number of British players competing in our professional Leagues is diminishing year by year. Why is this happening? It is certainly a well-paid job now. I have gathered some facts from the Burton upon Trent area, where I live. Every Saturday afternoon there used to be well over 60 teams competing as amateurs in the area, which extends to cover the Lichfield and Uttoxeter areas. Virtually no games now take place on that afternoon. The bulk of matches are played on Sundays, and many of the sides began as pub teams. I often watch matches near my home and, frankly, the physical condition of some of the players betrays their team's origins. Only about 40 teams now play locally, and the quality of football is certainly not up to the old standard. League club scouts were regular visitors in the old days, and most years one player went into League football to make a career for himself. Today this rarely happens.

Very close to my home is a large council-owned sports field where three games can be played at the same time. One pitch has excellent floodlighting available. The playing surface is kept in very good condition. Originally it was a lake, which was filled in as a tip by the council and with the ash waste from the local power station, then covered with soil and seeded. I have lived here for almost 10 years and have never seen a puddle of water on the surface. Recently a new block of changing facilities, toilets and showers was built on the very large car park at a cost of £250,000. Sadly, only one game takes place each Sunday, while on two or three nights each week training takes place under the lights. Surely local schools could take advantage of facilities such as these? One afternoon per week 12 to 16-year-olds could have inter-school competitive games. The youngsters would certainly enjoy it and it would give them the necessary break from their studies. Sporting facilities at most schools are diminishing each year.

One shining light has emerged in this area during recent years. The Burton Technical College allows teenagers one day a week off their studies for sporting activities. This was the brainchild of John Barton, the former Everton and Derby

County full-back, a lecturer at the college. Burton Albion have formed a youth team with these lads, and when Nigel Clough was the Burton Albion manager he actually coached them. One player, John Brayford, joined Burton Albion as a professional. He gained several caps playing for the non-League international team and drew the attention of League scouts. He was bought by Crewe Alexandra and became a regular in their first team. I had myself recommended him to League clubs. I am unaware of any similar arrangements with colleges anywhere else, but I would highly recommend it. The FA could attempt to promote such partnerships. John Barton has a job with the Football League Education and could advise them.

My own career as a scout is discussed later in the book, but my role as chief scout with Brian Clough and Peter Taylor was a different arrangement from most clubs. I had an advantage because for two years I was instructed by and received tuition from Peter, who was generally regarded as one of the best spotters of football talent that there has been in the game. I travelled with him to dozens of games and he pointed out the qualities that individual players possessed. At no time was I put under any pressure. The added bonus was that Brian Clough improved every player that was brought to him.

### Academies

There are 40 Academies of Football in this country at present, which are run completely separately from the senior part of their parent clubs. They take in boys from the age of eight to be coached in the skills of the game, with the aim that they will eventually be able to get a living from football. There are around 40 boys in each age group. Boys under the age of 13 must live within an hour's drive (around 35 miles) of the club, while for older boys the catchment area is extended. A contract is signed by the parents and the club and is reviewed every two years. I personally am not in favour of signing these agreements at such an early age, because of the restrictions imposed by the contracts. I understand that the boys are not allowed to compete in competitions for their own schools against other schools. I believe this is part of growing up, and nothing is more enjoyable at school than competing at sport against other schools with children of the same age, and being on the winning side.

Unfortunately, sports are disappearing from more and more school curriculums. Our home was in Repton for many years and the renowned Repton School was less than a mile away. This school has well above average sports facilities and many scholars from there have gained international sporting recognition. From football, household names such as Doug Ellis and Don Revie had their boys educated there. I often went along during the autumn to watch the school teams play, sitting on the wall overlooking the pitches. At one time Derby County had three of their young players attending the college, but they were not allowed to take part in competitive matches. Of course, the club were financing their education and entitled to make these stipulations. Incidentally, none of the three made the grade with the Derby County first XI.

The Aston Villa Academy has the most successful record for the number of boys that become professional. At the moment 33 per cent of graduates make it into the Football League, 9 per cent into the Premier League. Manchester City have the next best record, but all the rest have only averaged 1.5 per cent. However, Birmingham is the ideal catchment area as its concentration of population means that a greater number of lads are available to choose from. Only five or six boys each year graduate from the academies to the professional ranks.

Bryan Jones, the very successful head of the Academy at Aston Villa, originates from the Burton upon Trent area. As a teenager attending Burton Technical High School he received football coaching from Peter Taylor, who coached these school boys on two days of the week for a period of two hours. He had been recruited by the sports master at the school, who was a director of Burton Albion, Percy Davies. If any of the boys showed any real promise they were invited to play for the Burton Albion reserve side in the Burton and District Second Division. Bryan Jones joined Burton Albion after leaving school, playing as a striker. The youth team that Peter had assembled was very successful, winning every competition they were entered in, including the second division of the Burton league. At that time I trained with the Burton Albion players for my refereeing, and during this period I got to know Bryan very well. He must have taken on board much of Peter's coaching, just as I did.

# CHAPTER 1
# MY EARLY DAYS IN FOOTBALL

I was born in Burton upon Trent on 1 February 1927. My father was a carpenter, my mother a cinema projectionist. I was their second child; my older brother had died aged one of scarlet fever, a disease which in those days took many lives.

After Infants and Junior school I took the 11-plus and qualified to go to the Guild Street Central School. The sportsmaster there taught rugby, cricket, athletics and swimming. There was no soccer, which I and my pals loved, so we played on the recreation grounds in every spare moment. Boots were the only kit. We had coats for goalposts. In the summer we played cricket and swam: a highlight of the autumn was the Swimming Championships held at the Burton baths. When the baths were demolished after the war my 25 and 50yd sprint records still stood.

When war broke out our school was taken over by a Royal Artillery regiment and we shared premises with another school. I went to voluntary Saturday morning classes to learn shorthand and typing. I left school after Christmas, shortly before my 15th birthday in 1942, and started work in the cask office at the Ind Coope brewery offices, earning 17s 6d for a 48-hour week.

Our home at that time was a rented three-bedroom terraced house, owned by the tenants of the Star in the Victoria Ward in Burton. When our landlords retired my parents took on the tenancy of the pub and we moved in 1938. During the war beer was rationed and the pub could only open for three days each week. My father went back to his trade, working as a carpenter fitting cabs to army steel lorries at a nearby factory. This was a reserved occupation. In his absence I had to help my mother in the pub, looking after the beer cellar, tapping the barrels and connecting the pipes. When I was older I would serve behind the bar, playing darts with customers in quiet moments.

As a teenager I cycled a lot with my friends, going away for weekends and holidays to stay in youth hostels. Petrol was rationed so the roads were quiet.

Army call-ups meant that there were lots of local vacancies and so I changed my job, becoming a secretary at the local Gas Works offices. The wages were £2 per week for 48 hours.

As soon as I was old enough I volunteered to join the Royal Navy. On 1 September 1944, aged 17 and seven months, I began training at HMS *Royal Arthur*, the ex-Butlin's holiday camp at Skegness. On completion of the initial training I was posted to the Naval Barracks at Plymouth, then almost immediately sent to Belfast as part of the commissioning crew for a new Light Fleet Aircraft Carrier, HMS *Glory*. We soon went on to the ship and sailed to the Clyde to do our sea-going trials. Then the war in Europe ended and for two days we were allowed to go into Glasgow to celebrate.

We sailed to Malta to pick up our two Fleet Air Arm Squadrons to do landing and take-off trials. When these were satisfactorily completed we set sail, calling at Alexandria then through the Suez Canal to Trincomalee.

When my Chief Petty Officer was demobbed there was literally no one else but me to be the senior rating in the Captain's Office. I had to be upgraded to a Petty Officer. I was only 18, but there was nothing in the King's Regulations to prevent the appointment and I was promoted for a three-month period.

We were taking on supplies in Trincomalee Harbour in Ceylon (now called Sri Lanka) when it was announced that the war with Japan was over. We soon sailed to join the Pacific Fleet. Our first mission was to inspect the area close to Hiroshima, where we witnessed utter devastation. We were then ordered to Sydney, Australia, to undergo a major refitting to become a Troop Carrier. Over 1,000 double-decker bunks were installed in the hangers in no time at all and we sailed to collect ex-prisoners of war from the Malaysian Islands, all Australians and New Zealanders, taking them home firstly to Australia and then to Wellington. We immediately returned to the Malaysian Islands to collect British ex-prisoners of war for the long journey right across the Pacific Ocean via Hawaii to Vancouver, as the first part of their journey back home. I became extremely fit during this period playing deck hockey. The flight deck was completely empty and the pitch was situated between the two hangar lifts. The puck was made out of a circle of rope, the ends sewn together to form a circle, then soaked in tar and allowed to dry completely. We used primitive hockey sticks. The game was played at a very combative speed on the shiny steel deck, and the sea was calm for most of the journey. A knock-out cup was organised between the teams from the different messes, and the passengers who were physically able to get up on to the flight deck thoroughly enjoyed watching the games being played.

Our ship was later given to the Australian Navy as they had no aircraft carriers. Most of the crew were offered the chance to stay with the ship and transfer to the Australian Navy, but I could not wait to get back home to be demobbed. I was left behind with many others at Singapore Barracks to wait for a ship to take me back to Plymouth. I was there for about a month with no duties, so to pass the time I joined the Royal Naval Football Squad. Frank Scrine, the Wales winger, was in charge. He was capped three times for Wales when he got home. I played soccer on three occasions against other servicemen stationed out there, and this was when I first got a real liking for the game. I was eventually demobbed during the summer of 1947. Amazingly, according to the statistics on my release papers I had grown from a recorded 5ft 5in to 5ft 11½in, and my weight had increased from 10st 3lb to 12st.

My introduction to competitive football at adult level back home was during the 1947–48 season in the Burton & District Association League Second Division playing at right-half for the Municipal Officers Guild (MOG). We finished in fourth place the first season, but eight places lower the next year. After that I joined

Stapenhill FC with some of my close pals, and we duly won our league. I played at right-back for them.

I was invited to join Burton Albion as an amateur at the beginning of the 1951–52 season. The team had been formed the previous season, playing in the Birmingham Senior League. Billy Wrigglesworth (ex-Manchester United winger) was the manager and Bertie Mee was the trainer. He had played for Tutbury Hawthorn as an outside-left in the Burton and District League and I had played against him. He had apparently recommended that the Albion sign me to play at full-back. The ground was in Wellington Street adjoining Lloyds Foundry and the dressing rooms were 100 yards away in the men's shower room in the foundry. For the first time Burton Albion had entered a reserve team in the Burton & District League Division One. We won the league by 16 clear points, unbeaten throughout. I was ever present.

Bertie Mee, who would go on to manage Arsenal to an historic League and Cup double in 1970–71, was an important influence on me. Bertie lived in Tutbury on the outskirts of Burton upon Trent. As a player he had been at Derby County as an outside-left, but he had not made the grade. He went to the Etwall Rehabilitation Centre near Derby to study physiotherapy, a discipline which was in its infancy, and he joined Burton Albion to gain practical knowledge of football injuries. It was a stroke of good fortune for me to be under an experienced former professional footballer, and Bertie was brilliant with me. He altered my style of running, shortening my early strides, which put two or three yards on to my sprinting speed. As a result my game improved considerably. He also recommended that I take one cod liver oil capsule every day, which I have done ever since.

There had been a change of manager at Burton Albion and Bill Sneddon was in charge. I was offered professional forms playing part-time, but I refused. I had gained three Amateur caps playing for Staffordshire and took part in the North versus South trial game for the International team, which we won 3–0. I was hoping that I would be selected for the England Amateur XI squad for the forthcoming international, but 90 per cent of the squad was selected from the south to save travelling costs, as the game was being played in southern England. This influenced my decision to take up the offer from Burton Albion to turn professional, playing in the Birmingham Senior League. When I made my debut in the first team I was the only member of the side not to have experience with a Football League club.

At the end of the 1953–54 season I had an approach from Chesterfield Football Club offering me a full-time weekly contract of eight guineas in the first team, six guineas in the reserves and six guineas summer wages. My salary for the Gas Board was £60 per month, while football with Burton Albion earned me £5 a match, plus £2 for a win and £1 for a draw in the first team, £3 in the reserves, and £8–10 was brought in from a Sunday newspaper agency, bringing in over £30 per week. I turned the offer down.

One game stands out in my memory, an FA Cup tie at Bedworth in an early round. I was not in the selected XI, but at away games a reserve forward and a defender travelled in case they were required. On this occasion I was the reserve defender. Burton had its own motor bus for travelling, a 19-seater Bedford. Arriving at Bedworth I left my kit on the bus, not expecting to need it. With all of us crammed into a small dressing room, myself and the other reserve decided to go out to get some air. I was a superstitious player. Before a game I would not have anything to eat, and I always went to the toilet before putting my playing gear on. Having not eaten since breakfast time, and given that it was a cold autumn afternoon, I went to the burger stall and purchased a large beefburger with onions and mustard and tucked in. At about 20 minutes to three there came an announcement over the loudspeaker: 'Would Maurice Edwards report to the Burton Albion dressing room immediately'. I shot off to the dressing room. Reg Weston, the player-manager, said 'Get stripped, you're playing'. Apparently the club captain, 'Nobby' Hadfield, had a spasm in his lower back and could not move. There followed a panic call for the coach driver, Jock Middlemas, who was sent to get my bag. I got my kit on and dashed onto the pitch. The teams were lined up for the kick-off and there were over 3,000 spectators in the ground. My superstitions about eating went out of the window as I was pleased with my performance.

We were one up after about 20 minutes, Ray Russell scoring the goal. Shortly before half-time Jack Stamps, our centre-forward, suffered a broken leg when tackled. No substitutes were allowed then so we were left with 10 men. It was pouring with rain and the pitch was a quagmire. We had our backs to the wall. About five minutes before full-time, Bill Townsend, our goalkeeper, went to the edge of the penalty area to collect the ball and slipped in the mud. I covered behind on the goalline as the Bedworth forward with the ball advanced. 'If it goes past me I'll dive and save with my hands,' I decided, 'even if it gives a penalty away'. However, he shot wide of the post and we won 1–0. We did not get back to Burton until after 8pm, as we were waiting at the hospital for Jack to come out, complete with his plaster.

As a player you remember the good games, but you remember the stinkers as well. I was playing at Kidderminster in a Birmingham League game. It was a night match under floodlights at the beginning of February. There was a large crowd and it was very cold. The pitch was frozen but flat and my boots were fitted with leather studs. I weighed about 12 stone at the time and the conditions meant that I was having great difficulty turning and moving off from a standstill, and I could not make any sliding tackles. The outside-left against me was a 17-year-old Gerry Hitchens, weighing barely 10 stone and wearing gym shoes. We lost 1–3 and Gerry scored all three goals. Within a few days he had become a Football League player, later signing for Aston Villa and gaining seven international caps.

At work I was transferred from the East Midlands to the North Thames Gas Board to their training college at Fulham. On four nights a week I was attending evening classes at Westminster Technical College and Battersea Polytechnic, studying to become a Gas Engineer (Distribution). During this period I finished tuition on Friday afternoon and had Saturdays off, which allowed me to travel home to Burton for Saturday games. There were a few evening games in the spring and as we did not have floodlights it had to be an early kick-off, so I took a day's holiday leave to play.

During March 1955, while still working in London, I was approached by Guildford with a view to joining them. They were then top of the Southern League. It was left that I would go to see them before the start of the next season to discuss the offer. Unfortunately my career came to an end through injury before then.

In 1955 my reasonably short career came to an end in a Staffordshire County Senior Cup game against Hednesford United. We were winning 4–1. Towards the end of the game I was well forward with the ball and fancied my chance to score. Having never done so before, I decided to go and have a pop. While standing on my left leg preparing to shoot I was tackled from behind and was carried off with severe pain in my left knee. Next morning I was still in considerable pain and needed to go to the Burton Hospital for an examination by an orthopaedic surgeon. An X-ray revealed I needed surgery as the cruciate ligaments in the knee were damaged. In those days the injury was not repairable, unlike today, although a lengthy period of rehabilitation is still necessary. After my operation there was no stability in my knee joint and the surgeon informed me that my playing career was over. He warned me that if I was to damage that left knee again, it might result in it being stiffened for the rest of my life. Fortunately this has not occurred. At the time the muscles in my left leg were very wasted and I had to work extremely hard to build them up. It was a hard slog, involving weights and hours of jogging.

It was 19 weeks before I was able to return to my employment with the North Thames Gas Board at their college in Fulham and the evening classes at the two colleges. After successful completion of my studies I was transferred to the Camden Town District Office and given my own district to run. I changed my digs to a house at nearby Chalk Farm where were four other guests, all much older than myself. One was the Revd Foyle, brother of the famous book shop owner, while the others were all solicitors working in the City. My evenings were mostly spent jogging round Regent's Park on the running track.

My knee was causing me considerable concern and the muscles in my left leg were taking a long time to regain strength. I had developed a limp. One evening as I was going to White Hart Lane to see Spurs play I passed the Middlesex Rehabilitation Centre and Bertie Mee sprung to mind: I was sure that he had taken up an appointment there after qualifying at Etwall. I decided next day to see if I could trace him, as it was not very far from my digs. I located him and found the centre full of athletes, tennis players and rugby and football stars, all working on different types of apparatus. Once again I was deeply indebted to him, as under his guidance I spent many months on a rehabilitation programme involving weights and running. The muscles built up very well and I eventually lost my limp. Bertie's attention and advice were extremely helpful. My progress was so good that I wanted to play football again. I went as far as playing one game for Burton Albion reserves. By then they had moved to their new ground at Eton Park, and this was my only playing appearance there. Next morning my knee was very sore and swollen so I decided that this was really it for football. The same happened with golf: I paid for lessons to teach me to play left-handed to reduce the impact of the swivel action on my left knee, but I was unable to master it and had to give up.

Soon after this Bertie Mee was appointed physiotherapist at Highbury. He had been treating Arsenal players for their injuries for some time and they eventually decided to have their own physio. This turned out to be a wonderful move for both parties. In 1966 Bertie was appointed manager of Arsenal and he had 11 rewarding years in the job, becoming the first manager to land the League and Cup double in the same season, 1970–71. He was ably helped and supported by his non-playing staff.

While working in London I was able to go to Wembley to see the 1956 FA Cup Final, between Manchester City and Birmingham City. I will never forget the match, which ended in victory for Manchester. The outstanding player was Don Revie in midfield. He was fully in control from start to finish, and for many years after it was known as the Don Revie Final. After the game it was revealed that Bert Trautmann, in goal for Manchester City, had played almost the whole match with a broken neck.

The Burton Albion board of directors were very good to me when it became clear that I would not be able to play again. I was offered a Benefit Match, to be played at Eton Park, or the receipts from the Saturday night dance at the Town Hall that they had been allocated once a month (a sell-out virtually every time). As I was living most of the week in London, and it had been over 12 months since I last played for the Albion's first team, I opted for the night hop at the local Town Hall. It proved a great success and I received over £500 from the club, which was a tremendous amount of money in those days.

I was finding working in London arduous and lonely. Travelling home each weekend was stretching the finances considerably, although I held a good position at work and was quite happy with my job with the North Thames Gas Board. However, chances of further promotion seemed remote due to my age (I was the youngest in charge of a district in the office) and unlikely to happen in the foreseeable future. I decided to look for something near Burton upon Trent and I thought about running my own business. At that particular time it was difficult to borrow money for such a venture, and it came to my attention that a sub-Post Office in a good position in Burton had been for sale for some time without finding a buyer. I made enquiries and put in an offer for the premises, which was quickly accepted. With the help of a gift from my parents, the sale of my almost brand-new car that I had paid cash for and pension money from a plan I had been paying into for over 12 years, I was able to raise the necessary capital.

I handed in my one-month notice to the Gas Board and was summoned to headquarters to explain to the top Gas Engineer why I wanted to leave. He told me how much the board had spent on my education and training since I had been in London, and said that I had a bright future if I remained. I did not waver, however, and stood by my decision. He then amazed me by telling me that he would keep my job open for three months in case things did not work out.

My application for the sub-postmaster vacancy was accepted by the Post Office and I took over in September 1957. Having had only two days training at the work in a very busy office, I would have struggled badly had it not been for the existing staff. There was one very experienced part-time lady and a 17-year-old who had been there since leaving school. Both were very efficient and helped me to settle in quickly.

At the beginning of the 1958–59 football season, I was persuaded by a member of Burton & District Football Association to become a referee in the local leagues. I began as a Class 3 referee and progressed to become a Class 1 official in the minimum period possible. In my first season I was promoted to officiate in a semi-professional footballers' league, which was classed as a feeder league for referees to advance into the Football League. I honestly thought that I was a better referee than a player and I thoroughly enjoyed myself. Obviously the experience I had gained as a player was a big help. John Westmancoat, who at that time was the secretary of the Birmingham Football Association, privately told me that I had been recommended to go on to the Referees List of the Football League for the forthcoming season. I kept my fingers crossed. Unfortunately, the authorities reduced the age limit for qualification by 12 months, which meant that I would be six months too old. This was a huge disappointment, but I enjoyed refereeing so much that I decided to continue at the same level.

Shortly after the beginning of the new season I was appointed the main official for a second-round FA Cup tie between two non-League sides, which went very well. When I had begun refereeing I had obtained permission to train with the Burton Albion lads at Eton Park, taking part in the six-a-side practices and refereeing all their friendly matches.

My business venture was proving very successful and I needed more shop space. I purchased the wool shop next door and had the two premises joined together under one roof. The work was carried out by the late Sir Stan Clarke, a plumber, who had recently started up on his own in the building trade. He gave me a good price to do the work as he wanted a showpiece in the town. I also purchased a nearby newsagent, closed it and moved the trade into my premises. This was a sound move and I soon had to increase the staff to four full-time and four part-time assistants, plus 14 paperboys and girls. I was still managing without my own car, being determined not to have one until I could pay for it in full and have the one I wanted. After six years I bought a Jaguar Mark 2 for £1,500. The number plate was HFA 777.

# CHAPTER 2
# MEETING PETER AND BRIAN

None of us are aware of what lies around the corner, and I never imagined how my life was about to change. In July 1962, Peter Taylor joined Burton Albion from Port Vale as a goalkeeper to replace Bill Townsend (ex-Derby County) in the Southern League side. Bill was the manager and had decided to retire from playing. Peter moved into a council house in Winshill with his wife Lilian and two young children, daughter Wendy and son Philip. On training nights I got to know Peter quite well. He was a great talker and very interesting to listen to. Our conversations were usually about football and horse racing, and I quickly realised that he liked to gamble. We became friends, probably because we were of similar age while most of the others were much younger.

I only saw Peter make one appearance for the Albion. I remember that he threw the ball much farther than he could kick it and that he was a very nervy goalkeeper, who disliked having defenders in the box with him when the team was under pressure. He wanted plenty of space. He was 6ft 2in and 13 stone, but not the bravest of 'keepers. At the end of the season Bill Townsend, who had acquired a very good public house in a village on the outskirts of Burton, was given six weeks' notice by the chairman, Trevor Grantham. Peter was then offered the position of manager, which he accepted. It was an ambition of his to become a manager in the Football League. At 35 years of age, the chance to get into management had come rather earlier than he expected. He stopped playing himself when he took up the appointment.

At the start of the 1963–64 season several new faces attended training sessions. It was obvious that Peter's intention was to quickly build a side of his own, and to that end he had raided local clubs: Matlock Town, Loughborough Brush, Kidderminster and Hinckley United. Richie Barker, a professional draughtsman with an electrical engineering firm in Loughborough, who had previously been with the Albion as a striker with a very good scoring rate, came from Matlock Town, Les Green came from Nuneaton Borough for a fee of £750, and there were several others. George Pycroft, Peter's friend from school and youth days in Nottingham, was his scout. I could remember him playing for Peterborough (non-League) and Loughborough Brush, and he knew the players of good ability at that level. He was a big help to Peter in signing these new recruits. Another friend of Peter's from Nottingham, Brian Newton, played the odd first-team game and looked after the reserve team while also helping with the coaching.

Peter suffered an early setback, losing 1–0 in the second round of the FA Cup to Kidderminster, who were playing in the Birmingham League, a grade below the Southern League. One or two members of the board were calling for his blood. Peter was genuinely worried and a meeting was called by the chairman at his house for the Sunday afternoon. However, he was granted a stay of execution.

Peter, with the security of his three-year contract, purchased a newly-built Canadian-style bungalow by the side of the lake at the Newton Park Hotel in Newton Solney, between Repton and Burton. By this time I had got to know him quite well.

My extensive building alterations to the Post Office and private living quarters were now completed, and I had my own transport. After Easter, as the football season was coming to a close and with the annual drop in the amount of pools business, I was able to spend afternoons at flat race meetings, when they were within reasonable travelling distance. Peter would come along with me as often as he could. He was not a well-known figure in those days and he enjoyed his racing.

A sensible punter, prepared to wait until he really 'fancied one', he was a much heavier gambler on football results. He used his knowledge of the game to good effect. At the races I introduced him to a bookmaker course layer, who agreed with Peter that he would accept his football investments passed through me, which meant that Betting Tax was not deducted from his winnings.

In his contract with Burton Albion, Peter, with great foresight, had negotiated that the club would pay him a crowd bonus of one shilling for every paying spectator through the turnstiles over 2,300. Peter told me that this would be his available betting money. It was paid fortnightly by cheque and he asked me if I would kindly change it each other Friday for cash. The exact amounts were only known between the two of us. Usually there was just one home game gate included, but as his rebuilt side achieved success gates increased considerably, and were soon regularly over the 3,000 mark, bringing quite lucrative rewards.

I refereed all the friendly matches and practice games at the club. My instructions were to referee the games exactly as if they were normal matches, with full authority. I would have done that anyway. It was at around this time that I was first introduced to David Pleat, a fresh-faced teenager who used to come over to see Peter from Nottingham. He was a player with Forest at the time, but he had suffered a badly broken leg and was convalescing. They had both belonged to the same cricket club in Nottingham. I sat in the stand with David and he seemed, even at that early age, to have a great knowledge of the game. Much later Peter was instrumental in getting David his first taste of football management, recommending him to Nuneaton Borough in 1978. David has been highly successful and to this day he is extremely active. I still bump into him occasionally and we usually have a short, sensible chat about the game in hand. His knowledge and experience are widely used by the television companies and he is currently an advisor to Nottingham Forest.

In spring 1964, there was an exceptionally long spell of very low temperatures, with severe frosts each night. In those days before under-soil heating was popular, very little football was being played. The skies were cloudless, with full sunshine throughout the day, but by about 5pm the temperature fell. Malcolm Allison's Bath City were playing in the Southern League at the time and were due to play at Eton

Park one Saturday. When I arrived for my training session on the Thursday evening, Peter Taylor took me out on to the pitch to ask my opinion of the chance of the game being played on the Saturday, the forecast for the weather being for little change. Peter had a completely injury-free squad, and all the players were raring to go. The playing surface was flat, with no lumps or ruts to cause any problems, but very hard. Peter and I decided to meet the groundsman, Tom Eckleshaw, at 2pm on the Friday, which was when the referee would carry out his inspection on the match day and decide whether the game could go ahead. We walked all over the playing area. The overnight frost had gone, apart from a stretch of about two yards on the Popular side. This was because the sun was only just coming to shine on that part, where the corrugated roof over the supporters' space shaded the turf. We decided to cover this area. A local farmer was contacted and he brought down 10 bales of hay and many tarpaulin sheets. The area was completely covered with the hay and the tarpaulin placed on top, while the surplus was put on the penalty areas. Fortunately there was very little wind to disturb the cover. The two local radio stations were told to announce that the game would definitely take place.

At 9am on Saturday morning Peter, myself and the groundsman arrived and, with the help of several supporters, the covers were removed in the full sunshine. There was no sign of frost from under the covers: the hay had done the trick. The frost on the rest of the pitch was already beginning to disappear. At 10am Bath City were told to travel, and the radio stations were instructed to confirm that the game was on. At 1pm the referee arrived, changed into his football boots, did a few sprints and abrupt stops, then came over smiling, saying that he was satisfied. He congratulated the groundsman on the state of the playing surface. Tony Book, one of the Bath City players, also congratulated the groundsman. There was no other professional football played that day within a radius of 30 miles. The gate was over 4,000, and Burton won 3–1. Bath City were top of the Southern League at that time so Peter was over the moon.

That same season Burton went on to win the Southern League Cup against Weymouth. They were managed by Frank O'Farrell, who later became the manager of Manchester United. The home leg of the final was played before a record crowd of 5,806, an Eton Park record which stood until the ground's closure.

**Peter and Brian join Hartlepools United**

During October 1965, Peter came to see me to say excitedly that Brian Clough (Peter's big chum from his playing days at Middlesbrough) had called him to say that he had been offered the position of manager at Hartlepools United. Peter was meeting Brian the following day to discuss forming a partnership to manage the club.

The purpose of Peter's visit was to discuss the implications of taking the offer up. It would mean a cut in his weekly income of £24 a week, as he would lose for the money from coaching at the Burton Technical School and his crowd bonuses. My advice was that he should talk it over with his family, but I pointed out that he had recently signed a new three-year contract and that he had a beautiful bungalow. His playing side were doing exceptionally well, and I considered it only a matter of time before he was contacted himself about a manager's position in the Football League. Hartlepools United were struggling at the bottom of the Fourth Division and had applied for re-election again the previous season. None of this deterred Peter, who said that it was his great ambition to get into League football. He thought that a partnership between himself and Brian could not fail. I was well aware of the strong bond between them that had been forged in their Middlesbrough days.

Brian had remained on the coaching staff at Sunderland after his injury, coaching the youth team. Sunderland were managed by George Hardwick. When he was sacked Ian McColl was his replacement, and Brian also soon lost his job and so was out of work for a time.

The meeting between Peter and Brian, and their wives, was to be at a hotel near York Racecourse. Len Shackleton, the Sunderland and England inside-forward who later worked for the *Sunday People*, had recommended them to the Hartlepools chairman, remembering their days together in the North East.

They met as arranged and decided to give it a go, taking over on 29 October 1965. The chairman, Ernest Ord, would not allow Brian, who was only 30 years of age, to bring Peter in as his assistant manager, saying that the club could not afford it and there was not enough work for two of them. Instead, 'Trainer' was the title given to Peter to justify his existence to the club.

Brian and Peter got off to a good start at Hartlepools with three straight wins. At the end of the first season they finished seventh from the bottom of the Fourth Division. For the first time in recent years they did not have to apply for re-election, so considerable improvement had been achieved. During the season Peter rang me on several occasions just to keep me up to date. He said that several players had to go, as they were nowhere near good enough, and that Brian had passed his driving test so he could drive the team coach, to save on costs. I told Peter how Burton Albion were getting on, and he asked how my luck was with the horses. Peter, of course, could not afford to strike any bets.

One morning, shortly before the commencement of the 1966–67 season, Peter rang to ask whether I was still training with Burton Albion at Eton Park. I told him that I was. He then asked me to approach Les Green (Burton Albion's goalkeeper) on the quiet to ask whether he would play at Hartlepools if Brian made an offer for him. Peter had originally brought Les to Burton from Nuneaton. As luck would have it, I was due to referee the final warm-up game before the season's start at Eton Park on the Saturday. I decided that I would ask Les then. There were over a thousand spectators at the game. I waited until the ball went behind the net for a goal-kick, then followed Les and delivered my message. 'Peter rang yesterday to ask if you would play for him at Hartlepools if they made an offer to Burton for you,' I said. Without hesitation he said yes and after the game he came into the referees' room to bring me his home telephone number, which I passed on to Peter the same evening. A few days later he was transferred to Hartlepools United for an undisclosed fee. This was the first recruit that I helped them with.

**Peter introduces me to Brian Clough**

One Monday morning early in the 1966–67 season Peter rang for a chat. 'While you are out refereeing you must come across a player or two that would be good enough for our League,' he said. 'We're short of numbers, having sent one or two packing, but there's very little money available'. At the time I was officiating in quite a good standard of non-League semi-professional football.

'What a pity you didn't ring me last week,' I said. 'Do you remember Tony Parry, a young local lad that you signed on professional forms when you were at the Albion? He's from Burton, slight build, has pace, good control, he's 21 now and has come on a ton. He's as good a lad as I have seen and his skill on the ball is amazing. He's not a bit frightened in the tackle and has two good feet, both in the gym and out on the grass. I still play in the six-a-side training sessions and he is exceptional and has got into the Albion's first XI recently.

'I've told you about Bertie Mee, and how good he was with me. Well, I owed him a big favour so I wrote to him about this boy Tony Parry and said that Arsenal might like to take a look. Bertie has written back to me to say that if the Arsenal like the boy, they'll be only too pleased to sign him. He included George Swindon's (chief scout at Arsenal) telephone number in the letter and asked me to contact him, so I've to meet him at Burton Railway Station at 2pm next Saturday, to take him to Eton Park.'

Peter then asked 'How highly do you rate him?'

'He's the best inside-forward for a youngster that I have seen,' was my reply.

'What a coincidence,' said Peter. 'Here at Hartlepools we've taken on a 16-year-old who has huge potential, John McGovern. He took part in one of our recent Saturday morning trials for youngsters. A Grammar School boy, Brian was told by his headmaster that he was reluctant to agree to him going into football as a career, as he thought he could get A-levels and go to university.'

I wonder now whether that headmaster was still alive to see John lift two European Cups – not many people have that achievement on their CV.

The following Thursday morning, shortly after 11 o'clock, I was behind the counter in the Post Office with customers queuing in each position. It was the busiest day of the week. I looked up to serve the next customer, and in front of me was Peter Taylor. 'Can you spare a few moments? I have someone I would like you to meet'. I called for an assistant from the shop to come and take my place behind the counter.

A very smart young man in a blue blazer and grey flannels stood with Peter. 'Meet Brian Clough,' said Peter. Brian shook my hand warmly. 'Peter has spoken very highly of you, pleased to meet you,' he said.

'What brings you here?' I enquired. They said that they had come to see Alex Tait, the Burton Albion player-manager (a former Newcastle United player), who had a shop nearby. I gave them directions. 'It's just around the corner, across the road. It's a large pram and toy shop, you can't miss it. He should be there.'

The penny had not dropped as to why they were there. At about 2pm they came back to the Post Office and Peter said 'We've come to say cheerio, we're off. We've got Tony Parry in the car with us.' Away they went.

This was my first real experience of the speed at which they operated when bringing in new players. I was left with the task of ringing George Swindon, to save him the journey, and writing to Bertie Mee. I had a reply from Bertie thanking me and saying that they would have Tony watched playing for Hartlepools. He asked me to give him a call if a similar youngster turned up.

Tony and John McGovern soon appeared in the first team at Hartlepools, and I was invited up to the North East to see them play in an evening fixture at the Victoria Ground. I drove up during the afternoon, returning home the same evening. It poured with rain the whole time. I sat in the famous directors' box, with a bucket next to me catching the water dripping from the corrugated roof above. What I witnessed that night has always stuck in my mind: the sight of Peter in a tracksuit running on to the field with a bucket of water and a sponge. When I asked him what he would have done if there had been a serious injury to a player, he smiled and told me that they had made a donation to the St John's Ambulance Service, who had two of their men standing by.

In addition to the transfer fee of £2,000 that was agreed for Tony Parry, there was also a visit, in November, of the full Hartlepools first team to play a Burton Albion side at Eton Park. When they came down Les Green, Tony Parry and John McGovern were on view, plus a surprise: Brian Clough turned out as well. Having suffered no ill-effects from this match, Brian agreed to play for the Albion in another friendly game, against Port Vale two weeks later. I refereed both games. Opposite Brian as guest players for Port Vale were the legendary Sir Stanley Matthews CBE, MBE, aged 51, their general manager, and player-manager Jackie Mudie. Again it poured with rain the whole evening. I can remember how Sir Stanley shielded the ball, his close control making it impossible to take it away from him without fouling him, and how the other Port Vale players called 'Sir Stan' when they wanted to attract his attention. I did not have the opportunity to speak to Brian after the game; he was substituted for the second half because of the long drive home to Middlesbrough. Considering the atrocious weather, an excellent gate of 1,390 turned out to watch the stars in action.

Tony Parry passed away in November 2009 at the early age of 64 after a short illness, bringing back memories of him being the very first player who I recommended to a Football League club. He had later regularly attended Pride Park as an ex-player guest of Derby County and we had many chats together.

Peter told me that they were having problems with the chairman at Hartlepools, who had brought his son into the backroom staff and said that for economic reasons he wanted Brian to sack Peter. Shortly after this one of the directors, local councillor John Curry, who was a staunch supporter of Brian and Peter, persuaded the rest of the board to oust Ernest Ord as chairman.

At the end of the season Peter and Brian resigned from Hartlepools and moved on to a Division Two club. Angus McLean, the new manager, was to reap the rewards of the work that Brian and Peter had put into building the team by gaining promotion to Division Three the following season.

After the pools business had stopped for the summer season I had more leisure time to go flat racing. I made a good friend during one strange meeting on the Doncaster races car park, where I parked my Jaguar next to an almost identical one. The owner was in his 50s and had an insurance brokers business, with several of his clients being connected with horse racing. He was a large, well-built man, about 5ft 10in tall but about 16½ stone. As it turned out that we often drove the same route I offered to take him to future race meetings, picking him up from where our journeys met. We attended almost all of the midweek meetings during the summer.

One of my friend's clients was Lester Piggott. Before a race meeting at Newmarket we would usually go to Lester's home to deliver some freshly caught salmon from the River Severn, which was one of the foods that he could eat without having any weight worries. My friend usually had a coffee but I always stayed in the car. There were always stories about how careful Lester was with his money, and one tale has stuck in my memory. One morning Lester rang my friend to ask if he was travelling to Newmarket that day. 'Yes', came the reply. 'And I've got two beautiful salmon for you, seven pounds each.' Silence from Lester. Realising why, my friend said, 'Seven pounds in weight, that is.' Lester immediately replied, obviously relieved, 'They should be very nice, see you just now.'

This friendship lasted for over 12 years, until unfortunately my friend became ill and unable to drive, passing away shortly afterwards. The racing information that I gathered I used to pass on to Peter Taylor after he came to Derby. I may add that it did us both good financially during this period.

# CHAPTER 3
# LIFE BEGINS AT DERBY COUNTY

During the summer, one Sunday evening, I had a phone call from Peter. This was not unusual, but I did not expect to be told that Peter and Brian had accepted the Derby County job, Brian as the new manager and Peter as assistant manager. I knew that Tim Ward had not been offered a new contract, and that for some time it had been rumoured in the press that the Derby directors were not satisfied with the results, having finished 17th in Division Two. It had not crossed my mind, however, that Brian and Peter would be considered for running the club. The appointment was to begin on 1 June 1967.

Hartlepools United had finished eighth from the top of Division Four at the end of the previous season. Brian and Peter had made many changes to the playing staff, vastly improved performances and attendances were very encouraging. However, without contracts they were completely free to go.

Peter said 'As soon as we are settled in, I will be over to see you.' He came over after they had been at Derby a few days and explained to me how the move had come about. Len Shackleton had again been the one to do the recommending, suggesting

Brian and Peter as candidates to the Derby chairman, Mr Sam Longson. After only a very short meeting with Mr Longson and his directors the pair were duly appointed, with a promise of £70,000 available as transfer funds. Peter had apparently had to persuade Brian to take the job, as he was reluctant to leave the North East. Peter was keen to return to the Midlands to be among his family and friends, and fortunately for him the lure of a big club like Derby County was enough to convince Brian. They both moved into nice houses with their families, Brian at Ferrers Way, Darley Abbey, and Peter at Findern.

Peter went on to tell me that they would like me to become more involved. They wanted me to referee all the friendlies, practice games behind closed doors and pre-season games. It was their intention to commence Sunday morning trials at Sinfin training ground, and I was to officiate at those as well. Peter would be recruiting his own scouting staff to operate over the whole of the country. He had several contacts in mind, but was also keen for me to join the scouting staff. Any player I spotted that was above average I would bring along to a Sunday morning session. Peter's pal George Pycroft had been appointed chief scout and I had met him during the Burton Albion days.

Once the season got under way, the number of Sunday morning trialists increased week by week. Half-hour sessions started at 11 o'clock, usually finishing at about one. Lads arrived from all over the country, the general standard was good, and soon the sessions were stretching into the afternoon. Some lads were only on the pitch for a short time, while others stayed longer, some occasionally playing for two sessions, depending on what Peter saw in them. He was helped to assess the talent on view by two of the coaching staff and the local scouts. Brian often turned up during these trials with his two boys and their pet dog, and spent time talking to parents and trialists, but it was not his scene and he did not stay long. Some boys were invited back to be looked at again, while odd ones were signed to play for the club on the day. Jim Walker was picked up at one of these Sunday stints. He came from the Crewe area and was brought over for a trial by our scout in the Potteries area, Ron Astbury. Jim made over 50 appearances in the Derby County first XI and was the Aston Villa physio for many years after he finished playing. I sat with him at a Derby County reunion dinner at Pride Park recently. He currently spends two days with Sheffield United, two days at the Belfry golf club and two days in his surgery in Birmingham.

Another signing as an apprentice at the same time was Alan Lewis, a young left-back from Yorkshire, who signed professional at the end of the 1972 season and made two first-team appearances at 18 years of age. He was thought highly of, but Brian, showing what a strict disciplinarian he was, cancelled his contract the day that a tearful club landlady, who looked after several of our boys, came to see Brian to report a serious incident in her home. Brian would not stand any stupid behaviour from any member of staff.

During this period Peter began taking me along with him on scouting missions, at midweek evening games and Saturday morning reserve-team games in the Midlands. Usually he used a very low-profile approach, keeping away from spectators and hoping not to be recognised in his muffler and old cap. No one knew me. Over a two-year period I learnt a tremendous amount from him. This was my training, which went on to stand me in good stead. He taught me what to look for and points in a player that he did not like. He had a mental checklist, the most important aspects of which were: how well does the player receive the ball, from any height, first touch and to control it; what does he do with it; is he aware of players, both his own and opponents, around him; how comfortable is he when moving with the ball, does he use both feet; if a forward how well does he strike the ball, has he got pace, is he able to use both feet; as a defender how good are his clearances, what length does he achieve, can he move forward with purpose keeping full control of the ball; what is his heading ability, how high does he jump when heading; what are his stamina and mobility like? If a player fulfilled a lot of these criteria, Peter knew he was a serious prospect. He did not waste time once he thought that the target was not good enough, and he did not often go to watch a player again hoping to see an improvement. This very rarely occurred, and he knew his time was valuable.

Peter was not the best or the bravest goalkeeper in his playing days, but his judgement of 'keepers was superb. I think that he was fully aware of his own shortcomings and thus, when he saw someone who excelled in these areas he took notice. As often as he could we used to go along to see Peter Shilton play in goal for the Leicester reserve team. Shilton was a teenager at the time, but he was almost faultless. Peter Taylor was completely obsessed with him and told me countless times that the lad was going to be something special. How right he was! Most League clubs in those days played their reserve fixtures on Saturdays, usually a 3pm kick-off, but on some occasions they played at 11am, which suited us much better.

By strange coincidence, at that time I had a friend with a couple of greyhounds who used to race them at Coalville flapping track. Peter Shilton also owned greyhounds which regularly raced there, so I was often in conversation with him about the dogs and their chances. I never let on that I was scouting for Derby County, so football was never discussed.

Gordon Banks was the first-team goalkeeper at Leicester City and the England international custodian. David Nish was also a promising young player at Leicester City, so it was well worth the journey to see these reserve boys play. I must have seen Peter Shilton play more times than any other young footballer. I had actually become a fan without realising it.

Until Gordon Banks was sold to Stoke City for £60,000 Peter had only made the odd appearance in the first team. Even though he won 125 caps, in my opinion there should have been more. Ron Greenwood had a period when he was England manager of alternating Peter with Ray Clemence, who himself gained 61 caps.

In later years I did begin to think that Peter Schmeichel at Manchester United was slightly the better 'keeper of the two, but the difference was marginal. Those two were the best in the business.

## The signings commence

In July 1967, the rebuilding of Derby County commenced with the signing of John O'Hare, a young Scottish centre-forward from Sunderland. Brian had coached John from the age of 15 through his time as a youth-team player and John became a great servant for Brian. He cost £21,000 and made 308 appearances, gaining 13 caps for Scotland. What a bargain. John scored in his very first League game at the Baseball Ground and was a player that always gave his all.

The next recruit was Roy McFarland. One Monday Peter rang for his habitual chat. When there had been a good result on the Saturday I knew I would receive a call early. I asked him which game had he been to on Saturday and he told me that he had been on the long journey to Torquay to see newly-promoted Tranmere Rovers in Division Three. A young central-defender, Roy McFarland, was the target. At

Hartlepools the previous year, playing for Tranmere Rovers, 19-year-old Roy had impressed Peter greatly, and he told me that he had thought of him as soon as he and Brian were appointed at Derby. However, in Saturday's match Roy had not been outstanding, but he had been pitted against a very robust centre-forward who roughed him up a time or two. Tranmere were at home on Friday evening and Peter went to the game with Brian. This time McFarland's quality shone through and the pair stayed after the game and agreed a transfer fee of £24,500. Roy made 530 appearances for Derby, gaining 28 caps with England, and it would have been more had injury not curtailed his chances.

Peter and Brian's perseverance in negotiating for players was evident. Roy had left the ground by the time an agreement was reached with Dave Russell, the Tranmere manager, and Peter and Brian decided to go to his home, where they met his parents. Roy was already in bed. Brian and Peter explained that they had agreed the transfer with Dave Russell and now they needed Roy's signature. While they were waiting for Roy to come down they chatted to his father, an Everton supporter. When Roy appeared a problem arose because Roy had heard that Liverpool might be interested in him, and he was keen to join them. Brian then revealed some of the plans he and Peter had for Derby County. Roy wanted to have the weekend to think it over, but Brian said that he and Peter would not leave without a definite answer. Roy thought a moment then turned to his father for advice. 'Roy,' said his Dad, 'sign for Derby County. It seems they are going to go places and I've been impressed with these two. Liverpool must have watched you loads of times, but they've never been in touch.' Roy nodded, and Brian whipped out the forms and put a pen in his shaking hand. Peter always said that of all his signings Roy was the best. In later years I worked for Roy as a scout and got to know him well. He is a super guy for whom I have the greatest respect.

Besides the playing signings, new non-playing staff had also been brought in. Jimmy Gordon came from Blackburn Rovers as first-team trainer/coach. Jim had been with Brian and Peter when at Middlesbrough, where he started his career as a coach. John Sheridan came from Hartlepools as a coach and looked after the second team. Brian Newton (who was one of Peter's helpers at Burton Albion) also joined the coaching staff. Gordon Guthrie, the physiotherapist, had been at Derby when

Brian and Peter took over and he stayed on. He has been at the club for over 40 years and is still on the staff in 2009.

Alan Hinton was the next player to be brought in, from Nottingham Forest for £29,000. He made 316 appearances. A speedy wide player, he could play on either wing and had the best two feet I have ever seen. You could not tell, watching him play, which was his natural side. I asked Alan about it and he told me that he was naturally right-footed, so I asked him how he had developed his left so well. He told me that when he was with Wolves, he used to stay behind at the ground in the afternoon with the youth team. He would train wearing a boot on his left foot and a plimsoll on his right, hitting dead balls on the pitch and in the shooting alley, the concrete floor and walls under the North Stand at Molineux. It certainly worked. The accuracy of his crosses and his power were exceptional. It took a while for the Derby crowd to appreciate his ability with the ball as he rarely tackled, but Brian did not play him to do that. In the modern game he would be priceless.

Next there came a rare unsuccessful signing. Pat Wright, a full-back from Shrewsbury, cost £5,000 and made only 12 first-team appearances. He departed at the end of the season. His defensive qualities did not meet the required standard. Peter told me that he had not obeyed his golden rule of watching a player three times when deciding to sign Pat and he had only seen him once. Pat has done very well coaching young footballers and has made a career out of it. I bump into him on occasions at games.

Richie Barker, a striker, cost £2,500 from Burton Albion (he scored 157 goals for them) and signed on full-time, from being a draughtsman playing part-time football in the Southern League. Peter said that he would get goals anywhere. He made 45 appearances for Derby, scoring 14 goals.

Another early signing that Peter brought in was Arthur Stewart, a midfield player from Glentoran, who made 33 appearances before returning to Ireland. I cannot recall ever seeing him play.

Barry Cornforth, our scout in the North East, highly recommended a player called John Robson, who was playing in local youth football. Peter travelled all the way to see him play one weekend and came back with his signature. He made 211 appearances at left-back, completely justifying the urgency of his signing.

The following were already on Derby County's books when Brian and Peter arrived: veteran goalkeeper Reg Mathews, 34 years old, who had replaced Peter in goal at Coventry some years earlier; Colin Boulton, another goalkeeper, the son of a policeman from Gloucester, who was showing promise in the reserves; Peter Daniel (21), Ronnie Webster (23) and John Richardson (22), full-backs, who had come through the youth scheme; Alan Durban, a 26-year-old Welsh international, bought from Cardiff City for £10,000 as a forward four years earlier; and a fairly recent signing, Kevin Hector, a 23-year-old striker, bought from Bradford Park Avenue for £38,000 early the previous season. Together with the new signings the side was beginning to take shape. Brian and Peter were reasonably happy. However, the season ended with Derby in 18th position in Division Two, one place lower than the previous season. The vice-chairman, Mr Sydney Bradley, was soon asking questions, as money had been spent but no improvement was shown.

After Brian and Peter's discussions with the board, there was no panic. They seemed unperturbed and they said that the sun would soon be shining. One of their main aims was to get an 'old head' into the side, to steer the ship on the field and bring the best out of the youngsters. Peter's biggest disappointment was Kevin Hector, whom he thought should have scored more goals, and he attempted to arrange a straight swap of Kevin with Ken Wagstaff of Hull City. Apparently, when Hull City came to the Baseball Ground Wagstaff had been very good and Hull had won that game 2–1. However, their manager, Cliff Britton, would only take Roy McFarland as the player in exchange. There was absolutely no chance of this happening, as after his first season with Derby Roy was very highly rated. The matter was then dropped.

The next season Kevin began to deliver, an example of how Brian could improve players if they were willing to take on board what he said to them. By the time he finished at Derby Kevin had made 589 appearances, scoring 201 goals, and had won one Second Division Championship and two First Division Championship medals, plus two England caps.

## Promotion into Division One

The 1968–69 season began with the signing of Les Green, a goalkeeper from Rochdale. He made 129 appearances for Derby and had previously been signed by Peter at Burton

Albion and Hartlepools. Jimmy Greaves once told me, after his retirement, that Les Green had made the best save he had ever seen a goalkeeper make, in a match Jimmy had played in for Tottenham Forest against Derby in the early 1970s.

The priority, however, was still to bring in an experienced 'old head' before the start of the season. After lengthy discussions Peter and Brian decided to go for Dave Mackay, the Tottenham Hotspur legend. Brian set off the next day for London, as they had discovered, from the enquiries they made, that a proposed move for Dave back to Scotland with Hearts might not be finalised. Brian spoke to Dave at White Hart Lane and he agreed to come up to Derby for further discussions, to talk about the actual role he was wanted for. He was told he would be sweeping at the back alongside the young Roy McFarland and would be made skipper, in full charge on the pitch. He would not be running around, but would be the anchor man at the back. Dave was a little doubtful, as he had spent his whole career in midfield with a roaming role, but after a lengthy discussion he agreed to sign. He had actually thought that his playing days were over, but Brian convinced him that there was more to come. The £5,000 fee turned out to be one of the best-value transfers of all time. Dave made 145 appearances in three superb seasons and enjoyed it immensely. He proved to be the missing ingredient, and in one of his seasons, 1970–71, he played in every League game. He shared the Football Writers Association Footballer of the Year award with Tony Book of Manchester City, another great oldie, in the 1968–69 season.

Dave Mackay made his debut playing for Derby County alongside Roy McFarland in central defence, against Sunderland in a pre-season friendly on a Saturday evening at the Baseball Ground. I refereed the game and the two linesmen were from Burton upon Trent. The three of us regularly officiated together. The Derbyshire Referees Association objected to my being in charge, as they thought matches should be covered by Derbyshire officials, not those from the Birmingham Association. Until then they had always done it. Brian met six representatives from the Derby Football Association and the Derbyshire Referees Association to discuss the matter. Brian rejected their objections and gave them six complementary tickets for the game, saying 'See for yourselves whether you can find any fault with the handling of this game by Mr Edwards. If so, come back and I will listen to what you have to say.' They attended, but not another word was heard from them. Until I gave up refereeing I continued to officiate at all friendly matches that Derby County were involved in, both home and away.

Colin Todd played in that game for Sunderland. There was a good attendance and the new signings had generated much interest. During the game I had a few words with Dave Mackay: he was testing me with some banter. I quickly told him that the game was being handled as if it was a normal League match, and to pack it in. He was no more trouble. Brian and Peter were delighted with their team's performance.

The season opened with two 1–1 draws, bringing forward the need to make another vitally important signing. On the Tuesday evening we were due to visit Sheffield United at Bramall Lane. Peter rang to say that it was very important for him to attend the game and would I take him, as it was imperative that he was at the ground very early, before our team coach got there. I picked him up late afternoon at his home in Findern and on the way to Sheffield he told me that he wanted to be at the stadium early so that he could speak to Willie Carlin before the kick-off. This was the first time that I had heard Willie's name mentioned. Peter went on to tell me that Willie Carlin had played for Carlisle prior to joining the Blades, and that he and Brian had been in trouble with the FA for making an illegal approach to the player. They had been warned about their future conduct, and if there was a slip up now the FA would throw the book at them. We arrived at the ground just before six o'clock. Peter obtained our tickets from the office and we had to enter the ground through this way, as the turnstiles were not yet open. We made our way up into the stands. Our seats were about level with the halfway line. Peter left me and said that he would not be too long. The pitch was only lit by one set of floodlights and they were only partly switched on. I could hardly discern anyone on the ground. In the centre circle I could just pick out two figures, one tall, in a long coat, and a much smaller figure in a tracksuit. One or two others were kicking balls about in the far goalmouth.

Peter returned to his seat about half an hour before the kick-off. We left the ground some minutes before the end. Sheffield were winning 2–0. On the way home Peter told me that he had spoken to Carlin and that he was sure that he would sign for Derby before the weekend. Later in the week Peter rang to tell me that Carlin had signed for a £63,000 fee (he made 89 appearances), and he seemed very pleased with the transaction. The next Saturday, in another 2–0 defeat away at Huddersfield,

Carlin did not make his debut as the transfer was not quite complete. Derby had gained only two points out of a possible eight. On the Monday morning Peter rang me early: 'Give Ladbrokes a ring and ask what price we are to win Division Two this season. We are certainties, this is the final piece in the jigsaw'. I rang him back with the price offered: 100–6, a quarter of the odds to finish in the first three. 'Will you bet me £60 each way and the same for Brian?' Peter asked. I was very surprised as Brian rarely gambled. I thought to myself that I had better have a slice of the pie. I went and drew £360 out of my Lloyds bank account and placed the bet in Ladbrokes.

The same afternoon I went on my own to Wolverhampton races. At the bar I met Jack Taylor, an international and Division One referee. This was his local race meeting. He was a master butcher by trade and butchers were closed on Mondays, so he was there regularly. I joined him for a drink and a chat as I had met him recently when he was over at Burton giving a talk to the Referees Association. I related the story of the bets that I had struck that morning and the signing of Carlin, and said that Brian and Peter were convinced that they would definitely win Division Two.

Who should then walk in to the bar but Arthur Rowley, the manager of Sheffield United. He came straight up to Jack, but he did not know me from Adam. Jack introduced me to him by my Christian name only, making no mention of my involvement in football.

'Will you both join me in a bottle of Moet?' Arthur asked. 'I've just completed the best deal in football with Cloughie.'

'Cheers!' Jack Taylor replied. 'Tell us the story.' Arthur related exactly the same story as I had already told Jack. He went on to say that Carlin had been a bag of trouble at Sheffield, always getting booked, could not keep his mouth closed, been sent off three times. 'I can run faster than him,' he said. 'It pleases me to have pulled one over on Cloughie.'

During the afternoon I saw Alec Bird, a professional gambler from Manchester, whom I knew fairly well. I told him of the bet that I had struck with Ladbrokes on Derby County winning Division Two of the Football League and showed him the betting slip.

When Willie Carlin arrived at Derby he was firmly told by Brian what was expected from him and emphasis was put on his conduct on the field. Improvement was soon evident. The form of Derby County changed immediately and they went 14 games unbeaten. I have often wondered whether Arthur Rowley ever had any second thoughts about the Carlin transfer. He lost his job at the end of the season and Johnny Harris resumed the team duties.

In November John McGovern was signed from Hartlepools United. Brian and Peter knew his potential, having signed him as a 16-year-old when they were managing the club. This time he cost them £7,000.

### A new signing that cost absolutely nothing

I was still refereeing in the professional non-Leagues, which was mainly on Saturdays. On blank Saturdays I filled in with a Burton & District Division One game. After refereeing Linton United once or twice I took a liking to one of their team. He was useful on the ball, had great skill and continually scored goals. Jeff Bourne was 23 years old and worked on the coal face at a local pit. He was well overweight for a young man. I was given to understand that he was a heavy beer drinker, but his type of play and his skill in getting goals really impressed me.

I knew his fitness problems could be overcome if he put his mind to it. Peter Taylor, during my tuition period, had told me not to consider age or physique. Can he play? This is the most important assessment. I decided to invite Jeff to Sunday-morning trials at the Sinfin Lane training ground, if he fancied taking a shot at League football. He jumped at the chance. I told him that I would be refereeing the trial games, and gave him instructions about what time to arrive, where it was and what kit he should bring. When I arrived at the ground on the Sunday morning I made sure that Cliff Notley, who did all the organising of these trials, taking down the lads' names and addresses and sorting out the playing teams, was fully aware that Jeff was coming and what position to play him in, as a joint striker of a pair. I did not speak to Peter about him in advance. Jeff's trial period began and I kept as close to him as I could, continually giving him instructions, telling him when to hold on to the ball, when and where to pass and shoot. It worked a treat and he scored three good goals in the half-hour period, watched by Peter, who kept him on for a further half-hour session. After the game he was offered a contract to turn professional. Jeff accepted the terms without any hesitation, although it was a lot less than what he was earning down the pit. No transfer fee was involved: he did not cost the club one penny.

On Jeff's first Monday morning at the Baseball Ground, Brian set his eyes on him for the first time and remarked on his weight. He sent him to the Sinfin training ground with the instructions 'no ball work' and 'no drinking'. He was to help with hand-digging a trench around the pitch, which was to carry the cables for the floodlighting. It was four weeks before this work was completed and Jeff was then allowed to train with the others, do ball work and join in with the normal routines. By this time he had lost over two stone in weight and was soon included in the reserve team. He immediately started to score regularly and progressed into the first-team squad, where he was used mainly as an attacking midfield player. He made 70 first-team appearances, scoring 14 goals in League Division One and gaining a Division One Championship medal under Dave Mackay in the 1974–75 season. In 1976, after Colin Murphy became manager, he decided to accept an offer to play in Canada for the next six years, during which he had two short spells playing in the Football League, during the Canadian close season. Jeff was a fine example of how Brian could make a player out of raw material.

In February 1969 there was a very cold spell with few games taking place. The only fixture completed at the Baseball Ground was the win against Cardiff on 1 February. I had no matches to referee and was frustrated, so I asked if I could go to the City Ground to see Forest play Leeds United, who were Division One Champions elect. I could only get in standing at the Trent End as there were over 36,000 spectators and the rebuilding of the Main Stand had not been completed. I wanted to see Jim Baxter play. When I have read a lot about a player I like to form my own opinion of him.

The exclusive Victoria Club had recently been opened. The owners were George Aitken and his brother, Nottingham bookmakers. The Nottingham Forest team had been invited to one of the opening evenings, and a big gossip story that had rapidly spread among the sporting public was that Jim Baxter, having had too much to drink, had urinated on their luxurious carpet. It was well into the second half at the City Ground and Forest were kicking towards the Trent End. At the time Leeds were winning 1–0. Jim Baxter received the ball in the right-hand defensive quarter of Leeds United and ran with the ball towards the edge of the penalty area. A hush came over the crowd in anticipation. Suddenly, a very loud voice yelled 'Go on Jim, score and then you can come and piss on our carpet!' The Trent End erupted with laughter.

Leeds won the game 2–0. Before I went to the game, Peter told me to have a good look at Henry Newton in midfield. It was the first time I had seen him play and I thought he was Forest's best player. He was strong in the tackle and worked hard the whole game. Peter said 'I thought you would be impressed.'

The February lay-off caused a build-up of fixtures and Peter was worried about the amount of responsibility for getting goals that rested on Kevin Hector and John O'Hare. He felt that another strongly-built striker was required as a stand-by in case either became injured, as the results were now showing that the Championship was a strong possibility. No replacement had been signed after Richie Barker's transfer to Notts County. It was decided to sign Frank Wignall from Wolves for £20,000. This was entirely Peter's doing and Wignall made his debut on 1 March, coming on as a substitute for Willie Carlin and scoring. By the season's end he had made six appearances, scoring four goals, justifying the purchase. He played 54 League and Cup games before he was sold to Matlock Town in November 1971.

When League games resumed after the cold spell Derby County were only defeated once during the remainder of the season and won the title by seven clear points.

The winnings from the large bet that I had struck had to be collected from Ladbrokes. They had offered to pay me by cheque, but as it had to be divided I had asked for cash. I did not want to be seen collecting such a large amount so I persuaded a close friend, a bank clerk, to collect the returns of £4,110 in a leather case, as used by banks. I was waiting outside in my car. Few people knew of the investment. Soon afterwards I bumped into Alec Bird at Newmarket races. He immediately came up to me with a big smile and shook my hand vigorously. He told me then that he had put £600 each way on Derby County after seeing me at Wolverhampton. Alec never forgot this and he did me some very good turns in later years. He was a real gentleman, and at that time he was the bookmakers' most feared professional gambler. As an example, when I wanted an alternative betting account to the one I had with Ladbrokes, Alec suggested William Hill. On the application form I named Alec Bird to verify my application. The credit account was opened with a limit of £400. I had asked for a much larger sum and I rang Hill's for an explanation. They said that the connection with Alec Bird was the reason, and they said that they were worried that I might be asked to place some of his investments; however, at no time did he ever ask me to do this.

Soon after gaining promotion Peter told me that an approach to Nottingham Forest had been made via Matt Gillies to find out how much they would expect for Henry Newton. Matt put it to the Forest committee, but they had heard that Derby County had tried to swap Kevin Hector for Wagstaff at Hull and had been turned down, so they asked if they could have Kevin in part-exchange for Henry. Brian refused and said he was not available. Two days later Matt confirmed that the committee would not agree to Henry going to Derby for cash.

As a reward for getting promotion, Mr Sam Longson increased Brian and Peter's salaries. Their basic salaries were now £13,000 per year. At the first press conference Brian gave after news of this increase had leaked out, one reporter, feeling brave, asked 'Did you know, Brian, that your salary is twice the size of that paid to the Archbishop of Canterbury?'

'Young man,' responded Brian, 'I will tell you why. The Baseball Ground is full on Saturday, but on Sunday the churches are almost empty.'

### The rewards of Division One

Before the 1969–70 season began, the people of Derby had gone football crazy. Their idols were about to step into the Football League Division One for the first time since 1953, after a gap of 16 years. The ever-growing number of supporters had great expectations and the team certainly did not let them down.

The new Ley Stand had been completed, which had covered the whole length of the Popular side at a cost of £230,000, increasing the capacity to over 40,000. The average gate when Brian and Peter had first arrived was 16,000; they were now averaging 35,000. On 20 September 1969 the attendance record was broken when 41,826 witnessed a 5–0 drumming of Spurs, Dave Mackay's former club.

In the first game of the campaign in Division One, John McGovern became the first player to have played in all four Divisions of the Football League: what an achievement for a 19-year-old.

No new signings were made. Brian and Peter were satisfied with the present staff and, with the work that had been done at the ground and at the Sinfin training ground, there was no money available. Derby were unbeaten in the first 11 games. During the season John Rhodes, Peter Daniel, Arthur Stewart and Jim Walker were called on for odd games from the reserves. I was still refereeing and travelling to matches with Peter, scouting for possible new recruits. Now Derby were in the top flight higher quality players were required. We also assessed some of the teams we were due to play. On Saturdays Peter was usually with Brian at first-team matches.

It was the New Year before the first signing of the season was made, with Derby County's first six-figure purchase coming when Terry Hennessey, a Welsh international defender, joined from Nottingham Forest for £103,000. He made 82 appearances and stayed for just over four years, but he was plagued with injuries and absent for long periods. Terry had been bought to replace Dave Mackay, but he did not turn out to be one of Peter's best purchases. He had some outstanding performances, but others were below par. Terry was not strong mentally, and it is hard to detect that until you actually work with someone. First he picked up an ankle injury, then a knee condition. Brian and Peter did not think that he worked hard enough to get rid of these injuries and get back to full fitness. Terry lacked Dave's tenacity, courage and willpower. Dave, of course, was a very hard act to follow as he was someone very special. Nevertheless, Brian lost some faith in Terry and his last game for Derby was against West Bromwich Albion in January 1973, after which he had to retire through injury.

When Terry was signed Peter told me that the reserves needed strengthening in the central defence positions. He asked me whether I had seen anyone recently that could be brought in immediately. Tony Bailey came to mind. He was a local lad, in Burton Albion's first team, 23 years old and barely 6ft tall. He was not the most strongly built defender, but he read the game well, was strong in the tackle, jumped and headed well and had courage in the air. I thought he could play a bit of football, but would not make a top League performer. Peter paid Burton Albion £3,500 for him and he stayed with Derby for four years, making only one appearance in the first XI, against Leeds at Elland Road at Christmas 1971. He stood in for Colin Todd that day. Leeds won 3–0. It would have been hard for anyone to fill Colin's boots, however. Tony went on loan to Oldham, then moved to Bury for £6,000. In all he made over 300 appearances over six years, and injury brought his career to an early close.

Derby County finished in fourth place in Division One in 1969–70.

# CHAPTER 4

# SIGNINGS AND SCOUTING

Before the second season in the top flight began, a very important change was made to the non-playing staff. Club secretary Malcolm Bramley had been away from his desk for some time, apparently suffering from a mental breakdown and exhaustion. He claimed that attendances had doubled from 16,000 to 32,000 during the season, with no increase in the number of office staff. However, the 1969 accounts showed that there was a shortage of £3,000 in receipts from season ticket sales. Lodging allowances were being paid to apprentices rather than directly to landladies, some players' contracts had not been lodged correctly and £2,000, in £20 lots, that had been paid to Dave Mackay for programme contributions was outside the terms of his contract. All these irregularities were cited when the Football League later brought charges against the club.

In all this administrative chaos a replacement club secretary was urgently required. Jimmy Gordon suggested that Stuart Webb, the assistant secretary at Preston North End, would be the ideal candidate. Jimmy knew him well from his days there. Stuart had been a youth-team player at Preston but had not been offered a contract when he reached 18. However, he was offered a job in the office, where he had helped out as an apprentice. His good work had led to him becoming assistant to the secretary.

Stuart Webb was interviewed at the Midland Hotel and appointed very quickly. He was a dynamic young man and soon had the office converted to his way of working. He was an excellent addition to the non-playing staff and I found him of tremendous help to me. Brian and Stuart did not particularly get on, and were never close, but they had terrific respect for one another in the way that they did their respective jobs. However, they certainly each made sure the other knew who was in charge of their own domain. Brian wanted to handle some of the season ticket sales, but in the first alrercation between the two Stuart made his position very clear and told him that all players and staff relating to the footballing side of things was Brian's domain, and that he expected him not to touch anything concerning the administration or non-footballing staff.

This situation was quickly bourne out. One morning Stuart was in his office early, when there came a knock on the door. He opened it to see Special Constable Dunford stood before him. 'Can you tell me,' he said 'why my son Michael was given the sack yesterday?' After hearing Stuart's reply that he was unaware of the dismissal, the Special Constable explained 'Mr Clough dismissed him yesterday afternoon.'

Stuart went straight to Brian's office and gleaned that Brian had wanted to get into the safe in the office but Michael (who was in fact acting on Stuart's orders) had refused to hand over keys, for which Brian had sacked him. Upon hearing this, Stuart said 'You can't sack him, he's on my staff and nothing to do with you. I told you this two weeks ago. I'm recalling him.' True to his word, and despite Brian's displeasure, Stuart went to Michael's father and told him to send him back to work as soon as possible. Michael has since had an excellent career in the game and at the time of writing is in the position of chief executive at Birmingham City.

In April 1970 the FA and Football League announced the results of their investigations into the administrative irregularities at the club. Derby were fined £10,000 and banned from playing against European teams in any matches, competitive or friendly. The fourth-place finish in 1969–70 should have qualified them for a place in the Fairs Cup, but they could not enter the competition. Planned pre-season friendlies in France and Germany were cancelled.

Derby were invited to play in the Watney Cup. Peter and Brian accepted the invitation and the matches were played during the fortnight before the new season commenced. I was actually in the office when the two of them discussed how they intended to approach the competition. It was decided to play the full first team to get them in fine shape for the new season in the League. Brian said 'We're in it, let's give it our best shot.' We duly won the handsome trophy.

1 August a 5–3 victory away at Fulham, first round

5 August a 1–0 victory home to Sheffield United, semi-final

8 August a 4–1 victory home to Manchester United Final (United's full first team)

There had been concerns about risking the first-team players in these highly competitive games, but no injuries were sustained.

The League campaign began with a loss at Chelsea, which was followed by three wins and a draw. Peter was not satisfied and said we would have to introduce more pace and skill into the side.

## My appointment as chief scout

A dramatic change was soon made to my role with Derby County. I got a telephone call from Stuart Webb, the club secretary, saying that Brian wanted to see me in his office as soon as I could get over. There was no mention of the reason for the meeting. I said I would be there in an hour. With some apprehension I drove to the club. I met Brian in his office. It was just the two of us. He shook my hand. 'Sit down!' he said. He got straight to the point. 'I've had to sack George Pycroft on instructions from the chairman, Mr Sam Longson', he said. 'Mr Longson saw George shortly before kick-off at the last three home games, from his office overlooking the street by the main entrance in Shaftesbury Crescent. He said that he wasn't paying him to be there, he should be out looking for prospective players. Peter and I had not been fully aware of this – obviously our attention on match days is focused on our team preparation – so we have had little choice but to act on the chairman's instructions.' The chairman loved to have a go at Brian when he got a chance, particularly if there was a sound reason. He continued 'Peter has recommended that I offer you the job of chief scout of this club. He says that you know what we require and will be fully capable of doing the work. It will mean you packing in your refereeing, which you enjoy so much. I know how I missed playing when I had to finish. You will be directly responsible to Peter, he will tell you what he wants covering, there will be, of course, a monthly salary. Think it over!' I accepted straight away. Brian welcomed me on board and shook my hand and wished me the best of luck.

He then gave me some sound advice. 'If at any time you think you have stepped out of line with an approach to a player, don't sleep on it, tell me as soon as possible to enable me to kill it before it becomes serious, so that I can get it sorted out.' Peter came in and shook my hand and congratulated me. He said that occasionally I would be asked to do a match report on forthcoming opposition, although neither of them were believers in worrying about the opposition and the importance of match reports. All my work was to be top secret, only to be discussed with Brian or Peter.

### My first assignment

Stuart Webb had recommended to Brian and Peter that we go after Archie Gemmill at Preston, a young Scot with an Under-23 pedigree, who had been signed by them from St Mirren. Stuart had been the assistant club secretary at Preston when Archie had joined them over three years ago. Archie had pace and had consistently improved since he first arrived, and Stuart had continued to monitor his progress.

This was to be my first assignment as chief scout and on Saturday 19 September Peter told me to go to Villa Park, as Preston were the visitors and I would get a good look at Gemmill. At 12.30pm on Saturday, Peter rang to tell me that there had been a change of plans. He said that a definite decision had to be made that day as they had learned that Harry Catterick of Everton was about to make an offer to Preston for Gemmill. Peter was going to Villa and I was to go to Peter's match to do a report on West Bromwich Albion, who we were due to play the next week. It was a good move. Peter was very impressed with Gemmill's performance and he and Brian travelled up to Preston the same evening. They arrived at Deepdale in time for Alan Ball Senior's (the father of that wonderful footballer of the same name) return from Villa Park, and after discussions they agreed a transfer fee of £64,000. They then went to see

Archie Gemmill at his home for talks that went on for some considerable time. Negotiations were difficult. Archie himself was fairly quiet and reasonable, but Mrs Gemmill did not care for Brian, having formed an opinion of him from watching him on television. In the end Peter decided to make the journey home, leaving Brian to do the talking. Brian was determined not to go home empty-handed and slept at Archie's home, hoping to complete the deal on the Sunday morning. This proved worthwhile and Archie signed early in the morning, with his wife's consent. Brian rang Peter and said that he had got the signed contract and was on his way home.

On the Monday morning, Harry Catterick rang Alan Ball to arrange to go over to Preston to sign Gemmill. He was told that he was too late and that Archie had joined Derby County. This was another fine example of how Brian and Peter operated. The late change of plans had worked perfectly. If I had gone to Villa Park instead of Peter, even if I had made the same assessment, the signing would not have been completed so quickly and he would, in all probability, have become an Everton player. Peter said to me that Archie would develop into an even better player after a couple of months. He gained his first Scottish cap in 1971 against Belgium. I have always rated the signing of Gemmill as one of the major signings that Brian and Peter made during their partnership. Archie made 404 appearances for Derby and gained 43 full international caps for Scotland and two Division One Championship medals.

Willie Carlin, whose place Archie was to take, was sold to Leicester City for a £38,000 transfer fee in October. Carlin had done a tremendous job in getting us out of Division Two and established in Division One, but in football there is no room for sentiment and the time had come for Willie to move on. Although he was reluctant to go, for the club it was a shrewd deal: a new, younger arrival for only £26,000 expenditure.

### Peter taken ill

On the way to play Arsenal at the end of October 1970, Peter was taken ill in the coach while in London. It turned out to be an early warning of a heart problem. When he was ill again a couple of months later a heart specialist recommended that Peter take a few weeks' rest away from the club.

During Peter's absence Brian brought in Colin Boulton, the reserve-team goalkeeper, to replace Les Green, who had played in every game for the Rams since his arrival at the club. On Boxing Day 1970, at home to Manchester United in front of over 34,000 spectators, the final score was 4–4. Les Green was judged to have been mainly responsible for this surprise result, perhaps due to the Christmas festivities. Brian was furious and some unprintable words were exchanged between him and Les after the game. Les was dropped and Colin Boulton grabbed his opportunity with both hands, being ever present until he missed two games at the end of the 1972–73 season through injury. Les Green left the club at the end of the season and joined Durban City, the South African side. The whole saga was an example of how Brian handled behaviour that was deemed to be out of order. Players would be sidelined and moved on quickly to avoid disrupting the other players in the dressing room.

Brian also made one of his rare signings on his own judgement while Peter was away. Colin Todd joined us from Sunderland in February 1971 for £170,000, a record transfer fee at that time. He made 371 appearances, gaining 27 international caps and winning two Division One Championship medals with Derby County. Several clubs had attempted to sign him from Sunderland but had been turned away. Brian, with family and friends in the North East, knew that Sunderland were having a few financial problems. As soon as Alan Brown, who had returned as their manager, paid £100,000 for David Watson from Rotherham, Brian stepped in immediately with the offer for Todd.

Peter returned to active duty shortly after this. With Colin in the side Derby won the first game against Arsenal, but they lost five of the next seven games. Peter had told me that he would not have bought Todd and referred to him as a 'bread and butter player'. I am sure that this was because Brian had signed Colin and there was a little jealousy involved. I thought that Colin was a good acquisition. He had pace and strength and his ball control was excellent. Also, Brian had known him very well when he was coaching at Sunderland. Peter later changed his opinion, however, and agreed that there had been a big improvement in his play. I think that Peter secretly thought 'I wish I had brought him in'.

Peter asked me to go to Scunthorpe United, who were playing Stockport County in a Division Four match. The target was Kevin Keegan, playing for Scunthorpe, and I had instructions to make a thorough examination of his game. At the match

I recognised about six other scouts, two of them from top clubs. Keegan was playing in the right-half position. I made him about 5ft 6in height, slight of build, possibly 10 stone in weight. He kept wide right most of the time and his performance did not inspire me at all. He did not work hard enough, never challenged strongly for the ball and was reluctant to hold on to the ball and go wide forward down the wing. He parted with the ball far too quickly and gave me the impression that he did not fancy the physical part of the game. I decided not to recommend him in my report. Maurice Lindley, the Leeds United chief scout, sat next to me. Shortly before the game ended he asked me whether I had come to look at Keegan. I said I had and told him that I had not been impressed. Maurice said that Don Revie had sent him after having received a very good report, but he was not impressed either. I submitted my report to Peter next morning. Peter then revealed that he and Brian had been to see Keegan the previous Friday at Southend. 'We paid to go in and stayed at the YMCA to keep the visit very quiet, and we came away with exactly the same verdict,' he said.

During the close season Kevin Keegan was transferred to Liverpool for £140,000, the deal having been completed at Christmas. Bill Shankly had allowed him to stay at Scunthorpe until the end of the season, to ensure their survival in the Football League, as they were perilously close to having to seek re-election. The transfer had been a very closely kept secret. Our excuse for missing this great player was that we came on the scene after all the negotiations had been completed. I certainly never saw a glimpse of the player he became at Liverpool and in Hamburg.

The official date of Keegan's transfer was May 1971. In August of the next season he made his debut for Liverpool and he never looked back. We always referred to him as 'the one that got away'. George Pycroft had ribbed Peter about missing out on Keegan, after George had recommended him when he was available for £35,000, and he later stated that the falling-out they had as a result had led to his sacking from Derby County.

Sheffield Wednesday were playing in midweek against Santos, a Brazilian club, in a friendly at Hillsborough. Peter asked me to take him to the game, and on the way he said that we would learn something to our advantage that afternoon. We were not disappointed. The two Brazilian full-backs on view that afternoon were awesome. I could not take my eyes off them. They did not win tackles the way our defenders usually did, they pinched the ball with perfect timing. Their control on the ball was excellent, and their pinpoint passing set up endless attacks. They were superb. Peter could not stop talking about them on the way home. He remarked to me that David Nish of Leicester City was the only player in the country who would be able to do that job for us.

The Boxing Day 4–4 draw with Manchester United at the Baseball Ground was still in Peter's thoughts, although he had been off ill at the time. The return fixture at Old Trafford was to take place on Easter Monday. United were due to visit the Victoria Ground to play Stoke City towards the end of March and Peter wanted to watch the game, but the first team were away at Anfield and he had to travel with them. Thus he asked me to go to Stoke to do a match report.

Manchester United defeated Stoke City 2–1 with George Best scoring both their goals. This was the first time that I had seen 'Bestie' play in a game from the stands. He was fantastic. It was one of his outstanding performances. The playing surface was extremely heavy and it rained continuously. For one goal that he scored he collected the ball on the edge of his own penalty area, running with the ball almost the whole length of the pitch on the right-hand side, leaving in his wake several bewildered Stoke players. Nonetheless, I picked up on a couple of areas in the United defence that I thought were vulnerable and concentrated my report on these. At Old Trafford a wonderful result was achieved. We came away with a 2–1 victory, John O'Hare scoring both of the goals. I heard the news on my car radio on the way home from another game. It gave me a wonderful feeling as we had lost five games out of the last seven. Peter rang me that same evening, very pleased.

Derby County finished in ninth position at the end of the season, due to the very poor run up to Easter. Dave Mackay had been ever present for the first time in a season during his entire career. Some 34,000 supporters turned up to see his final game to say thank you. Dave Mackay had always been one of my idols from when he first joined Spurs. When he came to Derby I was over the moon and he gave magnificent service. I had asked if I could be present at this game, as it was the last game of the season. He left the field to tremendous 'thank you' applause from the spectators. What a player, what a man.

HMS *Glory* in Valetta harbour, Malta.

Hiroshima, Japan, shortly after the first atomic bomb raid by the Americans. In the foreground is the crater that was caused when the bomb exploded in the air immediately above.

Photograph taken on the extreme side of Hiroshima, where some shells of buildings remained, after some of the main roads had been cleared of debris. One strange observation that I made was that the railway station buildings were completely gone, but the railway track itself was hardly damaged.

# Instrument of Surrender

## of

# Japanese Forces in New Guinea, New Britain, New Ireland, Bongainville and adjacent Islands

I, the Commander in Chief of the Japanese Imperial Southeastern Army, hereby surrender to the General Officer Commanding First Australian Army all Japanese Armed Forces under my command in accordance with the Instrument of Surrender issued by the Japanese Imperial General Headquarters and Government and General Order No. 1, Military and Naval issued by the Japanese Imperial General Headquarters.

I will henceforth and until otherwise directed by you or your successor carry out the orders issued by you or your Staff on your behalf to the best of my ability and I will take action to ensure that my subordinate commanders carry out the orders issued by your representatives.

今村 均

草鹿任一
（南東方面海軍総指揮官）

General, Imperial Japanese Army

COMMANDER IN CHIEF
JAPANESE IMPERIAL SOUTHEASTERN ARMY

Received on board H.M.S. Glory off Rabaul at 1130 hours sixth day of September 1945.

LIEUTENANT-GENERAL
GENERAL OFFICER COMMANDING
First Australian Army

Photograph of the actual Surrender Document of the Islands in the Coral Sea by the Japanese Army General on board HMS *Glory*.

Anchored off Manila, where ex-POWs from the Phillipines have just embarked to commence their long voyage home to the British Isles, October 1945.

The converted aircraft hanger repatriated British Service personnel, who were photographed here resting with Red Cross nurses in attendance.

Me wearing Burton Albion's striped black and amber strip at the Wellington Street ground.

Burton Albion, August 1954. Standing, left to right: Dave McAdam, Maurice Hodgkin, Jack Stamps, Bill Townsend, Geoff Tye, Phil Aston. Kneeling: Phil Giles, Dave Neville, Reg Weston, Maurice Edwards, Les Evans.

Burton Albion's impressive Pirelli Stadium opened in 2007.

Wellington Street Post Office, 1958.

Wellington Street Post Office was modernised and enlarged in 1964. It is seen here with its present-day frontage, 2007.

Brian Clough and Peter Taylor recieve a welcome handshake from Sam Longson, the Derby County chairman, outside the Baseball Ground.

*Left:* Les Green was signed by Peter as his own replacement at Burton Albion. He later moved on to Hartlepools and then to Derby County.

3 August 1968 — Baseball Ground

DERBY COUNTY
White Shirts, Black Shorts

SUNDERLAND
Red and White Striped Shirts, White Shorts

Peter always said that Roy McFarland was his best signing.

Derby County, 1968–69. Back row, left to right: Pat Wright, Russ Bostock, Ron Webster, Colin Boulton, Les Green, Tony Rhodes, Barry Butlin, Jim Walker. Middle row: Alan Durban, Arthur Stewart, Richie Barker, John O'Hare, Kevin Hector, Alan Hinton. Front row: John Richardson, Peter Daniel, John Robson.

Derby County captain Dave Mackay holds the trophy high. The Rams are Division Two champions in 1969.

David Webb tackles Jeff Bourne in the six-yard box, as 'Chopper' Harris and Kevin Hector watch on. Both players finished in the net but no foul was awarded!

Peter witnessing the double signing of Tony Bailey (£3,500) and Terry Hennessey (£103,000).

Dave Mackay having received the Watney Cup from Sir Stanley Rous in 1970.

Brian had coached Colin Todd as a youth player at Sunderland before making him one of the few players to have been signed by Brian on his own.

Stuart Webb, the dynamic secretary.

Archie Gemmill delivering. Stuart Webb, Derby County secretary, recommended the player having known him at Preston North End. Peter saw him just once before completing a very speedy transfer, with Everton also hot on his trail. A little difficulty was encounted, but Brian overcame the problem.

Roger Davies was a bargain buy from Worcester City. The Derby County chairman was very displeased and even threatened me with the sack if Davies failed to deliver.

Early in the 1974 season Brian and Peter began seriously talking about their dissatisfaction with the board. Their resignations soon followed.

Cliff Notley and myself receiving commemorative medals at the celebratory dinner held after winning Division One, the Texaco Cup and the Central League.

Peter likened David Nish's play to the two Santos full-backs after the Brazilians' visit to England.

Tony Parry with John McGovern (behind) in the early days at Hartlepools. Each became legends in the North East and were later brought separately to Derby County.

For the first time I went on the club's end-of-season break to Cala Millor in Majorca for seven days. In the evening of the arrival day a Derby County XI played a Palma side. The only Derby County first-team players missing were those away on international duty. I refereed the game with two Majorcan linesmen. There was a good crowd in attendance, both holidaymakers and locals enjoying the occasion. I found it very hot and stuffy but the players enjoyed themselves. The refreshments went down well afterwards. Our share of the gate money went towards the cost of the holiday. Our evening meal was held at the 'Shack', as was usual on the first night, and guests were invited; some of the players had friends and relations over. The practice was that all meals for guests had to be paid for by the staff member who brought them along. Mr Sydney Bradley, vice-chairman, was in charge of the party and the collection of the monies. I had no guest. Mr Bradley came to me for my contribution, saying that any part-time members of the club were to pay in full. Mr Bradley did not know about my role with the club. Stuart Webb reimbursed me when he was told about it.

The holiday was the first I had taken away from my business for 10 years. The first evening we went out and I thought I was dressed alright – at least, no one said anything to me. The next morning Stuart Webb told me that he wanted to take me into town, and he took me to a gents' outfitters and bought me a pair of denim bell-bottomed trousers and a modern, dark-blue shirt to match, all on the club. He then said 'If you're coming out with us to the bars and dancing, you must look as though you belong to us.' When I went home I underwent a severe grilling.

## Aston Villa and Brian

While Peter was off ill there was a midweek Derby County reserve-team game at Villa Park. Brian asked me to go along with him and he picked me up at the shop on the way. I drove his car to Birmingham. Our reserves won the game 3–1 and after the final whistle Brian went to the dressing room to speak to the lads. He told me to wait in the visitors' reception room and have a cup of tea, and he would come for me when he was ready. After about half an hour Brian popped his head round the door and said that he was ready to leave. We walked along the corridor towards the car park and as we were passing the chairman's room out came Mr Ellis. Locking the door, he turned and in his charming way congratulated Brian on the victory.

'Well done Brian, you've got some very promising young lads.'

'That's very kind of you, Mr Chairman' Brian replied, equally as charming. He introduced me to Mr Ellis. There were only the three of us in the corridor. There was a short pause, then Mr Ellis said to Brian 'How would you like to come and work for a good big club, Brian?'

There was another pause and then Brian, in his majestic way, said 'Mr Ellis, that is a wonderful offer. I would jump at the chance, but seriously, do you think that you and I could work harmoniously together? I personally have considerable doubts'.

'Brian, you are probably correct,' said Mr Ellis, before shaking our hands and wishing us a safe journey home. On the way home in the car we did not discuss the exchange, and I never knew whether Peter was told about it.

In the book *Deadly* by Doug Ellis there is a chapter about Brian and Peter sounding Doug out about being offered the managership of Aston Villa. This took place when they were having a drink together at the Baseball Ground after the transfer of John Robson to Aston Villa from Derby County during December 1972. Unfortunately, John contracted meningitis and died young, his promising career cut unfairly short.

At that time Villa were in League Division Two and managed by Vic Crowe. Derby County had finished the previous season as Champions of League Division One. The story goes that a further meeting took place over lunch in a restaurant in Lichfield, which ended with Mr Ellis saying almost the same as Brian had said to him at Villa Park when I was with them. 'Look Brian, it would never work. There's only one boss at Villa Park and that's me – you and I could never work together.'

I was never told of these meetings, and until I read Mr Ellis's account of them in his book I had absolutely no knowledge of them, although Peter usually discussed behind the scenes happenings with me. Perhaps a reason for this was that relations between the Derby County board and Brian and Peter were a little strained at the time, mainly due to money.

# CHAPTER 5
# 1971–72 DIVISION ONE CHAMPIONS

**W**ith everyone back at the club for pre-season preparations, fully refreshed, the priority was to find a reserve goalkeeper to provide cover for Colin Boulton now that Les Green had left the club. Only friendly games were being played and no one was sure where a goalkeeper might be available. Peter had no one in mind, but wanted a promising young recruit.

Blackburn Rovers had been relegated to Division Three. We had a tip-off that their goalkeeper, Graham Moseley, who had just signed as a full professional from their youth team, was useful. At the same time Jimmy Gordon, the first-team trainer, suggested that a young lad at Middlesbrough (his old club) might be worth a look. The decision about which of them to follow up was left entirely to me. I decided to travel to Ewood Park first to watch Moseley. He was efficient and looked the part, but he did not have much to do. The Middlesbrough reserves were playing on a Wednesday afternoon and I decided to go and watch them too. Jimmy Gordon got permission from the boss to come with me. It was a good chance for him to visit some old friends. We travelled up in the morning, checking before leaving that the lad we were interested in would be playing. During the game he let in two goals, and he was not tall enough for my liking. Even Jimmy was disappointed. The following Saturday, the season proper having just begun, I went back to Blackburn to watch Graham Moseley a second time. This time he was downright impressive and he joined us for £18,000 two months before his 18th birthday.

It was April 1973 before Graham got his chance in the first team when Colin was injured. Before he left Derby he made 44 appearances.

Brian and Peter both forecast a good season ahead. The pre-season games had gone well, and they thought that the side would fulfil its potential. Only Roy McFarland was missing for the first three games due to an injury picked up while on international duty. Derby had a great opening to the campaign, going 11 games unbeaten, including knocking Dundee out of the Texaco Cup after home and away games, 8–5 on aggregate.

Peter was quite a nervous character, and this became very apparent during a scouting trip to Old Trafford. Four of us – Brian, Peter, Stuart and myself – travelled together in Brian's car. At the ground we sat three rows back from the front in the directors' box, and shortly before the game commenced Sir Matt Busby came down and introduced himself, shaking each of our hands and welcoming us all to Old Trafford. To my surprise, it was Brian who seemed to be overwhelmed by all this – he kept on whispering to Peter, 'Fancy Sir Matt Busby doing that. We're now being recognised by the top people.'

On the way home down the M6 it was all Brian could talk about, and his mind must have been elsewhere as his speed kept on creeping up to over 100mph. Terrified Peter, sitting in the front passenger seat, kept telling him to slow down, and eventually he screamed at Brian to pull over as he wanted to get out. Brian pulled into the first lay-by, and Peter jumped out, slammed the door and declared he was not going any further. Brian started to move off, but Stuart managed to persuade him to wait and promise not to exceed 70mph for the rest of the trip. After a short while Peter got back in the car, but hardly a word was spoken by anyone for the remainder of the journey back to Derby.

My first assignment of the season was to go to see Roger Davies play for Worcester City in the Southern League. Mick Walters, one of our scouts (skipper of Burton

Albion when they won the Southern League Cup when managed by Peter), had recommended that we sign Roger. I went along to see them play in their next two games, one home and one away. Roger scored in both of these matches. He had only been at Worcester City a month, having signed professionally for them from Bridgnorth Town at the beginning of the season. A 20-year-old centre-forward weighing 13 stone, he had good body strength. His skill on the ball was exceptional for such a big lad and he had pace and a good work rate, and was good in the air. I was convinced. I reported to Peter what I had seen, adding that he should go to see him as soon as possible, because obviously there would be competition from other clubs.

Worcester City were at home the following Saturday and Peter had decided that we would go together. I drove and we arrived at the St George's ground about an hour before the kick-off. Unannounced, we paid to go in, Peter complete with flat cap and muffler, and we went to the far end of the ground where there would be fewer spectators. As it turned out they were mostly youngsters and no one recognised Peter. Roger scored two goals, one of which was spectacular: he received the ball at his feet just inside the opponents' half, going down the slope, beating two or three defenders on the way to the edge of the penalty area, before side-footing the ball past the 'keeper.

Shortly after, with 10 minutes to go, Peter said 'Let's go'. As we arrived at the turnstiles, the gates open, Paddy Ryan, the chief scout for West Bromwich Albion, emerged from behind the pay box.

'What did you think of the big lad, Peter?' he enquired. Without stopping, Peter replied 'Not good enough for our League Paddy, he lacks class. Cheerio, we're off'. There were several other scouts close by, earwigging. In the car Peter said 'Let's go for a pot of tea at a café.' A short distance away we found a café and had tea and toast. Peter rang the Baseball Ground from the payphone in the café. He came away smiling. Brian had told him that they had beaten Stoke City 4–0, and that he was on his way down to meet us. I drove back to Worcester's ground. The place was almost deserted. Peter went into the office to see the secretary and I stayed in the car. The chairman and his brother (owners of a local building firm) were still there. After about an hour Brian arrived, driven by Michael Keeling, a club director. Roger Davies also returned. It was almost eight o'clock when Brian and Peter emerged from the offices. Peter came to me and said that Roger had signed, but it had cost £14,000. He had only expected to pay about £10,000, but apparently the shrewd brothers had pointed out that Arsenal, Coventry City and Portsmouth were all showing interest, offering trials. Peter went home with Brian and I drove back on my own, thoroughly satisfied with events.

The following Wednesday evening Derby County were playing Dundee United in the home leg of the Texaco Cup fixture. Roger was to be presented to the supporters prior to the kick-off. Peter told me that he wanted me to attend, never mentioning that the chairman was unhappy about the fee. He asked me to arrive early. I was there about an hour before the kick-off. I walked through the doors in Shaftesbury Crescent and at the bottom of the passage Mr Longson, the chairman, was waiting to greet me. 'Ee lad, I want to see thee in my office,' he said, in a stern Derbyshire accent. In I went. 'They tell me that this signing is your doing. £14,000 for a non-League player! Have you gone mad? It'll cost you your job, if he's not good enough. Don't you forget what I'm saying.' Brian and Peter were laughing when I came out. They had set me up.

That first season, when Roger was in the reserves, they won the Central League. At the beginning of the following season he went out on loan to Preston North End, but after only three months he was recalled due to his impressive performances there and injuries within our first team. His debut for us was in November 1972 away at Manchester City, in a 4–0 defeat. The team that day had four regulars missing: Webster, Durban, Gemmill and Hector. His next game was a 4–0 thrashing of Arsenal at the Baseball Ground, and he was soon picked for the first team on merit. His outstanding games were in the FA Cup, scoring at Peterborough and at home in the 1–1 draw with Spurs in front of almost 38,000 spectators. In the return leg at White Hart Lane, in front of another full house of 53,000, in extra-time Roger scored a memorable hat-trick. I had travelled with the team that night, and as there were no seats available I had stood the whole game at the end of the tunnel to the dressing rooms. I had a wonderful proud feeling watching Roger perform. These performances earned Roger an England Under-23 cap. After making 166 appearances and scoring 44 goals, he was sold to Brugge KV for £135,000. I cannot recall Mr Longson ever saying thank you. Roger is currently working at Pride Park as a PR officer.

Steve Powell, the 16-year-old son of Tommy Powell, made his debut for the Rams on 20 October 1971 in a Texaco Cup tie against Stoke City. He played three games in the League for the first XI during the season. He had been outstanding in the reserves, having come through from the youth team, and had set an age record.

At the beginning of December I was given the task of travelling up to Carlisle to watch a lad in his early 20s, a striker that they had taken from Crewe Alexandra (then in the Fourth Division) for a £12,000 fee, Stanley Bowles. Peter told me that there was considerable interest in him and he was linked to several clubs. I was greatly impressed. Although not tall, his skill and general standard was very good. As was our usual practice I checked thoroughly on his background. He was a Manchester boy and had been with Manchester City as a youngster. Joe Mercer, who was their manager in those days, let him go to Bury after some bad behaviour outside the club. He was only at Bury for a short while. I discussed what I had unearthed about Stan with Peter, who said that he would take a chance on him as Brian would soon sort him out. Peter made an approach to Carlisle but could not get Ian MacFarlane to consider less than £90,000 for his transfer. Brian was not too keen on his past history either, so it was decided not to proceed with the transfer. In September 1972, Queen's Park Rangers manager Gordon Jago paid £112,000 for Stan and his goals-to-games ratio during his time with them was better than 30 per cent. QPR were Division Two runners-up in 1972–73 and Division One runners-up in 1974–75, so Stan did very well with them.

**A rare scouting trip away with Brian**
By 8 January 1972, Derby County had only won two of their last four games, and had only won 1–0 at home against Chelsea on New Year's Day. This was causing some concern, as the reasons for the lacklustre performances were not clear. During the week it was decided that Peter and I should travel to Bournemouth on Saturday to take a look at their player Ted MacDougall. In the previous season he had scored 42 goals in Division Four, which had lifted Bournemouth into Division Three. He was still scoring regularly in Division Three but no one at our club had seen him play. We were to set off early on Saturday morning on our 400-mile round trip.

On Friday morning Peter rang to say that there was a change of plans for the weekend. They were going to try a new approach to the pre-match preparations of the first team, to freshen things up a bit. Brian was going to go with me to Bournemouth, leaving that afternoon if I could manage it. The proposed time of departure was 2pm from my shop, travelling in Brian's car and staying overnight in Bournemouth. The first team were due to travel to Southampton and stay overnight. Peter would join them at the Dell at 2pm on Saturday and tell them that Brian would be along later. Peter was going to give the team talk.

I told Peter that I would be able to go. Shortly after 2pm Brian arrived and walked into the shop. I was ready and waiting. 'Have you ever driven an automatic Merc?' he asked.

'No,' I replied, and he threw me the keys.

'You'll soon learn.' He went round to every member of my staff, greeting them with a smile and a few words, with his usual charm.

'I'll look after him,' he shouted, as we walked out of the door. When we got in the car he told me that he had only taken delivery of the car that morning. There were only 125 miles recorded on the clock. Before we reached Lichfield, a matter of 15 miles, Brian was fast asleep in the front passenger seat. He did not wake up until we were travelling round the Winchester bypass. I then asked where we were staying in Bournemouth.

'The Royal Bath,' Brian answered. 'The reservations are made in your name.' I had stayed at the hotel before and was able to drive straight there. On arrival we were met by two porters. One took our bags to the reception, the other took the car into the garage. We were guided to our respective rooms and arranged to meet in the lounge at 7.30pm. Before we went into dinner Brian said 'Peter's explained to you the reason for the change of plan?' I nodded. 'Let's hope it works,' he said.

This was the first time that I had been on my own with Brian for a long period. He went on to describe at great length why a partnership has to be with someone that you have complete faith in. He thought that this was crucial when important decisions had to be made. He was hopeful that the players would get a different approach to pre-match routine from Peter and that it would be successful. Brian was also pleased to get a look at MacDougall, as he thought he knew what a centre-forward was required to do. After the meal we had a couple of beers and went off to bed, agreeing to meet at nine o'clock the next day for breakfast in the dining room.

Next morning Brian appeared in a tracksuit. 'We'll go for a jog after breakfast', he said. Fortunately Peter had pre-warned me and I had taken tracksuit bottoms, a polo-neck pullover and gym shoes. We ran for about four miles along the seafront, to Canford Cliffs and back, talking generally and with him quizzing me about all kinds of things. This was an experience that I will never forget. I enjoyed it immensely. He was a naturally intelligent man, very interesting and completely relaxed. There was no tension and the time passed very quickly. We got on extremely well. He asked me the reason that I had never got into the Football League as a referee, and I told him that it was because of my age. It was a seven-year apprenticeship and I was a late beginner. He told me that I had always impressed him when officiating and said that he was sure that I would have reached the top grade. He went on to tell me that he had always told his players not to get involved disputing referees' decisions as there was nothing to be gained. I wonder what he would think of the happenings on the field of play now?

Back at the hotel it was time for a quick shower then into the lounge at 12.30 for a beer. The waiter brought the menu for lunch. Brian said 'My favourite, boiled beef and carrots. Have you tried it? It's delicious.'

Finishing our lunch, we packed our belongings into the car and set off for Dean Court, arriving about 10 minutes to three. The car park pass and tickets were in my name and we went straight to our seats. Brian did not want to go to the board room at half-time, nor did he want to know the score from Southampton. We left the game about five minutes before full-time. When we got into the car and began to move Brian asked what I had thought of MacDougall's performance as a centre-forward. I told him that I was not impressed and that he was not as good as John O'Hare or Roger Davies. Brian was of exactly the same opinion.

'Let's have the sports report on, its almost five,' he said.

I switched on and we discovered that Derby County had beaten Southampton 3–2. From the debate it seemed that it was a good result.

'Good old Peter, it's worked!' shouted Brian. 'After six, stop at the first village pub we come to for a beer, I need one.' At five past six we went into a very nicely set out village pub. There was not a soul inside, not even behind the bar. The radio was tuned in to the sports reports. Through the strings of beads in the doorway a middle-aged man appeared. He could not have been more surprised than he was when he saw Brian standing at his bar. All Brian said was 'Two halves of beer please'. Looking round he saw a dartboard. He asked me if I played darts and I said that I did. 'Let us play,' he said, asking the landlord for two sets of darts. 'We're playing for £1 a game, to make it interesting,' said Brian. I won the first game. 'Double or quits, come on,' Brian said. This game I won more easily, and he paid up. 'Why didn't you say that you could play like that?' he asked. I then told him that I had grown up in a pub. He said that he would never ever play me again, and he didn't. That is how much winning at anything meant to Brian.

Brian was soon fast asleep in the front passenger seat, and when I reached my house I had to wake him up. It had been a most enjoyable trip with an amazing man.

Frank O'Farrell eventually signed Ted MacDougall for Manchester United for £140,000 but it was a purchase that never fulfilled its potential.

We heard very good reports from Hartlepools about Tony Parry (bought by Brian and Peter from Burton Albion). He was now 27 years old and Peter decided to bring him to Derby County for a £6,000 fee in January 1972 as we were short of cover again. In February 1973 he made his debut, and in all he played six times for the first team. There were high hopes for him. At the end of the season he joined the annual trip to Cala Millor for seven days, but having had too much to drink one night he was guilty of serious misbehaviour in the hotel and was sent home in disgrace the next day by Peter. John Sheridan took him to Palma airport, bought a ticket for Birmingham and made sure he got on the plane. This was another example of the discipline that Brian and Peter exercised over all their staff. He never played for Derby County again after that.

One Tuesday in January, Peter rang to ask if could I pick him up at his home just after 6pm and then pick Brian up at his home, as he wanted to go with us to a game at Sheffield Wednesday. They were then playing in Division Two. Shortly before I left home I got a call from Brian, to ask what time I would be there. I said about half past six and he said he would not be home by then so he would make his own way to Hillsborough. I collected Peter and told him that Brian was running late. 'I bet he won't turn up,' Peter said.

In those days when we arrived at Hillsborough we were allowed into the ground car park through the large iron gates, which were manned by an elderly steward. On arrival Peter told him that we were from Derby County and he gave Peter the envelope with the tickets inside. Peter went on to tell the steward: 'I must warn you that a man in a Mercedes car will probably call here and tell you he's Brian Clough. Don't let him in – he's an impostor pretending to be Brian so he can get free admission. It happens regularly, so don't you let him in.'

It was a bitterly cold winter's evening. Once the game was underway, Peter turned to me. 'I told you Brian wouldn't be here'. Ten minutes before half-time Brian arrived, red-faced and out of breath. He was furious. He had arrived at about kick-off time, but the old man would not let him into the ground under any circumstances. He had parked his car about two miles away and run all the way back. We both burst out laughing. He glared at us. 'You pair of b*****ds!'

Shortly before the end of the game we all left together. We took him in my car back to where he had parked, and it was indeed a fair distance away.

Ian Storey-Moore became the next target from Forest, a wide attacking player with pace who possessed a wonderful goalscoring record. Peter was firmly fixed on bringing him to Derby County. He knew his capabilities very well. Ian was the best player in his position around at that time. From the outset the committee that ran Forest was determined not to lose another player to Derby. An agreed figure of £200,000 was well documented in the press, but Manchester United came on the scene, prepared to match the asking price. Ian was given the choice between the two clubs. I understand that he chose Derby County, as it would mean not having to move home, and at this time more honours were likely to be won at Derby. United were going through an unusually quiet period.

Ken Smales, the secretary of Nottingham Forest, was instructed by his committee not to sign the transfer forms under any circumstances. At the next home game, Ian was paraded in front of the Derby County crowd as their latest signing, but the ruse failed badly. Later that evening Ian and his wife, Carol, returned to their Nottingham home. Shortly afterwards two visitors were at the front door, Sir Matt Busby and Frank O'Farrell, the Manchester United manager, armed with a bunch of red roses for Carol. Ian, inwardly realising that Forest were determined not to let him join Derby, signed for United that same evening. The transfer went through without the slightest hitch. Unfortunately, after a very successful period playing in the first team, gaining international recognition and doing well, Ian severely damaged his leg ligaments. Although he worked hard to recover, the injury caused his career in League football to come to an end. During his stay at Manchester United no honours were won, while Derby County won the Championship in 1971–72 and 1974–75.

This saga ended with the Football League fining Derby County £5,000 for parading Ian in front of the Baseball Ground fans when he was not their player, which was classed as a breach of regulations.

With the continuous amount of good copy coming out of Derby County, journalists used to wait for hours in the press room under the Main Stand, supping tea, waiting in hope to get a few words from Brian, or a breaking story. Most of the dailies were canny; they used a good guy and an unpopular guy (with Brian) for writing sports stories. The ones who had upset Brian he would have nothing to say to, while the good early stories were released to the trusted.

## My 24 hours with Manchester United

On four occasions during my time in football I was offered a full-time appointment and only once did I verbally accept. My private Post Office business, with its security and financial rewards, meant that I had no need to make football my full-time occupation.

To my knowledge this story has never been told before. In February 1972, Peter rang me to say that he had been approached by Frank O'Farrell to become his assistant manager at Manchester United. At that time United was going through a very difficult period. Frank and Peter had known one another since they were both successful managers of clubs in the Southern League. Peter said that the offer was very good and that he was very flattered to have been asked. He had asked Frank if I could be recruited as his main assistant for scouting. I was sure that this was because he was nervous about being on his own and he wanted someone by his side whom he could trust. Frank had agreed, but only if I would join them on a full-time basis. This offer shook me for a few moments and I felt as if I had not the faintest idea what had been said. Manchester United! There could not be a bigger incentive to go full-time. I asked if I could talk it over with my family before making a final decision. Peter said that he had arranged to meet Frank in the car park by the canal at Willington, near Peter's home, the next Sunday morning.

By Sunday I had decided that I would join them, if I could be paid a minimum of £400 per week (that was the sum of money that my business was making me) and be allowed up to four months to sell my house and business and move up to Manchester. After his meeting with Frank, on Sunday afternoon Peter came over to my house to let me know how things were progressing. Frank did not foresee any problems with my requests, and it was all to go before the full board of directors in the morning.

Early on Monday afternoon Peter rang to say that the Manchester United board of directors had thrown Frank's proposals out. They had not given him any reasons why. Peter was extremely disappointed, but strangely it did not affect me. I was perfectly happy with my present arrangements, but at the same time I was mystified about why Frank's plan had been refused. After a couple of days turning it over in my mind, I decided to ring Alec Bird at his home at Nether Alderley. I knew that Alec was a very close friend of Mr Louis Edwards, the United chairman, and saw him regularly at their Lodge meetings. In fact, the house that Alec lived in had been purchased from Mr Edwards. I explained what had taken place at the meetings with Frank O'Farrell and asked whether he would be able to find out, discreetly, why the board had thrown the plan out.

A week later Alec called me back. Apparently all the members of the board had agreed to the proposed appointments, but Sir Matt Busby was very much against it, although he had no problem with the two men involved. Sir Matt's reasoning (he was probably spot on) was that Brian Clough would murder Manchester United in the media and on television for stealing his right-hand men.

I told Peter what had actually happened, and he thought it very likely that Brian would have had a go at them. There the matter was laid to rest. The story was never leaked and Brian never got an inkling of it. Manchester United were relegated into League Division Two at the end of that season and Frank lost his job, while Derby County went on to win the Division One Championship.

## Tickets for 'all ticket games' and train seats

With the continued success on the field, top-of-the-League matches, Cup games and later European Cup games had become all-ticket affairs. Supporters from the Burton upon Trent area and South Derbyshire, who gave Derby County tremendous support, were having difficulty in getting to Derby to purchase tickets when they went on sale at the Baseball Ground. I discussed the situation with Stuart Webb, the club secretary, who agreed to let me have 3,000 tickets for each game, for the standing enclosure, to sell at my shop. The restrictions were that tickets could not be put on sale until they were available on open sale at Derby, and each person could purchase no more than two tickets. I agreed to these terms and I had to pay for the tickets fully up front. These tickets were some of the 35,000 tickets that were made available for home supporters. On every occasion I was completely sold out. The newspaper department of my shop opened at 5am every day, including Sundays. I made sure that I had ample staff to cope with the extra demand each time. It brought me rewards, as well, because most fans picked up cigarettes, sweets, pop, stationery or greetings cards when buying their tickets, and many became regular customers even after I had left Derby County. It was such a success that Stuart arranged for one of the special British Rail trains that took fans to away games, often to London clubs, to leave from Burton station. For these I would have 100 tickets giving a seat on the train and a ticket for the game to sell. This again was very popular and appreciated by local supporters.

## A most memorable telephone call

As in previous years Peter, with one director, had taken the players (except those on international duty) and senior staff to Cala Millor in Majorca for an end-of-season break. Brian was in the Scilly Isles with his family. When we left England, all our fixtures had been completed and we were top of League Division One.

There were one or two outstanding games to be resolved, and the League table actually read:

|            | P  | W  | D  | L  | For | Ag | Pts |
|------------|----|----|----|----|-----|----|-----|
| Derby Co.  | 42 | 24 | 10 | 8  | 69  | 33 | 58  |
| Leeds Utd  | 41 | 24 | 9  | 8  | 72  | 29 | 57  |
| Man. City  | 42 | 23 | 11 | 8  | 77  | 45 | 57  |
| Liverpool  | 41 | 24 | 8  | 8  | 64  | 30 | 56  |
| Arsenal    | 41 | 22 | 7  | 11 | 57  | 38 | 51  |

Games still to be played: Leeds away to Wolves, Liverpool away to Arsenal

It was an unbelievable climax to the season. If Leeds drew or won away they would be Champions. Liverpool had to win to be Champions. In the event, Leeds lost 2–1 at Wolves and Liverpool drew 0–0 at Arsenal.

When we left England few people thought that Derby County had any chance of being crowned Champions. On the night that the matches were played the senior staff all stayed in the bar of our hotel, the Bahia. You could feel the tension. Some of the players drifted in and joined us. About 15 minutes before the games were due to end, Peter was called into the foyer of the hotel by a porter. A British journalist had rung Peter from Molineux and told him not to hang up, as at that moment Derby were Champions. When Peter did not return, one by one we crept into the foyer. There was complete silence, all eyes were glued on Peter. He was ashen white. This dreadful suspense lasted for 20 minutes that seemed like two hours. Suddenly he raised his free arm in the air and shouted. 'We've won it, we've won it!' The place erupted. Back in the bar the party started. The other guests at the hotel all joined in and the celebrations went on until the early hours of the morning. Not one sports journalist from the United Kingdom was in Cala Millor that evening.

Early next morning, shortly after breakfast, a Spanish television crew arrived to film us relaxing round the pool at our hotel. As the pool next door at the Castel de Mar, where the players were staying, was much bigger and would allow better filming we moved over there. No players had surfaced at that time, so five of the staff, including myself, swam for them in the pool as they wanted the film urgently so that it could be relayed out for the early news bulletins. When the pictures were shown in the UK it was said that we were Derby County players, but they were all still tucked up in bed. By the time of the evening meal, both the hotels were swarming with sports journalists from the British national press doing interviews with Peter and the players. The rest of the holiday seemed to drag for us all; we just wanted to get home to our relatives and friends.

The remarkable achievement of winning the League had been done with the use of only 16 players during the whole season, including three appearances by Jim Walker, two by Steve Powell and one by Tony Bailey.

It had been a wonderful season that ended in glory and celebration. After that, the winning of the Texaco Cup went almost unnoticed. This was a trophy played home and away that included teams from the Scottish Football League. Derby won the competition by defeating Dundee United, Stoke City, Newcastle United and Airdrieonians. Because of the large number of fixtures Barry Butlin was brought back off loan to play in these games. In the Texaco competition alone, over 100,000 spectators witnessed the games played at the Baseball Ground. Over the whole season more than one million spectators had been to the Baseball Ground, compared to 300,000 five years before.

### Footnote to the season: another record signing

During the summer of 1972, the annual Burton and District Tennis Championships had reached the final stages. The Men's Singles was an open event. One of my close friends, Ian Tate, had reached the final and was recognised as the best player in the Burton District. He was also a good class rugby player and a regular in the well-known Leicester Tigers. He had been educated at Burton Grammar School (well-known for producing top sportsmen) and was the nephew of the famous Sussex and England cricketer Maurice Tate.

Ian invited me to the final, saying that perhaps I knew his opponent, David Nish, the Leicester City footballer. The event was taking place on the council tennis courts at Shobnall Fields, only a mile from my house. My ears pricked up and I immediately thought 'I hope I get chance to speak to him on his own'.

When I arrived in the car park, who should pull up immediately alongside but David Nish himself. What a stroke of luck! I greeted David and he asked where the changing rooms were as it was his first visit.

'I'll walk with you,' I said. 'You're playing one of my friends.' I wished him good luck in the game and then went to my seat.

David won the final very impressively. He was well above average at tennis. I waited for him to receive the trophy, shower and get changed. I then walked back to the car with him. The many spectators had left by this time. I had decided to make an approach about joining Derby County. I would never get a better opportunity. I explained my job with Brian and Peter at Derby County and said that they would very much like him in their side for the start of the following season, to play as left-back. I asked him if he was interested. He said he was. The prospect of playing in the European Cup was very attractive. We exchanged telephone numbers and I told him to keep the conversation under his hat, promising that he would soon hear something officially from his club.

That evening I spoke to Peter in Majorca and told him everything that had transpired. Peter flew back from his holiday the following Monday very pleased, and before the end of that week David Nish joined Derby County for a fee of £225,000, a new transfer record. He made his debut on 26 August 1972 at Norwich and went on to make 237 appearances for Derby County, including 38 League appearances when they won the League Division One Championship, gaining a medal under Dave Mackay in the 1974–75 season. He was capped five times for England and but for illness it would have been more.

Brian, who was also away on holiday, did not know a thing about this transfer until it was all completed.

Unfortunately, David's career came to an end prematurely when he severely damaged his right knee ligaments, while still playing at Derby County. He would have been a great player with the modern ball. I met him recently at a Derby County reunion and I reminded him about the tennis. He told me that as a teenager he had had the chance to be a professional tennis player, but had chosen soccer.

# CHAPTER 6
# THE DERBY DREAM DIES

The 1972–73 season started with great hopes. For the first time in the history of Derby County they would be competing in Europe. It was also a first for Brian and Peter.

With the arrival of David Nish, and the emergence of Steve Powell, John Robson, who had been a great servant at full-back, was sold to Aston Villa for £90,000 as soon as Nish qualified to play in the third round of the European competition.

The first round was satisfactorily completed with a 4–1 aggregate victory over a Yugoslavia side, FK Zeljenicar, in Sarajevo. The second round was against Portuguese side Benfica and the first leg was played at Derby. The ground had been saturated with water during the day by the groundsman, on Brian's instructions, and to put it mildly the going was heavy. No members of the press were allowed into the ground until after 5pm. A 3–0 victory was the result and the score was 0–0 in the return leg. John McGovern's superb goal was one to be remembered. John told me that he had met Eusebio recently, and after 35 years he had brought up the condition of the Baseball Ground that evening. Eusebio said that the pitch that night was the worst that he ever played on.

The third round involved a long journey to Czechoslovakia to play Sparta Tranava, where the Rams lost by a single goal. They won the return leg 2–0, Kevin Hector scoring both of the goals at the Baseball Ground.

On 7 March, in the semi-final of the European Cup, Derby were knocked out over the two legs in controversial circumstances. The first leg in Turin resulted in a 3–1 victory to Juventus, before a 72,000 crowd; however, there were several unsatisfactory incidents prior to and during the game. The players and the team staff were staying at a hotel in the hills outside Turin, while the directors, senior staff and the press were staying in the city. Stuart Webb had arranged a dinner for the press and special guests at which Brian was to be the guest speaker. Brian was still in his tracksuit playing cards with several of his players when the time to go arrived. Being late for appointments was a bad habit of Brian's. Peter came and reminded him that they would be late for the dinner date and an argument followed between the two in front of the players, which was not a good thing before such an important game. Peter refused to go without Brian and went up to his room. Neither of them went to the dinner; I assume Stuart had to make the speech himself. Next morning, sensibly, they patched up their differences. The team was announced and with it came a big surprise: Tony Parry was included in the side instead of Alan Durban, to play in midfield. Peter had not seen the teamsheet the night before and he told Brian that playing Tony Parry in a game of such magnitude was ridiculous. At this late stage Brian decided to make the change. He told Alan Durban to go and put the number-four shirt on. This was in the last minute before the team left the dressing room. When Alan arrived on the pitch the teams were actually lining up, and the press were unaware of the change until the game was ready to begin.

John Charles, who had played for Juventus at centre-forward some years previously, travelled with the team to help with the language and familiarize the players with their surroundings. I had met John Charles at the wedding of one of my close pals, Dave MacAdam, in Leeds. Dave was in the Leeds United team when John joined them as an 18-year-old and Major Buckley, the Leeds manager, had put John in the same digs as Dave and instructed him to look after him.

John went to the Derby dressing room about half an hour before the kick-off to warn Brian and Peter that he had seen one of the Juventus subs, Helmut Haller, (who had played for Germany at Wembley in the 1966 World Cup Final) talking with the referee, Gerhard Schulenberg, also a German. At half-time the pair were talking as the two teams trooped off the field. Peter joined them to earwig, angry words were exchanged and Peter was arrested and kept in custody at the stadium until the two teams were back on the field to resume playing. Peter told me that he was in such a state he had completely lost his temper. Two of our most influential players, Roy McFarland and Archie Gemmill, were booked after innocuous tackles on Juventus players, which meant that they would miss the return leg at the Baseball Ground.

It could not be proved that Haller and the referee were in cahoots. The rules stated only that no players or team representatives were allowed to enter the referee's room. An official complaint was made to UEFA about the referee's handling of the game, but after an enquiry no apparent action was taken. However, shortly afterwards the referee became the owner of a brand new car and never officiated at international level again.

The second leg, two weeks later at Derby, finished 0–0. Juventus went through to the Final and there were no complaints this time. We had much more early possession of the ball in the game, but Alan Hinton unusually missed a penalty and later Roger Davies was sent off the field. Brian Glanville of the *Sunday Times* acted as the interpreter for Brian Clough (Glanville spoke fluent Italian) and even to this day he sometimes mentions in his articles the goings-on in Turin. One further interesting observation from these games against Juventus is that Fabio Capello, now in charge of the England international football team, played on both occasions.

One evening, while attending a game at Villa Park, I was sitting with Brian having a cup of tea when Bill Nicholson the Tottenham Hotspur manager, came into the room and sat with us. He congratulated Brian on winning the Division One title the previous season. Brian thanked him, then said that he wished that he was with a big club like Bill's. Bill replied that management of any London club was no great joy.

'In smaller towns and cities you know where your players are on the Friday evening before a home game,' he said. 'If they were out on the town, someone would tell you. In London we have no chance. Last Saturday morning Martin

Chivers didn't turn up until midday looking really rough. We'd made numerous attempts to locate him, but they can easily get lost in the big city. Morning pre-match preparations are virtually impossible to do.' Nowadays doormen, photographers and the media are always on the lookout for players, so it is not so easy to get away with it. The London nightlife certainly caused Bill a few headaches, and the following season he decided to leave White Hart Lane after 16 years of considerable success.

New signings were now at a minimum because of European restrictions on when signings had to be completed for a player to be eligible to play in the European Cup. For me it was a quiet time. The team was of such a high standard that it had become much harder to find new players who might gain a place in the first team. Fortunately there were no long-term injuries. I went abroad two or three times to assess forthcoming opposition, twice with Peter and once on my own. Brian was very wary of flying.

Behind the scenes, week by week, problems were arising between Brian and Peter. Brian's work away from the club, and the time he spent away from the Baseball Ground travelling and making television appearances, particularly on Fridays, were at the heart of the matter. When this had begun the chairman had been glad of the PR opportunity that the increased media attention brought.

At about this time Brian was offered a full-time position with ITV by Brian Moore, to be a football critic and an analyst of games, but he turned it down. However, Brian was also in demand for opening supermarkets and petrol stations, and these engagements meant that Peter was having to spend more time with the team. Peter occasionally made local public appearances himself, but he regularly turned down invitations to appear as a guest speaker. He was too nervous to attempt these on his own.

I could sense a real rift developing between Brian and Peter. When I asked Peter what the problem was he poured out the whole story. Unsurprisingly, money was the root of the trouble. He said that in Hartlepools days he and Brian had agreed that extra payments and bonuses outside of their contracts should be equally shared. I knew that football bonuses were always split; however, I did not agree with Peter, and told him so, that he should be getting a share of the TV money and the income from other activities. I argued that this money was earned by Brian's personality and popularity with the general public. I felt myself that these were his own earnings. In reply Peter said that Brian would not be able to carry on with his TV and promotional work if Peter did not stand in for him. Peter was spending more time with the team, particularly on Fridays. Stuart Webb had also let slip to Peter that the chairman had paid Brian an extra £5,000 without Peter's knowledge. Another factor was that at this time Peter was gambling heavily on football results. I knew because I was putting the bets on for him. He was having a run of poor form with these.

There was a marked deterioration in League performances on the pitch. I put this down to the emphasis that Brian and Peter put on the European games, and these differences that kept on arising between them. The existing playing squad was also not large enough to cope with the extra games.

There was a blank Saturday in the fixture list for the first team on 7 April. It was decided that eight of us would travel up to Scotland on a scouting mission to watch four games in the lower divisions of the Scottish Football League. There were two cars, Brian's and Michael Keeling's, with four of us in each car. We set off before lunch on the Friday morning: Brian, Peter, Jimmy Gordon, John Sheridan, Brian Newton, Cliff Notley, Michael Keeling and myself. We all went to a game at St James' Park during that evening, staying overnight in a hotel in Newcastle. On Saturday morning after breakfast we set off for Scotland, where we split into four pairs. One pair from each car was dropped off at the first venue selected, while the two left in the car went on to another game, returning later to pick up the pairs that were dropped off. These arrangements went without a hitch. I remember that I was at Stenhousemuir with Cliff Notley. The game was of a much poorer standard than I had expected, having not watched any Scottish games live before. I was of the opinion that they were not up to the standard of Burton Albion. We all drew a complete blank and did not see even one spark of talent. It was a completely wasted journey. We arrived home shortly before midnight.

As the season drew to a close, one morning Mr Arthur Whittaker, the bookmaker whose betting shop was opposite the Baseball Ground in Shaftesbury Crescent, came to see Brian. I was in his office at the time. Mr Whittaker was very concerned because one of the Derby County first-team players had run up a debt of £700 of losing bets. Attempts to get the player to pay up had failed. Brian reacted immediately. He was fully aware that things like this could cause players to lose form. He rang Stuart Webb, the club secretary, and asked him to bring £700 to his office as soon as possible. Stuart arrived quickly and the money was passed over to Mr Whittaker. Arthur was then told that as of that moment all staff and players of Derby County Football Club would be barred from his betting shop. Brian instructed Stuart to send out a letter to everyone with this information. His quick thinking and decisive action meant that there was never a leak of the story to the public. It was yet another example of how quickly Brian dealt with internal problems so that they did not become more serious. The player in question had to repay the money to the club, but I did not hear whether he was punished further.

### An offer to work for Don Revie

One Friday evening, 16 March 1973, I was enjoying a well-earned cup of tea, having just finished my work in the Post Office. I had been working on the weekly account balance since closing time and I was contemplating going to the chip shop next door to fetch fish and chips for a ritual Friday evening meal. The telephone rang and my immediate thought was that one of my customers had not received their evening paper, which would mean me turning out to deliver it. I picked up the telephone.

'Am I speaking to Maurice Edwards?'

'Yes,' I replied tentatively, as I did not recognise the voice.

'This is Don Revie,' the voice continued. My immediate reaction was that one of my friends was playing a prank.

'Come on Timmo, stop taking the piss,' I said. There was a low chuckle.

'Who are Derby County playing in the FA Cup tomorrow?'

'Leeds United,' I replied, realising that it really was the great Don Revie.

'We're staying at the Riverside Hotel at Branston. Have you eaten yet?' he asked. I said no.

'Would you join me for a meal here? There's something I'd like to discuss with you.'

'Thank you,' I said. 'I'll be there in about half an hour'.

Entering the lounge at the Riverside, I saw Don Revie on a settee on the far side of the room alongside a middle-aged gentleman. I went over. Don stood up and shook my hand, then introduced me to Les Cocker, his first-team coach, who had a pint of beer in his hand. I sat down and joined in their general conversation. One of the coaching staff came out of the dining room and told Don that the players had finished their evening meal. Did he want to have a few words before they retired to their respective rooms? Don excused himself and went into the restaurant, leaving me on my own with Les Cocker. I quickly realised that Les had been drinking for some time. His speech was slurred and he said 'Who the f*****g hell are you, what are you here for? There shouldn't be any part-timers in this game.' Half turning towards me, he fell off the settee full-length onto the floor, spilling his beer all over the carpet. At that moment Don returned and was not very pleased with what he saw. He called for two of his staff to take Les to his room, with instructions to lock him in and bring the key back. Don then apologised to me for Les's behaviour.

We then went into the dining room; there were just the two of us at the table. Our evening meal was ordered, together with a bottle of wine. I was still unsure what the meeting was all about. Don began by telling me that he had received one or two very reliable reports about my work with Brian and Peter. He had also heard from pressmen that the two of them were having a few problems and he asked whether these affected me in any way. I said that they did not and that I was completely out of internal affairs at the club. Differences were always happening in football and as long as I was not directly involved I ignored them. Don then came to the main reason for the meeting. 'I've got a proposition to put to you,' he said. 'I want you to come and work for me, to be my personal scouting rep. We would keep close secrecy between us, you would discuss your findings with me and no one else. You could continue working from home. I'm prepared to make you a good financial offer, certainly more than you are getting.' I was very flattered, if a little taken aback. I thanked him very much for the offer, but refused it. I went on to explain that I owed everything to Peter Taylor and without him I would not have achieved what I had in League football.

'Money doesn't come into it at all,' I said. 'I'll stay with them as long as they want me to be part of the team.' Before I left, Don produced a briefcase. Out came a large number of handwritten papers. He showed them to me briefly; they were reports on each of the Derby County players, very descriptive of their assets and shortcomings.

'This is how I prepare for all of our games,' he said. 'Who will be the main threat to Leeds tomorrow?'

'Archie Gemmill', I replied. He promptly pulled out the dossier on Archie.

'This is the reason why I'm keen to have you working for me,' he said. The last thing he said to me before I left was that he admired my loyalty to Brian and Peter.

'I wish some of my staff had the same principles,' he said. 'If you ever change your mind, give me a ring.'

His preparations for the game must have worked. Derby County were knocked out of the FA Cup the next day.

I never said a word to Peter or Brian about meeting Don or what had transpired. To this day I am not certain whether or not it was altogether genuine. At the back of my mind I wonder whether it was a ruse to take me away from Brian, to rob him of one of his main back-room assistants. At that time they were certainly bitter enemies, as later events went on to prove; however, I am sure that deep down they each admired what the other had achieved.

I must admit I was impressed by my meeting with Don Revie. I was proud to have been approached and I had enjoyed it immensely. When Peter and Brian inevitably split from Derby County, Don did telephone me to say that the offer was still open if I wanted it, but I remained loyal to my bosses.

Don Revie was appointed successor to Alf Ramsey as manager of the England team in April 1974. If I had decided to join Don Revie at Leeds United, when Brian was appointed their manager the first person to have been shown the door would have been me. When Don was appointed England manager he did not ask me to join him. In fact, I never once came face to face with him again, nor spoke to him on the phone. This contributed to my feeling that the original approach was intended to split up our camp at Derby County.

It is interesting to compare Don Revie's record with Brian and Peter's (when they were working together). Brian and Peter had 12 years at Derby County and Nottingham Forest; Don had 14 years at Leeds United. Brian and Peter won six major trophies and were runners-up twice, while Don won five major trophies and was runner-up 10 times. With all his thoroughness in preparation I concluded that Don erred on the side of caution. In my opinion at least five of those runners'-up medals should have been trophies. The main difference between them was that Brian and Peter's pre-match preparations were focussed on their own sides, whereas Don's were focussed on the opposition. In Brian's classic words 'Let the b*****ds worry about us.'

## Brian and Peter resign

At the start of the 1973–74 season, Peter had received a big tip-off about a schoolboy in the Doncaster area that had exceptional skills. He asked me to go up on a Friday evening to offer his mother and father an apprenticeship at Derby County when he left school.

Armed with his address I went up to Bawtry and knocked on the front door. I explained where I was from and was invited into the front room. Mr Rix listened to all that I had to say. He also told me that another club had already spoken to him. He asked whether I could come again the following week and they would give me a definite answer.

I duly went along the following Friday. When I arrived there was a brand new car outside. Once again I was invited into the front room, which had been completely refurnished and decorated, carpeted wall to wall. It was clear that my journey had been wasted. Mr Rix thanked me for the interest that we had shown, and asked that I pass regards on to Brian. To be fair, we were second on the scene. Graham, their son, joined Arsenal as an apprentice in 1974. He went on to make 464 appearances for Arsenal and won 17 international caps.

Mr Longson would never have agreed to gifts of this kind being given by Derby County in the quest to sign players. I took this new experience on board.

In late September 1973, Henry Newton became a Derby County player after Peter's third attempt to bring him to our club. He joined us from Everton for £100,000 and he was the only major signing for the new season. He only made three appearances under Brian and Peter, including a 1–0 victory away at Old Trafford. His total number of appearances for Derby was 156, including 36 during the 1974–75 season when they won the Division One Championship under Dave Mackay.

Each week something different occurred behind the scenes. Some of Brian's comments about other clubs, Leeds United in particular, which were aired on television and in the media, were very forthright. Complaints from other chairmen were upsetting the Derby County board, and away from football Sam Longson's friends in his village began to get at him about how rude and awful 'your Mr Clough' was.

I could sense that breaking point was not too far away. When Brian had first taken on this television work, Mr Longson had encouraged him, saying that it was good publicity for Derby County. Since then he had had a change of heart. Sam knew that there was a chance that he might be elected to the Football League Committee, and he thought that Brian's televised remarks were diminishing his chances.

Another incident took place after an excellent win away at Old Trafford 1–0, before a 43,000 crowd. Mr Jack Kirkland, a fairly new recruit to the boardroom, had seen Peter present at the game and asked, at the next meeting of directors, why Peter was on such a high salary when he just sat with Brian at games. Peter was made aware of this statement, and he did not take too kindly to it.

Mr Longson was not handling the situation very well and the other directors were worried that the FA would step in. Peter was getting worried and he told me of his concern. He had been shown a letter sent to Brian by Sam Longson telling him that he must give up his work on television and writing articles in the national press. On the following Sunday Brian and Peter decided that they would hand in letters of resignation, but they had not done this by the Tuesday.

Peter rang me at lunchtime. He wanted me to take him to Bury, a Division Four side, to see Derek Spence play. The centre-forward was of interest because of the number of goals he was scoring. 'Will you pick me up at home at 4.30? Kick-off is 7.30, but the chairman wants to come with us to see one of the directors of Bury, Canon Reg Smith.'

I had met Canon Smith some time before on the aeroplane that took the Derby County players and staff to an away tie in the European Cup. He sat next to me. He was a very jovial man, and that day he said to me on take-off, 'This is my first experience of flying. I suppose this is the nearest that I shall ever get to my gaffer!' In the car on the way to Chapel-en-le-Frith, where Sam Longson lived, Peter told me that we had been invited to have tea by Mrs Longson. When we arrived we were taken into a large conservatory where the table was well laid out, with china tea cups, sandwiches with the crusts taken off and serviettes. We were made most welcome.

When we left, I was driving and Mr Longson and Peter sat in the back. This was obviously what had been planned.

'Peter, I want you to take over as the manager of the club,' said the chairman. 'The directors and I have decided that Brian has to go. We feel that he has really overstepped the mark this time, and we're in no doubt that you are fully capable of running the football side of the club. We are prepared to give you a large increase in salary.'

Peter was superb at handling the situation.

'Forget it, Mr Chairman,' he said. 'In two weeks time the problems between you and Brian will have blown over and the two of you will be the best of friends again. I don't want to carry on this discussion; let's settle down and think about what we're looking for at Bury'.

When we arrived at Bury's ground Sam went into the directors' room and sat in their box to watch the match. Peter and I sat at the very rear of the directors' box. On the journey home no more was said about the situation at Derby, although the chairman did ask us what had we decided about Derek Spence. Peter told him that we would not be making an offer.

On 15 October, Peter and Brian handed in their written notices. I also sent in my written resignation. I did not attend any of the protest meetings; it really was no concern of mine. Strangely, all these problems had not affected the performances of the team. Derby County were actually lying in third place in the League, having won four, drawn two and lost one of the first seven games. Attendances were almost up to capacity and financially the club was in a healthy position, with over £200,000 in the bank.

### Dave Mackay's appointment as manager

Almost immediately Dave Mackay was appointed as manager of Derby County. He brought with him his assistant, Des Anderson. Dave had only been in charge at Nottingham Forest for 11 months, having begun his management career at Swindon Town for the previous year. His appointment at Derby was a very clever move by the chairman. The players had great respect for Dave Mackay and so did the supporters, which calmed the situation down very quickly.

Stuart Webb rang me the following week asking if I would come along to the Baseball Ground to see Dave. I went the following afternoon. Dave and Des had certainly done their homework. As I entered the manager's office I saw on the cocktail cabinet about 10 bottles of Mackeson, my drink in those days. I shook hands with both Dave and Des and I accepted a drink that was offered. Dave said that they wanted me to become their chief scout, on double the wages that I had been on. The meeting lasted about two hours and we discussed how they were going to take the club forward, and what my role would be if I joined them. The wages were not an incentive – my Post Office business was doing well – but I did enjoy my involvement in football at that level. However, I knew that Brian and Peter had already been approached by two League clubs, Birmingham City and Coventry City. I had great admiration for Dave and I was impressed with Des, who seemed a very likeable fellow. Over the years I have got to know them very well, and I am sure I would have enjoyed working for them. But I turned down their offer. I gave them my genuine reason: I intended to carry on working with Brian and Peter in the future when they were fixed up with another League club. I felt I owed them for taking me with them on their journey. I thanked Dave and Des for giving me the opportunity to join them and wished them every success. I have never regretted staying with Brian and Peter.

With two top-class additions to the side that they had inherited, Bruce Rioch and Francis Lee, Derby County again became League Division One Champions at the end of the 1974–75 season. During a game against Luton Town Roger Davies became the first Rams player to score five goals in a League game. I was delighted at the club's success. To this day I have a great affection for Derby County.

## Derby County lose Russell Osman

Despite my respect for Dave and Des, they did make a mess of their attempt to gain Russell Osman's signature. I took Russell along to Derby at the age of 13 and he attended coaching lessons, but he could not be put on forms until he was 16. Russell's parents, Rex and Diane, were friends of mine who at that time ran the Bull's Head in Repton. Rex had been a professional player with Derby County during the 1950s, making two first-team appearances, and was with the Rams for several seasons. He was captain of the reserves and we used to joke with him that he was only retained each season because of his golf – he was the major player in a very good club golf team.

Two of his sons, Mark and Russell, were educated at the Burton Grammar School. Rugby and cricket were the main sports taught there. Each of them in their respective years was captain of the England Schools Rugby Fifteen, an outstanding achievement. Almost every night they played soccer with the other boys in the village, and at the inn there was a very large car park, surrounded by three walls with a tarmac surface, which was ideal for developing skills. During this time I was refereeing in the Burton & District leagues. Both boys played for Repton Casuals, the village team, which was a very well-organised club. The club's youngsters were a very good side, winning several local trophies. I watched them playing on Sunday mornings and occasionally refereed their matches. I asked Rex if I could take Russell along to Derby County to be coached and to play with our youngsters. He agreed but disputed my choice: he was of the opinion that Mark, the elder of the two, was the better prospect. We had many a chat about it. Mark never went into League football.

John Sheridan, one of our coaches at Derby County, looked after the boys when they were in for coaching and training sessions. Russell had always played in the wing-half position when I had seen him. John, in his wisdom, moved him into central defence with considerable success. Russell continued to play football for Repton Casuals and rugby at school. Russell was 16 on St Valentine's Day 1975. This was the season that Derby became Division One Champions again. Dave Mackay and Des Anderson went to visit Rex (Russell's father) with the intention of completing the forms for Russell to officially become a Derby County player. I was not present in the Bull's Head that evening, but they went away without obtaining his signature. Rex and Di told me about the visit, saying that Dave and Des had arrived having had too much to drink and had offended Rex, who was a strong character and had asked them to leave the premises. What a loss to Derby Russell Osman turned out to be!

Frank Upton, a playing colleague of Rex's at Derby, was the chief scout at Aston Villa. He lived in the next village to Repton and heard what had happened when he called in for a drink one day. He arranged for Russell to go to Villa Park for a trial with other youngsters during the Easter holidays. A lot of boys were on trial that day and Russell was played out on the right wing. He did not have the pace for that position and he came away very disappointed. Frank Upton was furious when he was told the story of the trial. It was unfortunate, but Russell was never going to be a winger. He was not asked to return for a further trial. I told his father not to worry and forecast that a big club would come his way. I was then at Nottingham Forest with Brian, at the bottom of Division Two of the Football League. I spoke to Rex about taking Russell to Forest but he declined – he was still anti-Forest from his playing days.

Shortly after this, Tom Robson, brother of Bobby (who was then manager of Ipswich Town), came to see Rex to offer Russell a trial at Ipswich. Tom Robson was a mining engineer and had been transferred to Moira, only a few miles from Burton upon Trent. Working alongside him in the same office was Les Holland, a member of the Burton & District Football Association Committee. Bobby had told his brother Tom that Ipswich did not have a scout in that part of the country and that he should be on the look out for any talent. Tom quizzed Les about young footballers with a chance of getting into the professional game. Les told him about Russell and the rest is history. Russell signed for Ipswich on 1 March 1976. Later his parents, Rex and Di, went to live in the Ipswich area. Rex passed away suddenly in 2005.

Russell's prowess came as no surprise to me. He made over 600 League and Cup appearances, gaining 11 international caps. There cannot be many lads who have played international football and rugby union for England. On occasions Russell has popped in to see me as I have stayed in touch with the family. He does a wonderful amount of good for charities and in 2006 cycled from Lands End to John O'Groats.

# CHAPTER 7
# MOVING ON

At the end of October 1973, Peter rang to say that he and Brian had an appointment at the Waldorf Hotel in London with Mike Bamber, the chairman of Brighton and Hove Albion. He said that there was a strong possibility that they would take on the management of the club. The chairman did a good job and persuaded them to join Brighton. Peter was very upbeat about the move, but Brian was not as keen.

They took over at Brighton on 1 November 1973. The club was sixth from bottom of Division Three and the average gate was around 6,000. About six scouts that had been at Derby, including myself, joined up with them immediately. John Sheridan, the second-team coach at Derby, also joined them. Peter, with his wife Lilian, daughter Wendy and son Philip, moved to Brighton.

Brian and his wife Barbara viewed several houses, but the ones that they liked were too expensive for them and they eventually decided on a house that was under construction in the Hove district. Until its completion they would continue to live in Derby, and Brian would travel home on a Saturday after the game, his great friend Colin Lawrence picking him up from wherever they had been playing. He would return to Brighton on an early train each Monday morning and stay at the

Henry Newton was a hard-tackling midfield player. Peter attempted to sign him on three separate occasions, but on no account would Forest agree to him joining their neighbours. Eventually Newton was brought from Everton.

The 17-year-old Russell Osman at Ipswich Town. At the age of 13 I took Osman to be coached with the juniors. On his 16th birthday an attempt to sign him as a professional on a visit to his parents was badly handled by the management (Brian and Peter having left by that time). Twelve months later Osman joined Ipswich and achieved great success under Sir Bobby Robson.

Brian Clough on his first day at the City Ground, Nottingham. He was raring to go with his batteries fully charged after spending three months out of the game.

28th December 1974 **Nottingham Forest** at the City Ground

**1**
Middleton J.

**2**
O'Kane W.J.

**3**
Greenwood P.G.

**5**
Jones D.E.

**4**
Chapman R.D.

**6**
Richardson P.

**8**
Martin N.

**10**
Bowyer I.

**7**
McIntosh J.

**9**
Butlin B.

**11**
Lyall G.

Sub: Donnelly J.

# NOTTINGHAM FOREST v. MANCHESTER UNITED

DIVISION TWO. SATURDAY, 22nd MARCH, 1975. KICK-OFF 3 p.m.

## Nottingham Forest
Red Shirts. White Shorts

## Manchester United
White Shirts. White Shorts

Referee :
Mr. R. C. CHALLIS
(Tonbridge)

TODAY'S MATCH BALL
HAS BEEN KINDLY
DONATED BY
AN ANONYMOUS
FRIEND OF THE CLUB

Linesmen :
Mr. W. L. HARVEY
(Redditch)      (Red Flag)
Mr. M. R. BAKER
(Wolverhampton)
(Yellow Flag)

| | Nottingham Forest | Apps. | Goals | | Manchester United |
|---|---|---|---|---|---|
| 1. | JOHN MIDDLETON | 26 | — | 1. | ALEX STEPNEY |
| 2. | VIV ANDERSON | 11 | — | 2. | ALEX FORSYTH |
| 3. | PAUL RICHARDSON | 35 | 4 | 3. | STEWART HOUSTON |
| 4. | LIAM O'KANE | 40 | — | 4. | BRIAN GREENHOFF |
| 5. | DAVID JONES | 37 | 2 | 5. | STEVE JAMES |
| 6. | JOHN ROBERTSON | 13 | 1 | 6. | MARTIN BUCHAN |
| 7. | GEORGE LYALL | 37 | 4 | 7. | STEVE COTTELL |
| 8. | JOHN McGOVERN | 4 | — | 8. | SAMMY McILROY |
| 9. | JOHN O'HARE | 3 | 1 | 9. | STUART PEARSON |
| 10. | BARRY BUTLIN | 26 | 4 | 10. | LOU MACARI |
| 11. | IAN BOWYER | 35 | 7 | 11. | GERRY DALY |
| 12. | To be announced | | | 12. | JIMMY NICHOLL |

Brian presenting the 1975–76 Burton and District Division One Championship Trophy to Bob Stevens, captain of AFC 67 FC.

Charlie George signed for Derby County shortly before the 1976–77 season began after he and Arsenal had fallen out. Charlie had promised me that he would come to Forest if a First Division club failed to come in for him.

Frank Clark was signed from Newcastle United on a free transfer. Brian had shot off to the North East as soon as he heard of Clark's release and came back with his signature.

Colin Barrett was a snip at the price from Manchester City. Brian took some persuasion to sign him as he was put off by the small fee being asked. However, the tiny fee masked an outstanding ability.

Trevor Francis was the first player to cost £1 million. The preparation work for the transfer was done by Peter and myself three weeks beforehand and was the best-kept secret in the game. Only a handful knew when various stages of the move had been completed.

All smiles. Helen and Trevor Francis with Brian after the record signing.

Trevor Francis and Kenny Burns on international duty, May 1979.

John Robertson was already at Nottingham Forest on Brian's arrival at the club, but in truth he was going nowhere until Peter arrived. After some serious, hard talks, John adapted his game and became one of the finest wide players in the game.

Terry Curran was full of self-confidence and was never short of a few words to say.

Garry Birtles was a Nottingham lad. Most of the staff at Forest were critical of the £1,000 transfer fee paid to Long Eaton United – thank goodness Peter had great faith in my judgement.

Because of Kenny Burns' reputation for wildness and bad habits, on Peter's instructions I spent one month checking his private activities in the evening. Following my reports, however, Kenny was signed.

As a young player I saw Peter Shilton more times than any other. He was exceptional at 17 years old and kept on improving. At the time of writing he holds the record number of England Caps.

Martin O'Neill took some time to settle to Brian's managerial ways, but he eventually became a vital cog in the machine.

Chris Woods was a fine young goalkeeper who would have been first choice with any other club. Training with Peter Shilton helped him enormously.

Tony Woodcock was another player already on the books at Forest when Brian arrived. He was loaned out to Lincoln City, and this was followed by a spell at Doncaster. However, after a number of fees were put in for the player I was sent to Doncaster to check on his form. Tony was recalled the next day and put straight into the first team to become a regular starter.

John McGovern, with a captian's pride, holding the European Cup aloft.

A delighted John Robertson holding the European Cup aloft after making his 64th League and Cup appearance of the season.

The Forest squad in Madrid, celebrating the winning of the European Cup for the second time.

Niall Quinn and Kevin Phillips celebrate for Sunderland. A young, half-fit Kevin Phillips had not impressed on a scouting trip to Watford on behalf of Sunderland, but he was later signed for the club and went on to form a partnership with Niall Quinn which produced 43 goals in their first season together.

Courtlands Hotel. Barbara told me that she was looking forward to moving into their newly built house as it was very close to the sea.

Peter rang me regularly for a chat or to place a bet, and to tell me which matches to attend. He and Brian did not get off to a very good start at Brighton: they were very disappointed in the quality of the players that they had inherited and there were only 16 professionals on the books. It was imperative that they got some new blood in quickly and signings were soon made.

In one of Brian's early books he stated that four disappointing players, whom he named, had been recommended by Maurice Edwards and Dave Blakey (at that time Dave was chief scout at Burnley with Jimmy Adamson). After I read this I rang Dave to ask if he had recommended the players in question. Dave said that Peter had rung him for some recommendations, but he had been unable to come up with any names off hand. I personally had never seen any of the players in action and had certainly not made any recommendations.

Some time later I saw David Pleat at Leicester City's Filbert Street ground. I knew he was still in touch with Peter. I asked David if he had read Brian's book, in which he had blamed myself and Dave Blakey for four poor recruits at Brighton. I went on to say that neither of us knew anything about these players, who were all from London clubs. David Pleat grinned in his usual way and said that he had been the one to put the names forward, although he had told Peter that he should only sign them if he was absolutely desperate!

It was difficult to get Midlands players interested in going down to Brighton. The wages were not much better than they were being paid with their present clubs, but Brighton was well known to be one of the most expensive towns in the country to live in. I actually approached five players that would have easily got into their side, but they were not interested. Even playing for Brian Clough was not a big enough pull. The only player who signed a contract for Brighton was an 18-year-old goalkeeper from the Worcester area that I sent down for a week's trial.

Three scout meetings were held at Brighton during the season, and I attended all three. The earliest that I was able to leave home was about 7.30pm on the Friday evening, because of doing the weekly account for the Post Office. Usually I arrived at the hotel at about 11.30pm, after a long drive of 187 miles. The meetings were held on Saturday mornings, and the afternoon was spent at the Goldstone Ground to watch the first-team game. Obviously Brian and Peter were present at the meetings, and they entertained us in the evening. The chairman, Mike Bamber, always came round and had a few words with each of us; he was a very amiable man. I never heard Brian or Peter say a wrong word about him, and in fact in later years they referred to him as the best chairman they ever worked for. I set off home after lunch on the Sunday. It cost me £100 each visit to get a reliable friend to look after the newspaper side of my business, collecting the papers from the wholesalers each morning and opening the shop at a quarter to five, then staying until all the deliveries had been made.

Barry Butlin, a striker who had been at Derby County when Brian and Peter first arrived there, played for Brighton on loan from Luton Town for eight games, scoring five goals, to help save the team from relegation at the end of the season.

Brian never really settled in Brighton, what with the travelling backwards and forwards each weekend and having to live in a hotel on his own away from his family. This, along with the fact that the standard of football in Division Three, after what he had been used to, was relatively poor, meant that as the weeks passed by Brian began to lose interest and was becoming less involved with the day-to-day running of the club. Peter found that he was doing more and more of the work and occasionally poured his troubles out, telling me that he wished I was closer at hand. Brian took time off, with the chairman's permission, to go to America to see Mohammed Ali fight Joe Frazier for the World Heavyweight title in New York. Shortly after that he flew out to Tehran to have talks with the Shah about he and Peter becoming joint managers of the Iran national team. I heard very little about the visit, but I could not imagine them sitting on camels on the touchline watching a game of football. Peter, although he was a sun-worshipper, never seemed interested in going to Iran at all.

At the end of the season Brighton escaped relegation comfortably, results having improved greatly in the New Year. Brian's new house was not yet completed but would be before the commencement of the next season. John Sheridan decided to leave Brighton because he was struggling financially, despite a considerable rise in his pay.

## The epic of the famous 44 days at Leeds United

It was a telephone call with a difference. Peter rang to say that the Leeds United chairman, Mr Manny Cussins, and Mr Roberts, a director, were travelling down to meet our chairman, Mr Mike Bamber, at the Waldorf in London. Brian and Peter were also to attend. I said it sounded very promising, and Peter said he would ring to let me know what had happened. I spoke to him the following morning and he told me that the two of them had agreed to join Leeds United. Brighton were to receive £75,000 compensation as part of the deal. Peter and Brian wanted me to go with them. I jumped at the chance as I had been completely downhearted at Brighton, having had little success. It was agreed that I would travel up to Leeds one day during the next week.

On Sunday night I was in bed and asleep at 10pm as I got up at 4.30am to be ready to open the shop. My son John came into the bedroom and woke me up with the words 'Brian Clough's on the phone wishing to speak to you, Dad.' I did not believe him. 'Pick up the phone then,' he said. I lifted the bedside telephone to my ear.

'Maurice!' said Brian. 'I've woken you, I'm sorry, but have you heard the evening news? Your mate, the b*****d, is staying at Brighton. He's accepted an offer from Bamber to become manager. Hasn't he been in touch at all?'

'I haven't spoken to Peter since Friday morning, when he arranged to see me next week in Leeds,' I replied, still shocked.

'What are your feelings?' asked Brian. 'Will you stay at Brighton with Peter, or are you coming to Leeds with me?' I replied without hesitation.

'I haven't enjoyed my season at Brighton, I haven't achieved anything.'

'Good,' said Brian. 'When I've settled in next week I'll give you a ring from there, now go back to sleep.' I could not go back to sleep. I was so surprised, I could not take it in. How strange that Peter was staying at Brighton.

I sensed that Peter's decision to stay had come as a complete shock to Brian. He later told me that he had never settled down at Brighton, although Mike Bamber had been very good. I figured it out correctly in the end: Peter had been lured with a handsome signing-on fee out of the Leeds compensation money.

I went up to Leeds the following Friday. Brian showed me around and introduced me to several non-playing staff, the club secretary and the office girls, and my first impressions were good. Then, as he was about to introduce me to Maurice Lindley, the chief scout, he was called away, leaving us alone. We knew one another from being at football grounds together scouting. This was to be my first experience of what would unfold in the next few weeks. I held my hand out, intending to shake Maurice's hand, but he ignored the gesture completely.

'Welcome you!' he spat. 'You must be joking. You're here to take my f*****g job, you can piss off.' I tried to tell him that I would not interfere with his job: he would remain in charge of all the scouts all over the country and receive their reports. He would be liaising with me on reports that were recommending a player. I would then take over and go myself to see the player before making a decision on him. But he just did not want to listen to me. Little did he know that only a short time ago Don Revie had offered me exactly the same job.

When Don Revie took the England manager's appointment he took with him Les Cocker, the head coach at Leeds. To replace him Brian quickly brought in Jimmy Gordon from Derby County. Players John McGovern and John O'Hare followed, also from Derby. The early results were very disappointing and Leeds lost to Liverpool in the Charity Shield at Wembley. I understand that at this time Brian made a futile attempt to lure Peter away from Brighton, during a phone conversation in the early hours of the morning. Apparently, Brian discovered that Peter had been granted a £5,000 initial payment and given a lucrative two-year contract, and he fully intended honouring his chairman's persuasive agreement. He did not wish to take up the Leeds appointment. At the time neither of them mentioned this chat to me.

Almost a month later Peter rang me. He seemed a little embarrassed but he then began to quiz me about what was happening behind the scenes. He knew more than he was making out about the situation, however: a press member was marking his card. I sensed that he was feeling a little smug that there were major difficulties. Peter then asked me if I would still put his bets on for him. I said no problem, as I had not fallen out with him. From then on we were back to speaking every week, and he agreed to come up to see me once a month to settle up paying or drawing.

About seven members of the Leeds United first team were not prepared to give Brian a fair chance. Their ringleader was being coached every evening by Don

Revie, who made suggestions about what could be done to sabotage Brian's efforts. Don's dislike of Brian must have been very deep and he was certainly doing everything in his power to bring an early end to his reign at Leeds. There was, however, a 'mole' in the Leeds camp who kept Brian informed of the mafia-type operation that was going on, and Jimmy Gordon was also keeping his ear to the ground. Jimmy himself was not on the receiving end of any trouble. This was the worst period of Brian's career. He was completely on his own and powerless against the saboteurs. He told me the names of the seven bad guys and the mole, but I am not prepared to name any of them. A lot of water has passed under the bridge and there is nothing to be gained, but the culprits must have had it on their conscience.

Brian rang to say he had decided to bring a big name into the team to steady the ship, and could I come up with somebody. I thought for a while, then mentioned Duncan Mackenzie of Nottingham Forest. He certainly would not be fazed by the move. I had seen him twice recently, and thought that although he was playing in Division Two he would still be able to get goals in Division One. Peter had told me that his contacts in Nottingham rated him.

The transfer cost Leeds United £240,000 and was signed on 24 August 1974. Duncan made 81 appearances, scoring 30 goals, and was sold to Anderlecht for £200,000 when Jimmy Armfield decided to part with the three players Brian had brought in, so it was not too bad a signing. Mackenzie's record at Leeds was slightly better than at Forest, and Leeds recouped most of their original outlay.

In Peter's book he made reference to the signing of Duncan Mackenzie, saying that this was a bad move. He had previously called the signing of Colin Todd at Derby County a poor signing, although he later changed his mind. This was a reaction that Peter had to signings he had had no part in. He also said that Brian was wrong to bring in three new players so quickly, and should have let things settle first. Whether that would have made any difference to the outcome of the saga will never be known.

Brian kept in touch, ringing two or three times a week. He was becoming more and more depressed. Several times I went up to Leeds, but there was very little I could do. The results on the field were not showing any real improvement. Don's strategy was to make most of the players fearful of Brian's attempts to change things. This had certainly worked, and day by day the situation was getting worse.

It had become evident to me that Mr Cussins and his co-directors would soon have to step in. Brian had no intention of resigning.

The match played on Saturday 12 October 1975 against Luton Town, one of the less formidable sides in Division One, only resulted in a 1–1 draw and proved to be the final League game before the Leeds directors gave Brian the sack. The irony was that the Luton goal was a stunning effort from Barry Butlin, whom Brian had sold to Luton Town after loaning him out to Notts County. After the game Brian and Barry met in the passage near the dressing rooms in front of the waiting press. Brian flung his arms around the lad and presented him to the press, saying 'This is who you want to write about after that wonderful goal. He deserves it.' Barry played for Brian at both Brighton and later at Nottingham Forest.

On 15 October 1974, Brian was sacked. Don had achieved his objective. The episode convinced me that Don's offer to me of a job at Leeds was a serious attempt to harm Brian. I certainly made the right decision. The financial settlement that Brian received made him financially secure, but the shock of being dismissed was a bitter blow. I received all the monies due to me by post. Jimmy Armfield took over at Leeds and achieved moderate success, the team finishing as runners-up in the European Cup that season.

Was Mr Cussins right to take Brian to Leeds? This question could never be answered. Brian and Peter were the best management team in the country at the time, and if they had gone to Leeds together, as intended, the outcome might have been very different. History has shown that in football the two of them were better together than as individuals.

The rest of the year passed quietly and quickly. I was busy in the Post Office and my work there required my full attention. I had little time to reflect on the Leeds episode.

Peter continued to telephone me regularly with his investments and popped up to see me as promised. He asked me whether Brian had been in touch, saying he had had no contact with him at all. I did receive one telephone call from Brian during his off-duty spell. A couple of days before Christmas he rang to wish me and my family a Merry Christmas and I returned the compliments. He told me that he had been spending most of his time walking his dog in the nearby Derbyshire countryside and enjoying some time with his family. He enquired about 'my mate', and his parting words were that his batteries were now charged up and after Christmas he would be hoping for a football job to turn up.

## The beginning of eight years with Nottingham Forest

There were rumblings in the press that Allan Brown, the Nottingham Forest manager, was about to lose his job. The team had only won nine of the first 24 games of the season in Division Two. On the last Saturday of the old year they lost at home to neighbours Notts County and this was the last straw for the committee. Brown was dismissed from the club and Bill Anderson, the assistant manager, was put in temporary charge for an FA Cup tie at the City Ground, which resulted in a 1–1 draw against Tottenham Hotspur, a Division One side. It did not come as a surprise to me, and it had crossed my mind that Brian might be considered for the job.

On 6 January 1975, Brian was appointed manager of Nottingham Forest as replacement for the departed Allan Brown. At that time Forest were lying 13th in the Division Two League table. During that afternoon he rang me to ask me to go over to the City Ground the next day. It had been 115 days since his departure from Leeds United and I had only spoken to him once, just before Christmas. At the meeting he got straight to the point. He said that he wanted me to be the chief scout, doing exactly the same duties as I had done at Derby County but with him, in the absence of Peter. He offered me a salary, with the cost of any travelling expenses. I accepted and we shook hands. We had a general chat on what he hoped to do, but before he rushed into any signings he wanted a good look at what the players already there had got to offer. He asked if Peter had been in touch since Christmas. I said he had, but only to place a couple of bets on the football. He had not been up to see me for a few weeks. I then said, no doubt he'll ring in the next few hours to quiz me about what is happening over here, which raised a smile from Brian. He went on to say that he was fully charged up for any challenges and could hardly wait for the games to begin. I soon was on my way as he said that he had several more calls to make, but he seemed a very relieved young man.

Nottingham Forest, the second oldest club in the Football League, was unique. There were no directors. The club was run by a committee of nine, elected from the

200 Club members. The chairman was chosen from these nine men, to officiate for a period of two years. Mr Jim Wilmer was the chairman who made Brian's appointment and Mr Stuart Dryden was the vice-chairman. Mr Dryden was the main force that persuaded the committee to choose Brian, despite the reservations that several of them had about Brian's outspoken nature. At that time there was no waiting list to become a member of the 200 Club, the reason for which was probably the fact that the club had been relegated from Division One at the end of the 1972 season.

Brian immediately began appointing his own staff. Jimmy Gordon came in as first-team coach (he had been a coach at Middlesbrough when Brian was playing there, and later worked with Brian at both Derby County and Leeds United). Jimmy had been employed as a storekeeper at the Rolls-Royce factory since leaving Leeds United. John Sheridan, the second-team coach already at the club, remained (he had played for Brian at Hartlepools United and had been a coach for Brian at Derby County). Jimmy Gordon had asked Brian if John could stay, as he had great respect for his coaching work. John had been at Brighton with Peter Taylor but had returned to the Midlands because of the cost of living in Brighton. He is now the football coach at Nottingham University.

Out went first-team coach John McSeveney, and Bill Anderson, the assistant manager, resigned. Brian rang to ask me to go over to Nottingham on the Thursday morning, to meet the staff and have another look around. I was then introduced to Ken Smales, the secretary at Forest. He was the secretary the whole time I was with the club. I had never spoken to him before, although I remembered him from his county cricket playing days. He became a tremendous help to me at all times and I held him in high esteem. He was not as dynamic as Stuart Webb at Derby County, but was genuine, reliable and efficient. He was a quiet, intelligent man, and any problems that I encountered when travelling and attending matches when out scouting, he would quickly put right.

### The action on the field begins

The last side to be selected by Allan Brown that played against Notts County, losing 2–0, is printed in one of this book's picture sections. Only two players, Liam O'Kane and Ian Bowyer, were to become part of Brian's great success story at

Nottingham Forest. John Robertson, Martin O'Neill, Tony Woodcock and Viv Anderson were also at the club but were not selected.

Brian's first game in charge was a trip to White Hart Lane in an FA Cup replay on a Wednesday evening, 8 January 1975. Forest won 1–0. It was an excellent beginning, with Neil Martin scoring the only goal. The only change Brian had to make was to bring Martin O'Neill in playing on the wide left to replace Dennehy, who was injured. The following morning Brian rang me. He said little about the game but I could sense that the initial tension had been released. His main concern was that we urgently needed someone to play forward wide right side. At that time he had not seen John Robertson play.

On Friday morning Brian rang me to ask whether I would take him up to Liverpool that evening to see Bob Paisley about us taking Phil Boersma. I picked Brian up at about 3.30pm at his home in Darley Abbey, arriving at Anfield just after six o'clock. We went straight into the famous Boot Room, and the first person to greet us was Tommy Smith. Several of the first-team players were there and they made us most welcome. Bob Paisley was only the temporary manager at that time.

'Hello Brian, have you come for the job?' Tommy asked. Bob Paisley then walked in, greeting Brian with the same question.

'Have you come for the job, Brian?'

'You've got the job, Bob and doing well,' Brian replied.

'I don't want it, it's too big for me to take on,' Bob said. Brian put his hand on his shoulder.

'Don't be daft, you'll take it in your stride.' Tommy Smith brought each of us a welcome mug of tea. That season Liverpool finished runners-up and they were League Division One Champions for the next two years under Bob Paisley. Bob came over as a really nice guy.

After the early chit-chat, Brian said 'Can I explain the reason for our visit? I would like to sign Phil Boersma to come and play for us at Forest, if you are agreeable.' Bob said that if Phil was happy to move then he would allow it. Phil was called. He and Brian sat down and discussed the move privately. In the end, Phil said that he did not want to leave Liverpool, but very much appreciated being asked, and he wished Brian every success. Brian respected his decision, shook his hand and wished the lad all the best for the future. We stayed for a drink with Bob in his office. I had thoroughly enjoyed myself. It was the first time I had been behind the scenes at such a top club.

On the way home, Brian said 'How can you get anyone to leave a club like that? Weren't they a great bunch.' He was right. He then went on to explain the priorities for new recruits. He was looking for young players but with some experience, who could go straight into the side. There was a limited amount of money available, which had to be spent right to make progress.

The next day, Saturday 11 January, brought the first League fixture, away to Fulham. Brian made no changes to the side that had beaten Tottenham Hotspur earlier in the week. Once again it was a 1–0 win; this time Barry Butlin got the important goal. Brian had made a good start at his new club. Everyone was beginning to warm to him and the initial tension was evaporating.

On Sunday morning I got an early call from Brian, who said he still wanted somebody to play wide right. He said we would go up to Manchester to see Tommy (Docherty) at United, who might let us have a youngster. United were making one of their rare visits to Division Two, having been relegated the previous year. We arrived unannounced at their Mottram Hall retreat at about seven o'clock on the Friday evening. It was absolutely hilarious. About 15 of their players were there, and Brian and Tommy were in great form. Unfortunately our visit was fruitless, but what a night. I cannot remember ever having so many laughs.

**Two that we missed**

On 15 January I watched a midweek game at Eton Park in the Birmingham Senior Cup. Burton Albion beat Atherstone Town 4–2 and it was very entertaining. I came away that evening with two players on my mind. First was the young goalkeeper for Atherstone, Gerry Peyton. He was 18 years old and had an outstanding game, keeping the score down. Second was a Burton Albion player, Peter Ward, who was small for a striker, but sharp with quick feet. He scored a very good individual goal and caused the opposing defence many problems. The next day I discussed these two players with Brian. I said that they would not cost the earth, and that they were certainly players for the future. Brian explained that his urgent need was for players that could go straight into the first team, and said that we already had two young goalkeepers who were promising and highly thought of. As strikers we had Barry Butlin, Martin O'Neill and Neil Martin, so any money available had to be spent to bring in experienced players.

During this time Peter asked me if I had been to see any games. I told him I had seen a couple at Eton Park. He was looking for a striker to strengthen his playing staff. I told him about Peter Ward at Burton Albion. Peter was immediately interested, but I told him that I did not want to get involved because of my long connections with Burton Albion. I told him that Ken Gutteridge was the manager and suggested he rang him for a full run-down on Peter Ward. Soon afterwards Peter joined Brighton for £4,000. He did well and scored 21 goals in 50 outings. Ken Gutteridge himself left Burton Albion very shortly afterwards to become assistant manager at Brighton and Hove Albion. It was a big surprise locally, but not to me, as on two occasions during the last 12 months Peter had offered me the post, but I had turned him down.

I did Peter another good favour by marking his card about Brian Horton at Port Vale, for whom he paid £27,000. I had run the rule over him while I was at Leeds United.

Some time later, in April, Dave Blakey of Burnley rang to ask me whether I had seen a young goalkeeper good enough for them. Due to injuries they were desperate to find one. I told him that I would ring him back. This gave me time to speak to Brian to obtain permission to recommend Gerry Peyton to Burnley. He gave me the nod, saying that we were fine for goalkeepers. I rang Dave back and told him that the lad was playing for Atherstone and that Gill Merrick (the former Birmingham goalkeeper) was their manager. I said he was 18 and had been released from Aston Villa. I thought that playing under Gill was probably the reason for his improvement. Atherstone were due to play at home the next Monday evening. It was arranged that I would go to the game and meet Jimmy Adamson (the Burnley manager) outside the gates shortly before the kick-off. Jimmy paid for us both to go in and we watched the game from behind the goals. Gerry was faultless and Atherstone won 1–0. Five minutes from time I left the ground. Jimmy shook my hand and thanked me, and said he was staying to see Gill Merrick. That night Gerry

Peyton travelled with Jimmy to Burnley. The transfer fee was £1,000. Burnley sent me a small present for my help. Eighteen months later he was sold to Fulham for £40,000. During his career he played for nine League clubs, making over 600 appearances in League and Cup games, also collecting 33 Republic of Ireland caps. He later coached two clubs in Japan, where he met Arsene Wenger, who quickly brought him in to be the goalkeeping coach at Arsenal.

### First signings for Nottingham Forest

On 1 February, my birthday, Forest suffered their first defeat under Brian, 0–1 away at Oldham in the League. Two more defeats in the next 10 days included being knocked out of the FA Cup at the third attempt by Fulham. Brian said to me that he was going to bring in John McGovern and John O'Hare from Leeds: he knew exactly what he was getting. They cost £60,000, half what was paid when Brian took them to Leeds United from Derby County. John McGovern made his debut on 22 February at the City Ground against Cardiff City. The game ended in a draw. John O'Hare played in the next game at Oxford United. Again the result was a draw, this time 1–1.

John Middleton, John Robertson, Martin O'Neill, Ian Bowyer, Liam O'Kane, Tony Woodcock, Viv Anderson and Barry Butlin were all youngsters who Brian wanted to have a good look at. Most of them became very much a part of the Forest success story. Barry was an unusual member of the playing staff: he played for us for a total of eight seasons at three different clubs, but he had never been signed by Peter or Brian. He was always signed by the out-going managers.

The first serious casualty on the playing staff was Paddy Greenwood at left-back, who suffered a broken leg and never played for the club again. Paul Richardson was drafted into this spot from midfield. Brian Appleby QC had now taken over as the Nottingham Forest chairman and begun his term of office.

With the arrival of John McGovern and John O'Hare, Martin O'Neill had been dropped from the first team. In the reserves Martin had been scoring regularly and he thought he deserved a run back in the first team. Apparently in the dressing room the lads had said to him 'Go in and ask the boss why you haven't had your chance'. At a midweek reserve team game Brian was present and Martin scored two goals. This gave him courage. Very nervously he knocked on the manager's office door. 'Come in! Yes young man, what can I do for you?'

Martin, shaking, said 'Boss, can you tell me why I am still in the reserves? I feel that I am playing well and scoring goals.'

There was silence for a couple of minutes. Then Brian said 'I've seen you play recently. You're dead right you're playing well – that's the reason you're in the reserves, because you're "too good" for the third team!' Martin was out of the door in a flash. This was Brian at his wittiest.

Jimmy McCann, a 20-year-old youngster from the reserves, was given his debut as a striker alongside Barry Butlin in the last game of the season against West Bromwich Albion, resulting in a victory of 2–1. Barry scored both of the goals. Martin O'Neill was returned to first-team duty for this final game.

The season ended with the team finishing in 16th place in Division Two, with the average gate just over 13,000. Brian told me that he was reasonably satisfied with the progress that had been made, and that he could see daylight at the end of the tunnel. Although the team had finished in a lower position than the previous season, this was the same pattern that he had experienced at Derby County.

### The groundwork for a new signing

During February 1975 Brian took several telephone calls from an Alan Curran, who was the elder brother of Terry Curran, a young right-winger playing for Doncaster Rovers. Terry had been playing there just over 12 months, having been taken on by Maurice Setters when he was their manager, from non-League football with his local side Kinsley. Alan told Brian how well his young brother was playing, and said that Brian should have a look at him. One Monday morning I happened to be in Brian's office when he received such a call. Brian put his hand over the phone, looked at me and said 'Can you go to Doncaster on Wednesday night?' I nodded and Brian told Alan that someone would definitely be there. I went to the game. I had not seen Terry play before, and he possessed pace and good control, went down the touchline well and crossed the ball into the penalty area perfectly with power and precision. I reported my observations back to Brian, who said 'You'd better go again on Saturday, if he's that good, and take a second look.' Terry scored two goals, both from the edge of the box, low and well struck. This confirmed the opinion I had formed of Terry on my first visit.

The following Saturday Doncaster were due to play Barnsley away. The first team did not have a game, as their opponents were still in the FA Cup, so Brian said that he would come with me. Early on the Saturday morning he rang to tell me that he was going to Stoke, who were playing Forest's reserves in a match with an 11 o'clock kick-off, to see two of our young lads play. He said he would pick me up from the shop at around 1pm.

Brian was late as usual and we left my shop at 2.15pm. It was a one and a half hour journey to Barnsley. The M1 was not very busy and we made good time, but as we passed Chesterfield flashing blue lights chased us and a loudspeaker instructed us to pull on to the hard shoulder. Brian obeyed and two police officers came to the car. One of them said to Brian that he had been clocked at 94 miles an hour and asked him for his driving licence, which Brian produced without saying a word. The officer proceeded to book him. Brian only answered the questions that were put to him, took the ticket and said 'Thank you'. The officer said 'Watch your speed, have a safe journey. Good afternoon Mr Clough.' Brian said good afternoon and we carried on with our trip to Barnsley, arriving during the half-time break. Our seats were on the front row of the directors' box. Fortunately Terry was playing right under where we were seated and he was outstanding. He scored twice and Doncaster won 3–0.

Back at the City Ground on Monday Alan Hill, who had recently joined the staff, made enquiries about his availability. Doncaster wanted £140,000 for him. Brian said 'That is a ridiculous price, we'll sweat it out.' Terry's brother Alan rang later the same morning. He was fully aware that Brian had been to see him play at Barnsley. During the conversation Brian learned that Terry's contract with Doncaster ran out at the end of the season. Brian told Alan Curran that he would definitely sign Terry before the start of next season. 'Don't let him sign an extension to his present contract, to save complications,' he said. 'Keep the whole matter hush hush.'

Three or four weeks later Stan Anderson, the Doncaster manager (Brian played with him at Sunderland), rang Brian and accused him of tapping Terry up to join Nottingham Forest. Brian, in all truthfulness, told Stan that he had never spoken to Terry Curran, nor had any member of the Forest staff. Two weeks later Stan

Anderson rang Brian again, this time in a furious mood. Terry had refused to sign a new contract. Brian pleaded ignorance and told Stan that it was his problem. In the middle of May Alan Curran rang Brian to say that Doncaster Rovers had stopped Terry's summer wages and the lad had not got any money at all to live on. His summer wages were £25 a week. Brian asked him for Terry's telephone number and told him that one of our staff would get in touch with him. Brian rang me with the phone number and we discussed the money problem. He said that there was no way the Forest committee would sanction any payment of this kind to be made to Terry. I said 'Leave that to me, I will take care of it.' Brian said 'Be careful, the committee will go spare if any of this gets to them.'

On the phone I agreed to meet Terry every Friday evening at seven o'clock in the square at Bawtry. I used to park my car then get in the queue at the chip shop. Terry joined the queue behind me and I slipped him his £25. This went on for seven weeks and I paid out £175 of my own money. Brian asked 'How the devil are you going to recover that amount?'

'I'm in no great hurry for it,' I said. 'What if this season, in my expenses, I claim back some each month? I will soon recover the money.'

'That should be okay, if you're happy,' said Brian. 'I'll sanction and sign all the scouts' expense claims, and no one will query them.'

## Addition to the backroom staff

Brian had decided that someone was needed to deal with the paperwork and assist with the office work on the footballing side, and to liaise with the team of scouts. As a result Alan Hill was brought on to the staff from Derby County. He actually lived in Nottingham. A Barnsley lad, he was the goalkeeper for Rotherham United in the 1967–68 season when Tommy Docherty was their manager. He was transferred to Nottingham Forest, then under Matt Gillies, but unfortunately broke an arm during the home game against Everton on 28 February 1970 and was never able to play again. At Derby County he had been working as a youth development officer. He was recommended to Brian by Jimmy Gordon and his main duties were organising the scouts from all over the country, passing me any favourable reports on prospective signings and being a general help to Brian.

I had never met Alan before and when Brian introduced us he said that to begin with Alan would accompany me on scouting trips so that we would get to know one another well and know the type of player we were looking for. From then on we would be working closely with one another. Over the years we have become good friends and are still in touch. Alan is still very active within the game and he is still scouting. At the time of writing he is back at Forest with Billy Davies. When Brian retired from Nottingham Forest Frank Clark was appointed their manager. Alan Hill became his assistant manager and the two were later together in similar appointments at Manchester City, during a six-year period from 1993–99. At the time of writing he is back at Forest with Billy Davies.

## My attempt at the jackpot

At the end of the season Charlie George was having problems with Arsenal and I had heard from a good source that he would be available for transfer. Brian had said to me that he would like to come up with a big signing to help us push up into the top League. I suggested Charlie George, but Brian thought there was no chance that he would come down to our League. I said that I should go to see him, as we would never know if we did not try, and Brian agreed.

I had been given a horse that was a supposedly 'good thing' at Royal Ascot. I decided to combine going to the races with my trip to see Charlie. Peter Taylor had asked me to back the horse for him too. It was to be ridden by Lester Piggott, trained in Ireland and named Gay Fandango. I placed a very substantial bet at the course and decided to go to the very top of the Main Grandstand to watch the race. The view of the course was magnificent. I was the only person up there. Shortly before the off Vincent O'Brien came up and stood about two yards away from me. The horse won easily and I was the first person to congratulate the great Vincent O'Brien before he shot off down to the unsaddling enclosure.

I left the course early to avoid the traffic queues and travelled on to Enfield. I arrived at Charlie George's house shortly before six o'clock and knocked at the door, which was answered by Mrs George. I asked whether Charlie was at home and she said he was across the road at the pub helping his friend the landlord to get ready for opening time. I had a long chat with Charlie in the pub, telling him that

Brian would like him to come to Forest, and that if he was interested the wheels could be set in motion. Charlie told me that Arsenal had said that he could go to any club bar Tottenham Hotspur, and to thank Brian for the offer but he really wanted to stay in Division One (Forest were still in Division Two). However, if no one came in for him before the season started, he would seriously consider joining Nottingham Forest, liking the idea of playing for Brian.

The days ticked by. Shortly before the season was due to start Brian rang me one evening to say that Charlie George had signed for Derby. 'You've not marked Webby's card, have you?' he said. Until then I had forgotten about my meeting with Stuart some months before. During the period after the Leeds United debacle, when I was without a club, Stuart had come to see me about returning to Derby County. I had thanked him for the offer but said I was going to wait until Brian joined another club. Before Stuart left that day he asked me who my first target would have been if I'd gone back to Derby. I had said Charlie George. Apparently Stuart also heard, months later, that Charlie was still available. Dave Mackay was golfing near London, so Stuart rang Dave on the golf course and told him that the board had given the go ahead for Charlie to be signed. Dave went into London to do the necessary. It seems that what I had said to Stuart had registered. Charlie George was signed that afternoon.

# CHAPTER 8
# THE FIRST FULL
# SEASON AT FOREST

The 1975–76 season was Brian's first full season with Forest. Terry Curran came to pre-season training, supposedly on trial, then signed a contract. He did not appear in any of the friendly matches, but made his Nottingham Forest debut in the opening game of the new season, on 30 August 1975, at the City Ground against Notts County in League Division Two. The result was an unpopular 0–1 defeat. To my knowledge there were no repercussions from Doncaster over the signing, and Terry became a regular member of our first team.

I began to recover the money I had spent paying Terry's summer wages. As I did not want to be questioned about my expenses, I was careful not to over do it. I only included a couple of extra trips each month. Then there was a slight hitch. On one of my claims I had included a trip to Molineux. Alan Hill had also claimed for a trip there on the same night. One of the committee members spotted this and they refused to pay us both. When confronted Brian told the committee that he had sent Alan to the game himself, but he did not know why I was there. Brian rang me to tell me what had happened at the meeting. 'Why the claim?' he asked.

'This is my last-but-one claim, to recover the money I paid to Terry Curran during the summer.' I said.

'What do you suggest I tell the committee?' asked Brian.

'Tell them that I went to Molineux two weeks earlier (I had), but the player I had gone to see hadn't convinced me one way or the other, so I decided another visit was needed. Not having spoken to Alan, I didn't realise that he would be going to the game, or he could have saved me the journey.'

The committee accepted the explanation, but they said that Alan and myself had got to liaise better because the cost of two of us travelling in two cars to the same game was not acceptable.

It was almost Christmas before I was fully reimbursed. Terry Curran could have cost Nottingham Forest £140,000 in transfer fees. The committee was never told how the transfer had been handled and only Brian, Alan Hill and myself were involved. Even the club secretary Ken Smales had no knowledge of what had transpired.

Some time later, the FA were doing an investigation into transfers in and out of Nottingham Forest. The *News of the World,* along with other newspapers, had a team of sports reporters out interviewing players who had been bought and sold by Brian, looking for evidence to incriminate him.

One Sunday morning, at about 11 o'clock, I got a telephone call from a close friend. He said 'I knew that you would make the *News of the World* one day. Have a look at the front page!' We sold about 300 copies of the *News of the World* each Sunday. No one else had spoken to me about the article. I immediately got a copy and read the article, and the story was there. It was written by a reporter who had interviewed Terry Curran about joining Nottingham Forest from Doncaster Rovers. Terry had told him that the only money that had been paid to him was £25 per week for his summer wages, saying that a guy called 'Maurice' used to bring it to him each week, until he signed a contract to play for Forest. At the time the article appeared I was not working for Brian, and no one else has ever mentioned the article to me.

During the following summer I bumped into Terry at York races. This was the first time I had spoken to him since he joined Forest. After a short chat I asked him what had made him tell the *News of the World* reporter about me giving him the money each Friday evening in Bawtry. He said that the reporter had put him under intense pressure to tell him anything that he could remember about the transfer, but he could not remember my surname and had nothing else to tell him. The *Sunday People* had apparently later carried a similar report.

## More additions to the playing staff

During the close season Brian had heard from Doug Weatherall, sports reporter for the *Daily Mail* in the North East, that Frank Clark was going to be released from Newcastle United on a free transfer. At the first opportunity Brian travelled up to see Frank to discuss him joining Nottingham Forest, and an agreement was quickly reached. Frank was brought in at 33 years of age and proved an ideal signing. He had looked after himself and was in fine shape. With his knowledge and experience of the game he arrived at exactly the right time for us. An 'old head' was what Brian had been searching for; he had told me many times the previous season that one was needed in the side. Frank gave great service at left-back, going on to make 182 appearances for Nottingham Forest, collecting medals for a Division One Championship, two Football League Cups and a European Cup – not bad for a free transfer signing.

When Frank decided to call it a day he went back to the North East as assistant manager to Ken Knighton at Sunderland, later managing Nottingham Forest and Manchester City. He is still actively involved with the game as a representative of the League Managers' Association, and he lives in the Nottingham area.

Brian was still concerned about the midfield. He told me that he wanted to bring someone in to do a job similar to what Dave Mackay had done for us at Derby County, to give our midfield some education during a game. I slept on it and came up with Howard Kendall. I had recently seen him playing for Birmingham City reserves. I rang Brian and he thought it was a brilliant suggestion. He left it to me to fix up a meeting between them.

I spoke to Howard the same evening and told him exactly what Brian had in mind. He was extremely pleased with the offer, but he had been offered a coaching job with a Football League club which he was going to accept. He said it was his ambition to become a manager in the League and he hoped this would be a stepping stone. He asked me to thank Brian on his behalf. I reported back to Brian, who said 'Good luck to him, he deserves to get on.'

Howard Kendall soon joined Stoke City as a player-coach, which did lead on to him having a successful career in management. During three periods at Everton and one at Manchester City he gained several major honours.

Our next target was a central-defender. Brian said 'I want you to go to Maine Road to see Manchester City reserves this week and have a good look at Tommy Booth, he may do for us for a couple of seasons.' I had not seen Tommy play for several seasons, but it was soon evident that he would not be suitable. He was showing wear and tear, his pace had gone and he was taking things very easily. I could not possibly have recommended him. Once I had realised this I could focus on the other players on the field.

My attention was being continually drawn to the Manchester City left-back, who was doing all the right things. He was young, fresh-faced and fair-haired, with very good pace. He went forward quickly, had good control and a strong left foot and crossed the ball well. He could use his right pretty well too. I looked at the team sheet: Colin Barrett. I did not know of him and had never seen him play before. I stayed to the end of the game, then decided to make some discreet enquiries while I was still in the ground. There had been only one other League club scout present at the match.

I discovered that Colin had been with the club since he was a boy and had made his debut in the first team at the age of 20. He had made 69 appearances in League and Cup, and he had played in both full-back positions. He had also had some games at centre-half. Colin had been out of the game for some time due to breaking a leg, and this game was his first 90 minutes since his recovery. When I returned home I immediately went through his playing records, which matched what I had been told. Surprisingly he was now 23 years old – he did not appear that age on the field.

On Sunday morning Brian rang to find out how I had got on. I gave him the full report and said how impressed I had been with Colin Barrett's game. I said that there had only been one other League club represented at the game, but I knew that the way Barrett had played would soon create some interest. I said we should act quickly. Brian was pleased and said he would get on with it on Monday morning. After lunch Brian rang me to say that he had spoken to Tony Book, the Manchester City manager, and that Barrett was available at a fee of £30,000. He had arranged a meeting with Tony and his chairman, Mr Peter Swales, at an inn between Stoke and Uttoxeter for lunchtime on the Tuesday.

Michael Keeling, a friend of Brian's, drove him to the meeting. Michael had met Mr Swales several years back. On these occasions Brian was at his brilliant best. He told Mr Swales that he was prepared to pay the asking price, but, as he had not seen Colin play, and he was returning from a serious injury, he asked to have him at Forest for a week to satisfy himself. Brian said to me that the small transfer fee had made him cautious. Tony Book agreed with the proposal and Colin came for a week. Brian was impressed with the lad and he was duly signed. What a good signing it turned out to be. If it had not been for injuries he would definitely have gained full international recognition. Colin never gave Brian an ounce of trouble, and he described him to me as a 'model professional'. He played 99 League and Cup games, gained promotion to Division One and won a Division One Championship medal. The actual transfer fee had been £29,000. Torn medial ligaments and another spell out through injury curtailed his number of appearances and medals.

This signing has always given me the greatest satisfaction. Colin had that extra touch of class for a defender. Eventually he sustained further injuries and was unable to regain his place at Forest. He was later transferred to Swindon Town. To this day I have never spoken to him, although I understand he still lives in Nottingham.

### A chance meeting with Peter Shilton

The search was still on for a player to play wide on the right-hand side. Shortly before the end of the season I went to the Victoria Road Ground to see a Stoke City reserve game, an evening fixture. In the first half Sean Haselgrave impressed me. He had good pace and could cross the ball well; it was the first time I had seen him play. There was only a small attendance at the game. In the tea room at half-time, waiting for my turn in the queue for a cup of tea, a hand came down on my shoulder. I turned. It was Peter Shilton. I had not spoken to him since he had been with Stoke

City in goal. 'Maurice!' he exclaimed. 'What brings you here tonight, almost at the end of the season?' I told him we were looking for a good wide attacking player for the right-hand side, and said that Sean Haselgrave had impressed me during the first half. Peter said Sean would do well in our League. He had made over 100 appearances in the Stoke first team but was out of favour with Tony (Waddington). He thought Sean would be available for a reasonable fee.

I changed the subject. 'We're hoping to gain promotion next season. If we do, can I tempt you to join us at Forest?'

'I'd love to play for Brian,' Peter said. 'Will he have any money to spend?'

'I'm sure he'd bend over backwards to have you in our side,' I replied. 'He'd find some cash.'

Sean did just as well in the second half. I told Brian the full story, and Haselgrave became a Nottingham Forest player for a fee of £50,000. The following season he made his debut at Fulham on 21 August. He had suffered one or two niggling injuries, then gained a first-team spot when Terry Curran was injured. However, after six consecutive games he badly damaged both ankles and was out of the game for some time. He never regained his first-team place.

When Archie Gemmill joined Forest from Derby County, Sean was sold to Preston North End (by coincidence Preston had been Archie's first English League club). Forest recovered £25,000 of his purchase price from the sale. He had two very good seasons at Preston under Nobby Stiles before moving to Crewe and then York City, ending his career playing for Torquay United. In all he made 493 appearances in League football, but owing to injury only seven were for Forest. He eventually went back to Preston as a youth-team coach and obtained a UEFA (A) badge. I understand he is now employed as a coach at the Cardinal Newman College and is the English Colleges head football coach.

During the season Bryn Gunn, a full-back aged 17, and Peter Wells, a 19-year-old goalkeeper, made their debuts from the reserves and did well. The team finished in eighth position in the League. We were now moving in the right direction.

I was able to go to Cala Millor with the team for an end-of-season break. Brian, Alan Hill and myself were walking back to the hotel in the evening along the seafront, where a few yards in front of us there were a few people laughing. In the roadway Liam O'Kane and Sammy Chapman were on their stomachs, larking about pretending to be swimming. When they saw Brian they jumped up and walked away. Next morning they asked Alan whether the boss had made any remark. Alan told them that he had just smiled and seemed to dismiss the incident.

When the players reported back for pre-season training, a deputation of ladies came so see Brian to ask if he would allow two of the Forest players to take part in a charity swimming gala. He sent for Liam and Sammy, and told them what the ladies had come for. 'As I saw in Cala Millor, you two are good at swimming. I knew you'd fit the bill.' The pair quickly accepted. Brian rarely missed a trick.

### Peter and Brian together again

Towards the end of June, Peter came up to see me at the Post Office, suppposedly to say hello and collect some winnings that I had for him. I congratulated Peter on gaining fourth spot in Division Three with Brighton. Surprisingly he did not seem overjoyed. In fact, he was in very low spirits and said that he thought they should have gone up. He had lost some of his enthusiasm for life down there. He was always full of respect for the chairman, Mike Bamber, but he was completely exhausted and was having trouble with his immediate non-playing staff. He could not rely on them and he wanted to find someone he could trust to share the workload. It was all getting him down and he went on to say that he wished I lived much closer. His original two-year contract was almost over. He asked me again whether I would go down to Brighton full-time as his assistant. I told him that football life was too precarious for me, and that I would be foolish to give up what I had.

I then suggested to him that Brian might welcome him with open arms. Great strides had been made with the playing staff at Forest, all the dead wood had gone and next season we might be promoted to the top division.

'Why don't you bury the hatchet?' I asked. 'The time is absolutely right for you to come to Forest, and Brian is more focused on the job than I've ever seen him.' Peter shrugged his shoulders. 'I'm going to our apartment in Cala Millor tomorrow to join up with Lil and the kids. I need a month's rest and some sun, to recharge.

This will give me an opportunity to think seriously about next season and what we as a family want to do.'

Brian had often asked me whether I had spoken to Peter, always referring to him as 'your mate'. Recently he had become more inquisitive, asking how Peter seemed in himself, although at no time did he directly ask me whether Peter had mentioned working together again.

When Peter got back from Majorca he rang, supposedly to talk about his bets for the following football season. I had given my feeling that he and Brian should be reconciled a lot of thought. I was the obvious mediator, as I was the only one still close to them both. I had an ideal opportunity to bring the question up, and Peter would always discuss his private feelings on issues with me.

'Have you thought about letting bygones be bygones and joining us at Forest?' I asked. 'I reckon Brian would bend over backwards to get you back on board.' Peter's reply was quick and to the point. He said that he had thought about it, but no way was he going to be the one to make the first approach. If Brian rang him himself then he would meet him to discuss the possibility. I was delighted.

I could hardly wait for the first opportunity to dash off to Nottingham to see Brian. I explained what Peter and I had discussed.

'He wouldn't come,' was Brian's first reaction. 'He's had a very good season, things have gone well at Brighton, they only just missed promotion.' Obviously he had taken a big interest in how Brighton had performed. We discussed the idea for about half an hour and it became clear that neither man wanted to make the first move. It was just a matter of personal pride: I was convinced that both of them wanted it to happen.

'I'm not ringing Peter,' said Brian, after a short pause. 'He's the one that stopped speaking to me. Next time you speak to him, tell him to ring me at home. I would definitely be willing to discuss the move and fix a meeting to clear the air, with no strings attached.' I rang Peter straight away and told him to ring Brian that same night. Apparently, after sleeping on it, Brian flew over to Cala Millor to put the offer to Peter face to face and came back with the okay. Peter must have returned to his apartment there. I never asked about any of the details, I was just delighted that they were back working together again. When they told me about it, they each claimed that the other made the first move, although to my mind Brian going over to Cala Millor is the most likely story. Peter would have been nervous about making the first move.

A short time later, in July 1976, Peter resigned as manager at Brighton and Hove Albion, leaving the playing side in a healthy state, far better than when he first went there. Alan Mullery was appointed as his successor and took them up into Division Two at the end of the forthcoming season.

Shortly after Peter and Brian had made their agreement, they met Brian Appleby QC, the Nottingham chairman, and Stuart Dryden, vice-chairman, at the City Ground. A contract was signed. This was probably the most important signing I was ever involved with. Brian rang to say Peter had signed the contract, then Peter rang me and thanked me for my part in it. It was almost two years since they had spoken to each other. I was over the moon that they were back together again and I knew things would happen quickly at Forest now. However, even I did not imagine what they would achieve in the coming seasons, it was magnificent. I did follow my instinct, though, and had £100 each way at 20–1 on them winning Division Two. Nottingham Forest finished in third place, gaining promotion to Division One, winning me £400.

I was of the opinion that the ordeal that Brian had gone through at Leeds United, together with the large pay settlement he received from them, and the almost three months without having a job, had done him the world of good. He looked at things in a different light and seemed to have matured.

# CHAPTER 9
# BACK TOGETHER

The first priority was for Peter to get to know the players and assess their ability as he had not seen this Nottingham Forest squad perform. The backbone of the side was already in place: John Middleton and Peter Wells (goalkeepers), Colin Barrett, Frank Clark, John McGovern, Liam O'Kane, Sammy Chapman, Ian Bowyer, Terry Curran, Martin O'Neill, John O'Hare, Barry Butlin, G. Saunders and Sean Haselgrave. Viv Anderson came through from the reserves and Tony Woodcock had been out on loan, with Lincoln City and Doncaster Rovers, Brian doing Stan Anderson a good turn after the Curran saga.

Peter watched the first team while I carried on my scouting duties. He said that he was reasonably surprised at the quality of the first-team players but that we desperately needed a proven goalscorer and an experienced central-defender.

My first instruction from Peter was to go to watch Peter Withe, a striker with Birmingham City. He gave me a rundown of his attitude and fitness level. I went twice. Peter had had Withe all lined up to join him at Brighton from Wolves, but the news leaked out. Peter was not very happy about this, and Freddie Goodwin had topped Brighton's offer by £10,000, so he had lost him. Peter Withe became Peter's first new recruit. At £43,000 he seemed a good buy. He made his debut appearance on 25 September at the City Ground against Carlisle United. Forest won 5–1 and Withe scored one goal.

Peter Withe finished his first season with a tally of 20 goals, Forest gaining promotion from Division Two. In his second season Forest became Division One Champions; Withe's contribution was scoring 19 goals. Shortly after the commencement of his third season he was sold to Newcastle United for £250,000, making the club a handsome profit. He was replaced by at first by Steve Elliott and soon after by Garry Birtles, both from the Forest reserves.

Peter said that a centre-half was the priority because Sammy Chapman 'had shot it'. He brought in on loan the giant Larry Lloyd, a central-defender from Coventry, formerly in Liverpool's Championship side. He made his debut at Hull on 2 October, but after five appearances no transfer fee could be agreed, so he went back to Coventry.

Sammy came back in central defence after Larry returned to Coventry and stayed with the club until the end of the season, making 32 appearances. Shortly after that Larry was finally transferred permanently to Nottingham Forest. The fee was £55,000. He made his debut as a member of the playing staff on 4 December at the City Ground against Bristol Rovers. The Pirates had been his first League club, as he was born in Bristol. He went on to form a wonderful partnership with the equally strong Kenny Burns, winning a Division One Championship medal and a Football League Cup-winners' medal.

Early on in his career with Forest, Larry turned up for an away fixture to join the team coach dressed in an open-neck sports shirt and casual trousers, when every other player was dressed in club blazer and flannels. He was sitting on the coach waiting to leave when Brian, always the last person to arrive, climbed aboard and spotted him. 'Hey big fellow,' said Brian. 'Where are you going?'

'To Highbury, boss' replied Larry.

'Not dressed like that,' Brian replied. 'You know the rules. Go home, get dressed properly and get yourself to London. If you do you can play tomorrow. But don't claim any expenses!'

Larry took part in the game.

Rescued from falling into obscurity, Larry had five good seasons at Forest, creating a central-defensive partnership with Kenny Burns that was the best in the

English League and making 219 League and Cup appearances. He picked up one or two reprimands from the boss along the way, about the dress code and his weight, but they were all for his own good.

## The luck of the game

Letters recommending players to Forest were now coming in at the rate of over 100 per week. The legible, sensible letters were all distributed to the scout operating in the area concerned. The ones requiring further assessment were passed over to me for action.

One Saturday in October 1976, Burton Albion were playing in the FA Cup against Long Eaton at Eton Park. The game I was scheduled to attend, also in the FA Cup, was called off very late, so as I had no specific game to go to, I decided to watch Burton Albion. They won 5–0, so the 15-minute journey was not in vain. A young, slim lad playing centre-forward for Long Eaton, Garry Birtles, kept causing the Burton defence problems with his control and pace. He was completely on his own and had hardly any support from his teammates, but he never gave up. All weekend I kept thinking about what I had seen. It seemed unreal that in a side losing heavily it was the losing centre-forward who had registered with me. I did not mention what I had seen: Peter was still tied up with Brian and the Forest first team. I decided to pay another visit to Long Eaton during the next week for a second look. The game was a Derbyshire Cup game. The weather was awful, with heavy rain showers, and there were only a handful of spectators. I was able to watch the game from the comfort of my car, parked by the side of the pitch. The score at full-time was 1–1, so extra-time under floodlights was necessary. There were puddles all over the pitch. Just before half-time in the extra period, Birtles received the ball on the halfway line, sped off towards the goal and beat two defenders with control and pace. The 'keeper came off his line, and from the edge of the penalty area Birtles drove the ball past him, giving him no chance.

The following Saturday Long Eaton were away to Enderby Town. I had decided to go for a final look. During the morning Brian rang to say that Peter had gone to Oldham with the first team, and he asked where was I going.

'Enderby Town', I said.

'Where the devil's Enderby?' asked Brian.

'Near Leicester,' I replied. 'I'm leaving my place just before two o'clock.'

'I will be at your shop by then for sure,' Brian said. He arrived on time and passed me his car keys. 'Here, you know the way.' On the way he asked 'Who are we watching?' I told him that for the last two weeks I had been watching a young centre-forward who was worth another look. 'Interesting, I like judging centre-forwards,' said Brian.

I wanted to arrive just after the game had started so that spectators and well-wishers would not be surrounding Brian as we watched from the touchline. It was a bitterly cold October day and shortly before half-time Garry Birtles was carried off with a hamstring injury. The score was 0–0, and apart from some honest running and his control ability we had not seen much.

At half-time Brian said 'Let's have a Bovril to warm us up.' We learned then that Garry was not coming back on in the second half. Brian said 'Let's get off then.' On the way home, Brian came out with what became a well-known phrase when he was asked what he had thought of Garry Birtles when he first saw him: 'The Bovril was better than what I had seen'. Before he got out of the car he said 'If you fancy him I leave it to you, see their chairman and fix it up for him to come to the City Ground, I won't object.'

On the Monday I contacted the Long Eaton chairman, John Raynor, and agreed a transfer fee of £1,000, making arrangements for Garry to report to Alan Hill at Forest as soon as his hamstring had recovered. During the week I heard from Long Eaton that his injury was not as serious as first thought and that he would be able to join Forest the next Monday. I passed this information on to Alan Hill. Before the weekend I got a call from Alan Hill asking whether I was sure about Garry, pointing out that he had been on schoolboy forms with Notts County and they had released him as 'not good enough'. Two of our scouts operating in the Nottingham area had also said that they did not think he would be good enough and that he lacked the physical strength to cope with League football. I said that I had seen enough of him to bring him into our club, and that I believed he was worth signing.

On Sunday morning, Peter rang me. 'Garry Birtles,' he began. 'You've arranged for him to be signed by us and agreed to pay £1,000 fee. He's arriving at our ground in the morning to sign. The staff here are telling me that he isn't good enough.' I explained to Peter that I had personally watched him play three times and had seen enough to convince me. Peter went quiet for a few minutes, then he said to me, 'Get in touch with the Long Eaton chairman and tell him that we want to have Garry here at the City Ground for the week to have a good look at him. If we are still keen on signing him we will pay £2,000.' This was not a problem with John Raynor, the chairman. He had no doubts about Garry's ability, and he said that £2,000 would be most welcome.

Garry was played in the reserve team away at Coventry during the week. Peter went to the game himself, to make an assessment. He only stayed until half-time: he was convinced. The transfer was completed the next day and Long Eaton received £2,000. Garry made his debut at the City Ground against Hull City on 12 March 1977, but he did not appear for the first team again until the home game with Arsenal on 9 September 1978.

When Peter Withe was sold, Garry was brought in to replace Steve Elliott, in front of John O'Hare. He never looked back and, scoring on a regular basis, he kept his place. Peter had persuaded Brian to give Garry his chance, although reports from Ronnie Fenton, who was the second-team coach at Forest, were not very encouraging about him. Ronnie had been the manager at Notts County when Garry was released as 'not good enough'. Garry went on to win two European Cup medals, a League Cup medal and three international caps.

In October 1980, Garry was sold to Manchester United for £1.25 million. Brian asked the Nottingham Forest committee – I was unaware of this – to give me a present of £500. This was refused, as it was not in my contract to receive payments when a player that I had originally brought into the club was sold. One member of the committee was apparently heard to say, 'He's got more money than most of us and drives a new Jaguar.'

In later years I worked for Ian Storey-Moore when he was chief scout at Nottingham Forest. One day Ian said to me, when we were going to a game together, 'Maurice, I believe you saw Garry Birtles for the first time in an FA Cup game playing for Long Eaton at Burton Albion. I played in that game: we beat them 5–0 and I scored a hat-trick, why didn't you recommend me?'

I replied 'You were over 30, Garry was 21. If I had recommended you Brian would have sacked me.'

Some time ago I went to see Garry Birtles at the Pirelli Stadium, Burton Albion's ground. He was working for ITV, who were televising a game live. I had never talked to Garry before, but I wanted some details from him for this book. At first he did not believe who I was. A few weeks earlier I had written to him via the *Nottingham Evening Post*, but he had ignored it because he did not believe my story. When I recounted the initial games I had seen him play in he was convinced, but he told me that he was always under the impression that a scout living in Nottingham had recommended him, and Peter Taylor had clinched it. Peter, of course, had only seen him play the once, at Coventry during Garry's trial period at Forest, when the final decision was made whether or not to sign him. This was a fine example of how my work was carried out without any publicity within the club.

One of the young Forest players, Steve Elliott, a striker, was recommended by Brian to play in the England Under-21 squad. While he was away with the young hopefuls, Steve discovered that most of them were on much higher wages. When he returned to Forest he told Alan Hill that he was going to ask the boss for a raise. Alan advised against this, but Steve plucked up the courage to go and ask Brian. His request was refused, and Brian replied sharply that he would not recommend him for international duty again, if this was the sort of thing he was going to learn. Steve was never called-up again.

In the morning Peter and his dog used to arrive very early at the City Ground. He had stated to the staff that he could go through the morning post thoroughly without being disturbed, and this was the time when he could read *Sporting Life* without being interrupted or seen by anyone. He could select his football and racing bets for the day. Brian was fully aware of this but did not let on. One day, when Alan Hill and Brian were early, Brian said to Alan, 'Let's knock on Peter's door then listen to him rush his *Sporting Life* into a drawer, out of sight'. This duly happened, Alan said. As they went in there was no sign of a newspaper, but they had heard the rustling very clearly.

## My first sight of Tony Woodcock

One morning in October 1976, Brian, Peter and myself were together in Brian's office when his phone rang. 'Give me a couple of days and I will give you a definite answer', he said, putting the phone down. 'That was another call from Graham Taylor,' he said to us. 'Asking what price we want for Tony Woodcock. It's strange, Graham had Tony on loan last season and he keeps increasing his offer. Tony is on loan at Doncaster this season, I let Stan Anderson have him to sweeten him after the Curran episode. Three other clubs in the past week have also enquired about him. Has anyone been up to see him play at Doncaster recently?' We had not. When Brian arrived at Forest Tony had been playing for the reserves in midfield. Not having looked anything special, he had been sent out on loan to give him chance to grow stronger and mature. I checked and he had only played three times for Doncaster up to that day.

After a short discussion it was decided that I should go on the Saturday to watch him play at Doncaster. He played alongside the centre-forward and scored a goal for good measure. I was very impressed with his game. I had never seen Tony play before and he had pace, a good first touch, control and perpetual motion. In the Forest reserves he had been playing in midfield and at full-back, but this striking role at Doncaster seemed to suit his game ideally. I reported to Peter the following morning exactly what I had witnessed. Tony was recalled the next day. On the Wednesday Forest were in Scotland playing the second leg of the Anglo-Saxon Cup against Ayr United. Tony was included in the side and gave an impressive display, scoring one of the two goals, which earned him a place in the first team the next Saturday against Blackburn Rovers at the City Ground, which Forest won 3–0.

He never looked back and kept his place, scoring 16 more goals before the season ended. Forest were promoted to Division One that year. Tony gained his first of 42 international caps in 1978, and he also won a League Division One Championship medal for season 1977–78. Tony was sold to Cologne for £650,000 in 1979. He refused to sign for Tottenham Hotspur (their offer was £1 million) because he was set on playing in Europe. He continued to be selected for England while playing in Germany, where he still lives. Arsenal brought him back to England, paying over half a million pounds for him to return to Division One, teaming him up with his previous Forest teammate Viv Anderson. They both gained several international caps with the Gunners. Quite recently an ex-Arsenal player who was in the side at the same time told me the story that when Tony arrived, the day before a League game, they went out as usual to do some serious training. Tony told them that at Forest they rarely did a training stint the day before a match. Brian usually took them for a stroll along the River Trent instead. He often used to do very unusual things to take the stress away from the players before matches; his theory was to keep the brain active.

Barry Butlin was released to Peterborough United after Tony Woodcock took his place in the first team, after three years of valuable service.

### Two top Scottish players we didn't get

At the beginning of 1977, six of the staff, including Peter and Brian, went on a scouting mission to Scotland, hoping for more success than we had had on a similar journey when with Derby County. We did not have any scouts operating in Scotland at that time. We went in two cars to Edinburgh and stayed overnight. In pairs we went to three different games. Alan Hill and I went to Partick Thistle. We were very impressed with a tall young central-defender, Alan Hansen, who was only 21 years of age. Neither Peter nor Brian had seen anything special at their games. We discussed our findings with Peter. Hansen had been outstanding, his style of play was very similar to Roy McFarland, who had been fantastic for us at Derby County. I knew Peter would have been of the same opinion.

The next morning I went to the City Ground to report to Peter about how impressed we really were with Hansen. When I likened him to McFarland he became very interested and quizzed me for some time about his game. I pointed out that at the end of the previous season Partick had been promoted up to the Scottish Premier Division and that Hansen had been almost ever-present in the second half of that season. At the end of our chat Peter rang Partick Thistle to make an enquiry about his availability. Peter was told that an agreement had been reached with Liverpool, and that Hansen was staying with Partick until the end of the current season, to help them retain their place in the Scottish Premier League. Peter asked what he had fetched and was told over £100,000. He officially joined Liverpool in August and the published transfer fee was £110,000. What a 12-season career he enjoyed at Liverpool.

With Peter focussed on Scotland, we kept reading and hearing stories of the goalscoring exploits of Kenny Dalglish. I was sent up to Scotland on two occasions to watch him playing for Celtic and he scored on both occasions. His passing was top class, and he always gave the impression of goals to come. I gave my reports to Peter and he went up to see him play. Forest made enquiries to Celtic, but Peter said that the asking price of £400,000 was much more than the player was worth. He reminded me that he was 26 years of age and he did not think he would find the English Division One as easy to score in as the Scottish Premier. Dalglish went to Liverpool during the close season. Peter remarked to me that they had more money available than we did.

Peter did admit to me afterwards that he had been wrong about Dalglish, who had proved a better player than he had thought he would, and he wished that he had come to us. However, we were in Division Two at the time, although soon to be promoted to the First Division. Kenny would never have come, given a choice between us and Liverpool. Of course, Dalglish and Hansen went on to achieve great things for Bob Paisley.

### Promotion in Peter's first season

Promotion from Division Two was achieved after a very eventful season. Forest won the Anglo-Saxon Cup, beating Leyton Orient 5–1 on aggregate, and finished in third place in the League behind Wolves as Champions and Chelsea as runners-up. It was a very satisfactory ending to the season, Peter's first with Forest. For my part the season had flown by. I had been constantly involved and had also won £400 on the place finish.

The only disappointment to me was the loss of Alan Hill, who resigned from the club due to unfortunate circumstances. Alan had been invited by Radio Nottingham to be the guest in a phone-in request programme answering questions about Forest. Peter Taylor was in Germany with the pre-season tour squad. One supporter rang in and asked the question, 'Would Forest have been promoted if Peter Taylor had not joined Brian at Forest?' I did not hear the programme myself, but I understand that Alan replied 'Yes, in my opinion, as the nucleus of the side was in place before the season started. But Peter's arrival put the icing on the cake.'

By chance, Peter's daughter Wendy was listening to the programme and took a dislike to what was said. She told her father about it on his return from Germany and

Peter tackled Alan about it. Although Alan related exactly what was said on the radio, Peter would not accept it and from then on Peter gave Alan a hard time. Alan felt that he could not continue working for Forest under those conditions. It was some time before I knew exactly what had gone on. If I had been asked the same question I would possibly have given a similar answer. Peter had brought in Peter Withe and Larry Lloyd: both were certainly very good signings and fully justified, and they both made substantial contribution to the promotion gained from Division Two. Alan Hill is a very genuine person and would not intentionally hurt anyone's feelings. The existing squad were certainly moving towards being promoted, as only one game had been lost before Peter's two recruits made their debuts.

During July I decided to take my nine-year-old son to London to see some of the well-known historic places of interest. We left home early, going by train, which in itself was special to him. From his first taking an interest in football he had always been a keen Arsenal fan and I knew he would enjoy seeing Highbury. I told him that he would not be able to see any of the players, however, as they would be at the training ground at London Colney.

We arrived at the stadium shortly before midday and stood across the road opposite the main entrance looking at the huge ground. Don Howe appeared through the main doors and stood at the top of the steps. He called me over. I knew him from his managerial days at West Bromwich Albion and he had recently returned to Arsenal to join the coaching staff. He asked to why I was there, and I said that John was a very keen Arsenal supporter and that I had brought him to see the stadium. He asked if we would like a tour. We jumped at the chance and he took us all over. There were only a few people about, painters putting final touches to the structures for the coming season, and odd clerical staff. It certainly made our visit to London a day to remember. Don gave John some memorabilia which he treasured, he certainly made one small boy very happy. I sat next to Don in 2008 at Birmingham City's ground; he was still connected with Arsenal then.

# CHAPTER 10
# LIFE IN THE TOP
# FLIGHT

At a committee meeting shortly after the end of the season, Brian persuaded the committee to make extra funds available to prepare for life in Division One. Additional playing staff would be required. There had already been a big increase in sales of season tickets for the forthcoming season, and an all-round increase in gate receipts was expected.

Peter asked me to try to get in touch with Mick Channon, who was with Southampton, still in the Second Division, to see whether he fancied joining us now we had been promoted. Peter said that he was going on holiday, but that if he was willing to join us I was to let him know immediately. He said to me that Mick was just what we wanted, a regular goalscorer who had impressed greatly in the League and Cup games against Southampton the previous season. Mick was 28 and perhaps the money for the transfer would be of interest to him, as would the chance to play in Division One.

I obtained Mick's home telephone number and spoke to him one evening. He was very good with me and listened to what I had to say and to the offer of Division

One football, but he turned the offer down, saying that he was very happy with life at Southampton. He lived on his farm and was very fond of life with his horses. He asked me to thank Brian for offering him the chance to join Forest, but he had no desire to leave his present set-up.

To my surprise, a very short time afterwards Mick was transferred to Manchester City for £300,000, a sum which Forest had been willing to pay. Manchester City had finished runners-up to Liverpool in Division One. Peter had me up about it, doubting whether I had put over our story well enough.

Some 20 years later, when I was scouting for Sunderland, my chief scout was Tony Book, who had been manager of Manchester City when Mick Channon joined them. One day this crossed my mind and I asked him how he had managed to persuade Mick to join them. I explained the attempt I had made at that time to get him to join us at Forest. Tony laughed and said that he had spoken to Mick himself and had obtained the same story exactly. When he told the Manchester City chairman, Mr Peter Swales, about his failure, Mr Swales did the deal himself. At that time he was the chairman of the England International Selection Committee.

The irony for Mick was that he thought that he had a good chance of honours with Manchester City. Nottingham Forest won the Football League Cup at Wembley and also won the Division One Championship that season, and then went on to greater successes. Mick played his last game for England in October and was never picked again; the move from his home club seemed to have unsettled him. If we had bought him, how he would have reacted is anybody's guess. He returned to Southampton after a couple of seasons despite scoring 24 goals in 72 appearances. His love of horses led him to becoming a very successful racehorse trainer.

### A mission with a difference

The next assignment given to me was to do a spying mission on Kenny Burns, and here I did have success. Peter was in no doubt about his ability as a footballer, but press reports all wanted to paint a poor picture of Kenny, with problems off the field of play, including drinking and gambling. A well-known sports journalist in the Midlands, working for a morning national newspaper and living in Birmingham, told Peter and Brian that these stories were very misleading, as

Kenny was not like that. Peter asked me if I would do a private investigation into Kenny's behaviour as I would not be recognised as anyone connected with football in the Birmingham area. I learned that Kenny was a regular at the dogs and frequented the Kings Arms in Tamworth. For three consecutive weeks I trailed Kenny. It proved a very worthwhile exercise, given the magnificent results this surveillance achieved both for Kenny and Nottingham Forest. No one knew me from Adam. I set up camp each meeting at Perry Barr Greyhound Stadium, and Friday nights in the Kings Arms at Tamworth, completely on my own, keeping very close to Kenny on each occasion. I was there to observe all of Kenny's habits and transactions. I never saw him have more than two pints any evening, even ordering a shandy at times. As for his gambling, he did not bet on every race and his largest investment was £20. Usually he had a tenner on. At the dogs he spent much of his time kicking a ball about at the side of the stadium with the young lads, enjoying himself immensely.

In my report I said that he behaved himself immaculately on each occasion; that he looked a bit overweight was my only criticism. Brian purchased him for £145,000 from Birmingham City and he proved a wonderful investment for Nottingham Forest. On his arrival he did not go into the first team immediately; Brian put him through a strenuous training programme to get him into shape. When he was selected it was as central-defender alongside Larry Lloyd, which surprised Kenny himself, as well as everyone else. He had trained hard and responded so well to this central-defensive role, that at the season's end he was voted Footballer of the Year by the Sportswriters' Association. It was another of Brian's shrewd team placements.

## Championship year

Before the 1977–78 season commenced, Peter was very optimistic about our prospects for the coming season. The County Cup Charity game against Notts County was played at the City Ground before the start of the League fixtures. The game hung in the balance after Notts scored a goal almost from the halfway line. John Middleton, in goal, made a terrible hash of attempting to save: he got both hands to the ball and let it slip through into the net. Fortunately, Ian Bowyer levelled the scores to save many blushes. Peter was wild and he said that the goalkeeper would have to be changed if we were going to succeed.

Terry Curran had played in each of the friendly games, but before the season started Peter Taylor had a serious altercation with him. Peter had decided that Terry was going to be moved to play in midfield. When Peter told Terry, he complained that he had always been a striker. His scoring rate was 25 per cent in games played since his arrival. Peter said he thought that Terry would do a good job in midfield, but the argument worsened and cross words were exchanged. Terry never played in the first team again. I was very surprised. Terry had made 48 appearances for Forest scoring 12 goals, and had been a regular in the side that gained promotion from Division Two, even with two spells out through injury. However, falling out with the management was not a wise thing to do.

Terry was selected to play in the reserves at an away game. Peter was in charge of the team, everyone was in the coach waiting to leave bar Terry, and Peter said 'we will give him a quarter of an hour'. Shortly afterwards Terry arrived in the car park and headed straight towards the club office. Peter jumped off the coach and shouted to Terry, who waved a letter in reply. As Peter approached, Terry said 'It's my letter requesting a transfer – I'm not playing in the reserves.' Peter went back to the coach, sat down and opened the letter, at which point he burst out laughing. Showing it to the bus, he remarked 'It's his bloody gas bill – I hope he doesn't think I'm paying that!'

Terry was loaned out to Bury in October 1977, then sold to Derby County for £50,000. During his career he played for eight different League clubs, including Sheffield Wednesday, whom he joined for £100,000. During the 1979 to 1982 seasons, under the managership of Jackie Charlton, he scored 35 goals. When his playing career ended he had made 421 League appearances, scoring a total of 72 goals.

Peter knew that Terry would not be a great loss. John Robertson, who was a midfield player when Brian arrived at Forest, had now developed into a wonderful left-winger, and Martin O'Neill, who had been with the club since 1971 from Distillery in Ireland, was fully able to fill the wide right spot. These two had emerged as our key players. They are not doing badly today at Aston Villa either, where they are in management together. Some three weeks had passed when, one morning in Brian's office, I was with Peter and Brian when they were holding the inquest into their defeat at Arsenal by three goals. Brian said that he could not stand the performances of John Middleton any more.

Chris Woods, the young reserve goalkeeper, had been getting excellent reports, and was being seriously considered, but no change was made for the following game away against Wolves, which ended in a 3–2 win for Forest. John Middleton took the blame for the two Wolves goals. Again I was present in the office when his future was discussed. It was decided that Peter would notify all clubs that they were open to offers for John. Peter asked Brian what fee he should quote. They settled on £40,000, but would consider any offers. Brian reiterated that John had to go.

Just then, the phone rang. Brian answered, then looked up at Peter with his hand over the mouthpiece. 'It's Tommy Docherty, who's he after?' Tommy was put through to Brian and the conversation began.

'You're asking a lot, Tommy, he's our only experienced 'keeper, but if the money is right, with us, every player is available. Peter is with me, let me ask him.' Brian put his hand back across the mouthpiece. 'He wants Middleton, what shall I tell him?'

'Tell him that we would want £100,000,' said Peter, smiling. There was some chit-chat, then Brian said to Peter, with a smile and a wink 'Tommy says that the Derby board wouldn't let him have that kind of money for a 'keeper, the most he can muster would be £60,000.'

'Tell him yes if we can have Archie Gemmill as part of the deal,' said Peter, quick as a flash. Brian then said to Tommy 'We will do a deal, but you must top it up with Archie.'

The transfer was completed that afternoon and Gemmill moved to us for £20,000. Two superb deals had been done completely out of the blue. Archie gave two years' fine service, and while playing for Scotland in the World Cup side he scored a highly memorable goal during his stay.

As soon as Brian had finished his conversation with Tommy, my brain clicked into motion. I brought up the conversation I had had with Peter Shilton at Stoke some time ago. He was still in top form, and there were rumours that Stoke City were having financial problems. 'What do you feel about an approach to Stoke?' I asked. Peter Taylor was up in a flash. 'We must do it!' A record transfer fee of £250,000 was agreed the same afternoon, and Peter Shilton became the highest-paid player in the League. I cannot recall three better deals being completed in one day by any other club.

Manchester United had been interested in buying Peter Shilton but the fee was considered too high. Sir Matt Busby famously said 'Peter Shilton is too costly. Goalkeepers don't win you games.' I believe United learnt a lesson from this signing by Forest. Sir Alex Ferguson signed Peter Schmeichel from Brondby in August 1991 for £550,000, and how many games did Schmeichel win for them? I wonder if Peter Shilton ever crossed Sir Matt's mind when making that decision.

Archie Gemmill was given the number-seven shirt and Martin O'Neill was left out of the side. In November two away games were lost, both 0–1, to Chelsea and Leeds. Brian and Peter were quick to react. Ian Bowyer was taken out of the side, Archie Gemmill was given the number-eight shirt and moved into midfield and Martin was brought back into the side in the wide right position wearing the number-seven shirt. The changes proved a great success and a steady stream of good results followed. The side was playing the best football since Brian's arrival at Nottingham.

Martin O'Neill, in all his wisdom, chose completely the wrong time to pluck up enough courage to go to see the boss again. Apparently he was unhappy playing wide right and preferred his role in midfield. He honestly thought he was more suited to that position. Shaking a little, he knocked on Brian's office door. Brian shouted, 'Come in! Yes, son, what can I do for you?' Martin asked whether he could revert to wearing the number-eight shirt in midfield. There was complete silence for a minute or two, then Brian replied, in his indomitable way: 'Do you expect me to leave Archie Gemmill out of the side to accommodate your wishes? This next Saturday you can have a straight choice, the number-seven shirt or the number-12.' Martin was out of the office in a flash. He wore the number-seven shirt a further 150 times with considerable success, and he never mentioned it again.

The side only lost one game during the rest of that season and that was in the FA Cup sixth round, 0–2 at West Bromwich Albion. They had achieved a consecutive run of 42 games in the League without defeat. Peter and Brian must have got the positions of the players right.

### The England manager vacancy

In December 1977 Brian was interviewed at Lancaster Gate for the position of manager of the England international team. I said to Peter at the time that I would be extremely surprised if the 'gentlemen' at the FA had the courage to appoint Brian, although he really was the outstanding candidate. Brian came away from the interview feeling that it had gone exceptionally well, and believing that he and Peter would be appointed. Peter rang me and said that if appointed they would invite me into the England set-up as well. However, the excitement was soon over. The FA chose a well-respected gentleman, Ron Greenwood, to fill the position.

Ron caused no trouble but did not win anything major. He was replaced by Bobby Robson in 1982. In the same four-year period Brian won a Division One Championship, two Football League Cups and two European Cups. We shall never know how successful Brian would have been. Peter and Brian were appointed joint managers of the England Youth team as a consolation. I was not involved. After a while they gave it up as, with their work at Nottingham Forest, it was proving too much.

### Winning the Football League Cup

Shortly before Christmas Larry Lloyd broke a toe. Peter moved very quickly and signed David Needham from Queen's Park Rangers, a Division One side, for £140,000. David had previously played for Notts County and the signing raised a few eyebrows with the Forest supporters. However, his performances and the team results soon dispelled their fears, and he turned out to be another excellent signing by Peter Taylor.

At about this time, a young goalkeeper at the club was on his own in the players' dressing room. Brian rang down from his office. John Turner answered. 'Yes! Who do you want to speak to?' he asked, in a sharp voice.

Brian said 'Do you know who this is speaking?'

Realising, young John said 'Do *you* know who you are speaking to?'

'No,' replied Brian. The young goalkeeper put the phone down and scampered out of the room on to the pitch.

A major trophy was soon to come to Nottingham Forest. On 22 March 1978, after a replay at Old Trafford in which they beat Liverpool 1–0 having drawn the first game

0–0 at Wembley, they won the Football League Cup. Liverpool were the holders of the European Cup. John Robertson scored the only goal from the penalty spot. This was an outstanding achievement as Forest were without Peter Shilton, David Needham and Archie Gemmill (all three Cup-tied), and Colin Barrett and John McGovern were both out injured. The average age of the team was under 26 years. Chris Woods, in goal, aged only 18 years and four months, had been superb in every round.

Peter gave me five tickets for the replay. It was a very enjoyable night and one I will always remember. There were three of us, Edna, my son John and myself, plus our friend from Tarporley (a Manchester United season-ticket holder) and his son Nicky. In the main stand we sat next to Stan Boardman the comedian and his family, who were staunch Liverpool supporters. Stan had us all in hysterics throughout the game and the two young lads were mesmerised. Although his team had lost there was no animosity and he was full of praise for Peter and Brian and told me to congratulate them both on their success.

At Wembley, for the first game, Brian had asked the League management for permission for Peter Taylor to join him in leading the Forest team out on to the hallowed turf, in recognition of their partnership in bringing success to Nottingham Forest. Mr Hardaker, in his wisdom, refused his request. Peter was hugely disappointed.

Some time earlier, before the kick-off, Peter decided to go out on his own to sample the feeling and atmosphere of Wembley. A strange meeting took place in the tunnel leading to the pitch. Peter came face to face with Alan Hill, who was there working for the *Nottingham Evening Post*. They had not spoken to each other since Alan had left his employment at Forest. Alan now ran the Rancliffe Arms at Bunny on the outskirts of Nottingham. I had been to visit Alan there two or three times, but Peter had put Alan's premises out of bounds to the Forest players. Only Liam O'Kane ignored the order, and I never told Peter myself when I had been to visit Alan. Happily, this chance meeting at Wembley resulted in Brian getting the two together in his office. I do not know what transpired, but they shook hands and Alan made a most welcome return to his previous duties at the City Ground.

During the last 10 weeks of the season I had been sent out to do match reports on the upcoming opposition, with only the odd scouting mission. The scent of winning the League Championship was strong, so nothing was being left to chance. The good run continued until the end of the season and Forest were clear winners of League Division One and qualified to play in the European Cup competition in the following season.

I was invited to join in the team's seven-day celebrations at Cala Millor in Majorca, but I almost missed the flight from Castle Donnington. Peter had told me to be there for 9am, but this was the actual time that the plane was due to depart. I had been working in the newsagents, then a friend drove me to East Midlands Airport. When I arrived, at 8.40am, Ken Smales was waiting for me with my tickets, very anxious. I was whisked on to the plane and we were airborne at 10 past nine. The celebration dinner took place in 'The Shack' that evening, a restaurant specialising in fish meals which were first class. I had previously been to the same restaurant with Derby County, but this time I was not asked to contribute. It was a very enjoyable holiday, and it topped off possibly my most memorable and successful 12 months in football.

# CHAPTER 11
# EUROPEAN FOOTBALL

The first transactions of the 1978–79 season were Peter Withe's move to Newcastle (the emergence of Garry Birtles allowed this to happen) and Chris Woods' move to QPR. He had been brilliant in his occasional first-team appearances, but with Peter Shilton in such fine form it was not in his interests to hold him back. He had a superb career and gained 43 caps for England. He is now goalkeeping coach at Everton.

No one knew what was in store for Nottingham Forest in Europe. The draw had us lined up against Liverpool in the first round of the European Cup, the first leg to be played at the City Ground. The press and television pundits gave Forest little chance of progressing into the next round. The opening match resulted in a 2–0 home victory, which gave me great personal satisfaction, the two goals being scored by Garry Birtles and Colin Barrett. Over 38,000 Forest fans witnessed this outstanding beginning. It was followed by a 0–0 draw at Anfield, securing the passage into the next round.

I was sent to Greece to run the rule over our next opponents, AEK Athens. In round two the first leg was away on 18 October. We had achieved a 1–1 draw there in a pre-season friendly in early August, and this time goals from John McGovern and Garry Birtles gave us the victory. The return leg, before more than 38,000 fans at the City Ground, resulted in a comfortable 5–1 victory, Forest going through 7–2 on aggregate. Peter and I had both backed Forest to get through to the next round.

The regulations governing playing in the European Cup competition curtailed some of my scouting work as players we signed would not be eligible to play in Europe. The number of games I attended was about the same, but the standard of play at Forest was much higher than in the early days, so finding someone who would get a chance in the side was much more difficult.

Match reporting was not too intense for Peter and Brian as they did not require drawings of set plays or attacking and defending situations. They wanted me to concentrate on the strengths and weaknesses of individual players.

That season only 16 players were mainly used; four others played 12 games between them during the season in League and Cup games. We lost both Colin Barrett and Kenny Burns with knee problems during the early part of the season, but Forest came through without losing a game until the 2–0 defeat away at Liverpool, after 42 consecutive League games without a loss. We had been lucky that no other players had been injured.

With the satisfactory progress in the European Cup, Peter and Brian thought that there was a chance of us winning it; however, they decided that a top-class player was needed if we were to achieve this.

### Creating the first million-pound transfer

It was decided that Trevor Francis was to be the target. There were strong rumours in the press that Trevor was discontented at Birmingham City. He was being linked with Liverpool, Everton and Coventry City. It was the middle of January 1979. The date for signing a player to be eligible to play in the next two rounds had passed, but it was still decided to go ahead with an attempt to sign Trevor.

Peter was given the task of setting it all up. My instructions were that it was to be kept top secret, not a whisper to be leaked. The priority was to ascertain whether or not Trevor was interested in joining Nottingham Forest, without the press or Jim Smith, the Birmingham City manager, getting a sniff. I was given the telephone number of a Midlands sports journalist for a national daily who lived in the

Birmingham area. Contact with Trevor could be made with his help. The same journalist had been a tremendous help to us in signing Kenny Burns.

After giving it a lot of thought, I spoke to the journalist that evening and outlined how and where a meeting might take place between Trevor and Peter Taylor. I suggested the following Monday or Tuesday. He said that he would speak to Trevor to see if the proposed transfer would be of interest to him. The next morning he rang me to say that Trevor was definitely interested and that Tuesday would be the best night.

Trevor was asked to drive to the Burton Town Hall, arriving at 7pm, a distance of 50 yards from where I lived. My dark blue Jaguar would be parked in the parking area in front of the main building. He would park next to me and join me in my car. I would then drive him to my closest friend's house, which was outside Burton, the first of six houses leading to Bladon Castle. We would not pass the windows of any of the other houses. My friend was on his own in the house as his wife was away in London. Everything went perfectly to plan. Peter was already at the house when we arrived, and after shaking hands and making introductions, my pal and I disappeared to a pub on the main road, leaving Peter and Trevor to their discussions for a couple of hours.

We returned at about 9.30pm to be greeted by two smiling faces. They said that everything had been discussed. I drove Trevor back to his car. I had remembered how Sir Matt Busby and Frank O'Farrell had thought of Carol, Ian Story-Moore's wife, bringing her a large bunch of red roses when they successfully got him to sign for Manchester United. It was approaching Valentine's Day and my stock of goodies had arrived at the shop. There were some seven-pound boxes of Cadbury's milk chocolates and I gift-wrapped one with a label to Helen from Brian Clough and gave it to Trevor from the back seat of my car, saying that Brian had sent it for Helen. He told me to thank Brian.

Peter rang me shortly after I arrived home and said that he thought the meeting had gone very well. Trevor had seemed satisfied with what was on offer, and now we had to keep our fingers crossed. I told him about the chocolates and he thought it was a brilliant idea. Our friendly journalist had tipped me off that Helen, Trevor's wife, would be an important factor in his decision; however, I am sure that the progress that Forest were making in the European Cup was Trevor's main motivation for deciding to join us.

Next morning everything was passed on to Brian to set up the transfer deal. Brian did not make his initial approach until the last day of January, to make sure that it had been kept secret. He made his enquiry to the board via Jim Smith and a few days later an agreement was reached which went through without a hitch. On 8 February football history was made. Trevor Francis signed for Nottingham in a record million-pound transfer. I do not think Jim has ever known about our meeting with Trevor. I have read that Jim held out for the one million pounds, but Brian was always adamant that he did not pay above £999,995, saying Jim must have put the extra £5 in himself. I was never able to verify this story. With the taxes and bits and bobs the total sum was well over the million-pound mark. In the media there was much talk at the time of conflicts between Kenny Burns and Trevor at Birmingham City, and it was said that they would not get on with each other; however, no problems ever arose. They shook hands at their first reunion, when Trevor was introduced to the playing staff, and they realised that in the team they were good for each other.

Because he was Cup-tied, ineligible to play in the FA Cup, it was not until 3 March that Trevor Francis made his debut, away at Ipswich in a 1–1 draw. Garry Birtles was the scorer for Forest.

What became a nice little earner for me for several seasons then cropped up. A *Sunday Mirror* football correspondent persuaded me to let him have any snippets of information about transfers that I came across. I said that there was no way I would divulge any of our own activities, and he realised that, but he also knew that I must see and hear things about other clubs when out on my travels. The snippets were printed each week, along with others, under the reporter's assumed name.

**Further progress in the European Cup**

The day after Trevor made his debut I had what was possibly the longest day of my life. There had been a break of three months between the second and third rounds of the European Cup. Our opponents in the third round were the Grasshoppers in Zurich. The first leg was at home. I was asked to travel to watch them play in their last game, against Servette, before visiting the City Ground, to do an assessment of their side.

What a day it turned out to be! It was a Sunday. I got out of bed at four in the morning and fetched my supply of newspapers from the wholesaler on Burton railway station. I opened my shop at five and put up 15 rounds of Sunday newspapers for the paperboys to deliver. Two of my staff arrived at six so I could go. I changed my clothes, ate a couple of bacon sandwiches and checked with my staff that they would be able to handle everything in the shop, Sundays being the busiest morning of the week in a paper shop. I then set off on my journey. A friend took me to East Midlands Airport, where I took off on a British Midland flight to Amsterdam at 9.30am. I changed on to a Dutch flight to Zurich, arriving at about noon. I had lunch at the airport then walked to the stadium. It was a brisk, sunny winter's day and the scenery was eye-catching with the Swiss mountains covered in snow. The kick-off, under floodlights, was at three o'clock. The game was completely controlled by the Grasshoppers, who won 3–1, but I was not very impressed by the standard. The only player to give me concern was a striker, Raymond Ponte, who looked sharp and caused a few problems. He scored a good goal, but providing he was kept quiet I could not see any problem, they were well below our standard. I left at the end, with the feeling that we had nothing to fear on the following Wednesday.

I had another bite to eat at the airport while waiting for my return flight. I flew by Swiss Air to Brussels, where I changed onto a British Midland flight to Birmingham, arriving there just after midnight. I think I had the best part of an hour's sleep during the journey. I took a taxi from Birmingham to my house, arriving shortly before half past one. I had been on the go for over 21 hours, and was up again before five to begin another day's work. Later in the morning I went over to Nottingham to deliver my report. The journey had been very satisfactory, and Peter and I had a substantial bet on Forest to go through to the next round.

The first leg was at home and resulted in a comfortable 4–1 win by Forest. In the return match in Zurich a goal by Martin O'Neill gave us a 1–1 draw, a 5–2 aggregate, which made it all worthwhile.

In the semi-final we were drawn against Cologne. The first leg was at home and I was at the game. Forest struggled to get a 3–3 draw and at one time they were 2–0 down. I was of the opinion that Peter Shilton was to blame for the second goal, which for him was a rarity. The pitch was very heavy and did not suit our style of play. It was very difficult to run with the ball, but goals from John Robertson, Garry Birtles and Tony Woodcock put Forest in front. I thought Cologne's equaliser was deserved, however. I was very despondent leaving the ground, as I felt the replay was going to be very difficult.

The sporting press said we would struggle to get through to the Final. Cologne were the current German Champions. However, in a hard-fought game Forest did progress to the Final with a 1–0 win, Ian Bowyer scoring the goal. Archie Gemmill had an injury and had been replaced by Ian. This unexpected victory was in front of a 60,000 partisan crowd. I watched the game on television. I had not been to Germany prior to the games, as Peter had been to run the rule over Cologne. He always went to Germany on his own, as he stayed with his brother and relatives over there. To this day I have never been to Germany to watch football.

Peter seemed to be the only one giving Forest a chance before the game. The bookmakers were offering 4–1 to win the game at the Müngersdorfer Stadium, and Peter fancied them so much that he asked me to place a bet to win him £1,000, which I did. I missed out as I did not have the same confidence as him. I fought shy of having a bet.

Despite collecting 60 points in the League we finished runners-up to Liverpool in another tremendous domestic season.

Archie Gemmill was not selected for the European Cup Final. He had missed the last four League games through injury, but had declared himself fit. Ian Bowyer was kept in the side. Apparently Brian had promised Archie that he would play, then put him on on the bench. Archie afterwards made his feelings about this treatment very clear. He never played in another League game for Forest, and before the start of the next season Archie was sold to Birmingham City for £150,000. Martin O'Neill was left out because of injury, although he had also declared himself fit. He missed the Final but he kept his thoughts to himself. Archie was later asked to return to Forest but he refused, saying that too much had been said for the rift to be healed. Brian and Peter said that their decision was vindicated because they won the European Cup. Soon afterwards Martin broke down playing for Northern Ireland, so once again Brian's decision proved correct.

## The first European Cup Final

The Final was to be against Malmö, the Swedish team. I travelled with Peter to watch them. Coached by an Englishman, Bob Houghton, they played doggedly with very little flair. They seemed to be satisfied to nullify the opposition and hope to grab the odd goal, and in the game we saw they did just that. It was not very pretty to watch. Peter came away full of confidence; he could not see us being beaten if everyone kept their heads.

The Final was played at the Olympic Stadium in Munich in front of a capacity crowd of 57,000. It was to be Trevor Francis's first game in the competition as in previous rounds he had not been eligible. The plan was to go out and attack right from the beginning of the game, utilising the full width of the pitch to stretch their compact defensive approach. However, our team was feeling the pinch of a very hard competitive season. The forwards were continually falling offside and our lads had lost the edge of their game. However, just before half-time Trevor scored, with a very rare headed goal, to justify the enormous outlay on his transfer. It was not one of our better displays, but we came away with the right result. No substitutes were called on; the 11 starters completed the whole game. About 20,000 extremely happy Forest supporters had made the journey to Germany.

In their contract Brian and Peter had had written into it that each should receive a £5,000 bonus if they won the European Cup, but would not receive even one penny if they finished runners-up. Peter talked Brian into joining him in having £1,000 on Malmö at odds of 6–4, which Peter referred to as their insurance money. I placed the bet for them, but I did not bet myself as I did not have any incentive bonuses in my contract. They were both very happy. It was the first time I had seen Peter laugh after having a losing bet. Brian gave me a cheque in a few days, but I had to wait a while to get the whole amount off Peter. It was in cash, as his heavy betting was still a close secret.

This Final rounded off another absolutely wonderful season, which had begun with us winning the Charity Shield at Wembley 5–0 against Ipswich Town. This game was witnessed by 65,000 spectators. The Football League Cup had been retained by beating Laurie McMenemy's Southampton 3–2, also at Wembley, in front of a full house of 100,000. And, of course, we were runners-up to Liverpool in League Division One.

The total number of games played during the season by the Forest first team was as follows: 42 League, one Charity Shield, eight in the League Cup, three in the FA Cup and nine in the European Cup competition. John Robertson and Peter Shilton played in every one of these games plus 10 friendlies and two County Cup games. That is a total of 75 matches. Compare this with the appearances of the top players in the Premier League today. I have read that playing so many matches cannot be done and that physically it is not practical. Yet these two internationals also made appearances for their country that season, playing on many atrocious surfaces.

Attendances at all matches played during that season totalled over 1.25 million.

## 1979–80: two new signings

Before Peter and Brian left for their well-earned holiday, I was given the task of looking for a left-back. Colin Barrett was struggling badly after injury, and Frank Clark, in Peter's words, had 'shot it', but what a wonderful servant he had been, having taken part in 31 games the previous season. Before the start of the new season Frank went back to the North East, joining Sunderland as the assistant manager to Ken Knighton.

One beautiful sunny Friday evening in early July, my wife Edna and I decided to go for a drive in the country and call for a drink somewhere. We were in the vicinity of East Midlands Airport when a large jet flew overhead going in to land. This gave us the idea of going to the airport for a drink to watch the planes coming and going.

There is a saying that you never know what is around the corner. In the bar, which was packed with holiday-makers, we queued a while to get served. We managed to sit near the entrance, watching everything happening around us. Through the door came two couples and my attention was drawn to one of the men. It was Frankie Gray. I remembered Frankie from the infamous 44 days with Brian at Elland Road. He was in the reserves playing at left-back then, as an enthusiastic 19-year-old. I had never spoken to him there. He now was in the first team at Leeds United playing on the left side of midfield. I remembered Peter saying that the priority was to recruit a left-back to replace Frank Clark. I had seen Frankie play in the Leeds first team during the previous season and I quickly decided that he would be ideal in the left-back position for Forest. I remembered the Santos game at Sheffield Wednesday and I knew Peter would like his style. He was not the best tackler in the world but was very useful with the ball. Frankie and his friend went up to the bar and ordered drinks for their party. As they were being served, I leaned over Frankie's shoulder and said 'I'll pay for those.' He turned with a surprised look. 'When you've taken the drinks over to the girls, can I have a few words with you?'

He returned to me and thanked me for the drinks. We moved away from the bar, to as quiet a spot as I could find. I then explained that I was working for Brian at Nottingham Forest, and that I had been at Leeds with him during our short stay there. He did not remember me. I asked him whether he would consider joining us next season to play in the left-back position. Forest were covered in European Cup glory and had been runners-up in the League, while Leeds had only had a mediocre season. He seemed very interested, but he said that they were waiting for a flight to Tenerife for a two-week holiday. I said that was alright and that it could be done as soon as he got back if an agreement could be reached with Jimmy Adamson, the Leeds United manager. I agreed to telephone Frankie at his home on the Friday evening at eight o'clock in two weeks' time, when he should be back from holiday. We exchanged home telephone numbers, shook hands and I wished him a happy holiday. We returned to our respective drinks.

Over the weekend I rang Peter in Majorca and told him what had happened. He was in full agreement. I told Peter that Frankie had made over 190 first-team appearances for Leeds United. Peter remembered how well he had played when Forest defeated Leeds 2–1 at Elland Road near the end of the season. Peter said that he would be returning home from holiday at the weekend to prepare for the coming season, but he asked me to get in touch with Jimmy Adamson to find out what they would expect to receive for his transfer. He told me not to let them know we wanted him for the left-back position, so they would assume it was to play in midfield. I spoke to Dave Blakey, who was Jimmy's right-hand man, and asked him whether Frankie Gray would be available and if so at what price. They both owed me a favour for pointing them in the right direction when they signed Gerry Peyton for Burnley. The price Dave came back to me with was £400,000. I said it would be a week before Peter came back from holiday and that he would be dealing with it. When he returned to the City Ground Peter agreed the deal with Jimmy Adamson, but he was told that Frankie was away on holiday.

On the Friday evening when Frankie was due home I checked that his plane had landed on time. As agreed, I rang his home at Wetherby to tell him that the two clubs had come to an agreement on the transfer. I asked him to keep quiet and turn up for pre-season training as if nothing had happened and wait for Jimmy to call him into his office. He should not even tell his brother. Brian and Peter went up to complete the transfer and within a couple of days he was a Nottingham Forest player. In two very good seasons he played in 81 League and 39 Cup games, winning a European Cup and being a runner-up in the League Cup.

The other new signing was Asa Hartford from Manchester City for £450,000. He was bought to replace Archie Gemmill, who had left before the end of the previous season. This was Peter's first real mistake in the transfer market since joining us at Forest. Asa only made three League appearances: he made his debut at Ipswich, Tony Woodcock scoring the only goal, then played in two home games. Although all three games were won, he had fallen short of Brian and Peter's expectations. They then made one of their ruthless decisions. They liked Asa as a lad, and he was a current Scottish international, but he was not the player that they wanted. There was too much short ball with little variation, and he was not prepared to hit passes longer than 20 yards. His game had been misread and was not what they expected from a midfield player. I was not sure how much homework Peter had done on this signing. I certainly had not been asked to see him play on any occasion, so our usual pattern of scrutiny of an incoming player had not been followed. I felt that the reported interest by Everton had caused Peter to jump the gun. In Asa's defence, being asked to replace Archie Gemmill was a massive task.

Peter got out of jail by remembering that Gordon Lee, the manager of Everton, had been linked with signing Asa before they stepped in. Gordon was informed that Asa was available and the transfer went through immediately, Forest recovering almost all of the original outlay.

It was going to be extremely difficult to follow the successes of the previous season. Two players who would be greatly missed were Frank Clark and Archie.

Both had been wonderful servants, the type you want in the game. Trevor Francis would be an absentee, and Colin Barrett had not regained full fitness.

We were again in the European Cup and the Super Cup against Barcelona, home and away, together with the domestic Cups. Five pre-season friendlies in Europe was the chosen warm-up, during a 16-day trip away. Trevor Francis was absent because of a knee injury picked up during the summer playing in America. Brian had been afraid of this happening, but when Trevor had signed, it had been on the condition that he would be able to play in America during our close season. Brian had reluctantly agreed, as he did not intend losing Trevor's signature at this stage.

The season opened brightly with six wins and a draw, before losing away to Norwich 3–1. In the first round of the European Cup we were drawn against a little-known Swedish club, Oesters Vaxjoe, but we were unable to accrue much information about them. Over the two games we won by a comfortable 3–1 aggregate. Trevor Francis was able to return to the side much sooner than had been expected, but he was not risked in the European games. Our next opponents were the Romanian League Champions, Arges Pitesti. They were despatched with a 4–1 aggregate win. I had not been sent to see either of these early opponents; Peter had been over himself to assess them both.

In mid-November two shock defeats were suffered in the League, at home to Brighton and away to Derby County. These hurt Peter very much as both were his old clubs. This was the beginning of an unusual poor run and Forest did not win again until Boxing Day when they beat Aston Villa 2–1 at the City Ground.

### Another disappointing signing

Peter was still complaining about the lack of a left-sided attacking midfield player. In December 1979 Stan Bowles was signed from QPR for £250,000. I pointed out to Peter that we had withdrawn from a transfer for Stan in 1971, when we were at Derby County, because of the reports of his unreliability and gambling habits.

Stan's record at QPR was excellent, however. They had gained promotion to Division One and also finished runners-up in Division One. Tommy Docherty was their manager at that time and he convinced Peter that he was a reformed character. Peter had always admired his wonderful ball skills. Stan made his debut, now almost 31 years of age, on 22 December against Manchester United. We lost 3–0. In the next two games that Forest won he scored a goal. He made 24 appearances, scoring only two goals. He did not play in the first leg at home against Barcelona in the Super Cup, Forest winning 1–0, but he did travel to the second leg at the Camp Nou stadium which was a 1–1 draw, Forest winning the trophy.

Stan made one appearance in the third round of the European Cup, losing 1–0 to Dynamo Berlin at the City Ground, but he was not in the side when Forest won 3–1 away and proceeded to the semi-final. He had not turned up at the airport and the squad travelled with one short. Stan claimed that he had a fear of flying. He had also missed training several times and was still gambling heavily. Reports of his nights out up in Sheffield had also been filtering through.

Brian had reached breaking point. The irony was that if Stan had caught the plane, he would have played. When he was on the mat for not turning up he gave his reason as severe fear of flying. Brian was furious, but he had never really taken to Stan and did not rate him very highly as a player or a person. There was no room in his camp for problem players and Stan was transferred during the close season.

Charlie George was on loan from Southampton during January and February so Forest could assess his fitness, but when offered a contract Charlie refused it, saying he wanted to remain in the south. He then changed his mind, but it was too late: Brian had gleaned that he was suffering from a dodgy knee and would not complete the deal.

Brian had pet names for most of the players and staff at the club. He did not use them to their faces, but mostly they were humorously intended and you would recognise who he meant. One day the first-team squad were going off for a friendly game behind closed doors, something that happened frequently as a break from routine training. I was in his office when there was a knock on the door. 'Come in!' called Brian. Liam O'Kane popped his head round the door.

'What time is the coach leaving, Boss?' asked Liam.

'I don't know,' said Brian. 'Ask Clever Bollocks, he'll tell you.' This was the name Brian used for Martin O'Neill because he was attending college and training to become a solicitor. Liam left chuckling.

Brian referred to Alan Hill as 'Busy Bollocks' because he was always rushing all over the place. He always called me 'Peter's mate' when talking to the rest of the staff. There were some ruder names as well.

At this time Peter was not putting in the same work on the recruitment of new players as he had been. I was never sure whether to put this down to ill health or disagreements with Brian about the workload, but he was certainly not showing the enthusiasm I had been accustomed to.

### Further progress in the European Cup

Before the semi-final of the European Cup there came a trip to Wembley to play Wolverhampton Wanderers in the Final of the Football League Cup. Having held the trophy for the last two years, Forest suffered a 1–0 defeat due to a mix-up in the penalty area between David Needham and Peter Shilton in front of 100,000 spectators.

The home leg of the European Cup semi-final was played on 9 April against Ajax Amsterdam, Forest winning 2–0 with goals from Trevor Francis and a penalty by John Robertson.

For the second leg in Amsterdam I was invited to travel with the club. With the fame of Ajax and us going with a lead of two goals the media attention was enormous. I think the scribes fancied the venue as much as the game in hand. Our hotel was very near the notorious red light district. On the evening before the game, Brian, as usual, had dreamt up something surprising to take everyone's mind off the game. He took the whole squad to see the girls offering their trade. Outside the hotel he counted us all one by one. We walked down the notorious Canal Street with orders shouted to us that 'no one must stop'. We walked in a block, seeing the ladies sitting in the windows beckoning to us. It opened my eyes: I had led a very sheltered life.

During this stroll Brian, up to his mischievous best, got hold of the youngest member of the playing squad Gary Mills (brought along to gain experience) and told him to ask one of the ladies how much she charged for her services. He gave him a pen and a piece of paper to jot it all down. Gary, hugely embarrassed, went off and came back to Brian with the answer, to a round of applause from us all. This was just a ploy to relieve any tension building up in the players' minds. We returned to our hotel and were counted again before entering; there were no absentees. Brian then took us to a quiet pub nearby for two or three rounds of beers. We chatted to the locals for a short while, then headed back to our rooms in the hotel. Everyone seemed fully relaxed, and there were no signs of any tension.

The desired result was earned after a very hard rearguard action game. Forest lost by only one goal, which meant that they were through to the Final again. Peter did not have a bet; he had not been convinced that we would go through this time.

## The second European Cup

On 28 May 1980 Forest played Hamburg HV in the European Cup Final. Kevin Keegan was their star and at the time was rated the best player in Europe. Peter and Brian had tremendous respect for him. The Final was to be played in Madrid. If Forest did not win the Final they would not qualify for European competitions the following season.

Peter had been over to Germany on two occasions, once with Brian, to size up the opposition. He was confident that John Robertson would give their right-back Kaltz a hard night. Peter told me that the plan would be to string five across our midfield to keep Keegan's possession of the ball limited and hope that we could sneak a goal. It worked perfectly. John Robertson scored the all-important goal after only 20 minutes, then it was a supreme defensive performance from the whole team that brought the result.

The team that played was Peter Shilton, Viv Anderson, Frankie Gray, John McGovern (Capt.), John Robertson, Larry Lloyd, Kenny Burns, Martin O'Neill, Garry Birtles, Ian Bowyer and Gary Mills. The only substitute used was Bryn Gunn, who came on for Mills. This was to give the two youngsters invaluable experience.

Trevor Francis had ruptured an Achilles tendon during the 4–0 victory against Crystal Palace in April and was unable to play because of the injury. Stan Bowles had left the club. Martin O'Neill deserved his medal for the wonderful service that he had given the club. He had also missed out on the previous year's success because of injury.

I had again placed £1,000 on Hamburg to win for both Peter and Brian, as insurance money. They were once again on a bonus of £5,000 each for winning the

European Cup, but nothing if they did not. Both were more than happy to lose their bets. I watched the game on television in the old Dragonora Palace Hotel in Malta, on my annual holiday with my wife Edna and two children, Sarah and John. Also gathered round the television were about 20 Nottingham people on holiday in the hotel. Most were actually regular supporters at the City Ground. The Maltese are big supporters of English League football. Liverpool and Manchester United each have large supporters' clubs that are very active. Our celebrations round the pool went on until about 4am.

Forest finished the League campaign in fifth position. During this season Peter Shilton, Larry Lloyd, Garry Birtles and John Robertson had been ever present, making 65 appearances each. Kenny Burns had missed only one. For the second season running over 1.2 million spectators had been to see Nottingham Forest play.

# CHAPTER 12
# SEPARATE WAYS

A t the start of the 1980–81 season John O'Hare was released to a non-League club. He was having trouble with his ankles. This must have been a sad moment for Brian, as John had been with him as a footballer from the age of 15 when he coached him at the Sunderland Academy. John had been a wonderful servant, giving us 13 valuable years. Peter brought in two new signings to replace the departed Archie Gemmill and Stan Bowles.

Ian Wallace came from Coventry City for £1.25 million. He was a regular scorer in their side and had been there for four years since being bought from Dumbarton. His goalscoring record was good. I had gone with Peter to see him before the end of the previous season. He was small and lively, with bright ginger hair, and could turn on a sixpence. For the first three seasons he scored frequently, but in his last season at Forest he only scored three in 36 appearances. Peter made the excuse that Ian needed a big forceful centre-forward to play off, to supply him with knock-downs. I was always of the opinion that Ian was not one of Peter's better signings. After Peter's 'retirement' Brian sold him to the French club Brest. Sunderland soon brought him back into the Football League, but he only scored six goals in 34 appearances in two seasons for them, and the club were relegated during that period.

The second signing was Raimondo Ponte from Grasshoppers in Zurich for £230,000, a striker whom Peter had been impressed with during the two games against the Grasshoppers in the European Cup. He was purchased to replace John O'Hare. There was serious concern that our glory period was coming to an end and replacements were wanted. Trevor Francis was likely to be out for some considerable time. On a brighter note Peter was upbeat about a crop of five or six youngsters coming through from the reserves. Gary Mills, Bryn Gunn, Colin Walsh, Stuart Gray, Chris Fairclough and Stephen Hodge were mentioned.

However, the fears of a drop in performances were soon to become reality. Defeat by the Bulgarian side CSKA Sofia, in the first round of the European Cup and by Watford in the fourth round of the League Cup was in contrast to the success of recent seasons. The team also lost to Arsenal at Highbury and to Manchester United at home during this period.

In October, Garry Birtles was sold to Manchester United for a massive £1.25 million. With the departure of Garry, Peter persuaded Brian to buy Peter Ward from Brighton. In 1979, an attempt to get Peter Ward for £300,000 had failed, due to Alan Mullery stating that he was playing at the peak of his form and putting the price at £600,000. Brian and I had doubts about him being a consistent goalscorer in Division One, but Peter was adamant. Peter made the point, rightly, that he knew him better than either of us. The fee was £450,000. In two seasons in 33 League appearances he scored 11 goals and in 11 Cup appearances five goals. After Peter's retirement Ward only made two substitute appearances and was sold to Seattle Sounders, in Canada, who were at that time coached by Alan Hinton. Trevor Francis returned to the side during December as predicted by the medics, which was a welcome relief. He scored in his first League game back, at Sunderland, and three more in the next four games, to the delight of everyone. Martin O'Neill was sold to Norwich City for £280,000 in February, scoring in his last game for Forest. He had been at the club when Brian had taken over the management six years earlier. Peter told me many times that the successes achieved by Nottingham Forest had been down to the wonderful wide play from John Robertson and Martin O'Neill.

Martin was another player with whom I never came into contact. When I went away with the club after the season's end Martin was always away on international duty. Brian was wary of Martin, as he was of all 'intellectuals', but at the same time he admired him greatly as a player, which was the main factor.

Ian Bowyer, another great servant to the club, was sold to Sunderland. He will always be remembered for his wonderful goal in Cologne, which got us into the Final of the European Cup in Munich. Almost at the same time Larry Lloyd was allowed to leave to take up an appointment as player-manager of Wigan Athletic in Division Four.

The home game against Norwich on 28 March saw the debut of Jan Einar Ass (not surprisingly he asked for his name to be pronounced 'Oss'), a Norwegian central-defender, 25 years of age, who was signed from Bayern Munich. He had played the previous autumn at Wembley for his national team, and Peter and Brian had been to see him play in Germany on two occasions. I had not seen him play. They paid £250,000 for him to replace the departed Larry Lloyd. During the season five stalwart players had left during the rebuilding process. Four youngsters had been promoted into the first-team squad as forecast, and they were proving themselves: Gary Mills, Bryn Gunn, Colin Walsh and Stuart Gray.

Raimondo Ponte had been bought after being closely scrutinised as a person and a player. He could speak good English, and being Norwegian he should have had no trouble settling down in this country, but Raimondo found it very difficult to adapt his style of play to the English game. There was no room for passengers and he had to go, having scored only seven goals in 32 appearances. He went to play for Bastia in Sardinia. It was a big disappointment that he was not as good as expected, as he had been bought after a thorough examination. When mistakes on signings were apparent, Peter and Brian were ruthless. Gary Mills stepped into his shoes for the last few matches of the season.

It was a very quiet season for me with no rewards to show. I had travelled thousands of miles searching for young talent to come into the club without spotting anyone for the positions I had been given.

The final League position was a disappointing seventh with no trophies to be added to the trophy cabinet.

## More rebuilding of playing staff

The first signing of the 1981–82 season was Justin Fashanu from Norwich for £1 million. He was a 20-year-old striker, and I am sure Peter had not done his homework on this signing. All he talked to me about was Fashanu's wonderful volley, shown on television, against Liverpool, which earned him the Goal of the Year award in Norwich's relegation season. This goal had certainly influenced Peter. He made his debut at home to Southampton together with Mark Proctor in a 2–1 win. Trevor Francis scored both goals in what was his penultimate game, as he was to be transferred to Manchester City for £1.2 million. His goals would definitely be missed. The fee would balance the money paid out for Fashanu, but certainly not compensate for the loss of the player.

The dropped clanger was soon evident. Fashanu turned out to be a very disappointing signing and it was 10 games before he scored. He was only with the club for one season, making 36 appearances in League and Cup, scoring only four goals. Brian did not take to him one little bit, and there were stories about him visiting clubs and gay bars in the evenings. When challenged by Brian about his behaviour he denied these allegations, but his performances and efforts on the field were certainly not what was expected from a young player. He never buckled down to the job in hand. Brian loaned him out to Southampton but he did not last long there and was sold to neighbours Notts County for only £150,000. Brian was happy to get that. This must have been the only player they had purchased who had resulted in a major amount of money being lost.

Ass then picked up a bad injury, which meant a lengthy spell away. Willie Young, a 30-year-old, was purchased from Arsenal to take up the central-defensive role. Hans-Jurgen Roeber, almost 28 years old, a German who had been playing in America, was brought in to play wide out on the right. Gary Mills had been injured. Roeber was another player brought in without the right scrutiny. He played in 26 games, scoring only four goals. He was released by Brian at the end of the season.

Brian was sick for three weeks over the Christmas period and Peter was in complete charge. Performances were below the standard we had been used to. Forest were in a serious decline and the number of players coming and going had made it difficult to get a settled side. In the first FA Cup game of the season, in round three, Forest played Wrexham at the City Ground and it ended in a 1–3 defeat. Three of the newcomers were included in the side. Shortly after that Ian Bowyer was brought back from Sunderland to steady the ship.

Out of 11 of the final games that season, seven had been lost; in fact, in the last 24 games Forest had only scored 18 goals, five of those in the last two games, four of which were scored by 21-year-old Peter Davenport, who had just been brought into the side.

After the defeat by Manchester United 0–1 at the City Ground, Peter told Brian that he was going to resign and that he was having difficulty coping with the job. His impetuous nature caused him to rush in to this decision. I think that the mistakes that he had made with new signings, such as Ponte and Justin Fashanu, and to a lesser extent Wallace, were taking their toll. I had thought for some time that he was worried and nervous. He had not been as successful with his gambling on football as in previous years, and he seemed at a very low ebb. Nonetheless, his resignation came as a complete shock and he had not told me that he was considering it. When the two of them had signed an extension to their contracts he had said that they now had some leeway to bring the side back up to scratch. After his resignation the Nottingham Forest committee gave Peter a £25,000 cheque in recognition of his services to the club, and they also gave him the dark blue 2.8-litre Jaguar that he had been using for the last few months. The season ended with Forest finishing in 12th position, their lowest placing for five years.

At the end of the season, my wife and I and the two children went off to Cala Millor to stay for a week in the Taylors' apartment. Peter had promised it to us a few weeks before. One day, I was walking along the sea front as a familiar voice bellowed out 'Maurice! Maurice!' and Brian came running up to us in his shorts. He was staying with his family at his apartment, which was close to Peter's. We spent some time with them over the next few days, chatting and laughing. There was certainly no animosity about Peter's departure. Brian agreed with me that Peter's health had been deteriorating for some time and he was concerned.

**Life without Peter at Nottingham Forest**

By the beginning of the 1982–83 season, Peter Shilton had been sold to Southampton. His service to the club had been superb. To this day I have only seen one 'keeper I thought was better: Peter Schmeichel at Manchester United. Steve Sutton was given the task of following a great player. Steve had been with the club for some time, having been signed from Ashbourne, Derbyshire, as a teenager.

Colin Todd had been brought in to play in midfield. Brian had coached him as a youth at Sunderland and, of course, he had been a member of the very good side that was built at Derby County. In his second game at home against Manchester United he was sent off for a deliberate hand ball. With 10 men we lost 0–3. Hans Van Breukelen was brought in to replace young Steve Sutton after this defeat, making his debut in the 4–0 defeat of Brighton. This game also brought the welcome return of Garry Birtles. Brian had re-signed Garry after his unsatisfactory spell with Manchester United, at a much cheaper price. Garry showed how pleased he was to be home, scoring four times in his first five games back. He did not play in the 0–4 defeat at Villa Park, in which Ian Bowyer was sent off for a professional foul.

During October two young employees from Lloyds Bank came into my Post Office regularly. They always had a chat about football and asked me about the best bets on the coupon. They attended Burton Albion home games and they asked me whether I had seen Richard Jobson playing. He was a young player who had recently got into Burton's first team. 'He's good,' they said. 'You want to come and see him play, he's only our age.' I decided to go on the first Saturday they were at home. Jobson played with the number-four shirt on his back and I was impressed. He was about 6ft 2in tall and weighed about 12 stone, tackled well and had good pace.

On Monday morning, reporting to Brian, I told him that I had been to see Burton Albion. 'I was watching a boy that had been recommended to me,' I said. 'He's only played five times for them, he's been at university. He lives in a village just outside Burton. I don't want to tap him up round the back door though, my business is in Burton and if it leaked out I would get a lot of abuse from their spectators. Also I know one or two of the directors personally, and the club's been good to me since my playing days there.'

'Go and see Warnock [the Burton manager],' said Brian. 'Ask him if we can have him on loan for a couple of weeks, and tell him we'll pay a good fee if we think he's what we want.'

I made a big mistake. I did it the proper way and lost a valuable recruit. This was the first time I had spoken to Neil Warnock. I went to see him at the ground later that day. 'Tell Brian that he can't have him on trial at all,' he said. 'You must make your mind up and offer me a price. In fact, if you're prepared to pay £10,000, you can sign him now.' I reported back to Brian exactly what had been said.

'When are they next at home?' Brian asked, and I told him Wednesday night. This was the first youngster we had attempted to take on since Peter left the club and Brian was reluctant in case it was money thrown away. 'Right Maurice, John Sheridan, the reserve-team coach, will come with you to see him play at Eton Park. Make the arrangements to go with him'. I rang Warnock to tell him that we were coming to the game on Wednesday night and I asked him if Richard could wear the number-six shirt. He asked me why. I said 'He's naturally left-footed and will do things more quickly on that side, although he can use his right.' Warnock replied that he had picked the side and Richard would wear the number four.

John Sheridan and I went to Eton Park on the Wednesday evening. We stood on the Pop Side, level with the halfway line. Believe it or not, Burton Albion trotted out with Richard Jobson wearing the number-six shirt. He had a very good game, and was better than he had been when I had seen him play the previous Saturday. We left just before the end. I asked John what he thought and he said that we should take him as he was already good enough for our reserves.

As soon as I got home I rang Brian at home and told him that the verdict was a definite yes. 'Tell Warnock that Forest will pay the asking price,' Brian said. 'Bring him over as soon as possible, I will discuss wages etc. with him.' I immediately rang Eton Park and got an answerphone message: 'The office is now closed until nine in the morning'. I rang Neil Warnock the next morning, to tell him Forest would pay the £10,000, but he took great delight in telling me that Graham Taylor, the manager of Watford, had been at the game and had signed Richard Jobson when the match ended.

I immediately realised the connection. Warnock and Taylor had been together at Lincoln City. This definitely would not have happened if it had been any other club but Burton Albion, it would have been done the way Peter Taylor had taught me.

Richard had an excellent career in the game, playing for nine different League clubs and making 694 appearances. But for several bad injuries it would have been many more. I understand he suffered several lengthy lay-offs. His transfer fees totalled over £1 million over a 20-year period. He is now assistant manager to

Gordon Taylor, in charge of the Players' Union. The only satisfaction I got from the whole affair was that I was right in my judgement.

I later learned that Richard's father Mike was a Nottingham Forest supporter, so when I was writing this book I spoke to him about this occasion. The conversation was most interesting. He told me that a few days before the signing he had heard that I was interested in Richard for Nottingham Forest and he had come to my Post Office to confirm whether or not it was true. Apparently it was in his dinner hour from work, and owing to a large queue at the counter he could not get to see me, so he left.

When I told him the actual story he was astounded. He then went on to tell me what had occurred that evening. Neil Warnock had told his friend Graham Taylor about Forest's interest in Richard, and said that he should come up to Burton to watch him play as Forest were about to make a final decision. Watford had been promoted into Division One the previous season. The irony of it all was that Graham had lost his way to Eton Park and did not arrive until part-way through the second half. Whether or not he had time to form his own opinion I have no idea, but sometime after Richard had gone home, Neil Warnock and Graham Taylor followed him, driven by the Burton Albion chairman. They collected Richard and his father and returned to Eton Park. Mike Jobson, on the way back to the ground, asked Neil Warnock whether Nottingham Forest had been interested in signing Richard. Warnock replied that they had asked about him earlier, but had not followed it up.

I later spoke to the Burton Albion chairman socially one day, and he told me that he had been unaware of Forest's interest in Richard, which was interesting as he was a big fan of Brian's. It was only then that I learnt that Watford actually paid £14,000, although the purchase price had been quoted to me as £10,000.

At the end of his third season at Watford Richard was sold to Hull City for £40,000, then he moved to Oldham Athletic for £460,000. Howard Wilkinson then signed him for Leeds United, paying £850,000. I am pleased it turned out well for Richard. To this day I have never spoken to him.

Back at Forest Viv Anderson sustained a serious injury and Brian immediately brought in Kenny Swain to take his position at right-back. Young Chris Fairclough from the reserves was in the first team for the injured Willie Young at centre-half.

The results on the field were now showing vast improvement and the much-changed first XI were settling in.

## Peter appointed manager of Derby County

Another season was upon us. Peter spent the first month of it at his apartment in Majorca. When he came back, he told me that Derby County had offered him the manager's position. He had rung Brian to see whether the two of them might go, but he had been given a very firm 'No'.

Peter's appointment at Derby, which came only six months after he resigned at Forest, came as a huge surprise to me and many others. He would replace John Newman, who had only been in the job nine months and who had been sacked by the new chairman, Mike Watterson from Chesterfield. Stuart Webb, the club secretary, was obviously the one who had recommended Peter.

Peter immediately brought in Roy McFarland as his assistant manager and Mick Jones as first-team coach from Bradford City. This incurred a fine of £10,000 from the FA for an illegal approach and Derby were forced to pay £55,000 as compensation to Bradford.

Archie Gemmill signed as a player, immediately followed by John Richards, a striker from Wolverhampton Wanderers on loan for a period of 10 games. Bobby Davison was signed for £80,000 from Halifax as a striker and a prolific scorer. He proved a good signing.

In December, Peter rang me to ask if I would go with him to open a new shop in the Burton Cooper's Square Shopping Centre as he did not fancy going on his own. I had not spoken to him since his appointment. He picked me up at my home in Repton in his blue Jaguar, which had been a gift from Forest. On the way he told me that he now had two big cars as Derby County had provided him with a Ford Sterling. He said he was finding it expensive to keep the two on the road and asked me if I was interested in buying the Jaguar. It had only 23,000 miles on the clock and looked in perfect condition. I asked what price he wanted and he had no idea, so we agreed that he would take it to Wadham Kennings in Nottingham, from where it had come brand new. He would let them give him a price as if they were taking it off him with no part-exchange for another car. I said that whatever they priced it at I would give him £500 on top. He came back with the figure of £4,000 and I agreed that I would give him the full £4,500. We shook hands on the deal.

At that time Peter owed our bookmaker £9,000. He told me that I could have the car, keep the £4,500 and pay half of the debt off. I was pleased as the bookmaker had made some anxious remarks to me as he had not had any money for some months. Peter brought the car over to my house the following week, complete with the log book. He then told me that the log book was in his wife's name for tax purposes, having been a gift from Forest, and he therefore asked me to give him a cheque for the full amount, which I made out to Mrs L. Taylor. This meant that there would be no money for the bookmaker. Peter said that he had been promised a large cash-in-hand from Mr Watterson for agreeing to join Derby County, but this had not materialised.

As soon as I got the car I took it to my garage in Burton for a thorough check. All the mechanics discovered was that the brake pads needed replacing. This showed what a nervous driver Peter was. When they had to be replaced again, the car had completed 83,000 miles.

The next day Peter rang to say that a paperback book *With Clough by Taylor* had just been published. It had been ghostwritten by John Sadler, a journalist. Peter was also doing a series of articles about his time with Brian in *The Sun*, so he thought he would be able to get his hands on some cash. I was concerned about the money owing to the bookmaker as it was me who had introduced Peter to him.

Peter then asked me to join Derby County as the chief scout. I had been very happy working with Brian at Forest without Peter and we had been reasonably successful. Progress was being made. I asked Peter to give me a few days to consider the offer. Forest were in a far better position than Derby County, but after much thought I decided to go with Peter at Derby. The reason was purely the money that he owed my bookmaker friend. I thought I was more likely to get the money owing if I went: if I stayed at Forest the chances of getting the money would diminish. I wanted to go over to Brian to see him face to face, as it was only fair. He had always treated me well and it was going to be difficult, although Forest were now going in the right direction and the first team had begun to gel.

On the Monday of the next week I went over to the City Ground to see Brian, to tell him that I wanted to leave. I was with him for quite a long time. I explained that Peter had asked me to join him at Derby County. My reason for going was that the club was near the bottom of the Second Division, while Brian's lads were back on song and the team had been rebuilt. I also said that I felt indebted to Peter, and that without him I would never have been introduced to Brian or got into scouting. At no time did I mention gambling or the losses Peter had incurred. Brian was superb. He said that it had crossed his mind that I might join Peter. He shook my hand and thanked me for all the help I had given to him over the years and said he hoped we would remain friends. He thought Peter had taken on a massive job. 'Give my love to Edna and the bairns,' were his parting words.

A few years later I told him that one day I would tell him the real reason I went to Derby County with Peter, but the right opportunity never arose.

## Back at Derby County

On my first day back at the club it was nice to meet Stuart Webb again. He knew his job and we had always got on well together. In my first chat with Peter he told me that virtually all the money that was available had been used up. The chairman had not come up with the promised amount. Peter said he wanted me to cover the non-professional Leagues to see if there were any likely lads. Derby's League position had not improved, wins were extremely hard to come by and gates were below 15,000.

In January Paul Futcher joined the club from Oldham, along with Peter Hooks, a 23-year-old midfield player from Notts County. Just after the turn of the New Year Derby played 15 consecutive games without a defeat. They took Kenny Burns on loan from Forest for the run-in as there was no money to buy him. Kenny played in seven of the last nine games and was not on the losing side once.

From near disaster Derby County climbed up Division Two to finish in 13th position. Peter was reasonably happy.

The 1983–84 season soon came round. Peter had signed John Robertson from Forest behind Brian's back, and his book was in the shops. Brian had not even been aware that Peter was writing it. I did not see Brian but I understand he was in a furious rage, calling Peter all sorts of names. He sent Viv Anderson (injured at the time) and Mark Proctor to knock on the door of Peter's house saying that they had come to be signed for Derby County. Peter apologised to the two lads, who were apparently embarrassed and distressed, and they could not get away fast enough, walking all the way back to the City Ground. When Peter next rang he told me the story and was furious about it. It was at this time that Brian said he would never speak to Peter again, and I was sure that Peter would never have the courage to break the ice. Neither ever asked me if I had spoken to the other.

Derby had a disastrous start to this second season with Peter in charge. Of the first 14 games in the League and League Cup they only won two. Some new players came on to the scene: Dave Watson, a 37-year-old central-defender who had come back to England from playing in Canada; Graham Harbey, who was promoted from the reserves; Kevin Wilson, who had missed the first eight games, came back from injury; Andy Garner was promoted from the reserves to the first XI; Steve Devine, a wide-right player, joined from Wolves; and Kenny Burns was taken on loan again. However, the tide could not be stemmed. Gates had dropped to around 12,000. Mike Watterson, the chairman, had departed, leaving the club in a dire situation. The cash handout that Peter had been promised never materialised, and the Inland Revenue instigated winding-up petitions.

After a 1–5 drubbing away at Barnsley Peter left the club, never to return, blaming his ill-health. The winding-up petitions had been lifted after Stuart Webb secured financial help from Robert Maxwell. Roy McFarland took over until the end of the season. Despite not losing any of the remaining home games, and collecting 13 points, Derby could not gain a single point away from home. They were relegated to the Third Division, finishing in 20th position.

I had spent my worst 18 months in football. There had not been a penny available from start to finish. There was one player from non-League Telford United, who went on to make the grade in the League, that I could have got for £10,000, but there was no chance of the money. Peter did say later that it was a mistake not to have signed him. The only consolation I had was that Peter had given me £4,500 cash for our bookmaker from the sale of his book, halving his gambling debt. This, after all, had been my reason for going back to Derby.

I decided to leave the club. Stuart thanked me and said he was sorry. As a parting request I asked Stuart if he could get me four tickets for the Frank Sinatra concert at the Royal Albert Hall. My wife and I were big fans. He said that he thought he would be able to but that they would be expensive. He obtained them for me at a cost of £200 each, but we very much wanted to see him live. With two friends we had a wonderful evening. Anita Harris sat next to my wife. At that time she was a star in her own right, but she was in raptures over Frank. It was money well spent.

The following season, in Division Three, Arthur Cox was appointed manager at Derby County. He had just steered Newcastle United into the top division but had not been able to agree new contract terms with them. He appointed Roy McFarland as his assistant manager, and within three seasons they had returned Derby County to Division One.

# CHAPTER 13
# NEXT STEPS

It was Thursday 9 May 1985. I had not spoken to Brian since the day I had been to his office to tell him that I was joining Peter at Derby County, when out of the blue I got a telephone call in the evening. 'How are you? Have you spoken to your mate recently?'

'We're all fine, thank you,' I replied. 'It must be 12 months since I last spoke to Pete, he's spending a lot of his time in Cala Millor. It's nice to hear from you.'

'I was at Doncaster Rovers last night,' Brian said. 'Someone said that you were there too, but I never saw you.'

'Yes, I was there. You were probably in the directors' box,' I said.

'Who were you looking at?' asked Brian. 'And who are you working for these days?' Ian Snodin was my reason for being at the game, but I evaded the second question.

'Tell me,' said Brian, 'If you had been working for me, what would your report have said?'

'I would have given you an emphatic "no",' I replied. 'Ian isn't your type of player. He doesn't work hard enough, his vision's not the best, he's only got average pace. I can't see many goals in him, he's nowhere near your standard and you are three divisions above. He's definitely not worth the asking price of £450,000. I would say at 21 years old he might be worth £150,000, hoping that you would get more out of him, which you probably would, then you wouldn't lose any money.'

'These b*****ds I have here [Forest] working for me want me to buy him for that money. That settles it, he won't be coming to us. We've only two more fixtures left and the last one at home is on Saturday. Are you anywhere yet this week?'

'No, that was my last for the season,' I replied.

'Bring your John to the game on Saturday then,' said Brian. 'I'll put two tickets for the directors' box on the door. Don't rush off after the game though, I want to see you in my office.'

Everton, managed by Howard Kendall, were the visitors. They had just been declared the champions of League Division One. Good judges have said that this was the best side Everton ever had. Young Nigel Clough would be in Forest's line up and I was looking forward to seeing him. He had recently gained his place in the first team and had scored his first goal in the previous home game. The League table had Forest finishing in ninth position.

John and I duly went. We collected our tickets on the door, exactly as Brian had said, for the directors' box. Sitting next to me was Manchester United's chief scout, Tony Collins, who had managed Rochdale for eight years previously. Everton were to be United's opponents at Wembley in the FA Cup Final the next Saturday, and he was doing a match report on Everton. Forest won 1–0. There were signs that Everton had taken their foot off the gas now the League was over and Wembley was in their sights. It was the first Division One game I had seen all season. Nigel, in his early 20s, did well. Before I left my seat Tony Collins asked me whether I had noticed anything interesting. I told him that a major feature of the Everton defence was that the back four played very square, relying on the pace of Kevin Ratcliffe to cover behind. Forest had won the game with a through diagonal ball by Steve Wigley between the defenders, with Birtles, running behind, hitting the ball first time into the net. In the Cup Final Norman Whiteside scored the only goal from just such a through ball. I was sent a thank-you bottle of champagne.

I knew Brian would be in high spirits when he came into the committee room where John and I were waiting. The room was full of sports reporters and we had a very welcome cup of tea. After about half an hour Brian came in, greeted everyone and sat behind his small table. He was on top form. 'You all know Maurice!' he said to the reporters. 'Now let's have the questions.' Half an hour passed quickly. I clearly remember David Moore of the *Daily Mirror* (press officer at Pride Park at the time of writing) standing up and asking a question. Brian had known David since the early Derby County days when he was the programme editor. 'David, that is the most stupid question I have been asked,' said Brian. 'Go outside and stand in the passage at attention until I call you back.' David left. After 20 minutes Jeff Farmer of the *Daily Mail* stood up. 'Have you forgotten David, Brian?' A big grin appeared. 'Whoops! Open the door!' David was still standing at attention against the opposite wall. There was laughter all round. 'That's all now,' said Brian, bringing a halt to the questions. 'I have some business to do with Maurice. Goodnight gentlemen.'

I hadn't a clue what he wanted me for. Several things had crossed my mind, including the idea that he might ask me to go back to working for him. He picked up the phone and rang the dressing room. 'You can all come in now,' he said. In trooped Ronnie Fenton, Liam O'Kane, Alan Hill and Archie Gemmill; altogether there were eight of his staff in the room. 'Maurice, come and sit by me,' Brian said. He turned to the others. 'I've asked Maurice to come today to tell you b*****ds why we are not signing Ian Snodin.' I felt about 3ft tall. 'Go ahead,' said Brian to me. This was certainly unexpected. I told them exactly what I had said to Brian on the phone the previous Thursday. I was not involved with Nottingham Forest, and I did not change what I had previously said. I had formed my own genuine opinion of the player.

Before the start of the next season Ian Snodin was transferred to Leeds United, in Division Two, for the lesser sum of £200,000. Billy Bremner was the manager at Doncaster Rovers and Eddie Gray was the manager of Leeds, and they had played together at Leeds. Leeds did well out of the deal; they in turn sold him to Everton for £840,000, which did surprise me. Ian was converted to a right-back defender in an emergency and stayed there, but he suffered several injuries, at one point missing a whole season. In eight seasons he made only 148 appearances, costing over £5,500 per appearance. This was unfortunate for both the lad and the club.

Joe Royle then took him to Oldham Athletic who were playing in the newly formed Premier League, the old Division One.

## A surprise evening out with Brian

I had another surprise phone call from Brian early one Saturday morning the following June. 'Maurice, some help from you if you can,' began Brian. 'Brian Moore and his wife Betty are staying with us for the weekend and the weather forecast for today is sunny all day. Brian [Moore] likes to go racing. As you know I don't pay much attention to it, is there a race meeting on anywhere near today, what can you suggest?' I told him that there was an evening meeting at Doncaster that night, although it would be very crowded. It was extremely popular. 'Can you come with us and put us right?' asked Brian. I suggested that I contact the Doncaster racecourse office to see if we could get in the club enclosure. The two of them would not want to be smothered with well-wishers all evening. 'Right lad, I will leave it to you to arrange it. It seems a good idea.'

I rang the secretary's office and spoke to the secretary. I asked if I could have five tickets for the evening's meeting, explaining that I was coming with Brian Clough and his wife, and Brian Moore and his wife. I explained that if they were outside of the club enclosure their evening might be spoilt by public attention. He said that he could make the necessary arrangements and he fully understood the circumstances. He said he was looking forward to having them attend and to meeting them, and said he would leave the tickets on the door. I asked if we could park in the car park near the entrance with our two cars and he said it was no problem.

I rang Brian back and told him it was all laid on, I suggested that I took Barbara and Betty in my car, and that Brian follow in his car with Brian Moore. That was satisfactory. I had not been to Brian's house in Quarndon and he explained to me that it was opposite the cricket ground. We had to be on our way at five. I arrived there at five and we had a good journey, arriving at the racecourse at about six. The car park was almost next to the entrance and the steward was expecting us. We collected our complementary tickets for the club enclosure and up we went, to a very warm welcome from the secretary. Everyone was obviously pleased with their presence. I left them once they were all settled: the priority for me was to find some winners. During the evening I managed to glean information about two subsequent winners, and I took these tips back to the others. Fortunately, both won. The result was a wonderful evening. All five of us had won money, and they were very impressed with the hospitality they had received. After handshakes all round we set off on our journey home, arriving at Quarndon about 11pm.

On the Monday Brian rang me to thank me. He said that it had made the weekend for them – he himself had won £25 – and how much they had all enjoyed themselves.

**A short period not working for any one club**

I had by now sold my Post Office in Burton upon Trent. Two years later I got a letter from the Inland Revenue stating that I owed them a large sum of money in Capital Gains Tax. I had not been informed by my accountant that this would happen. They had been right back to 1957 when I first purchased the Post Office business. Fortunately, I had put money away in a savings account and had spent only a small amount of it, so I was able to pay it without a great deal of difficulty.

I learnt that if I purchased another similar type of business I could get a roll-over sum of money back. It was then that I bought a newspaper business in the village of Melbourne from Mr and Mrs Willie Carlin. Our intention was to stay there for four or five years, but we enjoyed our time in Melbourne. We got on with the villagers very well and the East Midlands Airport close by was beginning to grow quickly. The business did well and we stayed over eight years.

During this period I worked for about four different Football League clubs, but not in senior positions. I also spent two years scouting for a Maltese Division One club, attempting to take footballers over to Malta to play. It was very difficult. I only managed to get two to go over there, and they each came back after only one month. The pitches were very poor – mostly not grassed at that time – and wages were well below even non-League standards over here, so I gave it up.

One Sunday afternoon I was in bed in my home at Repton, having been up since 4am with the Sunday newspapers. Lil Taylor, Peter's wife, and his daughter Wendy came to our house. Lil stayed in the car and Wendy came to the front door and spoke to my wife Edna. She asked to see me, but she was told it was difficult unless it was very urgent. Edna was told that the asking price was £2,000 more than what I had paid for the car. Apparently they had been to Wadham Kennings in Nottingham and seen an almost identical Jaguar (second-hand) priced at £6,500. This was the asking price to sell to a buyer, not to purchase off a private owner. Edna explained how the price had been reached when Peter and I had done the deal. I understand that Edna and Wendy agreed to disagree, and Wendy and her mother left. Peter obviously was not aware of their visit and nothing further was heard from them.

Shortly after this my bookmaker friend asked me if I would contact Peter about the outstanding £4,500, as it had been almost two years since his last instalment. I went over to Tollerton armed with a letter to Peter stating the reason for my visit, intending to leave it if they were not at home. They were out so I posted the letter through their letterbox. Within half an hour of returning home Peter rang and gave me a few 'verbals', saying I should not have left the letter, because his wife knew nothing about it. He said she would have gone ballistic if she had read it. He warned me not to do it again, and said that when he had got the cash together he would bring it over. Both the bookmaker and Peter have passed away, and the outstanding sum of money was never paid.

## Two failed transfers

During the 1988–89 season I got a telephone call from Dave Mackay, who was managing Doncaster Rovers, then playing in the Fourth Division of the Football League. He asked whether I had been to any of Burton Albion's games recently. I said that I had been twice. He then asked 'How do you rate Steve Cotterill and John Gayle?' I said they had done well and would certainly get him goals. Doncaster had seen them too, and Dave asked me to go and see the chairman and offer him £15,000 for the pair. There was no more money available.

I went over to Eton Park the next day and saw Mr Sam Brassington, the chairman, and delivered the message. I personally thought there was a chance, as both had only been at the club a short while. Cotterill had cost £4,000 from Alvechurch and Gayle had been brought in on a free. Mr Brassington asked me to tell Dave that he was looking for much more than their offer, more like £25,000. I phoned Dave to give him this verdict and he thanked me, saying again that there was not another penny available.

Shortly after that the two were transferred to Wimbledon, playing in Division One of the Football League. The chairman of Burton Albion was apparently a friend of Mr Sam Hammam. Both players were sold on within four years: Steve Cotterill for £80,000 to Bournemouth, playing in Division Two, and John Gayle for £175,000 to Birmingham City. Both had good careers and are still working in the game.

In the transfer contracts with Wimbledon, Mr Brassington had written in further payments of £1,000 for a certain number of appearances in the first team, plus a percentage of any sell-on transfer fees Wimbledon obtained. It turned out to be a lucrative deal for Burton Albion, as the actual sum received was in the region of £120,000. This proved yet again that there is good talent to be found in non-League football.

### A classic signing of a young prospect

Another fine example of what Brian could achieve when given good prospective talent to work with was the signing of Roy Keane.

Noel McCabe, a postman working in Cork in the Republic of Ireland, was a part-time scout, trawling the area on his trusty motorbike looking for talented young footballers for Nottingham Forest. He made an approach to Cobh Ramblers about their young player Roy Maurice Keane. He was informed, however, that the Tottenham Hotspur scout was taking him to London for a trial period. Roy was turned down by Spurs and he returned home to Cork.

On hearing this Noel McCabe got on the phone to Alan Hill at Forest, saying that he would like to send Roy, with two more lads, over to Nottingham for trials. Arrangements were made for travelling and accommodation and the three duly arrived, taking part in training and a coaching programme plus a game at the end of the week. Unfortunately the game had to be cancelled owing to poor weather conditions. The lads returned home to Ireland, but Roy Keane, an 18-year-old, had caught the eye of Alan Hill, Liam O'Kane and Archie Gemmill. His attitude and ability had become apparent during the training sessions and it was decided that Roy should be invited back to play in a midweek game at Tranmere Rovers. Archie Gemmill was the coach with the team, and Alan and Liam travelled to Tranmere to make an assessment of Roy. He had an absolutely outstanding game playing in centre midfield. Back at the City Ground, Brian was told that they had certainly found a player, and his staff recommended that Keane should be signed. Brian said that he liked his staff to be positive in their decisions. All three who had seen Keane play were in full agreement about the lad. Brian said they would sign him as soon as possible.

Contact was made with the chairman of Cobh Ramblers and a meeting was arranged at Forest. He would fly over to Nottingham with Roy to complete the transfer. The discussion took place between Brian, Ronnie Fenton, Alan Hill and Roy, with the Cobh chairman, and the terms of the transfer were agreed. Ronnie, Brian's assistant manager at the time, was to deal with all the financial details. Brian then asked Alan to bring in a bottle of Scotch whisky to celebrate the deal. Brian signed the label and handed it over to the Cobh chairman. Brian told me that he seemed more pleased with the whisky than the deal agreed. The fee was £10,000 immediately, with a series of add-ons up to a total of over £100,000. The date of the signing was 12 June 1990, and he joined up with the rest of the Forest squad for the commencement of the 1990–91 season.

Roy's first game was in a pre-season Under-19 tournament, taking place in Haarlem, Holland. Forest reached the Final of this tournament, Roy playing in central midfield in the games leading up to the Final. For the Final itself it was agreed that he should play wide right in a 4–4–2 system. Their opponents were the mighty Barcelona side who had been the favourites from the start to win the competition. Keane had an outstanding game in the Final and was instrumental in Forest winning the tournament. On their return to the City Ground, Alan and Archie reported to 'the Gaffer', Brian's name to all the staff, 'We have some player on our hands.'

Brian was very anxious to see Roy play in a competitive game. As it was still pre-season he organised a match at Sutton in Ashfield, Nottinghamshire. Archie Gemmill was again in charge of the team, while Brian would travel separately, unannounced. Alan Hill picked Brian up at the Post House at Sandiacre, and they travelled together, arriving soon after the kick-off. Brian asked if 'the Irishman'

(Brian's name for Roy) was out on the pitch playing and Alan said no, but that he had definitely been in the squad that left the City Ground. At half-time Brian and Alan went for a coffee on the team coach. Brian instructed Alan to go to the dressing room and tell Archie that Roy was to be put on in midfield for the second half. However, the second half kicked-off without Roy Keane. Brian jumped out of his seat and shouted 'There's no Irishman!' He jumped over the low fence onto the pitch and asked the referee, Brian Saunders, to stop the game. Brian yelled to the bench 'Young Gemmill off, Irishman get on!' (Scot Gemmill was Archie's son.) Roy showed his qualities and Brian was very impressed with what he saw. After the game, Brian reminded Archie with a few choice words that when he gave orders, they were to be carried out.

The new season kicked-off with a 1–1 draw with Queen's Park Rangers at the City Ground. On the following Tuesday Forest were due to play Liverpool. Late in the morning Brian was informed that Steve Hodge had gone down with the flu and was not fit to play, and Franz Carr was doubtful. Brian asked Alan Hill who was available to play in midfield. Alan said that Starbuck and Keane were fit. Alan was instructed to arrange for them both to travel up to Liverpool and on the way to pick Brian up at his home in Quarndon. Alan arranged for Ronnie Fenton to drive them all up to Anfield. On arrival the rest of the team were out on the pitch deciding which boots to wear, with leather or rubber studs, when Brian asked Keane, who was still in the dressing room, what he was doing. Roy replied that he was helping Liam O'Kane with laying the kit out. Brian said 'That's great! But you see that number-six shirt son, you will be wearing that tonight.'

Roy sat down, went ghostly white and said 'What, me?' Brian said 'Yes, you son.' The rest of the team had now returned to the dressing room. Brian told them that 'the Irishman' would be making his debut, and that Phil would be in the side too, and that they were to look after them. As the bell rang in the dressing room for the players to make their way out on to the pitch, Brian said, in his inimitable way 'Irishman, come here', then proceeded to give him a big hug and a kiss, and said 'Go and enjoy it, son.' The match ended in a 2–0 defeat but it was the start of a wonderful career.

In only three seasons, Roy Keane made 154 appearances for Forest. Brian retired at the end of the 1992–93 season. Before the next season commenced, Nottingham

Forest's new manager, Frank Clark, and his assistant manager Alan Hill, sold Roy Keane to Manchester United for £3.75 million.

## My third time with Derby County

Roy McFarland was appointed manager of Derby County in October 1993. They were then in League One, the old Second Division. He had been assistant to Arthur Cox, who had had to retire due to a severe back problem. At this time Roy brought in Alan Durban as his assistant manager and I joined them as a scout. Ron Dukes was the chief scout. He was a good organiser, but I did not consider him the best judge of a player.

Obviously cash was still a problem with the club. In Roy's first season they got into the Play-offs to go into the Premier League, but they unfortunately lost to Leicester City in the Final.

During the second season Paul Kitson was sold to Newcastle United for £2.25 million, and Martin Taylor, the goalkeeper, broke a leg during October. Gary Charles and Tommy Johnson were both sold to Aston Villa for £2.9 million at the end of the year. Gordon Cowans was brought in but there were no big purchases.

Having not been involved in day-to-day work in football I was a not right up to date with what was happening in the game. Alan Durban asked me to go to Preston, who were in Division Three. I could not keep my eyes off a young midfield player: he controlled the whole game and scored a superb goal. My report was virtually all about him. Alan Durban rang me on the Monday and said he had my report. 'Did you not know that this player David Beckham is on loan from Manchester United to gain experience? He's rated the best youngster on Man U's books!' At that time I genuinely had not been aware of him. Ever since I have had a few chuckles to myself.

There were two players I did recommend. One was Robbie Savage, a slim 18-year-old midfielder playing for Crewe Alexandra in Division Three. He had been released by Manchester United, I presume because of his physique, but Dario Gradi could improve this type of incomer to his club. However, to be completely fair, Roy McFarland and Alan Durban went together the following Wednesday to see him play and rang to tell me that he had done well, but they doubted whether or not he would be up to the rigours of the higher divisions. I pointed out that he did not shirk anything and had never stopped working when I saw him. No action was taken to bring him on board. Nevertheless, what a career he has had in the game.

The other player was Emile Heskey. Playing for Leicester City reserves against Aston Villa reserves at Villa Park, he scored two goals in a 3–1 victory and worried the Villa defence to the extreme. He was only 17 years old and I listed his statistics in my report, along with a strong recommendation. Two days later I went into the Baseball Ground to see Ron Dukes. He said to me 'I've read your report from earlier in the week,' and fetched it out of his drawer. 'You like him because of his physique,' said Ron, 'big and strong'. I replied that his skill on the ball was excellent and that his pace and shooting power were also very good. Ron held the report up in front of me and tore it up. Emile Heskey has had an amazing career. Cloughie would have loved him at that age.

At the end of the season Alan Durban sent me to Burnley to see them play Sunderland at Turf Moor. The result was a 1–1 draw. This was Peter Reid's first game as manager at Sunderland. They finished the season in 20th position, just escaping relegation from League One. He had a tremendous reception from the travelling supporters from Sunderland as he walked to his place on the bench. I sent my usual type of report in to arrive on the Monday. Alan rang me and asked if I could go over to see him, which I did in the afternoon. He had on his desk my report. Then he put the team sheet in front of him and asked me to give him a complete run-down of every Sunderland player, with plusses and minuses. I spent about an hour with him. He thanked me and I left without him giving me a clue what it was for.

That season Derby finished in ninth position in League One. Considering the loss of four important players for the majority of the season and the fact that there had been no major newcomers, this was quite good. Nonetheless, Roy's contract was ended with no offer of an extension.

Jim Smith was appointed the new manager and brought in Steve McClaren as his assistant. Derby County finished in second place and gained promotion to the Premier League.

## Joining Sunderland FC

In this wonderful game of football there is a surprise around every corner. Before the beginning of the 1995 season I received a telephone call from Alan Durban. He had been appointed chief scout at Sunderland and wanted to know whether I would join their scouting staff and work the Midlands area. It suddenly dawned on me why Alan had wanted the Sunderland team report last season. I had heard nothing from Derby County since Jim Smith had taken over, and since I had not signed a contract I was free to join Sunderland.

All the scouts were invited up to Roker Park for a meeting. We were introduced to the senior staff: Peter Reid, his assistant Paul Bracewell, chief coach Bobby Saxton (Bobby had been a player at Derby County, but I had never spoken to him. Two years later he became assistant manager.) and Adrian Heath (whom I had attempted to sign as a schoolboy). Alan was the only one present that I knew well. Mick Buxton, who had been the previous manager, had been replaced when Sunderland had come perilously close to relegation into Division Two at the end of the previous season.

The first season under Peter Reid ended with Sunderland achieving promotion to the Premier League, topping the table by four points, ahead of runners-up Derby County. Unfortunately the Black Cats went straight back down at the end of the next season. The new stadium, to seat 48,000 spectators, was being built, and there was no money available to bring in players of the standard required in the top division. Niall Quinn, whom Peter had brought in from Manchester City, missed 26 games through injury, which did not help.

Towards the end of April Alan sent me to Chesterfield to have a good look at Kevin Phillips, who had returned to Watford's team after almost 12 months out through injury, having damaged his leg. When the game started he was on the bench as a sub having strained a muscle a couple of games before. He was brought on during the second period to try to get a goal. It had been a dour 0–0 game. He was a small lad, slightly built, who showed some nice touches on the ball and received it well. I thought he lacked the sharpness to break clear and to me he was not fully fit. I sent my report in to Alan. He rang and apologised for the fact that Kevin had only been a sub, but said he had also seen him twice recently and had come away with the same impression as me. Watford had not scored in either game and Kevin was obviously rusty.

Two or three weeks before the new season was due to kick-off, Alan went to a dinner at which he sat next to one of the Watford staff. He asked how Kevin was doing in pre-season training and was told that he was going like a bomb having done plenty of fitness work over the summer. If Sunderland wanted him, now would be the time to do the deal, before everyone saw him. On Alan's recommendation Sunderland paid £325,000 for him.

In League One, in 1997–98, Kevin Phillips made his debut at the Stadium of Light against Manchester City, scoring a goal in a 3–1 win. He had a wonderful first season, pairing up with Niall Quinn – little and large! – and they scored 43 goals between them. Sunderland finished in third place but lost out on promotion in the Play-offs. Magnificent attendances of over 40,000 were regular.

Alan Durban left the club and was replaced as chief scout by Andy King. He had plenty of experience and he knew the top level game well from his work at Everton. Shortly before the end of the season he was on a flight to Denmark. On the same flight was Peter Schmeichel. Manchester United had become champions of the Premier League with two games to go and Sir Alex Ferguson had given him permission to go home. Peter asked Andy who was he going to see, and Andy told him that he was going to watch a central-defender. Schmeichel asked 'How are you for a goalkeeper?'

'We could do with a good 'keeper,' Andy replied, 'we've kept only three clean sheets in the last 16 games'.

'You want to go to Odense,' said Peter. 'There's a lad there that's been at Old Trafford for a trial period, but the club can't make up their mind whether to offer him a contract. He's only 22 years old, I'm sure he is good enough.'

On Peter's recommendation Andy decided to go to see the lad. The outcome was that Thomas Sorensen joined Sunderland and became their first-team goalkeeper from the beginning of the 1998–99 season, only missing one League game. He was sold to Aston Villa before the 2003–04 season began, after making 171 appearances. The transfer fee was £2,225,000: not a bad day's trip to Denmark for Andy. At the time of writing Sorensen has become Stoke City's goalkeeper in the Premier League.

In 1998–99 Sunderland won League One by 18 clear points. Phillips and Quinn shared 41 goals. From the beginning of the New Year the team lost only one game. Home attendances continued to exceed 40,000. I had spent most of the season doing match reports, with some scouting, but I had not been involved with any of the new recruits.

A close friend of mine, an ex-Charlton centre-forward living in Wexford, Eire, rang me to tell me about a young 16-year-old, Michael Reddy, who he had seen scoring a lot of goals in junior football. He asked whether I could get over to see him play. Officially I did not deal with under-18s. Andy King had left Sunderland to become head coach at Swindon Town, so I got in touch with Tony Book, former player and Manchester City manager, who was the new chief scout at Sunderland, thinking that we would have a scout in Southern Ireland. We did not. Tony asked me whether my friend was a good judge, and when I said he was Tony asked me to get the full details of the boy and we would work from there. My friend told me that the lad was due to finish at grammar school, so arrangements were made for him to come to Sunderland for trials with our academy. The academy took him on and he was signed professional. He played in the reserves and graduated to the first team, playing in the Premier League in 1999–2000. He made eight appearances, scoring his first goal away at Middlesbrough. The club kept me informed and gave very rosy reports about how well he had progressed. A bright future was forecast for him and he gained a Republic of Ireland Under-21 cap. Unfortunately, he was dogged by several serious injuries, but Sunderland kept him on for seven seasons, loaning him out on occasions to speed his recovery. Michael was transferred to Grimsby and in two seasons he made 84 appearances and scored 22 goals, a 25 per cent strike rate. Another problem occurred with a further hip injury. Russell Slade had him at Yeovil in an attempt to get him playing again, but unfortunately he was forced to retire following a third hip operation. In 2008 he successfully completed his UEFA 'B' coaching course with the PFA. May he have different luck in this field.

Soon after the commencement of the next season in the Premier League, I was asked to go to West Bromwich Albion to look at a wide left player, Kevin Kilbane. He had been with them for just two years having been purchased from Preston North End. West Brom were playing in League One. Kevin did well, and I understand that he was watched another couple of times with satisfaction. He was bought for £2.5 million, twice as much as his club had paid for him. In 2003 Kevin was sold to Everton, then Wigan Athletic and most recently joined Hull City, along the way gaining over 100 international caps for the Republic of Ireland.

In 2001, I saw Jermaine Jenas at 17 make his first-team debut for Nottingham Forest. I had seen him twice in the reserves at the City Ground. He did okay, but did not get another game until the following season. I watched him in two of his first three games of the new season and was very impressed. I filed a report saying how good he was and recommending that we pursue him. Tony Book (chief scout) went to see him and he was also impressed. In early September Peter Reid put in a bid of £1.5 million for Jermaine Jenas. Paul Hart, the manager at Forest, turned the offer down and said he was looking for much more. Tony Book told me that this was the absolute maximum we could muster, as money was tight. Jenas continued to impress. It was an unusual surname, and I recalled having seen a Jenas playing for Burton Albion. He had been a striker, a good goalscorer, and enquiries revealed that it had been Jermaine's father, Dennis.

In February 2002, Bobby Robson, manager of Newcastle United, paid £5 million for Jermaine Jenas. He made his debut at home against Southampton in a 3–1 victory. Early in the 2005 season he joined Tottenham Hotspur for £7 million.

In the early part of the new season Peter Reid was sacked. We were all told verbally that we had finished at Sunderland. I was very disappointed as I had been impressed with the club. The season was ticking along when I had a telephone call from Sunderland asking me to go to a game for them. I told them that I was no longer with them. They asked me who I was with and I replied no one. I was told that as far as Sunderland were concerned I was still a scout, but they would confirm it. Shortly afterwards one of the directors rang me personally to tell me that I was still on the staff, and I should not have been told otherwise; however, he went on to tell me that they wanted me to join their academy staff searching for under-18s good enough for training to become League players. I agreed to do this for them and they kept me fully employed, using me two or three times per week. Many of the games were played in the late morning, which was not a problem for me as I had retired. During the year I managed to get two recruits into the academy. Jack

Witham also remained on the staff as a scout for the new manager, Howard Wilkinson, who had been at the FA, but he only lasted a few months. Mick McCarthy was put in charge having recently lost the Republic of Ireland position. Against the odds he got Sunderland back into the Premier League in his second season.

I heard an interview on Radio Five Live one evening that began with the interviewer praising Mick's achievement before introducing Mr Sanders, who held the purse strings at the Stadium of Light. He said, roughly, 'We'll see just how good he is now, as he'll have no money to spend.' This did not seem a nice way to talk about someone who had just secured the club promotion. Mr Sanders had also put the brakes on Peter Reid. After hearing these remarks I had a large bet that Sunderland would be relegated to Division One. Mick was barely given a chance, and they won only three games in the whole season.

This nine-year period had been very good for me personally. Collectively the staff that I had worked with as regards scouting were top class, and I believe that if there had been good funds made available most of the time then Sunderland would have been a major force in their superb stadium. The directors all treated us with great respect. Mr Sanders held the purse strings, though I never met him, and in my humble opinion his ultra-careful attitude stopped the club from rising to be among the elite – no manager can be successful when there are no funds available.

At around the time Mick joined Sunderland I lost my scouting job, although I doubt whether Mick had anything to do with it. The club had taken on two coaches to run the academy from Ajax football club, and they were establishing Dutch rules that no youths outside a 35-mile radius of the club would be taken in. I lived a three-hour drive away and so would be of no use to them. The new arrangement lasted one season and then the two ex-Ajax coaches were dismissed.

During my 12-month spell with the Sunderland academy, one morning I had a telephone call out of the blue. The gentleman explained that he was from a football agency and he had received a very favourable report about me. He went on to ask me if I would work for them recruiting players who I thought would make the grade at a reasonable level, both home and abroad. He offered me a salary of £10,000 per year plus expenses, and a bonus relating to the players' transfer fees. It would mean me working abroad at times, possibly being away for a week or more at a time. I said that if I had been offered this job 20 years ago I would probably have jumped at the chance, but I pointed out that I was in my 70s, and said my wife would not be very happy about me being away abroad for days. I thanked him for the offer. He apologised, saying that they had not realised my age. I have often wondered what Peter Taylor and I could have earned if agents had been allowed 40 years ago.

### A return to Nottingham Forest

Early in the 2003–04 season I was at Eton Park watching Burton Albion. I ran into Ian Storey-Moore, who was chief scout for Nottingham Forest. He asked me if I was still with Sunderland. I said 'No, I finished there at the end of last season and at the moment I don't have a club.' He asked me if I would consider working for Forest again. I did not have to think twice. I thanked Ian very much and said I would be willing to join their scouting staff. He rang me at home next day to confirm everything.

Paul Hart was the Forest manager, having been appointed after David Platt was dismissed in the summer of 2001. He was their fifth manager in five years. Dave Bassett, in his one year as manager, had put them back in the top division, but between them Ron Atkinson and David Platt, over a three-season period, had left the club in a financially precarious state. Some of their expensive buys had failed miserably. Paul was promoted to manager from the Youth Academy, where he had been a tremendous success. Several youths from the Academy were given the chance to prove themselves with the first team; there was little option, as there was no money in the kitty.

From the start I was told that there was a shortage of funds and all the scouting staff found it difficult to bring anyone into the club. Each time a player was suggested we were told that the money was out of the question. After 13 consecutive games without a win the fear of relegation crept in and Paul was dismissed in January. Joe Kinnear was appointed to replace him and enjoyed reasonable success, losing only two more games. Forest gained a better-than-hoped-for 14th place in Division One. Right up to the end of that season I had been kept busy, mainly doing match reports but also scouting.

The only player to catch my eye was Kris Commons playing for Stoke City. He had a mixed season, missing many games through injury, but he played in each of the last nine games of the season. I did not think he would cost a great deal in the transfer market. He was of diminutive build, had good pace and close control, and was mainly left-footed although he could use his right. I saw improvement each time I watched him. Ian, after seeing my reports, went along to form his own opinion. At the beginning of the following season Kris became a Forest player for £300,000, which was about what I thought he was worth. When he left to join Derby County at the beginning of the 2008–09 season he had made 138 League appearances. His transfer was under the Bosman ruling so no transfer fee was involved.

In 2004–05 the League renamed the divisions. Below the Premier League was the Championship, and below that League One and League Two. We were in the Championship. The Joe Kinnear magic was not in evidence and in December he resigned, giving ill-health as his reason. The team had not won a match in 10 games. Even at this early stage relegation was being discussed.

Gary Megson was brought in as the new manager on 10 January 2005. He had recently lost his job with West Bromwich Albion. I received a letter, signed by Gary, stating that owing to the financial situation at Forest the scouting staff were being dismissed. Gary hoped that things would improve and that he would be able to get in touch with the scouts again, but I never heard from him. The club were relegated to League One at the end of the season. After only 12 months at Forest Gary Megson departed in February 2006. To be fair he did not have a chance. A lack of finance will always get you in the end.

When I have gambled on football in pre-season I have always based my selections on clubs with funds rather than clubs with no money, and this has proved a successful strategy. When I first joined Forest with Brian in January 1975 they were almost at rock bottom, but in eight superb seasons he effected a total transformation and the empty shelves in the trophy room were filled. Brian was able to achieve success and balance the books, a rare gift indeed.

Since leaving Forest for the last time in 2005 I have not taken on a scouting job with any League club. I act as a freelance and am available to attend a game to give my opinion of a player. I still attend at least two League games each week and my opinions are continually sought. My only problem is the time it takes to drive to matches through the heavy traffic, so I now only attend midweek games that are close to home.

My estimate is that I have been to over 4,000 games during almost 40 years in football scouting, and I have enjoyed it. As I have said many times, you cannot prejudge what your next game is going to be like, and many lower League games turn out to be more interesting than those in the higher divisions. There is always hidden talent around the corner, waiting to be given a chance.

It has been a great pleasure to have worked with so many football household names and characters and I have many wonderful memories. I would like to make special mention of Dave Blakey, Tony Book, Alan Durban, Alan Hill, Andy King, Ian Storey-Moore, Roy McFarland, John Sheridan, Peter Shilton and the senior staff at Sunderland, Peter Reid, Bobby Saxton and Adrian Heath. It will soon be 60 years since I first joined a professional football club. I am still close friends with four others from those long-ago Burton Albion days: Maurice Hodgkin, Dave McAdam, Geoff Tye and Ray Bowering.

## Footnote: Burton Albion Football Club

In 2008–09 Burton had a memorable season, gaining promotion into the Football League over 100 years since the town was last represented at that level. I have always held them in high regard, taking a keen interest in their results and happenings over the years. Their progress has been steady. I give credit to the chairman, Ben Robinson, a Burtonian who has been successful in business. He has always run the club in ideal fashion, in my opinion, appointing a manager to run the team while he ensures that the rest of the operation runs smoothly. His heart is sincerely with Burton Albion.

Burton's old ground at Eton Park was 50 years old and looked it. Ben Robinson took a brave gamble and purchased ground from the Pirelli Tyre Company to build the Pirelli Stadium. After a few teething problems the playing surface is in tip-top condition and the gamble has paid off. First-time visitors are pleasantly surprised at the quality of the facilities.

The stadium was opened in 2005 by Mrs Barbara Clough and Sir Alex Ferguson, who brought his Manchester United side to play a friendly match. The site is in a wonderful position in the town, on the north side, approximately one mile from the railway station and serviced by five different bus routes. It is only four miles from the A50/A38 junction.

Ben Robinson brought in Nigel Clough as manager over 10 years ago. At the time Nigel had no experience as a club manager, but he nonetheless achieved continuous progress on the field. Nigel, having put together a side good enough to play League football, left to join Derby County in January 2009 with the Albion in a handsome lead at the top of the Blue Square Premier League. Roy McFarland took over to complete promotion.

To replace Roy McFarland the chairman appointed Paul Peschisolido and Gary Rowett. They were unproven in management but so far this bold move seems to be working very well.

On my travels I have visited about 90 per cent of all the League grounds in the country. The Pirelli Stadium is up there with the best of them in the way that visiting club representatives are looked after. Car parking and refreshments are supplied free of charge, and excellent seats in the centre of the main stand are allocated, which is valuable for those doing match reports. There is a trend among some clubs to withdraw this type of hospitality, which makes the job of compiling a match report much harder than it needs to be. At one ground I was sat behind the goal only four rows from the front, when there were empty rows up in the Main Stand. It is a shame that the job we are doing is not recognised properly among all staff at these grounds. There is always a chance that a visit by a scout might mean a big transfer fee for the host club – and I should know, I've created enough of them!

# EPILOGUE
# MY FINAL TRIBUTE

I n closing I wish to pay a sincere tribute to both Peter and Brian. They added something very special to my life. When you have to give up the sport you play due to an injury it comes as a severe shock. The younger you are, the more it hurts. Meeting Peter, then Brian, more than filled the gap that might have arisen. I feel extremely honoured to have been taken on board with them and I enjoyed the whole journey immensely. I am the only member of staff to have worked with them at every club.

Peter's natural gift for spotting the talents of players and sizing up how different teams functioned was immense. Fortunately, after spending hours with him, watching the same players and hearing his analysis, I was able to take it all in. His knowledge of players' skills and teams' tactical operations was second to none. He disliked discussing football with people outside the game, and he would not discuss it with directors either: he thought they should be busy running the club. Peter never liked the limelight and was always nervous of being on his own without a trusted partner. Being number two was his ideal position at a club. Peter's record throughout his career, until the last two years at Forest, was exemplary, and even the semi-failures that occurred towards the end were due to impetuosity, and his not feeling physically up to it. Peter struggled with adversities: this was why Brian was such a great partner for him. After Peter left his manager position at Derby County he hardly ever contacted me, and I never visited his new home in Widmerpool. I believe he spent most of his time in Majorca. I will always remain deeply indebted to him for the knowledge of this wonderful sport he gave me. In 21 years we never had one serious argument.

Brian was second to none in football. I have never met a man like him. He excelled in dealing with problems and problem players, and boardroom members were no trouble to him either. Peter never was happy with them because the vast majority are not football men, they are businessmen, who have been successful in their own field. My relationship with Brian was almost all on the football side. His great gift was that he was a born leader, and given a player with either proven ability or raw talent, providing they were willing to take his advice and instructions, he could improve him.

While under his charge 24 players gained international caps for their respective countries. The total number of caps won by these players while at Nottingham Forest alone was 283. During his managerial career he even improved seasoned players such as Dave Mackay (in the role he was given), Larry Lloyd, Alan Hinton, Alan Durban, Willie Carlin, Frank Clark and Kenny Burns. Over 50 other younger players became household names while under him. Brian did not have favourites, for him it was what they could do on the field, that was where he made his real judgement. Yes, he liked the players who never caused problems off the field. If you supplied the goods to him he would polish them and help them achieve their best. He was wary of all intellectuals. Any sport he participated in he always wanted to win.

When Nigel Clough came to Burton Albion as their player-manager, I saw Brian many times and had many good-humoured chats with him. I remember distinctly one occasion in 2003. Derby County had been relegated from the Premiership, and they were lying at the bottom of Division One (now the Championship). John Gregory had been sacked. I was sitting about six or seven rows back from Brian in the stand at Eton Park. During half-time, Brian turned round and shouted 'Maurice, let's you and me go to Derby and sort the b*****ds out. We could still do it!'

I saw Brian at Burton Albion with Ronnie Fenton only a short time before he passed away. He called me to him and we had a nice few words and a laugh.

Both Peter and Brian said a similar thing to me that has stuck with me. 'Nothing seems to change you,' they said. 'You're always placid, you treat everything calmly and easily cope with adversities.' I explained that for me, working in football was my relaxation. I put my business worries behind me, and my livelihood did not depend on my football. Neither of them ever put me under any pressure, but the two of them were always under pressure to keep up the results and team performances, to satisfy chairmen, press and the supporters. I admired them for that.

Peter's son Philip went into the newsagents' business in the Wardwick in Derby, and Brian's son Simon has a newsagency in West Bridgford, Nottingham. Brian's closest friend Colin Lawrence was a perfumery salesman visiting chemists and the cosmetic retailers. He purchased a very busy Post Office and newsagents in Park Farm, Derby, after visiting my Post Office in Burton. Colin has passed away, but his son Peter is still the sub-postmaster. One of Brian's brothers took over the newsagents in Duffield. I always think that these ventures were related to Peter and Brian seeing how successful I was with the one I owned.

I want to finish by saying what a great honour it was to have been a member of Peter and Brian's very successful team. I am glad to have been helpful on occasions, and to have had a hand in their achievements. I am also happy to have been associated with them both as a friend. I shall always be of the opinion that they passed away far too early, after illnesses that were brought on by their work and the stresses and the effort involved. However, both men will no doubt live on in thousands of people's sporting memories for many many years to come.

# Alternative Marketing Approaches for Entrepreneurs

# Alternative Marketing Approaches for Entrepreneurs

Björn Bjerke

*Linnaeus University, Sweden*

Edward Elgar
PUBLISHING

Cheltenham, UK • Northampton, MA, USA

Published by
Edward Elgar Publishing Limited
The Lypiatts
15 Lansdown Road
Cheltenham
Glos GL50 2JA
UK

Edward Elgar Publishing, Inc.
William Pratt House
9 Dewey Court
Northampton
Massachusetts 01060
USA

A catalogue record for this book
is available from the British Library

Library of Congress Control Number: 2017953169

This book is available electronically in the **Elgar**online
Business subject collection
DOI 10.4337/9781786438959

ISBN 978 1 78643 894 2 (cased)
ISBN 978 1 78643 895 9 (eBook)

Typeset by Servis Filmsetting Ltd, Stockport, Cheshire
Printed and bound in Great Britain by TJ International Ltd, Padstow

# Contents

# Preface

I have been interested in the subject of business for many years. My business education started more formally in the 1960s, when I was enrolled in Lund University Business School. My major subject was finance and my minor subject was marketing. I began to understand that this decade was something of a breakthrough for marketing as an orientation in theory as well as in practice. The industrial part of the world was booming, backed up by purchasing power among customers in consumer markets at an all-time high. It was in this environment that Philip Kotler published *Marketing Management* in 1967, a book which quickly became a bestseller and hard to avoid by anybody operating in the marketing field. At that time, I was also close to starting a business myself, with one of my classmates. We had the idea to name that business 4M (Marketing with More Modern Methods). But that thought was never realized.

However, while studying for my Bachelor's degree in Business, to improve my finances I started to work part-time as a night watchman in the neighbouring city of Malmö, and I did this for several years. At the end of the 1960s, the Swedish government issued a recommendation directed at companies or other organizations employing security people, implying that for anybody to call himself or herself a security officer, he or she should get some basic education and training in how to put out a fire, how to behave in a police-like fashion, how to be able to defend oneself, and other necessary skills to do the job well. So, an idea came to me. I saw a golden opportunity for starting a business to educate people in Sweden working in the field of security for them to live up to the government's recommendation, in case they could not provide any evidence that they possessed the formal requirements in question. I bought a non-active limited company and re-registered it in the name of SeEd (Security Education) Ltd, designed a two-week educational programme containing various security aspects, drew up contracts with people from the local fire brigade, police force, self-defence institutes etc., to provide me with teachers and admitted about twenty students with the adequate orientation as a first group, got it going and hoped for a bright future.

To my surprise, however, no people applied to enrol on my educational programme after the first admitted group. The reason turned out to be quite simple. Even though I had followed recommendations in my studies concerning how to start a business and how to support such a start with adequate marketing, all security companies in Sweden were boycotting the government's recommendations, refusing to 'waste money on unnecessary education'. So, I did not have the market that I expected, and was forced to terminate my company after just two months, having made a small personal financial loss.

I continued with business studies after my first degree, secured a MBA and doctorate in this subject and I was lucky (and ambitious) enough to be offered a permanent chair as professor in Business Administration at 'my' university in Lund in 1978. I made several friends (academics as well as practising outside the university) on the way. Guided by the idea that 'I do not find it satisfying to be professor in a subject that cannot be applied in practice', I started a consulting company with some of those friends that same year. We hardly had any clients to start with, but, spurred by the belief that market obstacles exist to be overcome, we combined our contact networks and were soon able to build a portfolio of consulting assignments to keep us as occupied as we wanted to be (and sometimes more than that). The name we gave our company was *Albatross 78*, justifying the choice of the name with symbolic statements like 'an albatross is the world's best flying animal; no other bird can stay that long in the air, and it never seems to give up'. We also became known after being asked to advertise in a book which listed all consulting companies in the country in the business field. On the background of our bird logo, we wrote the text: 'We are too busy to have the time to advertise'! The company exists still today, but I am no longer one of its owners.

One assignment that I acquired in the name of *Albatross78* started my solid interest in entrepreneurship. In the beginning of the 1980s, the Swedish shipyards could no longer compete with the Japanese and the Koreans, and had to finish business. One shipyard was situated in the harbour of a town 30 kilometres from Lund. Four thousand people employed there were given notice to quit. Including their families, around 6000 people were affected. To mitigate the social pain, the Swedish government at that time granted several millions Swedish krona to a fund which employed three people full-time, and I was asked to join part-time as a consultant. The objective of this group was to assist aspiring (or already active) entrepreneurs financially and with all possible support to establish businesses on the ruins of the shipyard, employing as many as possible of the former shipyard workers. The only restriction was that these new companies were not allowed to be involved in anything to do with boats. My task in this context was to give my opinion about who should be given support and who should not. During a period of about two years, we talked to about 1000 individuals, and were willing to try to start a business with the people given a notice to quit (and, as time went on, actually had to quit). We supported 100 new startups, employing around 1000 people (25% of the former shipyard employees; approximately 50% of them found a job on their own; 25% of them unfortunately had to be retired prematurely, sometimes given social benefits; two persons even committed suicide – the whole situation was one big social trauma). This was the start of my keen interest in entrepreneurship, an interest which I still have today. I have done much research and published several books in the subject before this one. I was appointed as the third full professor in Entrepreneurship at University of Stockholm in 1999, and I still work today (at the age of 76 years) part-time as professor in this subject at another university close to one of the islands in the Baltic Sea, where I now live.

I was the founder of one of the new companies started on the former shipyard. It was a subcontracting company, employing about 400 of those having to quit from the shipyard. My task (as its general director), together with a small group of white collar workers among the 400, was to find subcontracting assignments which were suitable to use the workers' technical skills. This company became very successful indeed. Through a lot of work and by using our connections, we were able to find work for all of these 400 during the rest of their working life. The company (like *Albatross 78*) started without any guaranteed customers, but (unlike *Albatross 78*) does not exist today – this was, however, the very idea on which it was built.

I started my fourth company about ten years ago. It is a partnership with my wife, and its purpose is to channel income I receive (apart from my pension) from selling books, providing guest lectures and being involved in consulting assignments (including the work I am doing part-time at the university). It is as successful as I want it to be without doing any kind of formal marketing. Through this company, I am able to make deductions for any cost that arise when pursuing my professional interests.

Being theoretically and practically interested in entrepreneurship, it is only natural to want to learn how to be a good marketer. As mentioned earlier, when studying for my Bachelor's degree at Lund University Business School, one of my areas of concentrated study was marketing. During the 1980s and the 1990s, I worked at several universities outside Sweden, from the University of Southern California in the west to Waikato University in New Zealand in the east, and, in between, King Fahd University of Petroleum and Minerals in Saudi Arabia and National University in Singapore, teaching subjects such as strategic management, business and culture, and international business alongside marketing. Focusing on entrepreneurship, I published about a dozen books on the way and presented papers in conferences all over the world almost every year. After having returned to Sweden at the end of the last century, I was financed for more than a decade by the Swedish Knowledge Foundation, leading a group of researchers and practitioners in the field of social entrepreneurship. I did this at the same time as being employed by Linnaeus University (with which I am still connected, even if only part-time these days). All in all, by starting four businesses of my own, teaching various business subjects and publishing books, presenting conference papers in the field of entrepreneurship in general and doing research on social entrepreneurship, I have learnt some crucial things about the relationship between entrepreneurship and marketing:

- Successful entrepreneurs are typically very good at marketing themselves.
- There is great variety in how entrepreneurs use marketing in practice.
- An obvious knowledge development of the academic subject of marketing (as well as of the subjects of entrepreneurship and leadership) increasingly shows the need to better and more intimately understand (and work closer with) customers and other users of what marketers, entrepreneurs and leaders are trying to achieve or produce.
- Some social entrepreneurs get good results without even using marketing in the usual sense.

This, combined with my experiences from starting four very different companies as described earlier, inspired me to write this book on the various and different ways to use marketing being an entrepreneur.

Öland, Sweden, July 2017

The author

# 1. Different times and realities – different thinking

## 1.1 SOME BASIC POSITIONS

One fundamental truth for me is that time never stands still. Changes are constantly going on, but at present more and more change seems to take place faster than before. Fewer aspects of life around us can, to our advantage, be looked at as fixed. This, however, is not a sufficient description of how I experience present times. Changes seem also to be of a different kind today. They contain *genuine uncertainty*, which cannot be reduced by more planning, for instance. The number of exceptions has also, as I see it, become higher, which makes it harder to forecast the future.

One consequence of these new conditions is that we must change our way of thinking and come up with new kinds of solutions to different problems; that is, we live in an *entrepreneurial society* today. One consequence of this is, of course, that it can sometimes be more important to get rid of old ways of doing things than find out new ones.

New ways of doing things have always been a major source of progress in society. However, due to the fact that today's changes are so many, so widespread and so different, we must all develop an *entrepreneurial mindset* to handle our situation, in everything from our families to institutions of our countries and their transnational obligations, businesses, and social and political agencies.

We can talk about *three kinds of entrepreneurial ventures* in a society:

- *Completely new independent businesses* offering new solutions to market customers. We can call them *independent business entrepreneurial ventures*.
- *Already existing businesses* offering new solutions to customers. We can call them *business intrapreneurial ventures*.
- New solutions that we demand and/or need as *market customers* or *as citizens*. We can call them *social entrepreneurial ventures*.

It is possible to talk about three sectors in a society and two kinds of entrepreneurs. The three sectors are:

*1*

- the *public* sector
- the *business* sector
- the *citizen* sector.

The two kinds of entrepreneurs are:

- *business* entrepreneurs. They operate in the business sector and they aim at satisfying customer demands.
- *social* entrepreneurs. They can operate in any sector of the society and they aim at satisfying somebody's needs.

By satisfying *demand*, I refer to such solutions which we are willing to pay for as customers in a market of some kind. By satisfying *need*, I refer to such solutions which make us feel more complete as members of a society (it can be anything from self-fulfilment, protection and care, to not feeling alienated or excluded as a citizen).

The four social entrepreneurs are:

1. Employees in the public sector who make social moves over and above what is required as employees while they are still employed there.
2. Business people, satisfying demand at the same time as satisfying social needs.
3. Entrepreneurs who are neither employed in the public sector nor belong to the business sector, but operate in the citizen sector, satisfying social needs in a business-like way. I refer to them as *citizen enterprisers*.
4. Entrepreneurs in the citizen sector satisfying social needs without doing this in a business-like way, and not even looking at themselves as operating in a market. I refer to them as *citizen innovators* (or *public entrepreneurs*).

I give social entrepreneurs a special place in this book. The citizen sector was strong in Western countries during the nineteenth century, but expansion during the twentieth century pushed it to the backseat during the major part of that century. During the last 30 years or so the trend has changed, however, which for three reasons has led to a revival of the citizen sector – sometimes called *the third sector* or *the social economy* (Murray, 2009):

- Consumers have increasingly become their own producers.
- Some social issues are harder to manage.
- Environmental issues have become more serious.

Consumers have, to a large extent, become their own producers; today they are more active in adding value themselves to what they need. Consumers have become *prosumers* (Toffler, 1980). Critical to members of society now is how different support and possibilities are designed to fill their day with content, rather than just buying all that is needed in completed form and/or being passive receivers of public service. The support economy has taken over from the commodity economy as an organizing principle in society (Maxmin & Zuboff, 2002). Production is no longer going on in a separate sector, generating products for other parts of society to choose from, but the whole arrangement in society is, to an increasing extent, built up around active users/citizens. These people are participating more and more in putting together, repairing and adding value to what they want and what they feel they need. A transformation of the relationships between consumers/users and markets has taken place. The process of production and supply is to a decreasing extent a *linear process* where the consumer is the end of the chain. Decisive middle hands are now those who have the knowledge, ambition and confidence to be more active in the society than others. Those are the ones who put the knowledge economy together and who develop it.

The institutional consequences are far-reaching. Systems are now organized around *citizens and their local communities*. Citizens have also become connected in a variety of shapes – through the Internet or by different kinds of events and in study groups – rather than built up around centralized institutions. This is a long way from the passive consumer and the mechanical worker of the early twentieth century. Modern society positions every household by itself *and* in cooperation as '*living centres*' in distributed systems – the vitality of the whole becomes dependent on the vitality of the individual innumerable components. This justifies asking new questions about what allows or prevents households from being participants, questions of what the relationships and possibilities look like, questions about which dwellings are to be built and where they are to be placed, questions about necessary working skills today, questions about tax design, to mention a few.

Pressure has increased on state-driven infrastructure which is supposed to provide social service. One type of pressure comes from the sheer size and growth of demand for such services. In many industrialized countries, there are dramatic rising trends in the number of immigrants and refugees, but also in internal phenomena such as obesity, chronic disease and demographic ageing, all of which have been described as time bombs.

These trends constitute a double challenge for existing structures. Firstly, there is a growing mismatch between traditional social service and new needs – for instance, in most countries, schools and dwellings were built up to service people already living within the country and hospitals to take care of emergencies rather than chronic diseases. Secondly, it has proven difficult to combine increased service needs with necessary cost-efficiency. Schools, hospitals, dwellings, nursing homes and prisons have cost structures, which, to a large extent, are of a fixed kind and difficult to reduce in a more work-intensive service.

As a result of this, these sections of society require an increasingly larger part of national resources. The major parts in economies in 2025 and beyond will not be cars, ships, steel, computers or personal finances, but instead health, dwellings, education and care. Public and citizen sectors will no longer be tributaries to the business sector but instead mainstreams of society and central for the employment and economy of the country as a whole.

There are two responses to these challenges. The most common has been to still try to design *technical solutions* to upgrade those institutions where service is given. In the case of hospital care, for instance, those industrial models, which once were associated with Ford and Toyota, have been adapted to try to speed up the patient flow through hospitals. Costs have been cut through outsourcing, by privatization in some cases and by repeated efficiency drives. Hospitals have become bigger and more specialized. Prices have been set on what once was free, and quasi-market arrangements have been established to bring in economic discipline among personnel and others. But the pressure has continued to increase relentlessly. In terms of health and some other social issues in general and environmental issues in particular, the most effective answers have been of a *preventive nature*, but these have proven to be very difficult to establish in the public sector and in markets as they look today.

Another approach has also been undertaken to try to cope with the problems. A number of attempts have *involved citizens and the civic society as partners in public service*; for instance, the assistance of parents, pensioners and other citizens in the governance of schools, representations of patients in hospitals and in dwellings by those who live in them.

To summarize, *active citizens* are presently central to many of the social issues. To those with chronic diseases, for instance, household communities and their supportive networks are central components of what have been the primary producers of service. The same goes for the integration of immigrants and refugees.

In these cases, citizens are active agents, not passive consumers. They need resources and abilities, support and relationships that existing social services struggle to provide. This could be called a *co-designed public service* and an acknowledgement of the role that the third-sector organizations play in providing service to citizens.

As public authorities have tried to involve citizens, it is obvious that the latter have radically changed attitudes in some respects. The French social analyst Gorz refers to the active involvement of the postmodern citizen as a new subjectivity, which is no longer moulded around the supply and demand of the economy in the traditional sense (Gorz, 1999). To the postmodern, individualized citizen, life becomes *a formation process*, where career must step back to different projects and where the picaresque becomes as important as following formal decrees (Murray, 2009).

This shift indicated a change from an economy dominated by concrete goods and services to an economy centred on service, information and communication – what is sometimes referred to as a *cognitive capitalism*. Means of production here become subordinated to the communication codes. In this world, images, symbols, culture, ideology and values take the driving seat. Development towards an individualized public service is also an aspect of these trends, as well as the shift in cultural policy from delivering finished cultural products to enabling an expressive life.

This is the personal cultural economy. But there is another significant development of cooperation. The disjunction between the existing sensitivity of the active citizen and the insensitive organizations that operated in an earlier period – companies, public bureaucracies, mass-political parties and the state church – has led to *a multiplication of different social movements and of citizens and local communities that take the issue into their own hands*. In several areas, these have long been leading social innovators.

These changes are not only influencing the 'rules of the game' within which different authorities and the public market operate. They have opened the very game itself to new social initiatives, to a more active role for citizens and local communities and to new value-based necessities. As movements, they gain support from different parts of society, both from those inside authorities and those outside. All activities in these movements start voluntarily and on a small scale, and they remain that way.

There is a clear movement in society that goes *from passivity to action*. And out of this comes a set of value-based initiatives, some within the citizen sector but some also in the market and in the public sector. This wave has developed its own form of network organization, its own mixture of paid work and voluntarism and its own culture. It is a source of a great variation of social innovations as well, which in many cases are focused on issues that authorities and the market have not been able to handle successfully. These developments are not completely determined by new technologies, but new technologies are doing much to reinforce and facilitate them. One characteristic of these systems is that they contain *a stronger element of mutuality*. These systems are part of what is often called *the social economy*, which is very important for these innovations and for the service and relationships that come out of them.

Issues that seem to be hard to solve today include *the environmental* issue. The present environmental movement is an example of the praxis and type of organization which exists with the new social movements and which also may be one example of the renewed social economy. Those who are involved have developed their own political economy with protests, production and consumption. They have created a wave of alternative technologies and of new forms of consumption and distribution.

There are consequently reasons why those entrepreneurs, with a social interest in mind, act outside or inside business to play a larger role in the society. But what does *the deployment period* look like, that period which is to bring us into the new society?

Social entrepreneurs are not a new solution by themselves, but a necessary part of it due to the remorseless growth of social and environmental issues which neither governments nor the markets are able to stem. These issues can no longer be confined with the economy of the state, but have consequences for the way production is organized in the market with or without the participation of citizens, and the way in which production and consumption take place at home.

The shift to a *network paradigm* is part of this answer and it has the potential to transform the relationships between both the organizational and institutional centres, and the citizens and their peripheries. The new distributive systems are not managing the complexity from the centre; this is done in a complex way increasingly from outside this centre – with local communities and service users and in work places, schools and local organizations. Those who are at the margin have something that those in the centre can never have – *knowledge of the details* – what are the specific time, place, events and, in the case of consumers and citizens, needs and wishes? This is the potential. But to realize this, a new kind of commitment is required with and for users.

This may seem important to citizens and to those who operate on the private market. But it is, in a way, of greater importance to authorities. For the moment, the economy is divided between a hierarchical and centralized state, companies and small local organizations, and informal associations and groups (which are often citizen-based). But the important thing is that the new techno-economic paradigm connected to the new social movement makes it possible to *combine the energy and the complexity of a distributive responsibility with the integrating capacity of modern societies*, which contain a strong citizen sector and intimate connections between this sector, the public sector and the business sector.

Essential structural reforms and institutional changes are necessary for a society of this kind to function effectively. New infrastructures, tools, platforms and means to distribute resources, new kinds of organizations are needed, and maybe above all *new ways to link the formal and the informal economies to each other*. The existing crisis provides possibilities for a social innovative activity to take place next to private innovation activities in society.

Sometimes our present society is referred to as a *postmodern society*. There are many ways to understand postmodernity. One generally accepted understanding is that there are no longer any generally valid solutions or models in society. As a consequence, progress cannot even be taken for granted anymore, nor can it be characterized in simple, straightforward terms. Constructive postmodern thinking (which is of some interest to this book), requires, and looks at it as progressive, thinking of several *alternative* theories of any specific phenomenon, for instance, to accept that there is more than one way to look at entrepreneurship or marketing.

One aspect in postmodern society is *the revival of place* (the economy can be seen in terms of space; the social is better seen in terms of place). This is related to a growing interest in *social entrepreneurs*. Associated with this is the more specific aspect that *interpretative thinking* has emerged alongside depicting and functional rational thinking as a research orientation. Constructionist dialogues contain a wide social potential; they open new spans of possibilities for understanding the world, the world of professional practice, our daily lives as well as society at large. Rational research criteria (which are dominating economic thinking) do not seem to fit the postmodern world very well.

Along the same line, there are more needs for *mythical and symbolic thinking* today. The mythical and the symbolic are more attractive when the world is experienced as complicated – as modern times are perceived by some. This has several implications for how to understand and how to use marketing and entrepreneurship. Many processes in and around social entrepreneurs, for instance, can be problematic to grasp in traditional marketing terms. 'Marketing' for social entrepreneurs must therefore sometimes be looked at with special spectacles, so to say, and sometimes replaced, for instance, by 'place vitalization'. Traditional marketing conceptual systems might generally sometimes be out of phase with postmodern thinking. For instance, whereas we can conceive freedom in the old days as a form of autonomy, in postmodern days, freedom may rather be conceived as being involved in finding opportunities (Maravelias, 2009).

We live in *a knowledge society* now. Dominant means of competition is now to have access to adequate knowledge. Knowledge is even seen by some as the only meaningful resource today. The challenge these days for leaders is to cooperate with knowledge followers. The competitive factor of knowledge is different from other competitive factors such as financial resources; for instance, it cannot be used up, and the more we share it, the greater it becomes. Another way to put it is to say that there is *a different view of capital invested in new ventures today*. This capital is less of a financial sort; instead we talk about capital invested in business processes, local databases, willingness to learn, vendor networks, contacts, etc.

It has already been mentioned that *relationships and networks are becoming more important*. Contemporary society is underpinned by all-encompassing networks; network is the primary symbol of our modern society. Understanding how these networks are working is the key to understand how our entrepreneurial society is working, and the greatest profits in this society are to a large extent to be found in researching and exploiting decentralized and autonomous networks, and building new ones.

In general terms, *technology* is involved in almost all aspects of modern life, and it seems to be moving faster becoming ever more advanced and complex. Also, technology plays a more *strategic* role than before. Looking at *media technology* more specifically, a new world is appearing. The Internet is something completely new in our history; a medium where almost anybody, after a relatively small investment in technical equipment and with a few simple manual operations, can be a producer as well as a consumer (prosumer again) of text, picture and sound. It is difficult to think about anything more democratic than this – on the Internet we are all authors and publishers, our freedom of expression is almost complete and our potential public is unlimited. The growth of this medium has been without comparison. The Internet is truly a frontier of opportunities for entrepreneurs; marketing through social media (such as blogs, podcasts, wikis and YouTube) contains gigantic possibilities today.

In the IT world, successful firms at the front of development come to the future first. The race is often more survival of the fastest rather than survival of the fittest. Language plays a huge role here. *Old words may gain a new meaning.* And when language changes, so does thinking. The IT society is not about the disappearance of physical things around us but their garnering new meanings. Talking about marketing of refrigerators these days, for instance, might not stress their ability to keep the milk cold, which we already take for granted, but perhaps its ability to communicate intelligently in a network.

The problem is no longer *lack of information* but *an abundance of it*. We experience more and more so-called *hyper-realities* (the result of too many realities presented today). Each of us are trying to filter all the visual and audial signals surrounding us, processing only those that we consider to be meaningful. There is a general scepticism, sometimes distrust, against the advertising that bombards us. We often feel that advertising rarely touches the more fundamental, spiritual and existential issues that the modern person is carrying, and is often therefore experienced as rather meaningless. In the postmodern world, we are searching for more symbolic, even mythical, dimensions in life. We therefore, sometimes, do not see that repetitive and banal advertising slogans have a justified or meaningful place anymore; we often rather perceive them as moments of irritation.

Finally, our society of today is also becoming more and more *service-based*. This leads to an increasing number of small ventures using very few established marketing procedures from yesteryear. The postmodern society is centred on service, information and communication. This is a world where images, symbols, culture, ideology and values take the driving seat. The most important success factor of a venture startup today is to have one or more change agents, who, at best insightful and visionary, take it upon themselves to realize new solutions and procedures. We refer to them as *entrepreneurs*.

## 1.2 THE FOCUS IN THIS BOOK

I was rather early clear about how I should organize this book. I believe that many entrepreneurial ventures (maybe most of them) start as copies of what already exists. I am of the opinion that the person who starts an entrepreneurial venture is an entrepreneur only in the *beginning* of the existence of this venture. After that, this person becomes (if he or she stays) more of a manager than an entrepreneur, the way I see it.

Nevertheless, startups can be innovative in two, partly different, ways. The *first* way is that they take place by following a specified sequence or structure, which is built up in a logical way, but where the components, by which the sequence or the structure is built up, could be innovative. This layout could be called *rational* (and is, consequently, based on a *rational philosophy*). The *second* way is such that even the very layout itself is (also) innovative. This layout could be called *social constructionist* (in my case, based on the social constructionist version of the philosophy of *social phenomenology*).

There is, in fact, a second non-rational marketing version emerging in theory as well as in practice. I became aware of this when looking at the knowledge development of the subjects of *entrepreneurship* (Chapters 2 and 3) and *marketing* (Chapter 4), which in both cases showed me that these subjects are increasingly interested in considering the receivers, i.e., customers or other users of what some venturesome people have achieved.

I have also made a study of the subject of *leadership* (Chapter 5), which in many ways is related to entrepreneurship and marketing, and found the same thing, i.e., that this subject also has been increasingly interested in the relationships to their 'users', which in the case of leadership refers to followers. This strengthened my ambitions even more and provided several new perspectives for my attempts to understand various 'marketing approaches for entrepreneurs'. Furthermore, leadership research seems to have developed further than entrepreneurship and marketing research in the application of the social constructionist approach (probably because leaders, in a way, are closer to their followers than are the entrepreneurs and marketers to their customers and other users outside their organizations).

To summarize, what I had learnt from the above gave me the idea of two different alternative ways to look at and apply marketing for entrepreneurs, which I wanted to discuss in this book. One of them is established as *marketing management*, and it is almost completely dominating marketing theory today. The other one was launched not so long ago and it is growing stronger and stronger. It could be called *bricolage*. With this as a background it is possible today to talk about two kinds of entrepreneurs. One consists of *the analytical and rational entrepreneurs* and the other consists of *the bricoleurial entrepreneurs*. These are discussed in Chapter 7.

Based on my research on social entrepreneurship and social entrepreneurs, which I have conducted during the past ten years or so, I have come to the conclusion that these entrepreneurs (particularly if they are of a non-business kind, which I refer to as social innovators or public entrepreneurs) think as well as act differently from business entrepreneurs in many respects (Chapter 3). It may even be difficult sometimes to name the field where they are operating a market, which obviously provides me with a reason to look differently at what could be called 'marketing'. In their case, it is more appropriate to talk about 'public places' instead of 'markets', of 'generators' instead of 'producers' and 'realizers' and 'place vitalizers' instead of 'marketers' (Chapter 10).

I also devote one chapter to review my methodological cornerstone (Chapter 6), which, in my opinion, the readers should know in order to understand my discussion of the two alternative ways presented in this book for entrepreneurs to think of and apply marketing.

To summarize: This book is about *two alternative kinds of marketing in the beginning of three kinds of business-orientated and/or social entrepreneurial ventures before these ventures have reached some clear and accepted form.*

Another fundamental pillar on which this book rests is that I believe that marketing an entrepreneurial activity is normally rather different from marketing established consumer goods or services.

Several other, more specific, orientations of mine have influenced and guided the writing of this book:

- *Entrepreneurial marketing* has been an established concept for several years. There is even an Entrepreneurial Marketing Interest Group in operation, arranging international conferences and research symposia for more than twenty years. This group has however focused more on how marketing can be made more entrepreneurial than on the subject of this book.
- I am not particularly interested in growth of a venture in this book. The way I look at it, growth has more to do with management than with entrepreneurship, i.e., more to do with exploiting an established concept than creating a new one. Nor am I particularly interested in strategic matters. It is my conviction and experience that entrepreneurs, unlike managers, rarely think strategically in the sense in which this subject is normally treated in the literature.
- Entrepreneurs exist in different shapes and varieties, for instance, as e-entrepreneurs, as student entrepreneurs, as techno-entrepreneurs or as male or female entrepreneurs. I rarely discuss different 'special types of' entrepreneurs in this book, with one exception already mentioned. I make a distinction between *business entrepreneurs* and *social entrepreneurs* (in the latter case, I have a special focus on that group of social entrepreneurs which I refer to as *public entrepreneurs*) due to my belief and experience that the values as well the principles guiding the two are generally different, and, in the case of marketing, specifically different.
- There are sometimes great differences between entrepreneurs emanating from different cultures (from a national point of view). I do not bring up such differences in this book. Marketing for entrepreneurs as discussed here is mainly valid for entrepreneurs in the Western world (if cultures in the Eastern world have been influenced by the logic among entrepreneurs in the Western world, this book may be of some value to them as well, of course).
- This book is about entrepreneurship, which to me is *not* the same as enterprise, small business, self-employment or innovation, even though there are relationships between entrepreneurship and all these concepts.
- Creativity and innovation are intimately related to entrepreneurship. However, I will not specifically discuss those aspects of venturing. I refer readers interested in these fields to special literature in these subjects.

## 1.3   THE OUTLINE OF THIS BOOK

The relationship between different chapters in this book can be seen in the Figure 1.1:

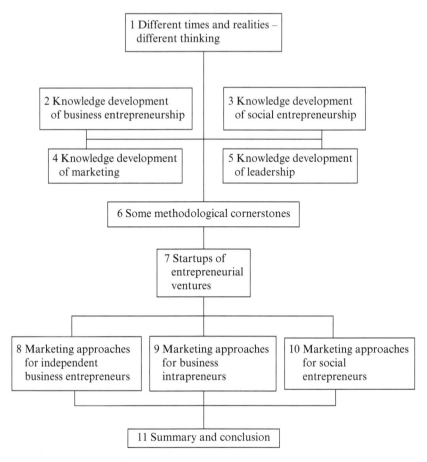

*Figure 1.1    The outline of this book*

# 2. Knowledge development of business entrepreneurship

## 2.1 INTRODUCTION

This chapter presents the knowledge development of the subject of business entrepreneurship, first in general terms and then my own opinion about the subject. The latter is important for the reader to better understand the message of this book.

I explore the knowledge development of business entrepreneurship in the following steps (which, by and large, follow the development of the subject over time):

- Business entrepreneurship as a function
- Personality traits of business entrepreneurs
- Business entrepreneurial thinking and behaviour
- Contextual theories of business entrepreneurship
- Results and effects of business entrepreneurship
- To better understand business entrepreneurship by understanding customers better.

Similar steps can be used to also show the knowledge development of the academic subjects of social entrepreneurship, marketing and leadership.

## 2.2 BUSINESS ENTREPRENEURSHIP AS A FUNCTION

As an academic subject, business entrepreneurship has existed for about 300 years (although I think that entrepreneurship as well as leadership have existed in practice as long as human beings have existed). During the first 250 years, only economists studied the phenomenon. They wanted to clarify which *function* business entrepreneurs have in an economy. The first person who gave them such a function (and, in fact, also gave the first profile to 'entrepreneur' as a concept) was Richard Cantillon (1680–1734). He claimed that business entrepreneurs function as middlemen in situations where one side wanted to have a task completed and the other side consisted of different resources (labour, capital etc.) that were needed to complete this task. In those days, there were risks associated with taking on such a task, in the sense that it could be relatively easy to calculate what it could cost to get the necessary resources in order to do the job, but more difficult to estimate in advance the amount of payment received when the task was completed. Cantillon therefore saw business entrepreneurs as *economic risk takers* (Cantillon, 1755/1955).

The meaning of the concept of business entrepreneur was widened as time went on. The nineteenth century was fertile ground for business entrepreneurship with the breakthrough of the Industrial Revolution, which led to many innovations and inventions. Even though researchers still did not study their personality, the idea arose that *business entrepreneurs brought together production factors and organized business firms.* The French economist Jean Baptiste Say (1767–1832) brought together much of the knowledge of business entrepreneurship at his time, and viewed the return to the business entrepreneurs as a profit, which he regarded as different from the return of capitalists' financial investments (Say, 1855).

Carl Menger (1840–1921) is one of the founders of the so-called Austrian school of economics. He established what is sometimes called 'the subjectivistic perspective' in this subject with his book, *Principles of Economics* (1871/1981). Menger saw the business entrepreneur as a change agent who *transforms resources to value-added goods and services* and who often creates circumstances leading to economic growth.

Say did not see any difference between the business entrepreneur and the business leader. Menger did so and in the beginning of the 1900s, it became more distinctly expressed that the role that the business entrepreneur fulfils in the economy is somewhat different from that of the business leader. The same opinion is also associated with the person who is often seen as the most influential classical scholar within business entrepreneurship theory, that is Joseph Schumpeter, who was born in Austria but worked his last twenty years at University of Harvard in USA. To Schumpeter, the critical function of the business entrepreneur was *innovation* – to introduce new products, processes or organizational units based on new combinations of the production factors in the economic value chain (Schumpeter, 1934). Schumpeter contributed many new ideas to the theory of business entrepreneurship, including:

- People stop being business entrepreneurs *when they have introduced a specific innovation*, that is, after having applied a new combination of the production factors for the first time. Business entrepreneurs may then continue as 'just' administrators of those businesses, which were based on their innovation.

- As business entrepreneurs are only entrepreneurs during certain periods of their lives, they *do not constitute any social class.*
- Business entrepreneurs *tend to appear in swarms,* and these swarms lead to a rise of the economy for a period. Business entrepreneurs are therefore important to economic cycles.
- The main mechanism in economic development is *creative destruction,* i.e., because of business entrepreneurs' interest in what is new, they destroy existing market mechanisms and build new ones.

During the economic period of the knowledge development of business entrepreneurship, few economists were interested in business entrepreneurship. The study of business entrepreneurship has never been part of the mainstream of economic research.

Around mid-1900, representatives of other subjects started to become interested in business entrepreneurship. These other subjects were mainly from the social sciences, but also from subjects outside this faculty such as law, history and philosophy. It is no exaggeration to claim that the interest in this subject at the tertiary level of education today is so big that there is hardly a university in the world that does not offer a course in entrepreneurship, innovation or the like.

Let us see how theories of business entrepreneurship have developed since the middle of the last century.

## 2.3 PERSONALITY TRAITS OF BUSINESS ENTREPRENEURS

One of the first scholars who came up with a picture of personality traits of business entrepreneurs was David McClelland. As stated by him, people in senior positions of an economy are motivated by three needs: (1) need to achieve, (2) need for power and (3) need for belonging. The relative importance of these three needs varies between different people. McClelland claimed that business entrepreneurs are primarily driven by the *need for achievement.* He also stated that societies where need for achievement is a norm are developing more dynamically than other societies, and wrote a classic book on this theme, *The Achieving Society,* which was published in 1961 and relates to the business entrepreneurship in the US.

Some personality traits which by tradition have been identified with business entrepreneurs (Bridge et al., 2009) are:

- achievement motivation
- risk-taking propensity
- locus of control
- need for autonomy
- determination
- initiative
- creativity
- self-confidence and trust.

Other personality traits which are often associated with business entre-preneurs (Timmons, 1999; Delmar, 2006; Zimmerer & Scarborough, 2005; Allen, 2010) are:

- responsibility
- opportunity obsession
- desire for immediate feedback
- future orientation
- tolerance of ambiguity
- over-optimism
- high commitment
- leadership.

Attempts to clarify personality traits among business entrepreneurs have endured much criticism, however. They have been unable to differentiate between entrepreneurial small-business owners and professional executives in more established organizations (Carson et al., 1995). Most of those factors believed to be entrepreneurial have not been found to be unique to entrepreneurs but common to many successful individuals (Boyd & Vozikis, 1994). Most business entrepreneurs do not possess all the enter-prise traits identified, and many of the traits are also possessed by those who could hardly be described as entrepreneurs (Bridge et al., 2009).

> Part of the problem with trait approaches arises from how the [business] entre-preneur and [business] entrepreneurship is defined. In the first instance, a focus only on the individual who establishes a new venture is arguably too narrow. It fails to recognise sufficiently the [business] entrepreneurial potential of people who work to develop and grow established enterprises. In addition, there is the difficulty raised by the fact, that [business] entrepreneurs are not an easily identifiable, homogeneous group. [Business] entrepreneurs, it appears, come in all shapes and sizes, from different backgrounds, with varying motivations and aspirations. They are variously represented and addressed in the literature as opportunists or craftworkers, technical entrepreneurs or so-called [business] intrapreneurs. (Carson et al., 1995:51–2)

## 2.4   BUSINESS ENTREPRENEURSHIP THINKING AND BEHAVING

Until the middle of last century, people were not interested in looking at business entrepreneurs as actual persons (not only to have a function in economic development). In the USA, the first business entrepreneurial course was introduced in 1947 by Myles Mace at Harvard Business School (Katz, 2003), even though business entrepreneurship education appeared first in Japan already in 1938 at Kobe University (Dana, 1992). Half a century later, this phenomenon had a more international breakthrough. One estimate in 2003 claims that the number of universities offering courses in business entrepreneurship was more than 1600 (Katz, 2003), of which more than half could be found in the USA (Fiet, 2001). Since then this number has continued to grow.

One example of a scholar who is interested in business entrepreneurial processes is William Gartner. Gartner is a sociologist and he claimed in a seminal article (1988) that it is not fruitful to ask who the business entrepreneur is. To him, the important question is: how are organizations created? He even defines business entrepreneurship as *the creation and establishment of new business organizations.*

The common objective when researching business entrepreneurial behaviour today is to look at a larger complex of variables, such as:

- ability to make judgements and decisions
- goal-orientated behaviour
- planning behaviour
- taking on responsibility
- creativity
- technical skills
- networking ability
- knowledge of project management.

Israel Kirzner is not the only one who has said so, but he is one of the first who clearly expressed the thought that business entrepreneurs are very alert to those [business] chances that appear, in order to realize his or her ambitions ('opportunity recognition'); that is, they are looking for unbalances in the economic system, which can be exploited in order to start business ventures (Kirzner, 1973). Peter Drucker claimed (1985:25) that 'the [business] entrepreneur always searches for change, responds to it, and exploits it as an opportunity'.

This is a dominant opinion today (particularly in the American view on business entrepreneurs), that business entrepreneurs are good at finding and exploiting business opportunities (Bjerke & Karlsson, 2013b). In Gaglio and Katz (2001:95), we can read that 'understanding the [business] opportunity identification process represents one of the core intellectual questions for the domain of [business] entrepreneurship'. Mariotti and Glackin (2010:13) assert that there is a simple definition of '[business] entrepreneur' that captures the essentials: 'A [business] entrepreneur recognizes [business] opportunities where other people see only problems.' As stated by Baron and Shane (2008:5), business entrepreneurship involves the core actions of identifying a [business] opportunity that is potentially valuable in the sense that it can be exploited in practical business terms and yield sustainable profits.

A business opportunity is seen by Barringer and Ireland (2006:28) as 'a favorable set of circumstances that creates a need for a new product, service, or business'. Coulter (2001:53) sees business opportunities as 'positive external environment trends or changes that provide unique and distinct possibilities for innovating and creating value'.

## 2.5   CONTEXTUAL THEORIES OF BUSINESS ENTREPRENEURSHIP

Gifford Pinchot III coined the term '[business] intrapreneur' (1985) to mean a business entrepreneur who generates new business ventures for an established firm, where he or she is employed. He defined a business intrapreneur as a person who takes on personal responsibility to create an innovation within a business organization.

David Storey was one of the first who showed (1980) that there are major differences between the frequencies in the establishment of new business firms in different regions of a country.

I mentioned already in Chapter 1 that we can talk about three sectors in a society:

- The public sector
- The business sector
- The citizen sector (or 'the third sector').

It is then possible to see three kinds of contextual entrepreneurs:

- *Entrepreneurs in the public sector*: People employed in different institutions in the public sector, who act for the common good over and above 'just being' employed there.
- *Business entrepreneurs*: Enterprising people, who are financially-driven, focus on demand in different markets and try to satisfy these

through new goods and/or services (possibly together with a broader social interest).

- *Citizen entrepreneurs*: Enterprising people who are idea-driven and direct their interest towards social needs through new activities (without being employed in the public sector or running a business). This can take place in *private places* (for instance, in sheltered workshops or by private care of elderly or by supporting parents) or in *public places* (for instance, in public squares, in public lecture events or on the Internet).

We may realize that 'increasing the connections between entrepreneurship and society, we get the chance to see the new multiverse of entrepreneurship with its variety of social, cultural, ecological, civic and artistic possibilities' (Steyaert & Katz, 2004:193).

It is also possible (also mentioned in Chapter 1) to separate two kinds of entrepreneurs, who in many ways think and act differently:

- *Business entrepreneurs* (those entrepreneurs in the business sector, who are primarily profit-orientated), who direct their activities towards a market.
- *Social entrepreneurs* (those entrepreneurs who act within the public sector or within the citizen sector plus those entrepreneurs within the business sector, who as well as their profit interest are also interested in solving social problems), who sometimes direct their activities towards a market, and sometimes towards other citizens; in the latter case it is sometimes difficult to characterize what is going on as taking place in a 'market'. The 'marketing' of social entrepreneurs can then have a very different content and can instead be characterized as 'place vitalization'.

Some entrepreneurship does not take place in separate sectors in the society but between two sectors. One example of this is cooperation between universities and industry, which is between the public sector and the business sector. It is called *academic entrepreneurship*. There are, as stated by Bengtsson (2006), trends in society which make higher education and research more important, and which create possibilities for business entrepreneurship in academic contexts. It has become commonplace for universities to start so-called *incubators*, which concentrate on the first phase of such academic business offshoots.

In general terms, it is possible, as stated by Kuratko and Hodgetts (2004), to classify business entrepreneurship research in two groups:

1. *Macro schools* (which focus on factors beyond the control of the business entrepreneur)

2.  *Micro schools* (which focus on factors which the business entrepreneur can control).

Socio-demographic circumstances can characterize business entrepreneurs to some extent:

–   Some *regions or communities encourage entrepreneurship* more than others because they have institutions ready to help small firms (Curran & Blackburn, 1991). Such localities are more favourably disposed to the notion of entrepreneurship (Bridge et al., 2009). These regions or communities are better at creating employment and positive developments.
–   *People who have self-employed parents* are over-represented among those who are themselves self-employed (Shapero & Sokol, 1982; Delmar & Davidsson, 2000).
–   *Education and work experience* influence business entrepreneurship. Two groups are over-represented in this respect (Delmar & Davidsson, 2000): (1) individuals previously self-employed, and (2) unemployed individuals searching for a way of earning a living. Education indicates a positive effect on self-employment, at least up to medium levels of education.
–   *Ethnicity*. Self-employment is often suggested as a way for immigrants to establish themselves in a new society. However, this differs widely between different categories of immigrants.
–   Those people who find themselves in an *in-between situation* in life seem to be more inclined to seek entrepreneurial outlets than those who are in 'the middle of things' (Dollinger, 2003). Examples of such situations, apart from immigration, are between military and civilian life, between student life and career, and between prison and freedom.
–   *Gender and age*. Running a business seems to be associated with gender to some extent – men start more businesses than do women. Business entrepreneurship is also conditioned by age. As stated by Brockhaus (1982), most businesses are started by people 33–45 years old (Landström & Löwegren, 2009).

However, no *single* socio-demographic variable has turned out to be a strong predictor of self-employment (Delmar & Davidsson, 2000).

## 2.6   RESULTS AND EFFECTS OF BUSINESS ENTREPRENEURSHIP

David Birch presented a pioneering work about the importance of small businesses in *The Job Creation Process* (1979). He claimed that in a country such as the US, most new jobs are created by small firms which have the ambition to grow fast (he referred to them as *gazelles*), while at the same time as big companies are decreasing the number of employment opportunities. Birch showed more specifically that small business firms, having not more than 100 employees, had created 80% of new jobs in the US in the beginning of the 1970s. This conclusion was contrary to the established, taken-for-granted understanding at that time that big companies are the drivers of the economy.

*Positive consequences for entrepreneurs* from starting a business are (Coulter, 2001; Zimmerer & Scarborough, 2005):

- to tackle opportunities
- to create one's own future
- to be able to use one's own abilities and talents more fully
- to have a higher degree of independence
- to be responsible only to oneself
- to gain financially
- to have fun
- to follow in the family footsteps.

The same authors stated some *negative consequences for entrepreneurs* from starting a business:

- change and uncertainty
- a multitude of sometimes contradictory decisions to make
- being forced to make economic choices
- risk
- uncertain financial flows
- much work
- possibility to fail.

## 2.7 TO BETTER UNDERSTAND BUSINESS ENTREPRENEURS BY UNDERSTANDING CUSTOMERS BETTER

For the sake of simplicity, I will refer to people acquiring the outcome of business entrepreneurs and marketers as customers, even though they may not be the final consumers. (I will return to this point in more detail in section 7.7).

It is possible to see a development where business entrepreneurs today are trying to understand their customers better, i.e., those people or organizations that are inclined to buy the products that business entrepreneurs have created and offer in a market.

Business entrepreneurs can only survive, of course, by servicing their customers. The latter have always been part of the picture for business entrepreneurs, of course, but surprisingly often only in an *implicit* way. It is not until the latest twenty years or so that the role of customers has become more explicit. Researchers have admitted that customers can sometimes participate more actively and even be co-creators in the business entrepreneurial process.

In the past, market customers showed themselves only as more or less demand in a market (Crane, 2013; Ruzzier et al., 2013). Research on consumer behaviour has been carried out over about fifty years, for sure, but this was not connected to business entrepreneurship until the end of the 1990s. This coincided with the raised interest in thinking in terms of *networking in the society* (Castells, 1998). Networking is now seen as being of great (sometimes even decisive) importance to business entrepreneurial activities. Some of these networks contain customers. Other actors can be business partners, banks, family members and/or friends.

The importance of networks for business entrepreneurs was first noticed in industrial cooperation and led to the wide dissemination of a branch of marketing called *relationship marketing* (Grönroos, 1994; Gummesson, 1999).

Networks have been found to assist small business entrepreneurial operations in their acquisition of information and advice (Birley, 1985; Carson et al., 1995; Shaw, 1997, 1998), in supplementary acquisition of internal resources (Aldrich & Zimmer, 1986; Jarillo, 1989; Hite & Hesterley, 2001), in their ability to compete (Brown & Butler, 1995; Chell & Baines, 2000; Lechner & Dowling, 2003) and in their development of innovative activities and results (Birley et al., 1991; Rothwell, 1991; Conway, 1997; Jones et al., 1997; Freel, 2000). Gibson (1991:117–8) claims that 'the more extensive, complex and diverse the web of relationships, the more the entrepreneur is likely to have access to opportunities, the greater the chance of solving problems expeditiously, and ultimately, the greater the chance of success for a new venture'.

So, 'networks' and 'networking' are seen today as important entrepreneurial tools to establish, develop and improve on small business and other operations in society. There are even those who claim that if there were no networking, there would be no business activities; furthermore, these people want to conceptualize the entrepreneurial process as *organizing oneself through personal networking* (Johannisson, 2000).

I will return to entrepreneurship and networking on several occasions in this book.

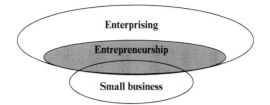

*Figure 2.1    Enterprising, entrepreneurship and small business*

## 2.8    MY VIEW ON BUSINESS ENTREPRENEURSHIP

### 2.8.1    The Difference Between Business Enterprising, Business Entrepreneurship and Small Business

Books about entrepreneurship do not always make a distinction between enterprising, entrepreneurship and small business, which I do. I *associate* entrepreneurship with being *enterprising*, which small (and even big) business is not always (even though it may once have been so). So, all small business can be entrepreneurial and even big business can be. Not all enterprising is entrepreneurial, as I see it: only some enterprising is (Figure 2.1).

The reason why an equals sign is often placed between enterprising and business entrepreneurship and between business entrepreneurship and small business is that all successful business entrepreneurship is enterprising to some extent. However, some enterprising as well as some small businesses can hardly be called entrepreneurial. Another reason why an equal sign is often placed between enterprising and small business could be that the subject of entrepreneurship, due to its popularity, has been associated with and allowed to contain an increasing number of activities in society.

To get a better focus on the subject, I think a distinction should be made between enterprising, entrepreneurship and small business.

### 2.8.2    Differences Between Business Entrepreneurship, Innovation and Self-employment

As in the previous case, business entrepreneurship, innovation and self-employment are often seen as approximately the same. The equality between business entrepreneurship and innovation can be traced back to Schumpeter (1934), who defined business entrepreneurs as individuals who come up with new combinations in the economic value chain of the

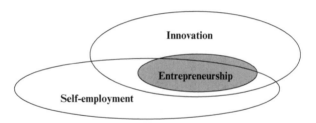

*Figure 2.2    Entrepreneurship, innovation and self-employment*

society; this is one way to look at innovation. However, not all innovation leads to business entrepreneurship.

More independence and self-fulfilment are often mentioned as important prime movers to becoming self-employed (EOS Gallup, 2004). To be a business entrepreneur can be favourable over and above just being self-employed, because it may lead to non-monetary merits such as more independence, broader use of own skills and the possibility to implement own ideas, i.e., more freedom (Sen, 1999).

Some self-employed people are innovative, but far from all are. However, I am interested only in innovative enterprising. Also, I exclude from my conceptualization of business entrepreneurship some variations of being self-employed. I do not include, for instance, activities such as specific changes of contract (for instance, going from being employed to becoming self-employed without any change in what you do) or internal, administrative or organizational changes that do not influence the market at all. Finally, we should keep in mind that much entrepreneurship takes place part-time, i.e., many people combine it with being employed or occupied in other ways. This complicates the figure a bit (Figure 2.2).

There are lots of definitions of business entrepreneurship (Hébert & Link, 1989; Thurik & Van Dijk, 1998). There is no single answer to the question of what the entrepreneurial phenomenon 'really' or 'exactly' is. Rather than looking for some essential 'true' definition of entrepreneurship, people often prefer to study different varieties and functions of entrepreneurship. If we bring together all business orientated entrepreneurial definitions, they show *two relatively distinct (but overlapping) phenomena* (compare Davidsson, 2004). The *first* of these is that some people, instead of working for somebody else, break out on their own and become self-employed. This often means some degree of innovation in the beginning and probably often requires a degree of innovative ability to survive. However, innovation must not be substantial in this context. There are many examples of self-employment, for instance, when a person educated in law starts a lawyer's firm, when a doctor participates in opening a private clinic or when somebody opens a shop or a restaurant, which may not have any notable innovative content.

The *second* phenomenon means a clearer renewal and development of a society, market or organization, based on actors at a micro level taking the initiative and having the perseverance to make things happen in a new way. 'Business entrepreneurship' here means the creation of new standing-alone economic activities and organizations ('independent business entrepreneurship') as well as the transformation of those economic operations that already exist ('business intrapreneurship').

My conceptualization of business entrepreneurship (as well as of social entrepreneurship) is more focused on the second phenomenon. As mentioned, I am interested in innovative business enterprising (or social enterprising).

### 2.8.3   Business Entrepreneurship and Management

I think there are important differences between *business entrepreneurship and management.* Some researchers look at business entrepreneurship as a kind of management. I claim, however, that management and business entrepreneurship are based on different logic and thinking.

> I make use of an analysis of entrepreneurship as distinct from management, the latter being focused on efficient stewardship of existing resources and social control, while the former is animated primarily by creativity, desire, playfulness and the passion for actualising what could come into being. (Hjorth, 2009:207)

I regard management as primarily a profession, where the point is to handle a more or less given situation (compare the relationship between the words 'management' and 'manual', that is, something that has to with your hands = handle). To handle what is needed as a manager, you need technical skills (such as reading an organization diagram, coming up with a budget, closing the books, etc.). As manager, you relate to the company where you are employed, and whether or not you are successful is judged by this employer. Entrepreneurship is more of an attitude, a view of life, being interested in coming up with something new. To do this, mental skills are needed. As an entrepreneur, you relate your new idea to the customer (in the market) or the user (in other parts of the society); whether or not you are successful is judged by this person.

Another view on business entrepreneurship is, like Wickham (2006:16), to claim that a *business entrepreneur is a kind of manager*, a person who handles a situation in an entrepreneurial way. Business entrepreneurial management is, as stated by him, characterized by three things: (1) a focus on change, (2) a focus on an opportunity and (3) a solid stress on management in all situations. Drucker (1985:131) asserts that no matter where in society entrepreneurship takes place, those rules that govern it are, by and large, the same; what works or what does not work is, by and large, the same, and this is also the case for innovation. He claims that there is a general set of concepts that could be called [*business*] *entrepreneurial management*. In a book on business entrepreneurship (Sexton & Bowman-Upton, 1991), there is a headline that reads 'The [business] entrepreneur – a special kind of manager'. Furthermore:

> Unless a new venture develops into a new business and makes sure of being 'managed', it will not survive no matter how brilliant the entrepreneurial idea, how much money it attracts, how good its products, nor even how great the demand for them. (Drucker, 1985:172)

Drucker (1985:23) asserts, furthermore, that anybody can make a decision to learn how to become a business entrepreneur and behave entrepreneurially in business. To him, business entrepreneurship is behaviour and not any personal characteristics, and is based on concepts and theories rather than on intuition. In line with this is the view that successful business entrepreneurship starts with creating a *good business plan.*

### 2.8.4   Two Views on Entrepreneurship Today

It is possible today to see two different views on entrepreneurship (compare with Bridge et al., 2009):

1. *The limited view*: Business entrepreneurship (and most of social entrepreneurship) is an economic phenomenon and is a matter of tracing and exploiting opportunities to become a business entrepreneur (or a social entrepreneur) and of creating something *new*, thereby satisfying *demand in different markets*, new or not. Entrepreneurs in all parts of the society should try to emulate those entrepreneurs who have been successful in business. Some representatives of this view are, for instance, Dees et al. (2001), Amin et al. (2002) and Dart (2004).
2. *The more extended view*: Entrepreneurship belongs to the whole society, not only to its economy, and is a question of creating something *new* (not necessarily in business) and thereby satisfying *demand in different markets and/or social needs in other sectors of the society*, new or not. To be a social entrepreneur is based on different logic from the one ruling in business. This view is represented by, for instance, Hardt (2002), Hjorth and Steyaert (2003), Johannisson (2005) and myself (Bjerke, 2013).

Some authors refer to this as the American (US) and the Scandinavian view (for instance, Bill et al., 2010). Even though there is some truth to it, this separation is a geographical simplification. There are many examples of what could be called the American view in Scandinavia and in other parts of Europe. There are also a few examples of what could be called the Scandinavian view in the US. Furthermore, it is possible to find both views in other parts of the world, for instance, in Canada, Australia and New Zealand. What is clear, however, is that the American view (what I prefer to call the limited view) is dominating everywhere.

The differences between the limited and the more extended view on entrepreneurship, and the frequent difference in how business entrepreneurship is seen in the US and in Scandinavia, becomes clear if you look at how the subject is defined in American and in Scandinavian books. Let me first look at some American examples:

> Entrepreneurship is a way of thinking, reasoning, and acting that is opportunity obsessed, holistic in approach, and leadership balanced. (Timmons, 1999:27)
>
> An entrepreneur is one who creates a new business in the face of risk and uncertainty for the purpose of achieving profit and growth by identifying opportunities and assembling the necessary resources to capitalize on them. Although many people come up with great business ideas, most of them never act on their ideas. Entrepreneurs do. (Zimmerer & Scarborough, 2005:4)
>
> Entrepreneurship is a dynamic process of vision, change, and creation. It requires an application of energy and passion towards the creation and implementation of new ideas and creative solutions. Essential ingredients include the willingness to take calculated risks – in terms of time, equity, or career; the ability to formulate an effective venture team; the creative skill to marshal needed resources; the fundamental skill of building a solid business plan; and finally, the vision to recognize opportunity where others see chaos, contradiction, and confusion. (Kuratko & Hodgetts, 2004:30)

Compare this with some Scandinavian definitions:

> Entrepreneurial processes are about identifying, challenging and breaking institutional patterns, to temporarily depart from norms and values in the society. (Lindgren & Packendorff, 2007:29; my translation)
>
> Entrepreneurship is tangible action as creative organizing in order to realize something different. (Johannisson, 2005:371; my translation)
>
> Entrepreneurship = to satisfy user values and/or needs – new or old – in new ways. (Bjerke, 2013:31)

### 2.8.5 Business Entrepreneurship = Behaviour?

It is obvious from the above that the more extended view defines entrepreneurship *less specifically* than does the limited view. In other words:

1.  The more extended view, unlike the limited one, does not find it necessary to specify what personality or which behaviour is *generally* associated with (successful) entrepreneurs.
2.  Results of entrepreneurship are, in the more extended view, normally not very radical. The limited view is more restrictive. Most entrepreneurship results, in the view of the former, are better seen as 'only' more or less constructive imitations of what exists already, and they do not have any major effect on our lives as customers or citizens.
3.  The limited view claims that entrepreneurs are extraordinary people; the more extended view does not do so.

Lindgren and Packendorff (2007:18) point out that there are *some weaknesses in existing business entrepreneurship research* (that is, what I refer to as the limited view on entrepreneurship):

- It suggests that entrepreneurship can be measured, predicted and stimulated in an objective and neutral way, which leads to a number of problems because the phenomenon of business entrepreneurship is characteristically complex.
- It almost always lets individuals embody business entrepreneurship, in spite of the fact that most business entrepreneurial acts are performed by people in cooperation.
- Business entrepreneurship is operationalized – lacking better data – as freshly registered new firms, which excludes a number of business entrepreneurial acts which take place within existing firms and/or do not lead to the start of traditional companies.
- Focus is too narrow, often excluding, for instance, women and ethnical minorities and what is referred to as the cultural sector.

### 2.8.6  To Behave out of the Ordinary and Act 'as if'

I am of the opinion that regarding entrepreneurs, maybe social entrepreneurs in particular (I will return to those in Chapter 3), with 'acting' eyes will lead to different results than if they are seen with 'behaviouring' eyes (Bjerke & Karlsson, 2013a). However, both perspectives are possible, and both are applied in entrepreneurship research.

**To behave**
If a human activity is seen as *behaviour*, it is looked at as observable, i.e., it can be perceived empirically consistent with classic behaviourism. 'Behaviour' is used by many social scientists as an umbrella term for all human activities. This may lead to confusion, however, if it is not clear

whether 'behaviour' or 'action' is referred to. I therefore suggest 'activity' as an umbrella term, and 'action' and 'behaviour' as two possibilities to look at human activities.

When looking at a human activity as behaviour, all non-observable aspects of this activity are neglected, as it is then necessary to try to explain using observable 'stimuli' and observable 'responses'. Every object in the environment then represents a potential 'stimulus'. In empirical research, an object is described as a 'stimulus' if it gives a behavioural reaction. 'Response' is defined as 'something a human person does' (Watson, 1970:6). To reduce human activities to observable processes should, as claimed by the behaviourist Watson and his followers, make a consistent application of (natural) science methods possible. The ambition with behavioural science is then to define behaviour causally within the framework of scientific theories such that, given specific 'stimuli', corresponding responses can be predicted in a deterministic way.

Theories of cognitive behaviour constitute a development of classic behaviourism, because behaviour is then no longer described only in terms of stimuli and responses. 'Stimuli' are here transferred *through* reflection, cognition and awareness, and not seen as behaviour until then. The *cognitive* (motives, needs, attitudes, levels of aspiration etc.) is seen as a perceptual filter for 'stimuli'. Stimuli are in turn described in terms of information. In these theoretical terms, human behaviour is explained as responses to stimuli, which are chosen selectively in the social and environmental milieu, pass through cognitive processes and become information.

In a behaviouristic view on entrepreneurship, scientific orientation is to see the environment as a cause. Entrepreneurs live here in a *world full of circumstances*, so to say. Bodies react in a deterministic way and their reactions are determined voluntarily only to some extent. Those who represent this view note that the subjective perception of environment sometimes differs from 'objective' facts. The reasons for *why* and *how* different perceptual filters appear are, however, not studied any further.

**To act**
From an 'action' perspective, the situation is seen in a different way. Action can be defined as 'intentionally effecting or preventing a change in the world' (von Wright, 1971:83). An action can also 'designate the outcome of this ongoing process, that is, the accomplished action' (Schutz, 1962:67). If a human activity is to be denoted an 'act', this is not only one aspect of 'reflexivity' which can be found in cognitive behavioural theories, but it also includes *an actively purposeful* result.

'Quasi actions' are described by Habermas (1984:12) as 'behavioural reactions of an externally or internally stimulated organism, and environmentally induced changes of state in a self-regulated system'. By this, Habermas means processes which can be described 'as if they were expressions of a subject's capacity for action', i.e., activities of a mechanism which itself is not capable of providing any cause of its actions. This can be compared with von Wright's distinction between 'quasi causal' (causal descriptions of intentional action) and 'quasi teleological' (intentional descriptions of causal processes in the sense of functional explanations) activities (1971).

Actions might be 'open, directed at the external world' (Schutz, 1962:67). Behavioural theory explains human activity as determined by stimuli, while action is purposeful and meaningful. In the latter case, the entrepreneur lives in *a world full of meaning* (not circumstances as in the case of behaviour). When concentrating on individuals' mental processes, cognitive behaviourism is inadequate when conducting research in a social milieu, because it assumes that the meaning context for socially relevant activities can be reduced to individual stimulus-behaviour. *It consequently cuts off the social context.* The context in the social world can only, as I see it, be considered if we look at members of society as purposeful and not just as 'responses'. Action theory provides a frame to do this. Behavioural theory does not.

Researchers as well as entrepreneurs could be regarded as news agents. One could question, however, whether it is adequate to see them as rational agents, in the sense that in an objective way they select the most effective roads forward to reach a clearly formulated goal, or that they constitute some kind of 'invisible hands' in Adam Smith's sense (1776/1991). They should be rather seen as business-driven (business entrepreneurial) or idea-driven (social entrepreneurs) 'visible hands'. This is partially what I refer to as the more extended view on entrepreneurship.

### 2.8.7   Two Metaphors

I have found it useful to discuss entrepreneurs by using *two metaphors*:

1.   Entrepreneurship means 'not only to be' and to 'act as if'.
2.   Entrepreneurs are involved with more parts of their body than just their brains.

To be an entrepreneur means basically, as I see it, 'not only to be', for instance, not only to be employed, not only to be a business manager, or not only to be a citizen, to take some examples. It is necessary, in my opinion, not only to continue the same but also to create *new* methods to satisfy users' demands or needs to be worthy of the epithet 'entrepreneur'. It is possible to see that to be entrepreneurial means not to be restricted in your actions by those resources that exist (and are expected to come), but to act in such an interesting way to others (among others, potential users of what you come up with) that new resources are generated, not only in terms of money but also in terms of voluntary help, time, cooperation and joy. It is the same as the difference that some make, already mentioned above, between being a *manager* (administrative and bureaucratic behaviour) and being an *entrepreneur*. The former means to operate within those resources you have and expect to get, the latter means to operate so that new resources will be created or *as if* new resources already are there.

To behave or act 'as if' does not, however, not only mean to act 'as if' you already have necessary resources. It can also be seen, for instance:

- To act 'as if' you can forecast the future better than others.
- To act 'as if' you are already on the road of success, even though you may not have arrived yet.

Gartner et al. (1992) express it such that entrepreneurship always has to do with something 'which is going on', and never with something 'which is finished'.

I have found another interesting metaphor to discuss all kinds of entrepreneurs, which is that to be successful, they should involve four different parts of their body, which are:

- the *brain* (to know)
- the *heart* (to be willing)
- the *stomach* (to dare)
- the *limbs* (to do things).

All these parts must be there. If any of the four is missing, the actual entrepreneurial attempt will not succeed. If you do not 'know', you will fumble blindly. If you are not 'willing', it will become an action against yourself. If you do not 'dare', something constructively will hardly come out of it. The fourth, that is, the 'limbs', means that you must *do things for them to take place.*

I am not using these two metaphors to indicate that I believe that I have been able to come with a better formula than others for what is required if you want to succeed as an entrepreneur. The metaphors should rather be seen as examples of a special way to work with pictures, what Max Weber calls *ideal types*. He also refers to them as *pure types*. One famous example of his ideal types is to make a distinction between traditional leadership, charismatic leadership and bureaucratic leadership. Weber asserts that you rarely find ideal or pure types in reality, but that combinations and deformed varieties exist (Weber, 1975).

### 2.8.8   My Conceptualization of Entrepreneurship – A Summary

To put some parameters on a phenomenon that can easily (and in many cases already have) exceed all borders (many warn against allowing entrepreneurship to mean almost anything, arguing that the concepts have been watered down that way, for instance, Jones & Spicer, 2009), I want to conceptualize entrepreneurship to such enterprise that leads to results which have some kind of *news value,* at least in some respect, and which are used by somebody who is not (only) the entrepreneur.

To leave some doors open, I prefer to talk about *conceptualizations* (from Latin *concipere* = summarize) than about *definitions* (from Latin *definire* = put limits to). Most American definitions of 'business entrepreneurship' tend to limit it to specific behaviour and to specific thinking. Some examples:

> [Business] entrepreneurship is the process by which individuals pursue opportunities without regard to resources they currently control. The essence of entrepreneurial behavior is identifying opportunities and putting useful ideas into practice. The tasks called for by this behavior can be accomplished by either an individual or a group and typically requires creativity, drive, and a willingness to take risks. (Barringer & Ireland, 2006:5)
>
> Entrepreneurship, as a field of business, seeks to understand how opportunities to create something new arise and are discovered or created by specific individuals, who then use various means to exploit or develop them, thus producing a wide range of effects. (Baron & Shane, 2008:5)
>
> An entrepreneur is one who creates a new business in the face of risk and uncertainty for the purpose of achieving profit and growth by identifying opportunities and assembling the necessary resources to capitalize on those opportunities. (Scarborough et al., 2009:21)
>
> [Business] entrepreneurship is a mindset or way of thinking, that is, opportunity-focused, innovative, and growth-oriented. [Business] entrepreneurship is also a set of behaviors. [Business] entrepreneurs recognize opportunity, gather the resources required to act on the opportunity, and drive the opportunity to completion. (Allen, 2010:3)

I do not want to put such limits on entrepreneurs by characterizing them in terms of separate features, behaviours or acts. It is my opinion that in order to succeed, entrepreneurs must not have a specific behaviour set-up, nor that they must be growth-orientated, which is common in the American type of definitions (see above). It is even the case that most business firms do not grow after having been started (or are even interested in growing) over and above a certain level (Davidsson, 1989; Wiklund, 1998).

Social entrepreneurial ventures are often more useful if they are locally connected and do not become too big (Nicholls, 2006:226). In other words, I want to conceptualize entrepreneurship only in terms of its effect, that is: *Entrepreneurship = to satisfy demands and/or needs (new or old) in new ways.*

### 2.8.9 Further Examination of the Limited View on Entrepreneurship

Most entrepreneurship theories are based on the limited view and *market-based*. Historically, business entrepreneurship discourse is based on economic discourse (Steyaert & Katz, 2004). These business entrepreneurship theories do not position themselves *in place or in time*, i.e., they are ahistorical and non-cultural (Bjerke, 2010). Some examples:

- Business entrepreneurs are achievement-motivated, have a risk-taking propensity, have an internal locus of control, have a need for autonomy, are determined, creative and self-confident and take initiative (Bridge et al., 2009).
- Many business entrepreneurs seem to think counter-factually, live more in the present and in the future than in the past, become more involved when making decisions and evaluating things, and under-estimate costs as well as time required in succeeding (Baron, 1998).
- Positive consequences for entrepreneurs of starting a business include creating one's own future, having a high degree of independence, being responsible only to oneself and following in the family's footsteps (Coulter, 2001).

Three things emerge from this type of theory:

- To look at *growth* as something primary (Coulter, 2001; Wickham, 2006; Allen, 2010).
- To see *opportunity recognition* as a distinct and fundamental entrepreneurial behaviour (Gaglio, 1997; Kirzner, 1979; Stevenson & Jarillo, 1990; Venkataraman, 1997).
- To view business entrepreneurship as a *(special) type of management* (Drucker, 1985; Stevenson & Jarillo, 1990; Wickham, 2006).

### 2.8.10 Further Examination of the More Extended View on Entrepreneurship

Progressive imitating and necessary mundane aspects of entrepreneurship is what Steyaert (2004) calls the prosaic in entrepreneurship. With a prosaic study of entrepreneurship, we leave the dominating focus on building models, which is usually supported in entrepreneurship research (Steyaert, 2000), and study the conversation process which is supporting the ordinariness of entrepreneurial processes.

> The point of departure of prosaic writing is the belief that everyday is the scene where social change and individual creativity take place as a slow result of constant activity. The daily effort of thousands of small steps makes after all a difference. . . . As prosaic has a sensitivity for the eventness of an event, for its creative moving ahead, it is highly suspicious of systems and all attempts that try to create all-encompassing patterns. In creating systems, there is a chronic double danger. One is the act of exclusion, things become driven out and end in a state of 'non-existence', and the unnoticed becomes even more unnoticeable. Another is that things which happen accidentally are meaningless (at least to the system being created) and not related but become somehow related, meaningful and are no longer accidental. (Steyaert, 2004:10)

The basic or at least a natural consequence of the more extended view on entrepreneurship is to make a difference between traditional ways of doing business and new business venturing – between 'managerialism' and 'entrepreneurialism' in Hjorth and Johannisson's terminology (1998). Business entrepreneurship has been reserved a place within management theory (and is consequently part of what I refer to as 'the limited view on entrepreneurship'), because it was seen among some management researchers as a given way to success. The discourse of business entrepreneurship became part of the view of management during the 1980s (Peter & Waterman, 1982; Kanter, 1983). It progressed on a broad front, including what was called Thatcherism and Reaganism in those days, and developing into the idea of making the employee an enterprising individual in the 1990s (Peters, 1994a, 1994b; du Gay, 1997). Enterprising (Burchell et al., 1991) represents the business entrepreneurial as consistent with managerialism (du Gay, 1997) and is therefore spread quickly to all places where managerialism has become the ruling basis for rationality (Hjorth & Steyaert, 2003:299). During the 1990s it was almost impossible to see any limits to what some scholars wanted managerialism to contain: 'attempts to construct a culture of enterprise have proceeded through the progressive enlargement of the territory of the market – the realm of private business enterprise and economic rationality – by a series of redefinitions of its objects' (du Gay, 1997:56).

The result became a target for management knowledge – the employees themselves. They were seen in business entrepreneurial terms and as parts of a business entrepreneurial company. All that could be governed, should then function as entrepreneurial management. To become successful and to contribute to the success of the company, almost any human activity should be built up by employees who develop a knowledge of themselves (Townley, 1995), a knowledge which centres around the management version of the entrepreneur. When Drucker (1985) expressed his wish to do for business entrepreneurship what he did for management in the 1950s – turn it into a successful discipline – he was prophetic both in terms of enterprising became the ruling power of the new technologies of the self (Martin et al., 1988; Townley, 1995; Deetz, 1998), and how business entrepreneurship as an academic discipline emerged during the 1990s (Katz, 1998). How to do something about your life was increasingly answered in business enterprising terms: manage your life as a business entrepreneurial venture and become an enterprising individual.

The more extended view on entrepreneurship sees no point in creating conceptual systems to explain entrepreneurship. What is needed, instead, is to invent a new way to understand entrepreneurship such that it includes more of society than just its economic parts.

Another aspect of the more extended view on entrepreneurship is not to have a focus on the discovery of opportunities but on the *creative process* itself, which is made clear by using the verb 'to enterprise' as something ongoing, that is, *entrepreneuring* (Steyaert, 2007). Entrepreneurial studies must then be based on a process philosophy (Steyaert, 1997) and can be called *the science of the art of the power of imagination* (Gartner, 2007). Two proponents of the more extended view on entrepreneurship, that is Hjorth and Steyaert, have used this as their starting point in their so-called movements books (Hjorth & Steyaert, 2004, 2009; Steyaert & Hjorth, 2003, 2006).

One important difference between the two views on entrepreneurship is that the more extended view inevitably looks at entrepreneurship as an activity embedded in *a special* (historical, cultural, economic) *context*. Entrepreneurship is, however, not determined by this context. It is rather a specific response to those limitations that are part of the specific context; it is a special way to *problematize* and *transform* these limitations.

Entrepreneurship can [then] be translated as an activity that takes advantage of the *Zwischenraum*, that is of the in-between space (*entre* = between, *prendre* = to take in French). This means that entrepreneurship is an activity that searches and actively creates the distance to what is seen as normal and habitual; it enters and actively creates the between-space as an intensive space and can thus reveal the becomingness of the world. It is further a creative activity in the sense that it connects and reconnects – assembles, dis-assembles and re-assembles – materials, ideas, and so on in a new way. Given rules, plans, norms, models and so on are *transformed* in the process of 'application'. Application, however, has to be understood in a new way. It is not a technical process or the execution of a programme that is fully determined. Rather, 'it would be a concept of application which generates something unpredictable in a totally different context, in contexts which no one can master in advance' (Derrida, 2000:28). *Application* can be rethought as the *space between* rules, regulations, and so on and the concreteness of the situation. (Weiskopf & Steyaert, 2009:196)

The more extended view on entrepreneurship also means that an understanding of business entrepreneurs cannot neglect those contexts in which they exist, and that entrepreneurs in different sectors of the society are guided by, at least partly, different logic. Nilsson (2003), for instance, makes a clear distinction between entrepreneurship research in the economy and other entrepreneurship research. This means, for instance, that business entrepreneurs are satisfying market values through new business ventures, while citizen entrepreneurs or entrepreneurs in the public sector are satisfying social values through new activities.

A criticism of the more extended view on entrepreneurship has come from the those supporting the limited view, which asserts that entrepreneurship research should limit itself and produce results in terms of what the critics call distinctly entrepreneurial, find its domain or so-called *core*, that is, claims that the subject should be consolidated (Venkataraman 1997; Low, 2001; Davidsson, 2003; Baron & Shane, 2008). The proponents of the more extended view, on the other hand, would be happy to support Johannisson (2005:28, my translation) in the following statement:

> To be enterprising in everyday life is to take initiatives, to take responsibility together with other people that something is done. Entrepreneurship is the antipodes to apathy and indifference. Some people picture entrepreneurship as extreme cheerfulness, intellectual malnutrition and a hysterical run for empty places to fill with its own content. It may be so. Nevertheless, an enterprising individual is recognizing his or her own humaneness, believes that he or she can do something about his or her own situation and is driven by being able to involve others in that project he or she is initiating. Entrepreneurship as persistent and creative business design, sometimes successful, becomes in this perspective just a special case of general enterprising.

### 2.8.11    Is it Possible to Combine the Limited and the More Extended View on Entrepreneurship?

Some concepts associated with the *limited* view on entrepreneurship are:

– There is a common profile among all entrepreneurs.
– Entrepreneurs are powered by a need for achievement.
– Entrepreneurship is an economic phenomenon.
– Entrepreneurs are looking for growth.
– Entrepreneurs must find an opportunity to become one.
– An entrepreneur is a kind of manager.

- Entrepreneurs should start with a good business plan.
- Entrepreneurship means extraordinary behaviour among extraordinary people.

Some concepts associated with the more *extended* view on entrepreneurship are:

- Entrepreneurs differ with context.
- Entrepreneurs are powered by imagination.
- Entrepreneurship belongs to the whole society, not only to its economy.
- You can be an entrepreneur without willingness to grow.
- Entrepreneurs start with the wish to become one.
- Entrepreneurs and managers think differently.
- An entrepreneur does not need a formal plan to start.
- Entrepreneurship means extraordinary actions among ordinary people.

The limited view on entrepreneurship is focused on explaining the consequences of a rational way to behave; the more extended view on entrepreneurship is focused on understanding consequences of a bricoleurial way to act.

Some scholars recommend a more extended view on entrepreneurship without completely neglecting the limited view. What should be kept in mind in a more extended view on entrepreneurship is, as stated by some entrepreneurship researchers, the following:

- Entrepreneurship is as much a matter of improving imitation as genuine creation of what is new (Johansson, 2010).
- It is too simple to claim that entrepreneurship needs freedom to thrive. It needs resistance to be triggered in the biggest degree to achieve great things (Berglund & Gaddefors, 2010).
- There is a risk in claiming that entrepreneurship requires spectacular action and that it excludes more mundane activities closer to everyday reality (Bill et al., 2010).

I normally prefer the more extended view on entrepreneurship. However, both views are observed in this book: the limited when discussing the managerial view on marketing for entrepreneurs, and the more extended view when discussing the social phenomenological view on marketing for entrepreneurs.

# 3.  Knowledge development of social entrepreneurship

## 3.1  INTRODUCTION

My view on social entrepreneurship, as previously mentioned, is based on talking about three sectors in a society (Figure 3.1).

These three sectors can be associated with three kinds of social entrepreneurs:

- entrepreneurs in the public sector
- business entrepreneurs with social visions
- citizen entrepreneurs.

Models similar to (but also different from) Figure 3.1 have been suggested by Augustinsson and Brisvall (2009) (Figure 3.2) and Nicholls (2006) (Figure 3.3).

The three new sectors and the hybrids are presented by Augustinsson and Brisvall in the following way:

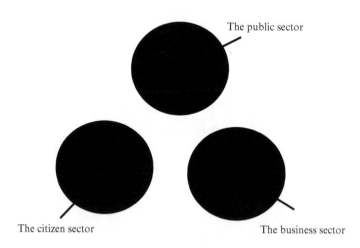

*Figure 3.1    The three sectors in society*

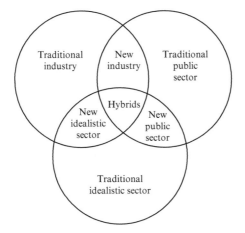

*Source:*    Augustinsson & Brisvall, 2009:25.

*Figure 3.2*    *Entrepreneurial sectors in society today*

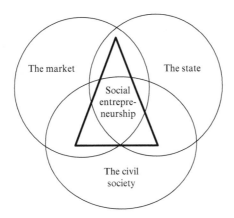

*Source:*    Nicholls, 2006:229.

*Figure 3.3*    *The three estates of society*

- *New industry*: These are entrepreneurs who challenge the traditional industry's lack of social and ecological considerations.
- *New public sector*: These are social entrepreneurs and citizen enterprisers who challenge sluggishness and bring new thinking to the traditional public sector.

*Table 3.1    Aspects of sector logics*

|  | Private sector | Public sector | NPVO sector |
|---|---|---|---|
| *Institutional pillars* | Normative | Regulative | Cognitive/Cultural |
| *Time perspective* | Short-term | Long-term | Short- and long-term |
| *Focal form of capital* | Financial | Human | Social |
| *Interaction rationale* | Calculative | Ideational/ Calculative | Ideational/Genuine |
| *Commitment* | Voice/exit | Loyalty | Involvement |
| *Control* | Output | Process | Culture |
| *Innovation* | Advancing technology | Ongoing, reforming | Mobilizing human resources |
| *Outlook* | Global | Local | Glocal |

*Source:*    Berglund et al., 2012:11.

- *The new idealistic sector*: These are the revivers within the idealistic sector who are using business methods and logics to challenge the power elite in non-governmental Sweden, from cooperative movements to public communities, to become entrepreneurial and self-going.
- *Hybrids*: These are the people who come up with new combinations of logic, methods and traces from all three new sectors to make money and save the world.

Figure 3.3 is rather self-explanatory. Another trans-sectorial idea is found in Table 3.1 (Berglund et al., 2012:11):

In Table 3.1 NPVO stands for 'non-profit voluntary' and social entrepreneurs are here seen as combining the other two sectors in the table. To stress their trans-sectorial role, the authors behind this table use the term 'societal entrepreneurs' instead of 'social entrepreneurs'.

The reason why I want to separate entrepreneurs into three clear sectors in the society is because I see clear differences, partly between social entrepreneurs and business entrepreneurs and partly between different kinds of social entrepreneurs, but above all between citizen innovators, citizen enterprisers and other types of social entrepreneurs, and not only in terms of their use of marketing, which is the subject of this book.

## 3.2   SOCIAL ENTREPRENEURSHIP – A YOUNG SCIENCE

The concept '*social entrepreneur*' appeared for the first time in the literature in Banks (1972). Such an entrepreneur can be defined like this:

> Social entrepreneurship is the use of entrepreneurial behaviour for social rather than profit objectives. (Burns, 2011:454)

One example of a Scandinavian definition is:

> A social entrepreneur is a person who takes an innovative initiative to develop functions which are useful for society. (Gawell et al., 2009:8; my translation)

There are many suggestions for *names for social entrepreneurs*. Some of the names below will later appear as *specific types of* social entrepreneurs:

- social entrepreneurs (Brinckerhoff, 2000)
- community entrepreneurs (De Leeuw, 1999; Johannisson & Nilsson, 1989; Dupuis & de Bruin, 2003)
- non-profit entrepreneurs (Skloot, 1995)
- civic entrepreneurs (Henton et al., 1997)
- idealistic entrepreneurs (Piore & Sabel, 1984)
- mundane entrepreneurs (Rehn & Taalas, 2004)
- public entrepreneurs (Hjorth & Bjerke, 2006).

There are also many suggestions to what could be *meant* by social entrepreneurs. Some suggestions are:

- social enterprisers
- entrepreneurs in the social economy
- participants in associations
- participants in protest movements
- business entrepreneurs devoted to Corporate Social Responsibility (CSR)
- cultural activists
- proponents of fair trade
- environmental activists
- managers of public events
- public entrepreneurs.

Even these could be specific types of social entrepreneurs.

We can summarize *differences between business entrepreneurs and social entrepreneurs* as in Table 3.2 (Johannisson & Nilsson, 1989:5).

*Table 3.2    Differences between business entrepreneurs and social*
*entrepreneurs*

| Business entrepreneurs | Social entrepreneurs |
|---|---|
| Look at society as a means to reach personal goals | Look at the development of society as an essential goal |
| Strengthen their own self-esteem and competence | Make conscious moves and assist in building self-esteem and competence with other citizens |
| Put themselves at the top of their organization | Participate as coordinator at grass-root level |
| Look at authorities and other stakeholders in society as obstacles and threats if they do not serve their own purpose | Approach authorities and external actors as potential supporters and supplier of resources |
| Exploit opportunities to build their own network | Use and build arenas where different networks can be connected |

*Source:*  Johannisson & Nilsson, 1989:5.

Nicholls (2010) argues that he can see *three types of social entrepreneurs* in the scientific discussion: (1) heroes that solve difficult social problems; (2) those who successfully use business entrepreneurs' methods to solve social problems, and (3) entrepreneurs with their own logic based on local community and social justice values.

So, social entrepreneurship is not an *unambiguous* concept. Furthermore, there is no (and there probably never will be) *neutral* view on what a social entrepreneur is doing, and what he or she should do. Among other things, there are always *political* aspects (Steyaert & Katz, 2004:180; Boddice, 2009:137). Social entrepreneurship is by its very nature a *political phenomenon* (Cho, 2006:36).

Social entrepreneurs are not new in society. We just have to think about historical figures such as Florence Nightingale and Mahatma Gandhi. What is new, however, is that the amount of social entrepreneurial activity is much bigger than ever before in history (Bornstein, 2004:3–6). There are, as stated by Nicholls (2006), studies in Great Britain that show that the number of new social entrepreneurial projects there *is larger* than the number of new business entrepreneurial projects. During 2003, it is estimated that 6.6% of the adult population of Great Britain was involved in some kind of new activity, which basically had a socially useful purpose. This was higher than what GEM (Global Entrepreneurship Monitor, 2007) estimated business entrepreneurial startup activities to be there during the same year, which was 6.4%.

Knowledge development of the subject of social entrepreneurship is rather short, and has not existed for more than twenty years or so. It is therefore difficult to characterize its knowledge development in the same six steps used to describe knowledge development of the older subjects of business entrepreneurship (Chapter 2), marketing (Chapter 4) and leadership (Chapter 5). However, we can classify what we have learnt about social entrepreneurship in the following four steps (the last four steps of the six used for the other three areas):

- social entrepreneurial thinking and behaviour
- contextual theories of social entrepreneurship
- results and effects of citizen entrepreneurship
- to better understand the citizen entrepreneurs by understanding users better.

I will return to the reason why I limit myself to specific types of social entrepreneurs in the last two sections.

We may ask why there is a citizen sector in society and how large it is. Westerdahl (2001) provides three proposals to explain why this is the case:

- *The vacuum hypothesis*: The stagnating of the public sector and (in some cases) decline in large areas of the business sector has created a space for other actors. As stated by Westerdahl, this hypothesis is the most important one of the three.
- *The global hypothesis (the identity hypothesis)*: At the same time as we are experiencing more globalization we also note a greater wish for local and regional identity.
- *The influence hypothesis*: We are experiencing an increased questioning of the public sector's handling of tax revenues connected with a wish of a greater influence over the way in which this is done.

These three hypotheses – if they are correct – show that the transformation of society currently under way in the Western world exhibits certain development features suggesting a probability that, whether by necessity or by voluntary commitment, certain social elements of the economy will assume increased importance for certain actors. This makes it possible for activities conducted under social-economic forms to expand. The extent to which these activities can make use of this potential for expansion is determined primarily by their strength, their competitiveness and the attitude towards them of other actors in society. (Westlund, 2001:435)

Estimated *employment* in the third sector is 8–10% in Western Europe (somewhat less in Sweden due to its large common sector and considerably more in, for instance, Greece). Between 1980–90, the increase of this sector was 40% in France, 36% in Germany and 41% in USA (Salomon & Anheier, 1994) and in twenty Western European regions the increase was 44% (Westlund & Westerdahl, 1997). All numbers are here very uncertain however (and in a sense misleading), among other reasons due to the large proportion of *part-time work in the citizen sector* (Vasi, 2009:169) and its many *volunteers*. The so-called not-for-profit sector in USA (which refers to all social entrepreneurs, not only those in the citizen sector) is much higher than in Europe and is estimated to be 7% of GNP (Burns, 2011:454).

> In almost all industrialised countries, we are witnessing today a remarkable growth in the 'third sector', i.e. in socio-economic initiatives which belong neither to the traditional private for-profit sector nor to the public sector. These initiatives generally derive their impetus from voluntary organizations, and operate under a wide variety of legal structures. In many ways, they represent the new or renewed expression of civil society against a background of economic crisis, the weakening of social bonds and difficulties of the welfare state. (Defourney, 2001:1)

Citizen entrepreneurs have their roots in *local service and development* (Grenier, 2009:199). Citizen entrepreneurship can even be seen as a universal attempt in a society to answer to the specific in local needs (ibid.). It is this local history that feeds their passion for creating activities which are important to society (Emerson & Twersky, 1996:2–3).

## 3.3 SOCIAL ENTREPRENEURSHIP THINKING AND BEHAVING

Areas in which social entrepreneurs have been operating are (Nicholls, 2006:228):

- poverty alleviation through empowerment (e.g., the micro-finance movement)
- healthcare, ranging from small-scale support for the mentally ill 'in the community' to larger-scale ventures tackling the HIV/AIDS pandemic
- education and training, such as widening participation and the democratization of knowledge transfer
- environmental preservation and sustainable development, such as 'green' energy projects

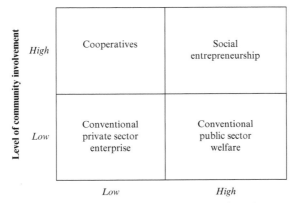

*Source:* Nicholls, 2006:230.

*Figure 3.4   One positioning of social entrepreneurship*

– community regeneration, such as housing associations
– welfare projects, such as employment for the unemployed or homeless and drug and alcohol abuse projects
– advocacy and campaigning, such as Fair Trade and human rights promotion.

Whatever way we look at it, social entrepreneurship is always about engagement (Figure 3.4).

Networking seems to be more important for social entrepreneurs than for business entrepreneurs. There are several reasons for this:

– The former does not offer *tangible goods and/or services* that can speak for themselves. They must constantly confirm their social entrepreneurial activities to those who support what they are doing and, above all, to the users of what they create.
– Social entrepreneurs exploit network relations in a *much broader field* (Dennis, 2000; Blundel & Smith, 2001; BarNir & Smith, 2002). They are looking for alliances and cooperative possibilities where they can most easily find them. Many social entrepreneurs work, *at the same time*, with local governments, welfare institutions, volunteering groups and banks. Further, social entrepreneurs use their networks not only to leverage resources and strengthen their own ventures, which is primary to business entrepreneurs, but also *to deliver impact and to create new social value* (Nicholls, 2006).

– Social entrepreneurs operate in *a more diversified and dynamically strategic landscape* than do business entrepreneurs (O'Gorman, 2006). Social entrepreneurs also often show *a much larger variation* in the form of organization under which they operate. Furthermore, economies of scale are *not as obvious* for social entrepreneurs as they are for business entrepreneurs. The former may often get maximum impact by remaining small and local and through deepening their activities, rather than broadening them (Nicholls, 2006).

– Social entrepreneurs are often looking for social space where traditional business activities and the public sector *have not* shown any major interest, and they improve on and create new social capital through institutional or gradual improvement and innovation. The urge to change the terms of engagement *for the benefits of their stakeholders* often marks social entrepreneurs out as quite distinct from business entrepreneurs (Nicholls, 2006).

– The ultimate aim (even if it may not be attainable) for social entrepreneurs is to do so well that *they are no longer needed.* This is not the case for business entrepreneurs (Nicholls, 2006).

– Paton (2003) asserts that social entrepreneurs and business entrepreneurs live *in different meaning-worlds.* To bring the business venturing mind to social entrepreneurship could undermine what is the strength of social entrepreneurs (Krashinsky, 1998), neglecting the dialogical and political praxis which is central to social entrepreneurship (Cho, 2006).

## 3.4 CONTEXTUAL THEORIES OF SOCIAL ENTREPRENEURSHIP

There is social entrepreneurship taking place in the public sector. One example is a business school which presents itself as entrepreneurial (Lundqvist, 2009). There is also social entrepreneurship in the business sector, for instance, a natural social responsibility with small business firms as stated by Sundin (2009). There are studies in Great Britain, on the other hand, which state that social contributions made by small business firms often stop with the economic ones (ODPM, 2003:Ch. 2). This can be summarized such, which I have said before, that all *entrepreneurial* activities that take place in the public sector and the citizen sector can be called social entrepreneurship, but *only some* entrepreneurial activities that take place in the business sector should be seen as social entrepreneurship.

Nicholls (2006:229) provides a list of contexts for social entrepreneur-

*Table 3.3    Contexts for social entrepreneurship*

| Origins | Social market failure | Means | Ends | Example |
|---|---|---|---|---|
| Grassroots | Lack of institutional support | Critical social innovation | Coordinated creation of social capital through local/ community action | Housing associations |
| Institutional | Changing social landscape | Normative social innovation | Social entrepreneur-ship champions new social institutions | Open University |
| Political | Retreat of centralised government control from society | Market socialism | Introduction of enterprise/ private sector market philosophy into public sphere | Public–private finance initiatives (e.g. London Underground) |
| Spiritual | Decline of church influence in society | Commercial-isation of congregation- and church-based activities | Revitalise role of faith in public affairs | CAFOD/ Fair Trade Foundation |
| Philanthropic | Lack of finance for development of social capital | Foundations coordinating charity giving as social entrepreneurial startup funding | Link business and social innovation | Skoll Foundation and community education |

*Source:*   Nicholls, 2006:229.

ship (Table 3.3). Referring to this table, I want to speak of social *entre-preneurs* only in the first case (grassroots), and to some extent the next three (institutional, political and spiritual); however, only before they have become too institutionalized. The fifth (philanthropic), I do not count as *entrepreneurial* at all, because it does not contain any *new* solutions (even though such attempts may be financed through this channel).

## 3.5   RESULTS AND EFFECTS OF CITIZEN ENTREPRENEURSHIP

The content of this section is valid only for such social entrepreneurs that I call citizen entrepreneurs; hence the restriction in the heading above.

It has been suggested that citizen entrepreneurs can express themselves in at least *three different ways* (Vasi, 2009:160–1):

1.  Some initiatives focus on *disseminating a package of innovations* needed to solve common problems. This form of entrepreneurial activity attempts to serve widespread needs because it assumes that 'information and technical resources can be reconfigured into user-friendly forms that will make them available to marginalized groups' (Alvord et al., 2002:10). Once such packages are constructed by various experts – a difficult task, because it requires substantial creativity to adapt materials and resources for low-cost usage – they can be disseminated by individuals and agencies with relatively few resources.
2.  Some forms involve *building capacities* to identify capacities needed for self-help. This approach is based on two assumptions: local groups possess the best knowledge about which issues are most important, and local actors may solve their problems if they have access to more resources and better capacity to act. Therefore, entrepreneurship directed at capacity building requires paying special attention to local constituents and resource providers.
3.  Some initiatives focus on *mobilizing grassroots groups* to form alliances against abusive elites or institutions. The assumption underlying this approach is that marginalized groups can solve their own problems if they have increased access to political institutions (Alvord et al., 2002).

Examples of how different groups in the society may need citizen entrepreneurial achievements is shown in Table 3.4 (Dees et al., 2002:143).

There are many negative trends in our society, such as lower participation in elections, higher contempt of politicians and decreased involvement in civic society. Whether social entrepreneurs in general, and citizen entrepreneurs in particular, will be able to *counterbalance* these negative trends is an open question.

One unsolved issue in social entrepreneurship (unlike in business) is how to measure its *effect*. A number of qualitative and quantitative measures have been suggested. The most recognized one is a model for 'social return on investment' (SROI) which was suggested by Roberts Enterprise Development Foundation (REDF) in the US (Emerson, 1999) and then refined in the UK by New Economics Foundation. These measures have, however, not in any

*Table 3.4    Communities likely to work with and need citizen entrepreneurs*

| Types of communities | Defining features |
|---|---|
| *Geographical* | Historically isolated and under-resourced or abused areas. |
| *Marginalized* | Stigmatized groups often viewed as nonconformist particularly with regard to work, personal and residential maintenance and sexual practices. |
| *Age groupings dependent on working population* | Populations segmented by virtue of their need for services, support and control they seem unable to provide for themselves. |
| *Special interest groups* | Affiliations that advocate for recognition, preservation or expansion of issues or entities that cannot speak for themselves. |
| *Groups that self-identify through religious, ethnic, racial or national membership* | Alliances built through a sense of common history, often shared hardships and hopes for a better future. |
| *Affiliate groups aligned through pursuit of similar activities* | Devotion to what are often leisure activities or specialized ways of carrying out particular types of work. |

*Source:*   Dees et al., 2002:143.

way been generally accepted. There are consequently few agreed-upon or even available benchmarks or 'best practice' for the effect of social entrepreneurship. The establishment of the effect of social entrepreneurial operations will, therefore, continue to be open for criticism and discussions.

## 3.6   TO BETTER UNDERSTAND CITIZEN ENTREPRENEURS BY UNDERSTANDING USERS BETTER

The reason why I only talk about citizen entrepreneurs here is because only those social entrepreneurs (and, above all, those citizen entrepreneurs who are called citizen innovators and in some cases social entrepreneurs in the public sector) provide something new concerning marketing for entrepreneurs. Other social entrepreneurs, that is, social entrepreneurs in the business sector and citizen enterprisers, are not using marketing very differently from business entrepreneurs, which I have already discussed. Furthermore, I talk about 'users', not 'customers' in this context.

As stated by Grenier (2009:174–5), it is possible to see *two kinds of citizen entrepreneurs*: 'citizen enterprisers' (for instance, Borzaga & Defourney, 2001; Martin & Thompson, 2010) and 'citizen innovators' (for instance, Steyaert, 1997, 2004; Bornstein, 2004). It is not easy to separate the two, however. Citizen enterprisers are also often interested in local issues, collective and private actions, local communities and local political struggle (Dey & Steyaert, 2010:98). In countries such as Sweden, the citizen entrepreneurial issue is different from many other countries. They are supposed to be managed there by the public sector. I am a Swedish scholar and therefore more interested in citizen innovators than of citizen enterprisers, that is, citizen entrepreneurs who act with the logic which exists in different *public places*. By public places I refer to *physical, virtual, discursive and/or emotional arenas* which, in principle, every citizen has access to and which, still in principle, every citizen should feel responsibility for. I refer to these people as *public entrepreneurs* rather than citizen innovators. They are usually not on the institutional decision makers' agenda (Hjorth & Bjerke, 2006:120). But notice that public entrepreneurs do not refer to entrepreneurs operating in the public *sector*, but in public *places*; places which, by the way, are often publicly owned (I refer to the former as *public sector entrepreneurs*). Citizen enterprisers, which have sheltered workshops, people's homes or the like as their operative location, do usually not operate in *public* places (and they often do not need to be innovative, and if not then they are not of interest to me). Protest movements traditionally operate in public places as well (for a discussion of Attac in Swedish as an entrepreneurial movement, see Gawell, 2009), but it is possible to make a distinction between *value creating citizen entrepreneurs* and *critical citizen entrepreneurs* (Nicholls, 2006:235). I am more interested in the former.

> [Citizen enterprisers] identify service gaps and efficiently mobilize resources to fill them. In doing so, however, they privilege addressing symptoms over resolving more fundamental root causes, such as social inequality, political exclusion, and cultural marginalization. (Cho, 2006:51).

Talking about public entrepreneurs in different citizen situations opens the door for a new discussion of entrepreneurs as a social force (Hjorth & Bjerke, 2006:99). Social entrepreneurs in general, and citizen entrepreneurs in particular, are commonly seen as people who are correcting unsatisfactory public service in society. It is a concept which is used today primarily when discussing how to 'fix' problems with a withering 'welfare state' (Dreyfus & Rabinow, 1982), including 'reinventing government' (Osborne & Gaebler, 1992). 'Public' entrepreneurs do not, however, devote themselves to such corrections, but to make more people in a society feel that they are part of that society instead of feeling alienated, that is, building *citizenry*. It is not a simple matter to determine what is meant by 'citizenry', but it can, in principle, be seen as 'a collective engagement (affective relation) that generates an assemblage (a project, a group of people)' (Hjorth, 2009:216).

So, public entrepreneurs do not try to make the public institutions' job better or to replace the market. There are even those who claim (for instance, Spinosa et al., 1997) that the concept of 'market' – in the sense of situations where supply and demand, and sales and buys take place – does not adequately catch those negotiation processes and those democratic structures that exist in a well-functioning citizen arrangement. It is therefore not surprising that established entrepreneurial and marketing models can only to some extent be used to understand who the citizen entrepreneurs are and what they do. Furthermore, theoretical views such as *convention theory* (Wilkinson, 1997; Renard, 2002) and *analysis of networks* (Callon, 1986, 1999; Latour, 1993) have challenged and provided new pictures of how economic mechanisms function in our world. (Convention theories are about how world trade of many fruits and vegetables are controlled more by governments and agreements than by market forces. Analyses of networks started with sociological, ethnographical studies during the 1990s of how, in practice, research is done in laboratories, and changed the widespread opinion at the time about the existence of a simple relationship between scientific knowledge and nature).

Public entrepreneurs are *citizens who involve other citizens in making some marginal phenomena more central (more public) in a society* (Bjerke, 2005; Bjerke & Dalhammar, 2006). Public entrepreneurs are primarily interested in getting other citizens and actors in the society together to reinforce what might be called our *citizen capital*. In a country such as Sweden, you might find values such as 'solidarity', 'representative democracy' and building more 'inclusiveness' to be part of this capital. This is, of course, of great importance for how those entrepreneurs use 'marketing', which is the main interest in this book. As we will see, it is even more appropriate sometimes to talk about 'place vitalization' rather than 'marketing' when these kinds of entrepreneurs act.

One might think that *social exclusiveness* (the opposite of 'inclusiveness') is a clear concept, but that is far from the case (Blackburn & Ram, 2006). Firstly, we should make a distinction between a 'strong' and a 'weak' version of the concept:

> In the 'weak' version of the concept, the solution consists of supporting excluded people's unprivileged conditions and support their integration in the mainstream of the society – Stronger versions of this concept are also stressing the role of those who lead to exclusion and consequently attempt to find solutions that decrease their power. (Blackburn & Ram, 2006:74)

Secondly, on the government part and from public institutions it has been claimed that the 'solution' would be to start more citizen enterprises, where the concept of 'enterprise' is seen as an essential factor in our new society. Unfortunately, this concept of 'citizen enterprises' is not very clear either. The concept might have been born in the USA, a country where 'enterprising' is of great importance. As I see it, in a country such as Sweden (and probably also in many similar countries today), an increase in so-called citizen enterprising is not enough. Citizen innovators, that is, public entrepreneurs, should be given more attention.

*Public places* are arenas for interventions in the society that link the institutional structured public sector with the mundane everyday practical maintenance of citizenry in civic society (Hjorth & Bjerke, 2006:109). This is where public entrepreneurs are operating. Local authorities, including local governments, can also act in these public places in different ways, for instance by (Bjerke & Karlsson, 2011:90):

- *Creating awareness in general*:
  a. Participating in arranging a public entrepreneurship day.
  b. Financing various publications on public entrepreneurship issues.
  c. Instituting a prize, 'The local public entrepreneur of the year'.
- *Participating in building public places, more specifically*:
  d. *Physically*: offering venues at a low rent; initiating 'Middle Age Weeks' and the like; arranging cultural exhibitions, music festivals and the like; opening an 'entrepreneurship office' accessible for *all* kinds of entrepreneurs, not only in business.
  e. *Virtually*: Presenting and discussing public entrepreneurs on the home page.
  f. *Discursively*: Starting a series of discussions and lectures on public entrepreneurship open to the public.
  g. *Emotionally*: Participating in discussions about what it means to be a citizen in the local community in question.

In complex societies, 'the civic society consists of the intermediary structure between the political system on one hand and the private sectors of the lifeworld and the functional systems on the other' (Habermas, 1996:373). This quotation and suggestions above to local communities to act in public places are aspects of 'governance', a concept which I will return to.

I believe that 'the public sphere' is at stake. We urgently need new ideas and tactics for imagining what the public should be today, and for exploring how we can act as citizens in order to enhance individuals' quality of life. My ambition is to contribute to this by elaborating on what I will call a public form of entrepreneurship which can create a new form of sociality in the public realm. The purpose of such a development is to re-establish the social as a force different from the economic rather than being encompassed by it. Entrepreneurship is then re-conceptualized as a sociality-creating force, belonging to society and not primarily to business. I also make use of an analysis of entrepreneurship as distinct from management, the latter being focused on efficient stewardship of existing resources and social control, while the former is animated primarily by creativity, desire, playfulness and the passion for actualizing what could come into being. Public entrepreneurship is a term thus meant to emphasize the creative and playful as central to entrepreneurial activity. (Hjorth, 2009:207)

Similarities between public entrepreneurs and the more extended view on entrepreneurship are obvious.

Citizenship is a composite concept that includes individuals and groups, and discussions of citizenship always have to deal with right, values and social practice in which forms of citizenship are practised (Petersen et al., 1999). Citizenship in today's society is less of an institution and more of an achievement. It is therefore a matter of identity. Spinosa et al. (1997) attempted to discuss the entrepreneurial aspects of citizenship. In their discussion, social changes are realized by 'virtuous citizens' as well as by entrepreneurs in co-creation with each other.

*Examples of public entrepreneurial activities* are (compare Thompson, 2002):

- remobilizing depleted social areas
- setting up agencies for support and advice
- re-utilizing of buildings and resources for social purposes
- providing 'suitability training'
- generating means for some common good issue
- organizing voluntary operations
- generating or supporting cultural activities that are not commercial
- generating or supporting sports activities that are not commercial.

## 3.7 THE IMPORTANCE OF A 'PLACE'

Public entrepreneurs act in public places. Let us clarify the concept of 'place', before we look at the role which entrepreneurs play in the development of a local community as a place.

The concepts of 'space' (*Raum* in German; *espace* in French) and 'place' (*Ort* in German; *lieu* in French) are basic components of the world, and we normally take them for granted. We notice the absence of space when we are pressured and the absence of place when we are lost (Tuan, 1977). Because we take them for granted, we normally deem them not worthy of separate treatment. What we also take for granted is, that we are 'put in a situation' in space and place to begin with, that space and place existed a priori of our existence on Earth. Just because we say that we cannot choose in this matter, we believe we do not have to think about such basic facts to start with (Casey, 1997). However, when we think about the two concepts, they may assume unexpected meanings and raise questions we have not thought to ask. The same thing happens to other concepts that we normally take for granted. For instance, we take for granted that we have a language and acquired a culture. But what does it mean, *really*, that we have a language and acquired a culture? In fact, space as well as place can be very complicated concepts, which is all the more confusing because, at first glance, they appear obvious and common sense. After all, it is impossible to think of the world without the two. To look at the world as space and/or place is to use dimensions to characterize the world into a special fashion and a special way to talk about and to understand the world. As stated by Cresswell (2004:27), 'by taking space and place seriously, we can provide another tool to demystify and understand the forces that effect and manipulate our everyday life'.

Looking at the world as a world of places, we see different things:

> Looking at the world as a set of places in some way separate from each other is both an act of defining what exists (ontology) and a particular way of seeing and knowing the world (epistemology and metaphysics). Theory is a way of looking at the world and making sense of the confusion of the senses. Different theories of place lead different writers to look at different aspects of the world. In other words, place is not simply something to be observed, researched and written about but simply part of the way we see, research and write. (Cresswell, 2004:15)

Space is normally seen as the more abstract of the two concepts. When we speak of space, we tend to think of outer space or possibly spaces of geometry (Cresswell, 2004). Space is something deterritorialized (de Certeau, 1984). It can be discussed without considering that it might contain social life, inhabited by actual identifiable people. Spaciousness is closely associated with the sense of being free. Freedom implies space, enough room in which to act (Tuan, 1977).

Space is generally seen as being transformed into place when it acquires definition and meaning. Brenner (1997:137) expresses it such: 'Space appears no longer as a neutral container within which temporal development unfolds, but, rather, as a constitutive, historically produced dimension of social practices'. Considering antonyms to place, we refer to words such as 'remove', 'take away', 'dislodge', 'detach' and 'take off' (Rämö, 2004). When space feels familiar to us, it has become place (Tuan, 1977).

Place is then a meaningful location, to which people are attached (Altman & Low, 1992).

Places are significant to human life. We might even say, like Cresswell (2004:33), that 'there was no "place" before there was humanity, but once we came into existence then place did too'. Places are being made, maintained and contested. All over the world, people are engaged in place-making activities. Nothing we do is unplaced (Casey, 1997:ix).

However, places are not isolated from each other. Cronon (1992) argues that we must pay attention to their connections. Relationships between people and places are as complex relationships between people, but of another kind. Places give meaning to people. This is where people learn to know each other and themselves. Places become points which stand out in every individual's biography and a set of feelings for different places develop through social interaction (Ekman & Hultman, 2007). Altman and Low (1992:7) phrase it such that 'the social relations that a place signifies may be equally or more important to the attachment process than the place qua place'.

Even though the term *homo geographicus* has been coined (Sack, 1997), place is more than geography. It is something, the meaning and usefulness of which is continuously created in social relations and networks, which are in meetings and flows between people and objects. This is something which has gained an increasing response within social as well as within human sciences (Ekman & Hultman, 2007). To put it differently, place is culturally defined (Casey, 1993).

The political geographer John Agnew (1987) has outlined three fundamental aspects of place:

1.  Location.
2.  Locale.
3.  Sense of place.

'*Location*' has to do with fixed objective coordinates on the Earth's surface (or in the Earth's case, a specific location vis-à-vis other planets and the sun). By '*locale*', Agnew means material setting for social relations – the actual shape of place within which people conduct their lives as individuals. By '*sense of place*', Agnew refers to the subjective and emotional attachments people have to place. Place can vary in size from being very large (e.g., the Earth, universe or nation), mid-sized (e.g., cities, communities and neighbourhoods), smaller (e.g., homes or rooms) or very small (e.g., objects of various kinds) (Altman & Low, 1992). It may even be something completely imaginary, such as *Utopia*. A place can be called a 'room for activities' (Massey, 1995b) or an 'arena' (Berglund & Johansson, 2008). 'Home' is an 'exemplary kind of place' (Cresswell, 2004:115).

It is possible to have a similar discussion about time. Places are never finished, but are constantly being performed (Thrift, 1996). Whereabout is always whenabout (Casey, 1993). The old Greeks separated *chora* (space) from *topos* (place, or rather, region), but also *chronos* (dated time) from *kairos* (valued time). Rämö (2000, 2004) makes a four-field classification from this, of obvious relevance to entrepreneurship. Being aware of the difficulties of separating time from space and place, however, I still do not discuss separate concepts and perceptions of time explicitly in this book. One excuse for this 'neglect' is possibly that in modern times we are so inured to the primacy of time that we rarely question the dogma that time is the first of all things. This modern obsession with time may have blinded us to the presence of place in our lives (Casey, 1993). More about entrepreneurship, space and place can be read in Bjerke and Rämö (2011).

In this book, I use the concepts of 'space' and 'place' in the same way as Hudson (2001) does. To him, 'space' is an economic evaluation of a situation based on its capacity for profit, while 'place' is a societal situation based on meaning. Spaces are therefore valued predominantly through the lens of production and consumption based on supply and demand, use of factors of production and operations on markets. Places, on the other hand, are situations of meaningful societal life where people live and learn; they are situations of socialization and cultural acquisition. Places are made up of a complex system of societal relations. While space is the situation of enterprise, place is the situation of societal life. Occasionally, situations thrive both as spaces for profitable business and as places with a rich societal fabric. Under these circumstances, the situation appears to combine the best of economic and societal life (Florida, 2002). In such situations, there is a synergistic relationship between space and place (Johnstone & Lionais, 2004).

Using the concepts of space and place when analysing entrepreneurship can have several advantages, as stated by Hjorth (2004), including:

a.  It brings into focus an often-neglected but basic element of everyday life.
b.  Power becomes naturally included in our studies, which is something that rarely happens in entrepreneurship research.

Paradoxically, place has been even more important in our modern society, with increased mobility (Ekman & Hultman, 2007). Today we can witness a multitude of what might be referred to as 'non-places', such as airports and other temporary dwellings, which Augé (1995) sees as different from genuine (what he refers to as 'anthropological') places. Our view on place has importance for such issues today as migration, cases of refugees and asylum.

It seems that place is more important to public entrepreneurs than space. Compare concepts such as public places, homes and work places with concepts such as expansion space and budget space.

Within the traditional, managerial approach to marketing, which is one of my two ways to look at the subject (marketing management), place constitutes that part of marketing mix which is used by a company to make its products available to the customers. One issue which is raised in marketing management is, for instance, how available a product should be, that is, how simple it should be for a customer to get hold of a specific product. Another issue which is normally put under the place category within marketing management is whether you, as a producer, should manage the whole so-called value chain of middle-hands yourself, or whether you should invite other actors into this chain.

From an interactionist perspective, Svensson and Östberg (2016) (in their case in terms of symbolic interactionism, which is close to that approach I use when discussing an alternative possibility to marketing for entrepreneurs, which is the social phenomenological one) discuss place as *something going on* under the following points:

● places as interaction and co-action
● enacted places
● negotiating and challenging places.

*Places as interaction and co-action.* A shop, seen as a place for instance, is often seen as a delimited thing, where you can go as a customer, do your shopping and then leave. A shop consists of walls, ceiling and a floor. The owner of the shop (or its personnel) is selling and the customers are buying there.

*Enacted places.* Places may require people who interact, but in order for a place to be one for selling and buying, it is necessary for people to interact consistently with certain rules and patterns. The shop must be *enacted*.

*Negotiating and challenging place.* One of the main points here is that the meaning of places is not something that is instilled only by those who put it up and by those who use it. The meaning of a place is a result of attempts to define and interpret it by several parties, that is, in this case of a shop the result of interaction between the owner of the shop (or its personnel) and/or its customers.

In a similar way in which I have discussed 'place' here, I will analyse the concepts of 'customer' and 'user' as well as the concepts of 'market' and 'value creation' in Chapter 7.

## 3.8    DEVELOPMENT OF A LOCAL COMMUNITY

An interesting area which is relevant to all kinds of entrepreneurs is the development of a local community. There is an increased interest in local communities. There are several reasons behind this:

- The bases of central control of an economy have changed – they have become smaller (MacKinnon et al., 2002).
- Small and medium-sized activities have shown themselves better at managing modern society in geographically concentrated areas – in spite of globalization in the world (Porter, 1998).
- Nearness between people has proven itself to reinforce productivity and innovation (ibid.).
- People come together in urban centres, and the economy of a country continues to concentrate itself to specific places. It seems that 'place' rather than the more abstract 'space' is essential for economic life (Florida, 2003).

*Three developments* have influenced local urban centres today, influences that should be seen as possibilities, not as threats (Hall, 2005):

- post-industrialization
- globalization
- migration.

*Post-industrialization.* With Daniel Bell's book *The Coming of Post-Industrial Society* (1974), the concept of the *post-industrial society* made a name for itself in public debate. In this classic work, Bell describes how American society is changing from an industrial to a service society. Information and communication technology, knowledge and a new organizational paradigm ('the network society') constitute important parts of this society. It is in 'hot', urban places, where ideas are created and disseminated (Sernhede & Johansson, 2005:10). In these urban centres, however, in parallel with the growth of a well-situated middle class which is adapting to the new knowledge-intensive economy, new types of poverty and 'social exclusion' exist. The middle class is developing a demand for new services (cleaners, gardeners, painters, crafts people, etc.). These are provided by the less educated workforce which has not been able to adapt to the new economy. Post-war welfare state is transformed by new urban development concepts, where, in the beginning, expansive industrial suburbs were part of a national effort for modernization, inclusion and social cohesion. However, nobody walking around in a city today can avoid meeting people begging. To those who bring themselves out to the peripheries of the large cities, meeting other kinds of stigmatization and alienation is even more tangible (ibid.:10–1). Reports about the conditions in many modern suburbs are not edifying. Many modern societies have developed, where the most exposed groups are no longer positioned at the lowest rung of the ladder. They have been placed outside the very ladder itself.

*Globalization.* The form of globalization which is referred to in contemporary globalization debates is a new global economy (totally different from colonial times), which started to develop during the second half of the 1970s. This new form is based on multinational corporations, on new forms of communication and on free flow of financial capital (Hall, 2005). Old relationships between periphery and centre are no longer valid as before. Division between developed and less developed regions at a global level is more complex today. Subordination, misery and hunger in so-called developing countries exist today in urban centres in the Western world. This new order is neither less cynical nor less brutal (Sernhede & Johansson, 2005:18).

*Migration.* Migration, the global relocation of people, has caught and transformed most cities in modern countries. Migration processes during the latest decades have brought the third world to all Western metropolises due to flight from devastating wars etc., and it is transforming the meaning and content of the EU.

Post-industrialization, globalization and migration are seen in cities and urban centres in the following way (Johansson & Sernhede, 2005):

1. Newly rich people are getting together in attractive suburbs ('the new underclass') and that part of population with money to spend settles down in the inner city (so-called 'gentrification').
2. It is more and more a matter of 'we' and 'they' now, that is, more of social exclusion for many.
3. The city is transformed from manufacturing, work and trade to tourist attractions and exclusive apartments.

The new, post-industrial economy, globalization and migration has not only created new class constellations, tensions and interfacial conflicts but also led to new strategies for how the dominating levels maintain and reinforce the social order. In a similar fashion, the subordinated and excluded develop new forms of resistance. All these tendencies are seen and are possible to read in the city space (Sernhede & Johansson, 2005:22; my translation)

Necessary *changes in local governments* today are (Öhrström, 2005:51ff):

a. To go from *service providers* to *leadership* ('community-manship'?)
b. To go from *administration* to *governance.*

c.  To go from *office management* to *acting on arenas, where venturing
    citizens* ('public entrepreneurs') *participate in various action nets.*

It is increasingly clear that it is not possible in a local community to
reach sustainable development by copying success elsewhere, but only by
connecting to and building new networks locally and outwards, and to
base these on what is unique and organic in the new situation, pointing this
out in all possible ways (so-called *'place marketing'*) (Ekman & Hultman,
2007). What has become a classic centralized government programme
in many countries should be replaced by attempts to create territorial
specializations which cannot be copied elsewhere. They circle around a
mix of specific local conditions which only exist in one place. Continuous
competitive advantages can be created that way (Öhrström, 2005:65).

Local governments are, in many ways, at the centre of development of
a new entrepreneurial society. Also, they need all sorts of entrepreneurs
within their area of interest. They have long tried to promote incoming
business entrepreneurs to create employment and economic growth.
Increasingly, however, they need to focus on other types of entrepreneurs
as well. Above all, their officials need to become more entrepreneurial.

Local government employees' intervention in their own development
could be called *municipal-community entrepreneurship* (Dupuis et al.,
2003:131). But another type of local entrepreneur, central to 'community',
is the 'ordinary' person (Thake & Zadek, 1997; Leadbeater, 1997), that is, a
'new breed of local activists who believe that energy and organization can
improve a community. They can be found organising street patrols to liber-
ate red-light districts, or running local exchange-trading schemes' (Rowan,
1997:T67). But they can also be some prominent member of a local centre,
attracting external investment, thereby improving the employment situation
without necessarily starting any business themselves. These people could be
called *community business magnets* (Vestrum & Borch, 2006:2). Community
business magnets 'entails innovative community effort as a catalyst for the
growth of local employment opportunities' (Dupuis & de Bruin, 2003:115).

Community business magnets could be defined as the mobilization
of resources to create a new activity, institution or enterprise, or an
enterprising environment, embedded in an existing social structure, for the
common good of individuals and groups in a specific region (Johannisson
& Nilsson, 1989). The community is an aggregation of people within a
rural area that are generally accompanied by collective culture / ethnicity
and possibly other shared relational characteristics (Paredo & Chrisman,
2006).

Table 3.5 (adapted from Zerbinati & Soutaris, 2005) presents a summary
of differences between independent business entrepreneurs, corporate

*Table 3.5   Some entrepreneurs and other actors of interest to local governments*

|  | Independent business entrepreneur | Corporate business entrepreneur | Public sector entrepreneurs | Community business magnets |
|---|---|---|---|---|
| *Institutional setting* | New business venture | Business venture | Public sector organization | Community |
| *Role and position* | Independent business people | Corporate executives | Politicians/common sector officers | Local public figure/regional developers |
| *Main activity* | Create and grow business. Usually invest own cash aspiring to create wealth for them and their investor. | Create values with an innovative project. No financial (but career) risk, but also less potential for creating personal wealth. | Create value for citizens by bringing together unique combinations of resources. Career risk and no financial rewards. | Facilitate and inspire entrepreneurship and renewal within their community. Limited focus on financial rewards. |

*Source:*   Adapted from Zerbinati & Soutaris, 2005.

entrepreneurs, common sector entrepreneurs (or municipal-community entrepreneurs) and community business magnets.

Citizen entrepreneurship becomes a way of reimagining the role of individuals within communities, where a sense of community has been 'lost' following the embrace of the market and neo-liberalism during the 1980s (Taylor, 2003). Community business magnets or community business entrepreneurs can play a decisive role for depleted communities (Johnstone & Lionais, 2004). Business magnets or community business entrepreneurs have several similarities with the bricoleurs, a concept which I have mentioned earlier and which I will discuss in more detail in Chapter 7.

Johnstone and Lionais (2004) use the term 'depleted community' to better understand the problems of communities affected by downturns in the local economy. To them, depleted communities are manifestations of uneven development. However, to these two authors, depleted communities are more than simply locations that lack growth mechanisms. They are also areas to which people retain an attachment.

> A depleted community, therefore, continues to exist as a social entity because it is shaped by positive social forces as well as by negative economic forces. While the economic signals are for people to move, the ties to community, the emotional bonds and the social benefits of living there create a powerful resistance to leaving. A depleted community, therefore, maintains a strong and active network of social relations. This can be understood in terms of the distinction made in the literature between *space* and *place*. (Johnstone & Lionais, 2004:218)

Florida (2002) argues, for instance, that certain features of place, such as tolerance to social differences, serve to attract highly creative economic actors who are drivers of wealth creation. In such locations, there is a *synergistic relationship between space and place*. Depleted communities do not enjoy this kind of synergy, however; instead, they suffer from economic stagnation and decline from social problems associated with economic decline.

Depleted communities may also be expected to have a diminished stock of entrepreneurs especially if, in the past, those communities relied on a limited number of growth mechanisms.

Community entrepreneurs and other actors working in depleted communities are likely to experience several obstacles to development, including venture capital equity gaps (Johnstone & Lionais, 1999, 2000), labour skills gaps (Massey, 1995a; Davis & Hulett, 1999) and a lack of business and financial support institutions (Johnstone & Haddow, 2003), as well as a lack of appropriate institutional weight (Amin & Thrift, 1994; Hudson, 2000). Because of these obstacles, conventional private sector development in depleted communities is less robust and less likely. As a consequence, depletion could be something of a permanent condition there.

> Redevelopment in depleted communities is not likely to occur through traditional private industry-led mechanisms. If redevelopment occurs at all, it will probably be through less traditional means. This does not imply that the entrepreneurial process is irrelevant; on the contrary, in areas where capitalistic relations are less robust, the entrepreneurial process will, as it is argued here, manifest itself differently. Depleted communities will act as hosts to alternative forms of entrepreneurship that are adapted to their particular circumstances. (Johnstone & Lionais, 2004:220)

Community business entrepreneurship can be distinguished from social entrepreneurship because it is focused on business organizations rather than charities, social ventures and purely social organizations. The process of community business entrepreneurship is neither entrepreneurship in the traditional business sense nor social entrepreneurship as commonly understood. It employs the tools of the former with the goals of the latter (Johnstone & Lionais, 2004).

Although the barriers to development might be the same as those faced by traditional business entrepreneurs (finance gaps, labour skills gaps, lack of business support institutions, etc.), community business entrepreneurs can adapt in a variety of ways to overcome these obstacles. Some examples from Johnstone and Lionais (2004):

- Community business entrepreneurs can accept unconventionally low rates of return from their projects because personal profit is not an objective.
- Community business entrepreneurs may also have a wider choice of organizational forms to employ when doing business.
- Also, once a project is undertaken, community business entrepreneurs have a different set of resources to call upon to achieve their goals. Among these resources is the access to volunteers.
- Another resource available to community business entrepreneurs is access to capital from neo-traditional sources. Community business entrepreneurs can overcome this by convincing local people, who would normally not invest in private businesses, to invest in their community businesses and organizations.
- Similarly, community business entrepreneurs can attract customers who will buy from them in preference to other (often non-local) organizations (Kilkenny et al., 1999).

A strong commitment to place consequently enables community business entrepreneurs to marshal a number of financial, professional and labour resources around their projects that would not be available to other, more traditional, business entrepreneurs. That is, community business entrepreneurs use the assets of community to overcome the obstacles of depletion.

Studies show that there are four main arenas within which citizen entrepreneurs can have a potentially critical impact (Grenier, 2009:183).

1. *Community renewal* (Brickell, 2000; Thake & Zadek, 1997). Citizen entrepreneurship is said to enhance citizen capital and build community. 'Community leaders and "citizen entrepreneurs" were to become the catalysts for overcoming the problems of run-down neighbourhoods' (Newman, 2001:145).
2. *Voluntary activity professionalization* (Defourney, 2001; Leadbeater, 1997). Citizen entrepreneurship is essential to reform a sector that is 'slow moving, amateurish, under-resourced and relatively closed to new ideas' (Leadbeater, 1997:50). In these accounts, citizen entrepreneurship appears as a kind of modernizing force within the voluntary and community sector, providing an impetus for change, new forms

of voluntary action, and a professional edge that will take the sector forward to further expand its role as a mainstream provider of social services.

3. *Welfare reform* (Leadbeater, 1997; Mort et al., 2003; Thompson et al., 2000). This is another envisaged citizen entrepreneurship as a timely response to social welfare concerns of the day and as an answer to the 'crisis of our welfare systems' (Leadbeater, 1997; Thake & Zadek, 1997). Citizen entrepreneurship is claimed to 'help empower disadvantaged people and encourage them to take greater responsibility for, and control over, their lives' (Thompson et al., 2000:329), and to counter dependence on welfare systems and charity (Leadbeater, 1997; Mort et al., 2003).

4. *Democratic renewal* (Favreau, 2000; Mulgan, 2006). Citizen entrepreneurship can be described as part of the democratization process in society – how people begin to take control of their own lives, the economy and society (Mulgan, 2006).

Two concepts which are of interest in this context are citizen capital and governance.

## 3.9   CITIZEN CAPITAL

It is important for citizen entrepreneurs through marketing and in other ways to build and exploit what I call *citizen capital* (a more common and more accepted term is *social capital*). This new capital concept was launched during the 1990s. The idea of citizen capital came from sociology, and it has proven particularly useful when analysing small firms and entrepreneurship (Westlund & Bolton, 2003). The very term citizen capital is commonly attributed to Jacobs (1961). As their main interest, analysts of citizen capital are concerned with the significance of relationships as a resource for action in the society (Nahapiet & Ghoshal, 1998). This reflects the growing concern over the role of citizen relationships in explaining and understanding business activity. A deeper view is that an actor's embeddedness in social structures endows him or her with citizen capital (Portes & Sensenbrenner, 1993; Oinas, 1999). In the literature, citizen capital is defined as the asset that exists on social relations and network literature (Burt, 1997; Leana & Van Buren, 1999). Citizen capital can be described as a consequence of how social processes work, where lack of cooperation leads to a decreased flow of information and resources (Bjerke & Karlsson, 2011:101). Citizen capital can reduce transaction costs (Putnam et al., 1993) or as Dosi (1988) puts it, by using middlemen that cannot be

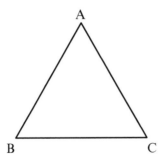

*Source:*   Coleman, 1990.

*Figure 3.5*   *Differences and relationships between human capital and citizen capital*

bought or sold on a market. Citizen capital can also reduce uncertainty (Fafchamps, 2000). To have access to citizen capital can be described as a catalyst for a useful social and economic interaction. All in all, citizen capital offers a way to understand how networks are functioning.

Citizen capital is, as stated by Bourdieu and Wacquant (1992:119):

> The sum of the resources, actual and virtual, that accrue to an individual or a group by virtue of possessing a durable network of more or less institutional-ized relationships of mutual acquaintance and recognition.

Coleman's (1990) definition is however on a different plane from the individual. In his book, he uses a diagram (Figure 3.5) to illustrate the difference between human capital and citizen capital.

As stated by Coleman (1990), human capital exists only in the nodes, with the individuals A, B and C. Citizen capital, on the other hand, is found on the sides of the triangle, that is, in the relationships between the individuals A, B and C. So, Bourdieu and Wacquant (1992) claim that citi-zen capital is *provided to individuals when they are part of a network*, while Coleman (1990) asserts that citizen capital exists *in the very relationships between people in a network*. The *difference* between human capital and citizen capital with Coleman is consequently that the former exists only within people, while the latter exists between people.

Fukyama (1995) defines citizen capital as 'the ability of people to work together for a common purpose in groups or organizations'. Leadbeater (1997) adapts this by suggesting a wider meaning to contain building something of real value for local communities or contexts. The citizen entrepreneur is using some kind of citizen capital – relationships, network, trust and cooperation – to get hold of physical and financial capital that can be of value to the local community.

Citizen capital can be seen as a *glue* as well as a *lubricant* (Anderson & Jack, 2002). When it is seen as a glue, it ties people harder together. When it is seen as a lubricant, it facilitates actions within a network. In the former case, citizen capital may consequently have a binding effect, by preventing deviants from acting and thereby having a negative effect on development. Powell and Smith-Doerr (1994:368) express it such:

> Sociologists and anthropologists have long been concerned with how individuals are linked to one another and how these bonds of affiliation serve as both a lubricant for getting things done and a glue that provides order and meaning to social life.

Citizen capital could also be called *network capital* (Anderson & Jack, 2002:196). Given that citizen capital is what ties people to each other (Putnam et al., 1993), 'capital' is a reasonable picture of the structural aspects of citizen capital. As is the case with financial capital, it is possible to see citizen capital as an asset and a necessary part of a structure. It also influences the structure and thereby its outcome. Furthermore, as a capital, it is tied to the network and becomes an integrated part of its structure.

Citizen capital is a productive asset, making certain specific results which, where citizen capital does not exist, would be impossible or more difficult (Coleman, 1990). In this perspective, citizen capital is created within the embeddedness process, both as a 'result' (a product of network) and as a 'means' (to facilitate what is going on). That embeddedness that takes place becomes an inevitable part of the social structure. However, networks can provide a mechanism for trust and legitimacy, but networks can also function to exclude or include – they can consolidate power without spreading it (Flora, 1998).

I regard citizen capital primarily not as a 'thing' but as a process. It is a process that is created to facilitate an effective exchange of information and resources – an artefact, which can only be studied considering its effects.

There is a close connection between the development of citizen capital and the corresponding growth of the third sector and the number of citizen entrepreneurs. The organization of the third sector has sometimes been called 'the organization of the civic society' (Salomon & Anheier, 1997). It is possible to talk about *civic capital* instead of citizen capital (Evers, 2001). If citizen capital is seen as civic capital, it points out the role of a wider group of political factors, both in terms of its general role in creating confidence and cooperation as well as its in-building orientation and behaviour of groups and associations in the society. Citizen capital is then seen both as an indicator of the development of the civic society (built by social as well as political action) and a way to debate civic engagement with an eye on economic development and governance (Evers, 2001:299).

> Citizen capital constitutes a resource that may be mobilized to a greater or lesser degree within a production process so as to improve its performance. But it is also an end in itself because it is a 'civic' capital contributing to a democratization process. Citizen capital is present in groups, networks and the local social fabric. Inasmuch as it is – at least partly – indivisible and thus cannot be appropriated by any single individual citizen capital constitutes a local quasi-public good. (Laville & Nyssens, 2001:317)

Westlund and Bolton (2003) see certain differences between citizen capital and other capital (Table 3.6).

## 3.10   GOVERNANCE

The concept of 'governance' has arisen on several occasions in this chapter. *Governance* is the name given to the more complex public decision process today.

Up to the 1970s, national states and political authorities could, through their elected advocates, more or less decide on the politics themselves. Today, due to the economic globalization the growth of EU, regions having more power and a demand for a deeper democratization process, government at different levels in a country that wants to keep up with the rest no longer has exclusive power. Within the EU in particular, politics is shaped through different networks, where representatives at the EU level as well as at the national level, non-profit organizations and business companies are made part of the process. Consequently, more parties are involved in different political decisions. A problem with governance experienced by some researchers, for instance, Blomgren and Bergman (2005), is that power becomes more blurred because politics is created in networks. This also makes political accountability more difficult.

As stated by Jessop (1997), governance is associated with a particular form of rule. Unlike the hierarchical rule provided by local state and the anarchy of the market, he argues that governance involves 'heterarchy', which might be defined as 'rule through diversity'.

The change from 'government' to 'governance' means a shift from an isolated public sector to a picture where the business and citizen sectors are part of and share responsibility and tasks.

*Table 3.6    Similarity and dissimilarity between citizen capital and other capital forms*

| Similarities | Dissimilarities |
|---|---|
| *Productivity* | |
| Citizen capital is sunk costs that might become obsolete. | Citizen capital expresses interests of actors, good or bad from society's perspective. It is not neutral with regard to society's interests. |
| Citizen capital can be put in good or bad uses (from society's perspective). | |
| *Vintage* | |
| Citizen capital consists of vintages. | The vintages of citizen capital are more comparable to a port wine than to other capital forms. The composition of vintages is decisive. There is no simple correlation between age and decreasing productivity. |
| *Accumulation and maintenance* | |
| Citizen capital is worn out if it is not intentional. | Citizen capital is a product of both investments and an unintended by-product of other activities. |
| Citizen capital is a result of past activities. | Accumulation of citizen capital does not necessarily need deliberate sacrifices for further benefits. |
| | Citizen capital is harder to construct through external interventions. |
| *Rights of possession versus public goods* | |
| Access to citizen capital is never completely public. Access demands connections to a network and/or certain skills. | Citizen capital is social, that is, it cannot be individually possessed. |
| *Complexity and levels of aggregation* | |
| Diversified citizen capital means less vulnerability to economic structural changes. | Citizen capital is the most diversified, least homogenous form of capital. |
| | Aggregating citizen capital belonging to different levels meets great methodological difficulties. |

*Source:*   Westlund and Bolton (2003).

Urban politics is no longer, if it ever was, a process of hierarchical government in which decisions by local politicians are translated straightforwardly by public bodies into social and economic change. Rather it involves a complex process of negotiation, coalition formation, indirect influence, multi-institution working and public-private partnerships. This diffuse and multi-faceted form of rule has come to be termed 'governance'. (Painter, 1998:261)

The new urban entrepreneurialism typically rests on a public–private partnership focusing on investment and economic development with the speculative construction of place rather than amelioration of conditions within a particular territory as its immediate (though by no means exclusive) political and economic goal. (Harvey, 1989:9)

We are probably moving from a welfare state to a new welfare mix where responsibility should be shared among public authorities, for-profit providers and third-sector organizations on the basis of strict criteria of both efficiency and fairness. (Defourney, 2001:2)

# 4. Knowledge development of marketing

## 4.1 INTRODUCTION

Knowledge development of the academic subject of marketing is presented in this chapter in the same steps as knowledge development of the subject of business entrepreneurship in Chapter 2, that is, in the following order:

- marketing as a function
- personality traits of marketers
- marketing thinking and behaving
- contextual theories of marketing
- results and effects of marketing
- to better understand marketing by understanding customers and/or users better.

The reason to follow this order is not to claim that knowledge development of marketing is the same in all respects as knowledge development of entrepreneurship. In fact, those subjects started quite differently, and also developed in separate directions from the beginning. The most important aspect of knowledge development of marketing as well as of entrepreneurship (which we saw in the last two chapters) and (as well as we will see in the next chapter) of leadership is that all of these disciplines, at present, find it increasingly important and constructive to gain a better understanding of those people who can benefit from using the results of what entrepreneurs, marketers and leaders are doing, which are customers, users and/or followers. If this understanding cannot be considered explicitly, they all find it useful to do it implicitly, at least. By this, I was supported in my opinion that a serious alternative approach to marketing for entrepreneurs is emerging, where customers and/or users are included more actively in the picture – that is, a social phenomenological alternative, next to the dominant rational alternative, which is marketing management.

## 4.2 MARKETING AS A FUNCTION

It is possible to talk about marketing as a function at three different levels:

1. Marketing as a function in society in general.
2. Marketing as a business or activity function.
3. Marketing as a sub-function.

I will look at the marketing as a function in society in general later in section 4.6. Studies of marketing have existed since the beginning of the twentieth century; although Adam Smith (Smith, 1776/1991) had already pointed at the importance of matching the needs of sellers and buyers in a free and competitive exchange, systematic research around marketing did not start until the beginning of the last century. As the marketing concept was developed in the US, with a focus on consumer goods in the beginning, it is natural to take the development in that country as a starting point for an outline of how the academic subject of marketing developed in the beginning – later supplemented by contributions from other countries.

At first, much marketing in practice was based on big companies in the US, such as International Harvester, Curtis Publishing and US Rubber around the time of the First World War. However, in 1881, the railway businessman Joseph Wharton had already donated a sum of money to University of Pennsylvania for them to develop The Wharton School of Finance and Commerce. The action took shape over the years, and in 1904 the course 'Marketing of Products' was started. In 1909, courses in advertising and the art of selling were added (Frankelius et al., 2015).

One could say that the knowledge area of marketing has oscillated from the integrated functional perspective to different sub-functions. When these sub-functions broke through can partly be derived from when they were first allocated their own books, which can be seen in the following list (Johansson, 1991):

- The Theory of Advertising (Scott, 1903)
- Science of Salesmanship (Estabrook, 1904)
- Credit and Its Uses (Prendergast, 1906)
- Scientific Sales Management (Hoyt, 1913)
- Retail Selling and Store Management (Nystrom, 1914)
- Commercial Research (Duncan, 1919)
- Marketing and Merchandising (Butler, 1923)
- Wholesaling (Beckman, 1926)
- World Marketing (Collins, 1935)

–   The Management of Marketing Costs (Culliton, 1948)
–   The Life Cycle and Consumer Behavior (Clark, 1955)

During the 1910s, the overall and integrated perspective was dominant, even though different sub-areas started to develop during this period. These sub-areas were, however, to a large extent treated in an integrated fashion.

During the 1920s and the 1930s, different marketing sub-functions and activities gained interest in education and research. Above all, there was a concentration on structural issues, and issues related to whether the use of middlemen led to higher prices or not were discussed to a large extent. During this period, the study area was also broadened to include industrial goods and services. So, for instance, Converse, in his book (Converse, 1936), has one chapter each on producer goods and services, even though the book is mainly discussing distribution matters.

During the 1940s, the leadership function gained a larger influence on marketing thinking. Market planning, market research and budgeting were important concepts. Problem solving and decision making became central areas, and the connection with behavioural sciences became closer.

Early 'marketing' research in the US followed, by and large, *a functional stream*:

> The commodity school proposed that marketing could best be understood by analysing the types of goods being exchanged, while the functional school asserted that the focus of analysis should be on the activities conducted in the course of the exchange. While institutional theorists appreciated the arguments advanced by their colleagues in these other two schools, they nonetheless believed that the marketing discipline could benefit by paying greater scholarly attention to the organizations that actually perform the functions required to move the goods from the producer to the consumer. (Sheth et al., 1988:73–4)

'For later development of marketing, the functional stream was probably the most important one of the three [mentioned in the above quotation]' (Bjerke & Hultman, 2002:26).

In the beginning of the 1900s, practitioners showed that demand was more complex than a simple function of purchasing power, due to advertising and personal selling. Furthermore, price was not a simple function of production costs even if the concept of marginal utility provided other aspects to the subject. Elasticity in demand considered other factors than just price elasticity alone. Price could be increased through promotional efforts, and production costs could be lowered through the benefits of large scale. The view of *middlemen* also became different – their role became more active and an increasing number of functions could be transferred to intermediaries. The overall concept of *distribution* then became *marketing*.

In early marketing theory, however, no major difference was made between separate sub-activities. The functional orientation in the subject built on identifying different parts of the marketing process, and finding out a structure to execute them in a combination. One author (Shaw, 1912) saw four such parts:

- sales
- assembling, assorting, reshipping or delivering
- risk sharing
- financing.

In principle, all organizations were assumed to consist of these parts, and all of them were supposed to be seen in a similar fashion. However, in practice it was not that simple. There are economies of scale in many of the above activities. Also, risk sharing and development of specialized channel structures could be seen functionally (for example, transporting and insuring) as well as geographically (for example, assembling, assorting and delivering).

From the 1950s, different marketing activities were understood as being related to one another. Exchange of goods and services associated with payments and change of ownership would take place only if time, place as well as assortment were appropriate. Marketing as a whole was expected to make sure that this was the case!

The functional stream was probably the earliest predecessor to the concept of *value chain*, later popularized by Porter (Porter, 1985).

The discussion on whether marketing is a specialist function (among several) in a business-orientated firm, or whether it is a more general philosophy for all organizations, is a commonly held discussion within the subject of marketing. As stated by Hunt (1976), the discussion on the limits and possibilities as far as marketing is concerned was boosted by an article that was presented by the Ohio State University during the 1960s. Marketing researchers at this university wrote that marketing represents 'the process in society by which the demand structure for economic goods and services is anticipated or enlarged and satisfied through the conception, promotion, exchange, and physical distribution of goods and services' (Marketing Staff of the Ohio State University, 1965:43–4). A few years later, Kotler and Levy (1969:15) broadened the discussion to suggest that marketing should also include non-business organizations. They asserted that no organization can function without having a marketing perspective, and 'the choice is whether to do it well or poorly'. Even Brown (1995:35) referred to this discussion of marketing as something broad and general, valid not only in the business world:

Marketing was an all-pervasive activity which applied as much to the selling of politicians, universities and charities as it did to toothpaste, soap and steel. As a consequence of dramatic, post-war social changes and the emergence of large complex professionally managed non-business organizations, such as museums, police departments and trade unions, it has become necessary to broaden the concept of marketing. Traditional notions of the 'product', the 'consumer' and the marketing 'tool-kit' had to be re-defined in non-business terms and attempts made to transfer the principle of effective marketing management – generic product definition, target group identification, customer behaviour analysis, integrated marketing planning, continuous feedback and so on – to the marketing of services, persons and ideas.

Brown (1995:35–6) continues:

Developing this theme Kotler (1972) went on to argue that it was necessary to extend the concept even further. There were, he maintained, three stages of marketing consciousness. The first represented the traditional view of marketing that it was essentially a business-oriented philosophy involving market transactions, the economic exchange of goods and services. Consciousness two held that marketing was applicable to all organizations that had customers or clients, even though payment in the normal sense may not take place. However, the third level of consciousness, deemed the 'generic' concept, contended that marketing was not only relevant to *all* organizations, be they churches, political parties or government departments, but to the relations between the organization and *all* of its publics, not only the consuming public. . . . he [Kotler] concluded that 'marketing can be viewed as a *category of human action*, distinguishable from other categories of human action such as voting, loving, consuming and fighting'. . . . Needless to say, not everybody shared Kotler's marketing megalomania.

Gummesson (1975) as well as Grönroos (1994) claimed that marketing is more of an overall management responsibility than a specialist function: contacts with the market are spread all over the firm and there is a large number of part-time marketers in all organizations (Gummesson, 1990, 1991). This means that individuals in different specialist functions also contribute to the firm's marketing efforts, directly or indirectly.

From the functional stream, it is possible to see the subject of *marketing* develop into *sub-schools*, which jointly can be labelled 'mainstream marketing'. Sub-schools constituting mainstream marketing today are:

- macro-marketing
- consumer behaviour
- managerial marketing
- marketing channels and distribution
- international marketing
- industrial marketing.

As in other research influenced by systems theory, the wider links between marketing and the environment are focused in *macromarketing* research (see, for example, Holloway & Hancock, 1964; Fisk, 1967). This area is defined by Hunt (1977:56) as follows: 'Macromarketing refers to the study of (1) marketing systems, (2) the impact and consequences of marketing systems on society, and (3) the impact and consequences of society on marketing systems'.

The importance and function played by middlemen in marketing was stressed rather early in the development of this subject. Among others, Butler (1923) coined the term 'utilities' in this context and separated elementary utility (what goods basically provide) form utility (to develop products and make them appealing to customers), place utility (buyers normally need products in other places than where they are produced, consequently transportation) and time utility (storage time between production and consumption). He asserted that middlemen could provide time and place utility more effectively than producers.

A general definition of marketing is to claim that the function of marketing is to reach objectives being set up, including determining the demands, needs and wishes that exist in those markets which are in focus, to deliver that satisfaction which is wanted there, and to do this more effectively than competitors.

The dominating marketing approach today is *managerial marketing*, which consequently is presented in this book as one of the two alternative ways of marketing for entrepreneurs, that is, the managerial approach. I will return to managerial marketing in more detail shortly.

## 4.3 PERSONALITY TRAITS OF MARKETERS

Research on the necessary personality traits to be a successful marketer provides very little over and above what we can read about personality traits of entrepreneurs in Chapter 2 or of leaders in Chapter 5, as I see it. One way to express the matter in question is (Smith, 2011):

> In order to make it as a successful marketer in a senior position, there are many traits of character that you must have. It is not just a matter of how to be able to understand and succeed in a marketing position as such, but what is more important is to be able to establish and implement the business plan of the firm from a sales and marketing perspective. Marketing managers of today are very different from marketing managers ten years ago. At the same time as they have a general ability to ensure that their group implement the marketing plan they intend to carry out, it is equally important to keep themselves updated with the latest in marketing techniques, changes in the economic and political environment and to have an ability to function in a partnership with professional sales people.

A successful marketing manager should have the following characteristics as stated by the same author:

*Vision.* A strong vision for what they want to achieve in terms of their brand in the short as well as in the long term, plus an ability to articulate this vision on various platforms and via different communication channels.

*Strategic thinking.* To have an ability to implement a marketing strategy, which is in line with the more total business strategy, and to 'think' strategically in all marketing aspects is not only something a marketing manager must have – it is also decisive negotiation skill. If a marketing manager is not a strategic thinker, he or she is simply not a qualified marketing manager and another role would be better for that person. A marketing manager needs to have a strong understanding of the market trends, be able to develop a goal-directed marketing strategy and reach the objectives of the firm.

*Business acumen.* The marketing department must be able to understand and to implement the total business plan. This means to understand what is essential and to be able to influence the business operation. To know the market, what makes it tick, change and develop is extremely important. A successful marketing manager can run business operations and encourage growth through innovative business solutions.

*Consumer focus.* A successful marketing manager needs to be very intimate with his or her consumers. He or she needs to be able to understand every aspect of the consumers' characteristics, wishes, dislikes and prime movers. To feel close to the consumers means in a way to share their bed, to accept their habits even if they may be experienced as heavy snorers, and to understand their sleeping habits. It might mean knowing that the first thing that a 'normal' consumer does in the morning is to pick up his or her I-phone, and that he or she sometimes wakes up in the middle of the night to have a drink or to go to the toilet. All outstanding marketing managers walk, so to say, regularly in the consumers' shoes in order to understand what it means to be a consumer in their case. They take in feedback and modify their goods and services accordingly. A marketing manager knows when and to whom to direct his or her efforts, and also has an ability to find the consumer, no matter where he or she is.

*Champion behind the brand.* To have a passion for one's brand means to eagerly find results. If you do not love your brand, you cannot market it. To inspire one's team, consumers and market to love one's brand means for a successful marketing manager to love one's brand, and to inspire their customers to see the passion that lives in every brand just like that.

*Personality.* A bit of personality can go far in marketing. When talking to an entrepreneur or a leader and asking about his or her favourite as far as a marketing manager is concerned, the answer will be something like 'he or she has a great personality, is straightforward and strategic, and has fun. People expect you to be good at performing, to be at the top of what you want to represent and to be innovative and self-confident'.

As with the case of entrepreneurs and of leaders, it is hard to find unique characteristics of marketers. Many managers, not being entrepreneurs, leaders or marketers, have similar traits.

## 4.4 MARKETING THINKING AND BEHAVING

What has dominated much of marketing thinking is the expression *4Ps*, which was coined by McCarthy (McCarthy, 1960) and later developed by Philip Kotler (1967). The original 4Ps stood for Product, Price, Place and Promotion; as time went by, these were supplemented by other Ps such as Policy, Personnel, etc. Perhaps having additional Ps meant that the idea behind this approach was no longer sustainable as a concept valid for all marketing areas.

- *Product* relates to the company's product, issued to become the 'correct' one for the market niche that has been selected. In practice, product means that combination of a good and a service – or other kind of value – which the company offers its customers.
- *Price* is about adapting the product's pricing so that the sales offer becomes attractive to the customer and profitable to the company. The price is also important as a differentiator and as a communication factor.
- *Place* is about all issues concerning how the product is to reach the customers in the chosen market niche, for instance, where it is sold and how logistics and distribution are to be organized.
- *Promotion* is focusing on how and through which market channel communication is to be designed.

During the 1950s and 1960s, the management-orientated marketing perspective became the dominating approach. Early contributors were, for example, Howard (1957), McCarthy (1960) and Buzzell (1964). The giant in marketing management, however, was Philip Kotler, who first published his *Marketing Management* in 1967 – it is probably the most widely read book in marketing. Due to its dominance, it is sometimes referred to as *the marketing Bible*.

With its origin in well-established theories of microeconomics, based on the assumption of an open market with pure transactions and influenced by recent findings in behavioural sciences, the managerial view of marketing became the *paradigm of marketing*. In the view of many commentators, one of its benefits is that the management paradigm offers a distinct guide to marketers in their actions and a framework that is rational and easy to understand.

One of the most widespread definitions of marketing, the official definition from the *American Marketing Association* (*AMA*), clearly demonstrates the managerial paradigm. The original version from 1935 was not changed until 1981. After that, reformulations took place more often:

- Marketing is the performance of business activities that direct the flow of goods, and services from producers to consumers (*AMA* 1935).
- Marketing is the (social) process of planning and executing the conception, pricing, promotion, and distribution of ideas, goods, and services to create exchanges that satisfy individual and organizational objectives (*AMA* 1981).
- Marketing is an organizational function and a set of processes for creating, communicating, and delivering value to customer and for managing customer relationships in ways that benefit the organization and its stakeholders (*AMA* 2004).
- Marketing is the activity, set of institutions, and processes for creating, communicating, delivering, and exchanging of offerings that have value to customers, clients, partners, and society at large (*AMA* 2007).

The 2004 definition lasted only for three years, compared to the decades that passed before the previous changes in definition. This probably reflects both the more changing business world and also a belief that a new definition can better cover such a complex field as marketing. For the academics involved in the new formulation in 2007, the definition probably reflects a different perspective. But, in reality, much of the discipline's *basic principles* remain as far as the function as well as the content of marketing is concerned, the way I look at it.

Well-known marketing terms in the managerial view on it are *marketing concept* (McKitterick, 1957); *market myopia* (Levitt, 1960); *marketing mix* (McCarthy, 1960; Borden, 1964); *marketing planning*; *segmentation* (Smith, 1956); *product life cycle* (Levitt, 1965); *market positioning* (Ries & Trout, 1981; *market orientation* (Narver & Slater, 1990) – the list of contributions from the managerial view on marketing is quite long.

Today, the managerial view of marketing is, among most scholars, still as valid as before (Kotler, 2015): To transform marketing strategy into marketing programmes, marketing managers must make basic decisions on marketing expenditures, marketing mix and marketing allocation. Then, the company has to decide how to divide the total marketing budget among the various tools in the marketing mix: product, price, place and promotion – all consistent with managerial marketing, which is very rational in its assumptions with a view on behaviour in accordance with the *economic man* in microeconomics.

Kotler (1986) suggests that marketers must also engage in *megamarketing*, where power and public relations are important. For instance, in blocked or protected markets, marketing should be more of a political nature:

> In addition to the four Ps of marketing strategy – product, price, place and promotion – executives must add two more – power and public relations. I call such strategic thinking megamarketing. Megamarketing thus takes an enlarged view of the skills and resources needed to enter and operate in certain markets. In addition to preparing attractive offers for customers, megamarketing may use inducements and sanctions to gain the desired responses from gatekeepers. (Kotler, 1986:119)

In situations where relationships between sellers and buyers act in any form of administrated system, or as Arndt (1979) calls it, 'domesticated markets', marketing changes character and becomes more of a political issue.

By following traditions brought up by Simon (1947) and Cyert and March (1963), many studies in marketing have followed a behavioural tradition to discuss internationalization; the so-called Uppsala School suggested, for example, a sequential pattern when internationalizing (for instance, Johansson & Vahlne, 1977).

## 4.5   CONTEXTUAL THEORIES OF MARKETING

One kind of contextual theory of marketing started from research on agricultural goods, and the conclusion that marketing in practice depends on the characteristics of the product being marketed and some of its knowledge is still with us today. Several systems for classification of goods have, for instance, been based on buyer habits, such as convenience goods, emergency goods and shopping goods (Sheth et al., 1988; here Charles Parlin is given credit for generating the initial classification system in 1912 published in *Department Store Report*, Volume B, October); convenience goods, shopping goods and speciality goods (Copeland, 1923); red, orange and yellow goods (Aspinwall, 1958); and shopping and non-shopping goods (Bucklin, 1962). Later classifications in this respect have also been suggested, based on behavioural sciences aspects such as perceived risk and expected effort from customers.

Some important special areas of marketing grew into prominence during the 1960s, 1970s and 1980s. Noteworthy among these are international, industrial (or business-to-business, B2B, as it is often referred to today) and service marketing.

The International Marketing Committee Review Board defined the field of *industrial marketing* (Industrial Marketing Committee Review Board, 1954). Early works in this area were done for example by Robinson et al. (1967); Webster and Wind (1972); Sheth (1973) and in Europe among others by Håkansson and other members of the IMD (Industrial Marketing and Purchasing) Group (for instance, Håkansson, 1982).

In *service marketing*, foundations were laid by scholars such as Richard Normann (1978, 1984); Evert Gummesson (1977, 1979); and Christian Grönroos (1979, 1983) in the Nordic countries as well as Robert Judd (1964); Lynn Shostack (1977); and Leonard Berry (1980) in the US. Much work done in this area can be contained in the managerial paradigm or in relationship marketing (more about this concept later). Much of service marketing and special conditions related to marketing of services are commonly regarded as a special area of marketing closely related to the differences between goods and services. These differences, however, can be questioned in the context of marketing today. In most marketing situations, what is offered to the market is a combination, having tangible as well as intangible components which are inseparable and where differences between these components are very blurred. Activities associated with marketing goods and marketing services are no longer useful to separate, at least not from a practical point of view, as no goods can be sold without services being involved. Every product is more or less service dominated.

Even the manufacturing industry 'is selling and exporting more and more services, either by services being integrated with the goods, or by selling them as supplements to the goods' (Anér & Rentzhog, 2012:13). The trend is referred to as *servicification*.

Models for firms' internationalization and international marketing behaviour are developed within *international marketing*. Neo-classical trade theory has been used to explain the pattern of movements of products across borders. Burenstam Linder (1961) claimed that home market demand was the driving force in the development of potential export products. Exports could be expected to be directed to similar foreign markets, and the more similar demand the structures in two markets, the higher the trade potential between the two countries. Vernon (1966) developed this thinking later into the *product cycle theory*.

International business research was mainly interested in big multinational corporations and their investments. Domestic market characteristics as well as internal firm characteristics were used to explain the selection of foreign markets and the establishment of foreign subsidiaries (Calvert, 1981).

In 1955, the researchers Katz and Lazarsfeld presented a book about marketing communication, which threw light on the phenomenon of 'word-of-mouth' in particular. This is the importance of what customers say to each other – what in our modern Internet-world is called *viral marketing* (Katz & Lazarsfeld, 1955).

## 4.6 RESULTS AND EFFECTS OF MARKETING

One consequence of marketing, which is often denoted, is measured in terms of growth and market share, and this has been the case during most periods of the knowledge development of the subject of marketing.

Many marketing planning models were developed in the 1950s and 1960s. At that time, big corporations were often bureaucratic and hierarchical in their structure (Webster, 1992) and large planning systems were natural both from a corporate perspective as well as from messages in various management seminars.

One example of the view of *benefits from marketing planning* can be found in Oxenfeldt (1966). He cited six such benefits that a firm can derive from setting up such a plan:

– coordination of the activities of many individuals whose actions are interrelated over time
– identification of expected developments
– preparedness to meet changes when they occur
– minimization of non-rational responses to the unexpected
– better communication among executives
– minimization of conflicts among individuals which, if individuals are on their own, would result in a sub-optimization of the goals of the company.

One book from around that time presents the advantages of marketing planning as follows:

The trend toward increased acceptance of marketing planning is a fundamental premise of business adjustment to present and future market patterns. As planning becomes a basic management technique and the cornerstone of management philosophy in designing market systems, practical methods of linking many market-related decisions and programs will be developed. The firm will be better able to capitalize on areas of market opportunity and profit, thereby achieving corporate goals in the market. (Kelley, 1972:54)

## 4.7   TO BETTER UNDERSTAND MARKETERS BY UNDERSTANDING CUSTOMERS AND/OR USERS BETTER

When markets changed, so did marketing. This will probably be so even in the future. Today, consumption patterns are changing and are becoming ever more complex. Old knowledge about customers will be – old! What is needed is continuous follow-ups and surveillance of the way in which the market is using and relating itself to the company's own products.

What will this lead to in terms of the future of marketing? Firstly, it will be increasingly important *to have good knowledge of one's customers.* Secondly, it will be more important than ever before for companies to *do well in terms of communication.*

What will be increasingly required is probably a fit between the company's values and those values which are centrally held among customers. This means that the image which a company has on the market (or on different submarkets) will determine which customers will be attracted by its own sales offers. Image should be seen quite broadly here, and it is necessary to be aware that it might be difficult to alter it to any great extent in the short term. If there is no fit, there is no way to make good business. The conclusion is that it is not enough to just know one's target groups and their wishes; it is also necessary to know one's own values and, most importantly, how one is perceived by the target group.

The need for information is well satisfied by the seller for the buyer in most areas. This relates to companies' advertising and other promotional efforts which take place to convey the message about their goods and services. But, in the other direction, from buyer to seller, the information flow is not equally natural and effective (Lekvall & Wahlbin, 2001).

It sounds obvious that communication in business should take place on the customers' and other users' conditions, but you only need to look briefly at a daily newspaper to realize that this does not always take place in practice. However, this means, in extension, that it might sometimes be necessary to have a good understanding of and close feeling for the receivers' way of thinking, and their way of using various symbols and codes in their language.

It is important, of course, that all communication outputs from a company give the same message and communicate at the same pitch. Communication outputs are here interpreted in a very wide sense. These cover the way telephone exchanges operate, how staff members behave on various occasions when in contact with customers and other target groups, the tone in demand notes and more. Even though this discussion has been going on for a very long time, there are, in my opinion, not many companies that have a complete control of their communication. Important to keep in mind here is that the company's communication should be 'true'. It must mirror those values which are real for a company. It is very difficult to build an image which does not correspond with reality. Sooner or later, customers will discover if that is not the case, and they will feel cheated. And you do not want to continue to do business with somebody who has cheated you.

Frankelius et al. (2015:13) claimed that one of three changes that has taken place within the subject of marketing in recent years is the concept of creating value by involving people outside the company (in their opinion, the other two changes are the new media landscape and that marketing should be seen as an integrated part of what a business is doing). Shimizu (2016) refers to this as *co-marketing* or *symbiotic marketing*.

> Marketing is, in a way, so much more than separate activities such as advertising campaigns, market surveys, segmentations, positional strategies and clever sales promotion at Christmas time. We claim that marketing should be understood as a social and interactive phenomenon, that is, as something which is created and exists in human interplay, between people when they interact. (Svensson & Östberg, 2016:9; my translation)

Wikström and Normann (1994:160; my translation) write the following: 'The role of a company does no longer limit itself to providing goods and services. It is rather a question of putting together a system of activities, within which customers can create their own values'.

An extension of this way of looking was the idea about value co-creation between the company and its customers. The customer becomes a co-producer or a co-creator, or the way Vargo and Lusch (2004:3) put it: 'The customer is always a co-creator of value.' In earlier perspectives, as stated by the same authors, the customers were rather seen as passive receivers of value.

To go back in time, buyer behaviour theories have been important contributions to marketing knowledge (for example, Katona, 1953; Howard & Sheth, 1969; Howard, 1963). Sheth et al. (1988) mention important concepts such as *perceived risk* (Bauer, 1960), *information processing* (Bettman, 1979), *reference group influence* (Bourne, 1965), *social class* (Martineau, 1958), *involvement* (Krugman, 1965), *psychographics* (Wells, 1975), *attitudes* (Hansen, 1972) and *situational influences* (Belk, 1974).

The focus on buyers and their needs is one of the most fundamental aspects of modern marketing. In the expanding economy of the 1950s and 1960s, the consumers' behaviour was already of utmost importance, and marketing was the business function to deal with this:

> Growing acceptance of this consumer concept has had, and will have, far-reaching implications for business, achieving a virtual revolution in economic thinking. As the concept gains ever greater acceptance, marketing is emerging as the most important single function in business. (Keith, 1960:35)

Other important concepts from behavioural sciences included in marketing were *cognitive dissonance* and *motivation*.

Many marketers emphasize a focus on customers. However, there can be a major difference between what you say and what you practise, e.g., to claim that you *are* marketing-orientated compared to actually *being* so (the same thing often goes for leadership when claiming that 'the employees are the most important asset in my firm') (Argyris & Schön, 1989).

As mentioned, one much discussed issue in modern marketing is its *marketing concept* (versus the *product concept* – this is related to the market orientation in a company). The marketing concept, as interpreted by Kotler (2001:12), 'holds the key to achieving its organizational goals and consists of determining the needs and wants of the target markets and delivering the desired satisfactions more effectively and efficient than competitors'. The marketing concept can be seen as a three-fold conceptualization concerned with:

1.   Orientation on customers and their needs.
2.   Long-run profitability as an objective rather than sales volume.
3.   Integration and coordination of marketing and other corporate functions.

On the other hand, the *product concept* (Kotler, 2001:11) 'holds that customers favour those products that offer the most quality, performance, or innovative features. Managers in these organizations focus on making superior products and improving them over time, assuming that buyers can appraise quality and performance'.

*Market orientation*, which can be understood as conceptualizing and operationalizing the marketing concept, is commonly regarded as critical for long-term success and superior performance at the marketplace (Kohli & Jaworski, 1990; Narver & Slater, 1990; Jaworski & Kohli, 1993) and is seen, if it exists, as part of a firm's culture, affecting both its learning capability and its strategic resources position. In the marketing literature, we can read that market orientation comprises three components (compare the marketing concept earlier):

1. Customer orientation.
2. Competitive focus.
3. Cross-functional coordination.

Kohli and Jaworski (1990:13) conclude: '[Market orientation provides] a unifying focus for the effects and projects of individuals, thereby leading to superior performance'.

Market orientation is regarded as directly relating to business performance. The components of market orientation influence a firm's 'core capabilities' such as customer service, quality, and innovation. These core capabilities may in turn affect aspects of the firms' 'competitive advantage' (consumer loyalty; new product success; market share), leading overall to positive business performance such as profitability and sales growth (Narver & Slater, 1990; Slater & Narver, 1994a, 1994b, 1995).

Langerak (1997) extends the constructs made by Narver and Slater, and looks at market orientation as the business philosophy that commits the organization to the continuous creation of customer value, doing this by encouraging four core skills (Langerak et al.,1997):

● customer orientation
● competitor orientation
● supplier orientation
● interfunctional coordination.

One fundamental theoretical discussion in marketing today is whether the concepts of *transactions or relations* are *the key* to what marketing is all about. The traditional US perspective (which is ruling today) is that research in marketing ultimately studies transactions driven by exchanges of value. On the other hand, contemporary schools among some researchers, especially in the Nordic countries and in the UK, claim that relationships to customers and others are the essence of the marketing discipline. No representative from the two perspectives, however, excludes the importance of the other, but supports the prominence of the own focus.

One leading advocate of the US research on *transactional marketing* (Kotler, 1972:48) writes that:

> The core concept of marketing is the transaction. A transaction is the exchange of values between two parties. The things-of-values need not be limited to goods, services, and money: they include other resources such as time, energy, and feelings.

Another leading US researcher (Hunt, 1983:12–13) states: 'that the basic subject matter of marketing is the exchange relationship or transaction. Marketing is the behavioural science that seeks to explain exchange relationships.'

Transactions are explained by exchanges of value. Oliver, in a book with the challenging title *Marketing Today*, says (Oliver, 1990:114):

> Despite the difficulty in defining the edge of marketing, the central focus is on exchange. An exchange is precipitated when a person recognizes that another person has something he would like to have. They both assign values to that which they currently have, and to that which they would like to have. If they both value what the other has, more than they value what they have themselves, then the exchange will be mutually beneficial. Fundamental marketing activities therefore include the need to understand what it is that buyers value, to design an offering so that it has those values, and to ensure that the values are communicated effectively.

Bagozzi (1974, 1975) goes so far as to claim that marketing can be regarded as the 'science of exchanges'; he asserts that marketing is a general business function of universal applicability and marketing is the discipline of exchange behaviour. Bagozzi was inspired by ideas from anthropology and sociology, and suggested that market transactions should be seen as complex exchange systems. He was partly elaborating the idea which was launched already a couple of decades earlier by Sidney Levy (1959) that market transactions to a large extent were symbolic.

Especially in the Nordic countries and in the UK, research in the marketing discipline has for a long time focused on different *relational aspects*. This does not necessarily mean, as already noted, that other aspects have been neglected, but a growing interest in relationships started early in that part of the world, for example within research in industrial marketing (Ford, 1990, 1998) as well as in service marketing (Gummesson, 1999). However, the number of relationship papers presented at US marketing conferences has been increasing rapidly.

One could say that *customer relationships* are part of the marketing core; promises are mutually exchanged and kept between buyers and sellers. As a result, customer relationships are established, strengthened and developed for commercial purposes. As an advocate for 'relationship marketing', Grönroos (1990:5) defines marketing:

> Marketing is to establish, maintain and enhance long-term customer relationships (often but not necessarily always long-term customer relations) so that the objectives of the parties involved are met. This is done by mutual exchange and fulfilment of promises.
> Furthermore, this definition can be accompanied by the following supplement: The resources of the seller – personnel, technology and systems – have to

be used in such a manner that the customer's trust in the resources involved and, thus, in the firm itself is maintained and strengthened. The various resources the customer encounters in the relation may be of any kind and part of any business function. However, these resources and activities cannot be totally predetermined and explicitly categorized in a general definition.

Several approaches to research where relationships are important exist in parallel, for example, the network approach (Johansson & Mattson, 1993), interactive marketing (Håkansson, 1982), direct marketing (Davies, 1992) as well as the concept of relationship marketing as introduced by Berry (1983). These approaches to marketing are often presented as alternatives to the managerial paradigm; it is even sometimes stated that the relationship perspective is more relevant in the modern business world of today. What these approaches have in common is the prominence of relationships as an important concept in marketing.

The idea of transactional marketing versus relationship marketing is sometimes seen as two ends of intended time of the involvement with individual customers (for instance, Grönroos, 1991; Gummesson, 1999). This view can be further illustrated by a view from Gummesson (1999:21):

> In order to conceptually incorporate transaction marketing in RM (relationship marketing), it can be seen as a zero point on the *RM scale*. The scope of the relationships can then be enhanced until a customer and a supplier are practically the same organization. No doubt we were misled by the authoritarian neo-classical economics in which markets are made up of standardized goods and anonymous masses who behave according to simplistic and distinct laws. Only the *price relationship* exists, and I call that the *zero relationship* on the RM scale.

As stated by Gummesson (1999), the relationship marketer should work with thirty different relations, which in turn can be divided into three different levels:

- *Market relations* – relations to customers, suppliers, retailers and competitors.
- *Mega relations* – relations to politicians and other important decision makers and moulders of public opinion, such as researchers, experts and journalists.
- *Nano relations* – relations within own organization and with owners, investors, internal customers, advertising agencies and more.

Interactions and relationships are, consequently, noted to some extent in marketing research since several years. But even if different contributions to marketing thinking may note interactions and relations as central phenomena in marketing situations, there are few authors who come to a halt at this observation, analyse how these relations *really* work and reflect on different consequences of them for society and people. It is possible to use symbolic interactionism in such a project, which, as stated by Svensson and Östberg (2016), uncovers several of those circumstances and phenomena which are hidden behind marketing as consistent with the managerial perspective. As the reader of this book will discover later, this is one part of the discussion about an alternative marketing approach which entrepreneurs can use, distinct from the more established managerial marketing.

Regis McKenna used the concept of 'relationship marketing' (RM) in a book title in 1991 (McKenna, 1991). He analysed some growing technology firms in Silicon Valley and showed how the marketing world had changed from the idea of massive advertising campaigns which were supposed to dictate to the customers what to buy, to a personal relationship building supported by computers, which assisted in keeping information about persons and about relations between the company and every customer.

It is possible to separate five components in the RM approach, as presented by Berry (1983) and others:

- focus on existing customers (supported by the thesis that it costs more to try to recruit new customers than to develop existing relationships)
- involve all colleagues in marketing (the importance of meeting customers)
- value-creating systems – services (customer and company are co-creating)
- value is defined by the experienced quality by the customer
- personal dialogue (rather than advertising, for instance).

The approach has several merits, but in the real world, the philosophy seems to have advantages as well as disadvantages; there are many different types of contexts and no marketing philosophy fits them all. Furthermore, there are signs that some customers are tired of all relations, which is understandable as it is almost impossible to buy a hot dog without being asked whether you are interested in joining a customer club. Another criticism against the RM approach could be that it does not clearly point at social and environmental responsibilities and similar matters. Like the classical marketing approach (the marketing mix), the approach focuses on customers, thereby running the risk that a number of other factors in the environment are neglected in the analysis.

As stated by Bjerke and Hultman (2002), this is too much of a simplification of how the two perspectives of RM and transactional marketing relate to each other. Since the two perspectives focus upon different aspects of marketing (unless, as I do in this book, you go further and look at them from the point of view of two strictly different philosophical perspectives), it is possible to claim that both could be needed if we want to understand marketing behaviour. The problem is, however, that while the conceptual framework for transactional marketing is more elaborated – especially as perceived by most people through the well-known managerial perspective – the conceptual status of RM is still rather loose and scattered. So, in order to get a more specific conceptual orientation of RM in modern times, the 'co-creational' aspect of it could be stressed – which I do in this book.

Business relations operate in general at many different levels, and RM can follow this pattern as well. Within the area of marketing, RM is, as we have seen, often referred to as focusing upon long-lasting relations with customers. However, a more extensive perspective can be taken as three different levels for RM can be identified (Li et al., 1997):

1.  *Integration of the development of long-term customer relationships with the traditional marketing activities.* Relationship selling is then marketing-orientated towards a strong, lasting relationship with individual accounts (for instance, Jackson, 1985); or, described differently, the goal of relationship selling is to earn a position of preferred supplier by developing trust in key accounts over a period of time (Doyle & Roth, 1992).
2.  *Relations as a change in the firm's strategic orientation.* Here, the conceptual aspects of customer relationships and its strategic consequences are in focus for marketing, supported by a well-known statement of Berry (1983:25): 'Relationship marketing is attracting, maintaining and – in multi-service organizations – enhancing customer relationships.'
3.  *General relationship management* is the third category. *Broadened RM* can be described as follows: 'Relationship marketing refers to all marketing activities directed towards establishing, developing and maintaining successful relational exchanges' in supplier-orientated, lateral, buyer-orientated and internal partnership (Hunt & Morgan, 1994:22). This can be defined as a type of management in RM, which orientates itself towards establishing close interactions with selected customers, suppliers and competitors. This creation of value is developed through cooperative and collaborative efforts (Parvatiyar & Sheth, 1994). To manage all types of business relations in the network would then be the key to success.

Another further development of RM which is possible to see today, is to study it from a perspective of a paradigmatic shift, in what is called *co-creation marketing*:

The meaning of value and the process of value creation are rapidly shifting from a product- and firm-centric view to personalized customer experiences.

Informed, networked, empowered, and active customers are increasingly co-creating value with the firm. The interaction between the firm and the consumer is becoming the locus of value creation and value extraction. As value shifts to experiences, the market is becoming a forum for conversation and interactions between customers, customer communities, and firm. It is this dialogue, access, transparency, and understanding of risk-benefits that is central to the next practice in value creation. (Prahalad & Ramaswamy, 2004c:5)

It is possible to see the development of co-operation between producer and customer to genuine co-creation marketing in the following way:

-   In their review of the literature on 'customer participation in produc-tion', Bendapudi and Leone (2003) found that the first academic work dates back to 1979.
-   From 1990 onwards, new themes are emerging: Czepiel (1990) suggests that customers' participation may lead to greater customer satisfaction; Kelley et al. (1990) are dealing with productivity, but suggest other ways to look at customer participation: quality, employee's performance and emotional responses.
-   Although not reviewed by Bendapudi and Leone (2003), the ground-breaking article by Normann and Ramirez (1993) suggests that suc-cessful companies do not focus on themselves or even on the industry, but on the value-creating system.
-   Michel et al. (2008) recognize the influence of Normann (2001) on their own work and acknowledge similarity between the concepts of co-production and co-creation: 'his customer co-production mirrors the similar concept found in Foundational Premise 6 (FP6)' (concern-ing the reading of FP6, see below). The authors suggest that Normann enriched the 'service-dominant logic', particularly through his idea of 'density' of offerings (for 'service-dominant logic', see below).
-   In a letter sent to the editor of the *Harvard Business Review* in reaction to an article of Pine et al. (1995), Schrage (1995) argues that not all customers are alike in their capacity to bring some kind of knowledge to the firm.
-   Wikström sees the role of customers as beginning to change (Wikström, 1996).
-   Firat et al. (1995) introduced the concept of 'customerization' (which is a buyer-centric evolution of the mass-customization process) and stated that it enables customers to serve as 'the co-producer of the good and service offering'. However, Bendapudi and Leone (2003) concluded in their article that 'the assumption of greater customiza-tion under co-production may hold only when the customer has the expertise to craft a good or service to his or her liking'.

- At the turn of the century, Prahalad and Ramaswamy (2000) produced another important piece of work, and built further on ideas from Normann and Ramirez (1993).
- In 2004, Prahalad and Ramaswamy (2004a) kept working on their original idea, published four years earlier. At the same time, Vargo and Lusch (2004) published on the service-dominant logic of marketing (see Tables 4.1 and 4.2). The process of value creation is covered in Foundation Premise 6 (FP6), which, in fact, is opposing the goods-

*Table 4.1   Goods-dominant logic vs service-dominant logic*

|  | Goods-dominant logic | Service-dominant logic |
|---|---|---|
| Value driver | Value-in-exchange | Value-in-use or value-in-context |
| Creator of value | Firm, often with input from firms in a supply chain | Firm, network partners, and customers |
| Process of value creation | Firms embed value in 'goods' or 'services', value is 'added' by enhancing or increasing attributes | Firms propose value through market offerings, customers continue value-creation process through use |
| Purpose of value | Increase wealth for the firm | Increase adaptability, survivability and system wellbeing through service (applied knowledge and skills) of others |
| Measurement of value | The amount of nominal value, price received in exchange | The adaptability and survivability of the beneficiary system |
| Resources used | Primary operand resources | Primary operand resources, sometimes transferred by embedding them in operand resources-goods |
| Role of firm | Produce and distribute value | Propose and co-create value, provide service |
| Role of goods | Units of output, operand resources that are embedded with value | Vehicle for operand resources, enables access to benefits of firm competences |
| Role of customers | To 'use up' or 'destroy' value created by the firm | Co-create value through the integration of firm-provided resources with other private and public resources |

*Source:*   Adapted from Vargo et al., 2008.

*Table 4.2     Conceptual marketing progress*

| Goods-dominant logic concepts | Transitional concepts | Service-dominant logic concepts |
|---|---|---|
| Goods | Services | Services |
| Products | Offerings | Experiences |
| Feature/attribute | Benefit | Solution |
| Value-added | Coproduction | Co-creation of value |
| Profit maximization | Financial engineering | Financial feedback/learning |
| Price | Value delivery | Value proposition |
| Equilibrium systems | Dynamic systems | Complex adaptive systems |
| Supply chain | Value chain | Value-creation network |
| Promotion | Integrated marketing communications | Dialogue |
| To market | Market to . . . | Market with . . . |
| Product orientation | Market orientation | Service orientation |

*Source:*  Adapted from Lusch & Vargo, 2006.

dominant logic versus the service-dominant logic, and the reading of which in this article was "The customer is always a co-producer". In Vargo and Lusch (2006), FP6 was reformulated to "The customer is always a co-creator".

Tables 4.1 and 4.2 summarize the goods-dominant logic and the service-dominant logic, which, as we know, was a decisive step towards increasingly talking about 'co-creation of value (and of marketing)'.

The Internet has fundamentally changed the logic of markets, and created new rules for marketing. As an example, small firms (and entrepreneurs) or genuinely niched products today have a much larger possibility of reaching customers, and this can be done all over the world today. *Digital marketing* has become a matter of course for marketing (Frankelius et al., 2015).

Generally, we can say that to a large extent, managers and researchers in marketing have ignored the customer, that agent who most dramatically has transformed the industrial system as we know it (Prahalad & Ramaswamy, 2004a).

There is more about knowledge development of the subject of marketing in Chapter 7, when I scrutinize four concepts of great importance to this book:

● market
● customer

- user
- value creation.

*The principles* behind the two marketing alternatives, which are the managerial approach and the social phenomenological approach (that is, the two orientations around which my discussion in this book about how marketing for entrepreneurs is built), will also be given in Chapter 7. Chapters 8–10 will then present how these two marketing alternatives can be designed as an independent business entrepreneur, as a business intrapreneur or as a social entrepreneur.

# 5. Knowledge development of leadership

## 5.1 INTRODUCTION

I also present my version of knowledge development of the academic subject of leadership. There are several reasons for this. One is that leadership is close to entrepreneurship as well as to marketing. You can talk about entrepreneurial leaders as well as market leaders, for example. Interestingly, knowledge development of leadership can be described in my six steps more clearly than the other two elements, which are:

- leadership as a function
- personality traits of leaders
- leadership thinking and behaving
- contextual theories of leadership
- results and effects of leadership
- to better understand leaders by understanding followers better.

What is interesting is that this subject is also increasingly stressing the *importance of followers for leaders*, maybe because followers in a way 'are closer to' their leaders than are entrepreneurs and/or marketers to their customers and other users. This will therefore provide me with several ideas about how to discuss the alternative version of marketing for entrepreneurs, which I will present alongside the more developed rational, managerial version, that is, the budding social phenomenological, co-creation version.

## 5.2 LEADERSHIP AS A FUNCTION

Leadership consists of two parties, who interact with each other, i.e., leaders and followers. Leadership can be defined as *the process, where the leader has the ability to frame and define the reality of those who are led*. To do so, the leader must make the situation meaningful and then transfer this meaning to their followers (Smircich & Morgan, 1982). By doing this, a feeling of solidarity and a shared feeling of meaning is created in organizations or other situations of being together (Bryman, 1997). If this feeling of being together is missing, followers tend to feel confused and a lack of belonging, because values and ideas are not exchanged, or people do not talk to each other (Smircich & Morgan, 1982).

## 5.3   PERSONALITY TRAITS OF LEADERS

Early research literature (until the late 1940s) followed the approach that leaders had certain personality traits. This approach was influenced, historically, by Theories of the Great Man (suggested by Thomas Carlyle, 1841) and was based on historical figures at his time. The primary studies concerning leaders' personality traits have been made, however, after the Second World War, and they were guided by the idea that some individuals had personality traits that made them more suitable to leadership positions.

Stogdill presented two summaries of leaders' personality traits, and he identified characteristics which often seem associated with great leaders such as: 'intelligence, task-orientation, power of initiative and persistency in handling problems, self-confidence and the willingness to take responsibility and occupy a position which implies dominance and control' (Stogdill 1948:45).

Gardner (1990) also presented a list of those personality qualities which a leader possesses, for instance, a need for achievement, the ability to motivate people, self-confidence, flexibility, courage, credibility, etc.

The personality approach identified important personality traits which were considered in a leadership role; these were criticized, however, as too simplistic and not convincing enough to be able to separate between successful and less successful leaders, and because it was difficult to identify enough measurable characteristics which, in fact, could represent what a leader is. We have seen the same for entrepreneurs and marketers.

The lack of answers to the questions that were raised by the personality-orientated studies on leadership prompted researchers to look for other conditions to understand leadership.

## 5.4   LEADERSHIP THINKING AND BEHAVING

Because of weaknesses in the research when trying to find personality traits among leaders, some researchers up to the end of 1960s suggested a kind of stylistic approach, and focused on behaviour among leaders. In the beginning, the theories were applied to military, political and industrial contexts.

The main assumption of this approach was based on the belief that it should be possible to identify *a behavioural pattern and a leadership style*, which was effective in a leadership role.

The first more specific studies concerning leaders' way of thinking and behaving were made in 1939 by Lewin, Lippitt and White, when they evaluated behaviour in five groups of children around ten years old under the influence of three leadership styles: autocratic, democratic and laissez-faire (Bass & Stogdill, 1990).

*Autocratic leaders* take decisions themselves: they tell the followers what they are to do, and they expect to be obeyed without any problems. They do not trust others, and their defence mechanisms trigger their tyrannical and rigorous behaviour. The main weakness of this leadership style is its great need for security and its apprehension of salary, reputation and career. *Democratic leaders* include their followers in the decision process: the main result is the outcome of a group discussion. *Laissez-faire leaders* give freedom to their groups: they do not interfere and do not participate in their work, because they avoid making decisions on their own. Even if the company is heading in an unwanted direction, they do not seem to bother about the situation: they just want to deliver decisions when superiors order them to.

Leadership experts such as De Pree, Bennis and Gardner claim that *there are characteristics which are typical for good leaders*. De Pree (2004) mentions three qualities of such leading figures: integrity, the ability to build and retain good relationships, and the ability to build a community context; in other words, a milieu where ideas are thriving, and where quality of life and performance are increasing.

Bennis also describes ingredients which are part of successful leadership and characterize a true leader: a guiding vision for the future, passion and, which is also mentioned by De Pree, integrity. To be an example in this respect, a leader must have a great degree of self-knowledge. To know yourself, your own strengths and weaknesses, is the key to being able to lead others (Bennis, 2009).

Bennis stresses two other points concerning leadership characteristics. First, he talks about maturity. Leaders are sharpening their qualities as time goes on, often as followers. Second, he asserts that a leader is not born, but developed in an environment, above all through devotion.

> Leaders are not produced during a seminar over a weekend, which many proponents of leadership theories seem to claim. I come to think of this as a kind of microwave oven theory: put in Mr and Mrs Average and out pops the ready-made Leader in sixty seconds. (Bennis, 2009:35–6)

Gardner brings up another aspect concerning leadership behaviour. Leaders function effectively by those stories they convey to their listeners and viewers/followers. These stories can be conveyed in different ways. As he looks at it, leadership is associated with arts: 'Leaders inspire others by the way in which they use the medium for artistic expressions that they choose, for instance, as a part of a sonata, as a gesture in a dance or as a mathematical equation with a theoretical physicist' (Gardner, 2011:9).

Gardner goes on to claim that leaders themselves must embody their stories and lead by good examples. They cannot expect that their followers would react otherwise or, to put it differently, *they should practise what they preach* (Gardner, 2011).

## 5.5 CONTEXTUAL THEORIES OF LEADERSHIP

The stylistic approach does not, on its own, identify the behaviour of universal leaders or give guidance in different situations. This approach led, therefore, to a consideration of situational and contextual factors which may influence the effectiveness of leadership.

Presenting contextual theories of leadership (until early 1990) came to symbolize a change in leadership research: the effectiveness depends on the leader, the follower, the task *and* the situation. This means that leadership does not only depend on what the leader is or does, but also on the type of followers that work in the organization, the type of task which is to be performed and the context where everybody involved is acting.

Among different contextual theories, one of the most important is Fiedler's contextual model (1967), which attempts to explain behaviour in a group as a result of interaction between two factors: *the leadership style* and *the influence of the situation*. This model brings up two kinds of leaders as stated by Bass and Stogdill (1990): *task orientated* (leaders are only interested in getting their tasks done), and *relationship orientated* (leaders perform their tasks by having good relationships with the group members). There are no perfect leaders; both of the above can be effective in their leadership style and should be adapted to the situation.

Furthermore, Hersey and Blanchard (1969) developed a model concerning contextual leadership, which is 'life cycle theory of leadership'. The model is based on the idea that the most effective leadership style varies in relation to *the degree of maturity with followers and the characteristics of the situation*, and it contains two dimensions, similar to the above: task dependence (direction) and relationship dependence (support). Hersey and Blanchard (1969) assert that an effective leader can make a diagnosis concerning a situation, understand the degree of maturity of the followers, and adopt the most suitable leadership style. It should be noted that the key concept in this theory is the degree of maturity of followers, which is defined as their willingness to take responsibility, their education, knowledge and also their experience related to the task which is at hand. Consistent with this model, there are four leadership styles – *delegating, supporting, coaching* and *guiding* – depending on the best fit with the degree of maturity among the followers: when they want to reach a higher degree of maturity, leaders should decrease the control of the people and the tasks (Bass & Stogdill, 1990).

It should be noted that those ways to function as a leader mentioned above have been surpassed by more modern research and new approaches. So-called 'new leadership theories' are *based on charisma, authenticity, inspiration and followers.*

## 5.6   RESULTS AND EFFECTS OF LEADERSHIP

Knowing oneself as well as story-telling are both elements of what is called *authentic leadership.* To be guided by one's own values is what makes a leader special. Authenticity is often seen as a crucial part of successful leadership. The theory of authentic leadership covers three levels (Caza & Jackson, 2011): firstly, the leader as a person, then the leader's role and function, and finally, the very phenomenon of authentic leadership itself.

George (2003) defines five characteristics of an authentic leader: he or she is carrying out a task with passion; he or she is leading others in a sympathetic way; he or she has lasting relationships with people; he or she shows self-discipline, and he or she is consistent. Furthermore, authentic leaders are 'committed to developing themselves because they know that becoming a leader takes a lifetime of personal growth' (George, 2003:12).

Many researchers have tried to provide a definition of authentic leadership, but no generally accepted definition has been created. Of course, authentic leadership is related to authenticity, somehow. However, not even the concept of authenticity is very clear. Walumbwa et al. (2008:94) suggest the following definition:

> A behavioural pattern with leaders which is based on and promotes positive psychological capacities as well as a positive ethical climate, which fosters a greater self-awareness, an internalized morale perspective, balanced information refinement and openness as one part of leaders, working with followers and which fosters a positive self-development.

This definition covers critical areas in authentic leadership, such as self-awareness and self-development. May et al. (2003) assert that authentic leaders are expected to have a capacity for a higher morality, which makes it possible for them to assess dilemmas from different points of view. Authentic leadership is shown in the fact that a leader is true to him- or herself, and above all it is so that somebody who is true to him- or herself is also true to his or her followers (Nyberg & Sveningsson, 2014). This can consequently be seen as a positive moral relationship between the leader and his or her followers, based on trust and commitment (Whitehead, 2009).

Some researchers take into consideration the importance of the context when studying authentic leadership. One may fear, for example, that a person's social responsibility will be reduced by rationalization, when a personal drive to be true to oneself is stressed too much. Authentic leaders are thought to be very much aware of the context in which they are functioning (Avolio et al., 2009); authentic leadership does not only depend on the positive psychological capacity of the leader; it is also determined by the specific organizational context (Gardner et al., 2005; Ilies et al., 2005).

The above definitions are primarily formulated from the leaders' perspective. The followers' perspective is equally important. Avolio et al. (2009:806) assert that authentic leaders:

> build confidence and gain respect and trust with followers by encouraging various points of view and building networks of cooperative relationships with followers and consequently lead in a way which the followers look at as authentic.

In other words, leaders can only be authentic when followers regard them as such. Authenticity can only be a perception of whether or not the leader is real and true. No leader can claim that he or she is authentic. Authenticity is something which is ascribed to somebody by someone else.

## 5.7 TO BETTER UNDERSTAND LEADERS BY UNDERSTANDING FOLLOWERS BETTER

In modern times of leadership research, the importance of followers is increasingly stressed. Followership means the ability to absorb supervision well, to make up one's mind to move in a specified direction, to be part of a team, and to reach the results that one is expected to achieve. Traditionally, *followership* refers to a role which a certain person can have in an organization (Riggio et al., 2008). More specifically, it is the ability of an individual to actively follow a leader (Forsyth, 2009). The study of followership is a decisive part to better understand leadership, as success and failure of an organization does not only depend on how well a leader can lead, but also on how well a follower can follow (Kelley, 1988). More specifically, *followers play an active role in success as well as in failure in groups and organizations* (Baker, 2007). How a follower is following is probably as important to measure in a process as how a leader is leading. The founding figure for the field of followership is asserted to be the researcher Robert Kelley (Riggio et al., 2008). He describes four main qualities of effective followers (Kelley, 1988). These are:

1. *Self-control*: This refers to the ability to think critically, to take control of own actions and to work in an independent way. It is important for followers to manage themselves as well as for leaders to have the ability to delegate tasks to these individuals.
2. *Commitment*: This refers to an individual who is committed to an objective, vision or purpose of a group or an organization. This is an important characteristic of followers as it helps to keep their morale and energy level high (as well as those of other members).
3. *Competence*: It is essential for individuals to own those skills and aptitudes which are necessary to fulfil the group's or organization's task. These people are refining these skills through knowledge development in classes or seminars and the like.
4. *Courage*: Effective followers stick to their convictions and maintain ethical standards, even if they have unethical or corrupt leaders. These individuals are loyal, honest and, not the least, straightforward with their leaders.

Kelley (1988) also identifies two underlying behavioural dimensions which assist in identifying the differences between followers and non-followers. The first dimension is whether the individual is *an independent critical thinker or not*. The other dimension is whether an individual is *active or passive*. From these dimensions, Kelley has identified five types of followers:

1. *The sheep*: These individuals are passive and require external motivation from the leader's side. These followers lack commitment and require constant guidance by the leader.
2. *Yes people*: These individuals absorb what the leader says and the task and objectives of the group or organization. These conformists do not question the leader's decision and actions. Furthermore, they will strongly defend their leader if they face opposition from others.
3. *The pragmatics*: These individuals are not drivers and they do not support controversial or unique ideas until the majority of the group has given their support. These individuals often stay in the background of a group.

4. *The alienated*: These individuals are negative and often try to stop or take down a group by constantly questioning the leader's decision and actions. These individuals often see themselves as being the rightful leaders in the organization, and they are critical of the leader and other group members.
5. *The star followers*: These exemplary individuals are positive, active and independent thinkers. They will not blindly accept decisions and actions of a leader until they have made a complete evaluation. Furthermore, these types of followers succeed without the leader being present.

Historically, followership has always been a part of leadership, of course, even if only in an implicit way. It is only, however, in the last decade that the leadership process has been studied such that *both leaders and followers are seen as essential parts* (Carsten et al., 2010; Collinson, 2006; Hoption et al., 2012; Sy, 2010). The study of followership is separate from previous approaches on leadership, in that followership is as worthy of study as leadership (Uhl-Bien & Pillai, 2007). One basic assumption in followership approaches is that *leadership cannot be completely understood without considering how followers and followership contribute to (or reduce) leadership* (Carsten et al., 2010; Dvir & Shamir, 2003; Hollander, 1993; Howell & Shamir, 2005; Sy, 2010).

We have normally not understood leadership as a process which is co-created in social and relational interactions between people (Fairhurst & Uhl-Bien, 2012). In such a process, leadership can also take place if there is followership – without followers and their actions there is no leadership (Uhl-Bien et al., 2014). However, we still know very little about these issues.

Problems with comprehending followership have been caused by the negative connotations of 'followers' and 'to follow' that may arise if we do not clearly clarify what constitutes a 'follower'. These negative connotations come from the leader-centric approach which has traditionally dominated leadership research (Hoption et al., 2012). This view romanticizes leadership and subordinate follower behaviour (Uhl-Bien & Pillai, 2007). The term 'followers' has sometimes been controversial because it entices the belief in passive, powerless individuals, who automatically do as the leaders say (Kelley, 2008). As a result, some scholars have argued instead for using terms such as 'collaborators', 'participants' and 'members/team members'. Gardner (1990), Rost (1993) and other researchers have even suggested taking away the term follower completely because of its negative connotations (for instance, Rost, 2008).

As Shamir (2007, 2012) asserts, however, if we eliminate 'followership', this means that we no longer study leadership. Instead, we study social phenomena more generally such as cooperation and coordination in a team. Shamir (2007) claims that a social phenomenon worth the name of leadership must contain 'disproportionate social influence' (i.e., connected to leaders' and followers' behaviours and identities). Shamir (2012) is careful to point out that this means that leadership *cannot completely* be 'separated' from followership (Pearce & Conger, 2003). 'If it is fully shared, I suggest we don't call it *leadership* because the term loses any added value' (Shamir, 2012:487; italics in the original).

For a social phenomenon to qualify as leadership, we must therefore be able to 'identify certain persons who, at least in a certain time, exert more influence than others on the group or the process' (Shamir, 2012:487). The clear implication is that *followers and followership are central to leadership* and that *the leadership process consists of a combination of leading and following behaviour*. We can even claim with some right that *it is in follower-ship behaviour that leadership is created* (Uhl-Bien & Ospina, 2012). Some assert that our leadership measurements suffer from a kind of attributional bias, that should make us question whether what we exploit is really a kind of halo effect, related to what we believe that leadership 'should' consist of rather than those theoretical concepts that we are actually measuring (Martinko et al., 2011; compare with Phillips & Lord, 1981; Rush et al., 1977; van Knippenberg & Sitkin, 2013).

The study of followership consequently means to investigate *the nature and influence of followers and followership behaviour or actions in the leadership process*. The leadership process then becomes a dynamic process which involves leaders and followers, who interact together in a context (Hollander, 1992; Lord et al., 1999; Shamir, 2012; Uhl-Bien & Ospina, 2012). This definition identifies followership in two ways, i.e., as a rank or position (a *role*) or as *part of the social process* (a constructionist approach).

*Role-based approaches.* Role-based approaches consider how individuals behave as leaders and followers in a context where there are hierarchical roles. The primary interest of role-based approaches is to improve the understanding of how followers (e.g., subordinates) work with leaders (e.g., bosses) in ways which contribute to or reduce leadership and the organization's outcome (Oc et al., 2013; Carsten et al., 2010; Sy, 2010). In this way, role-based approaches are interested in the question: 'What is the proper mix of follower characteristics and follower behaviour to promote desired outcomes?' (Graen & Uhl-Bien, 1995:223). The *social process approach* (Fairhurst & Grant, 2010) looks at followership from the other side as a relational interaction, where leadership is co-created in combined actions of leading and following (DeRue & Ashford, 2010; Fairhurst & Uhl-Bien, 2012; Shamir, 2012). While role-based approaches consequently study followership as a role and a set of behaviours or behaviour styles with individuals and groups, the constructionist approach studies followership as a social action process which is necessarily tied together with leadership.

Role-based approaches are consistent with Shamir's description of 'reversing the lens' in leadership research (Shamir, 2007). They consider *how followers are influencing leaders' attitudes, behaviours and outcomes.* These approaches identify followers as causal agents. The focus in these approaches is on follower characteristics and style, role orientation in followership, implicit theories of followership, follower identities and how follower identities and behaviours create leader attitudes, behaviours and effectiveness (Collinson, 2006; Lord & Brown, 2004).

The earliest role-based approaches are provided in typologies which identify follower characteristics and their styles. The first typology of that type was provided by Zaleznik (1965). This typology identifies four types of follower: (1) impulsive subordinates, (2) compulsive subordinates, (3) masochistic subordinates, and (4) withdrawn subordinates. It was introduced both to help leaders to better understand how they should manage their followers, but also to guide followers who aspire to leadership positions. As Zaleznik and Kets de Vries later expressed it: 'the person who aspires to leadership must negotiate the risky passage between dependency and assertiveness' (1975:167).

Even though Zaleznik provided the first typology, it is clear that the most quoted work concerning followership is the one that was presented by Kelley (1988). As I have already mentioned, Kelley defined the ideal follower as one who participates in a joint process to reach some common purpose (Kelley, 1988, 1992, 2008). He ascribes 'effective followers' a number of qualities, such as being self-motivated, independently solving problems and committed to the group and the organization. Effective followers are 'courageous, honest, and credible' (Kelley, 1988:144). Kelley's typology uses dependent–independent and passive–active as quadrants (i.e., alienated followers, exemplary followers, conformist followers, passive followers, and a 'centre' group, halfway between the two dimensions, who are called 'pragmatic followers') (Bjugstad et al., 2006; Hoption et al., 2012; Townsend & Gebhardt, 1997). Kelley advocates trying to make all followers become 'exemplary followers', arguing that the best followers are not passive sheep – they are actively engaged and exhibit a courageous conscience (Kelley, 1992).

Following Kelley, Chaleff published a practically orientated book (Chaleff, 1995). His premise was that the key to effective leadership is effective followership, which takes place when followers 'vigorously support' leaders in reaching organizational missions and visions. Chaleff identifies four different follower styles: implementer, partner, individualist and resource (Chaleff, 1995, 2003, 2008). His basic premise is that 'leaders rarely use their power wisely or effectively over long periods unless they are supported by followers who have the stature to help them do so' (Chaleff, 2003:1).

Another typology is presented by Howell and Mendez (2008). They suggest that there are different types of followers' role orientation and that they may influence the effectiveness of the relationship between leaders and followers. The first is followership as an *interactive role*, which supports and complements the leadership role. The second is followership as *a type of independent role*. This role orientation involves a high level of autonomy and, under positive circumstances, a high level of competence, which complement the leader's role (for instance, professional colleagues such as engineers, physicians, or university professors, who are working independently but contribute to the organization's objectives). The third type is more negative and consists of *another type of independent role*, that may consist of a follower who works at cross-purposes to the leader. The final follower role orientation is a *shifting role*, in which the individual alternates between the leader role and the follower role. For example, in collaborative teams, members in such roles may feel obliged to step up in a leadership role or feel that a less visible followership role is appropriate, depending on circumstances.

The idea that followers can hold different types of role orientations can also be seen in the work of Carsten and colleagues (Carsten et al., 2010, 2013). Carsten et al. (2010) offer the first formal empirical study concerning *followers' views of followership*. Their results identify different follower schema. Some followers report more passive views and look at their role as being obedient and deferent. Others report a proactive schema, and look at their role as having a partnership with leaders by feeling ownership of and responsibility for reaching organizational objectives (e.g., active co-contributors – Chaleff, 1995; Kellerman, 2008; Shamir, 2007).

The role-based approach to leadership is analogous with one of two alternatives to marketing for entrepreneurs, which is presented in this book and called managerial marketing.

*Constructionist approaches.* Constructionist approaches describe how people come together in a social process to co-create leadership and followership (DeRue & Ashford, 2010; Fairhurst & Grant, 2010). What characterizes constructionist approaches is that they, by necessity, constitute process approaches. They look at people as engaging themselves in relational interactions and in these interactions, leadership and followership are co-produced (for example, as continuing relationships, actions and identities) (DeRue & Ashford, 2010; Shamir, 2007).

These relational interactions do not necessarily follow formal hierarchical roles.

A constructionist approach imagines that leadership can only take place when leadership met by followership granting actions (DeRue & Ashford, 2010; Uhl-Bien & Ospina, 2012; Shamir, 2012), showing deference or obeying (Blass, 2009; Burger, 2009; Milgram, 1965, 1974), resisting or negotiating with others' wishes or influencing attempts (Fairhurst & Uhl-Bien, 2012). In this way, followership is not tied to a role but to *actions*. This approach permits us to consider that bosses do not always lead – they may also show deference to subordinates (Fairhurst & Hamlett, 2003; Larsson & Lundholm, 2013).

The constructionist approach shows that the relationships between followers and leaders could be so tight that it can be difficult to separate followership from leadership. This approach looks at followership as a necessary element in the co-construction of leadership, even though, sometimes, this is also the case in the role-based approach. One of the largest challenges in future studies of followership, if we want to apply the constructionist approach, is to get away from the semantics that arise in reductionist logics that cause us to hone in on 'the leader' as an individual or role and disregard the fact that 'follower actions' are crucial in the construction (or failure of construction) of leadership.

Consistent with the constructionist approach to leadership, if there are no followership actions, there is no leadership. The fact is that it is probably easier here (which is sometimes the case in the role-based view) to recognize leadership in *the actions with followers than what it is in leadership actions*, because individuals who try to be leaders can only be legitimized in the responses and receptions among those who are willing to follow them.

The constructionist approach to leadership is analogous to that alternative to marketing for entrepreneurs, which is presented in this book and called the social phenomenological approach. As we will see in Chapter 6, social phenomenology is one variation of constructionism.

For a framework to be counted as a theory, it must specify those relations which are suggested to exist between theoretical concepts (Sutton & Staw, 1995). Consistent with this, it is possible to identify two potential frameworks for studying followership. The role-based approach ('reversing the lens') is depicted in Figure 5.1.

A constructionist approach ('the leadership process') is shown in Figure 5.2.

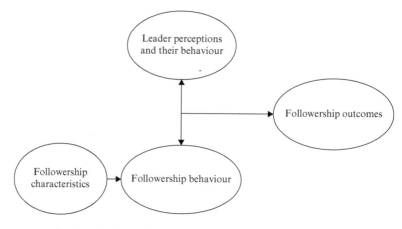

*Source:*   Uhl-Bien et al., 2014:98.

*Figure 5.1    Reversing the lens*

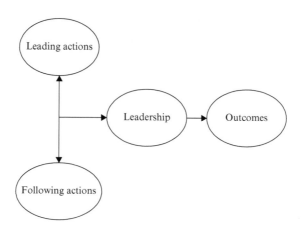

*Source:*   Uhl-Bien et al., 2014:98.

*Figure 5.2    The leadership process*

## 5.8   COMBINATIONS OF ENTREPRENEURSHIP, MARKETING AND LEADERSHIP

We have seen that the development of knowledge in entrepreneurship has followed a similar path to marketing and leadership, starting with functions, personality traits, thinking and behaviour, and continuing by looking contextually and at results and effects, finishing with the ambition today to better understanding customers, users and/or followers.

A person of interest is one who combines the best of entrepreneurship with the best of leadership, that is, *entrepreneurial leadership.* This could be defined as *a person who produces and assists in achieving new solutions to followers* (receivers or others). Entrepreneurial leadership is, for some, an increasing necessity (Santora et al., 1999; Pointer & Sanchez, 1994). It is an ability which should be valid in all contexts (Gupta et al., 2004).

# 6.   Some methodological cornerstones

## 6.1   INTRODUCTION

It is my conviction that researchers and writers of books with a scientific connection are influenced by those ontological and epistemological assumptions that they carry around. To understand what they are trying to say, I think it is necessary to know these assumptions. For this reason, I want to reveal my own paradigmatic assumptions in this chapter.

## 6.2   THE PARADIGM CONCEPT

The scientist mostly associated with the concept of *paradigm* ('model', 'pattern') today is Thomas Kuhn (1922–1996), who first presented his theories in *The Structure of Scientific Revolutions* in 1962. Kuhn was originally rather unclear about what a paradigm consisted of, which he admitted. In later editions of his book, however, he became more precise about his view of its components:

1.  *Symbolic generalizations*, which are typical expressions used within the scientific community – what might be called jargon – which are not questioned.
2.  *Metaphysical aspects*, that is, typical background thinking (which may vary along the whole spectrum from being heuristic to being ontological). These backgrounds function somewhat like symbolic generalizations, which offer suitable and acceptable analogies and metaphors. They also assist in determining what will be accepted as an explanation or an understanding, which also means that they determine which will be regarded as unsolved problems.
3.  *Values* for judging research results (e.g., that they should be formulated quantitatively), or theories (e.g., that they should be simple, consistent and probable) and scientific topics (e.g., that they should be related to specific social uses).
4.  *Ideal examples* – such as specific solutions to a problem – that scientists confront early in their careers and that can be found in 'recognized' scientific journals.

As stated by Kuhn, major changes in scientific thinking (scientific revolutions) involve a shift in paradigm and such changes are rare. Kuhn's thesis is that when scientists work consistently with a paradigm they take part in what he calls *normal science*, trying to solve the problems thrown up by the theories they hold. Science then becomes a kind of puzzle solving.

Sometimes, a scientific revolution occurs when the existing paradigm proves unable to cope with what appears to be an *anomaly* (deviation from the norm, from what is expected or from what should have happened consistent with existing scientific law). Existing assumptions become so inadequate that they collapse and are replaced by a new set of assumptions. A new paradigm is then in a process of development. Such shifts of paradigms cannot occur within normal science itself. That is why Kuhn talks about 'scientific revolutions'.

Paradigms are based on ultimate presumptions about what we study as researchers, which are certain assumptions about the quality of life and research. These assumptions can be conceived as different kinds of background 'philosophical' hypotheses, but not in the sense that they can be tested empirically or logically, as each paradigm is based on its own postulation of the constitution of reality and science. In consequence, data collected in that paradigm will be based on these assumptions. If we try to use data to test the assumptions mentioned, these data will only confirm their own assumptions in a kind of circular logic. These background hypotheses, or, as we might better name them, *normative theses*, can only be 'tested' reflectively. Furthermore, as different paradigms are based on more or less incompatible assumptions, there is normally no empirical or logical way to decide which paradigm is the best one. Also, looking at science paradigmatically, there is every reason to doubt the common opinion that knowledge develops in a simple linear and cumulative way.

Håkan Törnebohm (1919–2016) is a theorist of science. His works are mainly in the theory of physical science, influenced by Kuhn among others, but he has also, which is important in my case, developed theories of paradigms further in social sciences. One important difference between the development of natural sciences and social sciences of importance to him and to this book is that in natural sciences, old paradigms are replaced by new ones. In social sciences, on the other hand, paradigms live most of the time together side-by-side, and many social science methodological views do not even deserve to be called developed and mature paradigms.

Törnebohm's (1974) evolutionary position fits better with the purpose of this book than does Kuhn's revolutionary position. As stated by Törnebohm, a paradigm consists of:

- a conception of reality (a world view)
- a conception of science

- a scientific ideal
- ethical and aesthetical aspects.

*Conception of reality* is connected to philosophical ideas about how reality is constructed, whether reality exists in and of itself or through our mediation; for example, that reality is ordered and logical in causes and effects, or it has an inherent tendency to dissension with non-linear relations, or it is based on chaotic relations, or it is ordered as well as disordered at the same time.

*Conception of science* has to do with knowledge we have gained through research education, which provides our concepts or beliefs about objects and subjects we study, and our knowledge interests; for example, all kinds of pre-scientific concepts and models contained in entrepreneurship and marketing such as opportunity recognition, business plan, innovation, consumption, demand, need and others.

*Scientific ideal* is related to the researcher as a person – to his or her desires; for example, somebody perceives him- or herself as having the idea that science is something objective and not influenced by partial interests, or he or she claims that it is impossible to be impartial, or aims at changing some aspects of society.

*Ethical and aesthetical aspects* cover what the researcher claims to be suitable or unsuitable and to be beautiful or ugly; for example, people should not be observed without their knowledge, well-constructed diagrams and graphs are ideals of beauty, or scientific results justify the means used to achieve them.

There are many proposals in social sciences for classifying paradigms. Two classifications are by Burrell and Morgan (1979) and by Guba (1990). Burrell and Morgan discuss:

- functionalist paradigms
- interpretive paradigms
- radical humanist paradigms
- radical structuralist paradigms.

Guba explores:

- post-positivism
- critical science
- constructivism.

For the purpose of discussing marketing for entrepreneurs, I find it interesting to make a distinction between two paradigms only. They are:

- rationalism
- social constructionism.

There are several differences between these two scientific views which will be presented as we move on. One such fundamental difference is that rationalism aims at coming up with *explanations* and social constructionism at coming up with *understanding*, and that explanations are connected to *models* and understanding connected to *interpretations*. I will return to these concepts.

## 6.3 RATIONALISM

The presumption of an 'in here' world of subjectivity and 'out there' world of objectivity, creates riddles of great magnitude. Among the most profound, how do we as subjects acquire knowledge of the objective world? In philosophy, this is the problem of *epistemology*.

The ideal for most has been to demonstrate that – metaphorically speaking – the mind functions as a *mirror of nature*. Within the epistemological tradition, attempts to justify the view of the mind as mirror are typically identified as *empiricist*, that is, *all knowledge of reality emanates from our senses*. The classic version of empiricism can be found in Locke, Berkeley, Hume and Mill.

However, in their strong form, empiricist views of knowledge have never been wholly convincing for many scholars. First, the 'world as it is' does not seem to demand any particular form of categorization or thought. Nor can any convincing account be given of how 'abstract ideas' are built up from 'raw sensations'. Finally, how can the empiricist stand outside his or her experience to know whether there is a world being mirrored correctly? If all we have is the reflection in our minds, how can we be certain that what is 'out there' is producing this image?

Such doubts have given rise to a competing school of epistemology, commonly called *rationalism*. For rationalists, mental processes inherent within the individual play the role of fashioning our knowledge. To draw information from the world, it is proposed, we must use our common sense and approach reality with concepts already in mind. The world does not produce our concepts. Our concepts help us to organize the world in various ways.

The epistemology of rational thinking can be summarized following Törnebohm's categories provided earlier:

*Conception of reality.* Reality consists of objective as well as subjective facts. Such objective and subjective facts can be called *factual*. Even if we, through interference or through a change of mind, can make this reality appear in various forms, it is *basically* a stable construction.

*Conception of science.* Science provides pictures of this factual and stable reality. These pictures will improve, that is, become more and more correct and more valid as science progresses. Theories (as language) can be discussed in relation to how they are constructed (*syntax*), in relation to what they stand for (*semantics*) and in relation to their users (*pragmatics*). Because theories should be based on facts, their terms should be as syntactically and semantically correct as possible and – as far as possible – be made independent of pragmatic controversies. It is therefore often seen as ideal science when terms are defined operationally, based on logics and mathematics. Scientific knowledge should be logically separated from moral matters and ethics. This means that researchers can argue about which consequences different alternative actions will have in terms of formulated objectives, but deciding which objectives should be chosen is beyond its domain. There is also a sharp boundary between philosophy and research consistent with rationalism. Philosophy can be used as a basis for discussion, but it can never provide the truth.

*Scientific ideal.* Gradually, science will fill in as many 'empty spots' in our knowledge of reality as possible. Knowledge emerges best with the use of well-tested techniques, many of which have been picked up from the natural sciences. The result will be an increasing number of ever more refined, logical models, a good set of concepts and representative, generalizable cases. Knowledge is used to make better and better predictions of the consequences of various alternative actions that could be taken, and consequently to steer reality in a desirable direction.

*Ethical and aesthetical aspects.* These are relatively uninteresting questions to proponents of rationalism. It is instead seen as important to regard science as progress; as researchers, we do not have to take responsibility for how people use the knowledge that will be presented by the research.

As mentioned, one out of two versions of marketing for entrepreneurs presented in this book is based on rational thinking. The reason why I have chosen rationalism as one version to discuss marketing for entrepreneurs instead of the strong form of empiricism is that present mainstream marketing thinking, which is managerial marketing, is based on quite established terminology, strictly guiding the marketers – and it could be called rational. Most current marketing books assert to tell the reader how to succeed as a marketer in a rather normative way, using rational models and concepts.

## 6.4 KNOWLEDGE PROBLEMS

The prime importance we place on the self and the world can be traced to our cultural history. Most would credit the Enlightenment as the birthplace of our contemporary – modernist – belief about the self and the world. Enlightenment thinkers gave us the idea that individuals are capable of observing the world for what it is, and taught us to deliberate about the best course of action – which are the capacities to *observe* for ourselves, to *think*, *evaluate* and then *choose* our action. Neither royalty nor clergy could declare themselves superior in these universal capacities.

Knowledge was thus defined as private and personal, and not dictated by decree from on high. It is this legacy that stoked the fires of the French Revolution and formed the basis of what has come to be called cultural modernism. But did we generate this knowledge by ourselves, that is, the knowledge of our unique individual ability for conscious thoughts, self-determination and the freedom to determine our own future? The fact is that this heritage was given us by some great thinkers who lived at that time. There remain, however, problems today concerning the presumption of individual minds facing the world unimpeded, and creating a picture of it.

This means a belief in a private, interior consciousness ('me here') in contrast to an exterior world ('out there'). We presume the existence of a psychological world of the self (which perceives, deliberates, decides) at the same time as there is a material world (which exists outside of our thoughts). This arrangement seems self-evident. In philosophical terms, we find ourselves comfortably committed to a *dualist ontology* – the reality of the mind and of the world. Yet, dualist beliefs create problems as profound as they are insoluble. One thorny challenge is to comprehend how *a mental and a physical world can be causally related.* In present day terms, we may ask, how does 'a thought' ('I should send her a SMS') make its way into action ('picking up the phone')? How does a wish or an intention produce actual muscle movements? We have little difficulty in comprehending causality *within* the physical world or *within* the mental world. But can a 'thought' or an 'emotion' have a physical effect, and if so, how does the psychological impact on the physical? The question is how 'mind stuff' produces changes in material – or vice versa.

Another problem of knowledge is to provide answers to how, exactly, we know what we think, feel or want. 'We just do', you might say, but how? This is the *problem of self-knowledge* and it poses difficulties which are no less profound and intractable as those of dualism.

Further, if the idea of individual minds with knowledge of the external world is suspect, then what are we to make of our belief that knowledge based on experience is better than all subjective conceptions of this world, considering all the problems associated with the subjective–objective dualism? Such questions are closely related to the concept of truth. True statements about the world, we hold, reflect the world 'as it is', and not as we might 'wish it to be'.

Some thinkers today question the dualist ontology and the role of experience above. This leads us to the thinking and ideas of *postmodernism*.

### 6.4.1 Postmodernism

If our world, as it is now, is in a state of often rapid and sometimes constant flux, then what we need is not so much a careful review of past events, but rather a continuous and constructive analysis of the reality of today and the near future. An analysis is required that enables us to understand what is taking place right now from multiple standpoints, which will help us to become engaged in dialogues with others from varied walks of life and will bring to our notice a range of different possible futures. Most importantly, a social analysis of today should generate vocabularies of understanding that will help us to create the future together. The point of social analysis in the present state of the world is not, then, to 'get it right' about what is happening to us. Rather, such analysis should make it possible for us to 'see again and in a new way'.

Our present world is often described as *postmodern*. Postmodernism is a concept which generally refers to a longstanding development in critical theory, philosophy, architecture, art, literature and culture, which can be seen as either being generated from or as a reaction to modernism. Postmodernism has also been defined as groping for something new since modernism has run out of steam. But the meaning of postmodernism is not clearly defined, however, and is the subject of a continuing debate. Among other things, today it may be difficult to interpret *what is said*. *How it is said* is often considered to be clearer. 'The medium is the message' has become synonymous with postmodernism (McLuhan, 1964).

From a historical perspective, it is possible to see a chronological order from the modern to the postmodern. Malpas (2005) describes it as a transformation which has taken place during the last decades with the emergence of a new kind of capitalism, the development of information technologies such as the Internet and World Wide Web, the collapse of the Soviet Union which ended the Cold War, plus the growth of voices from different cultures to end the domination of the traditional white, male, European ideal. When describing modern and postmodern conditions, it is, however, important to be aware of the fact that what is modern and what is postmodern exist in parallel in different cultural and social layers in our era.

Postmodernism is often described as an objection to the idea that there are fixed values, one absolute truth and the simple existence of self, and thereby criticizes every opinion of objectivity. Instead, everything is seen as relational and contextual – the postmodern picture of the world is sceptical.

Within social sciences, postmodernism is regarded as a consequence of economic, cultural, technical and demographic changes and is characterized by concepts such as post-industrialism and neo-capitalism, which in turn are explained by the rise of a service society, the growing importance of mass media and the integration of the world economy. Other important concepts here are the information society, globalization, the global village and media theory.

As a cultural movement, postmodernism can be viewed as the Western society after modernism. As stated by the French philosopher and litera-ture theorist Lyotard, the most important distinction mark of postmoder-nity is *a scepticism against grand narratives.*

Because the term 'postmodernism' is used in many different ways, per-haps it is best for the purpose of this book to view it as pointing to a range of inter-related dialogues on our current knowledge condition, in particu-lar to another way of looking at marketing for entrepreneurs next to what seems to be the ruling view, that is, the rational and the modernist belief in objectivity and truth. It is no doubt fruitful to see the postmodernist thought as a topic which has a bearing on the alternative view of marketing for entrepreneurs which is presented in this book, that is, the non-rational one, and looking at reality as a social construction.

## 6.5   SOCIAL CONSTRUCTIONISM

As stated by Wenneberg (2001), there are three philosophical sources of inspiration underlying social constructionism:

1. Kuhn's concept of paradigm.
2. Wittgenstein's language philosophy.
3. Garfinkel's ethnomethodology.

> Social constructionism broadly defined rests upon several key philosophical assumptions concerning the constitution of social life through language and discourse. Significant themes include the semiotic and illocutionary character of human life, the drive for ethnomethodological integrity in social research and the focus on the mutual construction of meaning as the main unit of analysis. (Hackley, 1998:125)

Social constructionist approaches share one distinctive assumption which distinguishes them from cognitivist approaches in social research.

The former approaches are based on a theory concerning meaning, that originates in interactivity and is maintained as such. Interactivity means that meaning is a social construction between people, as opposed to a purely private cognitive construction in individual human beings. This entails not only a concern with subjective meanings as the products of private cognitive processing, but as ineluctably social constructions, which involve active selection, suppression and purposiveness. Meaning is constructed by drawing selectively upon discursive repertoires which are public. There is no conclusive version of social events which can lie outside of the discursive production of these events. The social constructionist approach takes subjective reports of events, emotions and cognitions to be multifaceted constructions which can be interpreted on many levels. The things we say serve a purpose of reassuring versions of our selves or of ideologies and power relations (Billig, 1987; Goffman, 1959). The versions of events we construct are invariably negotiable and are bound up with constructions of identity of self and social relations (Harre, 1998). We may achieve things through the illocutionary force of the words we utter, and these achievements may include the maintenance of a sense of meaning to ourselves (e.g. Billig, 1987; Goffman, 1959; Mauss, 1985; Miller & Hoogstra, 1992). The sense of meaning we maintain may entail sustaining a particular social relation, maintaining an ideology upon which we might depend for our reassurance, or creating and re-creating our very sense of self through (unconsciously) selective narratives or stories of self (Harre, 1998; Wetherell, 1996). These stories are not (necessarily) conscious fictions. Social constructionist qualitative research allows this sense of constructed meaning to be acknowledged in the research.

The phenomenon of human communication entails an element of indeterminacy (Cook, 1992). This implies that human communication in the construction of social life is richer and more open than is implied by a cognitive model of words as signifiers of private mental entities. On a social constructionist view, this richness can be brought out in social research which utilizes aspects of semiotics, speech act theory and ethnomethodology (Austin, 1962; Barthes, 1964; de Saussure, 1974; Garfinkel, 1974; Potter & Wetherell, 1987) to develop interpretations of social data (primarily, but not exclusively, words) which point to both the structure and the function of constructed meanings in discourse (Banister et al., 1994).

A research orientation which is based on the belief of reality as a social construction is sometimes called constructivism and sometimes constructionism. I prefer the latter. For one thing, constructivism is a branch of mathematics (Hacking, 1999). But more importantly for my preference for constructionism over constructivism is, that even within social sciences, there is a strong intellectual and therapeutic tradition often called 'constructivism'. It is a tradition with deep roots in rationalism, and represented in recent psychology by figures such as Piaget (1954) and Kelly (1955). Constructivists propose that individuals mentally construct the world of experience. In this sense, the mind is not a mirror of the world as it is, but functions to create the world as we know it. So far, constructivism and constructionism seem to be the same thing. However:

> Many scholars will use the words 'constructivism' and 'constructionism' inter-changeably. However, you can appreciate a fundamental difference [between the two]: for constructivists the process of world construction is psychological; it takes place 'in the head'. In contrast, for social constructionists what we take to be real is an outcome of social relationships. (Gergen, 1999:237)

*There are variations of social constructionism* (Sandberg, 1999). They include social phenomenology (Berger & Luckmann, 1981), ethnomethod-ology (Garfinkel, 1967), symbolic interactionism (Mead, 1934), discourse approaches (Foucault, 1972), post-structuralism (Derrida, 1998), cultural approaches (Geertz, 1973; Alvesson, 1993) and gender approaches (Keller, 1985; Harding, 1986).

There are, however, several similarities among all constructionist approaches (Wenneberg, 2001; Devins & Gold, 2002):

- Person and reality are inseparable.
- Language produces and reproduces reality instead of being a result of reality.
- Knowledge is socially constructed, not objectively given.

There are four basic working assumptions among social construction-ism researchers:

1. *Those terms by which we understand our world and our self are neither required nor demanded by 'what there is'.* This has to do with the failure of language to map or picture an independent world. Another way of stating this assumption is to say that there are a potentially unlimited number of possible descriptions of 'the situation in question' – and none of these descriptions can be ruled superior in terms of its capac-ity to map, picture or capture its features.
2. *Our modes of description, explanation and / or representation are derived from relationships.* Language and all other forms of representation are meaningful only in their relationships with people. Meaning and sig-nificance are born of coordination between individuals – agreements,

negotiations, affirmations. Nothing exists for us as intelligible people before relationships exist.

3.  *As we describe or otherwise represent our reality, so do we fashion our future.* Language is a major ingredient of our world of actions and therefore a part of building futures either as confirmation of what already exists or as part of what will be now.

4.  *Reflection on our forms of understanding is vital to our future well-being.* What shall we save, what shall we resist and destroy, what shall we create? There are no universal answers, only socially constructed ones.

Wenneberg (2001) claims that one can apply social constructionism with a higher or lower degree of radicalism. Of the following four levels, the last is the most radical:

1.  *As a critical perspective.* Everything in human existence can be questioned. Man is by nature more plastic and malleable than we normally think.

2.  *As a theory for the development, maintenance and modification of consciousness.* This can be called social phenomenology.

3.  *As an epistemological position.* This position claims that knowledge of reality is exclusively determined by social factors.

4.  *As an ontological position.* This position claims that reality *in itself* is socially constructed.

This book shows my preference for the epistemological level.

As stated by Norén (1995), there are three different interpretative approaches:

1.  *A metaphoric approach*, that is, to construct pictures, which not only catch what seems to be going on, but also open possibilities for new angles of interpretation.

2.  *An actors' approach*, that is, to construct pictures which stress the studied actors' own experiences and their points of view.

3.  *A social constructionist approach*, that is, to construct pictures which stress the researcher's way of understanding how a collection of actors produce and reproduce their own social reality.

I think it is possible to combine the last two approaches, or to put it another way, to subordinate the actor's approach to the social constructionist approach.

The paradigm of the social constructionism philosophy can be summarized following Törnebohm's categories as follows:

*Conception of reality*. Social constructionism assumes that reality, as it exists for us, is a social construction, mentally relating actors to other actors in this reality, where the researcher is one of the actors.

*Conception of science* of social constructionism is that all pre-scientific conceptions must be objects of reflection in all kinds of research. The social constructionism view claims that taken-for-granted concepts may become obstacles for real understanding and renewal. As social constructionism starts from the idea that a researcher always has self-reference to the society at large, that is, participates as one of the constructors of the social reality, it becomes natural that the *scientific ideal* of social constructionism advocates a scientific and consciously active interaction. This may mean everything from the language style of reports to actively interfering in the area being researched.

*Ethically* this is about taking responsibility for a person's part of the construction of reality, which the researcher cannot disclaim responsibility for, whether he or she wants it or not. *Aesthetically* it may be that the social constructionist view wants to produce descriptions and interpretations which are close to being artistic. The social constructionist view has an expressed concern in an innovative knowledge interest, that is, not only to describe but also to drive change.

Symbolic interactionism and social phenomenology are similar to each other. However, they also contain some important differences. Let us look at these two variants of social constructionism in some detail before I account for my choice between the two in this book.

## 6.6 SYMBOLIC INTERACTIONISM

Symbolic interactionism as presented here is taken from Svensson and Östberg (2016). One division in studying human beings and society is between psychology, which focuses on the individual and his or her inner world, and sociology, which concentrates on society, organizations, institutions and networks. Social psychology attempts to bridge this dualism by studying *the interplay* between the individual and the society. Mead (1934) is usually ascribed this thought and credited with being the founder of symbolic interactionism. Self is basically a social process and Mead refers to his science as social behaviourism, that is, a social variant of classic behaviourism (Watson, 1970).

The very point with a society and a group is, that they consist of people. This is one of the fundamental features of symbolic interactionism: what we understand to be a 'society' is nothing but social interactions and relations, constantly going on between people. In some sense, society appears every day through social events such as conversations, meetings, collective travelling, telephone conversations, mail correspondence, arguments, queuing in cars, discussions and lectures. We are created as individuals through social co-existence.

Apart from pointing out the importance of interactions and relations, symbolic interactionism stresses the importance of the use of symbols in social interaction. This is related to the idea of people as interpretative human beings, creating meaning. Sociality is what distinguishes human life, and a human being exists as a social creature. Social co-existence and interaction are *the bases of* rather than *the consequences of* the existence of separate individuals. Interaction – that is, an action which takes place *between* human beings – connects one or several people by their mutually interpreting an action, and by their response to these interpretations. Charon (1998:153) describes interaction in the following way: 'I act; you consider my act, and you act; I consider your act, and I act; you consider my act, and you act. This give-and-take process is what is meant by interaction.'

Consistent with symbolic interactionism, it is everyday interactions between people that constitute the body of what we call *the society*, and it is created and recreated by all of those interactions that take place every day. Within symbolic interactionism, this is sometimes referred to as talking about society as consisting of *co-actions*, which are chains of actions, where two or more people mutually interpret and adapt their actions to each other (Blumer, 1969). Co-actions are going on all the time, which keeps society constantly moving. Society is *taking place* all the time, over and over again.

'Everyday life is an interpreted life' (Asplund, 2006:47; my translation). Things, fellow beings and situations obtain their meaning and are defined through peoples' interpretations. By interacting with other people, we learn what things mean and how the world is functioning. Our interpretations of the world *are* the world, at least from a practical point of view. The world, as we perceive it, is more important to our actions than how the world is *in itself*. The meanings we give to things have tangible consequences for us, because our interpretations of things and situations guide us when we act and make decisions. What 'really' is the case is, in a way, less important for how we manage situations; even an incorrect interpretation has practical consequences.

Interpretations and definitions of objects and everyday situations, where we happen to be, are not neutral or objective descriptions of how things are and what they look like. All definitions of a situation are both political as well as ethical, in the sense that every situation creates expectations for how to behave in a specific situation and in its interactions (Heidegren & Wästerfors, 2008).

When we interact and co-act, we use symbols, and language is the most common symbolic system which is used in human communication. Other important symbols are signs, signals, pictures, body language, facial expressions and objects. Interpretations of these symbols are important activities in human social life; symbols do not speak for themselves. An action which is not symbolic is a reflex response; a symbolic action is an interpretation of an ongoing or a previous situation.

As said by Charon (1998), symbols are *meaningful*, which means that they always refer to something else (Nöth, 1990). A symbol is also *social*. It is shared by people. The meaning of a symbol is defined by people who interact and co-act with each other. There is no intrinsic, objective meaning of a symbol, but its meaning is the result of agreements between people who find themselves in a specific concrete context. A symbol is consequently something which is shared by several people. A 'private' symbol which nobody understands is rather useless for communicating with the outer world. Symbols are created and recreated daily by people who interact and communicate.

Symbolic interactionism maintains a *relational* view of the world (Israel, 1979), which means that things and persons become meaningful only in relation to other things and people. According to symbolic interactionism, to understand the world means to understand how objects and people relate *to each other*.

## 6.7  SOCIAL PHENOMENOLOGY

*The Social Construction of Reality* is a book written by Berger and Luckmann (1981), which is dedicated to the philosopher and social phenomenologist Alfred Schutz (1899–1959). The discussion in the book is about everyday reality ('life world') as a reality which is collective, but which is produced and reproduced by individual actors together with other actors, that is, developed and confirmed interactively. Reality is not 'objective' in the sense of constituting an entity independent of man. Instead it is 'objectified'; that is, it is seen and treated as objective, even though it is not.

Reality is developed and sustained by processes, which are intimately interconnected in a dialectic fashion. That process by which we create our own experience is called *subjectification*. This process is intentionally directed and leads to the idea that *humans are a subjectified reality*. When, through our common language, we make these subjectified experiences externally available, we talk about *externalization*. With externalization, we create the surrounding reality and can therefore say that *society is a human result*.

That process by which an externalized human act might attain the characteristic of objectivity is called *objectification*. Through objectification, externalization loses its subjectively significant structure and becomes a *typification*, that is, given an objectified significance structure. Typification is related to our way of attaching various labels and typical designations to – having different understanding of – people, things and events around us. Examples of such typifications could be 'refugee', 'entrepreneur', 'Englishman', 'souvenir' or 'networking'. We expect, and then take for granted, that what is typified behaves or takes place consistent with the understanding mediated by the typification. The typification is not completely objectified until it has gone through a process of *institutionalization* and *legitimization*. The process of objectification constitutes the basis for the assumption that *society is an objectified reality*.

The fourth and last of these processes in the socially constructed reality is called *internalization*. This stands for taking over the world in which others live. We are not born as members in this reality but become so via internalization with its primary and secondary socialization phases. This is the basis of the fourth assumption that *humans are a social result*.

*Primary socialization*, which takes place in childhood, is the most important phase for a person's development. Most of the 'objective' world that is accepted by a child is imparted by others. Therefore, knowledge being transferred becomes emotionally conditioned and identification becomes a necessary prerequisite. Children, for instance, identify themselves with a role or an attitude. It is in primary socialization that the first understanding of reality is founded. *Language* becomes the most important internalizing factor of primary socialization. Yet socialization is a continuous process that does not end with the primary phase but continues throughout a person's entire life as secondary socialization.

*Secondary socialization* mainly encompasses the internalization of specific institutional sub-areas. The content of this internalization depends on the complexity, the work specialization and the stage in life of a person. In this phase, the learning of professional language and role-specific knowledge associated with a person and what he or she is doing are often necessary. The learning situations of the two socialization phases are different to the extent that the degree of anonymity is considerably higher in the secondary phase. To summarize:

SUBJECTIFICATION => Humans are a subjectified reality
EXTERNALIZATION => Society is a human result
OBJECTIFICATION => Society is an objectified reality
INTERNALIZATION => Humans are a social result

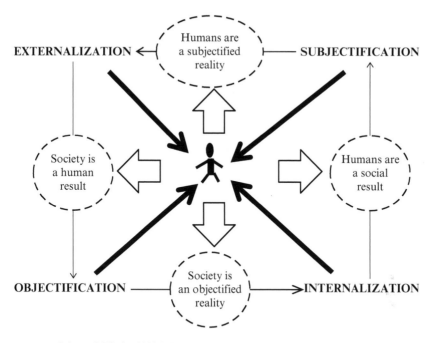

*Source:*    Arbnor & Bjerke, 2009:150.

*Figure 6.1    Social construction of reality*

Just as we have described how reality is socially constructed in a society, we can describe various organizations in the society. This means that we can talk about the socially constructed reality, say, of an entrepreneurial venture and can follow its construction using the four processes just mentioned. It is only a question of levels in the social order – a venture is only a small piece of the total social fabric. The development and self-movement of socially constructed reality at any level in the society is illustrated in Figure 6.1.

In the development and self-moving construction just described, the actors in the society construct their *finite provinces of meaning* which then reflect simultaneously both what is subjectified (personal) and what is objectified (common). The common set that emerges when all the finite provinces of meaning are combined in a society or any of its organizations constitutes the objectified reality for that aggregate. This is the reality in which we all live our daily lives as members of society. It is always there before us, its total existence is rarely or never in doubt, and only minor aspects of it are sometimes questioned. This objectified reality is what we call *everyday reality* (see Figure 6.2).

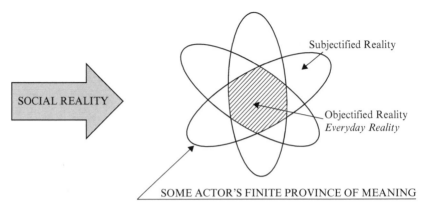

*Source:*   Arbnor & Bjerke, 2009:150.

*Figure 6.2   Social dialectics and everyday reality*

## 6.8   SYMBOLIC INTERACTIONISM OR SOCIAL PHENOMENOLOGY?

There is a 'hard' and a 'soft' version of social constructionism. *The hard version* is ethnomethodology, which focuses on micro processes (of which practically all are taken for granted and of which we are – in practice – unconscious), which make it possible for the life world to emerge and to be maintained at all. *The soft version* is symbolic interactionism and / or social phenomenology, which focus on how our life world (our everyday world) is constantly produced and reproduced by actors who are part of it. Both versions look at social reality as the only reality, which is developed interactively between us. Social phenomenology stresses more than symbolic interactionism that people carry language typifications to every social situation (which emerge, develop and, to a large extent, are confirmed in interactions between people) and that people (most of the time unconsciously) play with narratives and stories of self, what we could call *interpretative schemes* (another name could be *social intercourse scripts*), in which they place themselves in every specific situation. Which interpretative scheme they use depends on their intentionality at that place and at that time (intentionality means, consequently, to be controlled by a specific interpretative scheme). It is possible for an outsider, for instance a researcher, to interpret a specific social situation by extracting the pictures and typifications, by which the participants orientate themselves – which they may modify and, at least partly, clarify for themselves as well as for their environment – together with the interpretative scheme, which they

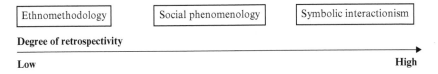

Figure 6.3    *Different degree of retrospectivity between social
constructionistic approaches*

externalize at that situation. I find it interesting to interpret entrepreneurs
consistently with the social phenomenological approach in the light of that
interpretative scheme by which they live – as entrepreneurs!

The scientific backgrounds to the two alternatives of marketing for
entrepreneurs which are used in this book, which are rationalism and social
phenomenology, can also be interpreted as separating (which I do) between
explaining and understanding. I look at these two concepts later in this
chapter. Furthermore, it is so, that interviews are common in the rational
managerial alternative for entrepreneurs' marketing, while dialogue is a
central concept within the social phenomenological alternative. A discussion about the concepts of interviews and dialogues ends this chapter.

To summarize, it is possible to see three alternative ways to use social
constructionism, which are:

–   ethnomethodology
–   social phenomenology
–   social interactionism.

These three have similarities (including a basic common view of the
construction of reality as social), but differences between the three can be
expressed in their degree of retrospectivity (Figure 6.3).

Ethnomethodology is concerned with unconsidered and unquestioned
background expectations and implicit rules that govern action in the life
world. Its method is to *focus on micro processes which make it possible for
the life world to develop and to be maintained*. Ethnomethodology has been
criticized for studying the consequences of our everyday conventions,
while ignoring the sources of these conventions:

> Ethnomethodologists forget to bring into their analysis the fact that ambiguity
> in human societies is partly eliminated by a whole range of tools, rules, walls and
> things, of which they just analyse some. (Latour 1998:18–19; my translation)
>
> Ethnomethodology never asks the central question: which are the supraindi-
> vidual structures that shape the actors' behavioural dispositions? (Alvesson &
> Sköldberg, 2000:43)

Ethnomethodology has been called 'the science of sense-making' (Gephart, 1993). Symbolic interactionism could be called social sense-making. Sense-making is conceptualized as *the reciprocal interaction of seeking information and constructing meaning with action* (Weick, 1995). Created meaning influences action. Reciprocally, action influences the meaning given to an action. One may conceptualize *action as meaningful behaviour* (Sanner, 1997).

Sense-making can provide special insights into uncertain and ambiguous situations, for example, when taking on a new and innovative activity related to an entrepreneurial venture. It is important for an entrepreneur to enact possibilities, and not be restricted by fixed ideas or definitions of what the situation is all about. The environment can be acted upon to widen these possibilities for an activity and include other actors. A broad network widens the environment through social constructions and then enlarges the room to act. Developing a problem to a possibility can be achieved through an entrepreneurial sense-making of reality (Sanner, 1997).

Sense-making concerns the future but tends to be retrospective. When people think of future actions, they think of similar actions they have already taken to anticipate and make sense of the consequences of the former (Gartner et al., 1992). One could say that 'they use the meaning they place in experience of their everyday life' (Schutz, 1967:73) as an *interpretative scheme* for their actions. We could also say that they, often unconsciously, *act consistently with a social intercourse script*, or if we put it differently, that they *enact a narrative*. Somebody might enact the narrative 'I will present myself as an unconcerned person' or 'incredibly experienced in relating to the opposite sex'. An entrepreneur might enact the narrative 'I have been around before' or 'I know what I am doing'.

Interpretative schemes, which we often take for granted (although without being able to tell somebody else their full content), make it possible for us to 'recognize', 'interpret' and 'negotiate' even strange and unanticipated situations and thus continue confirming and reconfirming meaning in interaction with others (Ranson et al., 1980). But these schemes also work as blinkers in a situation which should be looked at as new.

Sense-making, however, is more than a process of recalling existing interpretative schemes or playing out old narratives. If that were not true, no new learning could take place (Gioia, 1986). Instead, sense-making and construction of meaning involve associating new experience with existing knowledge, sometimes modifying existing schemes, scripts and narratives to incorporate new knowledge and, even if infrequently, dramatically restructuring existing knowledge or creating new knowledge by using intuition and revelation (Bartunek, 1984).

My choice in this book is social phenomenology. I am using symbolic interactionism with the addition that our experience of the world is directed by intentionality in a kind of *natural attitude*, where we take for granted that our (social) world is built up by assumptions of groups of event in our language, so-called *typifications*, assumptions which are rarely questioned, and which can also be controlled by *social intercourse scripts* (*interpretative schemes*), the content of which is influenced by our ambitions, in the case of this book being an entrepreneur. However, our typifications as well as our schemes, apart from being confirmed in social situations, can also be modified and changed through so-called *language development*.

I have mentioned a few times that I am presenting two alternative approaches of marketing for entrepreneurs in this book, of which one is the rational approach and the other social phenomenological. It will become clear that the former is naturally associated with 'explaining' and with 'interviews', while the latter with 'understanding' and 'dialogues'.

## 6.9   EXPLAINING AND UNDERSTANDING

To claim a clear difference between 'explaining' and 'understanding' may seem of little interest to some. However, it has become customary, though by no means universal, to distinguish between trying to build a picture of *events* and a picture of *acts*. It is suggested that the term 'understanding', in contrast to 'explaining', ought to be reserved for the latter.

Since the inception of the disciplines of social sciences, lines of controversy have been drawn between those who do and those who do not make a principal distinction between two presumed alternative modes of thought, which are the natural sciences and social sciences. Theorists rejecting any fundamental distinction between those modes could be called *explainists*. They assume that the methods which have proved their unparalleled value in the analysis of the physical world are applicable to the materials of the social sciences, and that while these methods may have to be adapted to a special subject matter, the logic of explanation in natural and social sciences is the same. Theorists who draw a distinction between 'understanding' and 'explaining' could be called *understandists* or *anti-explainists*. The critical element in anti-explainism is the insistence that the methods of natural sciences, however modified, are intrinsically inadequate to the subject matter of social sciences; in the physical world man's knowledge is external and empirical, while social sciences are concerned with interpretations and with various kinds of experience.

Many methodological and theoretical discourses within social sciences since the late nineteenth century have concerned modes of thought of 'understanding' and 'explaining'. These discussions reached a high point in the period before the First World War, and they have been part of social sciences ever since.

The controversy between explaining and understanding is deeply rooted in Western thought. In its most elementary sense it is based on a presumed intrinsic difference between mind and all that is non-mind. The controversy cannot be eliminated by choosing between explaining and understanding because, basically, they cannot be compared (just as different paradigms cannot). Most explainists, for instance, claim that everything, in the physical world as well as in the human world, can be explained, at least in principle; while understandists claim that understanding is only for humans. Furthermore, there is no third neutral position where you can choose between explaining and understanding in a business-like and impartial way. One must 'choose' at the same time as, by necessity, being positioned in either the explaining or the understanding camp. Which is really no choice at all!

To summarize, the explaining movement can be characterized by the three following statements relating to social sciences (Bjerke, 1989):

1.  Explanations produced by social sciences should be of the same type as natural sciences explanations, which are statements of conformity to law expressed in the form 'A leads to B'.
2.  Social sciences should, as far as possible, use the same type of methods as natural sciences as far as constructing and testing these explanations are concerned.
3.  Ideologies, myths and metaphysics have an extra-scientific content.

There are explanations of different kinds: (1) *deductive-nomological* explanations: a consequence of a general law; (2) *statistical* explanations: a consequence of a statistical law; (3) *causal* explanations: as an effect of causes; (4) *dispositional* explanations: an event has a disposition to happen; (5) *motivational* explanations: based on motives or purposes.

My preferred way of looking at explanations in this book is close to (3) and (5) above, which are causal ('due to'-explanations) and / or motivational explanations (also called teleological explanations – 'in order to'-explanations). This leads to my choice of managerial thinking as one of the two versions for discussing marketing for entrepreneurs.

No one today claims that only natural sciences should aim for explanations and that only social sciences should aim for understanding. In practice, attempts at both are made in both areas.

## 6.10 FURTHER EXPLORATION OF UNDERSTANDING

Many researchers are conscious of and accept the differences between the two approaches of explaining and understanding, although in everyday usage it is harder to distinguish between the two. While it seems relatively clear that 'explain' means, by and large, to figure out the external circumstances around what has happened or what is happening, there is, however, a wide variety of opinions as to what we could mean by 'understand'; for example, 'to understand' means to:

- find out more details
- access subjective opinions
- build a picture of the larger context in which a phenomenon is placed
- build a picture of relevant circumstances which have taken place earlier in a specific situation.

To me, none of these equates to understanding; they are each just more detailed, more circumstantial or deeper aspects of explanations. As I see it, one crucial difference between explaining and understanding, as far as the role played by the involved language is concerned, is that explanation sees language as *depicting* reality and understanding sees language as *constituting* reality.

Thus, explainists:

- look for factual (objective and/or subjective) data and use a depicting language,
- want to find causal or teleological relations, and
- build models

while understandists:

- deny that factual and depicting data exist (at least in the human world),
- want to look for actors' view on meaning, importance and significance and use a constituting and forming (even performing) language, and
- produce interpretations.

In this, *models* are deliberately simplified pictures of factual reality while *interpretations* are deliberately problematized pictures of socially constructed reality. It is natural for explainists to build models and for understandists to produce interpretations (Table 6.1 offers a summary).

*Table 6.1    Explaining and understanding – a summary*

| Explanation | Understanding |
| --- | --- |
| Uses a depicting language | Uses a constituting language |
| Believes in a circumstantial world | Believes in a meaningful world |
| Sees reacting human beings | Sees acting human beings |
| Aims to depict a naturally complicated reality in models; that is, to come up with patterns of causally- or motivationally-bound reality by finding out the most crucial external circumstances in such a situation and neglecting those circumstances which are of less importance | Aims to problematize a social-constructively simplified reality by using interpretations; that is, to construct pictures which contain that meaning which is seen and believed by people in a situation, which, furthermore, provide openings for further construction of social reality |

Understanding is only of interest:

• when studying human beings
• between human beings.

'It is possible to explain human behaviour. We do not try to understand an area of low pressure because it has no meaning. On the other hand, we try to understand human beings because they are of the same kind as we are' (Liedman, 2002:280; my translation). Bauman (1978) distinguishes between various kinds of understanding consistent with the theoretical ground on which it rests:

1. Understanding as the work of history (Marx, Weber, Mannheim).
2. Understanding as the work of reason (Husserl, Parsons).
3. Understanding as the work of life (Heidegger, from Schutz to ethnomethodology).

My way of looking at understanding in this book corresponds mainly to points (2) and (3) above, which leads to my choice of social constructionism as the second of two versions to discuss marketing for entrepreneurs.

In short, *understanding* to me means an insight into the *meaning with* (the purpose of) *an act* (meaning can never be quantified, nor reduced to any form of nature). Understanding to my mind calls for accepting that human beings are steered by *intentionality*. This is a concept which was developed by the founder of modern phenomenology, the German philosopher Husserl (1859–1938), who picked up the concept from one of his teachers, the German-Austrian philosopher and psychologist Brentano

(1838–1917). Like Brentano, Husserl claimed that all acts are governed by intentionality, that is, they are directed at an object in the wide sense of the term and they are always performed in a context. Our consciousness is permeated by our intentionality. We are always stretching ourselves, shaping what we perceive by using our intentionality (Bjerke, 1989).

A further distinction between understandists and explainists is that the former see no specific virtue in quantitative measures; they claim, as just mentioned, that *meaning cannot be quantified*!

> The interpretation of the meanings of actions, practices, and cultural objects is an extremely difficult and complicated enterprise. In order to know the meaning of certain overt movements, interpreters must understand the beliefs, desires, and intentions of the particular people involved. But in order to understand these, they must know the vocabulary in terms of which they are expressed, and this in turn requires that they know the social rules and conventions which specify what a certain movement or object counts as. Moreover, in order to grasp these particular rules, they also have to know the set of institutional practices of which they are a part, and how these are related to other practices of the society. Nor can interpreters stop here. The conventions and institutions of a social group presuppose a set of fundamental conceptualizations or basic assumptions regarding humanity, nature, and society. These basic conceptualizations might be called the 'constitutive meanings of a form of life', for they are the basic ideas of notions in terms of which the meanings of specific practices and schemes of activity must be analyzed. (Fay, 1996:115)

But Bauman (1978) asks how much one has to interpret in order to understand. He claims that one can say, for instance, that there is a difference in kind between those laws governing the objects of nature and the rules influencing human beings. The distinctive character of rules are meant to be grounded in certain psychological events which take place in the minds of people; nothing of a similar nature can be predicted upon natural phenomena.

This, indeed, seems like a valid argument, and for which we are prepared by the whole of our daily thinking and acting. Whenever we do not grasp 'directly' the meaning of other people's action, whenever we need to interpret action, we rely on concepts such as 'he wants to imply', 'she intends', 'he wants me to believe that' and so on – all referring the meaning of what has been said or done to mental processes of one kind or another. This we do only in the case of human action. We would certainly object to an attempt to describe the function of a machine in the same terms.

However, two very different things are confused here (Bauman, 1978). One is a statement of fact: no machine can write a book of Nobel Prize quality. The second, however, is a statement of interpretation: it is possible for a human being to write a book of Nobel Prize quality *because* of thought and emotions felt. Human action is unique because of the ability to make suppositions, to interpret the action of other humans via these suppositions, and to question the action of others on the same basis. 'Understanding' other humans' action, as against merely 'explaining' the conduct of inanimate objects, means ultimately extrapolating the method we use to account for our own action onto our accounts of the action of other objects whom we recognize as human. Recognizing them as humans, and extrapolating the method, mean in fact the same thing. Thus, perceiving an object as a human one boils down to assuming that the object has its own 'inner reality' structured in the same way as ours.

But now comes the crucial question: Do we really need to know what is going on in somebody else's head in order to understand them?

> Do we in fact need insight into the psychical process in the mind of the actor in order to *understand* his behaviour? Do we actually reconstruct this mental process when engaged in the effort of understanding? It is true that we normally refer to such mental processes when accounting for our *interpretation*. We articulate our version of other people's conduct in terms like 'he thinks that', 'he does not like it', 'he does not wish', 'he wanted to', 'what he meant was', etc., all implying that we have penetrated the 'inside' of our partner's mind and found the meaning of his behaviour there. The question is, however, whether these are only the terms which we use to couch our interpretation, or whether they are a true expression of what we have actually done. As a matter of fact we do not know what '*they*' think', 'intend', 'mean'. Or, at least, we do not know it in the same way as we know our own thinking, intending meaning. What we know is only their action, the sentences they utter, the prosodic features which accompany their speech, the 'paralinguistic' aspects of their behaviour. All these refer to what we can see or hear. When we speak of their thinking, intending meaning, we do not refer to what we see or hear, but to the manner in which we interpret what we see or hear. This common-sense-grounded manner of speech is regrettable, as it beclouds rather than reveals the true nature of understanding. It suggests that the activity of understanding needs what in actual fact it can well (and must) do without – knowing something which is essentially 'unknowable'. (Bauman, 1978:213–14)

So, when we interpret and try to understand other human beings, we do not need to have extrasensory, insightful or emphatic characteristics. It is enough to understand how to recognize oneself, that is, to have some cultural aspect in common with the other person (otherwise an understanding would not be possible at all). Furthermore, to understand what the other person means when he or she makes a specific remark, we do not need to enter the other person's consciousness. We 'only' need to agree with the other person about where and how this remark can be used, to know the 'language game' so to say.

That social phenomenological alternative (unlike the managerial alternative) of marketing for entrepreneurs, asserts that there is a good chance of succeeding if the entrepreneur is better in *understanding* the customer. One necessity in that case is to use dialogues instead of interviews.

## 6.11   INTERVIEWS AND DIALOGUES

There are differences between managerial and social phenomenological activities (say in marketing for entrepreneurs) in terms of using interviews or dialogues. Let us clarify some general differences between the two. A more detailed discussion can be found in Bjerke (2007).

The fact that interviews and dialogues are proven to be important in social science studies today is demonstrated by the fact that 90% of all studies are estimated to use face-to-face research of some kind (Briggs, 1986). Face-to-face research is the window of the world for the researcher (Hyman et al., 1975), but it is not always easy to use it well. Research face-to-face consists of encounters of a special kind: in a way, they mean meetings in everyday life, but with a research purpose relating to at least one of the participants (Curran & Blackburn, 2001).

The main purpose of an interview is to collect factual data of an objective and / or a subjective kind and, based on this data, try to describe and possibly explain factual reality. Objective data means true answers to questions of the type, 'How many employees do you have?', 'When did you last do your shopping here?'; the answers are not, when the question is asked, supposed to be dependent on any subjective whim, and the correctness of them could, in principle, be validated from sources other than from the respondent in the interview. Subjective (but still factual) describes answers to questions like: 'What is your opinion about . . .?' or 'What motivated you to visit this shop?' Data from subjective reality could be called private and cannot, unlike objective data, be validated from other sources of information.

The ambition of an interview is to create a true picture of part of objective and/or subjective – but nevertheless factual – reality. One important task for the interviewer is to avoid the interviewer effect, that is, to influence the answer in any direction. A possible metaphor is to 'draw a map' when looking for objective data and to 'fish' when looking for subjective data.

Some commentators see some problems with interviews:

> [There are] dilemmas facing interview researchers concerning what to make of their data. On the one hand, positivists have as a goal the creation of the 'pure' interview – enacted in a sterilized context, in such a way that it comes as close as possible to providing a 'mirror reflection' of the reality that exists in the social world. This position has been thoroughly critiqued over the years

> in terms of both its feasibility and its desirability. On the other hand, . . . social constructionists suggest that . . . the interview is . . . an interaction between the interviewer and the interview subject in which both participants create and construct narrative versions of the social world. (Miller & Glassner, 1997:99)

> From a more traditional standpoint, the objectivity of truth of interview responses might be assessed in terms of reliability, the extent to which questioning yields the same answers whenever and wherever it is carried out, and validity, that is, the extent to which inquiry yield the 'correct' answers. . . . When the interview is seen as dynamic, meaning-making occasion, however, different criteria apply. The focus is on how meaning is constructed, the circumstances of construction, and the meaningful linkages that are made for the occasion. (Holstein & Gubrium, 1997:117)

The alternative to an interview is a dialogue. The main purpose of a dialogue (which is radically different from an interview) is to try to understand the meaning in other people's language and cultural worlds. The way I look at it, understanding is not based on objective and/or subjective facts but on objectified and / or subjectified ideas (symbolic or typified language categories which are treated as objective and / or subjective, but without being so). Nor are they factual, but socially constructed (partly dependent upon and possibly created in the very dialogue itself). Compared with referring to interviews as *drawing maps* or *fishing*, it is possible, as a metaphor again, to refer to a dialogue as the *functioning of an author*.

> The interplay of questions and answers in a dialogue is close to what we might call an 'honest question'. To ask an honest question, you have to know that you don't know. And when you know that you don't know, you don't use a direct method, because that implies that you only want to know something more thoroughly in the way you already know it. (Arbnor & Bjerke, 2009:136)

Some questions related to interviews are:

- *Interview planning.* Most interviews are planned in one or several of the following aspects (Carson et al., 2001):
  - The *overall objective* with the interview should be formulated.
  - An *interview guide* should be written, if other people are helping with the interviews.
  - One should be clear about what *subject area* they want to clarify in the interview.
- *When does an interview start?* There are several opinions about the answer to this question (Emory, 1985; Carson et al., 2001):
  - When the interviewer feels that the respondent is ready.
  - When the interviewer has identified him- or herself as an interviewer and presented the purpose of the interview.

- – When, as an interviewer, we feel that the respondent wants to participate as a respondent, possibly by accepting that the interview will be recorded.
  – When all parties understand which degree of confidentiality and anonymity is to prevail.
- *Bases for a successful interview* (Emory, 1985):
  – The information looked for by the respondent should be accessible.
  – The respondent understands his or her role, that is, as a reporter of factual information.
  – The respondent should be motivated enough to participate constructively.
- *What characterizes 'good questions'* (Johansson Lindfors, 1993):
  – The questions are simply and clearly formulated.
  – Questions should not contain negations.
  – Questions should not be leading in any way.
  – A question should not contain more than one aspect at a time.
- *Reliability and validity?* In relations with interviews, questions concerning reliability and validity are commonly asked. Reliability means that those answers we receive do not depend on the circumstances around the interview. Validity means to be told the truth.

Some questions related to dialogues are:

- *Are dialogues more of an art than a science?* In a dialogue, the social context is a decisive factor to understand the data that we receive as researchers. In a dialogue, it is important to understand both *how* things are said as to understand *what* is said. Interpretations must therefore always be done by the researcher when taking part in a dialogue. We could ask whether these can be done scientifically or not. This question is not easy to answer. However, two comments could be made:
  1. That dialogue which takes place in a dialogue does not start from scratch. Much of it is confirmation of meaning, that is, a confirmation of what the participants brought with them when they entered the dialogue. The researchers also have 'interpretative baggage' when they enter.
  2. There is never an interpretation which is generally better than another. Nobody has interpretative precedence over others in a dialogue. The researcher's interpretation could be as good as any, if he or she is aware of the ground on which his or her interpretation is based.

- *How active should a researcher be in a dialogue?* For researchers to achieve something when participating in a dialogue, they should be well prepared in the meaning that they should have a good knowledge of what is to be discussed. Furthermore, dialogues often develop over several occasions. But, apart from this, how active a researcher should be must be decided from case to case. As a minimum, we should require that the researcher understands the forms related to the research settings in question as well as their content. 'The objective is not to dictate interpretation, but to provide an environment conducive to the production of the range and complexity of meanings that address relevant issues, and not to be confined by predetermined agendas' (Holstein & Gubrium, 1997:123). One could say that the researchers in a dialogue should use the social process as much as possible (they cannot escape from this process) without dominating it.
- *What characterizes a skilful researcher in a dialogue?* Some possible requirements for researchers to be successful in participating in a dialogue are that they should be:
  - Knowledgeable. To have a good knowledge of the subject which the dialogue is about, without trying to show off.
  - Clear. To talk a simple, distinct and understandable everyday language, not using academic language or professional jargon.
  - Sensitive. To be an active listener, to hear the nuances which are brought up and try to probe deeper into those nuances which seem important; to listen to emotional messages and to note what is said.
  - Critical. Not to take what is said for granted but to ask critical questions in order to move on.
  - Remembering. To remember what is said at different stages of the dialogue, partly not to repeat themselves but also to be able to relate the different stages to each other to develop them further as the dialogue continues.
- *Are there any limits to a dialogue?* There are several aspects of a dialogue which researchers should keep in mind (Silverman, 1993):
  - There is no absolute freedom. Social control also takes place in a dialogue. Realizing how this control takes place is part of the interpretation of the results of the dialogue.
  - It is difficult to avoid the tendency, as researchers, to believe that we have 'the answers' before they are given. It is naturally human (even for researchers) to make a pre-interpretation of situations in which they become involved. It may therefore be difficult to separate what has been taken for granted from what has been brought up as unique information in a dialogue.

   – It is difficult to interpret the interaction form and its content at the same time.

One may ask which type of face-to-face research is best. This is not possible to answer in general terms. It all depends on:

- the basic presumptions behind the research, in terms of the theory of science on which it is based
- the purpose behind the research.

The two groups of research face-to-face that have been discussed here, which are interviews and dialogues, as based on critically different and incompatible assumptions. An impartial choice between the two is impossible. There is no neutral position to take.

As mentioned earlier, it is natural to associate rational marketing with *interviews* and constructionist marketing with *dialogues*.

# 7.  Entrepreneurial startups

## 7.1  INTRODUCTION

This chapter discusses different kinds of entrepreneurial startups. First, there is a distinction made between rational and bricoleurial startups; secondly, between startups for business entrepreneurs (as independent units and as intrapreneurial ones) and for social entrepreneurs. Finally, there is a detailed review of four concepts, which are important in relation to the purpose behind this book. The concepts are 'market', 'customer','user' and 'value creation'. After examining the distinctive aspects of marketing for entrepreneurs and penetrating a fundamental phenomenon with which entrepreneurs' marketing is associated over and above what I have done already in terms of networking, I present some general fundamental (common as well as separate) principles behind the two alternative ways in which entrepreneurs can market themselves in my opinion, i.e., the managerial and the social phenomenological methods. The rest of this book is based on these principles.

## 7.2  RATIONAL AND BRICOLEURIAL THINKING

The anthropologist Lévi-Strauss (1966) separates two kinds of thinking from each other. One is associated with what he refers to as 'the rational engineer' and the other with 'the natural bricoleur'. The *engineer* tries to make his or her way with existing resources and, if needed, from what he or she can acquire in a professional network or buy / lease elsewhere, while the *bricoleur* has an inclination to make do with what he or she has alone and can get from other actors in his or her naturally existing network.

To behave rationally in an entrepreneurial case is to behave logically and consistently, considering those objectives and / or those means that exist and which you know that you can obtain (Stevenson & Jarillo, 1990; Sarasvathy, 2001). To act bricoleurially in the entrepreneurial case is to act naturally, considering your own talents and experience and in dialogues with friends, relatives and other contacts extend your citizen capital to widen your natural approach to various problems in your field of interest.

The word bricoleur (as well as entrepreneur) comes from French. In the old sense, the verb 'bricoler' applied to some external, natural movements, for instance, a ball rebounding, a dog straying or a horse swerving from its direct course to avoid an obstacle. In our time, a 'bricoleur' is someone who works naturally, almost instinctively without too much thinking, similarly to how a craftsperson works. This is unlike an engineer who rationally executes his or her profession, based on formal knowledge acquired, for instance by attending a professional school (Lévi-Strauss, 1966:16–17).

The bricoleur has no precise equivalent outside French. It describes a person who undertakes odd jobs and is a Jack-of-all-trades and professional do-it-yourself man or woman, but as Lévi-Strauss makes clear, this is a person of different standing from an 'odd job man or woman' or handy person. The bricoleur has a variety of skills, which, even if they are many, still are limited, due to the practical learning and experiences acquired in life. The engineer, on the other hand, acquires those skills and means that are necessary (for instance, by buying, cooperating with somebody else or hiring) to fulfil the purposes behind a project that he or she has taken on. In principle, there are as many skills and means available or acquirable as there are projects for an engineer. The skills and means of a bricoleur, on the other hand, cannot be defined in terms of a single project. The bricoleur collects skills and means to improve his or her own life, consistent with the principle that 'they may always come to be of some use' (Lévi-Strauss, 1966:18); i.e., without having one or several projects in mind, because, the way he or she looks at things, a bricoleur never knows exactly beforehand which type of projects he or she may become interested in. Nor does a bricoleur know, for natural reasons, to any larger extent how these projects will run and develop, especially if he or she want to become an entrepreneur (that is, *a genuinely new development* – and thereby unpredictable to some extent).

The engineer always tries to break free from limitations that exist at a given place and time. The bricoleur, on the other hand, feels that this is not always possible, but he or she may use a given context, place and time in a clever (or at least natural) way instead of achieving what he or she wants. The engineer chooses means from all directions rationally consistent with the needs of a specific project. The bricoleur chooses projects in a natural way, considering what skills and means he or she already has or could have access to in existing social networks, and which consequently are at hand. It is a big mistake, as stated by Lévi-Strauss (1966:21), however, to see the bricoleur's and the engineer's thinking as stages of more learning or acquiring better skills.

The importance of the relationships between a business venture and the environment for the improvement of the venture has been discussed for a long time. Penrose (1959) argued that firms which have very similar material and human resource inputs may offer substantially different services to the market because of differences in their abilities to understand possible use of various inputs. Open systems models started to be presented at about the same time (Boulding, 1956), suggesting the need for organizations to act differently in different environments. These open systems models were later developed by Katz and Kahn (1978), and Scott (1998) among others. However, none of these models provides any useful explanation of *how* such organization-specific processes take place or, above all, how organizations can *create something from seemingly nothing*. Theories of bricolage do so.

*Bricolage, creativity, improvisation and social learning often appear tightly linked together.* This differs from the traditional rational linear and objective planning focus within a social context. Bricolage is an important means of counteracting the tendency to enact limitations without testing them. This suggests that a social phenomenological approach to resource environments is sometimes more fruitful than objectivistic, factual, rational views, which hold sway in much contemporary entrepreneurship research (Baker et al., 2005) as well as in most contemporary marketing research today. The social construction of resource environment involves reframing or outright rejecting those definitions of resources that exist at present, and is fundamental to the process of bricolage. This opens new areas for entrepreneurship and marketing research by looking at networking as a natural part of entrepreneurship and marketing. In the literature, action faced with limited resources has been studied in terms of finance (for example, bootstrapping) and, to some extent, in terms of non-linear process design (Bhave, 1994). When defining resources at hand, we should also include resources that are available very cheaply or for free, even if others judge them to be useless or substandard; something which is rarely done in rational entrepreneurship and marketing research but which is done in bricolage theories. This also means that creating value through bricolage does not depend on the Schumpeterian assumption that some assets are withdrawn from one activity to be applied in another in order for development to take place – what he refers to as creative destruction – nor that business gain should be measured primarily by market share.

The bricoleurial version of entrepreneurship startups is particularly useful when looking at social entrepreneurship, especially that version of entrepreneurship which I refer to as public entrepreneurs (Chapter 10).

## 7.3    RATIONAL AND BRICOLEURIAL ENTREPRENEURIAL STARTUPS

The limited view of entrepreneurship tends to build *rational* models. This has had the consequence when referring to starting entrepreneurial ven-

**GOALS**                **STARTUP BEHAVIOUR**

*Figure 7.1   A goals-rational entrepreneurial startup*

**MEANS**                **STARTUP BEHAVIOUR**

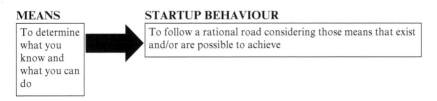

*Figure 7.2   A means-rational entrepreneurial startup*

tures of talking about *goals rationality* (as causation) or *means-rationality* (as effectuation) (Sarasvathy, 2001). Goals-rational entrepreneurial ventures start with rather explicit goals and ambitions, and the entrepreneur looks for alternative possibilities to fulfil these goals and ambitions. He or she then chooses the means that seem to provide the chance to achieve them.

A goals-rational person trusts his or her ability to forecast the future and to be able to acquire the means which are necessary to achieve his or her goals. Much of the limited view of entrepreneurship is based on this idea. Those who take this position assert that 'if I can forecast the future, I can steer it'. Goals-rational entrepreneurial startups are illustrated in Figure 7.1.

Means-rational entrepreneurial ventures are steered not so much by what the entrepreneur wants to achieve, as by those means that he or she has and can acquire to become an entrepreneur. The venture starts by determining these means. Those who take this position assert that 'if I can steer the future, I do not need to forecast it'. Means-rational entrepreneurial startups are illustrated in Figure 7.2.

Most business and social entrepreneurial startups, which take place according the limited view on entrepreneurship, are probably best seen as *rational* entrepreneurial startups. Other entrepreneurial startups, i.e., those which take place consistent with the more extended view on entrepreneurship, should preferably be looked at as *bricoleurial*, which means that something new is created by involving other actors in a process, where existing resources are transformed (Garud et al., 1998; Baker & Nelson, 2005). Bricolage is sometimes described as 'making do with what is at

*Figure 7.3    A bricoleurial entrepreneurial startup*

hand – at least to start with' (Lévi-Strauss, 1966:16–17; Miner et al., 2001; Weick, 1993). Bricolage is illustrated in Figure 7.3.

Kickul et al. (2010:232) describe bricolage as a set of actions 'driven by the pursuit of existing and often scarce resources that can be recombined to create novel and interesting solutions of value that affect their respective markets'. The concept of bricolage can help us understand how some emerging entrepreneurial ventures embrace challenges under conditions of tight resource constraints.

Rational models for how new entrepreneurial ventures begin look at the economic return that aspiring entrepreneurs expect. Bricolage focuses instead on more natural prosocial actions of entrepreneurs whose environments are typically resource-constrained and essentially present new challenges without providing new resources. Bricolage is often about exploiting physical, institutional, social or other inputs that other firms reject or ignore. Realizing greater impact through innovation may then depend on the extent to which entrepreneurs can apply and combine the resources they already have to attack new problems and possibilities (Baker & Nelson, 2005).

It may seem that means-rationality and bricolage are the same, but there are several differences. The basic distinction between the two is that means-rationality is based on rational epistemology (goals-rationality is also based on this), while bricolage is based on social constructional epistemology. In more practical terms, the following differences exist between means-rationality and bricolage:

●   Means-rationality attempts to provide a more correct picture of how business startups take place by *explaining them generally, using models*; bricolage attempts to *understand* business startups *by interpreting entrepreneurs as agents more specifically in social constructions.*

●   To take an example, somebody who is means-rational might prepare a meal using specified means, no matter when or where the meal is to take place. A bricoleur might start earlier (that is, before having a specific meal in mind) by collecting things, which he or she happens to come across and finds interesting due to an inclination or orientation – it might be, for instance, an interesting ingredient or recipe, which *might come to some use at some time or place.*

- *A bricoleur can be very clever in improvising.* To continue with the example of preparing a meal, a bricoleur, who looks at his or her situation not as factual but as something which can be constructed socially and thereby questions what different possibilities and limitations mean in a specific case, may use an ingredient in a clever way where it has hardly been used before.
- A model of a means-rational startup, whereby you know what resources you have, is generally valid and not tied to any specific time or place. A bricoleur, on the other hand, is bound to what is specified in terms of time as well as place, and must keep in mind where and when the event, in fact, is to take place.
- To extend the cooking scenario, an example of how a bricoleur can question apparent restrictions and who is ingenious as far as accomplishing a 'mission' is concerned (seemingly creating something out of nothing) is to collect some flowers that are growing in the garden at that specific time, which could be used as decorations (creating raw material), or to ask the guests to come earlier and assist in preparing the meal (creating labour).

In Figure 7.3, four bricoleurial startup actions are mentioned, which are 'testing limitations that are taken for granted', 'improvising', 'playing with what is at hand' and 'trying, modifying, accepting or rejecting'. Three comments can give a deeper understanding of what these actions might mean:

1.  Lévi-Strauss (1966) observes that bricoleurs accumulate physical artefacts, skills or ideas on the principle that they (like a normal person) may possibly come in handy, in contrast with 'the engineer', who rather acquires resources in response to well-defined demands of a specific project. The bricoleur regards their 'collection' as part of a practical repertoire for dealing with challenging new situations in life. Prior or existing results or elements of (own or others') failures are building materials for new challenges – a bricoleur does not build something new *on* the ruins but *with* the ruins of the old regime. Above all, existing citizen network contacts and the citizen capital they may bring contain resources for new entrepreneurial ventures (Baker et al., 2005).

2. Bricolage can mean combining and reusing resources for different applications from those for which they were originally intended or used. System designers may 'paste together a few components into "something", see how it looks, play with it, check if it works, evaluate, modify or reject. This bricolage activity is not directed to any specific solution or configuration in general because [no one] knows in advance what the final configuration is going to be' (Lanzara, 1999:337). Evolution is 'always a matter of using the same elements, or adjusting them, of altering here and there, of arranging various combinations to produce new objects of increasing complexity. It is always a matter of tinkering' (Jacob, 1977:1164–5). Bricolage means an 'ingenious reconciliation of existing organizational mechanisms and forms, picked according to subjective plans and interpretation' (Ciborra, 1996:104).

3. Making do implies a bias towards action and active engagement with problems, rather than lingering too much over questions of whether a workable outcome can be created from what is at hand. It also means by necessity a bias for testing received limitations. Many cases of bricolage are invoked during skilful acts of improvisation (Weick, 1993; Miner et al., 2001).

Bricolage can often start in spite of possible resource limitations, and most new entrepreneurial activities start small and local. Johnstone and Lionais (2004:227–8) provide examples of bricolage among entrepreneurs in so-called 'depleted communities', which succeed because of their local connections (mentioned in Chapter 3).

Based on the idea that reality is regarded as a social construction, networking as part of bricolage becomes a matter of genuine co-construction and co-creation, not just exchange of information (see section 7.9 later in this chapter). Baker and Nelson (2005:349) give several examples of this (Table 7.1).

> Bricolage notions of making do and using whatever is at hand links with a fundamental social shift of developing smart, sustainable, projects that are integral to social change. This represents a shift from a consumption-based to a conversation-based way of doing things better than through an improved understanding of existing resources, their form, function, and fungibility, thereby developing a more clever, creative means of developing goods and services aligned with market needs. (Kickul et al., 2010:237)

*Table 7.1   Clever bricoleurial steps to generate 'new' resources*

| Environmental domain | Description of bricoleurial activity |
| --- | --- |
| Inputs: physical | By imbuing forgotten, discarded, worn or presumed 'single-application' materials with new user value, bricolage turns valueless or even negatively valued resources into valuable materials. |
| Inputs: labour | By involving customers, suppliers and hangers-on in providing work on projects, bricolage sometimes creates labour inputs. |
| Inputs: skills | By permitting and encouraging the use of amateur and self-taught skills (electronics repair, soldering, road work, etc.) that would otherwise go unapplied, bricolage creates useful services. |
| Customers/markets | By providing goods and services that would otherwise be unavailable (housing, cars, billing system, etc.) to customers (because of poverty, thriftiness, or lack of availability), bricolage creates products and markets where none existed. |
| Institutional and regulatory environments | By refusing to enact limitations with regard to many 'standards' and regulations, and by actively trying things in a variety of areas in which entrepreneurs either do not know the rules or do not see them as constraining, bricolage creates space to 'get away with' solutions that would otherwise be impermissible. |

*Source:*   Baker and Nelson, 2005:349.

## 7.4   INTRAPRENEURIAL STARTUPS

There are two classical models of how intrapreneurial activities (which are entrepreneurial activities in existing business firms) arise, which seem to function fairly well even today. The first is a proposal from the person who first coined the term 'intrapreneur'. Pinchot III (1985) suggests that an intrapreneurial activity arises in four phases. These are:

1.   *The solo phase.* In the beginning, the intrapreneur builds the vision by and large on his or her own.
2.   *The network phase.* When the basic idea is there, most intrapreneurs can start to share it with some friends in their workplace and with some trustworthy customers. From their reactions, they receive opinions about the strengths and weaknesses of the concept. It is surprisingly easy to get others to contribute with their knowledge. To

be asked for an opinion implies that you are looked at as some kind of expert.

3.   *The bootleg phase.* As the network phase goes on, some people start to work closer with the intrapreneur in more ways than just giving encouragement and advice. Some kind of team is formed, but it still works 'underground', maybe at the intrapreneur's home or in some neutral place.

4.   *The formal team phase.* Increasingly, it becomes more of an intrapreneurial venture than just an idea with some individual(s) working with it. A formal intrapreneurial team, which eventually is established by the intrapreneur, is hopefully functionally complete, acting independently and perhaps coming together in a commercialization later.

The second model of an intrapreneurial process which does not contradict the first is provided by Kanter (1983), who suggests three stages. This second proposal is not as individually orientated as the first one. The three stages are:

1.   *Defining the project.* Some principles are established here, as well as suitable and possible procedures. This takes place by concentrating on the task at hand. At this first stage, political as well as economical information may be needed.

2.   *Building a coalition.* What is required to put together a working team and supporting networks can exist not only in the vertical and formal sources within the hierarchy, but also from all possible directions within the organization (sometimes even from outside).

3.   *Action.* This third stage contains several major activities, which are:

     a)   *Handle disturbances.* The leader (the intrapreneur, that is) patrols the borders of the project, so to say.

     b)   *Keep momentum.* Disturbances may come from outside as well as from inside.

     c)   *New reformulations.* It is a natural development in an intrapreneurial project that corrective arrangements have to made now and then, which may mean making internal changes or adding external components in order to handle new problems and new tasks. It may also mean ending some sub-activities which turn out to be less workable.

     d)   *External communication.* It may be critical that colleagues and those who support the operations are updated on the project and its ongoing results. When the project is finished, the results must also be published not only within the company but also among potential receivers. It is probably not until this change that marketing is considered in a more formal format.

These two proposals for starting intrapreneurial ventures look on the surface as rather rational, but can, if penetrated further, also be looked at in bricoleurial terms (this will be discussed further in Chapter 9).

## 7.5 SOCIAL ENTREPRENEURIAL STARTUPS

In terms of starting a venture, many social entrepreneurs are similar to business entrepreneurs (one type is even a combination of the two). If so, rational causation or effectuation models and bricoleurial thinking will function as a basis for explanation and understanding of social startups as well. Some social entrepreneurs are different enough, however, to deserve their own outline. This can be provided as a sequence (Figure 7.4) or as a circle (Figure 7.5).

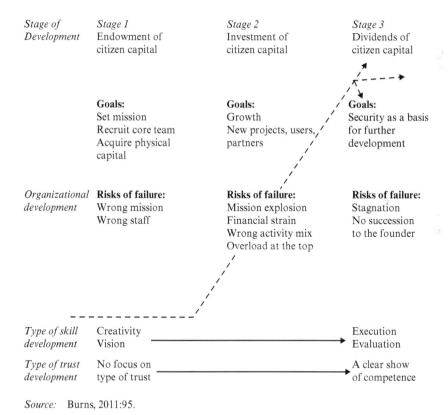

| *Stage of Development* | *Stage 1* Endowment of citizen capital | *Stage 2* Investment of citizen capital | *Stage 3* Dividends of citizen capital |
|---|---|---|---|
| | **Goals:** Set mission Recruit core team Acquire physical capital | **Goals:** Growth New projects, users, partners | **Goals:** Security as a basis for further development |
| *Organizational development* | **Risks of failure:** Wrong mission Wrong staff | **Risks of failure:** Mission explosion Financial strain Wrong activity mix Overload at the top | **Risks of failure:** Stagnation No succession to the founder |
| *Type of skill development* | Creativity Vision | | Execution Evaluation |
| *Type of trust development* | No focus on type of trust | | A clear show of competence |

*Source:* Burns, 2011:95.

*Figure 7.4 Life cycle of a social entrepreneurial operation*

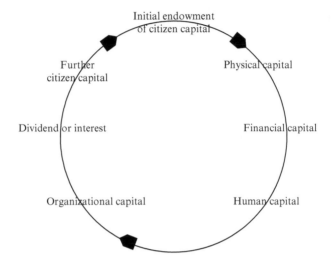

*Source:*   Adapted from Leadbeater, 1997.

*Figure 7.5   The virtuous circle of citizen capital*

The first proposal has been proposed by Burns (2011:95). It is presented in Figure 7.4 and it is, as I look at is, rather self-explanatory.

The second one is based on Leadbeater (1997) and it is presented as a *virtuous circle* (Figure 7.5).

Leadbeater's idea about social entrepreneurship as the development of citizen capital is that you already have access to such capital. The trick for the entrepreneur is to lever this up to gain access to more resources, firstly physical resources such as buildings, then financial capital to get the wheels rolling, and finally human capital in order to deliver.

Organizational capital is generated when the project begins to reach its goals and more resources are attracted. The resulting increase in cooperation and trust, which is generated in a successful project, can lead to new injections of citizen capital when the contact net and its contacts expand.

Both these proposals cover more of the entrepreneurial process than just the startup phase (which is my primary interest). However, the outcome of a social entrepreneurial venture is rarely about delivering a finished tangible product to a customer in a market, but more often about a citizen generating a service together with other citizens in an ongoing process, where it is hard to see the end of its 'development' and start of the 'delivery of a finished product'. This makes it harder to identify a discrete startup phase.

Public entrepreneurs are even more different from business entre-

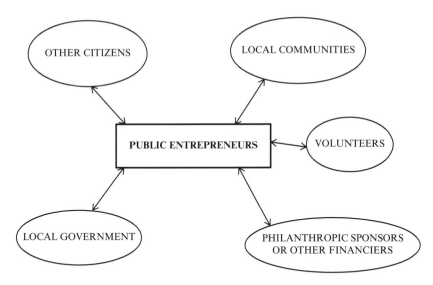

*Figure 7.6    Public entrepreneurs as catalysts in a value star for vitalizing public places with more citizenry*

preneurs and social entrepreneurs of a business-like type. They are not marketers, and they do not operate in a market in the normal sense of these terms. They are catalysts in vitalizing (public) places. Founders of museums, for example, are examples of public entrepreneurs: 'Good museums are a balanced combination of cultural [places] and social and community [places]. Today, museums have become "social condensers" for the community, almost taking the role churches once had. In an urban setting, they can be a catalyst for the revitalization of a derelict part of the city' (Bouchard et al., 2016:92–3). Public entrepreneurial startups would preferably be looked at as co-creation of 'more citizenry' in value stars (see section 7.11.1 for more about 'value stars'). Figure 7.6 illustrates one such star.

There are four concepts, the interpretation of which is important to understand differences between managerial marketing and social phenomenological marketing for entrepreneurs; that is, differences between my two marketing alternatives in this book. The four concepts are:

- market
- customer
- user, and
- value creation.

## 7.6   THE CONCEPT OF 'MARKET'

This book is about marketing for entrepreneurs. Marketing implies that there is a market – or, at least, a conception that there is a market, because market*ing* means to 'cultivate' a market (Frankelius et al., 2015) – *to bring something to a market*. But *what* is a market, *who* is a customer and / or a user of what is brought to the market, and *why*? Let us discuss this question one step at a time.

The concept of a market is not so easy to grasp as we may think. We might believe that our lives are full of markets, and that we are clear about what a market really means, how it functions and what are its basic assumptions.

In the traditional (and dominant) approach of marketing, that is, managerial marketing (which, as we know, is one of the two alternatives of marketing for entrepreneurs discussed in this book), a market is normally seen *as a space* (the concepts of 'place' and 'space' have been discussed in section 3.7). This is based on two assumptions (Svensson & Östberg, 2016):

- A market is something to work against, study, cover, analyse and cultivate as a mental conception.
- Exchange, price negotiations and agreements are actions between people having some common interests, rather than something that takes place *in* a tangible and physical place or creating a market as a place.

Markets *might* be referred to as (physical) places where goods, services and production factors are traded; for example, market squares, places for exchange of shares or currencies, galleries etc. This is also related to the origin of the concept. The Latin word *mercatus* means trade as well as the place where trade takes place (Aspers, 2011).

But markets today typically do not refer to physical locations:

> Markets need not be physical locations, where buyers and sellers interact. With modern communication and transportation, a merchant can easily advertise a product on the Internet or a late evening television programme, take orders from thousands of customers over the phone or online, and mail the goods to the buyers on the following day, without having had any physical contact with them. (Kotler et al., 2008:13)

In fact, in managerial marketing, physical places are normally not even referred to at all. A market means most often the total amount of money spent on some specific product during, say, one year in Europe (Frankelius et al., 2015:52). The concept of a market is then simply, 'where the price is determined in interaction between the two parties of buyers and sellers' (Eklund, 2010:339; my translation). This view of market lies behind Kotler et al. (2008:13)'s definition: 'We define marketing management as the art and science of choosing target markets and building profitable relationships with them.'

So, the concept of marketing means choosing markets and building strong relationships with those markets which have the highest profit potential, without pointing at some physical place, such as women between thirty and fifty years of age, the tourist market, or the market for I-phones. In other words, in managerial market,

> a market is a set of actual and potential buyers of marketing offering. These buyers share a particular need or want that can be satisfied through exchanges and relationships. Thus, the size of the market depends on the number of people who exhibit the need, have resources to engage in exchange, and are willing to offer these resources in exchange for what they want. (Kotler et al., 2008:12–13)

This is the same for some social entrepreneurs, that is, for those social entrepreneurs who behave in a 'business-like' fashion. Most social entrepreneurs act locally and look at their market as a 'place', however. Public entrepreneurs do not even operate in 'markets' at all, as I have mentioned. This also has consequences for how to conceptualize marketing associated with public entrepreneurial startups. This will be further developed in Chapter 10.

The traditional perception of 'market' evokes two clear conceptions, in other words. On one side, it represents an aggregation of customers. On the other side, it is an exchange space, where a company offers goods and services for sales to customers. Implicit in this view, there is a critical assumption that *companies can be self-governed* by designing products, developing production processes, constructing marketing messages and managing the sales channels with little or no interaction with customers. Customers come in here only at the moment of exchange.

In the traditional notion of the value-creating process, customers were 'situated outside the company'. Value creation was done by the company. The concept of 'value chain' summarizes the unilateral role that companies play in creating value (Porter, 1980). The company and the customer have distinct roles in production and consumption respectively (Kotler, 2002). 'The market, defined as customers, was a "target" for the company's supply' (Prahalad & Ramaswamy, 2004c:6).

It is obvious that the traditional market concept is company-centred. So is the value-creating process. Companies conceptualize the management of customer relationships as directing themselves to and managing the 'right' customers. Companies focus on the situation where the interaction is

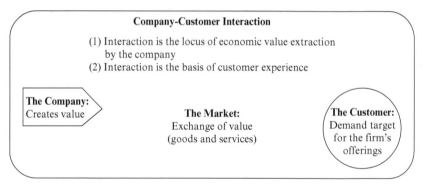

The market is separate from the value creation process

*Source:*   Adapted from Prahalad & Ramaswamy, 2004b:42.

*Figure 7.7    The traditional concept of a market*

happening – the exchange – as the space where economic value is extracted. The interaction between company and customers is not traditionally seen as a source of value creation (Normann & Ramirez, 1994; Wikström, 1996). The exchange and extraction of value are the primary functions of the market, which in turn is separated from the value-creating process. This can be seen in Figure 7.7. Communication goes from the company to the customer. The market is looked at as a situation where value is exchanged and the customer must be persuaded so that the company has the right to extract possible value from transactions.

In the view of the market which seems to emerge, the focus is instead more directly on the interaction between customer and company – *the role of the company and the customer converges.* The company and the customer are both cooperating and competing – cooperating in co-creating value and competing in extracting value. The market becomes inseparable from the value-creating process. (Figure 7.8).

Co-creation of value (which we will return to) challenges the distinction between supply and demand. When experience and value is co-created, the company may still provide a product. But focus is shifted to the character-istics of the total environment of experience. Now demand is contextual. We must look at the market as a *possibility for potential co-creating experi-ences*, in which individuals decide their willingness to pay for their experi-ences. 'In short, the market looks like a forum for co-creating experiences' (Prahalad & Ramaswamy, 2004c:12). New *experience-based approach to economic theory* will appear. Some of the key starting points are identified and summarized in Table 7.2.

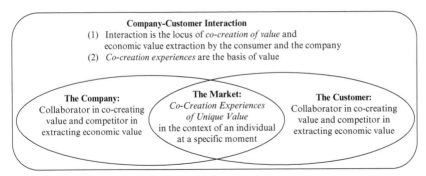

**The market is integral to the value creation process**

*Source:*    Prahalad & Ramaswamy, 2004c:10.

*Figure 7.8    The emerging concept of the market*

Svensson and Östberg (2016) discuss the market concept using symbolic interactionism through three themes:

- market as co-action
- market as a type of relationship
- market as an organizing principle.

*Market as co-action.* Based on the interactive relationship between humans and organizations which symbolic interactionism is based on, the market may look like, for instance, a tennis match. Players act and react and act again with sequential responses. Such an interactive business opportunity is, for example, made in an auction (Heath & Luff, 2007).

*Market as a type of relationship.* Using symbolic interactionism, we can also perceive a market as a place where relationships exist between two or more people. However, as in all relationships, there are prerequisites and rules for a market to function. A market provides possibilities which might not exist in other relationships, including exchange of goods and services. 'The value of the goods to be exchanged in markets are much more important than the relationship itself' (Powell, 1990:301–302). One meaningful result of a market is to be the owner of something desirable: a product or its payment.

A market, as a relationship, is based on what Erich Fromm refers to as *a having mode of existence*: 'In the having mode of existence my relationship to the world is one of possessing and owning, one in which I want to make everybody and everything, including myself, my property' (Fromm, 1976:21). Somebody who buys something in a market owns what is bought.

*Table 7.2    The market as a target for the company's offerings versus a forum for co-creation experiences*

| The market as a target | The market as a forum |
| --- | --- |
| The company and the customer are separate, with distinct predetermined roles. | The company and the customer converge; the relative 'roles of the moment' cannot be predicted. |
| Supply and demand are matched; price is the clearing mechanism. Demand is forecast for goods and services that the company can supply. | Demand and supply are emergent and contextual. Supply is associated with facilitating a unique customer experience on demand. |
| Value is created by the company in its value chain. | Value is co-created at multiple points of interaction. |
| Goods and services are exchanged with customers. | Basis of value is co-creation experiences. |
| Company disseminates information to customers. | Customers and customer communities can also initiate a dialogue among themselves. |
| Company chooses which customer segments to serve, and the distribution channels to use for its offerings. | Customer chooses the nodal firm and the experience environments to interact with and co-create value. The nodal company, its goods and services, employees, multiple channels, and customer communities come together seamlessly to constitute the experience environment for individuals to co-construct their own experiences. |
| Companies extract customer surplus. Customers are 'prey', whether as 'groups' or 'one-to-one'. Companies want a 360-degree view of the customer, but remain opaque to customers. Companies want to 'own' the customer relationship and lifetime value. | Customers can extract the company's surplus. Value is co-extracted. Customers expect a 360–degree view of the experience that is transparent in the customer's language. Trust and stickiness emerge from compelling experience outcomes. Consumers are competitors in extracting value. |
| Companies determine, define, and sustain the brand. | The experience is the brand. The brand is co-created and evolves with experiences. |

*Source:*    Prahalad & Ramaswamy, 2004c:13.

Tönnies (1887/1957; compare with Asplund, 1991) talks about two types of social communities, which are *Gesellschaft* and *Gemeinschaft*. Market is of the first type. Fellowship between friends and relatives is of the second type. One thing that makes friendship and confidence less important in a market compared to relationships in a local community is, that it is instrumental for buying and selling (Powell, 1990). This also has a bearing on to what extent governmental and legal regulations shape how a market is to function.

*Market as an organizing principle.* Consistent with symbolic interactionism, a market may be looked at as an organizing principle, that is, a way to plan, structure and assess the actions of the participants. In a bureaucracy, for example, the relationships are rather impersonal and formal (Styhre, 2009). In a market, on the other hand, relationships may be governed by individual contracts (Coase, 1937; Williamson, 1975) and competition (Blomqvist & Rothstein, 2000).

If you look at a market through social phenomenological eyes, it is possible to use the same results as through symbolic interactionism. However, one aspect is added, which is intentionality – an entrepreneur looks at his or her market possibilities, mainly implicitly as mentioned, through a contextual interpretative scheme, such as a social intercourse script 'not to repeat the same mistakes which the competitor made' or 'it should be understood that I have put my whole soul into what I am doing'.

We have seen that there are sometimes problems associated with interpreting what we mean by a 'market', when discussing places, where social entrepreneurs are acting, especially those situations where public entrepreneurs are in operation. As I mentioned before, we might in the latter case talk about 'place vitalization' rather than 'marketing'.

## 7.7   THE CONCEPTS OF 'CUSTOMER' AND 'USER'

For the sake of simplicity, I have usually referred to the person who receives the result which the entrepreneur produces as a 'customer' in the case of business entrepreneurs and some social entrepreneurs (that is, those operating in the public sector) in the business sector and those citizen entrepreneurs who are called citizen enterprisers, and as 'users' in the case of those citizen entrepreneurs who are called citizen innovators (which I refer to as public entrepreneurs). I will do the same thing for the rest of the book. Of course, I could be more careful and precise, and talk about customers, buyers, consumers, receivers and users. There are differences between them all, but, the way I see it, pointing out these differences would not add much to this book.

One important reason why I have limited myself to talk about 'customers' in the context of business entrepreneurs and some social entrepreneurs is, that I look at these people as being the first, when buying, to *co-create value* with a product. This concept seems to be important in modern marketing, and I will return to it in the next section.

During the last decade or so, customers have left their traditional roles and have become co-creators as well as customers of value, as stated by some researchers. Table 7.3 presents their development as visualized by some of these researchers through three stages and along several key dimensions.

One major reason for this change is the Internet. Because of this forum, customers have increasingly engaged themselves in an active and explicit dialogue with suppliers of goods and services. On top of that, the dialogue is no longer controlled by companies alone. Individual customers can direct themselves to and learn about companies either on their own or through knowledge shared with other customers. Customers can now even initiate the dialogue; they have moved from a position as viewers and have entered the stage.

The market has become a forum where customers play an active role in creating and even competing for value. The special characteristic of this market is that customers have become a new source of competence for the company. That competence which customers add is a function of that knowledge and those qualifications which they own, their willingness to learn and to experiment, and their ability to involve themselves in an active dialogue (Prahalad & Ramaswamy, 2004a).

To notice that customers are a source of competence is forcing the managers to put out a larger net; competence is now a function of knowledge which is available in the whole system – a heightened network of traditional suppliers, manufacturers, partners, investors *and* customers (see Table 7.4).

As an example of the above, more than 650 000 customers tested a beta version of Microsoft's Windows 2000 and shared their ideas to the software giant to change some of the characteristics of the product (Prahalad & Ramaswamy, 2004a).

The concept of the customer as a source of competence also starts to appear in less obvious industries such as medicine. Access to medical information on the Internet, in magazines and journals, on television and in newspapers helps patients to be part of the build-up of health care. Doctors may resent customers sharing their expertise, but they could make use of accepting it.

There is a danger of reducing the customer to a single individual, as this makes it difficult to understand how situations, social contexts and interactions with fellow human beings can influence the manager's perception of him- or herself and his or her actions. Furthermore, individualized psychological models give marketers a feeling of being able to control the

*Table 7.3* The evolution and transformation of customers

| | Customers as passive audience | | | Customers as active players |
|---|---|---|---|---|
| | Persuading predetermined groups of buyers | Transacting with individual buyers | Lifetime bonds with individual customers | Customers as co-creators of value |
| Timeframe | 1970s, early 1980s | Late 1980s and early 1990s | 1990s | Beyond 2000 |
| Nature of business exchange and role of customer | Customers are seen as passive buyers with a predetermined role of consumption. | | | Customers are part of the enhanced network; they co-create and extract business value. They are collaborators, co-developers, and competitors. |
| Managerial mind-set | The customer is an average statistic; groups of buyers are predetermined by the company. | The customer is an individual statistic in a transaction. | The customer is a person; cultivate trust and relationships. | The customer is not only an individual but also part of an emergent social and cultural fabric. |
| Company's interaction with customers, and development of goods and services | Traditional market research and inquiries; goods and services are created without much feedback. | Shift from selling to helping customers via help desks, call centers, and customer service programs; identify problems from customers, then redesign goods and services based on that feedback. | Providing the customers through observation of users; identify solutions from lead users, and reconfigure goods and services based on deep understanding of customers. | Customers are co-developers of personalized experiences. Companies and lead customers have joint roles in education, shaping expectations, and co-creating market acceptance for goods and services. |
| Purpose and flow of communication | Gain access to and target predetermined groups of buyers. One-way communication. | Database marketing; two-way communication. | Relationship marketing; two-way communication and access. | Active dialogue with customers to shape expectations and create buzz. Multilevel access and communication. |

*Source:* Prahalad & Ramaswamy, 2004a:76.

*Table 7.4    The shifting locus of core competencies*

|  | The company | Family/network of companies | Enhanced network |
|---|---|---|---|
| Unit of analysis | The company | The extended enterprise –the company, its suppliers, and its partners | The whole system – the company, its suppliers, its partners, and its customers |
| Resources | What is available within the company | Access to other companies' competencies and investments | Access to other companies' competencies and investments, as well as customers' competencies and investments of time and effort |
| Basis for access to competence | Internal company-specific processes | Privileged access to companies within the network | Infrastructure for active ongoing dialogues and diverse customers |
| Value added for managers | Nurture and build competencies | Manage collaborative partnerships | Harness customer competence, manage personalized experiences, and shape customer expectations |
| Value creation | Autonomous | Collaborate with partner companies | Collaborate with partner companies and with active customers |
| Sources of managerial tension | Business-unit autonomy versus leveraging core competencies | Partner is both collaborator and competitor for value | Customer is both collaborator and competitor for value |

*Source:*    Prahalad & Ramaswamy, 2004a:84.

customers (Schneider & Woolgar, 2012). Symbolic interactionism offers a possibility for a broader understanding of the complexity and unpredictability of the behaviour of the customers (I will return to 'users'). Three themes might then be discussed (Svensson & Östberg, 2016):

- the customer as product
- the social customer
- the relative customer.

*The customer as product.* It is possible to see the customer as a product of interactions which are part of the constitution of the consumption society. This makes it also possible to see the customer as a conscious person, a self-confident human being. In this interaction, entrepreneurs and customers are reflected in each other. This is different from the commonly held opinion that individuals come first and society comes as a product of them.

The individual is central in our consumption society and there is an equality between producers and customers (Firat & Dholakia, 1998; Slater, 1997). In consumption, we show each other and ourselves who we are, what we believe in, what we think of, where our loyalties are rooted and which ambitions and dreams we nourish (Belk, 1988). Marketing in the social fabric also makes us more like customers than, for instance, citizens.

*The social customer.* Consistent with symbolic interactionism, the customer is more of a social creature than just a person together with other persons in the same category. Consumption is a practice that binds human beings together and it is often a way to socialize. To go out with other human beings can indicate that we are customers together and that we can show our prosperity and status for each other through *conspicuous consumption* (Veblen, 1899/1934). This means that customers, as well as all people, are *interpretative* creatures.

*The relative customer: high and low consumption.* To be a customer is to function socially as well as relatively. Consumption is defined socially in relation to the consumption of other customers. Fellow human beings' consumption has an influence on our own consumption. Among other things, our consumption habits will show, socially, our *taste* (Bourdieu, 1984). However, in our modern society, it has been much more difficult to associate certain tastes with certain social classes than in earlier societies.

Social phenomenology stresses, maybe more than symbolic interactionism does, *co-creation* which takes place in and by the language we use, for instance, as customer, a language which they confirm and to some extent develop as so-called *typifications*. Language is here seen in a much wider sense than those symbols we not only hear (or read), but as we also see, not just as words but also in body language and in other signals in social contexts. This is, as said before, triggered by intentionality through those social intercourse scripts we use, for example, as customers.

Those social contexts (public places) where public entrepreneurs are operating are also part of the picture, of course. The activities of these entrepreneurs are going on with other citizens together and co-creatively – they all try to build more citizenry and less exclusiveness. The only difference between the public entrepreneur and other citizens in what they are engaged in, is that the former has a more conscious purpose, shown more explicitly in his or her social intercourse script (his or her interpretative scheme), and that he or she tries to externalize this to other citizens in so-called *language development*, that is, attempting to build a new understanding through partly new typifications in genuine dialogues, thereby supporting a positive and constructive citizen future. I stress again that what is going on in such contexts may be difficult to characterize as the public entrepreneur being a 'producer of goods and services', that other participating citizens are 'customers' (I therefore call them 'users' in such situations) and that the context, where it all takes place, is called a 'market' (I prefer to refer to it as a 'place' instead, as mentioned above).

## 7.8   THE CONCEPT OF 'VALUE CREATING'

Market-orientated companies have long been regarded as creators of *customer value* to attract and keep customers. Customer value then depends on how customers perceive benefits from a sales offer and sacrifices associated with buying it; that is, in the eyes of the customers, the following formula is valid:

*The value of a product = Perceived benefits from the product – sacrifices from buying it*

The value of products here is the customer's assessment of the extent to which goods or services satisfy his or her requirements of what is bought, by considering alternative solutions and costs associated with satisfying what he or she wants. Value in this case depends on a user's needs, expectations and experiences in relation to competing sales offers within a specific category. Perceived benefits can be derived from the very product itself, the service related to it and the seller company's image plus the relationship between buyer and seller (for instance, associated with the personal and professional friendship of the latter and the comfort value of working with a sales person you can trust). Perceived sacrifices are total costs associated with a purchase (monetary cost plus the time and energy involved, and possibly an added extra cost, a so-called opportunity cost, associated with not making the right decision).

The question is, however, *where value is created and by whom*. Traditionally (which is also the way managerial marketing looks at it), value creation is associated with the moment of buying (in a market etc.) and the value is perceived as company-centred; that is, a value of a product is created starting from the producer/seller. One alternative approach to value with the same focus associated with a product is that

*Table 7.5   Ways to transfer value between market actors*

| Category | Meaning | Example/comment |
|---|---|---|
| Give/receive | When somebody gives somebody else something without asking for something in return | Birthday gift; street kitchen soup; a gift to the Salvation Army |
| Violate/be violated | When somebody takes somebody else's property or even forces somebody else to do something of value | Read a history book |
| Find | When somebody finds something of value which is legally or sensibly possible to keep | Find a lamp that works on a city dump |
| Lend/borrow | When somebody is allowed to use somebody else's property, but without payment | Borrow the neighbour's bike |
| Sell/buy | Transferring a product exchanged for monetary means (money) | What normally takes place in markets |
| Rent out/rent | Sell or buy the right to use somebody else's property up to a certain point in time | Renting a car |
| Subscribe | Sell or buy the possibility to use a certain service during a certain time, but the arrangement does not usually influence to what extent the subscribed object is used or not | Broadband |
| Swap | Swap something without money being involved | Swapping apartments |
| Being part of a 'pool' | Co-owning something valuable which several persons can use together, consistent with some rules being agreed upon | Car pools; collective dwellings |

*Source:*   Frankelius et al., 2015:63; the author's translation.

it is determined by the amount of labour put into it, its *utility value* – in other words, the number of working hours socially needed for its production (Marx, 1867/1985).

However, the value of a product does not necessarily have to be transferred in a market when buying this product in the traditional sense (Table 7.5).

Another value related to a company is *owner value*. This is, for example, evident in small firms which are usually financed (at least in the beginning) by the owner's money (Bozkaya & van Pottelsberghe de la Potterie,

2008). The connections between customer value and owner value (with or without considering the society's norms and the natural environment) can be described as in Figure 7.9.

Traditionally, value calculation is based on a company's activities vis-à-vis the environment (from a business point of view) in what is referred to as the *value chain* (Figure 7.10).

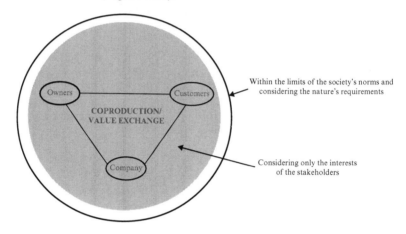

*Source:* Frankelius et al., 2015:593; the author's translation.

*Figure 7.9  Exchanging value from stakeholders' perspective*

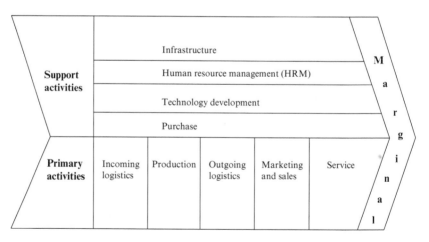

*Source:* Adapted from Porter, 1985.

*Figure 7.10  Porter's value chain*

The value chain was launched by Porter in the middle of 1980s. The purpose of the model is to maximize the marginal, that is, the difference between a company's revenues and its costs. Activities that take place within the company are divided into primary and secondary (see Figure 7.10). Primary activities comprise the chain from incoming logistics to service given to customers. Support activities comprise activities which facilitate or support the primary activities of the company. The value generated by the company constitutes the amount which the buyers are willing to pay for the product offered by the company. When the company can perform the various activities in a more efficient way, it can generate a higher value.

The understanding of companies and industries at that time was still very much based on ideas from industrialization, i.e., based on product and technology innovation. Many firms today, however, are not based so clearly on innovation of products and / or technology, but instead very often on new ways of making business. When Porter published his theories about the value chain, deregulations, globalization and technology development had already started to change the rules of the game – and those changes have continued. Instead of being one link of a linear chain where value was added step by step, Normann (2001) pointed out that many new companies are organizing other actors and stakeholders in *value-creating networks (stars)*. They put themselves as the hub in a business flow where all actors benefit from each other and where new ways of creating value take place (Figure 7.11).

At present, there is a much higher emphasis on the experience of consumption than on the actual mode of consumption (and buying), and modern customers are considered as actively participating in the experiences of products and brands, not just as passive receivers of advertising messages etc.

As noted in Chapter 4, development towards a more active participation of customers in the value-creating process has gone from relationship marketing to co-creation marketing (Figure 7.12).

Those who have developed 'co-creation marketing' as a basis for value creation are mainly Prahalad and Ramaswamy (2000, 2003, 2004a, 2004b, 2004c). They claim that the traditional perceptions of a market are challenged by the appearance of connected, informed, empowered and active customers. Customers now try to exercise their influence in every part of business system. Equipped with new tools and unsatisfied by available choices, customers want to interact with companies and 'co-create' value in that way (Prahalad & Ramaswamy, 2004b). The transformed nature of the interaction between customer and company as the possibility for co-creation (and co-extraction) of value is redefining the meaning of value and the value-creating process.

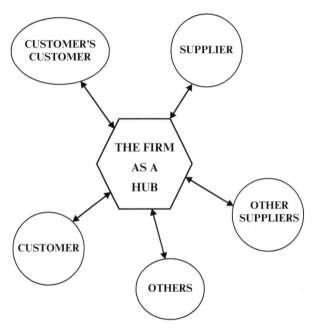

*Figure 7.11    The value-creating star*

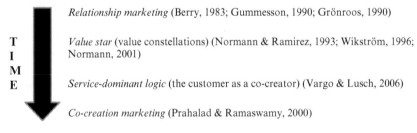

*Figure 7.12    From relationship to co-creation marketing*

The concept of market is on its way to changing and transforming the nature of the relationship between customer and company (Prahalad & Ramaswamy, 2004c:6). As customers become more knowledgeable and increasingly aware of their negotiating influence, more businesses will feel pressure to act in an implicit (if not explicit) position of negotiation. An auction is an example of a negotiation process (an online auction to book a hotel room or reserve a seat on an airplane, and purchasing goods on eBay's website are a few examples of this growing phenomenon). Equipped with a knowledge which they have acquired from today's ever clearer and more transparent business activities, customers are increasingly willing to negotiate prices and other transaction conditions with companies. We are on our way towards a world where value is a result of a negotiation between the individual customer and the company, even if still often implicitly.

The consequences of not noticing this shift can be serious. As long as companies believe that the market can be separated from the value-creating process, companies will have no other choice than to squeeze as many costs as they can from their 'value chain' activities. In the meantime, globalization, deregulations, outsourcing and mergers of industries and technologies will make it even more difficult for managers to differentiate their offers. Goods and services are facing commoditization more than ever before.

Companies must get away from the company-centred view which has been to try to co-create value together with customers by strongly focusing on personalized interactions between customers and the company. Furthermore, this action will demand marketers to escape their product-centred thinking and instead focus on those experiences which customers will try to co-create. It is necessary to challenge the traditional, fixed roles for both customers and companies, and try to investigate the power of a convergence of the production and consumption roles, i.e., convergence of the company and customer roles (Prahalad & Ramaswamy, 2000).

Top quality interactions that enable an individual customer to co-create unique experiences with the company are the key to unlocking new ways to create competitive advantages. Value must be created together by both the company and the customer (Table 7.6).

Before we discuss how marketing can be performed for entrepreneurs, it is useful to look further at an increasingly important part of modern marketing, that is networking.

## 7.9 NETWORKING AND ENTREPRENEURSHIP

Some say that Piore and Sabel brought *business networks* into entrepreneurship theories in their book of 1984 when they praised the industrial districts in northern Italy as an alternative economic model. They defined industrial districts as geographically concentrated operations that mainly consist of small firms which specialize in goods and services (often as part of an end product).

Today there is a more fundamental view of the importance of networks.

*Table 7.6    The concept of co-creation*

| What co-creation is not | What co-creation is |
| --- | --- |
| + Customer focus<br>+ Customer is king or customer is always right | + Co-creation is about *joint* creation of value by the company and the customer. It is not the firm trying to please the customer |
| + Delivering good customer service or pampering the customer with lavish customer service | + Allowing the customer to co-construct the service experience to suit her context |
| + Mass customization of offerings that suit the industry's supply chain | + Joint problem definition and problem solving |
| + Transfer of activities from the firm to the customer as in self-service | + Creating an experience environment in which customers can have active dialogue and co-construct personalized experiences; product may be the same but customers can construct different experiences |
| + Customer as product manager or co-designing goods and services | |
| + Product variety | + Experience variety |
| + Segment of one | + Experience of one |
| + Meticulous market research | + Experiencing the business as customers do in real time |
| | + Continuous dialogue |
| + Staging experiences | + Co-constructing personalized experiences |
| + Demand-side innovation for new goods and services | + Innovating experience environments for new co-creation experiences |

*Source:*    Prahalad & Ramaswamy, 2004c:8.


Our society can be looked at as a *network society. Networking is a natural part of marketing in the postmodern society.* Castells asserts that this is the first time in history that the economic unit has been other than the individual, the organization, the region or the sector. This unit is the network, where subjects and organizations are connected to each other and constantly being modified and adapted, supporting environments and structures.

The network society is a more open but also more human society. 'The network economy is based on technology, but can only be built on relationships. It starts with chips and ends with relations' (Kelly, 1998:179).

Consequently, the study of networks is popular today. However, there is considerable variation in what can be meant by 'network' and 'networking'. Competing definitions and perspectives often exist.

It is possible to talk about three important *parts* of a network (Hoang & Antoncic, 2003): (1) the content of the relationships, (2) the governance of these relationships and (3) the structure or pattern that emerges from the crosscutting ties.

*Relationships* (between people and between organizations) are viewed as the media through which actors gain access to a variety of resources held by others (Bjerke, 2013). Two such core resources for the actors are information and advice, which they can gain access to through their network. In the uncertain and dynamic conditions under which entrepreneurial activities occur, it is reasonable that resource holders (potential investors and employees) seek information that helps them to gauge the underlying potential of a venture, of which they are or want to be a part. Entrepreneurs, on the other hand, seek legitimacy to reduce possible perceived risks by associating with, or by gaining explicit certification from, well-regarded individuals and organizations. To be perceived positively based on your relationships in a network may lead to subsequent beneficial resource exchanges.

The second construct that researchers have explored is the *governance mechanisms* that are thought to underpin and coordinate network exchange (Bjerke, 2013). Trust between partners is often a critical element that in turn enhances the quality of the resource flows. Network governance can also be characterized by the reliance on 'implicit and open-ended contracts' that are supported by social mechanisms – such as power and influence or the threat of ostracism and loss of reputation – rather than legal support. These elements of network governance can give cost advantages in comparison to coordination through market or bureaucratic mechanisms.

The third construct is *network structure*, defined as the pattern of relationships that are engendered from the direct and indirect ties between actors (Bjerke, 2013). A general conceptualization guiding the focus on network structure is that differential network positioning has an important impact on resource flows, and hence, on entrepreneurial outcomes.

Similarly, Conway et al. (2001:355) talk of four core components that should be investigated when studying human networks and human networking (discussion in this section follows Conway & Jones, 2006:308–10):

- *Actors* – individuals within the network.
- *Links* – relationships between individuals within the network.
- *Flows* – exchanges between individuals within the network.
- *Mechanisms* – modes of interaction between the individuals within the network.

There are many dimensions that can be used to categorize individuals within a network, from general dimensions such as age, sex, family membership, nationality, ethnicity and education level, to more specific dimensions such as functional background (for instance, finance, marketing or design) or sectorial background. The choice from this breadth of dimensions should be informed by the nature of the network and the purpose behind studying it.

The nature of the links or relationships between the members within the network varies along several dimensions, of which the most relevant are (Conway & Jones, 2006:308–309):

- *Formality* – distinguishes between informal and personal links and formal links in a contract, for example.
- *Intensity* – indicated by the frequency of the interaction and the amount of flow or transactions between the two actors during a given time period (Tichy et al., 1979).
- *Reciprocity* – the balance of the flow over time between two actors through a given link. The link is 'asymmetric' or 'unilateral' when the flow is unbalanced (that is, by and large goes only one way), or 'symmetric' or 'bilateral' when the flow is balanced (that is, by and large goes both ways). Asymmetric links tend to lead to inequality in power relationships between two actors (Boissevain, 1974).
- *Multiplexity* – signifies the degree to which two actors are linked to each other through several role relationships (for instance, as friend, brother and partner); the greater the number of role relationships between two actors, the stronger the ties (Tichy et al., 1979). Boissevain (1974:30) also argues that 'there is a tendency for single-stranded relations to become many-stranded if they persist over time, and for many-stranded relations to be stronger than single-stranded ones, in the sense that one strand role reinforces others'.
- *Origin* – the identification of the event that leads to the origin of a link. It intends to incorporate facts such as the context in which the relationship arose and who initiated it.
- *Motive* – the functional significance of networking does not qualify for providing a convincing explanation of why it happened. When they discuss this issue, Kreiner and Schultz (1993:201) mean that 'one must determine the motives and perspectives of the actors who reproduce such patterns'.

Tichy et al. (1979) distinguish between four types of flows within a network, often named 'transaction content' in the network literature:

- *Affect* – the exchange of friendship between actors.
- *Power* – the exchange of power and influence between actors.

- *Information* – the exchange of ideas, information and know-how between actors.
- *Products* – the exchange of goods, money, technology or service between actors.

Individuals may 'exchange' any of these types of transaction content for another, for instance, power for money or information for friendship, even though in many cases, like in the last one, this can be more implicit than explicit. The flow between two actors within the network can vary widely between 'sender/provider' and 'receiver' as well as between other members within the network.

There are different ways in which individuals can interact with each other, for instance, talking to each other on the telephone, email, documents or meetings face-to-face. Kelley and Brooks (1991) dichotomize these interaction mechanisms into 'active', which refers to a personal interaction, either face-to-face or on the telephone, and 'passive', which refers to documents and other text material, where there is no direct relationship between 'provider' and 'receiver' of information. 'Networks do not emerge without considerable endeavor' (Birley et al., 1991:58).

Networks in general may also vary along different dimensions. Conway and Jones (2006:309–10) claim that the most relevant network dimensions of interest are often:

- *Size* – this dimension simply refers to the number of actors participating within the network (Tichy et al., 1979; Auster, 1990).
- *Diversity* – this network characteristic often refers to the number of different types of actors within the network (Auster, 1990).
- *Density* – the density of a network refers to 'the extensiveness of the ties between elements [actors]' (Aldrich & Whetten, 1981:398), which can be looked at as the number of existing links within the network divided by the number of possible links (Tichy et al., 1979; Rogers & Kincaid, 1981). Boissevain (1974:37) claims however that 'it must be stressed that network density is simply an index of the potential not the actual flow of information'; that is to say, it is a measure of the network structure and not of the network activity. Boissevain (1974:40) also asserts that 'there is obviously a relationship between size and density, for where a network is large the members will have to contribute more relations to attain the same density as a smaller network'. Furthermore, the network density tells us nothing about the internal structure of the network in itself, and as Boissevain (1974:40) points out, 'networks with the same density can have very different configurations'.

- *Openness* – there is often a distinction made between strong and weak ties. Strong ties are found in cliques and are associated with dense networks (which are relationships between individuals who are linked to each other more closely), whereas weak ties also link people outside the clique and consequently create 'openness' in the network, that is, they are boundary-spanning relationships or links spanning 'structural holes' (Burt, 1992).
- *Stability* – Tichy et al. (1979:508) define this dimension as 'the degree to which a network pattern changes over time'. Auster (1990) develops this further by talking about frequency as well as magnitude of the changes of members and links within a given network.

Another important aspect is that it is possible to distinguish *four levels in networks* (Fyall & Garrod, 2005:154):

1. Exchange of information.
2. Adaptation of activities.
3. Sharing resources.
4. Co-creation.

The further down one goes in these levels, the more is asked of the members within a network. Networking often stops at the top level. Furthermore, 'co-creation' is a natural way of looking at reality as socially constructed. It may seem like a paradox that while entrepreneurs are regarded as autonomous and independent, they are at the same time 'very dependent on ties to trust and cooperation' (Johannisson & Peterson, 1984:1).

So, 'networks' and 'networking' are important entrepreneurial tools to establish, develop and improve small businesses and other operations in society. However, I see a difference between discussing networking to improve existing operations (a discussion consistent with the limited view of entrepreneurship) and networking as part of being human and therefore, by necessity, part of being an entrepreneur (the more extended view of entrepreneurship). Discussions of the first kind often lead to technical issues such as what is a good or a bad network, what makes a network more functional, and so on. Typical discussions of networks consistent with the more extended view of entrepreneurship are as follows:

- A developed network is more valuable to a person who starts an entrepreneurial venture than to somebody who is running an ongoing venture.

- Membership of a network is advantageous for large as well as small entrepreneurial ventures, but it is more important for the survival of a small entrepreneurial venture.
- Networks make it possible for small entrepreneurial ventures to gain access to resources which are not possible elsewhere.

## 7.10 THE DISTINCTIVE ELEMENT OF MARKETING FOR ENTREPRENEURS

As mentioned, I think that marketing for entrepreneurs is distinctive enough from marketing in general for it to be discussed as a sole topic. It is often so, for instance, that much of the entrepreneur's future is uncertain, especially as I limit myself in my interest in entrepreneurship to cases where the new venture contains new aspects, and that the founding person is considered as an entrepreneur only in the beginning of the venture; that is, before the venture has got a clear and 'firm' shape, as perceived by the customers (or other users). As we know, I conceptualize entrepreneurship to only encompass such solutions *which are new in one way or another*. Copies of what exists already are consequently not of interest to me. The degree of innovation can be more or less obvious, of course, but I believe that 'new' results can only be achieved in, at least partly, new ways.

In the business world, the point is to gain customers, of course. Some practical questions, important to the small emerging business venture in the beginning of its existence, could be (Frankelius et al., 2015:56):

– How do I identify the makings of customers?
– How do I decide which to bet on first?
– Which customer value are the customers to be offered?
– How is this customer value to be produced in a competitive and sustainable way?
– How can I reach the customers and make them buy?
– How can I make it easy for customers to discover the company?

For social entrepreneurs (at least if they are of the public entrepreneurial kind), the situation is, furthermore, different from the business entrepreneurial situation in several respects as far as marketing is concerned:

- A public entrepreneur wants to co-create citizenry and reduce alienation in society together with other citizens.

- It cannot be expected that other citizens will want to pay for the results in the traditional sense of a customer. They will often, however, participate with voluntary contributions.
- Financing the activities of public entrepreneurs will often consist of sponsoring or donations, fund raising or other means of creating financial means.

It is possible, of course, to divide entrepreneurs into different groups considering, for example, their degree of novelty, forecasting possibility, uniqueness etc., but the fact remains that entrepreneurs often must acquire new habits and, at least partially, get rid of old ones.

One interesting aspect of living in the knowledge society of today is that networking has become more important and that networks have changed in content. This includes the importance of language as part of a foundation of change – to a large extent the result of new social media (blogs, podcasts, wikis, YouTube etc.).

For social entrepreneurs, the importance of 'the place' as such can be added.

Several new marketing approaches have been launched during the latest decades, some of which regard themselves as more entrepreneurial and may therefore be more suitable for entrepreneurs (Morris et al., 2002). Examples include *expeditionary marketing* (Hamel & Prahalad, 1992), *guerrilla marketing* (Levinson, 1993), *disruptive marketing* (Dru, 1996, 2002), *radical marketing* (Hill & Rifkin, 1999), *counterdisruptive marketing* (Clancy & Krieg, 2000), *buzz marketing* (Rosen, 2000), *viral marketing* (Gladwell, 2000) and *convergence marketing* (Wind et al., 2002).

There are several suggestions as to what new entrepreneurs should concentrate on. One example is what Wood (2016) refers to as '*content marketing*':

- Create a business blog.
- Use the right tools from the start.
- Quality content leads to better engagement.
- When you cannot create, repurpose.
- Find the right platform and influencers.
- Start everything with cornerstone content.
- Use rich images and videos in your content.

One interesting contribution to the innovative issue comes from Morgan (2009). He suggests eight principles which the small challenger should keep in mind to defeat those who are already established. The eight principles are:

1. *Ask naïve, but intelligent questions.* Those who have achieved great waves in any area are often newcomers to that area; for instance, Jeff

Bezos, who came from his knowledge in finance and changed how to sell books, and Eric Ryan, who left advertising to renew household cleaning. These people did not provide the right answers, but they asked the right questions.

2. *Make yourself known as a lighthouse identity*. The success for a newcomer consists of developing a very clear sense of what you stand for, so that customers are navigated by you, not you by the customers.

3. *Take thought leadership*. In every industry, there are two leaders. One is the brand leader, that is, the one with the largest market share. The other leader is the thought leader, that is, the one who has the highest 'sense momentum' in the eyes and mind of the customers and other users.

4. *Create symbols of re-evaluation*. Successful challengers capture the indifferent customers' and other users' imagination to the extent that the latter have a reason to re-evaluate what is important in new symbols being created by these challenges.

5. *Sacrifice*. Challengers have fewer resources in almost every aspect than the market leader. What they choose not to do, what they sacrifice, can therefore be as important to their success as what they choose to do.

6. *Overcommit*. Even though the challenger is forced to sacrifice much compared to the market leader, they should overcommit themselves in one or a few moves that they choose to make.

7. *Use communications and publicity to enter social culture*. Using communications is one of the few remaining sources of competitive advantage for the challenger – but only if systematically embraced as such within the company.

8. *Become idea-centred, not customer-centred*. Move your entrepreneurial skill from being customer-centred to concentrating on generating and applying new ideas that constantly refresh and renew the blood in the veins of the market.

We will return to these points later.

## 7.11 PRINCIPLES OF MANAGERIAL AND SOCIAL PHENOMENOLOGICAL MARKETING FOR ENTREPRENEURS

### 7.11.1 Principles for both Managerial and Social Phenomenological Marketing for Entrepreneurs

This chapter ends by presenting the principles for managerial and social phenomenological marketing for entrepreneurs; that is, principles of two alternatives discussed in this book, before the rest of the book explores how marketing can be pursued in three different entrepreneurial situations – for independent business entrepreneurs, business intrapreneurs and social entrepreneurs. I will first compare the principles of both the two alternatives, and then discuss the principles of the two alternatives individually. Much of what is said in these sections has been mentioned earlier in this book.

One might suggest that combining the advantages of the two alternatives might lead to a superior marketing approach. But it is not that simple. This is because the two alternatives, just like different paradigms, are based on *incompatible presumptions*. If, for instance, you try to transfer aspects of one of the two alternatives (say from managerialism to social phenomenology or reverse), *the content and signification change with the context.* The two alternatives cannot be compared in the same 'language', so to say. We will see several examples of this as we move on.

There are, in a way, also similarities between my two alternative ways to market for entrepreneurs. In my opinion, for an entrepreneurial venture to be called entrepreneurial, it must come up with innovative results. Further, as I believe that innovation cannot be achieved in a non-innovative fashion, both alternatives must contain innovative aspects. What unites the two alternatives, furthermore, is that both usually have the ambition to establish an operation which is to continue after the entrepreneurial start.

As far as their design is concerned, it is therefore necessary to use *different theoretical spectacles* to properly understand them. Whether this also refers to customers and other users is, however, a different, more practical, matter. In general, what I refer to as managerial marketing is based on what I earlier referred to as the limited view on entrepreneurship, and social phenomenological marketing is based on what I referred to as the more extended view on entrepreneurship. I want to stress, however, that even though I normally prefer the more extended view on entrepreneurship, my ambition is to present the two alternatives as fairly as I can. *One important difference* between the two marketing alternatives, and of great importance to marketing for entrepreneurs, is that managerial marketing naturally adopts management when he or she is applying marketing (thereby its name) to entrepreneurship, while social phenomenological marketing makes a distinction between management and entrepreneurship, and asserts that the former is not seen as an important part of marketing for entrepreneurs.

Managerial marketing has not changed in any basic respect for many years, and could be said to have started in 1967 when Kotler first published his book, *Marketing Management*. Its main features were ready-made. Social phenomenological marketing is, however, not much more than between ten and fifteen years old. It is still at a developing stage and cannot be associated so closely with one specific person, but rather to a stream of ideas, from *relationship marketing* (Grönroos and Gummesson) via *value stars* (Normann & Ramirez) and *service-dominant logic* (Vargo & Lusch) to *co-creation marketing* (Prahalad & Ramaswamy). In line with its own assumptions, it is not yet fully determined.

But I repeat, both alternatives must lead to new solutions consistent with my view of entrepreneurship. To what extent this means that *entrepreneurs must also be innovative in marketing* is an open question, however. To summarize, one can say that entrepreneurs who use managerial marketing aim at reducing the degrees of freedom that exist in the entrepreneurial situation by acquiring information to fill 'the empty spots' in their knowledge (as this approach to marketing looks at *reality as factual*, the idea here is that such information can be acquired through market surveys based on interviews, for instance in questionnaires), while entrepreneurs using social phenomenological marketing, looking at their reality as socially constructed, use the degrees of freedom to generate new understanding of the possibilities in the market by participating in different dialogues with customers or other users.

Managerial marketing is depictive and general (sometimes systems-orientated), while social phenomenological marketing is more formative and contextual (that is, actor-orientated). Managerial marketing aims to be explanatory and achieve as much control as possible; social phenomenological marketing searches for understanding and developmental possibilities based on such understanding. Managerial marketing is looking for *the right answers* – this is a useless criterion for social phenomenological marketers. Managerial marketing attempts to teach precisely what is required as a marketer; social phenomenological marketing can only teach a certain basic view and some ideas about how a design *might look*, based on this view.

A rational view claims that it must be possible to provide a complete picture of what is needed; a social phenomenological view claims that this is not possible. One way to express this is to say that managerial marketing can point a finger, while social phenomenological marketing wants to reach out a hand. These differences cause me to describe one type of entrepreneurial startup as rational (either causation or effectuation) and another as bricoleurial.

For both alternatives, words, language and terminology are important – in the managerial case as depicting and modelling tools, and in the social phenomenological case as formative and interpretative tools. It is therefore natural for pictures, symbols and even myths to be more important in the social phenomenological case than in the managerial case.

One could say that *the two alternatives live in different worlds of meaning and significance*. The managerial alternative lives in a *circumstantial* world, which is looked at as factual and where attempts are made to build consciously simplified pictures of what are considered to be the most decisive circumstances. These pictures are called *models*. With the social phenomenological view, where reality is looked at as socially constructed, the stance is instead that one lives in a *meaningful* world, where, in interaction with other human beings, the ambition is to come up with more constructive *interpretations* to be able to move on in a more positive direction. The two alternatives have consequently *very different views of the meaning of and the potential to plan*. The advocates of the managerial alternative attempt to forecast the future (and claim that this is possible) as far as the customers' demand are concerned; an advocate of the social phenomenological alternative finds difficulties in making meaningful forecasts and wants therefore to enter or create situations where learning can take place and where he or she can build common platforms with customers and other users (forums) for a constructive dialogical co-creation of common meaning and significations. One interesting aspect of this is that managerial marketers assert that *advertising may be of great importance*, while social phenomenological marketers think that it is more valuable to *spread their messages through various public relational actions and carry out discussions about their messages on Internet and in other social media*.

One way to express the differences in managerial and social phenomenological marketing activities is to say that *managerial marketers behave, while social phenomenological marketers act*. As is commonly stated, we live in a knowledge world today. It can therefore be useful to clarify how the two entrepreneurship marketing alternatives look at 'knowledge' and 'adequate learning' to behave and / or act in a sensible way, how to acquire such learning, how to build up a 'knowledge capital' and how to use it.

There is, as we know, a broader view of capital today. Traditionally, 'financial capital' was considered one of the most crucial production factors in an economy. Today, it is seen as necessary for entrepreneurs, among others, to build and spread the knowledge of their existence and what is possible for them to achieve and attain (this process is referred to as *governance* today); that is, to establish their significant presence and participation in the social capital (I prefer to call it *the citizen capital*), also referred to as *the network capital* in the modern *network society*. The importance of networking is not denied by any of the two alternatives of marketing which can used by entrepreneurs according to this book (both regard networking as a useful part of marketing). However, the two alternatives consider the content and use of networks somewhat differently. One difference is that managerial marketers assert that they function better (more rationally?) by using networking, while social phenomenological marketers look at networking as a natural way of life. Another difference is that managerial marketers claim that it is enough to use networks to exchange information with customers and other users, to adapt activities to other participants in the economic *value chain* or share resources with them, while social phenomenological marketers see it as constructive to co-create and co-extract experiences with customers, other users and various cooperating partners in so-called *value stars*.

The differences between the two alternatives in this respect is illustrated in Figures 7.13 and 7.14 (compare with Figures 5.1 and 5.2).

We have said many times that managerial marketing is rational in its approach and that it perceives reality as full of circumstances and facts. In

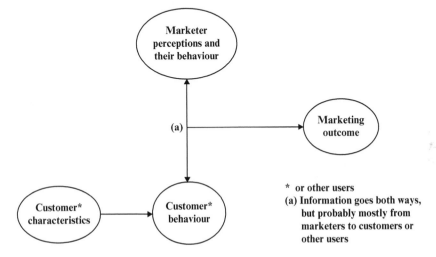

*Figure 7.13    Managerial marketing*

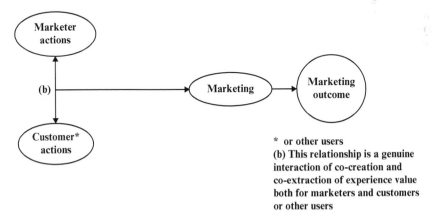

*Figure 7.14    Social phenomenological marketing*

this alternative, for instance, several *factual differences between goods and services are noticed.* For instance, services are looked at as:

- something which cannot be protected by a patent
- impossible to package
- something lacking tangible demonstration possibilities
- something which cannot be shown exactly the same way twice
- something which cannot be stored.

Managerial marketing claims, therefore, that there are enough differences between goods and services to see distinct divergences between marketing these two types of products.

Social phenomenological marketing asserts, on the other hand, that differences between goods and services are fluid and depend on how you look at them. This approach also claims that most goods are marketed with more or less of a service content. They describe this as *servicification.* Differences between marketing goods and marketing services are therefore not seen as distinctly here as in the managerial case.

The same point is valid for *industrial marketing* (B2B). Managerial marketing perceives enough factual differences in this area to claim that it differs from marketing consumer products. Those two areas of marketing are also at different positions in the economic value chain. Social phenomenological marketing does not see such clear differences. In this alternative, it is claimed, furthermore, that relationship marketing (which is a forerunner to the constructionist view of marketing) started in B2B and that two (or more) companies or other activities can be part of the same value star.

Managerial marketing has a much longer history than social phenomenological marketing. The former, unlike the latter, has become relatively clearly defined, and has changed its content only marginally but not its fundamental features. The postmodern school of thought, opposing ideas of fixed values, criticizing every opinion about objectivity and claiming that there are no longer any general solutions, does not fit well with the managerial marketing approach and has therefore not had any major effect on its arrangement. On the other hand, as postmodernism regards reality as relational and contextual (and which also has led to the renewal of the place, which we will return to), it is fully compatible with the social phenomenological alternative of marketing, and has influenced this approach. The 'postmodern entrepreneurial' concept is possible and even meaningful in social phenomenological marketing.

Managerial marketing aims at finding a model for marketing, which is valid independent of time, place or culture. This is, by the way, the same for all research and knowledge based on the rational philosophy. For social phenomenological marketing, it is quite the reverse. It is happy to be contextual because it is based on a constructionist philosophy, which requires individuals interacting with each other, for instance, a company with its customers in a market or a citizen innovator with other citizens in a public place. In the latter alternative of entrepreneurship marketing, furthermore, the market is often not so much seen as a target but as a forum (compare Table 7.2). In the former entrepreneurship marketing alternative, it is also an advantage to see the market as a space rather than as a place (place could only be valid if we talk about a market as, for instance, a market square). I assert that a space can be counted in terms of the number of heads, while a place can be measured in square miles.

The importance of a place is obvious when discussing the development of a local community. All entrepreneurs that could act there (for instance, independent business entrepreneurs, public sector entrepreneurs, community business magnets or social entrepreneurs in private or public places) could all gain advantages in their marketing by referring to their connections with the local community in question.

Let us summarize the paradigmatic content of the rational and social phenomenological philosophy according to Törnebohm (Table 7.7).

### 7.11.2 Principles for Managerial Marketing for Entrepreneurs

Let us look at some principles which are only valid for the managerial way of marketing for entrepreneurs.

As stated by Frankelius et al. (2015), a view of companies and its marketing which can be pictured in a *business model* (that is, deliberately simplified rational pictures of a business reality, which are looked at as factual) is based on a value chain in two parts (Margetta, 2002). The first part is related to these value-adding activities, which create what the company is offering; in other words, purchases, design plus manufacturing and supply if it is about goods, or performance if it is about services. This is extensively described by Porter (1985). The second part is about what can be associated with marketing; in this case, everything from market research and implementing market campaigns to sales and distribution. By having an overview of the whole business model and purposefully working for refining it, a company may gain advantages over competitors.

When talking about companies, running a business and marketing consistent with the managerial view, the *business idea* which underlies the company is often referred to. There have been many different opinions about the content of the business idea over the years. Drucker spoke (1954) about having a broad view of one's ambition with business activities, but

*Table 7.7    The rational and the social phenomenological paradigm*

|  | The rational philosophy | The social phenomenological philosophy |
|---|---|---|
| Conception of reality | Reality consists of objective as well as subjective facts. It is basically a stable construction. | Reality is a social construction, which mentally relates all actors to each other, where the researcher is one of the actors. |
| Conception of science | The scientific task is to provide us with pictures of the factual reality. | The scientific task can always be an object for reflection, and concepts that are taken for granted may become obstacles to real understanding and renewal. |
| Scientific ideal | Science ideally provides us with an increasing number of logical and rational explanations, a clear set of concepts and representative, generalizable cases, which can facilitate better forecasts of the future. | Science ideally leads to a language which can provide us with a good understanding, and it advocates a scientific and consciously active interaction with the environment. |
| Ethical and aesthetical aspects | These are relatively uninteresting issues in this case. | Ethically, the researcher can never disclaim the responsibility for his or her part in the construction of reality. Aesthetically, descriptions and interpretations which are near to the artistic ones are recommended. |

he used the term 'business purpose' rather than 'business idea'. Levitt (1969) also warned against having too narrow an orientation to what the company was doing, but the person who introduced the concept of 'business idea' is normally regarded as Normann (1975). His focus was not customers or customer needs, however, nor was it competitors, but rather the company's competence profile. He also asserted that a business idea does not exist until it is realized. Before that, it is just an 'an idea of a business idea'.

As stated by Frankelius et al. (2015), those behind the business idea concept that we normally describe today (consistent with managerial marketing) are Abell and Hammond (1979). They provided a model for articulating business ideas in three dimensions, formulated as three questions:

1. The customer concept dimension: *Whose need* is satisfied by the company?
2. The customer function dimension: *Which need* is satisfied by the company?
3. The problem-solving dimension: *How* to satisfy the needs?

The managerial marketing alternative views *customer satisfaction* as central. In 1991, Johansson (1991), who was a representative of managerial marketing, asserted that marketing in the future would be dominated by two issues, which would be necessary for the company to master. Firstly, companies would need to have a deep knowledge of their customers. Secondly, companies would increasingly have to improve at communicating.

Johansson predicted that a correspondence between the company's values and customers' values would become increasingly important. This means that the image you have in the market determines which customers will be attracted by your own sales offer. Image is here to be interpreted very broadly, and one should be aware that it cannot be changed to any major extent in the short run. The message is that it is not enough to know a company's target groups and its wishes; one should also know the company's own values and, above all, how it is perceived by these target groups.

Johansson (1991) also claimed that it is important to be clear about the customers' decision models and their decision processes, what they prioritize and how they take different factors into account, not only as a simple decision model, but as a model that considers emotional and psychological factors; who participates in the decision process, initiates it, influences in different phases, decides, buys and uses the goods or the services. If you do not have this knowledge, it is, according to managerial marketing, difficult to communicate one's message to those persons who are important in the decision process. Consumption becomes more and more complex with a mix of budget and luxury products. Furthermore, to an increasing extent, consuming is a way of communicating.

Some commentators claim, however, also consistent with managerial marketing, that marketing should create demand rather than reflect it. As Brown (2001:3) expresses it, customers should 'be excited, enticed and tormented by delightful unsatisfied desire'. He refers to this approach as *retro marketing* and adds that it is based on five principles: to be exclusive, to conceal, to reinforce, to entertain and to bluff. Being exclusive can be achieved by consciously holding back supply and postponing satisfaction. Customers are encouraged to 'buy while stocks last'. Those who are successful buyers are lucky that they belong to the selected few, the clear elite. The second principle with retro marketing – to conceal – aims at tickling potential buyers. The result is a heightened interest, encouraged by a diet of mysteries and intrigues. Even exclusive products need sales support, which leads to the third principles of retro marketing, which is to reinforce. This can be achieved such that customers talk about the 'cool' X or the 'hot' Y. To entertain is the fourth principle, which means to engage customers by marketing. As stated by Brown, 'the greatest mistake in modern marketing' is that marketing loses its sense for what is funny in trying to be too rigorous and analytical. The final principle is to bluff. This can be done by style and impudence.

Managerial management asserts that all of this can be managed, and a reduction in uncertainty can be achieved, by better planning. This alternative of marketing, even for entrepreneurs, is a two-stage process: (1) make basic decisions concerning the total expenses of marketing, its mix and its allocation to the different parts of the marketing mix, and (2) decide in broad outline how to use the allocated budget on the different parts of the marketing mix, that is, product, price, place and promotion. The marketing planning process offers a well-defined route from generating a business ambition to implementing and controlling the resulting plans. In real life, planning is never so straightforward and logical, of course. Different people can be involved in different steps of the planning process, and the extent to which they accept and are influenced by earlier planning processes varies.

It is admitted that there could be possible problems associated with too much planning:

–   political: frictions between participants
–   opportunity costs: possibilities missed from not planning
–   reward system: often short term
–   information about the future: may not exist
–   culture: may not fit the organization
–   personalities: possible personal clashes and pent-up antagonisms
–   shortage of knowledge and skills: how to do it.

That managerial marketing considers itself to be able to achieve so much and in such a detail is probably due to two things: firstly, it is intimately related to the management concept with all what that that entails, for example, being able to measure its effect more quantitatively, and secondly, it was developed in relation to mass marketing and not to marketing for entrepreneurs, which is the subject of this book. Furthermore, talking about entrepreneurs and their marketing, it is my experience that this literature rarely has that restriction I have, which is that an entrepreneur must come up with something which is new in some respect; the literature is otherwise often about starting new ventures, no matter how genuinely new they are.

Managerial marketing claims it is possible to use the same established basic marketing procedures in all parts of the society. Consequently, it is not specifically contextual and doesn't consider place or time. In all research based on the rational philosophy, the ambition is to build models and produce generalizable concepts. Managerial marketing has, therefore, constantly tried to extend its application area. The proponents of this approach mean, for example, that this type of marketing is also valid without any basic changes for industrial marketing and intrapreneurs. Proponents of the rational managerial marketing model, representatives for what I refer to as the limited view of entrepreneurship, also claim that the same approach also is valid for social entrepreneurs. However, the way I look at it, this model is not at all suitable for those citizen entrepreneurs which are called public entrepreneurs, as we will see.

The managerial marketing alternative is still influenced in some respects by microeconomic theory. It is based on *economic* rationality (*homo economicus*), even though Herbert Simon was awarded the Nobel Prize in Economic sciences in 1978 for the theory that we are rational in a limited sense due to a lack of complete information (March & Simon, 1958). Most managerial marketing alternatives also look at transaction as the building stone in marketing theory and (which is consistent with the limited view of entrepreneurship) assert that people must find an opportunity in the economy in order to become entrepreneurs. Such an opportunity can be detected through well conducted market surveys, or created through productive R&D efforts and / or aggressive management marketing.

The criticism of the management approach in marketing comes from several directions; it has, for instance, been criticized from a more general point of view by many authors (for example, Håkansson, 1982; Webster, 1992; Grönroos, 1994; Gummesson, 1999; Brown, 1995). The most basic criticism is whether it is relevant in situations other than for standardized consumption goods out of which it came.

### 7.11.3 Principles for Social Phenomenological Marketing for Entrepreneurs

Let us look at some principles which are valid only for the social phenomenological way to marketing for entrepreneurs.

Social phenomenological marketing is by necessity embedded in a historical, cultural and economic context. Marketing in this alternative can be looked at as a special way to problematize and transform the limitations in such a context. As entrepreneurship literally means to 'go in between', one could also express it such that social phenomenological marketing for an entrepreneur means to exploit the space of thought between concrete action in a specific situation and rules and regulations plus other limitations in the same situation. *Consistent with social phenomenology, the life world (everyday reality) is stressed*, not the theoretical abstract world, and concrete action constitutes *the prosaic in the creating everyday process of the entrepreneur*, that is, his or her constructive everyday imitations and successive improvements (in other words, that transformation process which happens in everyday reality). Rules and regulations plus other limitations in the situation can be interpreted as its *public room* (sometimes called the public sphere). Consistent with social phenomenology, entrepreneurial actions are directed by *intentionality*, that is, interpretative schemes and social intercourse scripts, which every human being is unaware of but implicitly carries around, and which function as a kind of invisible spectacles through which he or she looks at everyday situations in relation to every specific context.

Social phenomenology does not regard the entrepreneur as an extraordinary human being, or his or her marketing as something exceptional. In social phenomenology terminology, we can use the concepts which are introduced by Lévi-Strauss (1966), looking at the entrepreneur as more of a 'bricoleur' than of an 'engineer'; that is, he or she is directed by everyday language and 'natural' everyday images rather than by rational acquisition of those resources which the 'engineer' needs to handle a project, entrepreneurial or not. The bricoleur attempts to *construct meaning by interactive actions*, primarily with customers and other users of his or her realized or expected results (existing or expected new goods or services or other solutions to their perceived problems). This interaction goes on in dialogical form and, at best, the results are based on a language including, at least partly, new typifications, what social phenomenologically is referred to as *language development* (the idea is, in other words, that new components in the language should lead to new ways of looking at things, consistent with the basic idea of social phenomenology). These dialogues are part of the bricoleur's marketing and hopefully lead to the bricoleurial entrepreneur's results becoming more user-friendly.

One may ask whether social phenomenological marketing is more creative than managerial marketing. The answer is not a simple yes or no, and is more complicated:

– It is, as mentioned, not possible to directly compare the two marketing alternatives, but as managerial marketing is older and more established than social phenomenological marketing, the latter is less developed and not as clearly defined. Social phenomenological marketing also

does not claim, which managerial marketing does, that one best approach to marketing exists.
- There is not a crystal-clear picture of what it means to market oneself phenomenologically, and the possibilities for variation are still very wide. This means, for instance, that this alternative cannot be described or presented as unambiguously and distinctly as the managerial alternative.
- There are also many variations of social phenomenological marketing. In this alternative, nothing is absolutely true (there is always a 'both . . . and").
- Consistent with social phenomenological marketing, the entrepreneur does not take the market for granted – it is not discovered, so to say, and it does not exist in any objective sense. The entrepreneur disregards 'the market' as a factual reality, and accepts that it is more successful to develop through different social imaginations.
- Social phenomenological marketing is sceptical about one-sided and repetitive advertising, and claims that such marketing dilutes the public space. Arranging events and story-telling are more suitable to social phenomenological marketing.
- It is difficult to *measure* the effects of social phenomenological marketing.

The social phenomenological alternative of marketing is very much in line with the postmodern view of reality. The postmodern citizen is interested in issues concerning identity, the meaning of life and self-employment, rather than consumption of standardized products. Individual citizen life has become a *formation process* in this case. Postmodern marketing focuses on creating and confirming meaning in using goods / services rather than just buying them. To the postmodern marketer, the customer is actively participating in experiencing a brand and not simply in passively receiving an advertising message.

Social phenomenology leads naturally to marketing through networking. With this approach, marketing is nothing but a directed network. Companies of various kinds, financial institutions, governments at various social levels and all possible economic players are the nodes. Links are qualifying different interactions between these institutions and they may contain buys and sales, cooperative research and marketing, etc. The structure and the development of weighted and directed networks decide the outcome of all microeconomic processes.

When companies see an information explosion and an unexpected need for flexibility in a quickly changing market place, their business can be in the centre of a complete overhaul and possibly total turnaround. This does not mean a marginal reformulation of work descriptions for a few individuals. It is a completely new way of thinking about how to respond to the new business environment in the post-industrial era, which might also be called the information economy.

The most visible element in this new way of thinking is a shift from a tree to a net or a network organization – flat and with lots of cross-connections between the nodes. Project teams, alliances inside and outside the organization, and outsourcing are thriving. In trying to compete in a quickly moving market place, companies therefore shift from a static and optimized tree to a dynamic and mobile net, while they also offer a more flexible and versatile order structure.

Social phenomenologically, companies realize that they can never work on their own. They cooperate with other institutions and adopt successful business practices from other organizations. Co-creation is a result of an action initiative and a kind of economic strategy, which brings all parties together (for example, the company and some customers) to generate a mutually positively recognized result (Prahalad & Ramaswamy, 2004c). Co-created value emerges as personal, unique experiences for the customer (value-in-use) and ongoing revenues, learning and improved market-effective drivers for the company (loyalty, relationships and viral customer statements). Value is co-created with the customers, if and when a customer can personally convey his or her experiences from using those offers of goods and services that the company provides – during the period when they are used – to a level that is best suited to be able to be personalized in order to do the company's job or carry out its ambitions, and which allow the company to derive a higher value from its investments in goods and services as new knowledge, higher revenues / profit and / or superior brand values and qualities. Prahalad and Ramaswamy (2000) popularized the concept of co-created value. They further developed their arguments by building on experiences from companies such as Napster and Netflix, where they showed that customers no longer think it is enough to say yes or no to companies' offers.

Democracy is important to social phenomenological marketing. Traditional actions from companies and customers were traditionally assumed to have small consequences on the state of markets. Companies and other business activities were not looked at as interacting with each other but with 'the market', a mythical entity which mediated all economic interactions. Social phenomenological marketing aims for genuine co-creation.

Social phenomenological marketing fits citizen entrepreneurs, especially public entrepreneurs (true 'social phenomenologically co-creating entrepreneurs'). A good marketer here has a vivid imaginative ability.

# 8. Marketing approaches for independent business entrepreneurs

## 8.1 INTRODUCTION

Following on from the end of the last chapter, let us look more tangibly at how marketing can be designed for three different types of entrepreneurs: entrepreneurs who start up new business activities as independent business units (this chapter), entrepreneurs who develop new business activities within that company where he or she is employed or connected to in other ways, so-called business intrapreneurs (Chapter 9), and social entrepreneurs (Chapter 10). There are some initial points to make; let us call them some prerequisites to what has been said and what will be said:

- There is no way of providing a complete description of all possible uses of marketing for all entrepreneurs.
- Instead, I concentrate on providing some basic ideas that I think fit in with the three types of entrepreneurs. To clarify the differences between the three, there is no reason to provide any details but only to give an overview and some specific aspects of each type.
- The most important purpose of these three chapters is to illustrate differences between rational (managerial) and constructionist (social phenomenological) marketing. I sometimes think it is enough to provide some examples of how it could have been done or has been done in practice.
- The discussions are to show what could have been possible. I make no difference between thinking and acting in the sense that Argyris and Schön (1989) talk about 'espoused theories' and 'theories-in-use'; in other words, that people do not always practise what they preach.
- A reminder of the fact that, when talking about entrepreneurs of interest to me, I refer to people in the beginning of a new business or social activity who must produce innovative results.
- Much of what is said in the following three chapters can also sometimes be valid in more than one chapter. For instance, much of the content of

this chapter can also be applicable to business intrapreneurs (Chapter 9) and to some social entrepreneurs (Chapter 10).

As we have seen in this book, managerial marketing is based on the belief that the reality in which entrepreneurs operate is regarded as *factual and full of circumstances*, where you are, as marketer, supposed to do the following:

- Build *models* (that is, construct deliberately simplified true pictures of the most important factual circumstances which the interested participants can see in their reality).
- Produce *explanations* of this reality, that is, existing factual relationships between causes (of the causal type 'because of' and / or the motivational type 'in order to') and effects, by which entrepreneurs, their partners and their customers or users are influenced and which they can influence.
- Receive information through *interviews* (face-to-face or questionnaires) with customers or user receivers, information which is as true (objectively or subjectively factual) as possible.

The idea is, consequently, that fruitful interviews (or information gained in other ways) lead to fruitful models which in turn lead to fruitful explanations.

For social phenomenological marketing, as we know, the entrepreneurial reality is looked at as *socially constructed and meaningful*, and the marketer is supposed to do the following:

- Create *interpretations* (that is, constructions, consisting of problematizations in that language and with those values, which people who interact with you in markets or similar areas are using, or you use yourself, or both).
- Try to *understand*, that is, see how the entrepreneur and his or her co-actors fit in those language typifications, which you may arrive at by, for instance, describing them as the outcome of the dialectic social processes of objectification, subjectification, externalization and internalization.
- Obtain information through *dialogues* with customers / users and / or partners, which should be as constructive (that is, positively directed forward) as possible. These dialogues may possibly lead to a partly new language to build a different (and better) understanding, which the entrepreneur and his or her environment are co-creating in these dialogues. This is called *language development* (the idea is, of

course, that a new language should lead to new thinking and thereby new action).

The idea is, consequently, that fruitful dialogues (or information gained in other ways) are related to fruitful interpretations in a fruitful understanding.

We have also seen that managerial marketing and social phenomenological marketing differ, by asserting that the former is based on the limited view on entrepreneurship while the latter is based on the more extended view on entrepreneurship. In the former case, all entrepreneurs are considered, at least partly, similar, that they are driven by a need for achievement (which is primarily economically orientated), that they start by discovering (or creating) an opportunity to become an entrepreneur, that their behaviour has great similarities to management and that they look at it as advantageous to plan. Proponents of the more extended view are of a different opinion in these matters.

## 8.2 MANAGERIAL MARKETING FOR INDEPENDENT BUSINESS ENTREPRENEURS

Managerial marketing for independent business entrepreneurs starts from models for market planning of a management type, which at an early stage make it clear which prerequisites are at hand business-wise. This directing set of prerequisites can either consist of the entrepreneur's ambitions concerning time, objective and the extent of his or her future company (thinking which is referred to as causation), or of the entrepreneur's possibilities concerning his or her existing or acquirable knowledges and skills through his or her contacts etc. (thinking which is referred to as effectuation).

A review of those parts, which should be needed according to managerial marketing to create a complete conceptualization of managing either the goals-rational or the means-rational way to become an entrepreneur, can either be described as a sequence of decisions on the way there or an overview of all possibly relevant aspects which together and / or in cooperation would make you succeed.

In both cases, in my opinion it is necessary that their behaviour is related to innovative results, in small or in big terms. I consequently discuss only entrepreneurs as innovators, either as champions in parts of managerial marketing or as driving forces behind social phenomenological marketing. A review of which components are of interest, which questions it explores and which keywords are in focus at the beginning, is given in Table 8.1 (which is my adaptation of a table given in Frankelius et al., 2015:576).

*Table 8.1    The entrepreneur's business model as a managerial way of thinking*

| Component | Question | Keywords |
| --- | --- | --- |
| Sales offer | How is the company to create value? | Core competence and customer value |
| The market | To whom is the company creating value? | Sales organization and localization |
| Internal skills | Which are the company's internal competitive advantages? | Activities, processes, infrastructure and flows |
| Competitive skills | How is the company to position itself on the market? | Marketing strategy, differentiation factors |
| Economy | How is the company to make money? | Economic model (for instance, if sales is to take place over the counter or on Internet), accounting and business system |
| Personal factors (goals-rationally) | Which are the entrepreneur's ambitions in terms of objectives and business size? | Strategy and ambition |
| Personal factors (means-rationally) | Which knowledge and competence has the entrepreneur got and which contacts has he or she? | Knowledge and competence |

*Source:*    Adapted from Frankelius et al., 2015:576.

The model above is originally proposed by Morris et al. (2005) is useful for identifying factual essential components and breaking them down to concrete rules and from there control a company, new or old. In their model, Morris's author team tries to integrate the components of sales offer, market, internal skills, competitive skills, economy and personal factors.

The model is originally divided into three levels: overall level, business level and regular level. At all levels, you can find those six questions which are represented in Table 8.1, but the answers become more operative at lower levels. The idea is that the company, by working with the components at the different levels, is assisted to formulate and develop its model to create the business, operatively as well as consistently.

At the overall level, the foundation of the company is established, and the questions are used to find the main orientation of the company and to decide what to do within each component. At business level, the ambition is to find unique (innovative) combinations, which reinforce the company's competitive power. The business level also includes decisions on how to execute that which has been identified at the overall level. At regular level, decisions are made about tangible rules for how the sales offer is to be delivered so that the exchange creates value for the customer as well as for the company. Summary-wise, the business model with questions and answers becomes rather complex, consistent with the discussion above (Frankelius et al., 2015).

Note that in Table 8.1 in the component 'Personal factors', there are two parts, one with the subtitle 'goals-rationally' and the other with the subtitle 'means-rationally'. The idea is, at least at the overall level of the model, to choose one of the two as an entrepreneur if this model is used: the former one, if rationality starts from the entrepreneur's 'strategy and ambition' and the latter one, if rationality starts from the entrepreneur's 'knowledge and competence', consistent with the two alternative rational entrepreneurial startups presented in Chapter 7.

No matter which one of the two possible startup possibilities is chosen, the very implementation of a managerial marketing route for an independent entrepreneur may be built up from and follow two alternative *application models*. We may call one a *sequential* managerial marketing model and the other a *structural* managerial marketing model.

## 8.3   THE SEQUENTIAL MANAGERIAL MARKETING MODEL

The *sequential managerial marketing model* is presented in Figure 8.1.

The first step is for the entrepreneur to make up his or her mind about prerequisites that are at hand to start an entrepreneurial business venture in the first place. Consistent with the limited view on entrepreneurship, which corresponds with managerial marketing, the idea is that a business entrepreneurial venture starts with a person finding an opportunity to become an entrepreneur and claims, furthermore, that looking for opportunities to realize an entrepreneurial reality is a necessary, strong and basic entrepreneurial characteristic. An entrepreneurial opportunity is

*Figure 8.1   The sequential managerial marketing model*

considered as a factual and advantageous change in economic, technological, political and / or social conditions in the environment.

A potential business entrepreneur is therefore probably attentive to what is going on in his or her environment to be able to discover such opportunities. Based on the managerial approach that reality is to be perceived as full of real and factual courses of events, it is natural for an aspiring business entrepreneur under such circumstances to want to know which circumstances provide the prerequisites to start a new independent business venture. The independent business entrepreneur may try to obtain such knowledge through a formal environmental analysis. Such an analysis can be of one or several of the following six types (Frankelius et al., 2015):

– close surveillance of specific factors
– scanning without exact focus
– deeper penetrations of issues given beforehand
– explorative overviews
– forethought
– historical studies.

In most cases of independent entrepreneurial situations, however, such advanced environmental analyses are not made, in my experience. The acquisition of prerequisites to start independent business entrepreneurial ventures, including the opportunity to do so, is mostly more of an art than a science. The situation may be different for business intrapreneurs, which we will look at in the next chapter.

The next step in the sequential managerial marketing model (according to Figure 8.1), after having clarified the prerequisites, is to decide whether to go ahead goals-rationally or means-rationally. If one chooses the goals-rational way, and consequentially is mainly driven in one's planning by which results one wants to achieve, the managerial marketing approach is that the road ahead can be clearer and the success be more motivational (and above all be measurable) if the goal is operationalized as early as possible. If, on the other hand, the means-rational way is chosen, and consequentially mainly driven in one's planning by one's own qualifications and possibilities, this marketing approach holds that success is more likely if you causally clarify the relationships between where you are going and what is required to get there. Those means you do not have (or expect to gain access to on your own or through your contact), you must make plans for how to obtain. There is a rich variety of ways to achieve this, and there are no general rules for an entrepreneur in such a situation. What is required, however, is to be clever as well as creative.

As mentioned several times, I am only interested in entrepreneurs, who come up with *new* solutions, that is, who are innovative in their results. I am absolutely convinced that innovative results can never be achieved in a non-innovative way. I assert, therefore, that even managerial marketing for entrepreneurs, if it is to be part of my interest, *must contain innovative aspects*, even though this alternative of marketing is very clearly, logically and rationally built up. I will return to this issue.

The next step in the sequential managerial marketing model according to Figure 8.1 is to carry out strategic market planning. By strategy, one could mean that unique position which the entrepreneur wants to be in (and hopefully maintain) in the future. No matter which alternative of marketing an entrepreneur chooses, however, I think that an entrepreneur at a beginning stage in most cases is not particularly clear about this, even if he or she might have hopes as well as visions. However, he or she is probably much clearer of the next step in the sequential managerial marketing model, that is, how to construct the marketing mix and allocate funds to product, price, place and promotion. Considering the usual limitations in time as well as in other resources for an entrepreneur in the beginning of a new venture, it is probably wiser to select one part of the marketing mix and become overengaged on that part rather than be spread too thinly on all parts. I will return to this point at the end of this first section of this chapter, which is about *managerial* marketing for entrepreneurs.

The choice of focus in the marketing mix will influence the layout of the last step in Figure 8.1, the operative implementation plus the design of that feedback which follows the application of the whole sequence.

## 8.4   THE STRUCTURAL MANAGERIAL MARKETING MODEL

There are many varieties of the *structural managerial marketing model*, as with the sequential managerial marketing model. The different methods tend to illustrate different components that should be considered when the business entrepreneur is to become successful in a market, sometimes with a clarification of how these components are related and how they influence each other. One relatively accepted variety was launched by Osterwalder and Pigneur (2010) and is called *the canvas model*. The ways in which an entrepreneur is to create, deliver and extract market value are laid out as on a canvas. The model can be outlined as in Figure 8.2, a version which I have taken from Frankelius et al. (2015:578).

The model starts out from the perspective of the individual company, and like all models in managerial marketing, it assumes that the company

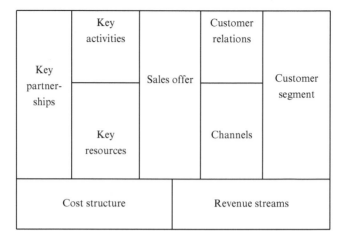

*Source:*   Based on Osterwalder & Pigneur, 2010; my translation.

*Figure 8.2    The Canvas model*

has a factual and a relatively stable structure – the model is probably easier to apply in more established companies than in completely new ones. It is therefore provided as an alternative in the next chapter also, as it is valid for intrapreneurs.

The canvas model is set up by a company which attempts to trim its flows of costs and revenues and improve its profitability while at the same time creating a higher market value for the company's entrepreneur. It could be described as 'a conceptual tool pointing at the logic behind how the company can or should make money on its sales offer, and it also works as a check list of what is important to keep in mind in such an effort' (Frankelius et al., 2015:577–8; my translation).

The canvas model focuses on the company's value offer and does so from two directions, that is, a market side and a production side. In the centre of the model, which is provided in Figure 8.2, is the sales offer. The customer and market side is made up of the company's *market and customer related activities*, and the chosen customer segment is in focus. Customers are reached and cultivated through the components of *customer relations* and *channels.* On the production side, its components are *key activities, key resources* and *key partnerships*. The costs and revenues of the business model are summarized in the components of *cost structure* and *revenue streams*. It is the customer and market side of the models which has the strongest connections to the literature around managerial marketing. Here value creation is focused upon, and it deals with the need and problems of the customer segment, that is, the benefit provided by the offer and which the customer finds it worth paying for. By identifying what it is that the customer wants, the company can satisfy a specific need by its offer and generate revenues that way (Frankelius et al., 2015:579).

Perceived market value is central in the entrepreneur's offer to explain success through managerial marketing models. It is also important that the company's opinion about what creates value somehow is checked against the customer segment, on which the entrepreneur is focusing. This can be done in this case through market research based on interviews and questionnaires of different kinds. Other benefits which a value offer can bring according to managerial marketing are to (Frankelius et al., 2015:580):

– help to do a specific job – can be about consulting or a commitment on a contract
– design – can be about special design which is aesthetically attractive, functional, user-friendly or environmentally sustainable
– brand building – by carrying and using specific brands, customers send signals to the environment about who he or she is
– cost saving – by customers using a scheduled maintenance system, for instance, he or she can save on their maintenance budget because the risk for break-downs decreases and the system makes sure the machinery is always 'well oiled'
– smaller risks – this can be about insurance systems or guarantee commitments which are part of the offer
– higher access – the company can offer online support, or use cooperating partners, with good access, which the customer can be part of
– user-friendliness – the company makes it simpler for the user to utilize the product
– the price – this is what decides which side of the business model is to be stressed the most, the value-creating side or the efficiency-side.

To summarize, one can say, when working with the company's offer, never to forget that customers pay for the experienced (or economically calculated) benefit. This is so when selling to a customer in general and when selling to companies in particular. Customers rarely buy just because it is fun or because they do not have other things to do. There are exceptions to this rule, about all in the customer market, and then as impulse buying and pleasure shopping, for instance. But if the reasons why the customer buys are strained, you end up most of the time with the customer experiencing some benefit with the purchase, even if it is an impulse buy. If it is about sales between companies, one must assume that a purchase made by the customer must be possible to calculate as an economical gain as margins when selling further, as higher efficiency, cost savings or other benefits, assisting the buying company to reach higher level of profitability short-term or long-term. (Frankelius et al., 2015:580–1; my translation)

## 8.5   ASPECTS OF BEING INNOVATIVE WHEN APPLYING THE MANAGERIAL MARKETING MODEL

A list of different ways in which an entrepreneur may be able to create value for his or her customer consistent with the managerial marketing model can include the following points (Frankelius et al., 2015:582):

– *Personal sales*: the company's sales person finds a customer and makes him or her buy.
– *Sales over the counter*: sale takes place in a shop or in a department store, where the customer chooses a product, brings it to the cash desk, pays and takes it home.
– *Sales of ticket*: this can be everything from bus, train or air ticket to charter trips and concert / event tickets. The customer pays beforehand and is allowed to consume the service / experience that has been bought when showing the receipt / ticket.
– *Broker models*: the company makes a profit by connecting seller and buyer, for example, real estate broker, stock exchanges, transaction brokers such as PayPal, auction houses or auction sites and other physical or virtual market places.
– *Advertising models*: examples are web portals such as Yahoo or Google, where a user can utilize a service for free and the company becomes an attractive advertising place because of its many users and good information about their profile.
– *Renting out*: the company owns machinery, cars, tools, competence, real estates, beds or other things which the customer can use during a limited time through paying a charge.
– *Services*: the company sells services, such as cutting hair or problem solving, and may either be paid at the same time as the service is provided or consistent with another agreement about how and when payment is to take place.
– *Subscription*: Examples are newspapers, journals, telephone, theatre tickets etc. The customer pays a charge in exchange for a specific or a running number of goods.
– *Licensing, royalty and franchising*: the customer may use a solution or a concept and pay compensation to the copyright holder.

– *Computer clouds and similar services*: the Internet is used as a base for these services. Customers and other users are given access to software, located in another server.

There is room here for combination, creativity and inventiveness – or innovation, which I regard as essential. There are many general suggestions as to how to try to make managerial marketing more innovative (Table 8.2).

As mentioned earlier, Morgan (2009) has several suggestions of creative moves, which could suit managerial marketing as well as social phenomenological marketing:

> While we might disagree on this implication or that implication of the changes around us, one thing is clear to everyone, it seems: Marketing or rather the transition that marketing is making, is now to be seen as a journey without map. We know, because influential CMOs have told us, that the old marketing model is broken, and certainly we have all lost confidence in it. What we *don't* yet know – because it is in a state of continual emergence and experimentation – is what the nature of the new model is that we are supposed to replace it with. (Morgan, 2009:xvii-xviii)

The starting point for Morgan (2009) is that the middle ground will be an increasingly dangerous place to be on. A successful business entrepreneur can therefore not be a player somewhere in the middle; *he or she must be at least a strong second position*. He also claims that there are important advantages to being an entrepreneur (and consequently be a newcomer in some way if an independent business entrepreneur). He or she does not have to be everything for all people, he or she can choose a place where to stand and something to believe in. Furthermore, he or she can concentrate on delivering his or her choice in a superior way.

Shortage of experience in a product category does not have to be a disadvantage, but can instead be a possibility for renewal, which allows new players to see fresh alternatives in the product category in question – alternatives which those who have been working there for years cannot see, because they have become too firmly rooted. The point is for an independent business entrepreneur not to think traditionally in that way which is flourishing in every product category and be caught by those details and perspectives which may obscure his or her judgements. One can simply ask 'Why not?' instead of 'Why?' There is no reason to belittle what a five-year-old child asks compared with what, for instance, research announces. Morgan (2009) refers to this as *intelligent naivety*!

> By intelligent naivety we mean in reality something more than 'do the opposite of what everyone else is doing'. We mean, very specifically, to bring a fresh and

*Table 8.2    Comparison between traditional managerial marketing and its more innovative possibilities*

|  | Traditional managerial marketing | More innovative managerial marketing |
|---|---|---|
| *Basic premises* | Facilitating transactions and market control | Sustainable competitive advantage through value-creating innovation |
| *Orientation* | Marketing as an objective, impassionate science | Central control for passion, enthusiasm, persistency and creativity in marketing |
| *Context* | Established, relatively stable markets | Imaginative, emerging and fragmented markets with a high degree of turbulence |
| *The marketer's role* | Coordinator of marketing mix; brand-builder | Internal and external change agent; category-shaper |
| *Market view* | Reactive and adaptive view of current market situation with gradual innovations | Proactive view, leading the customer with dynamic innovations |
| *Customer need* | Articulated, assumed, expressed by customers in questionnaires | Unarticulated, discovered, identified through lead-users |
| *Risk perspective* | Risk minimization in market actions | Marketing as a tool for calculated risk taking; stress on finding ways to minimize risks, managing them stepwise or sharing them |
| *Resource management* | Efficient use of existing resources, scarcity mentality | Reach leverage effects, creative use of others' resources; do more with less; actions not limited by resources accessible at the moment |
| *Development of goods/services* | Marketing supporting development of new goods/ services within R&D and other technical departments | Marketing is the home of innovation; customers are co-active producers |
| *The role of customers* | External source for information and feedback | Active participants in the company's marketing/decision making process and in their view of what product, price, place and promotion are and contain |

*Source:*    Morris et al., 2002:6.

dynamic set of questions to the category, a set of questions that deliberately breaks with the immediate past of the category and looks at what we can learn from other categories – both in terms of what we can bring that is new, and also in terms of which bits of so-called wisdom we need to *unlearn* in order to break through. (Morgan, 2009:38)

Sometimes it is *more important* to *ask the right questions than to provide the right answers*!

Customers do not navigate really successful business entrepreneurs. Instead, these entrepreneurs *navigate their customers*. They try to communicate clearly and unyieldingly where they stand and why they stand there. In human societies, products have always been some kind of communication. In uncertain times, which many of us think we live in today, it is possible to say, however, that some products have been not only a kind of communication but of navigation. Morgan (2009) refers to products which thrive in this uncertain environment as *having a lighthouse identity*.

That customers find the self-confidence of [products having a clear identity] appealing should be no surprise. In life, people are drawn to strength and to people of character who are true to themselves. In marketing life, in using goods as communication or even navigation, people are drawn to strong brands. This strength can come from . . . an intense projection of who you are. (Morgan, 2009:83)

The purpose of a strong identity is to invite and create a more intensive relationship between a product (or often its brand) and customers / users. Such a product succeeds because it offers the customer an emotional reward and / or relationship which previously established brands cannot match. Even though key aspects of the product mix may satisfy certain rational needs, new products tend not to succeed by only satisfying these rational needs (there are rarely any rational needs left in any mature category at any rate); by a lighthouse identity they offer instead a *realignment of the customers' feelings*.

There are two kinds of product leaders (or brand leaders) in every category. One is the market leader, the biggest player, the product the majority lives with – and the chance is that this is the product it has grown up with. But there is another type of product leader, which is *the thought leader*, the product (or the brand) which everybody is talking about. Even though it is not the biggest one, it is the brand which raises most attention. Successful business entrepreneurs should endeavour to create this kind of product leader.

They should try to reach thought leadership not only through product innovation or advertising strategy, but through *behaviour*: surprising the customer by consciously breaking one or two of those conventions (not all) which make up that category they entered or re-entered so late (Morgan, 2009:109–10).

Market leaders surround themselves with rules or conventions which control marketing of their product within a certain category. Customers have, in reality, expectations that they shall deliver and / or play in that category. But the point with these conventions is that they often have very little to do with understanding what the customer really wants, or rather *would like to have*; they have been invited by the marketers (and the market leader) for reasons which are now forgotten and which, without resistance, now have become dominant. In their turn, many secondary brands within each category supplement a comfortable but very unspectacular life by playing by the existing conventions, which are established by the market leader; and this repetition of established market leaders has in turn created customers' expectations on how a certain product is to be seen and marketed.

But an independent business entrepreneur (let us call him or her a *challenger*) enters a market late, almost by definition. And by entering a market late, you will have to differentiate yourself stronger. It is necessary to offer customers a strong reason for choosing what you offer, which is not easy. Although there are times when a genuine product innovation precedes the creation of a brand, it is more often the case nowadays that creation of a brand precedes the conceptualization of this product.

Category conventions offer a natural point of leverage to create this differentiation. The challenger must find a genuinely new insight into what the customer really wants – and then play accordingly, taking one or several of these conventions and consciously breaking them in the way in which the company markets itself.

It is important to stress that this kind of convention break is not simply about attracting attention to gain interest. But even if you really try to draw attention to yourself, the short-term objective is also to break a convention in order to communicate your identity and positioning, and to create a deepened customer relationship. In the long term, the objective is to provide a new framework in the category's area, particularly in the customer's choice criterion, which the challenger has defined him- or herself and is thereby to his or her own advantage. *Change the rules in the challenger's favour!*

Most people are quite content with where they are and what they do. They do not expect to change their opinion about what they consume, and in most purchasing moments, they already have a set of brands which they think with delight will suit their needs. Actually, the purchasing decision is often not a real decision – it is a habit. This is easy to forget.

For a challenger to reach an objective, he or she therefore needs to find a way in which to puncture customers' complacency. Some of this will obviously come from sustained free offer of samples and other ways in which to motivate change of behaviour. Some of it will be the result of brilliant communication. But, due to the fact that challengers are normally in a hurry, they will try to *find ways which create symbols of re-evaluation* – dramatic symbols or acts, which often involve startling presentations, which make customers sit up and re-evaluate their assumptions about those products they normally buy (Morgan, 2009).

As can be expected, common tactical means used by challengers involve attempts to surprise, or to attack the dominant complacency head on. Challengers may in such a case put things together which are not expected to belong together – such as art museums and discount stores, sloths and clocks, athletes and vegetarianism – where the juxtaposition makes it necessary to re-evaluate each item. Some business entrepreneurs may even need to arrange a sequence of symbolic re-evaluations to dislodge customers' complacency. However, as far as independent business entrepreneurs are concerned, their budget for promotional purposes is usually very small. Their fuel must then be idea power, ingenuity and passion.

In today's world of an abundance of information and media traffic, the greatest danger is not the customer rejecting the business entrepreneur's product, but neglecting it. To be rejected is to be noticed. In principle, this can be attended to relatively easy – you make a big change or you pull out – but complacency is a much more insidious and expensive problem. It is not enough, if that is the case, to invest more and more money – they will just give less and less return. The solution is, as stated by Morgan (2009), to *whole-heartedly concentrate* and sacrifice all that costs more than it is worth:

1. Concentrate the internal and external expressions of identity by eliminating activities that might dilute it.
2. Concentrate by changing the mind-set of the business entrepreneur and the organization from communicating vague general messages to more intensive, focused appeals (and thereby avoid being 'stuck in the middle').
3. Concentration generates a critical mass for the communication of that identity and differences by stripping away other secondary and unfocused marketing activities.

The independent business entrepreneur must understand that in the tough business world of today, he or she will face resistance. It is therefore important to overcome this resistance *before* it arises, and also to involve oneself more to achieve this – *to overcommit*. It does not help to just exert oneself enough to succeed in the most essential aspects; instead, he or she must overcome every possible source of inertia and lack of interest which one will inevitably will come across (internally or externally) when trying to translate the challenger's purpose and tactic into a constructive behaviour and a result.

This overcommitment is not just required in the language that the business entrepreneur uses to stress the advantages of the product to the selected market segment, but also in actions to show that he or she really means what he or she says – above all, to support the thought leadership that he or she intends to represent.

In my opinion, most market communication, just as television advertising, is rather banal. In many countries, it is even possible to pay for a television channel *free from commercials* today. Very few business entrepreneurs have a product to offer that sells itself without any efforts, which means that the business entrepreneur must look for possibilities to *create* news around what he or she is doing. Furthermore, a challenger has normally no other choice than showing him- or herself as special; differentiation is for an independent business entrepreneur a matter of survival as well as of reaching profitability. He or she has normally less financial means than the established competitor. *Clear and distinct* information is not enough in such a case – catching the target's imagination in different media must be the objective.

To just see all marketing as a simple aspect of the marketing mix is not enough. Interesting communication ideas and a consistent striving for the right publicity to get the word-of-mouth process going can be the most powerful business instrument that a challenger has access to today: the email culture, the emergence of social networks and different kinds of online connected local communities have created, like never before, a new level of possibilities for challengers with limited budgets to quickly build awareness and interaction around their product ideas among customers.

> Social media and networks have been around for hundreds of years – forums where people delighted in passing on and talking about news and ideas they have picked up – they just were called bars, cafes, and pubs. [However], there are critical new elements and opportunities that the digital world has brought to this opportunity to engage with social cultures (visual dynamism, interactivity, flow, accelerated community, and scaled momentum). (Morgan, 2009:194–5)

As stated by Morgan (2009), a business entrepreneurial challenger should not be primarily customer-centred. This is probably what most business enterprisers are, for obvious reasons. A successful independent business entrepreneur should, according to Morgan, be above all idea-centred and show this in all possible ways. To be successful in this endeavour, a great amount of creativity and innovative skill is required, which, as we know, is the focus of this book.

## 8.6 SOCIAL PHENOMENOLOGICAL MARKETING FOR INDEPENDENT BUSINESS ENTREPRENEURS

Due to its condition, social phenomenological marketing cannot be presented as simple models or algorithms either in a sequential or structural format, but rather as meta-principles and as process-orientated interpretations of starting points and fixed stars. Unlike managerial marketing, social phenomenological marketing cannot be taught or learnt as a set of average or typical explanations in a world of theories. This means, for instance:

- In social phenomenological marketing, it can be destructive, and even dangerous, to directly copy one's own or others' ways to succeed.
- It can be difficult in any quantitative way to decide whether one has been successful through social phenomenological marketing because to achieve this you assume that you act in a meaningful world instead of a world full of circumstances. Meaning cannot be measured in any traditional sense, but must be felt and experienced individually and contextually in actual cases, even if interactively together with other people.
- The concrete place (unlike the abstract space) is of importance here. A place is more or less specific. It contains, in the business entrepreneurial case, living individuals, who in interactive processes continuously create their existence. With this point of departure, the business entrepreneur cannot in any contemplative solitude figure out an abstract best plan, but must instead put him- or herself in (or rather often be part of creating) concrete situations of learning in order to communicate face-to-face with existing business partners and customers to generate an understanding of what is required to proceed in a more favourable direction. To express it as a game of words, the business entrepreneur must here learn more general principles for how he or she can be gradually more constructively specific.
- Social phenomenological marketing is related to the more extended view on entrepreneurship, which in the business entrepreneurial case means to stress one's own contextual learning process rather than

ready-made non-contextual knowledge of, for instance, decision making, picked up from other people who might claim that they have previously been successful and / or researchers who think they know and are willing to tell how to act without concentrating on what is specific in a particular case.

Language is extremely important in social phenomenological marketing and it is, more or less implicitly, part of all marketing consistent with this constructionist philosophy, including for business entrepreneurs. The reason is, of course, that reality is here seen as a social construction, that is, *built up by language typifications*, and not as in managerial marketing, where language is 'only' seen as a tool to *depict reality*. You may express it such that in rational philosophy, which managerial marketing is based on, language (in the wide sense of it, that is, not only written or spoken words, but also gestures and other body language) can be used to *better explain reality*. In social phenomenological marketing it is so, however, that (social) *reality does not contain anything else but language*. There is, of course, also a physical natural reality within social phenomenology, but this philosophy is only interested in *what can be understood* (that is, what can interactively take place between people). Explanations are not enough within its interest area. For example, you cannot 'understand' a metal, a tree or a planet, because as a human being, you have nothing in common with them. If, on the other hand, you use a specific metal or a certain kind of wood to construct something, you can start to talk about understanding (of the result). Knowledge of reality is created in social phenomenological marketing through *dialogues* ('through words') and not through *interviews* ('exchanging knowledge' – of factual reality).

Language used in social phenomenological marketing is constituted, as mentioned above, by *typifications*, which mean *taken-for-granted agreements* between people, which they use to understand their everyday reality. Typifications are treated as if they were *objective*, but they are not. They are *objectified* ('objective-made') and used as if they were objective. To understand partners and customers or other actors in the socially constructed reality, of which he or she is one component, one could say that a business entrepreneur using social phenomenological marketing *is problematizing partners' and customers' reality*; that is, he or she attempts to understand those values and conceptions which lie behind those typifications used by partners and customers.

To work symbolically through language and thereby transcend our biological limits is a hallmark of humanity, and can even be counted as the most significant feature of being human. Our acts are not only controlled by our intentions, but acts as well as intentions are controlled by the language we use. Genuinely new problems require genuinely new solutions, and I see *entrepreneurs as language makers* (to speak about them in analogy with watch maker and shoe maker) only when they achieve new solutions, and this requires that they use a language, which is, at least partly, new. This is what I have referred to as *language development*. As I see it, you do not find new solutions if you do not have a new language for it (Bjerke, 1989).

There are many examples of the magic and importance of language in our working life:

- Many companies try to make the concept 'employee' or 'worker' more humane by talking about, say, 'member of the crew', 'associate' or 'crucial key resource'.
- 'Restructuring' or 'rightsizing' are euphemisms used when companies cut down on their staff. They think it is too negative for anybody to be 'fired' or 'be given the sack'.

Understanding the importance of language in business contexts, including entrepreneurial situations, has been appreciated for a long time:

- The entrance to a company is its *language reality*. The symbols in this reality, including its language, offers in my opinion, a better understanding of any company than either its recorded plan or organization diagram.
- Every moment is a *symbolic* moment. Even to ignore this is symbolic.
- The vocabulary of a company can be its most important *asset*, but it can also be its major *liability*.
- To renew a company, that is intrapreneurship (which we will explore in the next chapter), may make it necessary to *change the central building blocks of their language*, that is, its memes, and to identify those who hold to the *relics* of its old language (Arbnor et al., 1980). Words rarely shake off their etymology and their origin. The point is to clarify the original ideas underlying the language being used in a company to reveal those who are still living in an outdated world.
- The ideal outcome for an entrepreneur would be, of course, to succeed so well that the name of their company is turned into a verb in common use. Two examples in the modern electronic world is 'to google' and 'to tweet'.

Many of the most important artefacts in the business world are symbolic. *Concepts* are incredibly important artefacts. They are:

memes often resulting from a long 'cultural' process, or they may be expressions of deliberate rhetorical innovation. When *Xerox* went from the copying machine company to 'the document company', or when *Mercedes-Benz* talked about selling 'mobility' instead of cars, these notions were highly significant as artefacts. When *Observer* (a very successful Stockholm headquartered company) launched concepts such as 'communication audit' and 'value-creating communications' they created mental analysts for reframing the company's business, which started as press clippings where they were the world's leader. The power of concepts is further proven by how extremely conserving they can be. When *IBM* set up a personal computer division and called it the 'entry products division' this, of course, reflected a whole world view out of touch with emerging reality. (Normann, 2001, p. 244)

In section 6.9, we talked about *entrepreneurs as active participants in sense making.* In this section, we have understood that entrepreneurs may also be called *language makers.* An interesting third variety of entrepreneurs as makers has been given by Spinosa et al. (1997), who talk about *entrepreneurs as history makers.* All these three conceptions of entrepreneurs as makers relate to their intimate connections to language, symbols and meaning, at least if a social phenomenological approach is applied, for instance to marketing.

Spinosa et al. (1997) assert that some people can be looked at as history makers, and claim that entrepreneurs belong to this group. This theory is based on the idea that we all experience anomalies or disharmonies in our lives. Most of us, however, do not do much more than just notice such situations. But there are those, as stated by Spinosa et al. (1997), who act when they face such situations and who present ways in which to challenge them. They do so by disclosing what the authors call 'the life styles' in the society. This can be done in three different ways:

- *Articulation* is the most familiar type of 'clarifying a style'. It occurs when a style, which so far 'is in the air', but is only at a potential stage, is brought into sharper focus. In articulating change, the style does not alter its core identity, but becomes more recognizable among customers/users of a good or service, the acquisition of which makes this life style possible. Articulation is the most common form of entrepreneurship as stated by Spinosa et al. (1997).
- *Reconfiguration* is a more substantial way in which a style can be focused. In this case, a marginal aspect of the practices coordinated by a style becomes more dominant. This kind of change is less frequent in everyday life than articulation. In the case of reconfiguration, a greater sense of integrity is generally *not* experienced (as in the case of articulation). Rather, one has the sense of gaining wider horizons.

- *Cross-appropriation* takes place when a part of society takes over a life style from another part of society, a style that it could not have generated on its own but that it finds useful.

Articulation, reconfiguration and cross-appropriation are consequently three different ways in which disclosed skills can work to bring about meaningful historical change of a disclosed reality. To what extent these changes could be called entrepreneurial in the innovative sense is debatable. In general, I look at articulation as not being an entrepreneurial act, but the other two might very well be so. All these three changes are called *historical* by Spinosa et al. (1997) because people sense them as a continuation of the past. Spinosa et al. (1997) are, therefore, contrasting their notion of continuous, marginal historical change with discontinuous change, and look only at the first ones.

To regard entrepreneurs as history makers fits with the social phenomenological way of applying marketing. One may ask, generally, why it is that our potential as history makers is discovered by so few? Spinosa et al. (1997) assert that there are three ways to understand this. All of them can be looked at as aspects of social phenomenology:

- Our common sense works to cover up our role as possible disclosers of new reality. Common sense is neither fixed nor rationally justified. The ultimate 'ground' of understanding is *simply shared, but not yet disclosed* practice – there is no understanding that exists only for the entrepreneurs.
- Once we have become habituated to a style, it becomes invisible for us. It becomes part of what we take for granted in our everyday reality. If someone behaves in a way that does not fit in with our dominant style, we can fashion his or her behaviour to fit with ours.
- Because we do not cope with the style of, for instance, our culture or our company or our generation directly – we simply *express this style* when we cope with things and with each other – we have no *direct* way to handle it or come alive to it and transform it. Our practices are designed for dealing with things but not for dealing with practices for dealing with things, and especially not for dealing with the coordination of practices for dealing with things. We do not normally sense our potential as disclosers, because we are more interested in the things we disclose than in the disclosing as such.

Through these three 'natural' tendencies to overlook our role as disclosers, we lose sensitivity to occluded, marginal, or neighbouring ways of doing things. By definition, an occluded, marginal or neighbouring practice is one that we generally pass over, either by not noticing its unusualness when we engage in it or by not engaging at all. Special sensitivity to marginal, neighbouring or occluded practice, however, is precisely at the core of entrepreneurship, as stated by Spinosa et al. (1997) (and may, as I see it, be disclosed through social phenomenological marketing). This sensitivity makes innovation more of an art than any rational managerial activity.

Spinosa et al. (1997) claim that three currently widespread ways of thinking about entrepreneurship (entrepreneurship as theory, entrepreneurship as pragmatism and entrepreneurship as driven by cultural values) are not enough for several reasons (this criticism is more relevant in the narrow view of entrepreneurship than in the more extended view):

- They are not genuinely innovative; to reduce entrepreneurship to a number of fairly stable and regular procedures places ourselves virtually outside of change.
- They only try to satisfy those needs that exist already or which can be discovered or created, without talking about how a person being an entrepreneur is changing the *general* way in which we handle things and people in some domain.
- They are deeply anti-historical.

Spinosa et al. (1997:66) claim that entrepreneurship is human activity at its best.

To go back to the ability to innovate as a necessary aspect of a 'true' entrepreneur, those views which are presented by Morgan (2009), which we have looked at before, may be seen with social phenomenological eyes. For example:

- Those naïve but intelligent questions that a challenging entrepreneur should ask him- or herself can be formulated in a language new enough (language development, as I call it) to lead to genuinely new thinking and thereby new actions.
- Language development does not only have to be the beginning of development of a new venture, but can also be used to clarify the challenger's identity, his or her thought leadership and his or her possibilities to be experienced as a 'lighthouse' for customers and other users to 'navigate' by.
- By a partly new language and other new symbols, successful challengers may make customers and others re-evaluate what is important in their way of life and then possibly favour new entrepreneurial challengers.

- Even though an aspiring business entrepreneur is usually short of financial resources, he or she may, as challenger, do all they can to enter the social culture.

The environment must be used by entrepreneurs to expand their venturing possibilities and to include other actors. A broad network extends the environment by new social constructions and, therefore, expands action space. One may believe that modern, ever more extensive electronic possibilities are decisive for these possibilities, but there are an increasing number of opinions to modify this statement. Turkle (2015), for instance, asserts that conversations face-to-face belong to the most human – at the same time as it is one of the most humane – things we can do as human beings, and which people involved in businesses, for instance, business entrepreneurs, should also be doing. It is, as stated by Turkle (2015), by giving each other our fullest attention (for instance, business entrepreneurs, their customers and business partners) that we learn to listen and develop our empathetic ability to really understand others' situation. She claims that face-to-face conversations are also necessary for that internal exchange of views we have with ourselves, to learn how to listen to and develop an empathy in relation to other people. Conversation, self-reflection and understanding our social environment are related.

As Turkle (2015) correctly points out, we try these days to get away from face-to-face conversations. We hide from each other, at the same time as we are constantly connected with each other. On the display in the telephone or on the computer, we are tempted to present ourselves in a way we would like to be. Of course, there are always aspects of acting every time people meet each other, in all contexts, but on the Internet, we always choose the moment ourselves and there it is very easy to clarify, edit, improve and revise. It is therefore questionable whether we really get to know each other, where we do it electronically. The same opinions are valid for most advertising we are exposed to. It is heavily made up and provides a glorified and biased picture of the supplier. Advertising gives no opportunity to counter or to create a constructive dialogue, and is surely one important reason behind that 'advertising weariness' which is so widespread today.

Through our mobile phones, computers and most advertising media, we run away from spontaneous and unconditional conversations where we play with ideas and permit ourselves to be completely present and vulnerable. These are precisely the conversations which promote empathy and intimacy and which strengthen our social (and business entrepreneurial) actions. In these face-to-face conversations, creative cooperation flourishes, which is necessary for a good family community and for developing learning as well as for successful businesses. Dialogical conversations face-to-face strengthen our relationships in networks at home, at school, in our working environment and in the public (Turkle, 2015). There is no better way to build confidence. '[Entrepreneurs] do not want their service to become just like any commodity. The best way to avoid this is to offer a relationship. And this requires conversations [face-to-face]' (Turkle, 2015:356).

A business entrepreneur should therefore act as much as possible as one of the participants in dialogical interactions – mainly 'on the floor' where customers and other users are, that is, walk around, and talk face-to-face with colleagues, business partners, customers and other users. Turkle (2015) presents some 'milestones' to guide such walking around:

- Slow down. Learn to listen to your own voice and to others'.
- Protect your creativity. Take the time you need and take time to be silent. Set your own agenda and keep your own pace.
- Create rooms which are promoting conversations face-to-face.
- Remember to do one thing at a time as your next trend. Productivity as well as creativity will increase that way.
- Talk to people you do not agree with. You learn more from people who do not agree.
- Follow the seven-minutes rule. It takes at least seven minutes before you know how a conversation will develop.
- Question the idea that the world consists of a number of apps. App-thinking starts from the idea that our actions function as algorithms, these actions lead to predictable results and are lacking in empathy anyway.
- Use the right tools. Those tools which are at hand, for instance a smartphone or a super-fast computer program, are not necessarily the right ones.
- Learn from moments full of conflicts. They may perhaps be possibilities to develop yourself.
- Remember what you know about life, above all those moments when you came closer to other people.
- Do not avoid the difficult conversations. Who said that life should be easy?
- Try not to think in terms of all or nothing. It is only the digital world which is built up by binary possibilities, and life is not a problem which requires a quick solution.

Modern technology is here to stay, along with the wonders and amazing possibilities of phones and computers. But the time has come for us to consider whether technology does not sometimes thwart other things which are important to us – above all face-to-face conversations for a dialogical and language developing empathetic purpose. When we have realized that this is so, we can do something about it. *We are able to embrace the technology as well as change its task in our lives*, for everyday use as well as for work. And we can admit that we sometimes need things which are rather hampered by social media, that is, close contacts with each other.

My opinion is that constructionism, for instance as social phenomenological marketing for business entrepreneurs, makes it possible for us to better handle those dialectical conditions which are often associated with postmodernism. Let us look in a constructionist way at some such dialectic conceptions and how they can be understood and exploited in marketing with the social phenomenology approach. Constructionism allows us exactly this 'both . . . and'! While the modern world can be described in extremes by using polar opposite differentials, for instance good *or* bad and pleasant *and* unpleasant, in the postmodern world marketers may experience *bipolar dimensions as juxtapositioned contrasts which are dialectically related to each other*, for instance, *both* good *and* bad and *both* pleasant *and* unpleasant. A few more precise examples:

- *Both the material and the symbolic.* Customers' experiences come from satisfying material needs as well from feeling the symbolic meaning they represent. As postmodern customers, we buy (or possibly not) the companies' image and activities as much as we (do not) consume their products. Luxury goods with a high symbolic value are sold in places with very high retailing prices. They are not only sold for their functionality but also for their symbolic values. There is a shift towards marketing any product for its symbolic possibilities. One key characteristic of postmodern marketing is the development of goods and services which display a new theme of an old product. This may possibly produce *hyper-realities* (*hyper* meaning exaggerated or extravagant). Postmodern markets may eventually be hyper-real; here conscious and demonstrative assets and fictitious improvisations are included.
- *Both the social and the individual.* Consumer goods have always meant more to us as customers than their function alone. But in the postmodern environment, a purchase of goods and services confirms not only who we are to ourselves, but also who we are to other people. There is social status involved in owning special kinds of goods and using special kinds of services. Our ownership of these products projects our meaning to other people in a cultural context. What is particularly different in postmodern environments is how easy it is to change oneself, and become another person. As marketers in the old

days may well have focused on rational buying motives, there is an increased acceptance and movement towards the idea that customers buy things they want, but because they do not want them. When the postmodern customer loses his or her contact with their local community in the traditional sense of it, and is short of time, they increasingly crave satisfaction through feelings they share with other people, whether or not this is genuine. This is denoted as *tribalism*. Furthermore, it is often so, that instead of having only one 'myself', acting in different buying situations, customers have many 'myselves' operating through different buying situations.

- *Both wish and satisfaction.* Whereas in the modern world the focus was on satisfying the customer, especially by appealing to functionality, in the postmodern era so that focus is shifting to customer wish. Not so much to satisfying wish, because wish can never be completely satisfied, but simply to let the customer recognize that the wish exists and experience its effects. Postmodern marketers notice the customer shift away from only satisfying functional needs. Even though advertising has long fed our wishes as customers, in the postmodern environment we want others also to see that our wishes are satisfied. In postmodern markets, such desire is accepted as well as acceptable for its own sake. The customer tolerates the message that it is good to wish something just to be able to experience it, not because you really need it. Consequently, appeals to customer wishes, unlike customers' rationalities, feel convincing because they appeal to the subconscious, often through sex appeal and through satisfying wishes which were previously taboo.

- *Both rationality and freedom.* Customers buy and consume goods and services because they have fun with them and enjoy them. That is a result of our customer experiences. But even if this might seem just like common sense, for many years researchers of customer behaviour stressed the fact that customers look for functionalities and the consequences of using the good/service as primary customer considerations. But those evaluation criteria which we use to choose product brands are also psycho-social (for instance, aesthetical aspects and play) rather than just economical. Inputs to buying decisions are based on consideration of time as well as money, hedonism unlike problem solving, thinking with the right side of the brain unlike thinking with the left side, explorative behaviour unlike behaviour collecting information, and type of personality unlike customer characteristics such as life style or social class. Inputs from the environment to these experiential considerations when customers take decisions stress the following:

- a syntactic shape of communication (how something is said) – unlike a semantic shape (what it means)
- non-verbal – unlike verbal stimuli
- subjective factors – unlike objective functions of a good or service.

Experience-based customer decision processes are looked at as particularly applicable to buyer situations involving customer experiences within entertainment, arts and recreation products. When we make decisions about what we consume, we might use different frames of references at different points in time to evaluate our experiences. Postmodernists claim that we are 'multiphrenic' – this is we suffer a kind of multiple personality (dis)order as customers where we might want something and not want it at the same time, we want different things at the same time, or we want very different things for one and the same purpose etc.

- *Both creativity and limitation.* In the postmodern world, opposite social forces exist. Because of this, we may ask whether advertising reflects reality or reality reflects advertising. In other words, do our needs reflect advertising or does advertising reflect our needs? There is, in a way, a counter-reaction by many citizens / customers against that kind of materialism which the advertising business has long tried to promote. Constantly advertising a product may lead to the idea that materialism in society is a good thing, that feeding material wishes is something which is worth our attention and our actions. For many, this will create what is called a psychological reactance (when a customer perceives his or her freedom to try to reach a specific decision alternative is blocked, completely or partially, he or she becomes very motivated to try to realize this alternative) at the same time as wishing to adopt another opposing frame of reference. To try to consume, starting from this new frame of reference, is a way to creatively restore that freedom which many postmodern customers feel that they run the risk of losing. This leads to the development of a new kind of tribalism, where customers build complete local communities around the symbolic consumption of goods and services.

## 8.7   INTERACTIVE CO-CREATION MARKETING

The primary proponent of managerial marketing, as stated by most commentators, is P. Kotler (1967, 2001, 2002, 2015). Those who most actively plead for a social phenomenological type of marketing, in my opinion, are C.K. Prahalad and V. Ramaswamy (2000, 2004a, 2004b, 2004c). We can call their view *interactive co-creation marketing*. It is based on a belief in the necessity in business today to consider the active participation of customers (which, as already mentioned, is my word for those who are 'receivers' of the activities and results of marketers, even though they do not have to be the final consumers and even though, in some cases (and above all when discussing social entrepreneurs), they do should not be called customers but rather vitalizers of a place together with the entrepreneurs themselves).

One important difference between managerial marketing and social phenomenological marketing (apart from their philosophical bases and the views and approaches which emanate from them) is *where value creation of a product takes place and who can profit on this* (compare section 7.8). With managerial marketing, value creation takes place in and by the company considering the position which it holds in the value chain, and this creation is *separated from the market*. Customers may *experience* the value of a product when consuming it, but its value is *extracted* mainly by the company (at least as costs and benefits), because it is looked at as the value-adding agent in the value chain. With social phenomenological marketing, on the other hand, value creation (as well as value extraction) takes place as a co-action between the company and its customers (as well as between the company and its suppliers and business partners) *in the market*. Co-creation and co-extraction are then better seen as value stars than value chains.

Co-creation of value challenges in a fundamental way the traditional distinction between supply and demand. When experience, together with its intrinsic value, is co-created, focus is shifted to the total experience environment, and new demand becomes contextual. The new approach to co-creation also generates a new competitive space for the company. To compete effectively, the company must then invest in building skills which are centred on co-creation through high-quality interactions between customers and company and personalized co-creation experiences (Prahalad & Ramaswamy, 2004b). While building new skills is critical, it is less difficult than changing one's dominating logic. If one does not make a shift from a company-centred to a co-creation perspective on value creation and co-extraction of economic value with informed, concatenated, empowered and active customers' local communities on one side and cost pressure which is forced by increased competition, company closedowns and product levelling on the other side, it will just be more difficult for companies to develop a sustainable competitive advantage. The future belongs to those who are able to successfully co-create unique experiences with customers.

Prahalad and Ramaswamy (2000) provide some advice for today's companies to follow in their marketing:

- Encourage an active dialogue.
- Mobilize customer communities.
- Mobilize customer differences.
- Handle person-based experiences.
- Handle multiple experience channels.
- Handle variation and evolution.
- Create customer experiences.
- Look at customers as competitors in value-extraction.
- Prepare the organization for customer competences in the new economy.

To engage in a dialogue with customers means that it becomes critical for companies to understand its purpose, meaning and quality from the customers' perspective. Companies will, furthermore, be forced to find ways in which they can add value to what they have learnt from customers, so that they can bring the dialogue forward and keep the interest of customers. Progressive internet companies have best adapted to this new form of dialogue. This is because the Internet has increased the customer's power as an interlocutor.

Another reality that companies must face is that, due to the Internet, customers find it easier in the new economy to establish virtual communities of their own choosing, and the strength of such communities emanates to a large extent from the speed at which they can be mobilized. Information is spread so quickly on the Internet, that we now have a new word for such exchange of words, that is 'viral marketing'. Previously, companies supported their image by using advertising and purposeful packages etc. But in the new market, positioning is developed with customers' collectively personalized experiences. Smart companies therefore find ways to mobilize customer communities.

As companies embrace the market as a forum, they become more vulnerable to customer differences. This is particularly true for companies selling technology-intensive products, which are sensitive to variations in customers' sophistication. Customers' experiences of technology products and their service, and with that, their judgements about these products, will vary of course, according to their skills. A user's degree of sophistication will also determine his or her tolerance of problems. Furthermore, globalization in the marketplace will also extend the variation in customers' sophistication.

To handle customer competences involves more than just participating in dialogues. Business companies must also realize that the customer is no longer interested in just buying a product (Prahalad & Ramaswamy, 2000). Furthermore, customers are no longer prepared to accept experiences suggested by the company. Increasingly, they will create those experiences themselves, both individually and together with experts and other customers.

To provide personalized experiences to the customers, the company must create opportunities for customers to experiment and decide what level of involvement they want, when creating a given experience with a company. Because the level of customer involvement cannot be determined in advance, companies must give customers as much choice and flexibility as possible in their choice of distribution channel and communication, and in design of their products.

The Internet is an incredibly rich channel for direct dialogues, even if not face-to-face. It has also led to the emergence of more effective business models. Some people claim, in fact, that virtual distribution channels made possible by the Internet will replace traditional channels in some industries due to their cost advantages. Most companies must, therefore, handle more distribution channels. One challenge will then be to guarantee that the nature and the quality of the personalized customer experience will be the same from channel to channel.

The biggest challenge for companies, however, is to develop the infra-structures needed to support a multichannel-based distribution network. For some business operations, the most pressing issue will relate to their information technology, which must be sufficiently developed to handle new communication and logistics channels. One of the critical elements in the information structure is the company's billing system, which is an invaluable source of customer information. The problem is that many companies who now must bargain directly with customers, lack com-petence concerning invoices, because their channel partners previously handled this task.

The challenges of building and integrating a virtual channel pale next to the challenges which the Internet channels meet themselves. It is no longer a question of e-commerce, but f-commerce – the fulfilment of goods and services, which cannot be downloaded. As one manager remarked: 'Anyone can sell a book on the Internet; delivering it to the individual expeditiously and at a very low cost is the problem' (Prahalad & Ramaswamy, 2000:82). To accomplish low-cost delivery in the new economy forces companies to combine its telecommunications and Internet infrastructure with a physi-cal infrastructure of its logistics and service operations.

Understanding that products are subordinated experience will force companies to give up their old assumptions concerning product develop-ment. Previously, companies had to understand how to use technology to generate variation among their products and to handle the way in which technology developed. Unfortunately, customers think that complicated operating instructions are annoying, and they judge a company's product not by its features, but by the degree to which a good or service gives them those experiences they want (Prahalad & Ramaswamy, 2000). But handling customer experiences is not the same as handling products, however. It is about handling an interface between a company and its customers; the range of experiences extends the company's products. The product must, therefore, develop in a way which makes future modifications and extensions possible, which in turn is based on customers' changing needs as well as the company's changing qualifications. But this is not easy.

To create expectations is not only a matter of traditional one-way communication from the market department by advertising. It is about involving customers in public debates, to educate customers as well as oneself. What complicates the matter is that, even if companies must look at customers as sources of competency, they must also realize that their customers become competitors, because they can now extract value in a way that was unthinkable only a few years ago.

In traditional market places, companies had far better access to information than their individual customers. This allowed companies to set prices based on their costs or their perceptions of which value their product had for their customers. But thanks to the Internet, customers and companies now have access to the same information – and this has led to a power shift. Equipped with this new knowledge, customers are now more willing to negotiate conditions and prices with companies. But it is not only the way in which customers assess and negotiate about prices that has changed: it is also the very price mechanism itself. From customers' perspectives, the advantage with this new way of experiencing products they acquire is, that prices really should reflect *the use for the customer* of products that have been bought. This does not mean that prices are lower, just that customers want to pay consistent with their needs rather than consistent with the company's needs. Marketers must get used to the idea that they are price takers as well as prices givers. Traditional price setting will not completely disappear. But as customers become more knowledgeable and understand that they have a choice and the power to negotiate, more and more companies will feel the pressure to adopt an implicit (if not even an explicit) auction process.

The organizational consequence of competing in a market as a forum will be rather challenging, and to involve oneself in a dialogue with a varying and changing customer base in several different channels will require high organizational flexibility. No part of the company can assume that its role in the organization is stable. As business ideas are revised and new challenges and possibilities are proposed, the organization will constantly have to reconfigure its resources. Departmental heads must create organizations in which resources can be reconfigured with as little effort as possible.

But creation of a flexible organization will impose psychological and emotional traumas on the employees of the organization, and this is a reason why startups have fewer problems in adopting new practices than established companies – it is easier to start something new than change something old. Marketers must be ready to handle these traumas at the same time as they identify business challenges. The new market place will reward people who are trained in cooperation and negotiation. Learning, teaching and transferring knowledge across boundaries will become essential skills. So, too, will the ability to attract – and keep – the right employees. In an era when the pace of change is irregular, the only way to stay ahead is to find people who are self-motivated to change themselves.

The ability to amplify weak signals, interpret their consequences and reconfigure resources faster than competitors will be the source of success. The point is not simply to 'run faster', but to 'think faster and smarter'. The new front for marketers is to create the future by harnessing competence in an extended network that includes customers (Prahalad & Ramaswamy, 2000). To take the new economy seriously, you must be part of what you play. In the traditional system, companies decide which goods and services they will produce based on deciding what is valuable to customers. In this system, *customers had a very small or non-existent role in value creation*. Today, there is an increasing uncoupling between the chances to value creation and differentiation, which is made possible by connected, active and informed customers, their expectations and the diminished power of the traditional market concept. The number of mobile phones and computers which exist in the world today creates an extended possibility to connect. A visit to the doctor today, for example, is qualitatively different from ten years ago. Patients want to be involved dialogically. They want to understand the risks and benefits of different kinds of treatments. They have access to more information than they have ever had before, independent of quality. Customers expect transparency. 'Don't keep things to yourself, give me the truth' is often the approach. Doctors may possibly not like this. It takes time. This will expose them and their expertise to external insight, and it is difficult today to hide behind authority. However, doctors have a better patient today. Because he or she understands and is involved now, the patient is more willing to accept treatments, which they have been part of *developing together*. What is necessary now is setting up an environment in which every patient (customer) can create his or her own unique personalized experiences. In that way, *products may be deprived of their character, but the co-creating experience cannot*.

How do you build systems for co-creation (and co-extraction) of value between company and customers? Prahalad and Ramaswamy base their

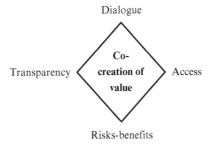

*Source:* Adapted from Prahalad & Ramaswamy, 2004c.

*Figure 8.3 Co-creating (and co-extracting) value*

thoughts about this on an interpretative design which they call DART (Dialogue, Access, Risks-benefits and Transparency) (Figure 8.3).

Dialogues are important elements of the co-creation approach. Markets can be viewed as situations of conversation between customers and company (Levine et al., 2001). Dialogues mean interactivity, involvement, and an ability and willingness to act on all sides. It is difficult to think of a dialogue between completely different sides with incompatible interests. For an active dialogue and possibilities for common solutions to take place, the company and customers must approach each other and be interested in problem solving. A dialogue must centre around subjects of interest to all – the customers and the company must have clearly defined roles concerning how to involve oneself.

But a genuine dialogue is difficult if customers do not have the same access and transparency to information. Companies have traditionally benefited from asymmetrical information from themselves to customers. Because of connections to information which exist everywhere, it is now possible for an individual customer to gain access to as much information as he or she needs from other customers, from local customer communities and from the company. Access as well as transparency are critical to meaningful dialogues.

More important is that dialogue, access and transparency can lead to a clear evaluation by the customer concerning risks-benefits with a specific route of action and decision. This is a personalized-based understanding of risks-benefits.

According to Prahalad and Ramaswamy (2004c), the possibilities for creating values are significantly increased for companies that can embrace the concept of personalized co-creation experience as a source of unique value. This differs from the concept of 'customers as innovators'.

The same idea is applicable to the conventional way to customize goods and services. In the original traditional company-centred approach to value creation, marketers focused on offering goods and services at the lowest possible price. This process led to mass-customization, which combined the benefit of 'mass' (production and marketing on a big scale and, therefore, low cost) with the equivalent from 'customization' (focus on single customers). Present focus on development and design leads to an increased range of choices for customers. On the Internet, for instance, the customer can customize goods and service in everything from business cards and computers to house mortgages and flower arrangements, by simply choosing from a menu of features.

To personalize co-creation experience means to develop individualized interactions and experiences. A personalized co-creation experience reflects how individuals choose to interact with that experiential environment, which the company facilitates – one which involves individual customers on their terms. This is a big challenge, which the company must accept. Once we forget 'the company-centred' approach to value creation and accept the 'co-creation' approach, the evidence of this shift is visible in a number of industries. For example, video games would not exist without active co-creation. Individuals construct their own experiences. Ebay and Amazon are further examples of this trend – both facilitate the process with personalized-based experiences. Both involve local communities and facilitate dialogue.

The transition from a company-centred view to a co-creation view has meant more than just minor changes to the traditional systems. Note what co-creation *is not*. It is neither the transfer nor outsourcing of activities to customers, nor a customization of goods and services. Nor is it to act around the company's different sales offers (for instance, La Salle & Britton, 2002; Peppers & Rodgers, 1993; Schmitt, 1999; Seybold, 1998). This kind of interaction between company and customers no longer satisfies most customers today. The change is much more basic. It involves co-creation of value by personalized interactions based on how every individual want to interact with the company. Co-creation puts the focus on *customer-company interaction as the locus of value creation* (Prahalad & Ramaswamy, 2004c). This new approach means that all points of interaction between customers and company are critical for value creation. Nobody can predict the experience a customer will have at any point in time. The task is therefore for the company to invent experience environments. The approach of co-creation of value is to challenge the conceptualization of a market as well as exchange of goods and services and an aggregation of customers. The traditional economic view has a clear focus on exchange of products between the company and customers.

In the co-creation view, all interaction points between the company and the customer are possibilities *for creation as well as extraction of value.*

> The co-creation view also challenges the market as an aggregation of customers for what the company can offer. In the new value co-creation space, business executives have at least partial control over the experience environment and the networks they build to facilitate co-creation experiences. But they cannot control how individuals go about co-constructing their experiences. Co-creation, therefore, forces us to move away from viewing the market as an aggregation of customers and as a target for the company's offerings. Market research, including focus groups, surveys, statistical modelling, video ethnography, and other techniques were developed in an effort to get a better understanding of customers, identify trends, assess customer desires and preferences, and evaluate the relative strength of competitors' positions. Within this framework, the ultimate concept in customer segmentation is one-to-one marketing. (Prahalad & Ramaswamy, 2004c:11)

While debates rage about the adequacy of this marketing method, its underlying vision of customers as goals (preys) is rarely questioned. But suppose the customers turn the tables? What would happen if customers were to start investigating companies, products and potential experiences in a systematic way? Is it enough for companies to 'sense and respond' to customers' demands? Do marketers need market foresight – besides market insight? Must they learn to anticipate and lead, and further, to co-create expectations and experiences?

In co-creation, the answers to such questions are crucial. Customer shifts are best understood by being there and co-creating with them. Companies must now learn as much as possible about customers by dialogues which are run at the level of the customers' sophistication. The information infrastructure must centre on customers and encourage active participation in all aspects of the co-creation experience, including information search, configuration of goods and services, fulfilment and consumption. Co-creation is more than co-marketing or engaging customers as co-sales agents. It is about developing methods to achieve a deep understanding of co-creation experiences so that companies can co-create customers' expectations and experiences together with them.

Co-creation transforms the market to a forum where dialogues among the customer, the company, customer local communities and company networks can take place. The transformation of relationships between companies and customers are shown in Table 8.3.

As we move towards a co-creation experience as a basis of value, the basic interaction between the company and customers is changing. It becomes a number of places where value creation happens; interaction can be anywhere in the system, not only in the traditional sales and service

*Table 8.3    Transformation of relationships between company and customers*

| From | To |
| --- | --- |
| + One-way | + Two-way |
| + Company to customer | + Customer to company |
| + Controlled by company | + Customer to customer |
| + Customers are 'prey' | + Customer can 'hunt' |
| + Choice = buy/not buy | + Customer wants to/can impose his or her view of choice |
| + Company segments and target customers; Customers must 'fit into' firm's offerings | + Customer wants to/is being empowered to co-construct a *personalized experience* around him- or herself, with firm's experience environment |

*Source:*    Prahalad & Ramaswamy, 2004c:12.

points. In the traditional approach of marketing, interaction takes place where the company markets its sales offers to extract economic value from the customers (based on that value which the company has already created in its value chain). This company-centred and product-centred view is deep-rooted and manifested in handling customer relationships, and it leaves little room for customers to co-create value.

Co-creation demands that the company as well as the customers make necessary adjustments. Both must recognize that the interaction between the two – the place where value creation takes place – is built on critical building blocks, for example. It must start from access and transparency. Companies have traditionally opposed transparency. The fight against product labelling is well known. To release information concerning possible risks is often compulsory today. Furthermore, transparency and access are of little value if the company does not create the infrastructure for a dialogue. This requires investment in technology, but more importantly in educating the employees in the company and changing their practice. How do companies involve themselves in a dialogue? How do they understand the underlying expectations from millions of customers and their utility functions? The infrastructure and the governance processes which have been developed in some industries is an indication of implicit negotiations (for example, Expedia, eBay and Amazon). Dialogues require us to invest time and effort to understand the economy of experiences and to produce systems to quickly come to agreements. Finally, companies must understand that the more educated customers are, the more likely it is that they will make intelli-

*Table 8.4    The building blocks of DART*

| Terms | Definition | Company consequences |
| --- | --- | --- |
| *Dialogue* | Interactive discussions between customers and company | Two-way communication instead of one-way sales tactics |
| *Access* | Allow customers to have data supply | Create value with the customer beyond the traditional value chain process |
| *Risks and benefits* | To handle risks and benefits between customers and company | Share the risk of product development with the benefits through communication |
| *Transparency* | Company information is available | Information barriers should be eliminated in order to gain confidence |

*Source:*    Prahalad and Ramaswamy (2000c:8).

gent choices and negotiate what is suitable for them. This does not take away the responsibility from companies to deny some choices. As we all know, the bartender has the duty to know when he or she should finish serving drinks.

Customers must also learn that co-creation works both ways. They must take some responsibility for the risks they consciously accept. Tobacco companies have a duty to educate customers about the risk from smoking and to develop cessation programmes. But if a customer insists on smoking, he or she must take the responsibility for his or her own actions. In cases where customers probably do not have the knowledge to make a correct choice, they will have to accept choices made for them by a neutral party. The objective is for governance to mediate aspects which are good for both parties, that is, both customers and company. This is most likely the next practical step in value creation.

Prahalad and Ramaswamy (2000c:8) define co-creation as 'Co-creation of value by companies and customers, allowing the customer to co-create the service experience to suit his or her context'. As mentioned, they claim that for co-creation to be applied, the building blocks should be prepared in advance (Table 8:4).

## 8.8   CONCLUSION

In this chapter we have looked at how independent business entrepreneurs can apply marketing. In the following two chapters, we will discuss how business intrapreneurs and social entrepreneurs can market themselves. This chapter is longer than the following two chapters, for the simple reason that much of what is covered in this chapter is also applicable to several parts of the following two chapters, particularly for Chapter 9.

# 9. Marketing approaches for business intrapreneurs

## 9.1 INTRODUCTION

'Intrapreneurship' is short for 'intracorporate entrepreneurship', and it means, consequently, *business venturing happening in existing business corporations.* In my case, I am only interested in business venturing which leads to new results (for the market and for customers) and only in the first part of the process, that is, before it is possible to see some clear results, even if only as a tangible layout of feasible thoughts and concepts.

As a company develops, it is not unusual, after its first successful business entrepreneurial success, to continue developing new entrepreneurial ventures. This could be supported by resources generated from the first one (Figure 9.1).

Following venture A, venture B *can differ in two ways*, however. One way (we may call it type I) means that venture B is different enough from venture A to refer to it as an almost different venture. The other way (we may call it type II) means that venture B is a modification of venture A (for instance, noticed by customers to satisfy some of their demand in a better way) (Figure 9.2).

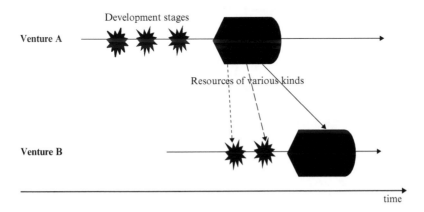

*Figure 9.1   Two ventures, where the first provides resources to the second*

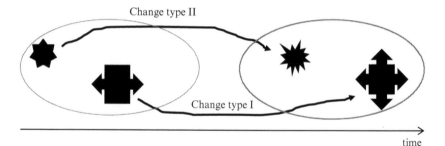

*Figure 9.2    Venture changes of two different types*

This chapter will only contain aspects of marketing for entrepreneurs which differ from what has been said in Chapter 8 (many aspects of Chapter 8 are applicable for this chapter). This means:

- The sequential model for managerial management is, in its design, the same. I will only discuss some aspects of how it could be adapted to business intrapreneurs.
- The structural model for managerial marketing presented in Chapter 8 (the canvas model) can also be used in the business intrapreneurial case. Even here, an adaptation for intrapreneurial circumstances must be made, of course. However, instead of discussing such adaptations here, I will present another structural model for managerial management which could be more useful for innovative business companies that decide to launch a new product. It is referred to as *the seven domains model or the 7D model* (Mullins, 2013).

Intrapreneurship could, perhaps, be a possibility for social entrepreneurs as well, of course. It is never discussed in such contexts, however. One reason is that intrapreneurship theories are developed exclusively for business-orientated ventures. Intrapreneurship, as we normally understand it, does not fit the social entrepreneurship situation very well, at any rate. Social entrepreneurial ventures typically thrive by being small, local and relying on one specific place only. If they develop, they preferably do so by deepening themselves in the area they are already operating rather than broadening themselves by offering more than one social solution or satisfying more than one social need.

## 9.2   SOME GENERAL ASPECTS OF BUSINESS INTRAPRENEURSHIP

Business intrapreneurship means, in practice, to go from one business entrepreneurial venture to another where, in principle, the latter is never *completely separated from, nor fully different from, the former*. As both take place under the auspices of the same company, it is impossible to move from one corporate culture to a completely new corporate culture. The culture of any company is an outcome of processes which have been developing inside the company as well as between the company and its environment over some time, depending on the age of the company. That history can never be eradicated. The new venture may be a reduced version of the old venture and may possibly be built on eliminating some old outdated habits, but *there is nothing that could be called a culture-free business intrapreneurship* the way I see it; otherwise, it would not be business *intra*preneurship! Some aspects of, say, the hierarchical system (or at least of the roles played by different individuals in the system), the political system and the social system will remain.

In other words, business intrapreneurship may build on the company's existing profile *or* attempts to break out of it. No matter which option will be chosen, *every company stands for something* in the eyes and minds of the employees and, more importantly talking about marketing, in the eyes and minds of the *customers*.

## 9.3   KEEPING THE BRAND ALIVE

Some companies have tried to keep their brands alive and have been quite successful in doing so, even thriving on it. Klein (2000) has some views on this, most of them of a negative kind. According to the traditional paradigm of business, all marketing stressed the sales of a product. But in modern times, sales of brands have a new dimension, which can only be described as spiritual (Klein, 2000:47). Advertising was about peddling goods and services, whereas brand trading in its truest and most developed version today is about business transcendence.

It may sound weird, but that it is the whole point. The products of the future are not those being presented as 'goods' or 'services', but those being presented as concepts: brand is experience, a lifestyle.

For a long time, some large companies have tried to free themselves from the habits of the material world, manufacturing and products to exist in another dimension. Anybody can manufacture a product, they reason. Such simple tasks can and should be outsourced to business entrepreneurs and subcontractors, whose only objective is to fulfil the order on time and within the budget provided (preferably in the developing world, where labour is indecently cheap, laws are loose at their edges and tax reliefs are legion). In the meantime, the head office can engage in the real business operation – to create a business mythology which is strong enough to endow these raw materials with a meaningful content just by giving them a name.

'The top layer – Coca-Cola, Microsoft, Disney etc. – consists of "players" in brain content. The next layer (Ford and GM) still consists of suppliers of clumsy things, even if cars are much "smarter" than what they were before' (Peters, 1997:16). With this wave of brain mania, a new type of company has arrived, which proudly tells us that brand X is not a product but a way of life, an attitude, specific values, a look, an idea.

The idea to sell the brave message of brands instead of a product means that the doors are open for an expansion without limits. After all, if a brand is not a product, it could be anything (Klein, 2000:50–1)!

The consequence of the advanced brand development, even if it has not always been the original purpose, is to knock the value culture to the background and make the brand the star of the stage. The objective is not to sponsor the culture but to be the culture. If brands now are not products but ideas and attitudes connected with certain values and experiences, why should they not be culture as well?

Many of the well-known brand companies aim at a spiritual reality on a level above sensibility and time, which frees themselves from the need to be associated with their earthly products. They dream instead of the deeper meaning of their brands – how they catch the feeling of individuality, and with the spirit of sports, wildlife and community. Together with the wish to shake the dust from their feet, those who take care of the administration of the brand identity – the marketing departments of the companies – start to look at the production as directly competing with their own activity, not as two processes in cooperation. 'Products are made in the factory, but brands are made in the brain' (Klein, 2000:241).

Ever since mass production created the need for launching brands, which slowly but surely has grown in status and has begun to play an increasingly important role in the companies, it is logical, more than two centuries since the Industrial Revolution, that companies have got the idea that launching brands could completely replace production (Klein, 2000:243). However, as stated by Klein (2000:283), the big brand companies have, however, become very skilled at escaping from most of their duties as employers by making their foremen imagine that their workers do not seriously need or deserve employment safety, reasonable pay and usual benefits. According to Klein, most major employers in the service sector treat their work force as if it was not dependent on their payment envelopes for something important in life such as rent and supply. Instead, the employers in the service and retail sectors look at their employees as children: students and pupils who are looking for a summer job, a temporary cash reinforcement or a short break on the way to a more satisfying and well-paid career.

## 9.4  BUSINESS INTRAPRENEURSHIP AND MARKETING

Like all entrepreneurs, it is possible to divide business intrapreneurs into different groups. There is neither opportunity nor reason to discuss such groups here, however. My aim is just to provide a few ideas about how business intrapreneurs may use marketing to bring their new ventures to customers successfully. These ideas are probably not valid to any extreme cases of business intrapreneurs, but hopefully still be of some interest.

An important circumstance for a business intrapreneur is that he or she has an established company as a backup, a company which has probably launched at least one business entrepreneurial success before. One aspect for a business intrapreneur to keep in mind is, therefore, to realize the consequences of such a previous success. It should at least provide some resources for a business intrapreneur, which the 'normal' first-time business entrepreneur does not have (see Figure 9.1). These resources may be tangible and / or intangible. The company's image and reputation may, of course, also be positive or negative or a mix of both. The business intrapreneur must consider these resources and that image and reputation in his or her marketing efforts. They might, for instance, be used for a more formal environmental analysis to build a better picture of the possibilities and external chances for the business intrapreneur.

What is useful for any entrepreneur most of the time is to gain knowledge and to improve on possibilities through networking. Business intrapreneurs are no exceptions. What is added in this case is the extra strength that might come from *networking within the company* to deepen or broaden his or her skills.

Even in the business intrapreneurial case, as in the independent business entrepreneurial case, it is necessary to separate managerial marketing from social phenomenological marketing. They are therefore discussed separately.

## 9.5  MANAGERIAL MARKETING FOR BUSINESS INTRAPRENEURS

We have learnt that managerial marketing is built on the following principles:

- It is based on the limited view on entrepreneurship.
- It looks at management as a central aspect of marketing.
- Its ideas started at the end of the 1960s and its form is well established.
- It favours transactional marketing over relationship marketing.
- It looks at reality as factual and full of circumstances.
- It aims at applying models, which are considered as reflecting the factual reality.
- It looks for explanations.
- It is based on a rational philosophy.
- It is useful for goals-rational or means-rational entrepreneurial startups.
- It believes in the advantages of planning and in possibilities of making useful forecasts.
- Its ambition is to control as much as possible.
- It values fact-finding through interviews and questionnaires.
- It looks at companies as being part of value chains.

Business intrapreneurial managerial marketing models can be either sequential or structural (as in the case of independent business entrepreneurial marketing models). The sequential version is presented in Figure 8.1. The only worthwhile addition is related to the second box in the sequence, which illustrates the possibility of heading the goals-rational or the means-rational way. It is likely in the business intrapreneurial case that the means-rational alternative is chosen more often, because the content of the sequence is probably not independent of the circumstances that the business intrapreneurial course of events is taking place in an existing company, controlling much of the means on which the business intrapreneur must rely.

The structural version is presented in the so-called canvas model (illustrated in Figure 8.2). As in the sequential version, the layout is applicable also in the business intrapreneurial case, but its content also has to be adapted to the new circumstances, of course.

Another structural version of managerial marketing is offered by Mullins (2013): the 'seven domains' or '7D' model, which is intended to be used for innovation-based business startups in earlier phases. It was presented first time in 2003 and it has since been launched in new editions. Mullins is a professor at London School of Economics and the model has, according to Frankelius et al. (2015) been derived above all by interviews with different venture capitalists. Mullins claims that most business plans that have been written should not have been written, and he bases this statement on his opinion that the business planning process should have started from another direction – by making sure that all the fundamental pieces were at place.

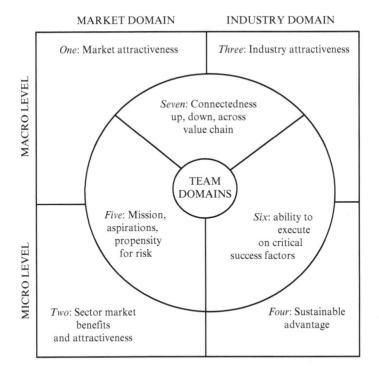

*Figure 9.3    Mullins' seven domains*

According to Mullins, seven domains can be used to analyse any business which is to be launched. Four of them look at the small-scale (micro) and large-scale (macro) aspects of the market and the industry, and three of them focus on the team of the company (Figure 9.3).

Mullins asserts that this model was created for entrepreneurs interested in starting new businesses. However, it can also be used within an organization to decide whether to pursue a new product or launch a new project. It is also designed to be used *before* writing a business plan. The idea is to look at each of the seven domains and ask key questions about each to have a clearer idea about how likely the business idea is to succeed.

The *market* is the group of people who are, or will be, buying the product. The *industry* is the group of sellers, most often organizations, that offer similar products. These are the competitors.

– *Domain One*: Market attractiveness. This domain looks at market attractiveness from a macro (large-scale) perspective.

- *Domain Two*: Sector market benefits and attractiveness. Realistically, it is unlikely that a venture will meet the needs of everyone in the market. A business intrapreneur will be more successful if he or she targets his or her idea at one market sector or segment, and aims to meet its demand fully.
- *Domain Three*: Industry attractiveness. This domain looks at how attractive the industry is on a macro level. Mullins suggests using Porter's five forces (Porter, 1980) to assess which factors affect the profitability of an industry.
- *Domain Four*: Sustainable advantage. Once a business intrapreneur has looked at the industry from a macro level, it is time to examine it closer.
- *Domain Five*: Mission, aspirations, propensity for risk. In this domain, located at the centre of the model, the business intrapreneur is going to analyse commitment – his or her own, and that of the team – to this idea.
- *Domain Six*: Ability to execute on critical success factors. A business intrapreneur needs to identify the critical success factors for the business, and think realistically about whether the team can deliver on this.
- *Domain Seven*: Connectedness up, down, across value chain. This last domain is about the connections of a business intrapreneur and how important they are for success in the venture.

Mullins admits that the model, at first sight, may look rather traditional and obvious. But he points also at some important distinctions which, in his opinion, often are forgotten or poorly understood in modern practice. One such distinction is that market and industry are not the same thing. Also, the team cannot be understood by just listening to what they say and reading their CVs. It is important to put their factual competencies, skills and risk willingness up against what is required in the business intrapreneurial project.

Ideas for how to become more creative and innovative as a managerial business intrapreneur can be seen in Table 8.2.

## 9.6   SOCIAL PHENOMENOLOGICAL MARKETING FOR BUSINESS INTRAPRENEURS

We have learnt that social phenomenological marketing is built on the following principles:

- It is based on the more extended view on entrepreneurship.
- It does not look at management as being a central aspect of marketing (it rather prefers leadership).

- It is not much more than 10–15 years old and still at a developing stage.
- It favours relationship marketing over transactional marketing.
- It looks at reality as socially constructed and full of meaning.
- It aims at finding interpretations, which are considered as formative and contextual.
- It looks for understanding.
- It is based on the constructionist philosophy.
- It is useful for bricoleurial startups.
- It sees some problems associated with planning and for making useful forecasts.
- Its ambition is to open as many possibilities as possible.
- It believes that useful conditions can be co-created through dialogues.
- It looks at companies as being part of value stars.

The above circumstances mean, of course, that success as a business intrapreneur using social phenomenological marketing will be very different from using managerial marketing. The building blocks of DART (Prahalad & Ramaswamy, 2004) are, as we know:

- Dialogue
- Access
- Risks-benefits
- Transparency.

They are undoubtedly as useful in the business intrapreneurial case as in the independent business entrepreneurial case. The business intrapreneur's success will depend, of course, very much on what experiences the company has in operating its marketing according to these principles. If it has not done so before, a major reconfiguration is necessary in terms of thinking as well as in modes of operation; a reconfiguration which will then have consequences not only on the new business intrapreneurial venture but also on all aspects of how the company carries out its business at present and in the future.

# 10. Marketing approaches for social entrepreneurs

## 10.1 INTRODUCTION

Many signs point at the fact that the number of social entrepreneurship activities has grown very strongly in our modern societies, and these activities have even taken on a leadership role in some areas. It is of interest, of course, to try to understand why this is so.

One obvious reason for this is that social entrepreneurs have *the best knowledge of local conditions*. They consequently respond better to local needs. In operation, social entrepreneurs are normally locally connected. It is even possible to say that social entrepreneurship has its roots in local service and development.

Other reasons can be discovered by analysing some current social trends. One trend comes from outside. There is a rise in immigration and, due to civil wars and social unrest in some parts of the world, many refugees are searching for better and safer places to live. But there is also a clear trend domestically in developed countries. Some chronic conditions, such as obesity and other unhealthy lifestyles, have risen close to an unmanageable level. This has led to much stronger pressure on public services than was previously the case.

Another reason is that citizens these days are more active supporters of themselves and their neighbourhoods; they are tired of being just passive receivers of public service and listening to political infighting. One obvious example of this is a greater interest among individuals and local communities to work for a healthier environment and to try to slow down its degradation as much as possible.

One can therefore talk about 'a co-created public movement' today. And the contributions coming from social entrepreneurs are certainly welcome here:

> Traditional welfare-state approaches are in decline globally, and in response new ways of creating healthy and sustainable communities are required. This is challenging our social, economic and political systems to respond with new, creative effective environments that support and reward change. From the evidence available, current examples of social entrepreneurship offer exciting new ways

of realizing the potential of individuals and communities in the 21st century. . . . There are benefits which social entrepreneurs can bring to communities. In the medium term, they can act as powerful models for reform of the welfare state, and in the longer term they can create and invest social capital. (Catford, 1998:96, 97)

Bornstein (1998:36) characterizes social entrepreneurs as 'pathbreakers with a powerful new idea, who combine visionary and real-world problem-solving capacity, who have a strong ethical fiber, and who are "totally obsessed" by their vision for change'.

One may ask whether postmodernism has anything to do with this development. This is not an easy question to answer, but we can say, at least, that life has become more of a *formation process*, that social entrepreneurs are some of the champions in *putting together and developing the knowledge society*, and that *there is a greater need for symbolic and even mythological aspects in life today*.

This chapter focuses on how social entrepreneurs can use marketing in promoting the results of their efforts. Most types of social entrepreneurs can use what has been said in Chapters 8 and 9, which there is no reason to repeat here. There is one type of social entrepreneur, however, which are the citizen innovators (what I normally refer to as public entrepreneurs), where there is even a problem to refer to anything they do as 'marketing'. I will therefore discuss only them in this chapter.

As mentioned previously, in my opinion all entrepreneurs, including social entrepreneurs, must come up with innovative results, and they participate as entrepreneurs only until the innovation is 'completed'.

## 10.2  A REMINDER

Social entrepreneurs are generally quite different from business entrepreneurs in thinking as well as in action; business entrepreneurs typically want to have a top position in their own ventures to steer and control the direction and outcome of these ventures – social entrepreneurs are typically happy to operate at grassroots levels and participate at the interface with other members of the society outside their ventures. The basic factor explaining the differences between business entrepreneurs and social entrepreneurs is that the former types are selling products in various markets, and trying to generate resources by customers paying for their demands being satisfied. The latter types are rather trying to satisfy needs that people might have and they must often compete for resources *before they can offer solutions to satisfy those needs*. In general, social entrepreneurs compete for resources, not for users. This statement contains two important aspects. When the economy is weak, non-profits and hybrid social ventures often starve for resources. On the other hand, the number of social entrepreneurial ventures is growing. The content of demands and needs may overlap, but they are usually different, often also such that those in need are unable to pay fully for their satisfaction. Business entrepreneurs look at society as a place to fulfil their personal goals; social entrepreneurs look at the development of society as an essential goal. This has major consequences for how many social entrepreneurs use marketing and networking differently from typical business entrepreneurs.

Social entrepreneurship research has not been carried out in any deeper sense much more than twenty years. However, it became clear quite soon that social entrepreneurs can express themselves in a variety of ways. Some possibilities are entrepreneurs in the social economy, participants in associations or sports clubs, cultural activists, proponents of fair trade, environmental activists and more. Social entrepreneurs may also operate in many areas. Some examples are micro-finance movements, support for mentally ill or disabled people, community regeneration such as housing associations, welfare projects helping homeless people or drug and alcohol abusers, human rights promotion and various protest movements.

Social entrepreneurs often foster social and environmental innovations. At the same time as governments are held back by the constant struggle between those who want to keep status quo and those who advocate change, which at best will lead to marginal changes, social entrepreneurship is exclusively built on fostering a positive change from a challenging point of view. To overcome that challenge, a transformation is needed. This is automatically facilitated in an environment where creativity and innovative skills are welcomed and supported. Social entrepreneurs take care of social inventions (fruits of creativity), whether or not they are their creator, and apply them (innovation) to achieve a solution to a problem and the transformative change which is associated with this. Whether or not this process is similar to the business entreneurial one is another matter. But there is a difference. The primary test of the value of a business innovation is its market share. Even though social entrepreneurs sometimes may have a market as well, the main test of its value is its potential to solve a social or environmental problem.

Social entrepreneurship facilitates transformation, and entrepreneurs are happy to be part of formation processes in the postmodern knowledge economy. Most of what is delivered to customers, clients or citizens from businesses and governments takes place through a transaction. Goods and services are exchanged through short-term transactional relationships. It works so far, but it does not lead to any long-term change or transformation. Social and environmental problems are not solved by transactions.

Some people seem to believe that an accumulation of transactions can lead to a transformation. A transformation requires systematic changes, however, which is what social entrepreneurs are focusing on to achieve a more permanent end to starvation and social environmental problems in a more sustainable way, for instance.

In a sense, social entrepreneurs are often more associated with their role than are many business entrepreneurs. Many of them put themselves so much into what they are doing and become so important for their ventures that they are more difficult to replace than business entrepreneurs. In section 2.8.7 I presented two metaphors, which I have found useful when trying to understand entrepreneurs. One of them is about the necessity for entrepreneurs to involve four parts of their body, the brain (to know), the heart (to be willing), the stomach (to have the courage) and the limbs (to do things). It is my experience after having studied social entrepreneurs for about ten years, that they are typically more involved with their heart than business entrepreneurs – to the extent that they often are passionate in what they are doing. Social entrepreneurs are, in a sense, more self-propelled than are business entrepreneurs. It is therefore not strange to find that they are hard to replace.

Furthermore, social entrepreneurs are typically more politically involved than business entrepreneurs. Political aspects are, by necessity, part of social entrepreneurship. One way in which social entrepreneurs show this in their marketing is that relationship marketing suits them better than transactional marketing. Social entrepreneurs build, maintain and use citizen capitals. Social entrepreneurs are also very contextual; they are embedded in their historical, cultural and social contexts.

In Chapter 1 I distinguished four different kinds of social entrepreneurs:

1. Employees in the public sector who make social moves over and above what is required as employees.
2. Business people, satisfying demand at the same time as satisfying social needs.
3. Entrepreneurs who are neither employed in the public sector nor belong to the business sector, but operate in the citizen sector, satisfying social needs *in a business-like way*. I refer to them as *citizen enterprisers*.
4. Entrepreneurs in the citizen sector satisfying social needs without doing this in a business-like way, and not even regarding themselves as operating in a market. I refer to them as *citizen innovators* (or *public entrepreneurs*).

Marketing (which this book is about) from the point of view of these four types of social entrepreneurs may differ widely. The first type (employees in the public sector) do not, as I see it, apply much marketing.

What they do, which is admirable in itself, is to come up with more innovative solutions to those welfare tasks which are part of their job. The second and the third type are natural marketers, but I do not think that a discussion of their marketing efforts can add anything to what has already been said in Chapters 8 and 9. What is interesting here, and what I will explore in this chapter, is what marketing means for public entrepreneurs. Such entrepreneurs do not even use marketing in any normal sense of the term, as we will see.

Generally, as has been said before, there are four areas in which citizen entrepreneurs (citizen enterprisers and citizen innovators/public entrepreneurs) can have a critical impact, and there are three different expressions in which they can show themselves. The four impact areas are:

- *community renewal* – being catalysts for run-down neighbourhoods
- *voluntary activity professionalization* – being a modernizing force within the voluntary and community sector, and taking the sector forward to further expand its role as a mainstream provider of social service
- *welfare reform* – being a response to the crisis of our welfare systems
- *democratic renewal* – producing a new form of citizenship, a new relationship between civil society and the state; a broader form of democratization.

The three different ways in which citizen entrepreneurs can show themselves are:

- *disseminating a package of innovation* – from 'experts' to individuals and agencies with relatively few resources
- *building capacities* – capacities needed for self-help
- *mobilizing grassroot groups* – to form alliances against power elites or institutions.

However, as mentioned, the two kinds of citizen entrepreneurs play distinctly different roles in connection with the above impacts areas and ways in which they show themselves. One kind is *citizen enterprisers*. Citizen enterprisers attempt to supplement public sector activities as far as welfare is concerned. They can do this, for example, by providing care for families in need, and elderly or disabled people (socially or otherwise) if or when the public sector is not able to cover all what is needed. This could be done, for instance, by organizing parents or those interested in caring for elderly people (often assisted by volunteers) to operate in the homes of families in need, by setting up sheltered workshops or building dwellings for housing incoming refugee lodgers. All these cases are supposed to be financed by public sector funding and they are done in non-public places.

I am not particularly interested in these citizen entrepreneurial activities here for two reasons. Firstly, even though they carry out invaluable tasks, they are often not particularly innovative, and are typically interested in getting paid for providing employment for themselves and their assistants; for this reason alone, these activities do not match my conceptualization of entrepreneurship. Secondly, they are operating more or less as a business and typically have a marketing method, which was well covered in Chapters 8 and 9 when I discussed marketing for independent business entrepreneurs or business intrapreneurs.

However, the other types of citizen entrepreneurs, that is public entrepreneurs, are very different from business entrepreneurs and even from other social entrepreneurs. They have a very specific attitude to and opinion of marketing and are therefore of great interest to me. Public entrepreneurs consist, as we know, of *citizens involving other citizens in building citizenry (sociality), which typically includes reducing social exclusiveness.* These entrepreneurs are not particularly interested in supplementing public sector duties or emulating business entrepreneurs, but *primarily interested in making some marginal phenomena more central (more public) in society.* They are typically guided, except for reducing exclusiveness, by values such as solidarity and representative democracy – and they show this by *operating in public places.* As mentioned, public places are defined as *physical, virtual, discursive and/or emotional arenas*, which, in principle, every citizen should have access to and feel a responsibility for.

In a democracy, the democratic importance of the public room is often stressed. Open and accessible places, where citizens can make demands, formulate and articulate needs or just reflect on how society is organized, are then acknowledged as democratically important along with other concepts such as free elections, universal suffrage and freedom of the press (Franzén et al., 2016). These are social aspects of special interest to public entrepreneurs. Typical public entrepreneurial activities include, as mentioned earlier:

- remobilizing deprived social areas
- setting up agencies for support and advice
- re-utilizing buildings and resources for social purposes
- providing 'suitability training'
- generating means for some common good issue
- organizing voluntary operations
- generating or supporting cultural activities that are not commercial
- generating or supporting sports activities that are not commercial.

Let us look at how public entrepreneurs use 'marketing'. They apply it in a completely different way from other entrepreneurs, as we will see.

## 10.3   SOME PUBLIC ENTREPRENEURIAL CASES

To start with, some questions should be of interest to public entrepreneurs, keeping the subject of this book in mind. Through marketing, how are public entrepreneurs able to:

–   build citizenry and prevent social exclusion?
–   involve other citizens in making some marginal phenomena more public?
–   mobilize individuals and citizens in local communities at grassroots level?
–   act physically, virtually, discursively and emotionally in public places?
–   revive a local community, professionalize voluntary activities and renew representative democracy?
–   build citizen capital to benefit many, and how to use it?

Let me try to provide some answers to these questions. This is best done, in my opinion, by first telling the story of some real public entrepreneurial cases that I have studied and worked with, to understand the specific role of public entrepreneurs and how different they are from other social entrepreneurs and, especially, from business entrepreneurs, not only in terms of marketing. More about the cases described briefly here can be read in Bjerke et al. (2007), and Bjerke and Karlsson (2011, 2013a). I will begin with some public entrepreneurial cases that I have studied in Sweden.

*Skateboard Malmö.* Malmö is the third largest city in Sweden with around 300 000 inhabitants, and is situated in the south of the country. It has become known as a centre for skateboarders in northern Europe. Two skateboard parks have been built there, one indoors called the Brewery and one outdoors called the Shipbuilding Berth. The origin of the names is simply that the indoors skateboard park is situated in a building, which was previously a brewery, and the outdoor park – 300 meters long and 75 meters wide – was once part of a shipyard, which closed around twenty-five years ago.

The Brewery was established by three social associations, of which one was a determined local community of skateboarders. This community has a passion for the culture of skateboarding and all that is related to that way of life. In their opinion, public servants and local politicians in Malmö didn't understand that supporting skateboarders should be counted as equivalent to sponsoring many other indoors and outdoors sports.

However, the combination of the community of skateboarders and the experienced social associations persuaded the city council of Malmö to change its mind and to support the wish from many social groups to establish an indoor skateboard park in their city. Before the Brewery, some real estate owners and their security guards had tried to chase the skateboarders out of their garage places; there was even a legal case, where a few skateboarders were accused of having damaged some cars while skateboarding inside one garage during the winter. After many discussions, the Brewery received some initial public financial assistance to build the park and did not have to pay any rent for using its premises, which was owned by the city. In return, the skateboarders acted as volunteers to set up the park, take responsibility for providing it with meaningful content, keep it clean and take responsibility, together with the social associations, for its proper running and development. The Brewery was inaugurated in September 1998.

The four public entrepreneurs, founders of the Brewery, were:

- Håkan Larsson: Chairman of one of the social associations (later headmaster of a folk high school with a clear citizen outlook).
- Ronny Hallberg: Consultant to another social association (later head of the Brewery).
- Nils Svensson: Informal head of the more active skateboarders.
- John Magnusson: A passionate skateboarder (who will appear later in this case study).

The Brewery is filled with skateboard ramps and is today considered as one of the best in Europe. It also contains a coffee shop, a shop where skateboarder products can be bought, and a workshop. It has around 1500 skateboarders visiting every week, paying a daily entrance fee. School classes and study groups also visit. Finally, public lectures and lots of different meetings are regularly held there. Using the Brewery as a model, several other skateboard parks were soon constructed: a huge one in Copenhagen in Denmark and several others in Swedish communities. For skateboarders living in Malmö and nearby, the Brewery has become the place to be. Many related activities have also been developed on the premises, for instance, new skateboard brands, self-made films, T-shirts, etc.

Because there were other forces behind the Brewery than just skateboarding, several other new activities have followed its premise, for example, a one-year project management education in cooperation with

Malmö University College. Also, a few years later, a public secondary school opened with skateboarding and dance included in its curriculum.

John Magnusson, who is the major public entrepreneur for the next stage of Skateboard Malmö, started work at the Brewery in the summer of 2002. He was employed as a member of a project, which was financed by the European Social Fund (ESF) after a successful application to the EU. At the end of the summer, he had a meeting with the city gardener of Malmö, Gunnar Ericson. Gunnar had heard from several sources in the city about a dream project among the skateboarders to build an outdoors skateboard park in that city, and he wanted to hear more about it from John. Gunnar explained that the local government of Malmö had plans to build an activity park close to the harbour. He liked the idea of an outdoors skateboard park and believed it could fit well in this activity park. The place he had in mind was one part of the former shipyard in the harbour, its shipbuilding berth.

Gunnar and John started to meet regularly and discuss how they could go on. Gunnar wanted to see a scale model of a potential outdoors skateboard park. To build such a model, therefore, John contacted several landscape architects to get ideas about which material to use to build such a model, material that could be put up in three dimensions and which would dry when having been used. It took John two weeks to build the model and for the material to dry. To get a better aesthetic feeling to his model, he bought artificial grass, trees and lamps in a modelling shop. He took a photo of the whole thing and sent it to the Technical Council, part of the local government, which eventually approved the outdoors skateboard project in one of its meetings.

To be able to continue, John contacted the reference group behind the project management education programme at the Brewery and asked if a group of students in that programme would be interested in working with the idea of the Shipbuilding Berth as a practical project in their education. John had one room at the Brewery, where he and other skateboarders collected magazines, pictures and all kinds of material which could be used to generate ideas about a possible design of an outdoors skateboard park. The group of students in question took over that room as a place to work with their practical project, which was to produce a design for a future outdoors skateboard park.

During the summer of 2005, what came to be considered as one of the best outdoors skateboard parks in Europe was built. The Brewery had gained the contract for its physical construction, having proven previously to be able to build such a thing, even if in concrete this time (instead of in wooden boards as in the case of the Brewery itself).

An international team of skateboard builders was handpicked, and they were formally employed by the Brewery. The Shipbuilding Berth was finished in November the same year. The whole of the summer of 2006 was filled with skateboard competition events – with the World Cup final Quicksilver as the most prominent one – and similar arrangements. Children, young people and the press made 'pilgrimages' to the Shipbuilding Berth in thousands to experience the new attraction. The success was a fact.

*The Future Hope – LSC B89.* This is a story of a soccer team. It began at the beginning of this century and is still continuing. It is a success story about a group of boys who love to play soccer more than anything else.

The boys started soccer training at a young age in the city of Lund in the south of Sweden (LSC B89 means 'Lund Soccer Club, Boys born in 1989'). As the years went by, the boys grew older and became more of a team. In the beginning, it was more child's play, but it soon became more serious.

The first milestone came with the Gothia Cup, an annual soccer event in Gothenburg, to which soccer teams come from around the world. The boys were twelve years old at the time and their expectations were high. Many dreamt of an international career. One of them was Joel Ekstrand, who was later selected as one of the players in the Swedish national team for 15-year-old boys. The team succeeded quite well in the Gothia Cup that year.

However, the first acid test came after having come back from the Gothia Cup in a local soccer tournament close to home. Here came the first signal that a good soccer team is something more than just a group of good players. The team lost their first two games. LSC B89 did not work as a team. The boys were sulky and the leaders did not show any good temper. But then something happened. A power amassed. Suddenly, everything was working. Through an incomparable effort, the boys won the rest of their games and ended up winning the tournament. Affected by this victory, new thoughts came up. Is it possible to do it again, and can the feeling be kept? At that time, one idea was born, which was that for a team to function well, the members' hearts must be there as well, not just their soccer feet. The boys, their parents and the leaders and trainers gave this a name. They called it 'The Future Hope'. The objective was to qualify for the premier national league for boys their age. A tough challenge!

A group of around thirty energetic boys full of hope was a fact. However, the resources were limited and consisted of two trainers and small financial means. The boys started to train more and were more willing to take the challenge. The driving idea was clear: 'B89 have more fun, the closest fellowship and the best team'. The team had also already started to see themselves as operating in the entertainment sector.

A year earlier, a team council had been elected, consisting of players, parents, leaders and trainers. The game season started. But the feeling and happiness of being a family did not come. The temporary euphoria of having won the local tournament disappeared. The boys lacked focus and the team lost its self-confidence. The trainers became impatient and the bad temper spread. The game results became worse. Some players left the team. Something had to be done. They felt stuck.

At a team council meeting, the players themselves came up with a suggestion of how to solve the problem. Somebody from outside had to come in to get the team back on their feet. Somebody who could infuse new courage and hope, and maybe look at the situation from another angle. This somebody was Balli Lelinge. He is the public entrepreneur in this story.

Balli Lelinge was employed by the local community of Lund and he was working with some primary schools in that town to reduce anti-social behaviour. He had developed his own methodology. His popular 'drama' lectures were part of the curricula in several of the primary schools in town. They were serious but they also contained a lot of laughter. Laughter and having fun was Balli's 'brand'. Laughter was exactly what was missing in the soccer team. Nothing was fun anymore.

Balli was rather critical after his first meeting with the team and its leaders and trainers. He knew from his own experience as a qualified soccer player that it was important for all the players to trust each other and to trust their leaders and trainers. His opinion after having met the team, its leader and trainers first time could be summarized as: 'The boys did not enjoy what they were doing. Everybody was afraid of failing – to be placed on the bench, outside the team. There were many good players in the group, but they could not make it as a team – and the trainers were too rigorous.'

Balli had many critics, but he defied them and started work anyway. Balli wove his exercises into the ordinary training. The team had never laughed that much before. The exercises proved how important it was to trust each other – and to talk to each other, both on the field and outside. He never said that they should win – the important thing was to have fun!

The reward came already after two years, when the team qualified for the highest league in Sweden for their age. Balli's guiding star had stuck: 'Act as if you already have reached your goal!'

*The Green Garden Room.* The Green Garden Room is a project aiming at cooperation between research, society and (public) entrepreneurship to develop Österlen region in the most southern part of Sweden (a region which to a large extent is devoted to horticulture) as a centre for knowledge, creation and therapy among all the fruit trees in the area. The driving force behind the project is Monika Olin Wikman, who lives in the area and loves the place. She is an active advocate for advertising the joy of Österlen to the public. She has worked in a team of three to promote this project. These three are the public entrepreneurs in this case. The other two are Ingrid Rasch and Göte Rudvall. Ingrid Rasch looks at art as an important public part of the development of a society and works actively to promote this. Göte Rudvall is an active pensioner with an interest in making adult education in a society more available.

Sustainable development and a good living environment are the benchmarks for this project, which aims in the long run to promote growth and employment. Part of the project is to study the prerequisites for creating this development.

The climate zone of Österlen is ideal for horticulture, and the varied landscape is attracting many entrepreneurs (of a business as well as of a social type) and cultural personalities to the region. A growing number of social entrepreneurs are creating personal and beautiful gardens in the region, in an ongoing dynamic process. Garden associations are founded, knowledge exchange takes place and the demand for common activities is increasing. Tourism in the area is based to a large extent on an exchange of gardens, where the public gains access to private gardens in exchange for knowledge and for creating models. Furthermore, several general activities are arranged in horticulture.

There is also a medical activity directed at rehabilitation, and there are entrepreneurs working with garden therapy. In rehabilitation medicine and its research, interesting projects based on gardens have been introduced. Important research results have shown, nationally as well as internationally, the positive effects of the green environments on health and wellbeing.

The three public entrepreneurs are working with the local political community in Österlen to find a strategy for local development, which is based on the following:

- good health
- space and time for human meetings and creativity, participation and spirit of community
- a rich cultural life
- an attractive way of living
- 'the slow city concept' as a common concept for these values.

The three public entrepreneurs have initiated several activities:

- A pilot study for a broad inventory of horticultural/employment activities, of tourism related to horticulture, health aspects associated with gardening, the relationships between culture and gardening, and of regular events, exhibitions, educations etc.

- Dialogical sessions with entrepreneurs of various kinds.
- Discussions, meetings and seminars with local and regional advocates.
- The build-up of a contact net.
- A collection of promising success stories, aiming at promoting Österlen as a horticultural centre.

The work continues.

*Centre for Public Entrepreneurship (CPE)*: This is an incubator for social entrepreneurship in general and for public entrepreneurship in particular, a platform for people who want to be part of changing the society for the better. This centre was started by the two public entrepreneurs Ingmar Holm and Ronny Hallberg (the latter also appeared in the story of the indoors skateboard park of the Brewery earlier). This centre is financed by different kinds of donations and grants, to a large extent due to its proven success.

In a sense, this centre became a reality as a continuation of many people's ambitions and needs to package social (mostly public) entrepreneurial possibilities and needs in the modern society. So, it is a cooperative project between many different social interests.

People behind this centre are members of the citizen sector of Malmö (where the centre is situated) and its surroundings. Ingmar Holm, who is a very driven public entrepreneur (as was Ronny Hallberg – he unfortunately died very shortly after the establishment of the CPE), was involved in two major projects before starting the centre, which were Association Öresund and Practical Bridges over Öresund (Öresund is the name of the strait between the cities of Malmö in Sweden and Copenhagen in Denmark, and a bridge was constructed between these two cities in 2000). The centre's objectives were:

1. To encourage cooperation between different public entrepreneurial interests in the region as a knowledge node and a support organization.
2. To visualize public entrepreneurs and the support they need at a societal, organizational and individual level.
3. To point out the importance of networking for public entrepreneurs.
4. To create possibilities for developing urban culture, social movements, media and communication nationally as well as internationally.

The CPE has been part of promoting and supporting hundreds of public entrepreneurial projects since it started in 2009, and is today described as a resource centre for individuals and organizations with an idea of how to develop society from a public entrepreneurial point of view. The centre supports social entrepreneurial initiatives in Scania (the most southern administrative region in Sweden) by offering mentorship and advice on finances, organization, social mobilization and communication, and access to their networks crossing over different social sectors. CPE is a place where knowledge, networks, mentorship and advice-giving are tools to support new development initiatives in the region. All of its services are free. The centre has just signed a three-year agreement of cooperation between the regional government of Scania, a major innovation institution in the Swedish government and the European Regional Development Fund. Its turnover is at present around 25 million Swedish kronor (around 2.5 million Euros).

*The Social Change In Practice (SIP) Network.* The SIP Network is a different and unique umbrella network, based in Växjö, a town in the south of Sweden. The SIP Network works for social change in practice by 'encouraging entrepreneurship and personal development for those who want to make the society more accessible and democratic' (a very public entrepreneurial ambition). They do this by using new media and modern technology, and by sharing knowledge and developing skills. One of its founders is Helen Hägglund, a genuine public entrepreneur. Within the SIP Network there are three organizations. Within and around the SIP Network, there are also several temporary and flexible networks, groups, project activities and individuals.

The SIP Network is not a legal entity of its own but a network created as an outlet for its common activities. Every organization within the SIP Network has then found its own purpose, but what is common for all of them is that they change the society for the better in large and in small ways, therefore it was given the name SIP, Social change In Practice.

Today the SIP Network operates in rural development, young entrepreneurship, democracy, international issues, education of adults and others, culture and digital media. They produce or facilitate publication of magazines and newspapers, public lectures, distance learning, folk high school courses, advertising and conceptual bureau activities, pilot and preliminary study projects, implementation programmes, coaching, establishment of activities, consulting and much more. Two development centres have been created within the areas of functional handicaps (Funkibator) and international issues (Globala Kronoberg), and they also run a subsidiary at a folk high school nearby.

The first organizations in SIP (Grrl Tech and Tech Group) started in 2000, and today these organizations have no fixed structure or traditions. The network has become a magnet for drive, burn, commitment and realization of ideas, in other words, social entrepreneurs. The operative culture thinks in new ways; it is exciting and it always permits experimenting, testing and thinking outside the box. The SIP Network is an organization for the future which has been created and 'owned' by young people and young adults who were already very digitally aware from the start. Digital and social media today permeate all that they do, and they invest heavily in development skills and scanning the environment within this area, both internally and externally.

At the head office, about forty people work together in an inspiring and creative office environment. The SIP Network operates in local, regional, national and international arenas. It is the only organization of its kind in Sweden.

Let us look at some other public entrepreneurial projects outside Sweden which I have studied, in Copenhagen, Berlin and London.

*The Project House at Bavnehøj.* The Project House in Copenhagen consists of five networks and organizations (Unfair, Supertanker's Metapol, Büro Detours, Gam3 and Republikken), which have developed with an integrated project workshop (on four floors), an open workshop and a culture stage (Remisen) for young people in Copenhagen. The concept fulfils objectives and ambitions which are presented by Copenhagen city government. One of its founders and a passionate public entrepreneur is Simon Prahm.

One ambition of those working in the Project House is to construct a creative environment at Bavnehøj, where young people can contribute to youth culture and involve themselves in the development of the city by realizing their own projects. They regard it as important that this is a place where young people can meet and take advantage of networks and organizations that have already succeeded in supporting and inspiring a participative youth culture.

As well as giving advice and plenty of space to a variety of young people full of ideas, they invite actors interested in youth culture from several different culture areas to rent smaller office spaces in the Project Workshop and places in Remisen. They are meant to function as sparring partners and 'cultural platforms' for the project activities of young people. They want to involve actors who understand and share their ideas and projects with young people and are generally able to contribute to the development of Bavnehøj as an exuberant place for creative and youth culture.

In the Project House, there are in principle three possibilities for the young people:

- *Project advice.* All young people can come to the Project House, discuss their project ideas and receive support to realize them. As well as allowing the applicant to consult the experienced project actors, the professional advisors of the local communities are also asked to get involved and give advice. The young people are also given support by working informally with more experienced participants in the Project House.

- *Project development.* Project groups may be allocated a place for project development in the house for a limited time. The support groups and the presence of established and semi-established cultural actors play an important role here. The idea is to build a real project incubator.
- *Project winding up.* In the Project Workshop as well as in Remisen, young people can try their abilities as culture producers. Some arrangements will be small and fragile, while some others will constitute major contributions. The young people create their own projects and will then enjoy the many 'project platforms' that exist in Remisen. The important thing is that Remisen remains an open stage which will contribute to and support young cultural actors as much as possible, including those who cannot be given a place at Bavnehøj.

The young people come to a house where they can develop and realize their projects, and where some of the most exciting young cultural networks in the city can back them up, inspire them and provide possibilities for common project activities. The new ideas and independence of the young people is also a reviving force to the more experienced culture and project networks. The Project House aims at actively working for cooperation with other cultural actors at Bavnehøj and intends to turn to the whole city with open arrangements and cooperative proposals, where young people can experience and create culture at premises and with a content which they launch themselves.

*Bolsjefabrikken in Copenhagen.* Bolsjefabrikken (which means 'candy factory', revealing what the premises were previously used for) is a place where an independent group of people run two culture houses in Copenhagen. One of the founders is a public entrepreneur and an artist, who likes to be called Benny. The facilities are used temporarily until the city council of Copenhagen has decided what to do with them. The facilities include an art gallery, a cinema, a library, a bicycle repair shop, a workshop for media, a café and much more. It is possible to eat there every Friday at a price of 20 Danish kroner (less than £2). People working and operating in Bolsjefabrikken do so by following and respecting certain rules:

- Respect your neighbours – they live here as well!
- No noise on the yard after 10 pm weekdays.
- You may paint graffiti on our buildings, but not on the neighbours'!

- You cannot stay the night.
- When you have something going on, stay afterwards and clean up your place!
- Clean twice as much when you have made a mess.
- Do not waste any electrical energy.
- Remember to accept and give each other a lot of hugs.

Below is a brief description of four public entrepreneurial projects in Berlin that I have studied.

*Street University*. Its main purpose is to help young people in deprived areas to increase their self-esteem by showing them that they can achieve something and that they are able to develop some status and dignity based on their abilities, skills and knowledge, not on their physical strength or health. The aim is to help them by the end to take their lives in their own hands and make it possible for them to begin a career (www.streetuniver sity.de).

*Künstlerhaus Bethanien*. This is a service activity, and its objective is to support contemporary art and contemporary artists. It is responsible for accommodating and helping international guests; to offer advice in general matters as far as art is concerned and practical matters related to this; to run workshops; to plan and to realize events, and to develop and organize cultural projects both in and outside Berlin. Künstlerhaus Bethanien is a workshop for projects and events. Its organizational structure has many layers (www.bethanien.de).

*RAW Tempel*. This is a non-profit organization which has about a hundred members and sixty-five projects. Its main purpose is to offer reasonably priced social and cultural events and activities. Since 1988 they have changed their structure to preserve the cultural style at present by participating in preserving valuable architectonic works. They are used by artists for cultural purposes with specifically expressed social goals. They also provide possibilities for rehabilitating young criminals (www. raw-tempel.de).

*Spreeufer für alle*. Regular peaceful demonstrations take place along the river Spree (which crosses the city of Berlin) as a protest against how expensive it is to find and use a place to exert one's culture in the city. Berliners are given the liberty to execute their art and music interests there. Without asking the city of council of Berlin for permission, these facilities are, by and large, rebuilt annually for the warm part of the year, and are much visited by those who live in Berlin and by tourists.

Below are details of two entrepreneurial projects in London, that I have acquainted myself with.

*Bike Works*. Bike Works' objective is to build sustainable societies by educating young people to support cycling in society. Their vision is to create a world where young people can get involved in their local communities to promote people's health and the planet. To achieve this, Bike Works' aims for the next five years are to:

- provide cooperative youth programmes which develop creativity, local communities and leadership
- rebuild and reuse bicycles and work towards environmental responsibility
- help more people to make cycling a part of everyday activities by making it more accessible and economically possible.

Their values:

- *Bicycling.* We think that bicycling is an accessible way of transport which is supporting general health, building confidence, encouraging consideration for the environment and strengthening the local community.
- *Young people.* We are committed to giving action power to young people. We provide young people with the possibility to grow as leaders, give back to the local community, work together and look at themselves as owners and creators of our common future.
- *Local community.* We work to build, support and include local communities. We welcome and respect variety in experiences, ideas and views and believe that cooperation is a powerful tool for social change.
- *Education.* We believe that we all teach and learn and we strive to be a place where we can work, learn and grow together. Through our work we foster creativity, critical thinking, curiosity and cooperation.
- *Availability.* We are convinced in our ambition to make bicycles available, economically possible and welcoming for people with all kinds of backgrounds, possibilities and income.
- *Environment.* We believe that respect and a connection to the world around us lead to more dignified local communities. To achieve this, we practise and encourage a limitation and recycling of waste, extend the lifetime of bicycles and teach waste management.
- *Social justice.* Inequalities in economic conditions and possibilities in our local communities will privilege some and marginalize others. We look at bicycles as a powerful tool, as a contribution to creating a more just and equal world.

*Bromley by Bow Centre.* This is an innovative local community organization in East London. It operates in some of the most deprived districts of the UK every week by supporting families, young people and adults of all ages for them to learn new skills, improve their health and welfare, find work and get the confidence to reach their goals and change their lives. At the core of the thinking in the centre is a belief in humankind and its capacity to achieve fantastic things.

Their ambition is to assist in creating a coherent, healthy, successful and lively local community and then eliminate 'deprivation' from Bromley by Bow. The centre has grown to become a very complex organization, which runs many projects at different places both by itself and in cooperation with others. The organization works with 2000 people every week and its service is tailor-made to the needs of the whole local community – families, young people, vulnerable adults and seniors. They support people in different projects and services in four different ways:

1.  They support people to overcome their chronic diseases and unhealthy lifestyles.
2.  They make it possible for people to learn new skills.
3.  They support people to become less dependent on financial support and to find a job.
4.  They provide the tools to create a more enterprising local community.

They provide a coherent breadth of services, available locally, where people need them and can access them. They feel proud of the quality of the service they provide and are determined in their ambition to provide the highest possible standard.

The centre is a hub for most of their services, and their beautiful buildings, situated in a green area, give a positive, inspiring and welcoming environment. They use the arts to build up the confidence in people and help them to express their creativity.

They constitute a major force to create local jobs, possibilities and welfare, and assist in raising the ambitions and support people in transforming their lives. They work to spread their experiences to other deprived local communities.

## 10.4   PUBLIC ENTREPRENEURS AND PLACE NEEDS

'Marketing' and concepts related to this, such as 'market', 'customer' and 'demand', do not seem to fit the public entrepreneurial situation very well. Market in the sense of a space, in which the entrepreneur is hoping to get a share and where buying and selling take place, is not a label that public entrepreneurs feel comfortable with. As mentioned earlier, these entrepreneurs act in public places, not in markets. They do not approach demanding customers, willing to pay for their goods and/or services. They would rather focus on people in need, who could be called users.

As we will see, public entrepreneurial marketing (if such a term would exist) does not consist of product development, distribution and promotion and the like as normally understood by marketers, but rather of *setting up dialogues in networks*, trying to understand how to satisfy some citizen needs and to do this co-creatively in a much deeper sense than what is typically the case for business entrepreneurs or business-like social entrepreneurs. These dialogues also happen face-to-face, generating a common understanding, a common way of thinking and a common language between participating citizens.

I have run many workshops with other researchers interested in understanding public entrepreneurs and with public entrepreneurs themselves. Some of my observations from these workshops are:

- Public entrepreneurs are skilled at understanding what is missing in empty or even destructive public places. They feel compelled to fill these places with meaningful content.
- Public entrepreneurs are convinced that they are doing the right thing, and they are surprised that more people are not doing what they are doing. They just do what they do naturally somehow (what I have referred to as bricoleurs), and they can have difficulties in describing in any detail or logical way what they have been doing or intend to do.
- Public entrepreneurs have no formal plan for their actions. If they had one, they would probably not succeed. They dare to have fun, and they would feel very uncomfortable working in a formal and / or bureaucratic organization.
- Obstacles for public entrepreneurs include nostalgic and reactionary individuals, who hang onto a firmly cemented and outdated version of the 'good' society which in their opinion once existed. These entrepreneurs are also very humble, and they regard their associates and partners as major contributors to what they have achieved.

Public entrepreneurs are not searching for venture opportunities to exploit but to problematizing the place where they feel needed (often by living in that environment themselves or having experiences of what it means to operate there). We may refer to this as a genuine empathy for their local community and an honest respect for their fellow citizens. Public entrepreneurs' perception of place needs were provided in section 10.3:

- In *Skateboard Malmö*, there was a need for a place for skateboarders to exert their passion without interfering with other public places in the city, such as streets and pavements meant primarily for traffic and pedestrians or, in the winter, garages for cars where the owners (of the garage and the cars) did their best to stop the skateboarders from being there.
- In *Future Hope – LSC B89*, the place is soccer fields, where a group of young boys had the need to excel.
- In the *Green Garden Room*, a group of public entrepreneurs saw the possibility of using a horticultural region as a place to satisfy cultural and medical needs.
- In *Centre for Public Entrepreneurship*, an incubator was set up to cater for different needs to be assisted, supported and coached by a huge number of aspiring social entrepreneurs (public or other), in an expanding and progressive city and its environment.
- In the *SIP Network*, the place is less geographically precise, but could be considered as any situation in the neighbourhood where public entrepreneurs see the need to 'change society in practice'.
- In the *Project House at Bavnehøj*, the place is the largest city in the Nordic countries, that is Copenhagen, where there was a huge need to support young cultural aspirations of various kinds.
- In *Bolsjefabrikken in Copenhagen*, the place is the same, but the cultural and artistic needs are somewhat broader.
- *Street University* provides a possibility to satisfy needs among young people in some deprived regions in Berlin, to increase their self-esteem.
- *Künstlerhause Bethanien* is a service organization to support needs among contemporary art and artists in Berlin.
- *RAW Tempel* is a non-profit organization, the purpose of which is to offer affordable and cultural solutions to satisfy similar needs in Berlin.
- *Spreeufer für alle* takes place annually on one side of the river Spree in Berlin (on the other side there are long rows of exceptionally expensive houses) for people to satisfy their need for exhibiting their local art and music.
- *Bike Works* feels the need to build a sustainable society in London and its environment, focusing on cycling.
- *Bromley by Row Centre* aims at supporting the need to build a better future for deprived districts in East London and its environment.

## 10.5   PUBLIC ENTREPRENEURSHIP AND SOCIAL PHENOMENOLOGICAL NETWORKING

Social phenomenology seems to be the proper starting point to approach and to understand public entrepreneurship. To begin with, public entrepreneurs have a very prosaic view of what they are doing, stressing everyday reality, that is, reality which is presumed to be socially constructed and maintained together with other citizens and which is built up by language typifications. In order to generate a new understanding of a social situation, in which they aim to satisfy some needs that other citizens have, public entrepreneurs are happy to develop some new typifications as concepts and images ('language development') to find new solutions for social problems.

In my experience, public entrepreneurs have something of their own vocabulary or their own understanding of the meaning of existing concepts, such as:

- social forums
- social climates
- freedom to try
- pride
- legitimacy
- authenticity
- vision.

They are also generally happy and sometimes even proud to be called 'public entrepreneurs'.

One reason why language is so important to public entrepreneurs is that they must be innovative in all that they do, not only in finding new solutions to different problems of interest to them, but also in implementing them. They seem to believe, at least implicitly, that to find a constructive solution to a new and different social problem, it is necessary to think differently, and for this a (partly) different language is required. Also, public entrepreneurs must often 'fight' with other people to get rid of old habits and learn new ones, which, again, requires the rejection of some old concepts and the thinking behind them.

Furthermore, that public entrepreneurs are typically short of resources. If they compete, it is not for users, but for resources to get started, most of the time in effective and sustainable ways. Public entrepreneurs must therefore often be creative inventors of resources (bricoleurs as they are). One could even say that it is necessary for them to have an extended view of resources (Figure 10.1).

If public entrepreneurs do anything which could be called marketing, it is networking. Only through networking can public entrepreneurs access their life blood. Public entrepreneurship is truly co-creation between different citizens. It might even be conceptualized as such. To bring people and organizations together to focus on a problem, to combine resources from a number of different places to implement solutions and to communicate

*Figure 10.1    An extended view of resources*

results effectively is what provide public entrepreneurs with power. These networks consisting of trusting each other are based on a common task and vision in relation to positive change. Public entrepreneurs embrace the concept of 'co-opetition', not competition (consequently Schumpeter's concept 'creative destruction' does not fit in here). Public entrepreneurs have networks in a much broader field than business entrepreneurs, they operate in a more diversified and dynamically strategic landscape, they act so that their stakeholders benefit from what they are doing, they try to do so well that they are no longer needed and they live in a world of meaning, not in a world of circumstances. Networks are more important for social entrepreneurs than for business entrepreneurs, if for no other reason than because they do not offer products which can speak for themselves. Social entrepreneurship activities must constantly justify themselves. Differences between emotional and calculative connections in networks are not so obvious or even so necessary to separate for social entrepreneurs as for business entrepreneurs. Confidence and trust are crucial for social entrepreneurs. Contacts in themselves are not enough, which might sometimes be the case for business entrepreneurs. Most social entrepreneurs work with a number of different stakeholders at the same time; they have multiple objectives, offer a limited range of services and their actions should be fully transparent and accountable. Networking, or building citizen capital, is a good way to gain knowledge about possible public entrepreneurial projects and to gain access to resources necessary to begin. A public entrepreneur must have three important things in mind:

1.  *With whom should I build alliances?* Public social projects should consider their ecosystems as 'parts of the game' and ripe for increasing the number of users that they can reach, expand necessary resources,

decrease costs for inputs and turn 'competitors' into partners in the game. As mentioned, *'competition' within public entrepreneurship is normally about resources*. If competitors have similar ambitions to the public entrepreneur, it is likely that they can see the advantages from sharing resources. If 'suppliers' can be convinced about what the public social project wants to achieve, they may very well go beyond their traditional supplier role and contribute to the success of the project. Competitors can sometimes be convinced that they are in fact complementary activities. To look at one's ecosystem this way opens up almost unlimited possibilities to build new alliances which will serve one's social project and boost the possibility of its success.

2. *Why is networking necessary and meritorious under the circumstances?* Public entrepreneurs use networks to gain advantages in the field. Four reasons for networks can be: resources shortage, growing competition for resources, increased social appetite to become more effective and an extended demand to show results.

3. *How should I design a meritorious network?* Successful networking is about successful relationships. Such relationships require attention to be directed at several factors (a common ambition, shared values, a shared vision or common goals, choosing leadership democratically, what stage the public social project is in, and the startup of several public social projects).

Public entrepreneurs build and exploit citizen capital through confidence and trust in networks (as we know, another name for citizen capital is network capital). As language and typifications are so important to public entrepreneurs, it is easy to understand that the generators for their progress come from dialogues with other citizens and with local interest and support groups of different kinds. The importance of networking and dialogues for success can be seen in all the cases provided in section 10.3:

- In *Skateboard Malmö*, the language among skateboarders is distinctive; for example, they give special names to their moves, such as 'kickflip', 'ollie' and 'grabs'. Skateboarding will even become one of the sports at the Olympic Games in Tokyo in 2020. The dialogues between John Magnusson and the city gardener, Gunnar Ericson, were necessary for the progress of the project, as were dialogues between students in the project management education team to build a model for the construction of the Shipbuilding Berth.

- In *The Future Hope – LSC B89*, the language used by the new trainer, Balli Lelinge, was special and engaging. For instance, he referred to one of his 'exercises' as 'the Beckham jump' and this was based on trust between the soccer players (David Beckham is a former world class UK soccer player, well-known among the young soccer players in LSC). The idea was that anybody in the team could run into a group of other soccer players in the exercising field at any time and just shout out as he jumped into the group, expecting to be caught in the arms of the others before he touched the ground.

– In the *Green Garden Room*, many progressive dialogues are held between members of the public entrepreneurs, local politicans in the area of Österlen, horticultural practitioners and medical experts, for instance.
– In the *Centre for Public Entrepreneurship*, dialogues between various interested parties and citizens in the region take place all the time, while developing the many public entrepreneurial projects led by the centre.
– In the *SIP Network*, its very existence relies on keeping networks and dialogues constantly going.
– In the *Project House at Bavnehøj* and *Bolsje fabrikken in Copenhagen*, the guarantee for success of all projects was that the public entre-preneurs were a member of at least one network, and constructively participating in its dialogues.
– In the three public entrepreneurial cases in Berlin and the two cases in London, the pattern is the same.

Public entrepreneurs regard themselves as hubs in constantly changing value star constitutions (Figure 10.2).

*Public entrepreneurs are genuinely social phenomenologically co-creating entrepreneurs.*

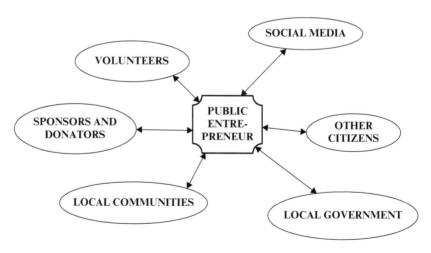

*Figure 10.2   A value star for a public entrepreneur*

## 10.6 PUBLIC ENTREPRENEURSHIP AND CO-CREATIVE PLACE VITALIZATION

'Marketing' for public entrepreneurship is different from marketing for business entrepreneurship and social entrepreneurship conducted in an enterprising mode. Not only is it different from the receiving side (from the point of view of customers or users), but also different from the 'generating' side. Public entrepreneurs are not producers of goods and / or services. They should regarded as *generators and utilizers, renewers and vitalizers of public places*. A reminder of two of my earlier points:

- A public place in a society is any place accessible to any citizen, and it is also a place which citizens should feel responsible for using in an ethical way to promote citizenry and sociality.
- Public entrepreneurs can operate in such places physically, virtually, discursively and / or emotionally to make social values such as inclusiveness more generally available and consequently reducing social alienation.

Prahalad and Ramaswamy (2004c) talk about DART (Dialogue, Access, Risks-benefits and Transparancy) to co-create more relevant market values between companies and customers. In the case of public entrepreneurship, I think it would be proper to talk about NERD to co-create citizenry between entrepreneurs and other citizens (Figure 10.3; Table 10.1).

Prahalad and Ramaswamy (2000) also provide some advice to follow for co-creative marketing (presented in section 8.7). In my opinion, such advice can easily be modified to fit the public entrepreneurial situation:

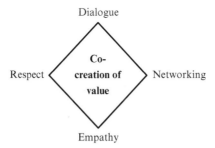

*Figure 10.3   Building blocks for interaction between public entrepreneurs and other citizens and local communities in order to co-create (and co-extract) value*

*Table 10.1    The building blocks of NERD*

| Terms | Definition | Public entrepreneurial consequences |
| --- | --- | --- |
| *Networking* | Interaction with all parts of the local individuals and associations | To understand his or her possible contributions as an entrepreneur |
| *Empathy* | To feel a deep commonality with other citizens | To get to know social needs outside him- or herself |
| *Respect* | To feel that nobody is superior or inferior as a citizen | To give to as much as to take from fellow citizens |
| *Dialogue* | Honest and open discussions between participating citizens | To listen and to talk, to understand the relevant and possible co-creation of social construction of reality |

- Encourage an active dialogue.
- Mobilize citizen communities.
- Mobilize citizen differences.
- Handle person-based experiences.
- Handle multiple experience channels.
- Handle variation and evolution.
- Create citizen experiences.
- Look at citizens as being as eager value-extractors as you.
- Prepare the public entrepreneurial project for the competences of other citizens in the new society.

## 10.7   CONCLUSION

This has been a chapter about how public entrepreneurs can promote their mission. As noted, there are difficulties in referring to this as 'marketing'. The reason is that this chapter has not discussed any business elite phenomena but a form of action that we all should engage in from time to time; it is not about system-changing or creative destruction to build something new at the same time as washing away what has been, but about small but real improvements of what is already in place in everyday life. It is not about autonomous market-share building but about common citizenry and freedom for individuals in a society, to involve each other in getting to know what is essential for civic inclusion and democracy.

# 11. Summary and conclusions

In this book, I have presented two fundamentally different ways to apply marketing for three types of entrepreneurs, i.e., independent business entrepreneurs, business intrapreneurs and social entrepreneurs. The book was written from my background of more than thirty-five years of studying the subject academically, conducting research in related fields in the meantime, presenting papers in conferences around the world, publishing several books and articles, and starting four businesses of my own.

One thing I have learnt during these years is that using marketing for entrepreneurs is different in several respects compared to using marketing for an established business or social venture. I have also come to understand that there are several ways of applying marketing successfully, not only by using the established version based on the management marketing model. Finally (which is also seen in this book), some entrepreneurs, in particular of the social kind, succeed without using marketing in its normal sense. I have tried to demonstrate this in the book.

One of my many interests is philosophy. I can therefore see in marketing theory, as well as in emerging reality, a new marketing paradigm emerging which includes customers and users of goods and services more tangibly, even to the extent that customers and users are involved in the developing and consuming process as co-creators and co-extractors of the value, which is embedded in all products being offered. From a philosophical point of view, I refer to this paradigm as social phenomenological marketing.

By looking at and practising marketing in different ways, it is my conviction that we can understand each other better in terms of what we do as researchers, as well as gain a better understanding of what it means to be marketers, customers and users – and how to live better and more comfortably in an increasingly changing and more demanding society.

# References

Abell, D.F. & J.S. Hammond (1979), *Strategic Market Planning: Problems and Analytical Approaches*, Englewood Cliffs, NJ: Prentice Hall.

Agnew, J. (1987), *The United States in the World Economy*, Cambridge: Cambridge University Press.

Aldrich, H.E. & D. Whetten (1981), 'Organisation-sets, action-sets, and networks: Making the most of simplicity', in P. Nystrom & W. Starbuck (eds.), *Handbook of Organizational Design*, Vol. 1, New York: Oxford University Press.

Aldrich, H.E. & C. Zimmer (1986), 'Entrepreneurship through social networks', in D.L. Sexton & R.W. Wilson (eds.), *The Art and Science of Entrepreneurship*, Cambridge, MA: Ballinger.

Allen, K.R. (2010) (5th edition), *New Venture Creation*, International edition, Mason, OH: South-Western.

Altman, I. & S.M. Low (1992) (eds.), *Place Attachment*, New York and London: Plenum Press.

Alvesson, M. (1993), *Cultural Perspectives on Organizations*, Cambridge: Cambridge University Press.

Alvesson, M. & K. Sköldberg (2000), *Reflexive Methodology: New vistas for qualitative research*, London: Sage.

Alvord, S., D. Brown & C. Letts (2002), 'Social entrepreneurship and social transformation: an exploratory study', Working Paper No. 15, available from *Social Science Research Network Electronic Paper Collection*, Hauser Venter for Nonprofit Organizations.

Amin, A. & N. Thrift (1994), 'Living in the global', in A. Amin & N. Thrift (eds.), *Globalization, Institutions and Regional Development in Europe*, Oxford: Oxford University Press.

Amin, A., A. Cameron & R. Hudson (2002), *Placing the Social Economy*, London: Routledge.

Anderson, A.R. & S.L. Jack (2002), 'The articulation of social capital in entrepreneurial networks: a glue or a lubricant?', *Entrepreneurship and Regional Development*, July-Sept, 193–210.

Anér, E. & M. Rentzhog (2012), *Everybody is in Services – The Impact of Servicification in Manufacturing on Trade and Trade Policy*, Stockholm: Kommerskollegium.

Arbnor, I., S.-E. Borglund & T. Liljedahl. (1980), *Osynligt ockuperad: en arkeologisk studie av nutidens ledarskap*, Stockholm: LiberLäromedel.

Arbnor, I. & B. Bjerke (2009) (3rd edition), *Methodology for Creating Business Knowledge*, London: Sage.

Argyris, C. & D.A. Schön (1989), 'Participatory action research and action research compared: A commentary', *The American Behavioral Scientist*, **32**(5), 612–23.

Arndt, J. (1979), 'Toward a concept of domesticated markets', *Journal of Marketing*, **43**(Fall), 69–75.

Aspers, P. (2011), *Markets*, Cambridge: Polity.

Aspinwall, L. (1958), 'The characteristics of goods and parallel systems theories', in E.G. Kelly & W. Lazer (eds.), *Managerial Marketing*, Homewood, IL: Richard D. Irwin.

Asplund, J. (1991), *Essä om Gemeinschaft och Gesellschaft* [Essay about Gemeinschaft and Gesellschaft], Gothenburg: Korpen.

Asplund, J. (2006), *Munnens socialitet och andra essäer* [The sociality of the mouth and other essays], Gothenburg: Korpen.

Augé, M. (1995), *Non-Places: Introduction to an Anthropology of Supermodernity*, London: Verso.

Augustinsson, E. & M. Brisvall (2009), *Tjäna pengar och rädda världen* [Make money and save the world], Stockholm: Bookhouse Publishing.

Austin, J. (1962), *How to Do Things with Words*, London: Oxford University Press.

Auster, E. (1990), 'The interorganizational environment: network theory, tools, and Applications', in F. Williams & D. Gibson (eds.), *Technology Transfer: A Communication Perspective*, London: Sage.

Avolio, B.J., W.L. Gardner, F.O. Walumbwa, F. Luthans & D.R. May (2009), 'Unlocking the mask: A look at the process by which authentic leaders impact follower attitudes and behaviors', *The Leadership Quarterly*, **15**, 801–23.

Bagozzi, R.P. (1974), 'Marketing as an organized behavioral system of exchange', *Journal of Marketing*, **38**(4), 77–81.

Bagozzi, R.P. (1975), 'Marketing as exchange', *Journal of Marketing*, **39**(4), 32–9.

Baker, S.D. (2007), 'Followership: The theoretical foundation of a contemporary construct', *Journal of Leadership & Organizational Studies*, **14**, 50–60.

Baker, T. & R.E. Nelson (2005), 'Creating something from nothing: Resource construction through entrepreneurial bricolage', *Administrative Science Quarterly*, **50**, 329–66.

Baker, T., E. Gedljovic & M. Lubatkin (2005), 'A framework for comparing entrepreneurship processes across nations', *Journal of Business Studies*, **36**, 492–504.

Banister, P., E. Burman, I. Parker, M. Taylor & C. Tindall (1994), *Qualitative Methods in Psychology: A Research Guide*, Buckingham: Open University Press.

Banks, J. (1972), *The Sociology of Social Movements*, London: Macmillan.

BarNir, A. & K. Smith (2002), 'Interfirm alliance in the small business: the role of social networks', *The Journal of Small Business Management*, **40**(3), 219–32.

Baron, R.A. (1998), 'Cognitive mechanisms in entrepreneurship: why and when entrepreneurs think differently than other people', *Journal of Business Venturing*, **12**, 275–94.

Baron, R.A. & S.A. Shane (2008) (2nd edition), *Entrepreneurship. A Process Perspective*, Mason, OH: Thomson.

Barringer, B.R. & R.D. Ireland (2006), *Entrepreneurship. Successfully Launching New Ventures*, Upper Saddle River, NJ: Pearson Education.

Barthes, R. (1964), *Elements of Semiology*, New York: Hill and Wang.

Bartunek, J.M. (1984), 'Changing interpretive schemes and organizational restructuring: The example of a religious order', *Administrative Science Quarterly*, **29**, 355–72.

Bass, R.A. & I. Stogdill (1990) (3rd edition), *Bass & Stogdill's Handbook of Leadership: Theory, Research, and Managerial Applications*, New York: The Free Press.

Bauer, R. (1960), 'Consumer behavior as risk-taking', in R.S. Hancock (ed.). *Dynamic Marketing for a Changing World*, Proceedings of the 43rd Conference of the American Marketing Association, 389–98.

Bauman, Z. (1978), *Hermeneutics and Social Science*, London: Hutchinson.

Beckman, T.N. (1926), *Wholesaling*, New York: The Ronald Press Co.

Belk, R.W. (1974), 'An exploratory assessment of situational effects in buyer behavior', *Journal of Marketing*, **38**, 156–63.

Belk, R.W. (1988), 'Possessions and the extended self', *Journal of Consumer Research*, **15**(September), 139–68.

Bell, D. (1974), *The Coming of Post-Industrial Society: A Venture in Social Forecasting*, New York: Basic Books.

Bendapudi, N. & R.P. Leone (2003), 'Psychological implications of customer participation in co-production', *Journal of Marketing*, **67**(1), 14–28.

Bengtsson, L. (2006), *Entreprenörskap och företagande i akademiska miljöer* [Entrepreneurship and enterprising in academic contexts], Lund: Studentlitteratur.

Bennis, W. (2009), *On Becoming a Leader*, New York: Basic Books.

Berger, P.L. & T. Luckmann (1981), *The Social Construction of Reality*, Harmondsworth: Penguin.

Berglund, K. & A. Johansson (2008), *Arenor för entreprenörskap* [Arenas for entrepreneurship], Stockholm: Stiftelsen för Småföretagsforskning.

Berglund, K. & J. Gaddefors (2010), 'Entrepreneurship requires resistance to be mobilized', in F. Bill, B. Bjerke & A.W. Johansson (eds.), *(De) mobilizing the Entrepreneurship Discourse. Exploring Entrepreneurial Thinking and Action*, Cheltenham, UK and Northampton, MA, USA: Edward Elgar Publishing.

Berglund, K., B. Johannisson & B. Schwartz (red) (2012), *Societal Entrepreneurship. Positioning, Penetrating, Promoting*, Cheltenham, UK and Northampton, MA, USA: Edward Elgar Publishing.

Berry, L.L. (1980), 'Services marketing is different', *Business*, May-June, 24–30.

Berry, L.L. (1983), 'Relationship marketing', in L.L. Berry, G.L. Shostack & G.D. Upah (eds.), *Emerging Perspectives in Service Marketing*, Chicago, IL: American Marketing Association.

Bettman, J.R. (1979), *An Information Processing Theory of Consumer Choice*, Reading, MA: Addison-Wesley.

Bhave, M.P. (1994), 'A process model of entrepreneurial venture creation', *Journal of Business Venturing*, **9**(3), 223–42.

Bill, F., A. Jansson & L. Olaison (2010), 'The spectacle of entrepreneurship: a duality of flamboyance and activity', in F. Bill, B. Bjerke & A.W. Johansson (eds.), *(De)mobilizing the Entrepreneurship Discourse. Exploring Entrepreneurial Thinking and Action*, Cheltenham, UK and Northampton, MA, USA: Edward Elgar Publishing.

Billig, M. (1987), *Arguing and Thinking: A Rhetorical Approach to Social Psychology*, Cambridge: Cambridge University Press.

Birch, D. (1979), *The Job Generation Process*, Cambridge, MA: MIT Program on Neighborhood and Regional Change.

Birley, S. (1985), 'The role of networks in the entrepreneurial process', *Journal of Business Venturing*, **1**, 107–17.

Birley, S., S. Cromie & A. Myers (1991), 'Entrepreneurial networks: their emergence in Ireland and overseas', *International Small Business Journal*, **9**(4), 56–74.

Bjerke, B. (1989), *Att skapa nya affärer* [Creating new business ventures], Lund: Studentlitteratur.

Bjerke, B. (2005), 'Public entrepreneurship – marginal made central', paper presented at *Enterprise & Innovation Conference*, University of Waikato, New Zealand.

Bjerke, B. (2007), 'Face-to-face research: Interviews, conversations and dialogues', in B. Gustavsson (ed.), *The Principles of Knowledge Creation. Research Methods in the Social Sciences*, Cheltenham, UK and Northampton, MA, USA: Edward Elgar.

Bjerke, B. (2010), 'Entrepreneurship, space and place', in F. Bill, B. Bjerke & A.W. Johansson (eds.), *(De)mobilizing the Entrepreneurship Discourse.*

*Exploring Entrepreneurial Thinking and Action*, Cheltenham, UK and Northampton, MA, USA: Edward Elgar Publishing.

Bjerke, B. (2013), *About Entrepreneurship*, Cheltenham, UK and Northampton, MA, USA: Edward Elgar Publishing.

Bjerke, B. & C. Hultman (2002), *Entrepreneurial Marketing. The Growth of Small Firms in the New Economic Era*, Cheltenham, UK and Northampton, MA, USA: Edward Elgar.

Bjerke, B. & T. Dalhammar (2006), 'Public entrepreneurship – definitely different', paper presented at *UIC Research Symposium on Marketing and Entrepreneurship*, Chicago, IL.

Bjerke, B., D. Hjorth, H. Larsson & C.-J. Asplund (2007), *Publikt entreprenörskap. Det marginella görs centralt* [Public entrepreneurship. The marginal is made central], Malmö: Folkbildningsföreningen.

Bjerke, B. & H. Rämö (2011), *Entrepreneurial Imagination – Time, Timing, Space and Place in Business Action*, Cheltenham, UK and Northampton, MA, USA: Edward Elgar.

Bjerke, B. & M. Karlsson (2011), *Samhällsentreprenör. Att inte vara och agera som om* [Social entrepreneur. To just not be and to act as if], Malmö: Glokala folkhögskolan i [Folk High School] Malmö (Att bygga den Glokala staden 3 [Building the Global City 3]).

Bjerke, B. & M. Karlsson (2013a), *Social Entrepreneur. To Act as If and Make a Difference*, Cheltenham, UK and Northampton, MA, USA: Edward Elgar Publishing.

Bjerke, B. & M. Karlsson (2013b), 'Why are some people behaving or acting entrepreneurially more than others? Looking at opportunities as part of entrepreneurial behaviour or action in more than one way', *Journal of Business and Economics*, **4**(6), 465–74.

Bjugstad, K., E.C. Thach, K.J. Thompson & A. Morris (2006), 'A fresh look at followership: A model for matching followership and leadership styles', *Journal of Behavioral and Applied Management*, **7**, 304–19.

Blackburn, R. & M. Ram (2006), 'Fix or fixation? The contributions and limitations of entrepreneurship and small firms to combating social exclusion', *Entrepreneurship and Regional Development*, **18**, 73–89.

Blass, T. (2009), 'From New Haven to Santa Clara: A historical perspective on the Milgram obedience experiments', *American Psychologist*, **64**(1), 37–45.

Blomgren, M. & T. Bergman (2005), *EU och Sverige – ett sammanlänkat statsskick* [EU and Sweden – a linked form of government], Malmö: Liber Förlag.

Blomqvist, P. & B. Rothstein (2000), *Välfärdsstatens nya ansikte: Demokrati och marknadsreformer inom den offentliga sektorn* [The new face of the welfare state: Democracy and market reforms in the public sector], Stockholm: Agora.

Blumer, H. (1969), *Symbolic Interactionism: Perspective and Method*, Englewood Cliffs, NJ: Prentice Hall.

Blundel, R.K. & D. Smith (2001), *Business Networking: SMEs and Inter-Firm Collaboration, a Review of the Research Literature with Implication for Policy*, Report to Small Business Services PP03/01, Department of Trade and Industry, Small Business Service, Sheffield.

Boddice, R. (2009), 'Forgotten antecedents: entrepreneurship, ideology and history', in R. Ziegler (ed.), *An Introduction to Social Entrepreneurship*, Cheltenham, UK and Northampton, MA, USA: Edward Elgar Publishing.

Boissevain, J. (1974), *Friends of Friends: Networks, Manipulations and Coalitions*, Oxford: Basil Blackwell.

Borden, N.H. (1964), 'The concept of the marketing mix', *Journal of Advertising Research*, Advertising Research Foundation, Inc. (June), 2–7.

Bornstein, D. (1998), 'Changing the world on a shoestring', *The Atlantic Monthly*, **281**(1), 34–9.

Bornstein, D. (2004), *How to Change the World. Social Entrepreneurs and the Power of New Ideas*, Oxford: Oxford University Press.

Borzaga, C. & J. Defourney (eds.) (2001), *The Emergence of Social Enterprise*, Oxon and New York: Routledge.

Bouchard, C., M. Bossier & C. Howald (2016), 'Private art museum report', in *Larry's List Ltd. & AMMA* (eds.), Manchester: Cornerhouse Publications.

Boulding, K.E. (1956), 'General systems theory: the skeleton of science', *Management Science*, **2**, 197–208.

Bourdieu, P. (1984), *Distinction. A Social Critique of the Judgment of Taste*, Cambridge, MA: Harvard University Press.

Bourdieu, P. & L. Wacquant (1992), *An Invitation to Reflexive Sociology*, Cambridge: Polity Press.

Bourne, F.S. (1965), 'Group influences in marketing and public relations', in J.V. McNeal (ed.), *Dimensions of Consumer Behavior*, New York: Apple-Century-Crofts.

Boyd, N. & G.S. Vozikis (1994), 'The influence of self-efficacy on the development of entrepreneurial intentions and actions', *Entrepreneurial Theory and Practice*, Summer, 53–77.

Bozkaya, A. & B. van Pottelsberghe de la Potterie (2008), 'Who funds technology-based small firms? Evidence from Belgium', *Economic Innovation and New Technology*, **17**, 97–122.

Brenner, N. (1997), 'Global, fragmented, hierarchical: Henri Lefebvre's geographies of Globalization', *Public Culture*, **10**(1), 135–67.

Brickell, P. (2000), *People before Structures: Engaging Communities Effectively in Regeneration*, London: Demos.

Bridge, S., K. O'Neill & S. Cromie (2009) (3rd edition), *Understanding Enterprise, Entrepreneurship and Small Business*, New York: Palgrave Macmillan.

Briggs, H. (1986), *Learning How to Ask: A Sociolinguistic Appraisal of the Role of the Interviewer in Social Science Research*, Cambridge: Cambridge University Press.

Brinckerhoff, P.C. (2000), *Social Entrepreneurship. The Art of Mission-Based Venture Development*, New York: John Wiley & Sons.

Brockhaus, R.H. (1982), 'The psychology of the entrepreneur', in C.A. Kent, D.L. Sexton & K.H. Vesper (eds.), *Encyclopedia of Entrepreneurship*, Englewood Cliffs, NJ: Prentice Hall.

Brown, B. & J.E. Butler (1995), 'Competitors as allies: a study of the entrepreneurial networks in the US wine industry', *Journal of Small Business Management*, **33**(3), 57–66.

Brown, S. (1995), *Postmodern Marketing*, London: Routledge.

Brown, S. (2001), 'Torment your customer (They'll love it)!', *Harvard Business Review*, Oct. 8, 74–88.

Bryman, A. (1997), 'Leadership in organizations', in S.R. Clegg, C. Hardy & W.R. Nord (eds.), *Handbook of Organization Studies*, London: Sage.

Bucklin, L. (1962), 'Retail strategy and the classification of consumer goods', *Journal of Marketing*, **27**(October), 50–55.

Burchell, G., C. Gordon & P. Miller (eds.) (1991), *The Foucault Effect: Studies in Governmentality*, Chicago, IL: University of Chicago Press.

Burenstam Linder, S. (1961), *An Essay on Trade and Transformation*, New York: John Wiley.

Burger, J.M. (2009), 'Replicating Milgram: Would people still obey today?', *American Psychologist*, **64**(1), 1–11.

Burns, P. (2011) (3rd edition), *Entrepreneurship and Small Business. Start, Growth and Maturity*, New York: Palgrave Macmillan.

Burrell, G. & G. Morgan (1979), *Sociological Paradigms and Organizational Analysis: Elements of the Sociology of Corporate Life*, London: Heinemann.

Burt, R.S. (1992), *Structural Holes. The Social Structure of Competition*, Cambridge, MA: Harvard University Press.

Burt, R.S. (1997), 'The contingent value of social capital', *Administrative Science Quarterly*, **42**, 339–65.

Butler, R.S. (1923), *Marketing and Merchandising*, New York: Alexander Hamilton Institute.

Buzzell, R.D. (1964), *Mathematical Models and Marketing Management*, Boston: Harvard Business School Press.

Callon, M. (1986), 'The sociology of an actor-network', in M. Callon, J. Law & A. Rip (eds.), *Mapping the Dynamics of Science and Technology*, Basingstoke: Macmillan.

Callon, M. (1999), 'Actor-network theory – the market test', in J. Law & J. Hassard (eds.), *Actor Network Theory and After*, Oxford: Blackwell.

Calvert, A.L. (1981), 'A synthesis of foreign direct investment theories and theories of the multinational firm', *Journal of International Business Studies*, Spring/Summer, 43–59.

Cantillon, R. (1755/1955), *Essai sur la nature de commerce en general* [Essay on the general nature of commerce], London: Fletcher Gyles.

Carlyle, T. (1841), *On Heroes, Hero-Worship, and The Heroic in History*, London: James Fraser.

Carson, D., S. Cromie, P. Mc Gowan & J. Hill (1995), *Marketing and Entrepreneurship in SMEs*, Hemel Hempstead, UK: Prentice Hall International (UK) Ltd.

Carson, D., A. Gilmore, C. Perry & K. Gronhaug (2001) *Qualitative Research Methods*, Thousand Oaks, CA: Sage.

Carsten, M.K., M. Uhl-Bien, B.L. West, J.L. Patera & R. McGregor (2010), 'Exploring social constructs of followership: A qualitative study', *The Leadership Quarterly*, **21**(3), 543–62.

Carsten, M.K., M. Uhl-Bien & A. Jaywickrema (2013), '"Reversing the lens" in leadership research: Investigating follower role orientation and leadership outcomes', presented at *Annual Meeting, Southern Management Association (SMA)*, New Orleans, Louisiana: USA.

Casey, E.S. (1993), *Getting Back into Place: Toward a Renewed Understanding of the Place-World*, Bloomington, IN: Indiana University Press.

Casey, E.S. (1997), *The Fate of Place: A Philosophical History*, Berkeley, CA: University of California Press.

Castells, M. (1998), *Informationsåldern. Ekonomi, samhälle och kultur: Band I: Nätverkssamhällets framväxt* [The information age. Economy, society and culture: Book I: The emergence of the network society], Gothenburg: Daidalos.

Catford, J. (1998), 'Social entrepreneurs are vital for health promotion – but they need supportive environments too', Editorial, *Health Promotional International*, **13**, 95–8.

Caza, A. & B. Jackson (2011), 'Authentic leadership', in A. Bryman, D. Collinson, K. Grint, C. Jackson & M. Uhl-Bien (eds.), *Sage Handbook of Leadership*, Thousand Oaks, CA: Sage.

Chaleff, I. (1995), *The Courageous Follower: Standing Up to and For Our Leaders*, San Francisco, CA: Barrett-Koehler Publishers, Inc.

Chaleff, I. (2003) (2nd edition), *The Courageous Follower: Standing Up to and For Our Leaders*, San Francisco, CA: Barrett-Koehler Publishers, Inc.

Chaleff, I. (2008), 'Creating new ways of following', in R. Riggio, I. Chaleff & J. Lipman- Blumen (eds.), *The Art of Followership: How Great Followers Create Great Leaders and Organizations*, San Francisco, CA: Jossey-Bass.

Charon, J.L. (1998) (6th edition), *Symbolic Interactionism: An Introduction, an Interpretation, an Integration*, Upper Saddle River, NJ: Pearson Prentice Hall.

Chell, E. & S. Baines (2000), 'Networking, entrepreneurship and micro-business behaviour', *Entrepreneurship and Regional Development*, **12**, 195–215.

Cho, A.H. (2006), 'Politics, values and social entrepreneurship: a critical appraisal', in J. Mair, J. Robinson & K. Hockerts (eds.), *Social Entrepreneurship*, Hampshire, UK and New York, USA: Palgrave Macmillan.

Ciborra, C.U. (1996), 'The platform organization: Recombining strategies, structures, and surprises', *Organization Science*, **7**, 103–18.

Clancy, K.J. & P.C. Krieg (2000), *Counterintuitive Marketing: Achieve Great Results Using Uncommon Sense*, New York: Free Press.

Clark, L.H. (1955) (ed.), *Consumer Behavior: The Life Cycle and Consumer Behavior*, New York: New York University Press.

Coase, R. (1937), 'The nature of the firm', *Economica*, **4**, 386–405.

Coleman, J.S. (1990), *Foundations of Social Theory*, Cambridge, MA: Harvard University Press.

Collins, V.D. (1935), *World Marketing. A Complete Guide to World Marketing Merchandising and Selling of the New Era*, Philadelphia: J. B. Lippinett Company.

Collinson, D. (2006), 'Rethinking followership: A post-structuralist analysis of followership identities', *The Leadership Quarterly*, **17**(2), 179–89.

Converse, P.D. (1936), *Essentials of Distribution*, New York: Prentice Hall, Inc.

Conway, S. (1997), 'Informal networks of relationships in successful small firm innovation', in D. Jones-Evans & M. Klofsten (eds.), *Technology, Innovation and Enterprise: the European Experience*, Basingstoke: Macmillan.

Conway, S., O. Jones & F. Steward (2001), 'Realising the potential of the social network perspective in innovation studies', in O. Jones, S. Conway & S. Steward (eds.), *Social Interaction and Organizational Change: Aston Perspectives on Innovation Networks*, London: Imperial College Press.

Conway, S. & O. Jones (2006), 'Networking and the small business', in S. Carter & D. Jones- Evans (eds.) (2nd edition), *Enterprise and*

*Small Business. Principles, Practice and Policy*, Harlow, UK: Pearson Education.

Cook, G. (1992), *The Discourse of Advertising*, London: Routledge.

Copeland, M. (1923), 'The relations of consumer buying habits to marketing methods', *Harvard Business Review*, **1**(April), 282–9.

Coulter, M. (2001), *Entrepreneurship in Action*, Upper Saddle River: NJ: Prentice Hall.

Crane, F.G. (2013) (2nd edition), *Marketing for Entrepreneurs. Concepts and Applications for New Ventures*, Thousand Oaks, CA: Sage Publications, Inc.

Cresswell, T. (2004), *Place. A Short Introduction*, Oxford: Blackwell.

Cronon, W. (1992), 'Kennecott journey: The paths out of town', in W. Cronon, W. Miles & J. Gitlin (eds.), *Under an Open Sky*, New York: Norton.

Culliton, J.W. (1948), *The Management of Marketing Costs*, Boston: Harvard University Press.

Curran, J. & R.A. Blackburn (1991), *Paths of Enterprise*, London: Routledge.

Curran, J. & R.A. Blackburn (2001), *Researching the Small Enterprise*, Thousand Oaks, MA: USA: Sage.

Cyert, R.M. & J.G. March (1963), *A Behavioral Theory of the Firm*, Englewood Cliffs, NJ: Prentice Hall.

Czepiel, J.A. (1990), 'Service encounters and service relationships: Implications for research', *Journal of Business Research*, **20**(1), 13–21.

Dana, L.P. (1992), 'Entrepreneurial education in Europe', *Journal of Education in Business*, **68**(2), 74–9.

Dart, R. (2004), 'The legitimacy of social enterprise', *Non-profit Management & Leadership*, **14**(4), 411–24.

Davidsson, P. (1989), *Continuing Entrepreneurship and Small Firm Growth*, doctoral dissertation, Stockholm School of Economics.

Davidsson, P. (2003), 'The domain of entrepreneurship research: some suggestions', in D. Shepherd & J. Katz (eds.), *Cognitive Approaches to Entrepreneurship Research*, Amsterdam: Elsevier.

Davidsson, P. (2004), *Researching Entrepreneurship*, New York: Springer.

Davies, J.M. (1992), *The Essential Guide to Database Marketing*, Maidenhead: McGraw-Hill.

Davis, C. & L. Hulett (1999), 'Skills needs in the resource-based sectors in Atlantic Canada', presented at *Skills Development in the Knowledge-Based Economy*, Moncton, Canada.

de Certeau, M. (1984), *The Practice of Everyday Life*, Berkeley, CA: University of California Press.

Dees, J.G, J. Emerson & P. Economy (2001), *Enterprising Nonprofits. A Toolkit for Social Entrepreneurs*, New York: John Wiley and Sons.

Dees, J.G., J. Emerson & P. Economy (2002), *Strategic Tools for Social Entrepreneurs. Enhancing the Performance of Your Enterprising Nonprofit*, New York: John Wiley and Sons.

Deetz, S. (1998), 'Discursive formations, strategized subordination and self-surveillance', in A. McKinley & K. Starkey (eds.), *Foucault, Management and Organization Theory*, London: Sage.

Defourney, J. (2001), 'Introduction. From third sector to social enterprise', in C. Borzaga & J. Defourney (eds.), *The Emergence of Social Enterprise*, Oxon and New York: Routledge.

De Leeuw, E. (1999), 'Healthy cities: Urban social entrepreneurship for health', *Health Promotion International*, **14**(3), 261–9.

Delmar, F. (2006), 'The psychology of the entrepreneur', in S. Carter & D. Jones-Evans (eds.), *Enterprise and Small Business. Principles, Practice and Policy* (2nd edition), Harlow, UK: Pearson Education.

Delmar, F. & P. Davidsson (2000), 'Where do they come from? Prevalence and characteristics of nascent entrepreneurs', *Entrepreneurship and Regional Development*, **12**, 1–23.

Dennis, C. (2000), 'Networking for marketing advantage', *Management Decision*, **38**(4), 287–92.

De Pree, M. (2004), *Leadership is an Art*, New York: Crown.

Derrida, J. (1998), *Rösten och fenomenet* [The voice and the phenomenon], Stockholm: Thales.

Derrida, J. (2000), *Also ich tot wäre. Ein Interview mit Jacques Derrida* [Consequently, I would be dead. An interview with Jacques Derrida], Vienna: Turia+Kant.

DeRue, S. & S. Ashford (2010), 'Who will lead and who will follow? A social process of leadership identity construction in organizations', *Academy of Management Review*, **35**(4), 627–47.

de Saussure, F. (1974), *Course in General Linguistics*, London: Fontana.

Devins, D. & J. Gold (2002), 'Social constructionism: a theoretical framework to underpin support for the development of managers in SMEs?', *Journal of Small Business and Enterprise Development*, **9**(2), 111–19.

Dey, P. & C. Steyaert (2010), 'The politics of narrating social entrepreneurship', *Journal of Enterprising Communities*, **4**(1), 85–108.

Dollinger, M.C. (2003) (3rd edition), *Entrepreneurship, Strategies and Resources*, Upper Saddle River, NJ: Prentice Hall.

Dosi, G. (1988), 'Sources, procedures and microeconomic effects of innovation', *Journal of Economic Literature*, **36**, 1126–71.

Doyle, S.X. & G.T. Roth (1992), 'Selling and sales management in action: The use of insight coaching to improve relationship selling', *Journal of Personal Selling and Sales Management*, **12**(Winter), 59–64.

Dreyfus, H.L. & P. Rabinow (1982), *Michel Foucault – Beyond Structuralism and Hermeneutics*, London: Harvester Wheatsheaf.

Dru, J.M. (1996), *Disruption*, New York: John Wiley and Sons.

Dru, J.M. (2002), *Beyond Disruption*, New York: John Wiley and Sons.

Drucker, P. (1954), *The Practice of Management*, Amsterdam: Elsevier.

Drucker, P. (1985), *Innovation and Entrepreneurship. Practice and Principles*, London: Heinemann.

du Gay, P. (ed.) (1997), *The Production of Culture – Cultures of Production*, London: Sage.

Duncan, C.S. (1919), *Commercial Research*, New York: The Macmillan Company.

Dupuis, A. & A. de Bruin (2003), 'Community entrepreneurship', in A. de Bruin & A. Dupuis (eds.), *Entrepreneurship: New Perspectives in a Global Age*, Aldershot: Ashgate Publishing Limited.

Dupuis, A., A. de Bruin & R.D. Cremer (2003), 'Municipal-community entrepreneurship', in A. de Bruin & A. Dupuis (eds.), *Entrepreneurship: New Perspectives in a Global Age*, Aldershot: Ashgate Publishing Limited.

Dvir, T. & B. Shamir (2003), 'Follower development characteristics as predicting transformational leadership: A longitudinal field study', *The Leadership Quarterly*, **14**(3), 327–44.

Eklund, K. (2010) (12th edition), *Vår ekonomi – En introduktion till samhällsekonomin* [Our economy – An introduction to the economy of the society], Stockholm: Norstedt.

Ekman, R. & J. Hultman (eds.) (2007), *Plats som product* [Place as product], Lund: Studentlitteratur.

Emerson, J. (1999), 'Social return on investment: exploring aspects of social creation', *REDF box set 2*, Chapter 8, San Francisco, CA: Roberts Enterprise Development Foundation.

Emerson, J. & F. Twersky (1996), *New Social Entrepreneurs: The Success, Challenges and Lessons of Non-Profit Enterprise Creation*, San Francisco, CA: Roberts Enterprise Development Foundation.

Emory, C.W. (1985) (3rd edition), *Business Research Methods*, New York: Irwin.

EOS Gallup (2004), 'Flash 160 "Entrepreneurship"', survey for Directorate General Enterprise – European Commission, Brussels: EOS Gallup.

Estabrook, P.L. (1904), *Science of Salesmanship*, Dallas: University Textbook Co.

Evers, A. (2001), 'The significance of social capital in the multiple goal and resources structure of social enterprises', in C. Borzaga & J. Defourney (eds.), *The Emergence of Social Enterprise*, Oxon and New York: Routledge.

Fafchamps, M. (2000), 'Ethnicity and credit in African manufacturing', *Journal of Development Economics*, **61**, 205–35.

Fairhurst, G.T. & S.R. Hamlett (2003), 'The narrative basis of leader-member exchange', in G.B. Graen (ed.), *LMX Leadership: The Series*, Charlotte, NC: Information Age Publishers.

Fairhurst, G.T. & D. Grant (2010), 'The social construction of leadership: A sailing guide', *Management Communication Quarterly*, **24**(2), 171–210.

Fairhurst, G.T. & M. Uhl-Bien (2012), 'Organizational discourse analysis (ODA): Examining leadership as a relational process', *The Leadership Quarterly*, **23**(6), 1043–62.

Favreau, L. (2000), 'The social economy and globalization: an overview', in J. Defourney, P. Develtere & B. Foneneau (eds.), *Social Economy North and South*, Belgium: Catholic University of Leuvren and University of Liege.

Fay, B. (1996), *Contemporary Philosophy of Social Science*, Oxford: Blackwell Publishers.

Fiedler, F.E. (1967), *A Theory of Leadership Effectiveness*, New York: McGraw-Hill.

Fiet, J.O. (2001), 'Education for entrepreneurial competency: a theory-based activity approach', in R.H. Brockhaus, G.E. Hills, H. Klandt & H.P. Welch (eds.), *Entrepreneurship Education*, Aldershot: Ashgate Publishing Limited.

Firat, A.F., N. Dholakia & A. Venkatesh (1995), 'Liberatory postmodernism and the reenchantment of consumption', *Journal of Consumer Research*, **22**(3), 239–67.

Firat, A.F. & N. Dholakia (1998), *Consuming People: From Political Economy to Theaters of Consumption*, New York: Routledge.

Fisk, G. (1967), *Marketing Systems: An Introductory Analysis*, New York: Harper & Row.

Flora, J.L. (1998), 'Social capital and communities of place', *Rural Sociology*, **63**, 481–506.

Florida, R. (2002), *The Rise of the Creative Class*, New York, NY: Basic Books.

Florida, R. (2003), 'Cities and the venture class', *City & Community*, **2**(1), March, 3–19.

Ford, D. (1990) (red), *Understanding Business Markets: Interactions, Relationships and Networks*, London: Academic Press.

Ford, D. (1998) (ed.), *Managing Business Relationships*, Chichester, UK: John Wiley & Sons.

Forsyth, D.R. (2009), *Entrepreneurship Education*, Aldershot: Ashgate Publishing Limited.

Foucault, M. (1972), *The Archeology of Knowledge*, London: Routledge.

Frankelius, P., C. Norrman & A. Parment (2015), *Marknadsföring. Vetenskap och praktik* [Marketing. Science and practice], Lund: Studentlitteratur.

Franzén, M., N. Hertting & C. Thörn (2016), *Stad till salu. Entreprenörsur banismen och det offentliga rummets värde* [City for sale. Entrepreneurial urbanism and the value of the public room], Gothenburg: Daidalos.

Freel, M. (2000), 'External linkages and product innovation in small manufacturing firms', *Entrepreneurship and Regional Development*, **12**, 245–66.

Fromm, E. (1976), *To Have or to Be?* New York and London: Continuum.

Fukyama, F. (1995), *Trust: The Social Virtues and the Creation of Prosperity*, London: Penguin.

Fyall, A. & B. Garrod (2005), *Tourism Marketing – A Collaborative Approach. Aspects of Tourism 18*, Clevedon, UK: Channel View Publications.

Gaglio, C.M. (1997), 'Opportunity recognition: Review, critique and suggested research directions', in J. Katz & R.H. Brockhaus (eds.), *Advances in Entrepreneurship, Firm Emergence and Growth*, Greenwich, CT: JAI Press.

Gaglio, C.M. & J.M. Katz (2001), 'The psychological basis of opportunity identification: entrepreneurial alertness', *Small Business Economics*, **16**, 95–111.

Gardner, H. (2011), *Leading Minds*, New York: Basic Books.

Gardner, J.W. (1990), *On Leadership*, New York: The Free Press.

Gardner, W.L., B.J. Avolio, F. Luthans, D.R. May & F. Walumbwa (2005), '"Can you see the real me?" A self-based model of authentic leader and follower development', *The Leadership Quarterly*, **16**(3), 343–72.

Garfinkel, H. (1967), *Studies in Ethnomethodology*, Englewood Cliffs, NJ: Prentice Hall.

Garfinkel, H. (1974), 'On the origins of the term "ethnomethodology"', in R. Turner (ed.), *Ethnomethodology*, Harmondsworth, UK: Penguin.

Gartner, W.B. (1988), 'Who is the entrepreneur? is the wrong question', *American Journal of Small Business*, **12**(4), 11–32.

Gartner, W.B. (2007), 'Entrepreneurial narrative and a science of the imagination', *Journal of Business Venturing*, **22**(5), 613–27.

Gartner, W.B., B.J. Bird & J.A. Starr (1992), 'Acting as if: differentiating entrepreneurial from organizational behavior', *Entrepreneurship Theory and Action*, **16**, Spring, 13–30.

Garud, R., A. Kumaraswamy & P. Nayyar (1998), 'Real options of fool's gold. Perspective makes the difference', *Academy of Management Review*, **3**(2), 212–4.

Gawell, M. (2009), 'Samhällsentreprenörskap för en global utveckling'

[Social entrepreneurship for global development], in M. Gawell, B. Johannisson & M. Lundqvist (eds.) (2009), *Samhällets entreprenörer* [The entrepreneurs of the society], Stockholm: KK- stiftelsen.

Gawell, M., B. Johannisson & M. Lundqvist (eds.) (2009), *Samhällets entreprenörer* [The entrepreneurs of the society], Stockholm: KK-stiftelsen.

Geertz, C. (1973), *The Interpretation of Cultures*, London: Fontana Press.

George, B. (2003), *Authentic Leadership: Rediscovering the Secrets to Creating Lasting Value*, San Francisco, CA: Jossey-Bass.

Gephart, R.P.J. (1993), 'The textual approach: risk and blame in disaster sensemaking', *Academy of Management Journal*, **36**(6), 74–81.

Gergen, K.J. (1999), *An Invitation to Social Constructionism*, Thousand Oaks, CA: Sage Publications.

Gibson, D. (1991), *Technology Companies and Global Markets: Programs, Policies and Strategies to Accelerate Innovation and Entrepreneurship*, Lanham, MD: Rowman and Littlechild.

Gioia, D.A. (1986), 'Symbols, scripts and sensemaking: Creating meaning in organizational experience', in H.P. Sims & D.A. Gioia (eds.), *The Thinking Organization*, San Francisco, CA: Jossey-Bass Publishers.

Gladwell, M. (2000), *The Tipping Point: How Little Things Can Make a Big Difference*, New York: Little, Brown and Company.

*Global Entrepreneurship Monitor*. Executive Report, 2007.

Goffman, E. (1959), *The Presentation of Self in Everyday Life*, New York: Doubleday Anchor.

Gorz, A. (1999), *Reclaiming Work*, Cambridge: Polity Press.

Graen, G.B. & M. Uhl-Bien (1995), 'Relationship-based approach to leadership: Development of leader-member exchange (LMX) theory of leadership over 25 years: Applying a multi-level multi-domain perspective', *The Leadership Quarterly*, **6**(2), 219–47.

Grenier, P. (2009), 'Social entrepreneurship in the UK: from rhetoric to reality?' in R. Ziegler (ed.), *An Introduction to Social Entrepreneurship*, Cheltenham, UK and Northampton, MA, USA: Edward Elgar Publishing.

Grönroos, C. (1979), *Marknadsföring av tjänster. En studie av marknadsfunktionen i tjänsteföretag* [Marketing of services. A study of the market function in service companies], doctoral dissertation, Swedish School of Economics and Business Administration, Helsinki, Finland.

Grönroos, C. (1983), *Strategic Management and Marketing in the Service Sector*, Cambridge, MA: Marketing Science Institute.

Grönroos, C. (1990), 'Relationships approach to marketing in service contexts: The marketing and organizational behavior interface', *Journal of Business Research*, **20**, 3–11.

Grönroos, C. (1991), 'The marketing strategy continuum: A marketing concept for the 1990s', *Management Decision*, **79**(2), 7–23.

Grönroos, C. (1994), 'Quo vadis, marketing? Toward a relationship marketing paradigm', *Journal of Marketing Management*, **10**, 347–60.

Guba, E. (1990), *The Paradigm Dialogue*, Beverly Hills, CA: Sage.

Gummesson, E. (1975), *Marknadsfunktionen i företaget [The marketing function of the company]*, Stockholm: Norstedts.

Gummesson, E. (1977), *Marknadsföring och inköp av konsulttjänster* [Marketing and purchasing consulting purchases], Stockholm: Stockholm University.

Gummesson, E. (1979), *Models of Professional Service Marketing*, Stockholm: LIBER/MTC.

Gummesson, E. (1990), *The Part-Time Marketer*, Stockholm: Norstedts.

Gummesson, E. (1991), 'Marketing revisited: The crucial role of the part-time marketers', *European Journal of Marketing*, **25**(2), 60–7.

Gummesson, E. (1999), *Total Relationship Marketing: From the 4Ps – Product, Price, Promotion, Place – of Traditional Marketing Management to the 30Rs – The Thirty Relations*, Oxford: Butterworth-Heinemann.

Gupta, V., I.C. MacMillan & G. Surie (2004), 'Entrepreneurial leadership: developing and measuring a cross-cultural construct', *Construct of Business Venturing*, **19**(2), 241–60.

Habermas, J. (1984), *The Theory of Communicative Action*, Cambridge: Polity Press.

Habermas, J. (1996), *Between Facts and Norms*, Cambridge, MA: MIT Press.

Hacking, I. (1999), *Social konstruktion av vad?* [Social construction or what?] Stockholm: Thales.

Hackley, C.E. (1998), 'Social constructionism and research in marketing and advertising', *Qualitative Market Research: An International Journal*, **1**(3), 125–31.

Hall, T. (2005) (3rd edition), *Urban Geography*, London: Routledge.

Hamel, G. & C.K. Prahalad (1992), 'Corporate imagination and expeditionary marketing', *Harvard Business Review*, **69**(4), 31–43.

Hansen, F. (1972), *Consumer Choice Behavior: A Cognitive Theory*, New York: Free Press.

Harding, S. (1986), *The Science Question in Feminism*, London: Cornell University Press.

Hardt, M. (2002), *Gilles Deleuze. An Apprenticeship of Philosophy*, Minneapolis, MN: University of Minnesota Press.

Harre, R. (1998), *The Singular Self: An Introduction to the Psychology of Personhood*, London: Sage.

Harvey, D. (1989), 'From managerialism to entrepreneurialism: the transformance of governance to late capitalism', *Geografiska Annaler*, **71B**, 3–17.

Heath, C. & P. Luff (2007), 'Ordering competition: The interactional accomplishment of the sale of fine art and antiques at auction', *British Journal of Sociology*, **58**(2), 63–85.

Hébert, R.F & A.N. Link (1989), 'In search of the meaning of entrepreneurship', *Small Business Economics*, **1**(1), 39–49.

Heidegren, C.-G. & D. Wästerfors (2008), *Den interagerande människan* [The interacting human being], Malmö: Gleerups.

Henton, D., J. Melville & K. Walesh (1997), *Grassroots Leaders for a New Economy. How Civic Entrepreneurs are Building Prosperous Communities*, San Francisco, CA: Jossey-Bass.

Hersey, P. & K.H. Blanchard (1969), *Management of Organizational Behavior – Utilizing Human Resources*, Upper Saddle River, NJ: Prentice Hall.

Hill, S. & G. Rifkin (1999), *Radical Marketing: From Harvard to Harley, Lessons from Ten that Broke the Rules and Made it Big*, New York: HarperCollins.

Hite, J. & W. Hesterley (2001), 'The evolution of firm networks: from emergence to early growth of the firm', *Strategic Management Journal*, **22**(3), 275–86.

Hjorth, D. (2004), 'Creating space for play/invention – concepts of space and organizational entrepreneurship', *Entrepreneurship and Regional Development*, **16**(September), 413–32.

Hjorth, D. (2009), 'Entrepreneurship, sociality and art: re-imaging the public', in R. Ziegler (ed.), *An Introduction to Social Entrepreneurship*, Cheltenham, UK and Northampton, MA, USA: Edward Elgar Publishing.

Hjorth, D. & B. Johannisson (1998), 'Entreprenörskap som skapelseprocess och ideologi', in C. Czarniawska (ed.), *Organisationsteori på svenska* [Organization theory in Swedish], Malmö: Liber Ekonomi.

Hjorth, D. & C. Steyaert (2003), 'Entrepreneurship beyond (a new) economy: creative swarms and pathological zones', in C. Steyaert & D. Hjorth (eds.), *New Movements in Entrepreneurship*, Cheltenham, UK and Northampton, MA, USA: Edward Elgar Publishing.

Hjorth, D. & C. Steyaert (eds.) (2004), *Narrative and Discursive Approaches in Entrepreneurship. A Second Movements in Entrepreneurship Books*, Cheltenham, UK and Northampton, MA, USA: Edward Elgar Publishing.

Hjorth, D. & B. Bjerke (2006), 'Public entrepreneurship: moving from social/consumer to public/citizen', in C. Steyaert & D. Hjorth (eds.), *Entrepreneurship as Social Change*, Cheltenham, UK and Northampton, MA, US: Edward Elgar Publishing.

Hjorth, D. & C. Steyaert (eds.) (2009), *The Politics and Aesthetics of Entrepreneurship. A Fourth Movements in Entrepreneurship Books*, Cheltenham, UK and Northampton, MA, USA: Edward Elgar Publishing.

Hoang, H. & B. Antoncic (2003), 'Network-based research in entrepreneurship. A critical Review', *Journal of Business Venturing*, **18**, 165–87.

Hollander, E.P. (1992), 'The essential interdependence of leadership and followership', *Current Directions in Psychological Science*, **1**(2), 71–5.

Hollander, E.P. (1993), 'The toxic triangle: Destructive leaders, susceptible followers, and conducive environments', *The Leadership Quarterly*, **18**(3), 176–94.

Holloway, R.J. & R.S. Hancock (1964), *The Environment of Marketing Behavior: Selections from the Literature*, New York: John Wiley & Sons.

Holstein, J.A. & J.F. Gubrium, J.F. (1997), 'Active interviewing', in D. Silverman (ed.), *Qualitative Research Theory, Method and Practice*, Thousand Oaks, CA: Sage.

Hoption, C.B., A.M. Christie & J. Barling (2012), 'Submitting to the follower label: Followership, positive affect and extra-role behaviors', *Journal of Psychology*, **220**, 221–30.

Howard, J. (1957), *Marketing Management: Analysis and Decisions*, Homewood, IL: Richard D. Irwin.

Howard, J. (1963), *Marketing: Executive and Buyer Behavior*, New York: Columbia University Press.

Howard, J. & J. Sheth (1969), *The Theory of Buyer Behavior*, New York: Wiley.

Howell, J & B. Shamir (2005), 'The role of followers in the charismatic leadership process: Relationships and their consequences', *Academy of Management Review*, **30**(1), 96–112.

Howell, J. & M. Mendez (2008), 'Three perspectives on followership', in R. Riggio, I. Chaleff & J. Lipman-Blumen (eds.), *The Art of Followership: How Great Followers Create Great Leaders and Organizations*, San Francisco, CA: Jossey-Bass.

Hoyt, C.W. (1913), *Scientific Sales Management*, New York: George B. Woolson & Co.

Hudson, R. (2000), *Production, Places and Environment: Changing Perspectives in Economic Geography*, Harlow, UK: Prentice Hall.

Hudson, R. (2001), *Producing Places*, London: Guilford Press.

Hunt, S.D. (1976), 'The nature and scope of marketing', *Journal of Marketing*, **40**(July), 17–28.

Hunt, S.D. (1977), 'The three dichotomies models of marketing: An elaboration of issues', in C.C. Slater (ed.), *Macro-Marketing: Distributive Processes from a Societal Perspective*, Boulder, CO: Business Research

Division, Graduate School of Business Administration, University of Colorado.

Hunt, S.D. (1983), 'General theories and the fundamental explanada of marketing', *Journal of Marketing*, **47**(Fall), 9–17.

Hunt, S.D. & R.M. Morgan (1994), 'Relationship marketing in the era of network competition', *Marketing Management*, **3**(1), 19–28.

Hyman, H.H., W.J. Cobb, J.J. Feldman, C.W. Hart & C.H. Stember (1975), *Interviewing in Social Research*, Chicago, IL: University of Chicago Press.

Håkansson, H. (1982) (ed.), *International Marketing and Purchasing of Industrial Goods – An Interactive Approach*, Chichester, UK: John Wiley & Sons.

Ilies, R., F.P. Morgeson & J.D. Nahrgang (2005), 'Authentic leadership and eudaemonic well-being: Understanding leader-follower outcomes', *Leadership Quarterly*, **16**(3), 373–94.

Industrial Marketing Committee Review Board (1954), 'Fundamental differences between industrial and consumer marketing', *Journal of Marketing*, **19**(October), 152–8.

Israel, J. (1979), *Om relationistisk socialpsykologi* [About relationistic social psychology], Göteborg: Bokförlaget Korpen.

Jackson, B.B. (1985), *Winning and Keeping Industrial Customers*, Lexington, KY: Lexington Books.

Jacob, F. (1977), 'Evolution and tinkering', *Science*, **196**, 1161–6.

Jacobs, J. (1961), *The Death and Life of Great American Cities*, New York: Random House.

Jarillo, J. (1989), 'Entrepreneurship and growth: the strategic use of external resources', *Journal of Business Venturing*, **4**(2), 133–47.

Jaworski, B.J. & A.K. Kohli (1993), 'Market orientation: antecedents and consequences', *Journal of Marketing*, **57**(July), 53–70.

Jessop, B. (1997), 'The governance of complexity of governance: preliminary remarks on some problem and limits of economic guidance', in A. Amin & J. Hausner (eds.), *Beyond Markets and Hierarchy. Third Way Approaches to Transformation*, Cheltenham, UK: Edward Elgar Publishing.

Johannisson, B. (2000), 'Networking and entrepreneurial growth', in D.L. Sexton & H. Landström (eds.), *The Blackwell Handbook of Entrepreneurship*, Oxford: Blackwell Publishers Ltd.

Johannisson, B. (2005), *Entreprenörskapets väsen* [The essence of entrepreneurship], Lund: Studentlitteratur.

Johannisson, B. & R. Peterson (1984), 'The personal networks of entrepreneurs", presented at *Third Canadian Conference of the International Council for Small Business*, Toronto.

Johannisson, B. & A. Nilsson (1989), 'Community entrepreneurs: networking for local development', *Entrepreneurship and Regional Development*, **1**, 3–19.

Johansson, A.W. (2010), 'Innovation, creativity and imitation', in F. Bill, B. Bjerke & A.W. Johansson (eds.), *(De)mobilizing the Entrepreneurship Discourse. Exploring Entrepreneurial Thinking and Action*, Cheltenham, UK and Northampton, MA, USA: Edward Elgar Publishing.

Johansson, J. & J.-E. Vahlne (1977), 'The internationalization process of the firm – a model of knowledge development and increasing foreign market commitments', *Journal of International Business Studies*, Spring/Summer, 23–32.

Johansson, J. & L.-G. Mattson (1993), 'The markets-as-networks tradition in Sweden', in G. Laurent (ed.), *Research Traditions in Marketing*, Dordrecht: Kluwer.

Johansson Lindfors, M.-B. (1993), *Att utveckla kunskap* [To develop knowledge], Lund: Studentlitteratur.

Johansson, S.-G. (1991), 'Marknadsföringsbegreppet – förr, nu och framöver' [The marketing concept – before, now and in the future], in A. Ewerman, O. Holm & T. Nordlinder (eds.), *Reflektioner människa och marknad* [Reflections on human and market], Stockholm: RMI- Berghs.

Johnstone, H. & R. Haddow (2003), 'Industrial decline and high technology renewal in Cape Breton: exploring the limits of the possible', in D. Wolfe (ed.), *Clusters Old and New: The Transition to a Knowledge Economy in Canada's Regions*, Kingston, Quebec: McGill-Queen's University Press.

Johnstone, H. & D. Lionais (1999), 'Identifying equity gaps in a depleted local economy', presented at *Canadian Council for Entrepreneurship and Small Business Annual Conference*, Banff, Alberta, Canada.

Johnstone, H. & D. Lionais (2000), 'Using Pareto distributions to better characterize equity gaps and improve estimates of informal venture capital', presented at *Frontiers of Entrepreneurship Research Conference 2000*, Kauffman Center for Entrepreneurship Leadership, Babson College, Wellesley, MA, USA.

Johnstone, H. & D. Lionais (2004), 'Depleted communities and community business entrepreneurship: revaluing space through place', *Entrepreneurship and Regional Development*, **16**, May, 217–33.

Jones, O., C. Carduso & M. Beckinsale (1997), 'Mature SMEs and technological innovation: entrepreneurial networks in the UK and Portugal', *International Journal of Innovation Management*, **1**(3), 201–27.

Jones, C. & A. Spicer (2009), *Unmasking the Entrepreneur*, Cheltenham, UK and Northampton, MA, USA: Edward Elgar Publishing.

Judd, R.C. (1964), 'The case of redefining services', *Journal of Marketing*, **28**(January), 58–9.

Kanter, R.M. (1983), *The Change Masters: Innovation and Entrepreneurship in the American Corporation*, New York: Simon & Schuster.

Katona, G. (1953), 'Rational behavior and economic behavior', *Psychological Review*, **60**(September), 307–18.

Katz, D. & R.L. Kahn (1978) (2nd edition), *The Social Psychology of Organizations*, New York: John Wiley & Sons.

Katz, E. & P.F. Lazarsfeld (1955), *Personal Influence: The Part Played by People in the Flow of Mass Communications*, New York: The Free Press.

Katz, J.A. (1998), 'A brief history of tertiary entrepreneurship education in the United States', presented at *Entrepreneurship Education Workshop*, Esbri, Stockholm.

Katz, J. (2003), 'The chronology and intellectual trajectory of American entrepreneurship education – 1876–1999', *Journal of Business Venturing*, **18**, 283–300.

Keith, R. (1960), 'The marketing revolution', *Journal of Marketing*, **24**(January), 35–8.

Keller, E.F. (1985), *Reflections on Gender and Science*, New Haven, CT: Yale University Press.

Kellerman, B. (2008), *Followership: How Followers are Creating Change and Changing Leaders*, Boston: Harvard Business Press.

Kelley, E. (1972), *Marketing Planning and Competitive Strategy*, Englewood Cliffs, NJ: Prentice Hall.

Kelley, M. & H. Brooks (1991), 'External learning opportunities and the diffusion of process innovations to small firms: the case of programmable automation', *Technological Forecasting and Social Change*, **39**, 103–25.

Kelley, R.E. (1988), 'In praise of followers', *Harvard Business Review*, **66**, 142–8.

Kelley, R.E. (1992), *The Power of Followership*, New York: The Double Day Business.

Kelley, R.E. (2008), 'Rethinking followership', in R. Riggio, I. Chaleff & J. Lipman-Blumen (eds.), *The Art of Followership: How Great Followers Create Great Leaders and Organizations*, San Francisco, CA: Jossey-Bass.

Kelley, S., J. Donnelly & S.J. Skinner (1990), 'Customer participation in service production and delivery', *Journal of Retailing*, **66**(3), 315–35.

Kelly, G.A. (1955), *The Psychology of Personal Constructs*, New York: Norton.

Kelly, K. (1998), *Den nya ekonomin. 10 strategier för en uppkopplad värld*

[The new economy. 10 strategies for a connected world], Stockholm: Timbro.

Kickul, J., M.D. Griffiths & L. Gundry (2010), 'Innovating for social impact: Is bricolage the catalyst for change?', in A. Fayolle and H. Matlay (eds.), *Handbook of Research on Social Entrepreneurship*, Cheltenham, UK and Northampton, MA: USA: Edward Elgar.

Kilkenny, M., L. Nalbarte & T. Besser (1999), 'Reciprocated community support and small town-small business sector', *Entrepreneurship and Regional Development*, **11**, 321–46.

Kirzner, I.M. (1973), *Competition and Entrepreneurship*, Chicago, IL: University of Chicago Press.

Kirzner, I.M. (1979), *Perception, Opportunity, and Profit*, Chicago, IL: University of Chicago Press.

Klein, N. (2000), *No Logo. Märkena, Marknaden, Motståndet* [No logo. Taking aim at the brand bullies], Stockholm: Ordfront Förlag.

Kohli, A.K. & B.J. Jaworski (1990), 'Market orientation. The construct, research propositions, and management implications', *Journal of Marketing* (April), 1–18.

Kotler, P. (1967), *Marketing Management: Analysis, Planning, and Control*, Englewood Cliffs, NJ: Prentice Hall.

Kotler, P. (1972), 'A generic concept of marketing', *Journal of Marketing*, **36**(April), 46–54.

Kotler, P. (1986), 'Megamarketing', *Harvard Business Review*, **64**(March-April), 117–24.

Kotler, P. (2001), *A Framework for Marketing Management*, Upper Saddle River, NJ: Prentice Hall.

Kotler, P. (2002), *Marketing Management*, Englewood Cliffs, NJ: Prentice Hall.

Kotler, P. (2015), *Marketing Management, Global Edition*, London: Pearson Education.

Kotler, P. & S.J. Levy (1969), 'Broadening the concept of marketing', *Journal of Marketing*, **33**(January), 10–15.

Kotler, P., G. Armstrong, V. Wong & J. Saunders (2008) (5th edition), *Principles of Marketing*, Upper Saddle River, NJ: Pearson Prentice Hall.

Krashinsky, M. (1998), *Does Auspice Matter? The Case of Day for Children in Canada*, New Haven, CT and London: Yale University Press.

Kreiner, K. & M. Schultz (1993), 'Informal collaboration in R&D: the formation of networks across organizations', *Organization Studies*, **14**(2), 189–209.

Krugman, H. (1965), 'The impact of television advertising: Learning without involvement', *Public Opinion Quarterly*, **29**(Fall), 349–59.

Kuhn, T. (1962), *The Structure of Scientific Revolutions*, Chicago, IL: University of Chicago Press.

Kuratko, D.F. & R.M. Hodgetts (2004) (6th edition), *Entrepreneurship. Theory, Process, Practice*, Stanford, CT: Thomson South-Western.

Landström, H. & M. Löwegren (eds.) (2009), *Entreprenörskap och företagsetablering. Från idé till verklighet* [Entrepreneurship and business etablishment. From idea to reality], Lund: Studentlitteratur.

Langerak, F. (1997), 'The effects of market orientation on business performance in industrial markets', doctoral dissertation, Erasmus University, Rotterdam: Holland.

Langerak, F., H. Commandeur, R. Frambach & M. Napel (1997), 'The moderating influence of strategy on the market orientation-performance relationship', in W.M. Pride & G.T.M. Hult (eds.), *Enhancing Knowledge Development in Marketing*, 1997 AMA Educators' Proceedings, **8**, Chicago, IL: American Marketing Association.

Lanzara, G.F. (1999), 'Between transient constructs and persistent structures: Designing systems in action', *Journal of Strategic Information Systems*, **8**, 331–49.

Larsson, M. & S. Lundholm (2013), 'Talking work in a bank: A study of organizing properties of leadership in work interactions', *Human Relations*, **66**(8), 1101–29.

La Salle, D. & T.A. Britton (2002), *Priceless: Turning Ordinary Products into Extraordinary Experiences*, Boston: Harvard Business School Press.

Latour, B. (1993), *We Have Never Been Modern*, Boston: Harvard University Press.

Latour, B. (1998), *Artefaktens återkomst* [Return of the artefact], Stockholm: Nerenius & Santérus Förlag.

Laville, J.-L. & M. Nyssens (2001), 'Towards a socio-economic approach', in C. Borzaga & J. Defourney (eds.), *The Emergence of Social Enterprise*, Oxon and New York: Routledge.

Leadbeater, C. (1997), *The Rise of the Social Entrepreneur*, London: Demos.

Leana, C.R. & van Buren, H.J. (1999), 'Organizational social capital and employment practices', *Academy of Management Review*, **24**, 538–54.

Lechner, C. & M. Dowling (2003), 'Firm networks: external relationships as sources for the growth and competitiveness of entrepreneurial firms', *Entrepreneurship and Regional Development*, **15**(1), 1–26.

Lekvall, P. & C. Wahlbin (2001) (4th edition), *Information för marknadsförings-beslut* [Information for marketing decisions], Lund: Studentlitteratur.

Levine, R., C. Locke, D. Searls & D. Weinberger (2001), *The Cluetrain Manifesto: The End of Business as Usual*, Cambridge, MA: Perseus Publishing.

Levinson, C. (1993), *Guerilla Marketing: Secrets for Making Big Profits from Your Small Business*, Boston: Houghton Mifflin Company.

Lévi-Strauss (1966), *The Savage Mind*, Chicago, IL: The University of Chicago Press.

Levitt, T. (1960), 'Marketing myopia', *Harvard Business Review*, **38**(November/December), 45–6.

Levitt, T. (1965), 'Exploit the product life cycle', *Harvard Business Review*, **43**(November/December), 81–94.

Levy, S.J. (1959), 'Symbols for sale', *Harvard Business Review*, **37**(July-Aug), 117–24.

Li, F., B.A. Greenberg & T. Li (1997), 'Toward a general definition of relationship marketing', in W.M. Pride & G.T.M. Hult (eds.), *Enhancing Knowledge Development in Marketing*, 1997 AMA Educators' Proceedings, Vol. 8, Chicago, IL: American Marketing Association.

Liedman, S.-E. (2002), *Ett oändligt äventyr* [One eternal adventure], Stockholm: Albert Bonniers Förlag.

Lindgren, M. & J. Packendorff (2007), *Konstruktion av entreprenörskap. Teori, praktik och interaktion* [Construction of entrepreneurship. Theory, practice and interaction], Stockholm: Forum för småföretagsforskning.

Lord, R.G., D.J. Brown & S.J. Freiburg (1999), 'Understanding the dynamics of leadership: The role of follower self-concepts in the leader/follower relationship', *Organizational Behavior and Human Decision Processes*, **78**(3), 167–203.

Lord, R.G. & D.J. Brown (2004), *Leadership Processes and Follower Self-Identity*, Mahwah, NJ: Lawrence Erlbaum Associates Publishers.

Low, M.B. (2001), 'The adolescence of entrepreneurship research: specification of purpose', *Entrepreneurship Theory and Practice*, **25**(4), 17–25.

Lundqvist, M. (2009), 'Den tekniska högskolan på den samhällsentreprenöriella arenan' [The institute of technology on the social entrepreneurial arena], in M. Gawell, B. Johannisson & M. Lundqvist (eds.), *Samhällets entreprenörer* [The entrepreneurs in the society], Stockholm: KK-stiftelsen.

Lusch, R.F. & S.L. Vargo (2006), 'Service-dominant logic: reactions, reflections and refinements', *Marketing Theory*, **6**, 281–8.

MacKinnon, D., A. Cumbers & K. Chapman (2002), 'Learning, innovation and regional development: a critical appraisal of recent debates', *Progress in Human Geography*, **26**(3), 293–311.

Malpas, S. (2005), *The Postmodern*, London: Routledge.

Maravelias, C. (2009), 'Freedom, opportunism and entrepreneurialism in post-bureaucratic organizations', in D. Hjorth & C. Steyaert (eds.), *The Politics and Aesthetics of Entrepreneurship. A Fourth Movements in Entrepreneurship Book*, Cheltenham, UK and Northampton, MA: USA: Edward Elgar.

March, J.G. & H.A. Simon (1958), *Organizations*, New York: John Wiley & Sons.

Margetta, J. (2002), 'Why business models matter', *Harvard Business Review*, **80**(5), 86–92.

Mariotti, S. & C. Glackin (2010) (2nd edition), *Entrepreneurship*, Upper Saddle River, NJ: Prentice Hall.

Marketing Staff of the Ohio State University (1965), 'Statement of marketing philosophy', *Journal of Marketing*, **29**(January), 43–4.

Martin, F. & M. Thompson (2010), *Social Enterprise: Developing Sustainable Businesses*, Basingstoke: Palgrave Macmillan.

Martin, L.H., H. Guttmann & P.H. Hutton (1988), *Technologies of the Self – A Seminar with Michel Foucault*, Amherst, MA: University of Massachusetts Press.

Martineau, P. (1958), 'Social class and spending behavior', *Journal of Marketing,* **23**(October), 121–9.

Martinko, M., P. Harvey, D. Sikora & S. Douglas (2011), 'Perceptions of abusive supervision: The role of subordinates' attributional styles', *The Leadership Quarterly*, **22**(4), 751–64.

Marx, K. (1867/1985), *Kapitalet* [The capital], Lund: Arkiv förlag/A-Z förlag.

Massey, D. (1995a), *Spatial Divisions of Labour: Social Structures and the Geography of Production*, London: Macmillan.

Massey, D. (1995b), 'The conceptualization of place' in D. Massey & P. Jess (eds.), *A Place in the World*, Oxford: Oxford University Press.

Mauss, M. (1985), 'A category of the human mind: the notion of the person: the notion of self' in M. Carrithers, S. Collins & S. Lukes (eds.), *The Category of the Person*, Cambridge: Cambridge University Press.

Maxmin, J. & S. Zuboff (2002), *The Support Economy*, New York: Viking Penguin.

May, D.R., A.Y.L. Chan, T.D. Hodges & B.J. Avolio (2003), 'Developing the moral component of authentic leadership', *Organizational Dynamics*, **32**, 247–60.

McCarthy, E.J. (1960), *Basic Marketing: A Managerial Approach*, Homewood, IL: Irwin.

McClelland, D. (1961), *The Achieving Society*, Princeton, NJ: D. van Nostrand.

McKenna, R. (1991), *Relationship Marketing. Successful Strategies for the Ages of the Customer*, New York: Addison-Wesley.

McKitterick, B. (1957), 'What is the marketing management concept', in

F. Bass (ed.), *The Frontiers of Marketing Thought and Action*, Chicago, IL: AMA.

McLuhan, M. (1964), *Understanding Media: The Extensions of Man*, Cambridge, MA: MIT Press.

Mead, G.H. (1934), *Mind, Self and Society from the Standpoint of a Social Behaviorist*, Chicago, IL: Chicago University Press.

Menger, C. (1871/1981), *Principles of Economics*, translated by J. Dingwall & B.F. Hoselitz, New York: New York University Press.

Michel, S., S.L. Vargo & R.F. Lusch (2008), 'Reconfiguration of the conceptual landscape: A tribute to the service logic of Richard Normann', *Journal of the Academy of Marketing Science*, **36**, 152–5.

Milgram, S. (1965), 'Some conditions of obedience and disobedience to authority', *Human Relations*, **18**(1), 57–76.

Milgram, S. (1974), *Obedience to Authority: An Experimental View*, New York: Harper & Row.

Miller, J. & B. Glassner, (1997) 'The "inside" and the "outside": Finding realities in interviews', in D. Silverman (ed.), *Qualitative Research Theory, Method and Practice*, Thousand Oaks, CA: Sage.

Miller, J. & L. Hoogstra (1992), 'Language as a tool in the socialisation and apprehension of cultural meanings', in T. Schwartz, G. White & C. Lutz (eds.), *New Directions in Psychological Anthropology*, Cambridge: Cambridge University Press.

Miner, A.S., P. Bassoff & C. Moorman (2001), 'Organizational improvisation and learning. A field study', *Administrative Science Quarterly*, **46**, 304–37.

Morgan, A. (2009) (2nd edition), *Eating the Big Fish*, Hoboken, NJ: John Wiley & Sons.

Morris, M.H., M. Schindehutte & R.W. LaForge (2002), 'Entrepreneurial marketing: A construct for integrating emerging entrepreneurship and marketing perspectives', *Journal of Marketing*, Fall, 1–19.

Morris, H.M., M. Schindehutte & J. Allen (2005), 'The entrepreneur's business model: Toward a unified perspective', *Journal of Business*, **58**(6), 726–35.

Mort, G., J. Weerawardena & K. Carnegie (2003), 'Social entrepreneurship: towards conceptualization', *Nonprofit and Voluntary Sector Marketing*, **8**(1), 76–88.

Mulgan, G. (2006), 'Cultivating the other invisible hand of social entrepreneurship: comparative advantage, public policy, and future research priorities', in A. Nicholls (ed.), *Social Entrepreneurship: New Models of Sustainable Social Change*, Oxford: Oxford University Press.

Mullins, J.W. (2013) (4th edition), *The New Business Road Test*, London: Prentice Hall.

Murray, R. (2009), *Danger and Opportunity. Crisis and the New Social Economy*, National Endowment for Science, Technology and the Art: UK.

Nahapiet, J. & S. Ghoshal (1998), 'Social capital, intellectual capital and the organizational advantage', *Academy of Management Review*, **23**, 242–67.

Narver, J. & S.F. Slater (1990), 'The effects of market orientation on business profitability', *Journal of Marketing*, **54**(October), 20–35.

New Economics Foundation (2004), *Social Return on Investment: Valuing What Matters*, London: New Economics Foundation.

Newman, J. (2001), *Modernising Governance: New Labour, Policy and Society*, London: Sage.

Nicholls, A. (2006), 'Social entrepreneurship', in S. Carter & D. Jones-Evans (eds.) (2nd edition), *Enterprise and Small Business. Principles, Practice and Policy*, Harlow, UK: Pearson Education.

Nicholls, A. (2010), 'The legitimacy of social entrepreneurship: reflexive isomorphism in a pre-paradigmatic field', *Entrepreneurship Theory and Practice*, July, 611–33.

Nilsson, N. (2003), *Entreprenörens blick* [The entrepreneur's look], doctoral dissertation, Department of Business Administration, University of Gothenburg.

Norén, L. (1995), *Tolkande företagsekonomisk forskning* [Interpretative business research], Lund: Studentlitteratur.

Normann, R. (1975), *Skapande företagsledning* [Creative business leadership], Malmö: Liber.

Normann, R. (1978), 'Kritiska faktorer vid ledning av serviceföretag' [Critical factors at leading service companies], *Utvecklingsstrategier för svenskt servicekunnande* [Development strategies for Swedish service knowledge], Stockholm: SIAR.

Normann, R. (1984), *Service Management*, Chichester, UK: Wiley.

Normann, R. & R. Ramirez (1993), 'From value chain to value constellation: Designing interactive strategy', *Harvard Business Review*, July-August, 65–77.

Normann, R. & R. Ramirez (1994), *Developing Interactive Strategy: From Value Chain to Value Constellation*, Chichester, UK: Wiley.

Normann, R. (2001), *Reframing Business: When the Map Changes the Landscape*, Chichester, UK: Wiley.

Nyberg, D. & S. Sveningsson (2014), 'Paradoxes of authentic leadership: Leader identity struggles', *Leadership*, **10**, 437–55.

Nystrom, P.H. (1914), *Retail Selling and Store Management*, New York: George B. Woolson & Co.

Nöth, W. (1990), *Handbook of Semiotics*, Indianapolis: Indiana University Press.

Oc, B., M.R. Bashshur & C. Moore (2013), 'Stooges and squeaky wheels: How followers shape leader fairness over time', *Working paper.*

Office of the Deputy Prime Minister (ODPM) (2003), 'Business-led regeneration of deprived areas: a review of the evidence base', *Research report.*

O'Gorman, C. (2006) (2nd edition), 'Strategy and the small business' in S. Carter & D. Jones- Evans (eds.), *Enterprise and Small Business. Principles, Practice and Policy*, Harlow, UK: Pearson Education.

Öhrström, B (2005), 'Urban och ekonomisk utveckling. Platsbaserade strategier i den postindustriella staden' [Urban and economic development. Place-based strategies in the post-industrial city], in O. Sernhede & T. Johansson (eds.), *Storstadens omvandlingar. Postindustrialism, globalisering och migration. Göteborg och Malmö* [The transformation of big cities. Post-industrialism, globalization and migration. Gothenburg and Malmö], Gothenburg: Daidalos.

Oinas, P. (1999), 'Voices and silences: the problem of access to embeddedness', *Geoforum*, **30**, 351–61.

Oliver, G. (1990), *Marketing Today*, Hemel Hempstead: Prentice Hall.

Osborne, D. & T. Gaebler (1992), *Reinventing Government: How the Entrepreneurial Spirit is Transforming the Public Sector*, Reading, MA: Addison-Wesley.

Osterwalder, A. & Y. Pigneur (2010), *Business Model Generation*, New York: Wiley.

Oxenfeldt, A.R. (1966), *Executive Action in Marketing*, Belmont, CA: Wadsworth.

Painter, J. (1998), 'Entrepreneurs are made, not born: learning and urban regimes in the production of entrepreneurial cities', in T. Hall & P. Hubbard (eds.), *The Entrepreneurial City*, Chichester, UK: John Wiley & Sons.

Paredo, A.M & J.J. Chrisman (2006), 'Toward a theory of community-based enterprise', *Academy of Management Review*, **31**(2), 309–28.

Parvatiyar, A. & J. Sheth (1994), 'Paradigm shift in marketing theory and approach: The emergence of relationship marketing', in J. Sheth & A. Parvatiyar (eds.), *Relationship Marketing Theory. Methods and Applications*, Atlanta, GA, Center for Relationship Marketing, Emory University: USA.

Paton, R. (2003), *Managing and Measuring Social Enterprises*, London: Sage.

Pearce, C.L. & J.A. Conger (2003), *Shared Leadership: Reframing the Hows and Whys of Leadership*, Thousand Oaks, CA: Sage.

Penrose, E.G. (1959), *The Theory of the Growth of the Firm*, New York: Wiley.

Peppers, D. & M. Rodgers (1993), *The One to One Future: Building Relationships One Customer at a Time*, New York: Doubleday.

Peters, T. (1994a), *The Pursuit of WOW! Every person's guide to topsy-turvy times*, London, Sydney and Auckland: Pan Books.

Peters, T. (1994b), *The Tom Peter Seminar. Crazy Times Call for Crazy Organizations*, London, Sydney and Auckland: Pan Books.

Peters, T. (1997), *The Circle of Innovation*, New York: Alfred A. Knopf.

Peters, T. & R. Waterman (1982), *In Search of Excellence*, London: Harper and Row.

Petersen, A., I. Barns, J. Dudley & P. Harris (1999), *Poststructuralism, Citizenship and Social Policy*, London: Routledge.

Phillips, J.S. & R.G. Lord (1981), 'Causal attributions and perceptions of leadership', *Organization Behavior and Human Performance*, **28**(2), 143–63.

Piaget, J. (1954), *The Construction of Reality in the Child*, New York: Basic Books.

Pinchot III, G. (1985), *Intrapreneuring*, New York: Harper & Row.

Pine II, B.J., D. Peppers & M. Rogers (1995), 'Do you want to keep your customers forever?', *Harvard Business Review*, March-April, 15–23.

Piore, M.J. & C.F. Sabel (1984), *The Second Industrial Divide. Possibilities for Prosperity*, New York: Basic Books.

Pointer, D.D. & J.P. Sanchez (1994), 'Leadership: a framework for thinking and acting', in S. Shortell & A. Kuluzny (eds.) (3rd edition), *Health Care Management: A Text in Organization Theory and Behaviors*, New York: Delmar Publishers.

Porter, M. (1980), *Competitive Strategy: Techniques for Analyzing Industries and Competitors*, New York: The Free Press.

Porter, M. (1985), *Competitive Advantage*, New York: The Free Press.

Porter, M. (1998), 'The Adam Smith address: location, clusters, and the "new" microeconomics of competition', *Business Economics*, January, 7–13.

Portes, A. & J. Sensenbrenner (1993), 'Embeddedness and immigration: notes on the social determinants', *American Journal of Sociology*, **98**, 1320–50.

Potter, J. & M. Wetherell (1987), *Discourse and Social Psychology*, London: Sage.

Powell, W.W. (1990), 'Neither market nor hierarchy: Network forms of organization', *Research in Organizational Behavior*, **12**, 295–336.

Powell, W.W. & L. Smith-Doerr (1994), 'Networks and economic life', in N. Smelser & R. Swedberg (eds.), *Handbook of Economic Sociology*, Princeton, NJ: Princeton University Press.

Prahalad, C.K. & V. Ramaswamy (2000), 'Co-opting customer competence', *Harvard Business Review*, January-February, 79–87.

Prahalad, C.K. & V. Ramaswamy (2003), 'The new frontier of experience innovation', *Sloan Management Review*, Summer, 12–18.

Prahalad, C.K. & V. Ramaswamy (2004a), 'The co-creation of value in "invited commentaries" on "evolving to a new dominant logic in marketing"', *Journal of Marketing*, **68**, 18–27.

Prahalad, C.K. & V. Ramaswamy (2004b), *The Future of Competition: Co-creating Unique Value with Customers*, Boston: Harvard Business School Press.

Prahalad, C.K. & V. Ramaswamy (2004c), 'Co-creation experiences: The next practice in value creation', *Journal of Interactive Marketing*, **18**(3), 5–14.

Prendergast, W.A. (1906), *Credit and Its Uses*, New York: D. Appleton-Century Co., Inc.

Putnam, R.D., R. Leonardi & R.Y. Nanetti (1993), *Making Democracy Work. Civic Traditions in Modern Italy*, Princeton, NJ: Princeton University Press.

Rämö. H. (2000), *The Nexus of Time and Place in Economical Operations*, doctoral dissertation, Department of Business Administration, Stockholm University.

Rämö, H. (2004), 'Spatio-temporal notions and organized environmental issues: an axiology of action', *Organization*, **11**(6), 849–72.

Ranson, S., B. Hinings & R. Greenwood (1980), 'The structuring of organizational structures', *Administrative Science Quarterly*, **25**, March, 1–17.

Rehn, A. & S. Taalas (2004), 'Acquaintances and connections – *Blat*, the Soviet Union and mundane entrepreneurship', *Entrepreneurship and Regional Development*, **16**, May, 235–50.

Renard, M.-C. (2002), 'Fair trade quality, market and convention', *Journal of Rural Studies*, **19**, 87–96.

Ries, A. & J. Trout (1981), *Positioning: The Battle for Your Mind*, New York: McGraw-Hill.

Riggio, R.E., I. Chaleff & J. Blumen-Lipman (2008), *The Art of Followership. How Great Followers Create Great Leaders and Organizations*, San Francisco, CA: Jossey-Bass.

Robinson, P.J., C.W. Faris & Y. Wind (1967), *Industrial Buying and Creative Marketing*, Boston: Allyn & Bacon.

Rogers, E. & D. Kincaid (1981), *Communication Networks*, New York: Free Press.

Rosen, E. (2000), *The Anatomy of Buzz: How to Create Word of Mouth Marketing*, New York: Double Day.

Rost, J.C. (1993), *Leadership for the Twenty-First Century*, New York: Praeger.

Rost, J.C. (2008), 'Followership: An outdated concept', in R. Riggio,

I. Chaleff & J. Lipman- Blumen (eds.), *The Art of Followership: How Great Followers Create Great Leaders and Organizations*, San Francisco, CA: Jossey-Bass.

Rothwell, R. (1991), 'External networking and innovation in small and medium-sized manufacturing firms in Europe', *Technovation*, **11**(2), 93–111.

Rowan, D. (1997), 'Lastword: glossary for the 90s', *Guardian*, Guardian Weekend, 15 February, T67.

Rush, M.C., J.C. Thomas & R.G. Lord (1977), 'Implicit leadership theory: A potential threat to the internal validity of leader behavior questionnaires', *Organizational Behavior and Human Performance*, **20**(1), 93–110.

Ruzzier, M.K., M. Ruzzier & R.D. Hisrich (2013), *Marketing for Entrepreneurs and SMEs. A Global Perspective*, Cheltenham, UK and Northampton, MA, USA: Edward Elgar Publishing.

Sack, R. (1997), *Homo Geographicus*, Baltimore, MD: John Hopkins University Press.

Salomon, L.M. & H.K. Anheier (1994), *The Emerging Sector Revisited: An Overview*, Baltimore, MD, John Hopkins Institute for Policy Studies: USA.

Salomon, L.M. & H.K. Anheier (1997), 'The civil society sector', *Society*, **34**(2), 60–5.

Sandberg, J. (1999), 'Konstruktioner av social konstruktion' [Constructions of social construction], in S.-E. Sjöstrand, J. Sandberg & M. Tyrstrup (eds.), *Osynlig företagsledning* [Invisible business leadership], Lund: Studentlitteratur.

Sanner, L. (1997), *Trust Between Entrepreneurs and External Actors. Sensemaking in organizing new business ventures*, doctoral dissertation, Department of Business Administration, Uppsala University.

Santora, J.C., W. Seaton & J.C. Sarros (1999), 'Changing times: entrepreneurial leadership in a community-based non-profit organization', *Journal of Leadership Studies*, **3**(3/4), 101–109.

Sarasvathy, S. (2001), 'Causation and effectuation: toward a theoretical shift from economic inevitability to entrepreneurial contingency', *Academy of Management Review*, **26**(2), 243–63.

Say, J.B. (1855) (4th edition), *A Treatise on Political Economy*, Philadelphia, Lippincott: Grambo & Co.

Scarborough, N.M., D.L. Wilson & T.W. Zimmerer (2009) (9th edition), *Effective Small Business Management. An Entrepreneurial Approach*, Upper Saddle River, NJ: Pearson International Edition.

Schmitt, B.H. (1999), *Experiential Marketing: How to Get Customers to Sense, Feel, Think, Act, and Relate to Your Company and Brands*, New York: Free Press.

Schneider, T. & S. Woolgar (2012), 'Technologies of ironic revelation: Enacting consumers in neuromarkets', *Consumptions Markets & Culture*, **15**(2), 169–89.

Schrage, M. (1995), 'Customer relations', *Harvard Business Review*, July-August, 154–6.

Schumpeter, J.A. (1934), *The Theory of Economic Development*, Cambridge, MA: Harvard University Press.

Schutz, A. (1962), *Collected Papers*, Vol. I, ed. and intr. M. Natanson, Haag: Martinus Nijhoff.

Schutz, A. (1967), *The Phenomenology of the Social World*, Evanston, IL: Northwestern University Press.

Scott, D.L. (1903), *The Psychology of Advertising in Theory and Practice*, Boston: Small, Maynard & Company.

Scott, W.R. (1998) (4th edition), *Organizations: Rational, Natural, and Open Systems*, Upper Saddle River, NJ: Prentice Hall.

Sen, A. (1999), *Development as Freedom*, Oxford: Oxford University Press.

Sernhede, O. & T. Johansson (2005) (eds.), *Storstadens omvandlingar. Postindustrialism, globalisering och migration. Göteborg och Malmö* [The transformation of big cities. Post-industrialism, globalization and migration. Gothenburg and Malmö], Gothenburg: Diadalos.

Sexton, D.L. & N.B. Bowman-Upton (1991), *Entrepreneurship. Creativity and Growth*, New York: Macmillan Publishing Company.

Seybold, P.B. (1998), *Customers.com: How to Create a Profitable Business Strategy for the Internet and Beyond*, New York: Times Books.

Shamir, B. (2007), 'From passive recipients to active co-producers: Followers' roles in the leadership process', in B. Shamir, R. Pillai, M. Bligh & M. Uhl-Bien (eds.), *Follower-centered Perspectives on Leadership: A Tribute to the Memory of James R. Meindl*, Charlotte, NC: Information Age Publishers.

Shamir, B. (2012), 'Leadership research or post-leadership research: Advancing leadership theory versus throwing the baby out with the bath water', in M. Uhl-Bien, & S. Ospina (eds.), *Advancing Relational Leadership Research: A Dialogue Among Perspectives*, Charlotte, NC: Information Age Publishers.

Shapero, A. & L. Sokol (1982), 'The social dimension of entrepreneurship', in C.A. Kent, D.L. Sexton & K.H. Vesper (eds.), *Encyclopedia of Entrepreneurship*, Englewood Cliffs, NJ: Prentice Hall.

Shaw, A. (1912), 'Some problems in market distribution', *Quarterly Journal of Economics*, **12**(99), 703–65.

Shaw, E. (1997), 'The real networks in small firms', in D. Deakins, P. Jennings & C. Mason (eds.), *Small Firms: Entrepreneurship in the 1990s*, London: Paul Chapman Publishing.

Shaw, E. (1998), 'Social networks: their impact on the innovative behaviour of small firms', *International Journal of Innovation Management*, **2**(2), 201–22.

Sheth, J.N. (1973), 'A model of industrial buyer behavior', *Journal of Marketing*, **37**(October), 50–6.

Sheth, J.N., D. Gardner & D.E. Garrett (1988), *Marketing Theory, Evolution and Evaluation*, New York: Wiley.

Shimizu, K. (2016), *Co-Marketing (Symbiotic Marketing) Strategies*, Souseisha Book Company: Japan.

Shostack, G.L. (1977), 'Breaking free from product marketing', *Journal of Marketing*, April, 73–80.

Silverman, D. (1993), *Interpreting Qualitative Data*, London: Sage.

Simon, H. (1947), *Administrative Behavior*, New York: Macmillan.

Skloot, E. (1995), *The Nonprofit Entrepreneur*, New York: Foundation Center.

Slater, D. (1997), *Consumer Culture and Modernity*, Cambrige, MA: Polity.

Slater, S. & J. Narver (1994a), 'Market orientation, customer value, and superior performance', *Business Horizons*, March-April, 22–8.

Slater, S. & J. Narver (1994b), 'Competitive strategy in the market focused business', *Journal of Market Focused Management*, **II**, 59–74.

Slater, S. & J. Narver (1995), 'Market orientation and the learning organisation', *Journal of Marketing*, **29**(July), 63–74.

Smircich, L. & G. Morgan (1982), 'Leadership: The management of meaning', *The Journal of Applied Behavioral Science*, **18**, 257–73.

Smith, A. (1776/1991), *The Wealth of Nations*, London: Everyman's Library.

Smith, M. (2011), 'Traits of a successful marketing manager', *Melbourne: Marketing Eye*.

Smith, W.R. (1956), 'Product differentiation and market segmentation as alternative market strategies', *Journal of Marketing*, **21**(July), 3–8.

Spinosa, C., F. Flores & H. Dreyfus (1997), *Disclosing New Worlds*, Cambridge, MA: MIT Press.

Stevenson, H.H. & J.C. Jarillo (1990), 'A paradigm for entrepreneurship: entrepreneurial management', *Strategic Management Journal*, **11**, 17–27.

Steyaert, C. (1997), 'A qualitative methodology for process studies in entrepreneurship. Creating local knowledge through stories', *International Studies of Management and Organization*, **27**(3), 13–33.

Steyaert, C. (2000), 'Entre-concepts: conceiving entrepreneurship', presented at *RENT- conference XIV*, Prague.

Steyaert, C. (2004), 'The prosaic of entrepreneurship', in D. Hjorth & C. Steyaert (eds.), *Narrative and Discursive Approaches to Entrepreneurship*.

*A Second Movements in Entrepreneurship Books*, Cheltenham, UK and Northampton, MA, USA: Edward Elgar Publishing.

Steyaert, C. (2007), '"Entrepreneuring" as a conceptual attractor? A view of process theories in 20 years of entrepreneurship studies', *Entrepreneurship and Regional Development*, **19**(6), 453–77.

Steyaert, C. & D. Hjorth (eds.) (2003), *New Movements in Entrepreneurship*, Cheltenham, UK and Northampton, MA, USA: Edward Elgar Publishing.

Steyaert, C. & J. Katz (2004), 'Reclaiming the space of entrepreneurship in society: geographical, discursive and social dimensions', *Entrepreneurship and Regional Development*, **16**, May, 179–96.

Steyaert, C. & D. Hjorth (eds.) (2006), *Entrepreneurship and Social Change. A Third Movements in Entrepreneurship Book*, Cheltenham, UK and Northampton, MA, USA: Edward Elgar Publishing.

Stogdill, R.M. (1948), 'Personal factors associated with leadership: A survey of the literature', *Journal of Psychology*, **25**(1), 35–71.

Storey, D. (1980), *Job Creation and Small Firms Policy in Britain*, UK: Centre for Environmental Studies.

Styhre, A., (2009), *Byråkrati: Teoretiker, kritiker och försvarare* [Bureaucracy: Theorists, critics and defenders], Malmö: Liber.

Sundin, E. (2009), 'Det dolda samhällsansvaret – omsorgsmotiv i småföretag' [The hidden social responsibility – caring motives in small firms], in M. Gawell, B. Johannisson & M. Lundqvist (eds.), *Samhällets entreprenörer* [The entrepreneurs in society], Stockholm: KK- stiftelsen.

Sutton, R.I. & B.M. Staw (1995), 'What theory is not', *Administrative Science Quarterly*, **40**(3), 371–84.

Svensson, P. & J. Östberg (2016) (2nd edition), *Marknadsföring, människor och interaktion* [Marketing, humans and interaction], Lund: Studentlitteratur.

Sy, T. (2010), 'What do you think of followers? Examining the content, structure, and consequences of implicit followership theories', *Organizational Behavior and Human Decision Processes*, **113**(2),73–84.

Taylor, M. (2003), *Public Policy in the Community*, Basingstoke and New York: Palgrave Macmillan.

Thake, S. & S. Zadek (1997), *Practical People, Noble Causes: How to Support Community-based Social Entrepreneurs*, London: New Economics Foundation.

Thompson, J. (2002), 'The world of the social entrepreneur', *International Journal of Public Sector Management*, **15**(5), 412–31.

Thompson, J., G. Alvy & A. Lees (2000), 'Social entrepreneurship – a new look at the people and the potential', *Management Decision*, **38**(5), 328–38.

Thrift, N.J. (1996), *Spatial Formations*, London and Thousand Oaks, CA: Sage.

Thurik, A.R. & H.K. van Dijk (1998), 'Entrepreneurship: visies en benaderingen' [Entrepreneurship: points of views and approaches], in D.P. Scherjon & A.R. Thurik (eds.), *Handboek ondernemers en adviseurs in het MKB* [Handbook for enterprisers and advisors to SMEs], Dordrecht, the Netherlands: Kluwer Bedrijfsinformatie.

Tichy, N.M., N.L. Tushman & C. Forbrun (1979), 'Social network analysis for Organisations', *Academy of Management Review*, **4**(4), 507–19.

Timmons, J.A. (1999) (5th edition), *New Venture Creation. Entrepreneurship for the 21st Century*, New York: Irwin McGraw-Hill.

Toffler, A. (1980), *The Third Wave*, London: Collins.

Townley, B. (1995), '"Know thyself": self-awareness, self-formation and managing', *Organization*, **2**(2), 271–89.

Townsend, P.L. & J.E. Gebhardt (1997), *Five-star Leadership: The Art and Strategy of Creating Leaders at Every Level*, New York: Wiley.

Tuan, Y.-F. (1977), *Space and Place. The Perspectives of Experience*, Minneapolis and London: The University of Minnesota Press.

Turkle, S. (2015), *Reclaiming Conversation. The Power of Talk in a Digital Age*, New York: Penguin Books.

Tönnies, F. (1887/1957), *Gemeinschaft und Gesellschaft* [*Community and Society*], East Lansing: Michigan State University Press.

Törnebohm, H. (1974), *Paradigm i vetenskapens värld och i vetenskapsteorin* [Paradigms in the world of science and in scientific theory], Department of theory of science, Gothenburg University.

Uhl-Bien, M. & R. Pillai (2007), 'The romance of leadership and the social construction of followership', in B. Shamir, R. Pillai, M. Bligh & M. Uhl-Bien (eds.), *Follower-centered Perspectives on Leadership: A Tribute to the Memory of James R. Meindl*, Charlotte, NC: Information Age Publication.

Uhl-Bien, M. & S. Ospina (2012), 'Paradigm interplay in relational leadership: A way forward', in M. Uhl-Bien & S. Ospina (eds.), *Advancing Relational Leadership Research: A Dialogue Among Perspectives*, Charlotte, NC: Information Age Publishers.

Uhl-Bien, M., R.E. Riggio, K.B. Lowe & M.K. Carsten (2014), 'Followership theory: A review and research agenda", *The Leadership Quarterly*, **25**, 83–104.

van Knippenberg, D. & S.B. Sitkin (2013), 'A critical assessment of charismatic-transformational leadership research: Back to the drawing board?' *The Academy of Management Annuals*, **7**(1), 1–60.

Vargo, S.L. & R.F. Lusch (2004), 'Evolving to a new dominant logic for marketing', *Journal of Marketing*, **68**(1), 1–17.

Vargo, S.L. & R.F. Lusch (2006), 'Service-dominant logic: What it is, what it is not, what it might be', in R.F. Lusch & S.L. Vargo (eds.), *The Service-dominant Logic of Marketing: Dialogue, Debate, and Directions*, Armonk, NY: ME Sharpe.

Vargo, S.L., P.P. Maglio & M.A. Akaka (2008), 'On value and value co-creation: A service systems and service logic perspective', *European Management Journal*, **26**, 145–52.

Vasi, I.B. (2009), 'New heroes, old theories? Toward a sociological perspective on social entrepreneurship', in R. Ziegler (ed.), *An Introduction to Social Entrepreneurship*, Cheltenham, UK and Northampton, MA, USA: Edward Elgar Publishing.

Veblen, T. (1899/1934), *The Theory of the Leisure Class*, New York: The Modern Library.

Venkataraman, S. (1997), 'The distinctive domain of entrepreneurship research', in J.A. Katz & R. Brockhaus (eds.), *Advances in Entrepreneurship, Firm Emergence and Growth*, Vol. 3, Greenwich, CT: JAI Press.

Vernon, R. (1966), 'International investment and international trade in product life cycle', *Quarterly Journal of Economics*, **80**(May), 190–207.

Vestrum, I.K. & O.J. Borch (2006), 'Dynamics of entrepreneurship culture', presented at *ESU2006 Conference*, University of Tampere in Hämeenlinna, Finland.

von Wright, G.H. (1971), *Explanation and Understanding*, London: Routledge & Kegan Paul.

Walumbwa, F., B. Avolio, W. Gardner, T. Wernsing & S. Peterson (2008), 'Authentic leadership: Development and validation of a theory-based measure', *Management Department Faculty Publications, Florida International University*, **24**(1), 89–126.

Watson, J.B. (1970), *Behaviorism*, New York: Norton.

Weber, M. (1975) (2nd edition), *Makt og byråkrati* [Power and bureaucracy], Oslo: Gyldendal Norsk Förlag.

Webster, F.E. Jr (1992), 'The changing role of marketing in the corporation', *Journal of Marketing*, **56**(October), 1–17.

Webster, F.E. Jr & Y. Wind (1972), 'A general model for understanding organizational buying behavior', *Journal of Marketing*, **36**(April), 12–9.

Weick, K.E. (1993), 'The collapse of sensemaking in organizations: The Mann Gulch disaster', *Administrative Science Quarterly*, **38**, 628–52.

Weick, K.E. (1995), *Sensemaking in Organizations*, Thousand Oaks, CA: Sage.

Weiskopf, R. & C. Steyaert (2009), 'Metamorphoses in entrepreneurship studies: towards an affirmative politics of entrepreneuring', in D. Hjorth & C. Steyaert (eds.), *The Politics and Aesthetics of Entrepreneurship. A*

*Fourth Movements in Entrepreneurship Books*, Cheltenham, UK and Northampton, MA, USA: Edward Elgar Publishing.

Wells, W.D. (1975), 'Psychographics: A critical review', *Journal of Marketing Research*, **12**(May), 196–213.

Wenneberg, S.B. (2001), *Socialkonstruktivism – positioner, problem och perspektiv* [Social constructivism – positions, problems and perspectives], Solna: Liber AB.

Westerdahl, S. (2001), *Business and Community*, Gothenburg: Bokförlaget BAS.

Westlund, H. (2001), 'Social economy and the case of Sweden', presented at *Uddevalla Symposium 2001, Regional Economies in Transition*, Vänersborg, Sweden.

Westlund, H. & S. Westerdahl (1997), *Contribution of the Social Economy to Local Development*, Östersund/Stockholm: Department of social economy/Koopi.

Westlund, H. & R. Bolton (2003), 'Local social capital and entrepreneurship', *Small Business Economics*, **21**, 77–113.

Wetherell, M. (1996), 'Life histories/social histories', in M. Wetherell (ed.), *Identities, Groups and Social Issues*, London: Open University Press, Sage.

Whitehead, G. (2009), 'Adolescent leadership development: building a case for an authentic framework', *Educational Management Administration & Leadership*, **37**, 847–72.

Wickham, P.A. (2006) (4th edition), *Strategic Entrepreneurship*, Harlow, UK: Pearson Education Limited.

Wiklund, J. (1998), *Small Firm Growth and Performance*, JIBS Dissertation Series No. 003, Jönköping International Business School.

Wikström, S. (1996), 'Value creation by company-consumer interaction', *Journal of Marketing Management*, **12**, 359–74.

Wikström, S. & R. Normann (1994), *Kunskap och värde – Företaget som ett kunskapsproducerande och värdeskapande system* [Knowledge and value – the company as a knowledge-producing and value-creating system], Stockholm: Fritzes förlag.

Wilkinson, J. (1997), 'A new paradigm for economic analysis? Recent convergences of French social science and an exploration of the convention theory approach with a consideration of its application to the analysis of the agro-food sector', *Economy and Society*, **26**(3), 305–39.

Williamson, O.E. (1975), *Markets and Hierarchies: Analysis and Antitrust Implications: A Study in the Economics of Internal Organization*, New York: Free Press.

Wind, Y.J., V. Mahajan & R.E. Gunther (2002), *Convergence Marketing: Strategies for Reaching a New Hybrid Consumer*, Upper Saddle River, NJ: Prentice Hall.

Wood, M. (2016), '7 content marketing tips for new entrepreneurs', *Wikipedia* (accessed Feb. 2017).

Zaleznik, A. (1965), 'The dynamics of subordinacy', *Harvard Business Review*, **43**(3), 119–31.

Zaleznik, A. & M.F. Kets de Vries (1975), *Power and the Corporate Mind*, Oxford: Houghton Mifflin.

Zerbinati, S. & V. Soutaris (2005), 'Entrepreneurship in the public sector: a framework for analysis in European local governments', *Entrepreneurship and Regional Development*, **1**, 3–19.

Zimmerer, T.W. & N.M. Scarborough (2005) (4th edition), *Essentials of Entrepreneurship and Small Business Management*, Upper Saddle River, NJ: Prentice Hall.

# Index